Clash of Arms

Clash of Arms

How the Allies Won
in Normandy

Russell A. Hart

University of Oklahoma Press
Norman

Library of Congress Cataloging-in-Publication Data

Hart, Russell A.
    Clash of arms : how the Allies won in Normandy / Russell A. Hart.
        p.   cm.
    Originally published: Boulder, Colo. : Lynne Rienner, 2001.
    Includes bibliographical references and index.
    ISBN 0-8061-3605-7 (alk. paper)
    1. World War, 1939-1945—Campaigns—France—Normandy. I. Title.

    D756.5.N6H345 2004
    940.54'2142—dc22

                                                          2003063411

1   2   3   4   5   6   7   8   9   10

To Mum and Dad, Stephen, Sharon, Allison, Oscar, and Clio

Contents

Illustrations

Maps

Tables

Photographs

Foreword

D. E. Showalter

Defining operational effectiveness and determining how it is established are once again among the central questions of military history. Temporarily eclipsed by a focus on the general social, cultural, and economic factors of warmaking, the issue of combat performance is increasingly recognized as the sine qua non of armed forces, even those with a domestic, constabulary orientation.

That subject is particularly vital in the context of World War II. Since 1945 a virtual cult of the *Wehrmacht* has emerged among its former enemies. Books, magazines, and films pay tribute to its fighting power. Even when acknowledging its weaknesses at the levels of strategy and policy, even when accepting the role of Nazification in its effectiveness, this school continues to praise in particular the German Army's virtuosity at operational and tactical levels. At times it seems as though the German generals allowed the Allies to win the war out of kindness. Allied military performance is generally treated condescendingly. The British and American armies in particular are dismissed as lacking fighting spirit, tactical skill, and operational virtuosity, depending on numbers and material superiority to win victories by the low common denominator of attrition.

Recent challenges to this paradigm fall into three categories. One approach, exemplified by Ken Tout's narratives of the fighting in the Anglo-Canadian sector, stresses the difficulties of conducting offensive operations, going so far as to argue that the normal result of attacks is either defeat or a too-costly advance, and that the outcome of battle should be judged against an expectation of failure. A second perspective, illustrated by the work of Stephen Ambrose, proffers anecdotal arguments that Allied soldiers were in fact motivated to fight, and fought well throughout the northwest Europe campaign. The focus of the third challenge is expressed in the title of one of its best-known examples. Keith Bonn's *When the Odds Were Even* argues that under conditions when their air and artillery superiority were nullified, U.S. divisions by 1944–1945 were in fact more effective than their German opponents.

The end result of this revisionism too often resembles the kind of ongoing dispute better associated with the relative capabilities of sports teams—more of a pastime than an intellectual or professional exercise. It is in that context that *Clash of Arms* makes a seminal contribution. Making extensive use of both archival and published sources, Hart establishes a comparative two-stage model that includes the Western Front's three major combatants: the German, the American, and the Anglo-Canadian armies. In general terms he establishes the importance of such factors as geography and domestic politics. Germany, a continental power, was fighting on its own ground, and in contexts of preparation that dated back to the Weimar Republic. The Allies on the other hand were geostrategic islands, who had to devote as much attention to getting to Europe as to staying there once they landed. Neither the U.S., British, nor Canadian governments, moreover, was willing to devote resources to military preparation between the world wars in ways acceptable to even a democratic German government, much less Adolf Hitler's Reich.

At institutional levels, Hart stresses the importance of adaptability. By 1944, none of the major combatants in Western Europe was an easy enemy to defeat. The outcome of battles and campaigns depended to a corresponding degree on learning the operational lessons one's adversary taught. And that in turn depended heavily on prewar approaches to doctrine. Were those fundamentally flawed, appropriate adaptation to circumstances became questionable. The German way of war was essentially artistic, emphasizing individualistic virtuoso performances at all levels. Cooperation, particularly among the services, was correspondingly discounted. More seriously, the "artistic" paradigm was significantly vulnerable to a Nazi ideology that encouraged replacing rational calculation with wishful thinking in such crucial matters as the military capabilities of "racially inferior" opponents—Americans in particular.

On the other side of the line, the Americans followed a managerial/scientific paradigm. They took advantage of late entry into the war to study German methods and develop responses to them. If their operational "machine" did not work, they repaired it or redesigned it, paying little regard to feelings or traditions. This gave them a flexibility, and eventually a fighting power, significantly greater than their Anglo-Canadian allies, who followed what might be called an artisanal model of warmaking. Incorporating respect for tradition and low-risk, trial-and-error methods of adaptation, the "British way" reflected both prewar doctrinal shortcomings and wartime lack of resources compared to both the Germans and the Americans. In the end, both the Americans and the Anglo-Canadians proved able to outfight their German adversaries—but as much because of German shortcomings as their own positive qualities. Hart's conclusion, that modern war offers no shortcuts and seldom rewards improvisation, merits application well beyond the parameters of this single monograph. *Clash of Arms* is a must read for anyone concerned with the creation and maintenance of combat effectiveness, whether in the twentieth or the twenty-first centuries.

Acknowledgments

I wish to thank the following people for the help, advice, encouragement, training, and support without which I would never have completed this project. My adviser, Williamson Murray, was a source of continual encouragement and intellectual stimulation. I am deeply indebted to my colleagues at Ohio State University—Mark Grimsley, Joe Guilmartin, Allan R. Millett, and Geoffrey Parker—for their keen insights and enthusiastic support. The following offered valuable assistance and friendship: David Bercuson, Jeremy Black, Peter Dennis, Walter Dunn, Anthony Fletcher, Holger Herwig, John English, and Gerhard Weinberg; Geoff Megargee, Jeff Marquis, Anthony Milburn, Rich Muller, Jeff Roberts, and Dave Thompson; Chris Cook, Leo Daugherty, Stephen Glick, and Louis Rotundo. I am also indebted to Dennis Showalter for his support and willingness to write the foreword for this book.

I owe a debt of gratitude to the hard-working staffs of several archives who have assisted me. Particular thanks go to Robin Cookson at the National Archives Records Service; Kate O'Brien and Patricia Methven at the Liddell Hart Centre for Military Archives, Kings College, London; Anthony Richards of the Imperial War Museum; as well as the personnel of the Public Record Office, the Imperial War Museum, the National Archives, the Canadian National Archives, and the United States Military History Institute. At Ohio State University, David Lincove and the library staff were enormously helpful.

The author and publisher acknowledge the kind generosity of the trustees of the Imperial War Museum for access to the collections held by the Department of Documents as well as Viscount Montgomery of Alamein, CBE, and the Montgomery Collections Committee of the trustees of the Imperial War Museum for use of the the field marshal's papers. The author and publisher also acknowledge permission from the trustees of the Liddell Hart Centre for Military Archives, Kings College, London, to quote from the Alanbrooke and Liddell Hart Papers. Crown copyrighted material in the Public Record Office is used by permission of the controller of Her Majesty's Stationery Office. Additional excerpts from documents are used by permission of the National Archives of Canada.

The research and writing of this study was financed in part by the following grants and awards: Ohio State University Presidential Fellowship; Ohio State University, Department of History, Ruth Higgins and Philip Poirier Awards; and the Ohio State University, Graduate School, Alumni Research Award. Without this generous financial support this work could not have been completed.

At Lynne Rienner Publishers, thanks go to Dan Eades, Leanne Anderson, Steve Barr, and the entire editorial team for their invaluable assistance in shepherding this study through to publication. The final product is all the better as a result of their endeavors.

Finally, special thanks and affection go to my brother, Stephen Hart, my parents, and my sister, all of whom remain an inspiration. I also send appreciation to Gary Huckle and Chris Packham for many years of friendship. Nor can I ever repay the debt of gratitude I owe Allison Gough, whose love and friendship has endured throughout the long process of completing this work.

Any errors of fact or of interpretation are solely my responsibility.

—*Russell A. Hart*

Chronology: 1918–1944

11 November 1918	Armistice ends World War I
1919	Ten-Year Rule promulgated by Great Britain
1920	National Defense Act (United States)
1923	British Army forms Royal Tank Corps
1927	Britain forms Experimental Mechanized Force
1935	Germany forms its first panzer divisions
1936	German reoccupation of the Rhineland
1937	Canadian War Scheme Three
1938	Austrian *Anschluss*
August 1938	Munich crisis—Germany occupies the Sudetenland
March 1939	Germany overruns the rump Czech state
April 1939	British Army forms Royal Armoured Corps
1 September 1939	Germany invades Poland
3 September 1939	Anglo-French declaration of war
April 1940	German *Weserübung* invasion of Denmark and Norway
10 May 1940	German invasion of the west
June 1940	Italy enters the war
July 1940	Independent Armored Force formed in United States
13 August 1940	Canadian Royal Armoured Corps activated
September 1940	U.S. Selective Service Bill enacted
9 December 1940	Western Desert Force launches Operation COMPASS
7 February 1941	Battle of Beda Fomm
6 April 1941	German invasion of Yugoslavia and Greece
11 April 1941	Rommel besieges Tobruk
15 June 1941	Wavell launches Operation BATTLEAXE
21 June 1941	National Resources Mobilization Act in Canada
22 June 1941	German invasion of the Soviet Union

5 July 1941	Auchinleck replaces Wavell in the Middle East
September 1941	Louisiana Maneuvers (United States)
November 1941	Carolina Maneuvers (United States) and Operation CRUSADER
6 December 1941	Soviet winter counteroffensive begins
7 December 1941	Japanese attack on Pearl Harbor
6 April 1942	Anglo-Canadian raid on Dieppe
April 1942	Anglo-Canadian Exercise TIGER
26 May 1942	Battle of Gazala
20 June 1942	Fall of Tobruk
30 June 1942	First Battle of El Alamein
10 July 1942	Battle of Ruweisat Ridge
30 August 1942	Battle of Alam Haifa
23 October 1942	Second Battle of El Alamein
8 November 1942	Operation TORCH invasion of northwest Africa
23 November 1942	German Sixth Army encircled at Stalingrad
13 December 1942	Battle of Agheila
23 January 1943	Fall of Tripoli
22 February 1943	Manstein retakes Kharkov
6 March 1943	Battle of Medenine
1 April 1943	Battle of Wadi Akarit
4 April 1943	Exercise SPARTAN
8 May 1943	Axis resistance in Tunisia ends
July 1943	Allied Operation HUSKY invasion of Sicily
August 1943	Operation AVALANCHE landings at Salerno
September 1943	First U.S. Army begins assembling in Britain
3 November 1943	German Directive 51 to repulse the Second Front
November 1943	Montgomery takes command of 21st Army Group
31 December 1943	Rommel appointed commander in chief, Army Group B
January 1944	Anzio landings in Italy
15 February 1944	Carpet bombing of Monte Cassino
March 1944	Operation STRANGLE in Italy
20 April 1944	Crerar takes command of First Canadian Army
May 1944	Operation DIADEM in Italy

Introduction

*The soldier is the most conservative creature on earth. It is really danger-
ous to give him an idea, because he will not adopt it until it is obsolete,
and then will not abandon it until it has nearly destroyed him.*
                                                                    —J. F. C. Fuller[1]

*The Army possesses no inherent right to conceal the history of the U.S.
affairs behind a cloak of secrecy. . . . The history of the Army in World
War II must, without reservation, tell the complete story of the Army's participation.*
                                                        —Dwight D. Eisenhower[2]

How well did the militaries of the Western Allies—Great Britain, Canada,
and the United States—as well as their enemy, Nazi Germany, perform in
the European Theater of Operations (ETO) during World War II? How flexible and adaptable were they? How—and how well—did they learn from
their combat experience, and what impact did their ability to adapt have on
the course and outcome of the war? These questions constitute the core of
this book and they are examined in two parts. The first part of the work
explores how the Western Allied and the German militaries prepared in the
1919–1944 period for their decisive confrontation in World War II in the
ETO, the 1944 Normandy Campaign. The second part examines the performance of these four militaries in Normandy between June and August
1944, where the audit of war tested the effectiveness of their preparation.
    Victorious militaries are dynamic institutions that adapt to battlefield
conditions, which are both often impossible to predict and difficult to replicate in peacetime, to ensure victory in war. The military profession is
unique because it is unable to practice realistically its profession in peacetime. Militaries must prepare for future war at an indeterminate date,
against an uncertain enemy, with untested doctrine, tactics, organization,
and ordnance.[3] The audit of war thus invariably proves peacetime military

preparation deficient. The ability of armed forces to adapt during wartime and on the battlefield is, therefore, a key ingredient in the creation of military effectiveness and in the preservation of national security.

The question of how armed forces adapt and innovate during wartime is thus fundamental to this study. Implementing change in wartime is a complex, multifaceted, interrelated activity that involves most functions and facets of a military institution. To enhance its battlefield effectiveness a military has to consider its own strategy, doctrine, tactics, organization, training, and equipment. Equally, it must consider the same characteristics for its opponent. It must also first recognize the need for change as well as value change. Since modification inherently enters the realm of the unknown, powerful evidence that the potential gains outweigh possible drawbacks must exist for military institutions to make fundamental changes. Consequently, combat experience provides the greatest stimulus for adaptation. Not only do armed forces require combat experience but, to adapt effectively, they also require mechanisms to determine, disseminate, and distill "lessons learned" to adapt effectively. Yet, discerning accurately through the fog of war what actually happens on the battlefield is extremely difficult.

The character of the 1914–1918 battlefield, for example, and the lessons to be drawn from it were difficult to discern between the wars and have remained that way. In the interwar period only Germany developed an accurate understanding of the nature of warfare on the Western Front during World War I and historians have only recently come to appreciate that conflict's complexities.[4] Moreover, necessary modifications must be disseminated both to new recruits in training and to veterans in the field. Not only must basic training be reorganized, but units in the combat zone must also retrain in the field amid ongoing combat operations.

Innovation is also inherently nonlinear: different kinds of adaptation bring varying degrees of improvement in combat effectiveness. Strategic shifts and doctrinal refinement are most likely to bring the greatest benefit, while improved organization, tactics, and weapons typically bring less substantial, and more ephemeral, rewards. Input-output yields also vary from combatant to combatant. The process of innovation is nonlinear because it involves numerous actors, complex technologies, and marked uncertainty incapable of simple reduction or quantitative analysis.[5]

The issue of how military institutions adapt has considerable historical significance. While economic, industrial, and demographic strength have played major roles in determining the outcome of modern wars, militaries still have had to win on the battlefield.[6] The relative success and rapidity with which rival military institutions have enhanced their combat effectiveness has shaped the course and outcome of modern wars. National assessments of the origin, nature, and extent of perceived threats have also had a significant influence on whether military institutions innovate successfully.

In the absence of powerful, immediate, and clearly perceived threats, military institutions sometimes find it difficult to generate in peacetime the necessary impetus for sweeping reform. At the same time, wartime events can also act as major obstacles to effective adaptation. Most innovation is thus evolutionary: adaptation emerges gradually and incrementally through trial and error, experimentation, evaluation, and refinement. A complex process of organizational culture, strategic requirements, combat realities, and capacity to adapt shapes innovation. Prevailing military culture more greatly affects the capacity for innovation—the adaptability—of military institutions than individual personalities.[7] In the 1919–1945 period both the U.S. and German militaries generally possessed a culture that promoted creativity and innovation, while British and Canadian military culture, on the other hand, often militated against effective adaptation. Indeed, the military history of the twentieth century demonstrates that organizational and institutional rigidity are major obstacles to effective innovation.

Moreover, the more narrow and specific a military problem, the easier it is for military institutions to solve the problem by innovation or adaptation. Germany addressed and solved the tactical and operational problems associated with static, bloody trench warfare during the latter stages of the Great War, though at the price of strategic myopia that the war could still be won. The British Army, on the other hand, failed to develop broad military proficiency until late in World War II because the fundamental problem was its entire approach to war and the absence of a coherent, realistic doctrine grounded in its extensive Great War experience. The problems that afflicted British operations during World War II were, therefore, not amenable to easy or quick correction.

That this was the case is illustrated by the contrasting British and German experiences with armor. Britain failed to adopt armor effectively between the wars because there was no place for tanks in an imperial defense force that aspired to hold on to its existing empire and that sought to defeat aggression through a protracted strategy of attrition that took advantage of Britain's demographic, financial, and industrial strength.[8] The interwar German military, on the other hand, was institutionally predisposed to innovation because Germany was determined to escape the consequences of its defeat in World War I, and wrest what most Germans still considered to be its rightful place in the sun. Committed to aggression, the Germans were able to adapt (though not without difficulty) the tank to traditional offensive-oriented Prussian strategic tenets to forge the blitzkrieg approach of strategic deep penetration and maneuver by combined-arms mechanized forces.[9]

Many factors affect the ability of military institutions to adapt in wartime: capabilities, strength, and tenacity of the opponent; time constraints; military commitments; and resources. Less quantifiable, but equally important, considerations include a military institution's character—its morale, culture, and social prestige. One also has to distinguish between adaptation and change. Effective adaptation involves reforms that contribute to final victory or to enhanced military effectiveness, whereas change is modification that brings no discernible improvement in performance. However, adaptability and flexibility per se do not guarantee victory. Superior quality militaries can lose wars, and have done so. In fact, the history of modern warfare indicates that overwhelming numerical superiority typically prevails in the long run over a more militarily effective opponent. Armed forces can rarely sustain sufficient battlefield superiority in the long run, because of the very process of adaptation, to outweigh a significant numerical or material inferiority.[10]

The quest for military effectiveness and the importance of flexible armed forces capable of rapid adaptation is of greater significance today than ever before as we enter the new millenium. In the destabilizing post–Cold War era the ability of military establishments to adapt rapidly to unanticipated threats, despite downsizing and financial stringency, is not only at an unprecedented premium, it may well even be the defining factor in national security in the twenty-first century. The recent information revolution has engendered a new bout of rapid military innovation that appears bound to continue into the next century. At the same time, the international community has entered a new era where strategic and political threats are more indeterminate. Military institutions must innovate with much less funding, within greater uncertainty, and in the face of rapid technological change.

The experience of past conflicts can provide valuable pointers to the militaries of tomorrow. However, despite its significance, historians have only recently begun to examine the issues of how and with what success the combatants adapted and innovated during World War II. Moreover, much of the scholarship that has sought to evaluate the performance and military effectiveness of the protagonists is unsatisfactory. Not only have few studies been comparative in nature, but various forces have distorted existing scholarship in a number of significant ways.[11] First, since 1945 scholars have extolled the military capabilities of the World War II German army—the *Heer.* This process began with the eyewitness memoirs that deluged the English-speaking world early in the Cold War.

Allied memoirs acknowledged, typically with grudging admiration, the battlefield superiority of German soldiers over Western Allied troops. This trend toward inflating German military capabilities gained momentum as Anglo-American histories of World War II became refracted through a lens imposed by the ideological imperatives of the Cold War. These imperatives led Anglo-American historians to downplay the brutality of the war, to sanitize the conflict, and to extoll German military prowess at a time when the West desperately sought to rehabilitate a new democratic, rearmed West Germany as a bulwark against communism. During the Cold War the

Western Allies quickly forgot, even repudiated, wartime principles. The Western Allies rehabilitated alleged war criminals who were valuable in the war against communism, played down the enormous Soviet sacrifices that had guaranteed Allied victory, and largely accepted without scholarly challenge the unrepentant and distorted apologia of nazi generals for their genocidal struggle against bolshevism and European Jewry.[12]

The Cold War need to counter and undermine communism thus subtly distorted Anglo-American interpretations of World War II. These imperatives led historians to inflate German battlefield skill and to focus blame for Germany's defeat on Hitler, thereby denigrating Soviet military effectiveness and minimizing its decisive contribution to Allied victory.[13] Cold War scholarship, therefore, extolled the martial achievements of the wartime *Heer:* quantitative analysis concluded that on a man-to-man and unit-to-unit basis the Germans consistently outfought their opponents.[14] In toto scholarship created an image of a mighty German army skilled in operational art, tactics, and fieldcraft.[15] Some political commentators even went so far as to argue that the World War II German army offered a paradigm of military effectiveness.[16]

Such evaluations are both narrowly focused and unbalanced because they fail to present a comprehensive evaluation of the *Heer* as a fighting force. What existing scholarship has often overlooked is that Germany had to outfight its enemies because its leaders had committed the nation to war against overwhelming, and ultimately insurmountable, odds. Thus the German Army throughout the 1919–1945 period structured itself to maximize its immediate combat power. But such an orientation had its price, which was the *Heer*'s inadequate staying power: the German army maximized its immediate combat power only at the expense of its underlying strategic and logistic base.[17]

Moreover, comparing the *Heer* and its opponents at any fixed point in time during the war is inherently misleading because Germany had begun rearmament several years before its opponents. A more balanced assessment would compare armies at the peak of their efficiency and accomplishments. A comparison between the 1941 *Heer* and the 1945 U.S. Army, for example, narrows considerably the performance gap.[18] For, as this book illustrates, during the latter stages of the war the U.S. Army did not simply overwhelm an increasingly outnumbered enemy but ultimately learned to outfight it too.[19]

The Cold War distorted Western understanding of the character of the German military in other significant ways. The need to rehabilitate West Germany as a bastion against communism also led historians to deemphasize the impact and role of nazi ideology within the German military. During the Cold War, Anglo-American historians readily accepted the claims of former German generals that most of the German military remained both apolitical and innocent of atrocities that were supposedly committed by a minority of Nazi fanatics. Until the emergence of the new military history in the 1970s and 1980s, scholarship presented a sanitized view of the German armed forces as a thoroughly professional and largely apolitical military force.[20] The West's need to present a united front against communism also muted critical Anglo-American appraisal of Allied wartime combat effectiveness. The authors of the numerous Allied official histories, for example, were generally selected because of their sympathy toward their own respective military institutions and their aims, values, and reputations. Thus the official histories often lacked critical analysis of Allied performance.[21]

The end of the Cold War in the late 1980s has finally allowed historians to reexamine World War II divorced from the Cold War's ideological imperatives. Historical understanding of the war began to change in three significant ways. First, fueled by the opening of Soviet archives, historians have begun to reevaluate—and reemphasize—the enormous Soviet contribution to Allied victory. Recent scholarship has emphasized the Red Army's adaptability and growing combat effectiveness and has demonstrated that the war on the Eastern Front was far less one-sided than the German generals had us believe.[22] Second, historians also began to present more balanced assessments of the character, capabilities, and effectiveness of the *Heer.* Recent scholarship has stressed the continuity of poor German strategic planning and decisionmaking throughout the 1914–1945 period and the weakness of German battlefield intelligence.[23] New studies have also reemphasized the role of ideology, and specifically the pervasiveness of nazism, within the German military.[24] Recent research on the Eastern Front, for instance, has illustrated the process of intense nazification that occurred to condition the *Heer* for an ideological and racial war of extermination. These studies have demonstrated that most of the German army in the east, the *Ostheer,* either directly participated in, or were complicit in, nazi atrocities.[25]

Third, historians have begun to reappraise the performance and combat effectiveness of the Western Allies. Recent works have thus been much more critical of Allied performance than the official histories.[26] These studies have emphasized the Allies muddling through to victory via overwhelming resources and massive firepower.[27] Yet this scholarship has largely failed to differentiate among the relative combat capabilities of the U.S., British, and Canadian militaries. Only in the past five years has pioneering research suggested that the U.S. Army adapted more quickly and better, and therefore ultimately performed more effectively than its Anglo-Canadian counterparts.[28]

Another major weakness of the existing literature on World War II is that few works have attempted to integrate analysis of the effectiveness of military organizations into operational narratives. How, for example, did doctrine, tactics, organization, and manpower policies actually affect the course of combat on the Normandy battlefield? The character, conduct, and outcome of any campaign can only be understood with reference to the organization, military thought, culture, doctrine, equipment, training, and leadership of the protagonists as forged by historical experience and refined by the ordeal of war.

The second part of this study thus evaluates the performance of the U.S., British, Canadian, and German militaries in the 1944 Normandy Campaign. This was the major campaign of the war in the European theater and it tested the efficacy of each combatant's preparation as well as their ability to adapt in the field. These chapters explore how prevailing doctrine, tactics, equipment, organization, and manpower policies—the sum of each armed forces preparation—shaped the outcome of the struggle, while simultaneously examining the actual process of adaptation by the combatants on the Normandy battlefield.

The 1944 Normandy Campaign is a particularly appropriate case study through which to examine the theme of wartime military adaptation. During its time span two non-European powers, the United States and the Soviet Union, eclipsed the European great powers and emerged as the two superpowers of the postwar era. The Normandy campaign, therefore, witnessed not only the defeat of Nazi Germany but also the decline of Europe. Great Britain, while ostensibly a victor, effectively emerged from the war a loser, a fate starkly illuminated by the 1956 Suez debacle. The second front thus represented Britain's last opportunity during the war to preserve at least a semblance of its former greatness through feats of arms on the battlefield. The Normandy Campaign, therefore, offers an excellent case study of institutional barriers to flexibility and the historical importance of adaptability for the effective preservation of national security.

Moreover, existing literature on the Normandy Campaign reflects the prevailing deficiencies in the scholarship on World War II. Two special limitations plague the voluminous literature on the campaign. The first is the lack of scholarly comparative analysis of Allied performance in Normandy. Indeed, a "British school" has powerfully informed Anglo-American scholarship on the campaign. This school has elevated British accomplishments, exaggerated the success of Field Marshal Montgomery's theater strategy, and criticized the American effort for amateurism and for failing to heed the advice of the more experienced British.[29]

The second limitation is the unsatisfactory character of literature on the German defense of the west. Anglo-American works are often either poorly grounded in primary research, or else the credibility of the sources is suspect.[30] Other scholarship is problematic because its avowed purpose is an explanation of German defeat—and no military looks good in defeat. Historians have thus focused on supposed German combat weaknesses without concomitant attention to the grave logistic deficiencies that were, as this book illustrates, central to German defeat.[31] German literature, on the other hand, sometimes fails to rise above nazi apologia. Recently, Omer Bartov has illustrated how defeat led German Eastern Front veterans to revise and to rewrite their perceptions of that struggle. It is evident that a complex mix of defeatism, fear, admiration, and bitterness similarly distorted German recollections of the Normandy Campaign.

Several major conclusions underpin this project. The first is that the 1944 Normandy Campaign offers a paradigm of military adaptability. This study concludes that—contrary to conventional wisdom—the U.S. military proved more flexible than its Anglo-Canadian allies and thus generally adapted more quickly and more effectively. Consistently, U.S. forces rapidly and accurately identified deficiencies that hampered their performance. Just as quickly, through trial and error, American troops devised solutions to the problems that confronted them, disseminated these lessons learned, and retrained in the field during ongoing combat operations to enhance combat effectiveness.

The study also contends that the institutional flexibility of the U.S. military was an important ingredient in Allied victory in Normandy. For the Anglo-American armies early in the war were far from being war-winning instruments, and even in June 1944 their combat power remained limited. By the end of the Normandy Campaign the U.S. military had developed an all-around military proficiency. Conventional wisdom maintains that the Americans prevailed through overwhelming superiority rather than skill. This study's findings, however, confirm the conclusions of recent scholarship that the U.S. Army became increasingly skilled and perfected its mastery of both combined-arms warfare and of the air-land battle during the Normandy Campaign.[32] The book thus concludes that the flexibility and creativity of the U.S. military played an important role in the transformation in the global balance of power that resulted from World War II.

A second major conclusion is that the tenacity of the German defense of Normandy must also be explained in ideological terms. This study contends that conventional interpretations of the campaign are unbalanced because they deemphasize the role of ideology. In reality two German armies fought in the west: one, a cohesive core of nazified Eastern Front veterans fleshed out with equally indoctrinated young volunteers and recruits; the other, an older occupation army bypassed by the indoctrination experienced in the east and softened by four years of comfortable garrison duty and higher neglect. This study also concludes that it is inappropriate to view the World War II German army as a paradigm of military effectiveness. The evidence demonstrates that logistic deficiencies and ideological prejudices played a major role in the German defeat in Normandy. This work thus reintegrates ideology into our understanding of the character of the German military and illustrates that nazi ideology powerfully shaped German planning and preparation for, as well as conduct of, the Normandy Campaign. In reality, nazism proved a double-edged sword in terms of

German military effectiveness. It imbued German resistance with tenacity, but it also bred racial arrogance that led Germans to inflate their own capabilities and to underestimate those of their enemies. In sum, nazi ideology hampered German adaptation throughout the war.

The study also illustrates that considerable integration both between nations and services ultimately characterized the Allied war effort, but that integration between individual arms of those services proved most problematic because this was where parochialism was strongest. It also illustrates that among the Axis forces the reverse was true. Nazi Germany proved least effective at strategic cooperation with its Axis partners; German interservice coordination remained poor; and only within services—and most notably in the army—was coordination good. The net effect of this was that the Allies possessed considerable all-around strength, while German strength remained narrowly limited to its army, and even more narrowly to the effectiveness of its armored forces, the soundness of its doctrine and equipment, the quality of its training, and the professionalism of its officer corps. While confirming an overall German tactical and operational superiority, German excellence was nonetheless narrowly confined to battlefield performance and further restricted to a battle-hardened elite. In the fields of strategy, logistics, and intelligence the German army's effectiveness was poor indeed. Ultimately these larger weaknesses outweighed the German military's limited strengths.[33]

This book also offers generalized conclusions about the nature of wartime adaptation and its connection to military effectiveness. It illustrates that the most difficult dimension for adaptation is at the strategic and doctrinal levels. This study demonstrates that militaries whose peacetime doctrines are essentially sound can adapt, given sufficient combat exposure and in the absence of major defeat. Where an armed service's basic doctrine, however, lacks fundamental soundness—as was the case with the British and Canadian Armies between the wars—not only is effective adaptation less likely, defeat may follow. Without modification of fundamentally flawed doctrine, improvements in organization, training, tactics, and weaponry can only bring incremental improvement in combat effectiveness.[34] This reality helps account for the relatively slower pace of effective adaptation in the Anglo-Canadian armies of World War II.

The factors that contribute to and the processes involved in innovation are inherently difficult to discern, and few patterns, let alone a model, are discernible because innovation is complex and ambiguous.[35] By exploring the strategic framework, organizational structures, and doctrine of each army, it becomes apparent that a complex blend of personalities, intellectual trends, societal influences, and societal standing of the military affects innovation.[36] Yet in the absence of an overwhelming demographic or industrial superiority, victory in modern warfare belongs to the armed forces that learn most quickly and most effectively from their mistakes and adapt to new environments, refining doctrine, improving weapons, and modifying tactics in the process. The triumph of the Allies in World War II demonstrates this reality. Although constant German adaptation and innovation delayed defeat and increased the price of victory, the Allies progressively enhanced their combat effectiveness during the war to erode the qualitative edge the Germans possessed in 1939. Ultimately the law of numbers prevailed, and Allied numerical and material superiority overwhelmed Nazi Germany. At the same time, the considerable flexibility and adaptability exhibited by the U.S. military played an important role in the Allied triumph over the evil of National Socialism. For during the last year of the war the U.S. Army did not simply overwhelm an increasingly outnumbered and outgunned enemy, but it learned on the battlefields of Normandy to outfight the nazi war machine.

Notes

1. J. F. C. Fuller, *Memoirs of an Unconventional Soldier* (London: Ivor Nicholson & Watson, 1936), 151.

2. Dwight D. Eisenhower, memo of 20 November 1947 quoted in Martin Blumenson, "Can Official History be Honest History," in Robin Higham, ed., *The Official Histories: Essays and Bibliographies from Around the World* (Manhattan: Kansas University Press, 1970), 40.

3. Michael Howard, "Military Science in the Age of Peace," *Journal of the Royal United Services Institute* 119 (March 1974), 3–9.

4. Timothy Lupfer, *The Dynamics of Doctrine: The Development of German Defensive Doctrine during the First World War* (Fort Leavenworth: Combat Studies Institute, 1981); Timothy Travers, *The Killing Ground: The British Army, the Western Front, and the Emergence of Modern Warfare, 1900–1918* (London: Allen & Unwin, 1987); and *How the War Was Won: Command and Technology in the British Army on the Western Front, 1917–1918* (London: Routledge, 1992); Bruce Gudmundsson, *Stormtroop Tactics: Innovation in the German Army, 1914–1918* (New York: Praeger, 1989); David T. Zabecki, *Steel Wind: Col. Georg Bruchmüller and the Birth of Modern Artillery* (Westport, Conn.: Praeger, 1994); Hubert C. Johnson, *Breakthrough: Tactics, Technology, and the Search for Victory on the Western Front in World War I* (Novato, Calif.: Presidio Press, 1994).

5. "Innovation: an Introduction," in Allan R. Millett and Williamson Murray, eds., *Innovation in the Interwar Period* (Washington, D.C.: Office of Net Assessment, Department of Defense, 1994), iv-vi.

6. Allan R. Millett and Williamson Murray, eds., *Military Effectiveness* (Boston: Allen & Unwin, 1988) 3 vols.; John Cushman, *Challenge and Response: Military Effectiveness, 1914–1945* (Washington, D.C.: National Defense University, 1988).

7. Military culture is best defined as the sum of the intellectual, cultural, social, professional, and traditional values of an officer corps.

8. Robert H. Larson, *The British Army and the Theory of Armoured Warfare, 1918–1940* (Newark: University of Delaware Press, 1984); Brian Bond, *British Military Policy Between the Two World Wars* (Oxford: Clarendon Press, 1980).

9. Burton H. Klein, *Germany's Economic Preparations for War* (Cambridge, Mass.: Harvard University Press, 1957); Alan Milward, *The German Economy at*

War (London: Athlone Press, 1965); Larry Addington, *The Blitzkrieg Era and the German General Staff, 1865–1941* (New Brunswick, N.J.: Rutgers University Press, 1971); James S. Corum, *The Roots of Blitzkrieg: Hans von Seeckt and German Military Reform* (Lawrence: Kansas University Press, 1992); Jehuda L. Wallach, *The Dogma of the Battle of Annihilation: The Theories of Clausewitz and Schlieffen and Their Impact on the German Conduct of Two World Wars* (Westport, Conn.: Greenwood Press, 1986).

10. Millett and Murray, *Military Effectiveness,* passim.

11. Martin van Creveld's *Fighting Power: American and German Army Performances in the Second World War* (Westport, Conn.: Greenwood, 1978) compares American and German performance but unduly focuses on organizational aspects. The notable exception is Millett and Murray, *Military Effectiveness,* which examines the military effectiveness of twelve nations in the period 1914–1945. For bias in World War II scholarship, see John Keegan, *The Battle for History: Re-fighting World War II* (New York: Vintage Books, 1996).

12. Heinz Guderian, *Panzer Leader* (London: Joseph, 1952); Erich von Manstein, *Lost Victories* (Chicago: H. Regency Co., 1958); Friedrich von Mellenthin, *Panzer Battles: A Study of the Employment of Armor in the Second World War* (London: Cassell, 1955); Frido von Senger und Etterlin, *Neither Fear nor Hope* (London: Macdonald, 1960).

13. The classic example of this is Earl Ziemke's *Stalingrad to Berlin: German Defeat in the East, 1943–45* (Washington, D.C.: Government Printing Office, 1968).

14. Trevor Dupuy's quantitative evaluation of the performance of World War II combatants contended that on a man-to-man and unit-to-unit basis the Germans consistently outfought their opponents. Trevor N. Dupuy, *Numbers, Predictions, and War* (Englewood Cliffs, N.J.: Prentice-Hall, 1977).

15. Max Hastings, *OVERLORD: The Battle for Normandy* (London: Joseph, 1984); Creveld, *Fighting Power,* passim.

16. Trevor N. Dupuy, "The Current Implications of German Military Excellence," *Strategic Review* 4, 4 (Fall 1976).

17. Williamson Murray, *The Change in the European Balance of Power: The Path to Ruin* (Princeton, N.J.: Princeton University Press, 1984).

18. Peter Mansoor, "Building Blocks of Victory: American Infantry Divisions in the War Against Germany and Italy, 1941–45," Ph.D. thesis, Ohio State University, 1995, 9–11; John Desch, "The 1941 German Army/The 1944–45 U.S. Army: A Comparative Analysis of Two Forces in Their Primes," *Command Magazine* 18 (September–October 1992), 54–63.

19. Michael Doubler, *Busting the Bocage* (Fort Leavenworth: U.S. Army General Staff and Command College, 1988); and *Closing with the Enemy: How G.I.s Fought the War in Europe, 1944–45* (Lawrence: Kansas University Press, 1994); Peter Mansoor, "The Development of Combat Effective Divisions in the U.S. Army During World War II," M.A. thesis, Ohio State University, 1992; and "Building Blocks of Victory," Ph.D. thesis, Ohio State University, 1995.

20. Manstein, *Lost Victories,* passim; Guderian, *Panzer Leader,* passim; von Mellenthin, *Panzer Battles,* passim.

21. For discussion of the issues involved in writing official history, see Martin Blumenson, "Can Official History Be Honest History?" in Higham, ed., *Official Histories,* 38–47; Sir J. R. M. Butler, "The British Military Histories of the War of 1939-45," ibid., 511–515; Kent R. Greenfield, "Scholarship and the U.S. Army in World War II," ibid., 551–552; B. H. Liddell Hart, "Responsibility and Judgement in Historical Writing," *Military Affairs* (Spring 1959), 35–36.

22. Recent scholarship on the Eastern Front has emphasized rapid Soviet

adaptation in operational art and excellence in battlefield intelligence and deception, thus questioning the long assumed German battlefield superiority. David Glantz, *Soviet Military Deception in the Second World War* (London: F. Cass, 1989); *Soviet Military Intelligence in War* (London: Cass, 1990); *From Don to the Dnepr: Soviet Offensive Operations, December 1942–August 1943* (London: Cass, 1990); David Glantz and Jonathon M. House, *When Titans Clashed* (Lawrence: University of Kansas Press, 1995); Walter S. Dunn, Jr., *Hitler's Nemesis: The Red Army, 1930–1945* (Westport, Conn.: Praeger, 1994).

23. See Millett and Murray, *Military Effectiveness,* passim; Cushman, *Challenge and Response,* passim; and David Glantz, *Soviet Military Deception,* passim.

24. Klaus Jürgen Müller, *Das Heer und Hitler: Armee und national-sozialistisches Regime, 1933–1940* (Stuttgart: Deutsche-Verlags Anstalt, 1969); Christian Streit, *Keine Kameraden: die Wehrmacht und die sowjetischen Kriegsgefangenen, 1941–45* (Stuttgart: Deutsche-Verlags Anstalt, 1978); Omer Bartov, "Indoctrination and Motivation in the Wehrmacht: the Importance of the Unquantifiable," *Journal of Strategic Studies* (March 1986), 16–34; *The Eastern Front and the Barbarization of Warfare* (New York: St. Martin's, 1988) and *Hitler's Army: Soldiers, Nazis, and the Third Reich* (Oxford: Oxford University Press, 1991); Hannes Heer and Klaus Naumann, *Vernichtungskrieg: Verbrechen der Wehrmacht, 1941–1944* (Hamburg: Hamburger Edition, 1995).

25. Historians have generalized about the ideological character of the entire German military based on these few, narrow works on the *Ostheer.* Yet no exploration of the ideological character of any other wartime German Army has yet emerged. For the available literature see note 24 above.

26. Russell Weigley, *Eisenhower's Lieutenants* (Bloomington: Indiana University Press, 1982); Max Hastings, *OVERLORD: The Battle for Normandy* (London: Joseph, 1984); John English, *The Canadians in Normandy: A Study of Failure in High Command* (Toronto: Praeger, 1990).

27. John Ellis, *Brute Force: Allied Strategy and Tactics in World War II* (New York: Viking Press, 1990).

28. John Sloan Brown, *Draftee Division: The 88th Infantry Division in World War II* (Lexington, Ky.: University Press of Kentucky, 1986); Doubler, *Busting the Bocage* and *Closing with the Enemy;* Mansoor, "The Creation of Combat Effective Divisions"; and "Building Blocks of Victory."

29. John Keegan's *Six Armies in Normandy,* one of the few comparative works on the campaign, is flawed by its reliance on secondary sources. Exponents of this British school include Bernard L. Montgomery, *Memoirs* (London: Hutchinson, 1947); Chester Wilmot, *The Struggle for Europe* (London: 1952); Henry Maule, *Caen: The Brutal Battle* (London: Purnell, 1976); John J. Sweet, *Mounting the Threat: The Battle of Bourguébus Ridge, 18–23 July 1944* (San Rafael, Calif.: Presidio Press, 1977); J. J. How, *Normandy: The British Breakout* (London: W. Kimber, 1981); John Keegan *Six Armies in Normandy* (New York: Viking, 1982).

30. Scholars have, for example, extensively relied on translated postwar German prisoner of war accounts, most of which were written from memory and often contain glaring errors. Moreover, the reports reflect a spectrum of biases from unrepentant nazi apologia and self-serving hagiography to fawning ingratiation. In addition, the quality of translation was typically poor. Alan Wilt's excellent *Hitler's Atlantic Wall* (Ames: Iowa University Press, 1975) is well grounded in primary research but only analyzes the German defenses rather than the army that manned them.

31. See the author's "Feeding Mars: The Role of Logistics in the German Defeat in Normandy, 1944," *War in History* 3, 4 (Fall 1996), 418–435.

32. Brown, *Draftee Division;* Doubler, *Busting the Bocage* and *Closing with the Enemy;* Mansoor, "The Creation of Combat Effective Divisions," and "Building Blocks of Victory."

33. Millett and Murray, *Military Effectiveness;* Charles Cruickshanks, *Deception in World War II* (Oxford: Oxford University Press, 1979); Martin van Creveld, *Supplying War: Logistics from Wallenstein to Patton* (Cambridge: Cambridge University Press, 1977); Glantz, *Soviet Military Deception in the Second World War.*

34. Recent scholarship has demonstrated how flawed doctrine was central to both French defeat in 1940 and the American failure in Vietnam. Robert Doughty, *The Seeds of Disaster: The Development of French Army Doctrine, 1919–1939* (Hamden, Conn.: Archon Books, 1985); Andrew F. Krepinevitch, *The Army and Vietnam* (Baltimore: Johns Hopkins University, 1986).

35. Stephen P. Rosen, *Winning the Next War: Innovation and the Modern Military* (Ithaca, N.Y.: Cornell University Press, 1991), 1–53.

36. Williamson Murray, "Armoured Warfare: the British, French, and German Experiences," in Millett and Murray, eds., *Innovation in the Interwar Period,* 4.

PART 1

Preparation: 1919–1944

1

The Interwar Period

The United States

The American struggle for independence bred an innate distrust of military institutions and a belief that martial values were alien to American democracy. Thus, historically, armed forces have had an ambiguous position in American society and a standing army only emerged in the early nineteenth century after bitter political struggle.[1] Thereafter, cultural distrust of the military combined with prevailing notions of governmental thrift ensured that the United States maintained only a small, neglected peacetime army prior to World War II. Historically, the United States, safe in its geographic isolation, forwent large, expensive military forces and accepted the risks that this entailed as it relied instead on mobilizing its great demographic and industrial strength when confronted with imminent war.

The United States also had limited military experience. Between its foundation and World War II, the nation fought nine wars, few of which were long or costly, though peacetime neglect sometimes brought initial reverses. Even World War I was not a total war for the nation; the late entry into the conflict in April 1917 ensured that it was not until late 1918 that U.S. ground forces took significant offensive action in the Meuse-Argonne campaign. Rather, the army's most enduring experience was of policing the frontier and Indian fighting. Indeed, the only event to prepare the army at all for total war was the Civil War (1861–1865). These contrasting experiences of frontier skirmishing and bitter civil strife shaped a unique American way of war in the twentieth century.[2]

During the 1920s, the country reverted to isolationism in the belief that its geographic separation and economic self-sufficiency protected it from external threat. Thus the nation demobilized in 1919 and thereafter maintained minimal ground forces for domestic defense and to preserve civil order. Yet the interwar U.S. political environment made the maintenance of effective military forces all but impossible as successive Republican presidents pursued "sound business principles" of low taxation and low government expenditure and downsized the military, a process greatly accelerated by the Great Depression of the 1930s. Moreover, the government directed most of its meager defense funds to the navy, the country's traditional first line of defense. The interwar army thus suffered such unprecedented neglect that it became less combat ready than at any time in its history.[3]

The 1920 National Defense Act (NDA) established a 280,000-strong regular army of nine infantry and two cavalry divisions backed by the Organized Reserves and the National Guard. Underfunding ensured that the army could not even maintain this modest establishment. It remained at half strength for most of the interwar period, while the neglect of the Reserves and National Guard left them totally unfit for modern war. Financial stringency also forced the army to adopt desperate and pernicious economy measures. It reduced commissioned and noncommissioned officers in grade, rationed fuel, curtailed training and maneuvers, and slashed unit establishments. Such economy inexorably sapped combat effectiveness.[4]

At the same time, doctrinal controversy, which divided the interwar army between competing doctrines of annihilation and of mobility, further limited the army's combat effectiveness. Basic doctrine emphasized hard fighting as the key to victory, since the military's experience suggested that the only proven way to defeat an enemy was to destroy its army through the application of mass and concentration as had General Grant during the Civil War and General Pershing in the Great War. Doctrine thus advocated a strategy of annihilation. While the army's tactics and organization emphasized such application of mass and overwhelming power to crush the enemy in battle, its weapons and training reflected its tradition of frontier fighting and were thus more suited for tactics of mobility and maneuver.[5]

Doctrine reflected the nation's military experience and thus was offensive in orientation. But limited combat experience ensured that neither doctrine nor tactics emphasized speed, surprise, or rapid exploitation. The art of deception was virtually nonexistent, and tactics did not seek to exploit specific enemy weaknesses. Interwar doctrine also upheld 1914–1918 conceptions of combined-arms coordination that viewed infantry as dominant and armor and artillery as supporting arms. Based on its Great War experience, the U.S. Army was well aware of the theoretical need to integrate arms, units, and weapon systems on the modern battlefield. It proved far more difficult, however, for the interwar army to decide exactly what missions arms of service, types of units, and weapons would have in future war, let alone put theory into practice.

The biggest difficulty the interwar army faced, though, was that it gained no practical experience with which to test the validity of its doctrine, organization, and tactics. Inevitably, therefore, the audit of war during World War II demonstrated that the doctrine was flawed. However, central to the wartime army's eventual military effectiveness was that combat revealed that most of its doctrine was basically sound because, unlike Great Britain, the United States had both examined and preserved its Great War experience. Thus the deficiencies that remained could be—and largely were—corrected during the course of the war.

Controversy also raged in the interwar army over the future role of mechanized forces and of air power. During 1918–1920 the U.S. Army had fielded its own Tank Corps, but the NDA abolished it and reassigned armor to the infantry. This decision and the limited experience of tank warfare during World War I hindered development of armored doctrine between the wars.[6] In the late 1920s, the army emulated the British Experimental Mechanized Force (EMF) and created the 7th Cavalry Brigade (Mechanized). As in Britain, the U.S. military initially envisaged mechanized cavalry as fulfilling traditional cavalry roles of reconnaissance and exploitation. However, unlike the British EMF, the 7th Cavalry Brigade became permanent and, despite severely limited manpower, equipment, and funding, demonstrated the potential of armored forces to carry out independent operations.[7] At the same time, the offensive orientation of U.S. doctrine enabled the army to assimilate tanks into existing doctrine more effectively than Britain proved able to. However, even though the army recognized the potential of armor between the wars, resource constraints denied it an effective tank force prior to 1941. These limits also ensured that the army lacked antitank capability; it remained wedded to the outdated belief that artillery should provide antitank defense, which stifled development both of antitank weapons and of effective means of employing them.[8]

Unlike the Tank Corps, the U.S. Army Air Corps (USAAC) survived and developed as a distinct organization between the wars. Its interwar quest for independence not only left it reluctant to cooperate with the ground army, but led its adherents to push the independent strategic potential of air power at the expense of the tactical support of ground forces. Thus it remained committed to building up a force of long-range heavy bombers to attack enemy industry and destroy its warmaking potential. While it gave some thought and resources to battlefield interdiction, the USAAC made almost no preparation for close air support of ground forces between the wars. So at the outbreak of World War II, the USAAC was largely incapable of directly assisting U.S. ground forces on the battlefield.[9] Its failure to develop a tactical support capability reflected that while accepting in principle the need for integration of arms within services, the interwar U.S. armed forces remained hostile to interservice coordination and cooperation, a reality reflected in the largely unimpressive joint exercises the services occasionally held between the wars.[10]

If the army's combat branches suffered badly between the wars, its support services deteriorated even further. Alongside the inevitable decline in logistic capabilities caused by financial cutbacks, the army had to contend with the disdainful attitude of many combat officers toward support services. In consequence, between the wars the army utterly lacked the logistic base for extended overseas operations. Throughout the 1920s and 1930s the army also faced serious manpower problems. Officer quality declined because low pay and slow promotion forced many talented officers to resign; and some that remained lost their edge and neglected their professional development. Slow promotion also created an elderly officer corps. Thus at the start of World War II, many army officers were of questionable competence and physical condition. At the same time, poor pay and societal distrust of the military meant that the army experienced even greater difficulty recruiting enlisted men. The Depression temporarily ended the army's recruitment difficulties but by the late 1930s the army once again experienced problems in obtaining sufficient volunteers.[11]

The army also had a poor training record between the wars as economy sapped the quality of instruction and led to the abandonment of multidivision maneuvers. As a result, U.S. troops were simply too poorly trained to conduct mobile offensive warfare. In the absence of realistic threats to U.S. security, the interwar army possessed negligible capabilities and could not even properly defend the country's coastlines, let alone project military power overseas. Since at no point between the wars did the army conceive of its mission as involving combat in Europe, the military undertook no planning or preparation for a European war.[12]

Despite these many obstacles to the maintenance of effective military forces, the interwar army possessed several strengths that allowed it to improve rapidly its wartime combat effectiveness. A key strength was the army's intellectual vitality and creativity as military thought continued to develop at service schools between the wars. Indeed, the U.S. armed forces displayed originality and flexibility in adapting new weapons and technology despite severe budgetary constraints.[13] Fort Knox, Kentucky, developed basic mechanized warfare principles that stood the test of time and the Field Artillery School at Fort Sill, Oklahoma, made equally important advances in fire direction techniques, including the use of forward observers and modern radio communications, which allowed massed artillery fire far more rapid than was possible in World War I.[14] This creativity extended to weapons too: the army developed a rugged 105mm howitzer and the Garand rifle, both of which saw service throughout World War II. At the same time, the Signal Corps developed radar as advanced as any in the world, while the Christie suspension resulted in some of the fastest tanks produced between the wars. The U.S. armed forces' most notable interwar advances occurred in communications intelligence, particularly code breaking.[15]

The armed services achieved these technological and tactical innovations despite severe fiscal restraints that often meant weapons and equipment for these emerging operational doctrines either did not exist or existed only in rudimentary form. This record of intellectual vitality and technical adaptation reflected the interwar army's resourcefulness and ingenuity in the face of adversity. Despite enormous obstacles that prevented maintenance of combat effective ground forces between the wars, the military culture exhibited a creativity and flexibility that augured well for the challenges of war that awaited it.[16] Nonetheless, when war broke out in Europe in September 1939, the U.S. Army remained small, understrength, underequipped, and outdated in equipment, organization, and doctrine. Only three of twenty-seven divisions were at all battleworthy, and even these remained at half-strength. Divisional organization was bulky and unwieldy. The army had only a single tank brigade and lacked antitank capability; it also had no clear operating procedures with air power.[17] As a result, in September 1939 the United States was incapable of deploying and supporting its land forces overseas.

Great Britain

Britain's maritime location and imperial aspirations ensured that its army chiefly fought small, uncostly wars in distant territories during much of its history. In 1914, however, Britain sent an expeditionary force to France and was drawn into the bloodiest and most devastating conflict in its history. The Great War cast a shadow that profoundly shaped the development of the British Army throughout the 1919–1945 period. Indeed, the legacies of this conflict hampered the army's performance throughout World War II and contributed directly to the dramatic string of military reverses that Britain suffered between 1939 and 1942.

Although the British Army had distinguished itself in World War I— first with its stoic defense and then with the offensive actions that defeated the German Army on the Western Front in 1918—operationally it proved slow to learn and found tactical effectiveness elusive. British operations were rigid and inflexible, and rarely used surprise.[18] The army's command structure hampered reevaluation of prevailing doctrine and tactics and thus it adapted at an incremental rate. The pace of innovation picked up during 1917–1918 as reform slowly emerged, largely from the bottom up. As a result, the army underwent a partial tactical revolution in 1918, though reform remained piecemeal. Thus, by 1918 the army had mastered the break-in battle but not the breakout.[19]

The root cause of the slow pace of change was the absence of a British doctrine of war.[20] Lacking doctrine, the army fought doggedly in defense but struggled to master the offense. Moreover, the army's class-oriented and hierarchical culture promoted loyalty above honesty, thus hampering appraisal of performance. Training too was unsophisticated and did little to foster the independence and initiative required for innovation.[21] At the same time, the army's regimental system promoted parochialism that hampered battlefield cooperation by infantry, cavalry, and gunners. The army learned the fundamental principles of modern warfare slowly, and at great cost, on the fields of Flanders.

The legacies of World War I powerfully shaped British strategy, operations, and performance throughout World War II. The Great War had been a disillusioning, misleading, and costly experience for Britain, and it left the nation not only economically and financially weakened but psychologically scarred. Most significant of all, the interwar army never escaped the haunting psychological legacies of the slaughter in the trenches as the British people discovered after the war the true cost of the terrible battles of attrition that had preceded final victory. Defense and casualty conservation— the avoidance of undue losses—became the twin pillars of British strategic and operational thought throughout the 1919–1945 period.

The material, psychological, and strategic legacies of the Great War, as well as the social and political character of interwar Britain, created a climate hostile both to the maintenance of combat effective forces or to military reform.[22] The war had significantly eroded Britain's economic, demographic, and military strength, precipitating both massive demobilization after 1919 and sweeping cuts in defense spending.[23]

The slaughter in the trenches had a profound psychological impact on interwar Britain. An intellectual crisis, manifested in pacifism, wracked the nation. Society questioned whether Britain had really emerged victorious from the Great War, and such profound doubts led to widespread questioning of whether force could solve the disputes inherent in international relations. Many Britons placed undue faith in the ability of the nascent League of Nations to resolve international disputes peacefully. Thus was born the "never again" ethos, an instinctual rejection of the wisdom of preparing for another major war. Pacifism and the "never again" sentiment forced the services to justify not only defense spending but even their very existence. Popular antimilitarism between the wars fueled both defense cuts and a climate inimical to military reform.

Domestic political concerns also contributed to Britain's reluctance to fund defense between the wars.[24] The ideological antimilitarism of the Labour and Liberal parties and the Conservative Party's credo of commercial growth and limited government all promoted defense cuts. Such government parsimony led to the introduction of the Ten Year Rule in 1919, which mandated that defense estimates be framed on the assumption that there was no likelihood of war for the following ten years. The implementation of the rule stifled preparation, crippled Britain's armaments industry, and contributed directly to the decline in British military efficiency. It was impossible for the army to maintain its effectiveness.[25]

The Great War also had significant strategic ramifications as Britain abandoned the costly continental commitment it had undertaken in 1914 and reverted to the maritime strategy that had formed earlier British foreign policy.[26] Such a policy relied on continental allies and economic blockade by the Royal Navy as Britain's first line of defense; the army reverted to policing the empire. But to defend the empire required a large fleet and, after 1918, also an air force, which left insufficient defense allocations to maintain a sizeable home army for continental service. Indeed, commentators argued that a continued continental commitment would actually reduce Britain's independence by tying Britain to French strategy.

Britain's interwar strategic and international policies, therefore, profoundly shaped the condition, character, and capabilities of its army. The abandonment of a continental commitment left the army with no clear mission between the wars, and controversy thus raged within it as to what role it should prepare for. The army's lack of a clear mission hindered the maintenance of effective combat forces in the United Kingdom between the wars. Imperial policing compartmentalized and dispersed the army in garrisons around the globe and reduced the home army merely to service overseas garrisons. It lacked balance, mobility, or the capability for rapid deployment to the continent. Moreover, expanded British overseas commitments in the 1920s stretched the army even thinner.[27] Finally, this system made it difficult for the army to concentrate a field force in Britain in the late 1930s in response to rising German and Italian threats.

Interwar British governments, the Treasury, much of the army, and most of the public thus opposed contingency planning for another continental commitment between the wars. In the face of political and popular sentiment, it was impossible for the army to forge any kind of expeditionary force. Even in the late 1930s, when it became clear that another such commitment was unavoidable, British politicians and military theorists opposed the re-creation of a national conscript army and supported instead "limited liability."[28] Shaped by Great War experience, the proponents of limited liability argued that Britain must avoid being sucked into another protracted ground war on the continent. Instead, they argued that Britain should rely on its traditional blockade—now reinforced by air power, with heavy bombers able to strike deep into enemy territory to shatter the vulnerable morale of enemy civilians and destroy the enemy's will to fight. The advocates of limited liability argued that technological advances, especially mechanization and the rise of air power, made a large land army redundant and that Britain should instead rely on a small, elite, professional armored force.

In this political, economic, and cultural climate the army had difficulty even in subsisting. A decline in funding inevitably brought a decline in efficiency. The interwar army regressed, mentally stagnated, and proved reluctant to study the lessons of World War I or to preserve its experience by formulating coherent doctrine. Nonetheless, in the 1920s the army remained appropriately structured given its strategic priorities, and reform continued, despite scarce funding, at an attenuated rate. The army both revised its manuals and initiated limited mechanization.[29] In the early 1930s, though, regression set in as the nation plunged into severe economic depression, and the army's combat effectiveness dwindled accordingly. Unprecedented economic difficulties aggravated the psychological, material, and strategic legacies of the Great War as the Depression focused national and political attention on domestic socioeconomic issues and deepened popular hostility toward the military. The Depression engendered further sweeping reductions in defense spending, polarized political and military thought, instilled fear and uncertainty in the military, and exacerbated the conservatism inherent in peacetime armies. The result was the stifling of military reform.

But such external factors as government parsimony and popular anti-militarism fail to explain adequately the army's deficiencies at the start of World War II. The army did share much of the responsibility for the disasters of 1939–1942. At the root of the army's inadequate preparation for continental warfare, and hence dismal early war performance, was its view of World War I as aberrant. The army's assumption that it would never again have to fight another major continental war ensured that it saw little rationale or relevance in studying the lessons of the Great War. And in the face of inevitable personnel turnover between the wars, the army lost whatever expertise and experience it had slowly and painfully gained on the fields of Flanders.

The army was also neither structured, nor possessed mechanisms, to derive, disseminate, and retain combat experience. It did not have a continental-style general staff with which to preserve institutional knowledge. It was not until 1932 that the War Office examined the lessons of the Great War. This was too late to revamp doctrine and transform training prior to the outbreak of World War II.[30] Even when the army finally studied its Great War experience, it misinterpreted the lessons of the war because it evaluated its performance to validate traditional strategy. Thus the War Office erroneously concluded that the naval blockade that had eroded German civilian morale was the key to Entente victory, whereas, in reality, it had been the combination of sustained military action on land and blockade that defeated Germany.[31] This misperception validated traditional British foreign policy and reinforced the "limited liability" proponents' misguided claim that a peripheral strategy, relying on naval blockade and aerial bombardment, could defeat a major continental power in a future conflict.

The most significant lesson the army drew from the Great War was that adherence to a strategy of attrition had brought victory, and it concluded that the struggle demonstrated that modern industrialized nations could only be defeated by protracted attrition.[32] It made little effort to contemplate other alternatives or to evaluate how potential enemies had interpreted the lessons of the Great War and adapted in response to them. The army's conclusion that victory in 1918, however costly, vindicated the adherence to a strategy of attrition ensured that Britain remained wedded to this doctrine throughout the 1919–1945 period. The army made minor modifications to prevailing doctrine to absorb such new technology as armor and air power but refused to reexamine, rethink, or revise strategic fundamentals. The major reverses the army suffered during 1939–1942 illuminated the vulnerability of a such an attritional strategy to the new German blitzkrieg warfare that aimed to overwhelm quickly unprepared militaries before they could mobilize their demographic, industrial, and financial strength. The British Army was therefore unable to discern clear lessons and a path to follow between the wars. Its failure to examine quickly and thoroughly its previous experience and then to preserve such knowledge shackled even the limited preparation that the army was capable of.

Most serious of all, however, the British people's association of the slaughter in the trenches with the doctrine of the offensive meant that offense was repugnant and unacceptable to the army between the wars. As a result, what passed as interwar strategy was one of defense. The British military had erroneously concluded that the strategic defensive inevitably meant operational and tactical defense as well. This was a serious error, for such a posture surrendered the strategic initiative to potential aggressors, insidiously eroded morale and fighting spirit, and bred caution and hesitancy.[33] These were characteristics that the 1939–1945 army never entirely eradicated. In the aftermath of World War I, few politicians, soldiers, or civilians contemplated British involvement in another major war. The improbability of major war in the 1920s buttressed both the intellectual sway of the "never again" ethos and economic pressures for military retrenchment.[34] Anticipating no mission that could lead to war, the interwar army lacked the impetus for preparation, let alone reform or innovation.

The army's Victorian culture also contributed to its inadequate preparation between the wars: soldiering was an honorable part-time occupation rather than a full-time profession that required extensive training and education, and officership remained the preserve of elite society. Such a culture was unreceptive to criticism, and thus the army leadership discouraged critical analysis of its performance and equated criticism with disloyalty.[35] The War Office, for example, only disseminated a condensed and censored version of its 1932 study of the army's Great War performance.[36] Army culture also disparaged preparation and intellectual study, especially of military theory. Thus the army remained reluctant to evaluate honestly its capabilities and instead extolled pragmatism and improvisation. Army culture so militated against honesty and creativity that it slowed the pace of innovation throughout the 1914–1945 period.[37] Although the interwar army remained intellectually alive—vigorous debate continued in the army's professional journals and at staff college courses—this activity was uncoordinated and unfocused, and the army itself made little effort to develop doctrine.

Lack of a mission, ambivalence to professional development, lack of strategic threats, dispersion of the army for imperial defense, and fiscal stringency all forged indifference toward maneuvers between the wars. The army conducted large-scale maneuvers only twice, which demonstrated that the army was less well prepared than it had been in 1914. In fact, the War Office used troop unreadiness to justify abandoning maneuvers amid the financial stringency of the 1930s.[38] The absence of large-scale peacetime exercises prevented the army from identifying the manifold deficiencies in its doctrine, training, tactics, organization, and equipment.

Popular antimilitarism also ensured that despite the high unemployment of the Depression, the interwar army experienced major recruitment problems. The Great War had destroyed the flower of British youth, and slow promotion, low pay, and lack of societal recognition of officership as a profession meant that the officer corps failed to attract the talented and energetic. Inevitably, officer quality declined between the wars as the army effectively abandoned evaluation of fitness to command.

Rapid technological change between the wars posed additional problems for the army as it strove to modernize despite minimal funding. The interwar army's loss of boldness and aggressiveness ironically occurred at the very time when technological change restored mobility and offensive power on the battlefield. The army's lack of a mission and its determination to forget the experience of World War I engendered indifference toward technology between the wars, which meant that the army had the poorest record of the three services in adapting modern technology to the battlefield.[39] The army of 1939 remained largely equipped as it had been in 1918, and its failure to keep pace with technological change contributed directly to the serious reverses that it suffered early in World War II.

The most significant area in which Britain failed to adapt modern technology between the wars was armor. Britain had pioneered armored warfare in the Great War, and the tank had played a significant role in a number of major battlefield victories during 1917–1918.[40] But the technical limitations of tanks ensured that they had only tactical, not strategic, capabilities in World War I. Britain led thinking on armor into the mid-1920s, producing the leading theorists J. F. C. Fuller and B. H. Liddell Hart. In 1923 Britain formed its armor into a separate arm, the Royal Tank Corps (RTC) and in 1927 created the world's first wholly mechanized formation—the Experimental Mechanized Force (EMF). In the late 1920s, the RTC also produced its first doctrinal manuals on armored warfare, and in the Vickers Medium tank Britain possessed the most advanced armored vehicle of its day.[41]

But, from the late 1920s, Britain both lost its lead in armored warfare theory and British tank design fell behind that of its neighbors, with the result that early in World War II the army proved unable either to master armored warfare or to find an effective counter to German mastery of armored warfare. British armored warfare doctrine went awry in the late 1920s for several reasons. Part of the reason lay in financial constraints, army conservatism, and the army's mission.[42] Reduced spending and the return to imperial policing militated against both tank development and effective organization and employment of armor. Tasked with imperial defense, the army had no rationale or impetus to create a large, expensive tank arm or to develop a coherent, offensive, armored warfare doctrine, and the government withheld the resources to do so.

Historians have also often argued that socially conservative British officers maintained an unsound faith in the horse as a instrument of war, despite the lessons of the Great War. Many of these landed, rural officers possessed limited understanding of industrial society or modern war, a provincialism that failed to raise officers above the narrow confines of regimental life. Recent scholarship, however, has demonstrated that the army was less conservative about mechanization than previously assumed.[43] Rather, the creation of the RTC and the EMF demonstrated that by the mid-1920s the army had accepted the tank as a valuable weapon of war.[44] The real explanation for Britain's loss of its leadership in armored warfare is more complicated.

Clearly, the extremism of many tank enthusiasts that armor was a independent strategic instrument capable of winning wars unaided hindered creation of effective armored forces between the wars. The enthusiasts' claims for the strategic independence of armor not only hampered development of integrated, combined-arms mechanized forces but challenged the framework of British strategic doctrine. The army, therefore, rejected Fuller's call for an elite armored force, and instead embarked on the more sensible, cautious approach of gradual, broad mechanization. While this approach meant that by 1939 the army was the only field force in the world whose transport was fully motorized, it also entailed the disbandment of the EMF.

The crux of Britain's failure to harness armored warfare between the wars, however, was its rigid opposition to modifying basic strategic doctrine to encompass the potential of armor. The tank controversy in interwar Britain was more about the adoption of a new and radically different concept of strategy rather than about the adoption of a new weapon. The army was willing to adopt the tank but only to fit it into established strategic doctrine, without consideration of how armor could or might change such doctrine. Britons also saw the tank as a product of the Western Front and as such it had limited applicability outside total war, which was unthinkable in the 1920s. The technological limitations of armor also justified much of the criticism by reactionaries, for, until the late 1930s, a gulf existed between armored warfare theory and practice. The army's development of armor remained cautious and constrained by its prudent unwillingness to unbalance its force structure and thereby undermine its ability to pursue a strategy of attrition.[45]

Britain's lead in armored warfare evaporated during the Depression. On the surface this period appeared as one of accelerated progress. The RTC expanded and issued its first doctrinal manual, the EMF conducted four major exercises, Britain created its first tank brigade, and even in 1934 it still had the largest, most tactically advanced, and best trained tank force in the world. But during these years armored warfare theorists made no doctrinal progress. Rather, a reaction set in against armor as the Depression fueled insecurity and financial stringency, which bred conservatism and slowed the pace of mechanization. As a result, the army wedded the tank to infantry support and ultimately disbanded the EMF.[46]

Most significant of all, by 1934 the "cavalry concept" of armored warfare, which viewed the tank as a surrogate for horsed cavalry, had become firmly entrenched. The cavalry concept conceived of armor as being employed en masse and without supporting arms for raiding, reconnaissance, patrolling, and pursuit in the light-cavalry tradition, and as a counterattack force against enemy penetrations in the heavy-cavalry tradition. While progressive in 1934, by 1937 the cavalry concept of armored warfare was obsolete because it viewed armor as a narrow, specialized weapons system rather than as a versatile and broadly applicable weapon. This view of armor specialization led the army to procure multiple tank types for narrow, specialized missions—for example, a light tank for traditional cavalry reconnaissance and raiding missions and a heavy tank for counterattacking.

The cavalry concept triumphed for a variety of reasons, but mainly because the army mechanized the cavalry (to protect regimental structure) rather than expand the RTC in the 1930s. The cavalry changed its mode of transport but not its mission or its habits. Moreover, armored warfare proponents generally supported mechanization of the cavalry and the armor concentration that the cavalry concept engendered because they believed massed tank forces would both guarantee the independence of armor and allow it to demonstrate its strategic capabilities. Thus the army went to war with a unique, untested, and fundamentally flawed conception of armored warfare that envisaged the employment of armor en masse in a cavalry role.[47]

This conservative view of the role of armor partly reflected the army's regimental structure. Regimentalism promoted professional socialization among officers and fostered unit morale, esprit de corps, pride, and cohesion, all of which contributed to the battlefield doggedness and tenacity displayed by wartime British soldiers. But it also promoted regimental tribalism and parochialism that hindered interarms and interservice cooperation. During World War I the regimental system's benefits outweighed its drawbacks, but interwar technological change necessitated greater interarms and interservice cooperation. The interarms rivalry the regimental system brought about not only hindered development of common doctrine and standardized training, but it also stifled intellectual thought. As a result, the army's theoretical preparation between the wars lacked rigor and failed to raise officers beyond the confines of regimental life.[48]

That imperial defense rarely required interarms and interservice cooperation did little to promote cooperation either: the interwar British armed services coordinated poorly. The Royal Air Force (RAF), after its bitter fight for independence and then for continued survival, was reluctant to cooperate with the army or navy. The army's culture and finances left it reluctant to cooperate with the RAF; and the equally vocal demands of armor and air power enthusiasts that their respective arms were decisive instruments of war crippled development of air-ground coordination. Thus in September 1939, the three services were largely incapable of conducting an integrated war effort. The inadequacy of British interarms and interservice coordination in 1939 was a serious deficiency that contributed directly to the military disasters that befell Britain during the early war years.

That Britain in the early 1930s was incapable of deploying an overseas expeditionary force was in many ways inevitable and unavoidable. Britons erroneously believed that there would be time to prepare for war if a crisis developed. The emergence in the 1930s of three powerful potential enemies in distant theaters (Germany, Italy, and Japan), however, confronted Britain with unprecedented strategic threats at a time when the nation's power had been greatly diminished. After Hitler's rise to power in 1933, the government overturned the Ten Year Rule. Yet even then Britain rearmed casually, unhurriedly, and tardily because the forces that had fueled military neglect in the 1920s hindered rearmament in the 1930s. The legacies of earlier neglect, government rearmament policies, and the army's culture and mission all militated against effective reform.

Britain also failed to orient rearmament toward the threats it faced. The government rearmed to deter aggression rather than to prepare for war and so it reequipped the air force and navy, which were perceived to have a deterrent effect.[49] Fear of the bomber also led to major enhancement of Britain's neglected antiaircraft defenses. These rearmament priorities ensured that the army received little increase in funding. Thus the government geared military preparation in the late 1930s to create the illusion of strength, purpose, and resolve to deter aggression rather than to forge an effective field force. Such pursuit of deterrence led the government during the spring of 1939 to introduce peacetime conscription for the first time and to double the Territorial Army, initiatives that hampered creation of an expeditionary force.[50] Not only did these measures, designed to demonstrate the government's resolve, neither deceive nor deter Hitler, they placed a great strain on available resources and delayed establishment of a viable expeditionary force. Conscription caused chaos in the armaments industry, disrupted army reorganization, and forced abandonment of the major exercises scheduled for the summer of 1939 while doubling the Territorial Army further dissipated already meager resources.

Earlier neglect also hampered rearmament in the late 1930s. Interwar governments had allowed Britain's military-industrial base to run down.[51] The loss of production facilities as well as design and development expertise retarded rearmament and contributed to Britain's loss of leadership in armored warfare. When rearmament began in earnest in 1939, lack of production facilities hampered reequipment of the army and condemned it to fight during 1939–1942 with inferior, and often obsolete, weaponry. Despite its best efforts, Britain never completely closed this quality gap during the war, and the army's inferiority in armaments both fueled the disasters of 1939–1942 and delayed ultimate victory.

This gap had become most pronounced in armor by September 1939. Closely tied with Britain's loss of leadership in armored warfare doctrine was a parallel loss of its primacy in tank design. Despite British invention of the tank during World War I and continued design leadership during the 1920s, in the 1930s British tanks fell behind French, German, and Soviet designs. The dwindling of design and production expertise resulted in technical problems and mechanical unreliability that badly hampered British tank development.[52] Technical limitations thus contributed to Britain's loss of leadership in armored warfare. Budgetary constraints shaped procurement too and led to development of cheap light tanks, tankettes, and tracked carriers suitable for colonial service. It was only after 1936 that Britain energetically pursued heavy-tank projects, too late to create an effective heavy-tank force prior to the outbreak of war.[53]

The most significant cause of Britain's tank development going awry in the late 1930s, however, was the emergence of the view, already noted, of armor specialization that led it to procure multiple tank types whose functions and capabilities overlapped. While partly a consequence of lack of foresight, the multiplicity of tank types that Britain produced was more the result of deliberate design than of confusion. Such multiplicity reflected the army's view of the tank as a specialized vehicle performing a variety of functions, as the cavalry had done. It also reflected the absence of holistic doctrine, thus blinkering the army to the broader applicability and potential of armor. This philosophy of armor specialization dissipated meager financial resources and overstretched limited design and production facilities. In 1936, for example, Britain pursued development of four distinct tank types: a light tank for reconnaissance and raiding missions by mechanized cavalry; a medium tank for flank protection; an infantry tank to provide firepower for foot soldiers; and a close-support tank for indirect artillery support. Such diversification exacerbated the severe design and production difficulties that the British tank arm faced as a result of nearly twenty years of neglect.

Loss of design and production expertise, the resultant technical problems, and dissipation of resources meant that Britain was unable to produce a tank in the 1930s that combined mobility and firepower.[54] By 1939 Britain had clearly fallen behind in armored warfare: the German Army had by then incorporated tanks into its operational and tactical doctrine and consolidated its armor into mechanized corps. Britain's inability to develop a quality battle tank in turn drove doctrine to support those tanks that Britain could produce. By the outbreak of war tank doctrine emphasized two types of warfare—fluid and positional—that required two types of tanks—fast, mobile cruisers and slow, heavily armored infantry tanks.

During rearmament in the late 1930s, the British tank arm saw unprecedented expansion and an influx of new equipment. The army formed a Mobile Division in 1938 (redesignated the 1st Armoured in 1939) and combined the RTC and the mechanized cavalry into a new Royal Armoured Corps (RAC) in April 1939. The outbreak of war caught the RAC in mid-expansion, at which point it comprised eight weak mechanized cavalry regiments equipped with light tanks, the understrength 1st Armoured Division, the ragtag Egyptian Mobile Division, and the Army Tank Brigade. On paper these developments appeared progressive and significant reforms. But in reality, this expansion and reorganization was less effective than it appeared, and in September 1939 the RAC still lacked well-organized, trained, and equipped armored forces. At the root of this deficiency lay the army's unswerving adherence to a defensive strategy that prevented any change in thinking about armored warfare. British armored forces remained poorly organized, equipped, and trained for offensive action. The ascendancy of the cavalry concept ensured that the army structured and equipped the Mobile Division not for an attack role but for reconnaissance and pursuit missions. The division's organization also reflected both the prevailing view of armor specialization and the confused and multifarious mission of tanks within existing strategic doctrine, containing different tanks designed for disparate tasks. The division lacked an all-arms composition and was very tank-heavy and unwieldy. The army's failure to exercise with armor between the wars, however, ensured that it remained blind to the deficient organization of its armored forces.

The amalgamation of the RTC and the mechanized cavalry was also a dubious reform. The army merged these branches largely to alleviate the huge intellectual and practical problems the cavalry faced in adapting to mechanization. The decision was a compromise that allowed cavalrymen and tankers to coexist in separate but equal status. The creation of the RAC around the mechanized cavalry, however, further entrenched the cavalry concept of armored warfare; while the move undoubtedly improved the mechanized cavalry's proficiency, it hampered the effectiveness of the RAC throughout the war.

In September 1939 Britain went to war with two mechanized divisions that had never exercised as integral formations, and the lack of concern the army displayed for the operational inexperience of its armored forces clearly demonstrated that it still failed to see the revolutionary potential of the changes it had wrought. During the frantic expansion, reorganization, and reequipment of 1938–1939, the RAC inevitably focused on basic training and did not participate in large-scale maneuvers that might have revealed glaring flaws in tank quality, armored organization, or doctrine. The absence of a strategic doctrine that contemplated the offensive employment of armor meant that at the outbreak of war Britain had no established, coherent armored doctrine, little understanding of how mechanized forces could—and would—revolutionize warfare, nor any properly constituted armored forces. Thus, in the frenzy of rearmament, the army missed the lesson that the Germans and Soviets drew from their involvement in the Spanish Civil War—the need for close cooperation between arms. Only in the Middle East, where Percy Hobart had turned a ragtag body of troops into an embryonic mobile division (later redesignated the 7th Armoured), did Britain possess in 1939–1940 a well-trained and offensive-minded armored formation.[55]

Meanwhile, the backbone of the army remained the infantry that provided the bulk of the forces that garrisoned the empire. This dispersion was a major obstacle to modernization and reequipment and prevented the establishment of a powerful, well-equipped, and modern infantry force at home in the late 1930s. Although modest reform and reequipment occurred after 1935, Britain entered World War II without infantry organized, trained, or equipped for offense. Lack of political direction to prepare for continental service also grievously hindered interwar innovation in the Royal Artillery, which had proven the most flexible, adaptable, and innovative arm in World War I. Then, the gunners had rapidly adopted the airplane for aerial reconnaissance and the wireless for improved communication and control.[56] By 1918 the Royal Artillery had become especially adept at counterbattery work. Nonetheless, real limitations still existed in artillery capabilities. Lack of range and mobility and crude communications meant that massed artillery could smash a breach in enemy lines but could not provide continuous support throughout an attack.[57]

Memories of the slaughter in the trenches adversely influenced development of British artillery doctrine, tactics, and organization between the wars. Innovators and reactionaries alike agreed that trench warfare was an aberration and that future war would never see massed artillery fire. Instead, the interwar Royal Artillery prepared for "open" warfare and emphasized mobility and more rapid gunnery. It discarded most of its heavy artillery and expanded the obsolete mobile horsedrawn field batteries of the Royal Horse Artillery that undertook imperial policing. Interwar artillery doctrine rejected wartime experience of mass and concentration and instead came to stress economy of force, surprise, and precision.[58] Nevertheless, important reforms continued during the 1920s. The army opened a new central School of Artillery at Larkhill, which played an important, if inadvertent, role in the development of tactical gunnery doctrine between the wars. Larkhill partially preserved the Royal Artillery's Great War experience, and a central school promoted both uniform doctrine and reform. In addition, motorization of the artillery was begun in the 1920s and was complete by 1939.[59] The army also formed light artillery brigades equipped with 3.7-inch pack howitzers to provide close support in imitation of the German and Soviet infantry guns developed in the 1920s. Moreover, in 1925 the army developed the pioneering 18-pounder self-propelled Birch gun, which, despite major limitations, was years ahead of its time. Most important, artillery doctrine remained progressive in the 1920s: early armored warfare doctrine in 1929, for example, recognized the need for artillery support of armored forces.[60]

During the Depression, though, the Royal Artillery slipped into the conservatism that gripped the rest of the army.[61] Uncertainty over its future role, the triumph of the cavalry concept of armored warfare, and financial cutbacks eroded its efficiency as stagnation and regression set in. In 1931, revised doctrine relegated artillery support of armor to an ancillary role. The army also scrapped the Birch gun, which it deemed too slow and unreliable for mobile warfare and developed instead a close-support tank that extended the army's multifarious tank inventory. The addition of infantry mortars and antitank guns also killed the light-brigade concept in the 1930s.[62] The demise of the self-propelled gun, close artillery support, and tank-artillery cooperation crippled artillery performance early in World War II. The scrapping of close-support artillery prevented development of coherent antitank doctrine and inevitably sucked field artillery toward dangerous and improper forward deployment in an antitank role, a trend reinforced by the transfer of responsibility for antitank defense to the Royal Artillery in 1938.[63]

Yet having failed to appreciate the potential of armor, the army devoted few resources to antitank defense between the wars. In 1939 the mobile 2-pounder (40mm) gun, the mainstay of the army's antitank arsenal, had limited effectiveness against the second generation of German medium tanks, the Panzer III and IV. Lack of antitank capability forced the artillery to deploy field guns forward in an antitank role during 1939–1942, thus compromising the ability to provide indirect fire support. The disappearance of the close-support gun led to emergence of a passive, static, and defensive antitank doctrine that was primarily the responsibility of artillery.[64]

Financial constraints also hampered development of new ordnance between the wars and the Royal Artillery's lack of modern, long-range, mobile artillery was a major limitation in 1939. The only new weapon designed between the wars was the excellent 25-pounder field gun, which proved one of the most rugged and dependable artillery pieces of World War II. However, the 25-pounder was a compromise designed to replace the

18-pounder gun and 4.5-inch howitzer. It thus lacked the punch of the 105mm howitzers that entered German and U.S. service between the wars or the velocity to be a good antitank gun. Moreover, it was in short supply at the outbreak of war, while new medium and heavy guns fell victim to interwar economy measures. Britain thus entered World War II with only a few, largely obsolescent, medium and heavy guns, a deficiency that compromised artillery counterbattery and defensive fire capabilities. Finally, most lacking was a self-propelled gun to provide mobile fire support for armored forces.[65]

Financial constraints had also hampered improvements in artillery fire control and communications methods. The army had introduced its first field radios in 1928, but lack of funds meant that they only became available in quantity in 1938.[66] Funding constraints also ensured that mechanization progressed slowly. By 1939 mechanization and radio communications had progressed sufficiently to create artillery that was more mobile and flexible than its 1918 predecessors, but artillery fire control and communications failed to keep pace with the rapidity and mobility that armor had injected into modern warfare.

The Royal Artillery also went to war in 1939 with a defective organization. In 1938 the army reorganized divisional artillery brigades, both as an economy measure and in an abortive effort to increase mass-fire capabilities. It introduced a new organization of three field regiments of two batteries divided into three troops of four guns. This reform had two beneficial consequences: it established the regiment as a tactical fire unit (which allowed quicker fire) and attached permanent observers (which brought improved accuracy). However, it also had serious flaws, for it reduced the number of batteries per division from nine to six, which meant that it was no longer possible for divisions to provide simultaneous fire support for each infantry battalion. It also prevented the semipermanent battery-battalion affiliation that promoted proficiency through close association. In addition, economy measures left only one troop in each battery equipped with an observation post (the other two troops had to fire blind) and led to the abolition of artillery survey parties, both of which were retrograde steps that compromised the ability of gunners to provide rapid defensive fire.[67]

British artillery doctrine had recovered somewhat in the late 1930s. The revised *Field Service Regulations* (1935) reemphasized the massed employment of artillery and the importance of signals communications.[68] Consequently, the artillery went to war in better shape than the other arms. In September 1939, it had progressed far in mechanization and had gained some radio communications. Its ordnance was largely obsolescent but mobile, the quality of its training and the caliber of its manpower was good, and its morale was high. But the most serious problem that afflicted the interwar Royal Artillery was its fatal misapprehension that future wars would not require massed fire, thus leading it to assume a novel direct-fire antitank role without an effective antitank weapon and denuding it of the medium and heavy artillery required for effective fire support. Its orientation toward positional warfare with meticulous fire plans was another serious deficiency, for it simply lacked the expertise and organization to perform in fast-paced mobile operations. Its structure and training emphasized massed predicted fire that was only possible after extensive survey and registration, which prevented rapid, mobile action. Its defective organization and lack of rapport with infantry and armor further hampered its ability to make its presence felt on the modern battlefield. Nevertheless, the Royal Artillery made an important achievement between the wars that paved the way for it to become once again the most adaptable and innovative British arm during World War II. It devised a basic gunnery technique and created a uniform and sound doctrine, both of which served with very little modification throughout the war.[69]

If the combat arms suffered serious neglect between the wars, financial stringency led to even greater neglect of army support services. Provision for antiaircraft defense was utterly inadequate, and the logistical base for extended operations overseas did not exist. What distinguished Britain from Germany, however, was that even though it lacked the resources, Britain—having learned from its mistakes in the Great War where initial neglect of logistics had undermined British operations—carefully considered the logistics of a future war. With adequate attention given to the theoretical supply needs of its armed forces, Britain quickly achieved excellent logistic support for its military operations during World War II.[70]

Intelligence failures also hindered British rearmament in the 1930s. Interwar Britain remained ill informed about the capabilities and intentions of possible enemies. This was a function of both financial constraints and of structural flaws. British intelligence consistently misevaluated German military capabilities and the threat they posed to British interests.[71] Poor understanding of military developments in Germany prevented accurate assessment of German potential and goals. For example, Britain was aware that Germany had created armored divisions and consolidated them into corps, but the British military did not identify any strategic implications of Germany's adoption of an armored warfare doctrine. In fact, the British military misperceived how the Germans intended to employ armor, believing tanks would be used in dispersed packets to infiltrate Allied lines in a replay of the storm troop attacks of 1918.[72] Thus the British Army would disperse its armor along the front in reserve to counter infiltration by small groups of enemy infantry and armor. Moreover, British military and intelligence agencies failed to evaluate how German history since 1914 had shaped military developments in Germany between the wars. The British Army was prepared to refight the war of 1914 with the tactics and ordnance of 1918.

During the September 1938 Munich crisis, Britain still possessed negligible military capabilities. The War Office rated only two divisions operational, and even these remained undertrained and underequipped. Britain, therefore, acquiesced to the partition of Czechoslovakia to postpone war and buy time for rearmament. After Munich, changing public and parliamentary opinion pushed the government into greater defense expenditures, and, finally in February 1939, Britain renewed its continental commitment to France and Belgium, gave its armed forces an unequivocal mandate to prepare for war, and ordered six divisions readied for continental service.[73] That the army had only six months to prepare the British Expeditionary Force (BEF) left it with no choice but to assume the defensive in the west. The army required planning, resources, and time to fix its interwar neglect—but none of these did it possess. That the BEF had less than a year for serious preparation does much to explain the debacle that befell British arms in France during May 1940.

Finally the army began to prepare a modest expeditionary force. But without long-term planning this effort was unbalanced. Britain initially decided to commit the BEF to the northeastern flank of the French Army on the Belgian border in a replay of its deployment in 1914. But here the similarity ended, for the 1914 BEF was a much better prepared fighting force than its 1939 equivalent. Simultaneous rapid reequipment and massive expansion was simply impossible to achieve in a few months, especially given simultaneous introduction of conscription and expansion of the Territorial Army. In 1939 Britain, therefore, cobbled together an unbalanced expeditionary force short on supporting arms and service elements from a ragtag peacetime army. Dispute within the army over the wisdom of another continental commitment, government parsimony, and the running down of the military-industrial base all hampered preparation of the BEF. Moreover, the government had also to channel resources to home defense, especially antiaircraft defenses, as well as the navy and air force. Yet even after February 1939, peacetime habits died hard and the Chamberlain government remained hostile to the notion and expense of a continental commitment. Circumstances, therefore, severely circumscribed the army's endeavors to fashion an expeditionary force.

Army rearmament made some progress during summer 1939. The Mobile Division was reorganized as the 1st Armoured, and belated reequipment finally began to transform it into a combat formation. The onrush of events, however, left the army little time to contemplate broader theoretical and doctrinal issues. As a result, the army's operational concepts in 1939 were inapplicable and outmoded for modern war—a situation that was hardly surprising given the lack of awareness of future wartime strategic objectives. The army went to war while in the throes of massive expansion and equipped for imperial defense; it was intellectually and organizationally ill prepared to meet the German Army on the continent.

At the same time, regimental tribalism and the absence of holistic doctrine led each branch to prepare for war in a narrow, parochial, and idiosyncratic fashion as each considered problems and developments through a narrow single-arms view. Given the largely unavoidable circumstances the army found itself in at the start of the war, it was crucial that the wartime army learn on the job to improve its combat effectiveness. However, the interwar army failed to examine problems analytically or thoroughly; nor did it examine, verify, or refine doctrine, tactics, or organization through trial and error. Without central direction, doctrine, training, and capabilities varied widely not only from arm to arm, but from unit to unit. Thus while the Royal Artillery had partially preserved the lessons of the Great War, the infantry had largely jettisoned its institutional knowledge. In fact, most regiments did not perform realistic training nor possess common doctrine between the wars because the army's approach remained idiosyncratic and individual, rather than uniform.[74]

The interwar British military's most effective innovations were defensive in orientation because defensive technology best fitted Britain's strategic posture. The British armed services enhanced their signals intelligence capability and developed defensive-oriented radar. Britain had lagged behind Germany in radar technology prior to 1940, but the British armed forces applied radar much more effectively. The RAF, in particular, adapted its thinking to utilize radar effectively and developed the Chain Home early-warning system that played an important role in the winning of the Battle of Britain.[75] Just as geography and policy promoted offensive-oriented innovation in the interwar German military, so it promoted defensive-oriented innovation in the British armed forces.

The army that went to war in September 1939 was in the middle of expansion from a minimal base and was thus in poor condition. Its senior leadership lacked even peacetime operational experience. Moreover, mechanization since the mid-1930s had made the experience of earlier exercises largely irrelevant in 1939. The army lacked coherent doctrine and tactics, and training quality varied dramatically from unit to unit.

Britain also went to war without commitment to, mechanisms for, or experience of, interservice cooperation. The RAF viewed the direct support of ground forces as dangerous and unprofitable and therefore to be conducted only as a last resort. Instead, wedded to a heavy bomber force, which it saw as a independent strategic instrument capable of winning wars in its own right, the RAF was only prepared to aid the army indirectly by achieving aerial superiority and by providing occasional reconnaissance and interdiction missions when other priorities permitted.[76] The interwar RAF rejected the need for specialized close-support aircraft, formations, and training. Its belief in the strategic independence of the bomber force and the preferment the RAF consequently received placed the air force in competition with the other services in national strategy.[77] The Royal Navy, too, despite a long tradition of overseas expeditions, failed to develop a specialized amphibious assault capability between the wars. It remained wedded to the Mahan doctrine of big surface fleet engagement to the detriment of the growing submarine and aerial threat. Between the wars, therefore, the services prepared for separate wars: the army, to defend the empire; the navy, for surface war against Japan in the Far East; and the RAF, for a continental European bombing campaign. In fact, the army's caution contrasted strongly with the offensive-mindedness of the RAF and the Royal Navy. Indeed, one of the key weaknesses of the other two services between the wars was their excessive offensive orientation. The RAF's fixation with strategic bombing and the invincibility of the bomber led to the neglect of Fighter Command, while the Royal Navy's commitment to the battle fleet and Mahan fleet action led to neglect of antisubmarine forces. The contrasting strategic postures of the services was both cause and effect of the lack of coherent strategic doctrine. The three services' reluctance to cooperate and coordinate their war efforts contributed directly to the disasters of 1939–1942.

In retrospect, the Ten Year Rule did serious damage to British defense capabilities and ability to innovate between the wars. Interwar neglect— financial, intellectual, material—impeded British military effectiveness throughout World War II. Up to 1937, home and imperial defense still took priority over support to allies on the continent. Thus, strategic and political factors partly account for the failure of the British Army to innovate between the wars. In the final analysis, Britain's strategic, political, financial, and social condition between the wars made the army's inadequacies at the start of World War II to some extent unavoidable. Popular antimilitarism in Depression-torn Britain constrained defense spending, and financial stringency in turn crippled efficiency and hampered reform. The British Army thus went to war in September 1939 with very limited combat capabilities and was clearly no match for the *Heer.*

More perplexing, however, was the army's inability to catch up with the German lead during the war. The root cause lay in the army's character, culture, structure, experiences, and most especially in its amateurism and lack of doctrine. The army's sluggishness in enhancing its wartime combat effectiveness in part derived from a military culture that undervalued educational and professional development. The army discouraged criticism of prevailing doctrine and got less out of training and maneuvers because it lacked the determination to learn honestly from them. Moreover, it lacked mechanisms to derive and then to disseminate combat experience throughout the army. Battle experience was rarely absorbed into revised training. At the same time, in the absence of clear, realistic doctrine and in the face of its rigid, but distorting adherence to a strategy of attrition, the army found it difficult to draw appropriate lessons from early war experience against a backdrop of bitter and disastrous defeat. The army not only failed to emulate its Great War achievements, but during 1939–1942 suffered repeated and unprecedented setbacks that brought Britain close to defeat.

Canada

Canada's unmilitary tradition and the resulting reluctance of its government and people to fund defense expenditures created a climate inhospitable to the maintenance of effective military forces between the wars. At the same time, resentment at the heavy loss of Canadian life during the Great War, pessimism that force could solve the tensions inherent in international relations, and the impact of the Great Depression further eroded Canadian defense spending and stifled possibilities for military reform. As a result, the interwar Canadian military experienced difficulty in simply existing. At the outbreak of war in September 1939, Canada possessed negligible military capabilities and few Western nations were as unprepared for war. Given this unpromising start and the unwillingness of the Canadian government to commit troops to combat for domestic political reasons, it was only late in World War II that the Canadian Army developed military proficiency.

Because of its geographic position and political character Canada has long had an unmilitary tradition.[78] Canada's military, which originated from the French militia levied in the seventeenth century, had fought in only one conflict, the War of 1812.[79] In consequence, the Militia dwindled. Nonetheless, Canada made an unparalleled effort to support Great Britain during the Great War. The Canadian Expeditionary Force (CEF), rapidly and haphazardly dispatched to the Western Front, grew into a four-division corps. Forced to learn the mechanics of modern warfare on the fields of Flanders, the CEF adapted relatively quickly, though at a heavy price in lives. Raised from scratch, the CEF evaded the parochialism of the militia, acquired a permanent, cohesive force structure, and received ample manpower reserves. This allowed it to innovate tactically and organizationally by adopting and refining British methods. It pioneered, for example, development of concentrated machine gun and trench mortar tactics, and the Canadian Independent Force of 1918 was the world's first combined-arms mechanized formation.[80] The CEF relied heavily on artillery to smash enemy resistance, rapidly adopted the airplane for aerial reconnaissance, and developed a counterbattery sophistication. Thorough planning, preparation, and training forged Canadian fighting efficiency, and consequently the CEF distinguished itself repeatedly during the Great War, becoming one of the Germans' most feared opponents. Indeed, it was the CEF that spearheaded the August 1918 operations that broke the German front.[81]

Canada's participation in World War I, however, did not convince its people of the need for peacetime military preparedness. To the contrary, the high cost of victory both exacerbated Canada's historic isolationism and fueled pacifism between the wars. The never again ethos gripped interwar Canada even more powerfully than it did Britain. Such influences merely reinforced Canada's historic unwillingness to finance peacetime military preparation.[82] Canada demobilized in 1919 and reverted to its traditional militia. The Great Depression brought further sweeping cuts in defense spending after 1929.[83] Since Canada's geostrategic position presented few potential aggressors, no rationale existed for large defense expenditures in a period of severe economic crisis. The Canadian military thus suffered serious and sustained neglect from which it lost its expertise, its excellence, and even the essence of its profession. Little of the knowledge of modern warfare, gained at such a high price in Canadian lives on the Western Front, survived this neglect in the face of inevitable personnel turnover.[84]

In the face of pacifism, the Depression, and the prevailing small-war mentality, the Canadian government provided the barest minimum of funds to keep the mechanism of defense alive as the government allowed the nation's military-industrial complex to run down.[85] The heavy cost of victory in World War I fueled antimilitarism between the wars and the Depression reinforced anti-institutional sentiments, spawned labor and political unrest, and intensified disenchantment and distrust of the government. The French Canadians of Quebec, in particular, remained as bitterly hostile as ever to cooperation in imperial defense. Not surprisingly, Canadian politics thus focused on domestic issues and interwar governments displayed little understanding of, or concern for, strategic and national security issues.[86]

Emphasis on home defense, public concern over the growing Japanese threat in the Pacific, lack of popular consensus on the need for military preparedness, and lack of consultation with Canada's prospective allies, let alone joint planning, all prevented the maintenance of effective military forces in the interwar period. The government inevitably subordinated military considerations to what was politically feasible: Canadian politicians and treasury officials thus resisted increased defense expenditures throughout the 1930s.[87] The standing of the military in Canadian society was a further obstacle to military preparedness. Few Canadians viewed the military as a prestigious, respectable, financially rewarding, or honorable profession. The militia's chronic understaffing was thus not only a function of stringent financial restraints, but also reflected its low social prestige, even during the high unemployment of the Depression years.

The interwar militia consisted of a small, permanent professional cadre, the Permanent Active Militia (PAM), and a larger, part-time Non-Permanent Active Militia (NPAM). Underfunded and undermanned, the militia barely preserved Canada's military experience.[88] While the PAM comprised dedicated career soldiers, the NPAM mustered for a mere ten days of annual exercising and undertook almost no collective training.[89]

The militia's theoretical fifteen divisions existed on paper only; the largest formation it could actually field was the brigade. Its force structure—dominated by infantry and cavalry but lacking artillery, armor, supporting arms, mobility, and a logistic tail—quickly became unbalanced and outdated. It was also utterly ill equipped to fight modern war: it possessed no modern antiaircraft guns, almost no tanks or armored cars, no medium or heavy artillery, and few infantry weapons, let alone many motor vehicles.[90] The equipment it did possess was of Great War vintage and had become both obsolete and worn out by the 1930s. Such was the extent of the military's neglect between the wars that in the absence of any realistic threat to Canadian security, that it was barely possible for the Canadian military to even defend Canada. The establishment of an expeditionary force for service in Europe was clearly impossible.[91]

Resistance by the Canadian government, treasury officials, and citizens severely circumscribed the militia's endeavors to enhance its capabilities in the late 1930s in the face of increased threats to Canada's national security. Modest increases in annual defense spending materialized after 1937 as the Canadian government prudently invested in coast artillery, warships, and planes to bolster its domestic defense capabilities. But the government directed most funds toward the Pacific, where the prospects of a Japanese-U.S. war were growing, in the belief that the Royal Navy could protect Canada's Atlantic seaboard. These logical defense priorities brought about a proportionate decline in funding for the militia during the late 1930s.[92] The militia could thus achieve few substantive reforms. There was no expansion of the PAM, though in 1936 the NPAM finally reduced its number of paper formations, began very limited mechanization, and expanded artillery and services.[93] In addition, the government extended the militia's annual training from ten to eleven days, but even this most modest of improvements had to be bitterly fought for. The decline of Canada's military-industrial complex also seriously hampered rearmament in the late 1930s. Lack of a domestic arms industry made Canada dependent on Britain for all its ordnance, save small arms and some field artillery. But since Britain had also embarked on crash rearmament it had no modern weapons to furnish to Canada. What British hardware Canada did acquire was obsolete. In the financial, political, and cultural climate of the late 1930s what appears most remarkable was that the militia managed to enhance its capabilities at all.[94]

Only in the late 1930s did Canada begin rudimentary planning for possible involvement in a European war. War Scheme Three of 1937 called for the dispatch overseas of a three-division-strong "Mobile Force" but identified no possible deployments or missions.[95] By 1939 revision had curtailed the Mobile Force to two divisions, but no progress had been made in identifying deployments or missions. Thus, when Canada declared war on Germany on 10 September 1939, a full week after Great Britain, Canada both lacked concrete plans on how to aid Great Britain and remained incapable of projecting military power beyond its frontiers.

Germany

Germany's long military tradition, the military's domination of politics and society, and the bitter legacy of defeat in 1918 stimulated substantial reform and innovation between the wars that paved the way for the tremendous German battlefield triumphs of 1939–1942. Germany's tradition as a military state, dating from 1870, created a climate conducive to innovation between the wars, and the military dominated German politics and society down to 1945.[96] This political and social ascendancy had encouraged military innovation, but it had also dragged Germany into a global conflict in 1914 that the nation could not win.

Despite overwhelming odds, the Imperial German Army outfought its opponents, defeated Russia, crippled the French Army, and forestalled defeat for four years. Such battlefield success was largely a consequence of the Imperial Army's tactical and operational flexibility. It innovated defensively, developing elastic defense in depth based on reverse-slope positions and rapid counterattack by local reserves, reforms that contributed directly to Allied failure to overcome trench warfare.[97] The army also developed new, offensive tactics; it pioneered the employment of poison gas and became proficient in its use.[98] During late 1917, it also developed new infantry "storm troop" tactics of infiltration and surprise that, when coupled with new artillery support methods, broke the deadlock on the Western Front during the German spring 1918 offensives.[99] German military innovation in World War I thus both prolonged the struggle and increased the price of Allied victory, but ultimately sheer numbers prevailed.

After defeat in 1918, the Treaty of Versailles imposed the democratic Weimar Republic on Germany and reduced its ground forces to a 100,000-man volunteer internal security and frontier defense force (*Reichswehr*) forbidden to possess planes, tanks, antiaircraft and antitank guns, heavy artillery, or chemical weapons.[100] Versailles also severely restricted German heavy weapons and prohibited armaments importation or production.[101] Throughout the interwar period, however, German politicians and generals alike remained committed to rebuilding a modern, strong army to reshape Europe politically.[102] The rise of Adolf Hitler and the National Socialists to power in 1933, therefore, brought no fundamental shift in German purpose, only in speed and determination: throughout the interwar period the German military possessed a clear political mandate to prepare for war. Such a mandate created a climate conducive to adaptation and fueled military innovation. Despite its intentions, the Treaty of Versailles thus failed to emasculate German military power as Germany resisted the treaty throughout its sixteen years' existence. Germany first evaded treaty restrictions by dismantling and hiding weapons and by smuggling ordnance overseas.[103] Thereafter, the *Reichswehr* covertly rearmed as it developed forbidden weapons abroad and then secretly inside Germany.[104] It also maintained secret troop and weapons reserves well in excess of treaty limits.[105]

Defeat and the Versailles restrictions spurred the *Reichswehr* to search for new ways to prevail against potential aggressors. Toward this goal it extensively analyzed the lessons of the Great War. The *Reichswehr* recognized that poor strategic decisionmaking and political guidance were central to German defeat, but it made little effort to reorganize or reform at the political-strategic level.[106] Examination also demonstrated that the highly trained Imperial General Staff had created a flexible command tradition that allowed individual initiative within the framework of a uniform and universal doctrine. This tradition had enabled the army to adapt tactically and operationally during World War I. Study also demonstrated the importance of firepower superiority and quality training for successful offense— and that the army's commitment to retrain in the field had allowed it to adapt to changes in the nature of the war.[107] The lessons of World War I thus reinforced the army's belief in its flexibility, tactical superiority, and mobility.

Germany also extensively examined the air war and concluded that strategic bombing attacks by Zeppelin airships and Gotha and Riesen aircraft had failed. Study revealed that Germany had proven innovative in the air war, developing pioneering specialized ground-attack aircraft and employing them as integral elements of the storm troop attacks launched during the spring 1918 offensives in the west. The *Reichswehr* thus concluded that the Great War had demonstrated a future tactical role for aircraft in direct support of ground forces, alongside strategic bombing. Germany, therefore, emerged from the Great War with a more realistic appreciation of the capabilities of air power.[108]

Scrutiny also revealed Germany's technological inferiority as Germany had lost the wartime technology race, and its failure to develop an effective tank, in particular, had contributed to defeat.[109] The *Reichswehr,* therefore, was determined to remain at the forefront of interwar weapons development, despite treaty restrictions, and to replicate the technical achievements of potential enemies. The lessons that Germany drew from the Great War in terms of the efficacy of its tactical mobility and flexibility, the superiority of its training and conduct of air operations, and its strategic and technical failings, led the *Reichswehr* to develop modern technology between the wars. At the same time, forced disarmament robbed Germany of the kind of large weapons stockpiles that hindered interwar arms development among the victorious Entente powers. The *Reichswehr* secretly developed modern weapons overseas by absorbing and enhancing foreign technology.[110] As a result, during the 1920s Germany produced many modern, high-quality weapons, including a rapid-fire light machine gun, a novel general-purpose machine gun, unrivaled modern infantry guns, a first-rate light field howitzer, a quality heavy cannon, excellent light and heavy antiaircraft guns, a mobile light antitank gun, and modern armored cars. Such were the quality of these weapons that most remained in production through 1945.[111] The *Reichswehr*'s record of technological innovation also extended beyond weaponry to include modern portable shortwave radios and the Enigma encoding machine.

The political and cultural climate of interwar Germany promoted both militarism and military innovation. Many Germans felt angered and betrayed rather than revolted by defeat and the slaughter in the trenches.[112] Cultural militarism and nationalism ensured that the military remained widely respected and admired in Germany after 1918 despite defeat, and therefore it had to justify neither itself nor defense spending. Rather, its social prestige grew as it acted as a bulwark against communism. The standing of the military in German society allowed the *Reichswehr* to focus on its political mandate for reform. Despite economic difficulties, Weimar Germany also maintained high levels of defense spending: financial constraints never shackled military reform in Germany nearly as much as they did in Britain, France, and the United States. In fact, the *Reichswehr* spent more on defense per combatant than any army in the world.[113] At the same time, the *Reichswehr*'s weakness also ensured that it was the best informed army in the world in the 1920s concerning the organization and capabilities of potential rivals.[114] Such intelligence helped the *Reichswehr* to stay ahead of other powers in the arms and technology races. For example, it standardized the 105mm howitzer as the mainstay of its artillery in the 1920s, well ahead of other nations.

One of the *Reichswehr*'s key strengths was its determination to integrate the experiences of the Great War into revised doctrine. In the early 1920s it published a new doctrinal manual, *Command and Battle,* which presented a holistic, modern, integrated approach to warfare. Steeped in the Prussian military tradition and the lessons of the Great War, it stressed concentration, the offensive, deep penetration, speed, encirclement, flexibility, and interarms cooperation.[115] Moreover, the *Reichswehr* modernized its doctrine to accommodate interwar technological change. As more capable tanks and aircraft appeared, it introduced in 1933 a new *Troop Leadership* (*Truppenführung*) manual, which placed greater emphasis on mobility as mechanization got under way within the army.[116] The clear exposition of a progressive, comprehensive, realistic, and flexible doctrine in the *Truppenführung* lay at the heart of German military effectiveness during World War II.

The key strength of German doctrine was that it conceptualized both the tactical and operational levels of war, it integrated the traditional infantry and artillery arms, and that it was farsighted and flexible enough to absorb evolving armored warfare and air power concepts. Moreover, German doctrinal emphasis on mobility, decentralization, speed, surprise, and exploitation, ensured that Germany entered World War II with realistic, balanced, and offensive-oriented doctrine. The quality of its doctrine gave the army an edge that contributed to its spectacular military triumphs early in the war.

During 1919–1933 the *Reichswehr* restored German military excellence by building on the recognized strengths of the Imperial Army. Historically German training was intensive, thorough, and emphasized regular exercising.[117] During the 1920s, the *Reichswehr* achieved an unrivaled reputation for the quality of its training because excellence in instruction was one area in which it could compensate for treaty limitations on its size and equipment. It resumed annual maneuvers as early as 1922, and from 1925 troops participated in biannual week-long exercises.[118] Frequent and extensive live-fire maneuvers tested both the capabilities of weapon systems and the viability of doctrine and tactics, improved interarms cooperation, and brought valuable operational and command experience. In these exercises the *Reichswehr* experimented with motorized troops and dummy tank units, simulated air attacks, and practiced passive air defense and anti-tank techniques. Maneuvers also emphasized envelopment, offensive defense, camouflage, and concentration of force in the attack.[119] These exercises quickly became sophisticated and the army's skill on maneuvers unsurpassed: by the 1930s the army had begun to devise operational and tactical methods for employing mobile forces.

Thorough and rigorous evaluation after each maneuver provided recommendations for reform that the army quickly acted upon.[120] Through these exercises the *Reichswehr* progressively improved its organization and the proficiency of its motorized units, familiarized troops with the need for interarms cooperation, and explored the practical problems of mechanized warfare. The Versailles denuding of German military strength and concern about Polish aggression also led the *Reichswehr* to maximize its immediate fighting power.[121] To achieve this it revived traditional Prussian strategic tenets of surprise, encirclement, and annihilation battle and married them to modern technology. Thus Weimar Germany forged a small but high-quality and well-trained army capable of limited mobile warfare, not only to defend the nation but also one day to overturn the peace settlement. Versailles, therefore, ironically imbued speed, flexibility, mobility, and offensive spirit in the *Reichswehr.*

The interwar period also saw refinement of German defensive doctrine. Treaty restrictions prevented the *Reichswehr* from conducting the defense in depth that the Imperial Army had developed during the latter stages of the Great War. Instead, it developed the approach of elastic defense employing delaying tactics (*hinhaltender Widerstand*) in which outnumbered German forces would conduct a delaying withdrawal, utilizing terrain advantages, speed, and concentration to inflict crippling losses on the enemy. The *Reichswehr* recognized that to prevail against a more powerful opponent via delaying defense required combat arms to coordinate closely to ensure that the sum of their fighting power was greater than that of the individual parts. *Reichswehr* doctrine and training thus inculcated appreciation of the need for arms to cooperate closely.

The man most responsible for molding the *Reichswehr* was its first commander in chief, Hans von Seeckt. Seeckt believed that an offensive defensive by fast-moving forces could offset numerical and material inferiority. Thus during 1919–1926, he began to motorize the army and to inculcate mobility and the offense. In stressing maneuver war, Seeckt drew on the extensive German mobile operations on the Eastern Front during World War I. Forced by the Versailles Treaty to retain a large and, by Western standards, anachronistic cavalry force, Seeckt modernized the German cavalry arm and transformed it into a mobile, offensive, semimotorized, combined-arms force for deep-penetration operations.[122] The speed, mobility, and offensive orientation that Seeckt and Versailles brought to the *Reichswehr* was central to Germany's dramatic victories early in World War II. As important in the long term was the *Reichswehr*'s initiation of limited mechanization during 1929–1931, which owed itself to von Seeckt's successor, Wilhelm Groener.[123]

Nevertheless, at the time of Hitler's accession to power in 1933 the *Reichswehr* remained a lightly equipped, horse-drawn, ten division garrison force. But the experimentation and innovation of the 1920s bore fruit in the late 1930s and eased the burden of massive, ill-planned expansion and rearmament that Hitler embarked upon. For the efforts of the 1920s had created a *Führerheer,* an army of leaders, which allowed expansion into a modern, large, offensive-oriented field force in the late 1930s far more quickly than was otherwise possible. Hitler's rise to power accelerated the pace of reform; during 1933–1935 clandestine expansion and broad rearmament began despite Versailles. Hitler covertly tripled the army and put into production the weapons developed by the *Reichswehr* in the 1920s.[124]

In 1935 Hitler renounced the Versailles Treaty, reintroduced conscription, and began simultaneous massive rearmament and military expansion. In July 1935 the Reich Defense Law redesignated the German armed forces as the *Wehrmacht,* and the German Army as the *Heer.* The fruits of *Reichswehr* research, design, and technological innovation reached the army in the late 1930s, with the result that the *Heer's* elite mechanized spearhead possessed a technological edge during the early years of World War II. Moreover, the *Reichswehr*'s evasion of treaty restrictions allowed the *Wehrmacht* to expand at an otherwise impossible pace. The Great War weapons it had secreted away, and the interwar design, development, testing, and training it had conducted allowed the *Heer* to train large annual intakes in the mid-1930s until sufficient new production became available. (But because expansion outstripped production, mobilization divisions went to war in September 1939 equipped with World War I weapons.) At the same time, Germany's military culture facilitated rapid military expansion; few Germans opposed the reintroduction of conscription, and political and public sentiment supported rearmament.

Nevertheless, the *Heer*'s cohesion and combat effectiveness initially was eroded during expansion as formations reorganized, divided, absorbed recruits, and redivided in turn, as the *Heer* underwent a twentyfold expansion in six years. During 1935–1936 the army completed its second stage of expansion to thirty-six divisions, but growth temporarily eased in 1937 as the army struggled to complete a fivefold expansion in only three years. Rapid and massive expansion brought rushed training in the late 1930s that sank below traditionally high German standards. Even though Hitler pushed the pace of expansion and rearmament, his strategic goal of global dominance had little impact on the development of German tactical or operational doctrine.[125] In fact it was Freiherr Werner von Fritsch, the army commander in chief, Ludwig Beck, the chief of the General Staff (CGS), and Erich von Manstein, the deputy CGS who were the generals chiefly responsible for the development of the new *Heer*.[126] An important key to the *Heer*'s wartime success was its receptiveness to ideas outside the main rearmament effort as senior commanders gave wide latitude and freedom to innovators to develop novel weapons, tactics, and doctrine. This quality led the army to develop a tank arm, the air force tactical aviation, and the navy a submarine force—novel arms that subsequently proved to be Nazi Germany's most effective military instruments.

Most significant of all, Germany usurped Britain's position as pioneer in armored warfare between the wars. Germany had lagged behind Great Britain in the development and employment of tanks in World War I and Versailles had forbidden the *Reichswehr* from possessing armor. However, this did not stop the German military from secretly building and testing tanks; and it examined, absorbed, and refined British ideas on armored warfare to develop its own armored doctrine between the wars.[127] The nazi rise to power energized mechanization because many leading Nazis favored motorization. In October 1934, a mobile troops command and Germany's first independent mechanized formations emerged based around the *Reichswehr*'s motor transport troops (*Kraftfahrtruppen*) and its semi-motorized cavalry arm.[128] In 1935 the establishment of Germany's first three panzer divisions followed. This development was a natural evolution of German strategic, operational, and tactical thought rather than revolutionary change. For the panzer division concept was a logical outcome of the trends of mobility, offense-mindedness, and deep penetration in

German doctrine and operational art. This reality helps explain why Germany more easily and effectively absorbed armor between the wars than did Britain.

From their genesis the panzer divisions were interarms, rather than simply tank, units that trained to cooperate together.[129] This emphasis on interarms coordination reflected both the lessons drawn from the Great War on the effectiveness of storm troop tactics and the *Reichswehr*'s efforts to maximize its fighting power. In August 1935 the *Heer* conducted its first large-scale tank maneuvers; it also closely scrutinized British evaluation of their Experimental Mechanized Force and learned more from its exercises than the British did.[130] Though modeled on the British EMF, the *Heer* came to recognize through regular exercises the strategic potential of its mechanized forces.

After 1936, the expansion of the panzer arm lost some momentum because it both generated opposition and invited grasping hands. Such opposition, however, focused on the viability of deep-penetration operations rather than on the value of the tank. In fact, broad acceptance of the utility of the tank throughout the army led Germany to raise two independent panzer brigades for infantry support, four light divisions for reconnoitering and raiding, and four motorized infantry divisions to hold captured ground. Recognizing the strategic potential of mechanized warfare, the *Heer* consolidated these formations into three motorized corps in January 1938.[131] Historians have argued that the early wartime success of German armored forces was due in part to a German refusal to build this new arm around cavalry as occurred in the British Army. However, historians have understated the role that the cavalry played in the genesis of the panzer arm. Not only was the *Heer*'s first mechanized division built around cavalry, but cavalry provided most of the personnel for Germany's first armored divisions.[132] The key difference was that the *Reichswehr* trained its cavalry during the 1920s as a mobile, combined-arms, deep-penetration force.[133] Thus the incorporation of German cavalry into the armor force proved far less detrimental than it was in the case of the more conservative British Army. In 1933–1935 Germany produced its first two tanks—the Panzer I and Panzer II—light, mass-produced training vehicles intended to be quickly superseded by larger battle tanks. Early German tanks were light, undergunned, poorly armored, and possessed poor communications and optics.[134] Equipment shortages, inexperience, and rapid expansion all hindered development of German armor in the 1930s, so that it was not until 1938 that the first medium tanks, the Panzer III and Panzer IV, entered service and lack of expertise meant that production was slow.

The tremendous German victories of 1939–1941 notwithstanding, German rearmament in the late 1930s was neither easy nor particularly effective. It was hurried and poorly planned, and the regime failed to gear rearmament toward a strategic blueprint. Rather, Germany pursued rearmament in breadth but not depth. Each service pursued independent, uncoordinated, and virtually unlimited rearmament. Such a policy inextricably bound the *Wehrmacht* to nazism and its racial-political goals but did so at a heavy price. Broad rearmament coupled with the construction of the Westwall fortifications almost bankrupted Germany during 1938–1939, and it was only the annexation of Austria and Czechoslovakia that prevented German financial and economic collapse.[135] Moreover, several inescapable strategic limitations curbed German rearmament, most significantly Germany's dependence on raw material imports, especially petroleum products and heavy metals, and its shortage of foreign exchange.[136] Within these limitations Germany prepared for war to the maximum extent possible.[137] Unconstrained rearmament promoted innovation but simultaneously removed central direction, engendering interservice rivalry as well as duplication in weapons development and force structure. The character of the National Socialist regime with its numerous competing authorities merely fueled the interservice rivalry inherent in all military organizations.

Massive, unplanned rearmament gave the West a false impression of German strength that contributed to Western appeasement and the Munich agreement. Moreover, the Nazis manipulated propaganda with decisive success to inflate Western perceptions of German military strength. In reality, German rearmament was window dressing: raw material and foreign-exchange limitations placed a ceiling on rearmament. Expansion consistently outstripped both production and training facilities. Even in the spring of 1939, for example, the army remained seriously deficient in weapons, especially mortars and heavy artillery, and only had an estimated fifteen days' worth of munitions.[138] The massive rearmament increased Germany's dependence on raw material imports, which left Germany severely short of petroleum reserves.[139]

While Germany's ambitious and expansionist foreign policy goals created a fertile environment for military innovation, both policy and geography directed innovation toward offensive ground warfare to prevent a repetition of Germany's World War I defeat. The army widely adopted radio to allow rapid, effective communications among its fast-moving offensive army, and, indeed, Germany developed the best radios in the world between the wars. But it failed to capitalize on the potential of radar because this technology's value was largely defensive, and the orientation of German preparation was overwhelmingly offensive.[140] Hitler expanded the *Heer* at a tremendous pace (see Table 1.1), but forced expansion fragmented and rushed training and reduced its quality.[141] Massive expansion of combat units also unbalanced the army's force structure, restricted its operational flexibility, and left it extremely short of nondivisional army troops and support services.[142]

Table 1.1   Expansion of the *Heer,* 1933–1939

Year	Armies	Corps	Divisions
January 1933	2	0	10
January 1934	2	10	24
January 1935	3	10	29
January 1936	3	12	39
January 1937	4	13	39
January 1938	6	19	51
January 1939	6	22	51
September 1939	11	26	102

Source: Tessin, *Formationsgeschichte,* 14.

The German military's tradition of open, honest, and critical self-examination, though, limited the detrimental effects of excessive expansion. Even in the middle of massive growth and restructuring, the *Heer* continued regular and extensive exercising. The July 1935 exercises saw the first maneuvers by an entire mechanized division and demonstrated the potential of armored warfare.[143] In September 1936 the largest German maneuvers since 1913 took place, and in the following year an even larger exercise was held.[144] These maneuvers revealed many flaws in German preparation and led to a reversion to basic training. The Czechoslovakia crisis led to a scaling back of the 1938 maneuvers, though troops exercised intensively in preparation for war with Czechoslovakia.[145] Moreover, the *Heer* evaluated in detail its combat readiness and mission potential and it gathered extensive intelligence. Hard work and sensible application characterized German military preparation, and such professionalism minimized the deleterious effects of forced expansion.

Such efforts notwithstanding, the *Heer* experienced considerable prewar growing pains. It had a severe and insurmountable officer shortage, which reinforced the army's traditional reliance on its noncommissioned officers (NCOs).[146] Yet the shortage of NCOs in the late 1930s was even more acute. The *Heer* thus went to war in September 1939 underofficered, a situation that steadily worsened throughout the war. Rushed training and its offensive orientation left troops inexpert at defense, while constant turnover in personnel delayed the acquisition of combat readiness and eroded cohesion.

One strength of the German military in 1939 was that it had gained recent operational experience from the German Condor Legion's participation in the Spanish Civil War (1936–1939).[147] The *Wehrmacht* learned important lessons in Spain where the *Luftwaffe* conducted the first large-scale strategic airlift in history, pioneered carpet bombing at Guernica, first used the Junkers Ju-87 *Stuka* dive bomber in a tactical ground-support role, and developed an embryonic command and control system for air-ground attack.[148] The ground fighting also provided important lessons, including the notable antitank capabilities of the German 88mm heavy antiaircraft gun, as well as both the potential and limitations of Germany's first generation of panzers. Germany's peaceful annexations of Austria (1938), the Sudetenland (1938), and the rump Czech State (1939) gave the *Wehrmacht* further operational experience. These campaigns were instructive rehearsals that identified numerous and glaring deficiencies in German equipment, training, and organization, but the annexations witnessed progressive improvement in German mobilization.

Confusion and chaos had accompanied mobilization for the 1938 Austrian *Anschluss*.[149] After-action reports were highly critical of doctrine and troop performance, training, and discipline. Undertrained reserve forces mobilized in disorder, march discipline was poor, and the German advance into Austria fell well behind schedule as formations straggled into Vienna. Moreover, SS, police, and *Luftwaffe* units that had not jointly exercised with the army caused major disorder.[150] Postcampaign analysis revealed that the most serious deficiency was inadequate fuel provision for the mechanizing *Heer*.[151] Due to the intensive German preparations for war with Czechoslovakia and the absorption of lessons learned from the *Anschluss*, the 1938 annexation of the Sudetenland went more smoothly. The occupation of the Czech state in March 1939 witnessed further improvement in German mobilization.[152] These operations all provided the first practical German experience with armor and ironed out many kinks in German organization, preparation, and mobilization.

Despite historical focus on the development of the panzer arm in the 1930s, most of the *Heer* remained infantry. An integral, if often underrated, element of the German blitzkrieg success was the skill, quality, and aggressiveness of German infantry. Although often depicted as a conservative opponent of armor, CGS Ludwig Beck, rather than opposing development of armor, favored balance that led to parallel enhancement of the German infantry in the 1930s. This contributed both to the German triumphs of 1939–1942 and to the protracted defense of 1943–1945.[153] Examination of the lessons of the Great War demonstrated that the German infantry had collapsed in 1918 under the strain of war. The *Reichswehr* thus revamped the infantry and von Seeckt imbued the infantry with his doctrine of mobile offense to build an aggressive infantry arm. Training emphasized individual initiative, the highest caliber squad leaders, and maximum physical fitness.[154] Interwar German infantry also routinely practiced small-unit tactical drills involving assault groups and flexible ad hoc groupings that forged a cohesive, disciplined, and flexible infantry arm prepared for fast-paced, combined-arms offensive warfare. Recognizing the infantry as a battle-winning instrument in its own right, the *Reichswehr* also improved infantry mobility and firepower: it introduced new infantry guns, antitank weapons, and machine guns, as well as modern radios.[155] It also motorized heavy weapons, communications, and headquarters. The German infantry that went to war in 1939 was better equipped and trained than its counterparts.

There was, however, little that was revolutionary about the German artillery arm in the 1930s. The Treaty of Versailles had reduced the German artillery arsenal and banned mobile heavy artillery.[156] As a result, the artillery arm struggled to meet expansion needs in the 1930s. It was slow to motorize, and overexpansion meant that even in 1938 heavy artillery remained both largely horse-drawn and in short supply (see Table 1.2).[157] Nonetheless, in the early 1930s it raised experimental motorized and chemical mortar batteries. Moreover, the mobile 105mm light field howitzer standardized in the 1930s proved well suited for the fast, mobile operations envisaged by the Germans. Emphasis on fast-paced, offensive maneuver war, though, obviated the need for a centralized artillery arm. In fact, the organization of German artillery reflected skepticism that massed artillery fire could make a decisive contribution to offensive warfare. Instead, the *Heer* envisaged the decentralized forward employment of artillery at the battalion and regimental level to disrupt and to harry, rather than shatter, an enemy already outmaneuvered and unbalanced by fast-paced ground offense.

Table 1.2   Growth of German Artillery Arm, 1933–1938

Year	Horse-drawn Battalions		Motorized Battalions		Total
	Light	Heavy	Light	Heavy	
1933	24	—	—	—	24
1934	66	21	1	7	95
1935	70	21	4	21	116
1936	86	30	8	24	148
1937	114	33	10	30	187
1938	107	36	31	54	228

Source: Tessin, *Formationsgeschichte,* 41–48.

The popular image of excellent air-ground coordination created by the blitzkrieg notwithstanding, in September 1939 the *Luftwaffe* had very limited capability to support the *Heer* and lacked an effective system for close air support. Like other air forces, it remained principally committed to strategic bombing and direct support of ground forces remained a tertiary mission. But the lessons of World War I had led it to devote greater resources to creating an air superiority fighter force; and Germany's geostrategic position compelled the *Wehrmacht* to approach air-ground cooperation with greater open-mindedness and less interservice rancor than other militaries.[158] *Luftwaffe* doctrine thus advocated a more integrated approach to war and recognized the need for air power to assist the land battle. Nevertheless, close support remained subsidiary to the air superiority, interdiction, and strategic bombing missions that dominated *Luftwaffe* rearmament in the 1930s.[159]

The Spanish Civil War had given the *Luftwaffe* practical experience of the problems of air-ground coordination from which it drew important lessons. The static warfare that had dominated that war due to well-matched ground forces led the Condor Legion to develop a primitive close-support capability. Although demonstrating the accuracy of the Stuka dive bomber as a precision bomber, the *Luftwaffe* gained no experience of close support of fast-moving mechanized forces in mobile warfare in Spain. Thus, in September 1939, the *Luftwaffe* had only a very limited close-support capability. For the Polish campaign, it allocated to direct support a single wing of obsolete aircraft relegated to this task because they were unsuited to more important missions. Moreover, the *Luftwaffe* lacked tested procedures for operating in support of armored forces, and structurally the German system of air-ground coordination was poor. Thus serious tactical, organizational, equipment, and training weaknesses limited conduct of the air-ground battle.[160] Expansion of the air force and navy also fueled interservice rivalry as these services sought to acquire ground force capabilities. Göring's quest to expand the *Luftwaffe*'s sphere of control led to a bitter, but ultimately successful, struggle with the army over antiaircraft artillery and airborne forces. The army and navy, too, clashed over control of coast defense and coast artillery.

In September 1939, Hitler mobilized a "window front" *Heer* in which Germany committed all its ground forces to the field. The German order of battle displayed an impressive 103 divisions, but all were understrength and underequipped.[161] Only half the army comprised trained combat troops, the rest were reservists and *Landwehr* (the World War I veterans who had undergone hasty refresher training). German reserves were almost nonexistent and supply stocks negligible—a mere six weeks' supply of munitions.[162] Not only was everything in the shop window, but the army was heavy on "teeth" and short on "tail" because Hitler committed everything in an effort to quickly overwhelm Polish resistance.

The outbreak of war, however, found Germany unprepared for protracted war, and its armed forces were weak long-term instruments of aggression because Germany lacked the raw materials and industrial capacity necessary for prolonged war. Moreover, despite its aura of modernity, most of the *Heer*, like German society, remained horse-drawn.[163] The strategic weakness of the German petroleum industry, the relatively unmotorized nature of German society, the limited supply of armor, and adherence to an as yet unproven tank doctrine all placed real constraints on the extent of mechanization. The limited size of the German armored force in

September 1939, therefore, reflected genuine strategic constraints rather than conservative opposition to change.

Nonetheless, Germany had started rearmament several years before its neighbors, and although the *Wehrmacht* suffered from many deficiencies, it remained better prepared than its rivals. In September 1939, Hitler thus gambled that this imperfect instrument could quickly overwhelm Germany's underprepared neighbors before they could mobilize their resources, rearm, and eliminate the German lead. The result—which materialized as much by default as by rational planning—was the blitzkrieg strategy of the early war years that transformed the global balance of power.

In conclusion, Germany's strategic and political environment created a climate conducive to innovation between the wars. However, factors beyond the strategic and political environment allowed the German military to innovate effectively in the interwar period: a combination of personalities, experiences, and the character of German military culture made the interwar German military receptive to new ideas.[164] The root of the brilliant German successes of 1939–1941 thus lay in the bitter experience of defeat in 1918 and in the army's determination to learn the operational and tactical lessons of the Great War. The interwar German military explored and disseminated these lessons diligently, flexibly, and with receptivity to new ideas. Moreover, its awareness as to who Germany's future enemies were and where they would be fought both eased the task of innovation and focused it toward offensive ground warfare. The result was the blitzkrieg.

Blitzkrieg theory presented less of a challenge to the German military because it believed that Germany had fought the Great War with correct principles, and armor offered a solution to the problems that had brought Germany defeat. Intellectual and doctrinal accommodation of the tank was thus easier in Germany than in Britain. This reality explains why by 1939, despite opposition in both countries, armored warfare had become a tenet of German doctrine but failed to get similarly established in Britain. Accommodation of armor within a realistic combined-arms doctrine allowed Germany to succeed during 1939–1940 despite the fact that Germany had devoted no more resources to mechanized forces than its enemies. The key distinction, though, was that the *Heer* allowed innovators greater freedom to develop radical, yet effective, means of employing new weapons. Moreover, the *Heer* trained for fast, offensive, combined-arms, mobile warfare and to ruthlessly exploit a breakthrough. By September 1939 the *Heer* was the only ground force in the world with an armored force, albeit small, capable of independent strategic operations. This edge—when combined with the realism and offense-orientation of German doctrine, the quality of training and leadership, and the army's professional willingness to evaluate honestly its performance and to retrain to improve its proficiency—allowed Germany to achieve a spectacular series of military triumphs over underprepared opponents during 1939–1942 that shattered the global balance of power.

Notes

1. Richard H. Kohn, *Eagle and Sword: The Federalists and the Creation of the Military Establishment in America, 1783–1802* (New York: Free Press, 1975).
2. The United States initially suffered reverses in both the War of 1812 and the 1898 Spanish-American War. Harry L. Coles, *The War of 1812* (Chicago: Chicago University Press, 1965) provides the best monographic summary of that conflict, as does James MacPherson's *Battle Cry of Freedom* (New York: Oxford University Press, 1988) for the Civil War. Lester Langley's *Banana Wars: An Inner History of American Empire, 1900–1934* (Lexington: Kentucky University Press, 1983) examines U.S. intervention in the Caribbean. On World War I, see Paul F. Braim, *The Test of Battle: The American Expeditionary Forces in the Meuse-Argonne Campaign* (Newark: University of Delaware Press, 1987). On the American way of war, see Russell F. Weigley, *Eisenhower's Lieutenants* (Bloomington: Indiana University Press, 1981) 2 vols.
3. Defense spending between the wars averaged 2 percent of GNP. Russell F. Weigley, *History of the United States Army* (New York: Macmillan, 1967), 402–403; Paul Kennedy, *The Rise and Fall of the Great Powers* (New York: Random House, 1987), 275–343.
4. Between 1919 and 1932 infantry strength declined 63 percent. On interwar conditions see Ronald Spector, "The Military Effectiveness of the U.S. Armed Forces, 1918–40," in Allan R. Millett and Williamson Murray, eds., *Military Effectiveness* (Boston: Unwin Hyman, 1988) II, 70–72; John K. Mahon, *History of the Militia and National Guard* (New York: MacMillan, 1983), 172–174; J. E. and H. W. Kaufmann, *The Sleeping Giant: American Armed Forces Between the Wars* (Westport, Conn.: Praeger, 1996), chap. 2; Shelby Stanton, *World War II: Order of Battle* (New York: Galahad Books, 1984), 2–13.
5. "The ultimate objective is the destruction of the enemy's armed forces in battle." FM 100-5, *Field Service Regulations (tentative), Operations, 1939,* para. 91. The interwar *Manual for Commanders of Large Units* stressed the mobility doctrine. On the development of this strategy of annihilation see Weigley, *The American Way of War* (Bloomington: Indiana University Press), 1977, chap. 14; Mark Grimsley, *The Hard Hand of War* (Oxford: Oxford University Press, 1995).
6. Dale E. Wilson, *Treat 'Em Rough: The Birth of American Armor, 1917–1920* (Novato, Calif.: Presidio Press, 1989); John L. S. Daley, "From Theory to Practice: Tanks, Doctrine, and the U.S. Army, 1916–1940," Ph.D. thesis, Kent State University, 1993), chaps. 3–7; Mildred H. Gillie, *Forging the Thunderbolt: A History of the Development of the Armored Force* (Harrisburg, Pa.: Military Service Publishing, 1947); Timothy K. Nenninger, "The World War I Experience," *Armor* 78, 1 (January–February 1969), 46–51.
7. During the August 1939 Plattsburg maneuvers, the 7th Mechanized Brigade defeated several infantry divisions and proved "the decisive force" in the exercise. Daley, "Theory to Practice," 765–800.
8. The 1939 infantry division had twenty-four 37mm M2 antitank guns that were virtual copies of the German 3.7cm Pak 36. John Weeks, *Men Against Tanks: A History of Anti-Tank Warfare* (New York: Mason/Charter, 1975), 92.
9. Robert F. Futrell, *Ideas, Concepts, Doctrine: A History of Basic Thinking*

in the United States Air Force, 1907–62 (Maxwell Air Force Base, Ala.: Air University, 1971), 31–62; W. F. Craven and J. F. Tate, *The Army Air Forces in World War II* (Chicago: University of Chicago Press, 1948) I, 17–74; William A. Jacobs, "Tactical Air Doctrine and AAF Close Air Support in the European Theater, 1944–45," *Aerospace Historian* 27, 1 (March 1980), 35–49; Lee Kennett, "Developments to 1939," in Benjamin F. Cooling, ed., *Case Studies in the Development of Close Air Support* (Washington, D.C.: Office of Air Force History, 1990), 23–43; Thomas H. Greer, *The Development of Doctrine in the Army Air Arm, 1917–41* (Washington, D.C.: U.S. Air Force, 1985); Kent R. Greenfield, *Army Ground Forces and the Air-Ground Battle Team* (Washington, D.C.: Historical Division, AGF, 1948); Richard Muller, "Close Air Support: The German-British-American Experiences, 1918–41," in Allan R. Millett and Williamson Murray, eds., *Innovation in the Interwar Period* (Washington, D.C.: Office of Net Assessment, DOD, 1994), 215–300.

10. Spector, "American Military Effectiveness," 85; Greenfield, *Air-Ground Battle Team,* 17–19; Kennett, "Developments to 1939," 56.

11. On average it took thirteen years to rise from first lieutenant to captain in the interwar army. Robert K. Griffith, Jr., *Men Wanted for the U.S. Army: America's Experience with an All-Volunteer Army Between the World Wars* (Westport, Conn.: Greenwood, 1982), 87–95.

12. Kaufmann & Kaufmann, *Sleeping Giant,* chaps. 4–6.

13. Spector, "American Military Effectiveness," 87.

14. By the late 1930s, the response time of U.S. artillery regiments was down to three minutes. Riley Sunderland, "Massed Fire and the FDC," *Army* 8 (August 1958), 54; Janice E. McKenney, comp., *Field Artillery: Regular Army and Army Reserve* (Washington, D.C., USACMH, 1992), 268–270.

15. The best known interwar U.S. intelligence coup was the breaking of Japan's "purple" diplomatic cipher by U.S. Army Signal Intelligence. The Naval Communications Security Unit (OP-20-G) also partially broke Japanese naval codes. Ronald Lewin, *The American Magic: Codes, Ciphers and the Defeat of Japan* (New York: Farrar, Straus Giroux, 1982); Ronald Spector, ed., *Listening to the Enemy: Documents on Communications Intelligence in the War with Japan* (Wilmington, Del.: Scholarly Resources Inc., 1988).

16. Spector, "American Military Effectiveness," 88.

17. For example, in 1938 fourteen of thirty-eight infantry regiments lacked a battalion. Stanton, *World War II: Order of Battle,* 13. Manuals TR 440-15, *Fundamental Principles of the Employment of the Air Service* (1926, revised 1935) and FM 1-5, *Employment of the Aviation of the Army* (April 1940) provided only general and broad guidelines.

18. Timothy Travers, *How the War was Won: Command and Technology in the British Army on the Western Front, 1917–1918* (London: Routledge, 1992), chaps. 8–10; Stephen P. Rosen, *Winning the Next War: Innovation and the Modern Military* (Ithaca, N.Y.: Cornell University Press, 1991); Paul Kennedy, "Britain in the First World War," in Allan R. Millett and Williamson Murray, eds., *Military Effectiveness* (Boston: Allen & Unwin, 1988) I, 31–79.

19. Travers, *How the War Was Won,* passim; Paddy Griffith, *British Fighting Methods in the Great War* (London: F. Cass, 1996).

20. Dominick Graham, "Sans Doctrine: British Army Tactics in the First World War," in Timothy Travers and Criston Archer, eds., *Men at War: Politics, Technology, and Innovation in the Twentieth Century* (Chicago: Precedent, 1982).

21. Kennedy, "Britain in the First World War," 66.

22. On the interwar political and social climate in Britain, see Charles L.

Mowat, *Britain Between the Wars, 1918–1940* (London: Metheun, 1955); Robert Graves and Alan Hodge, *The Long Week-End: A Social History of Great Britain 1918–1939* (New York: Norton, 1963).

23. By 1922 defense spending was 5 percent of its 1918 level and during 1923–1933 the army received only 9 percent of defense funds. Robin Higham, *Armed Forces in Peacetime: Britain 1918–1940, A Case Study* (Hamden, Conn.: Archon Books, 1962), 326–327; M. M. Postan, *British War Production* (London: HMSO, 1952), 6.

24. Literary examples of interwar antimilitarism include Guy Chapman, *Passionate Prodigality* (London: Nicholson & Watson, 1933); Robert Graves, *Goodbye to All That* (London: Jonathan Cape, 1929) and Erich Remarque, *All Quiet on the Western Front* (London: Heinemann, 1929).

25. David Fraser, *And We Shall Shock Them! The British Army in the Second World War* (London: Hodder and Stoughton, 1983), 6; R. P. Shay, *British Rearmament in the Thirties* (Princeton, N.J.: Princeton University Press, 1977), 14–17.

26. Michael Howard, *The Continental Commitment* (London: Maurice Temple Smith, 1972).

27. Britain confronted insurrection in Ireland, maintained occupation forces in the Rhineland and Turkey, and held the League of Nations mandate in Palestine. Michael Carver, *Twentieth Century Warriors: The Development of the Armed Forces of the Major Military Nations in the Twentieth Century* (London: Weidenfeld & Nicholson, 1987), 24.

28. The leading advocate of limited liability was Basil Liddell Hart in his *The British Way in Warfare* (London: Faber and Faber, 1932), 12–56.

29. War Office, *Field Service Regulations* I-III (London: HMSO, 1929–1935); War Office, *Infantry Training, 1932* (London: HMSO, 1932).

30. Brian Bond and Williamson Murray, "The British Armed Forces, 1918–1939," in Millett and Murray, *Military Effectiveness* II, 121.

31. The most trenchant exposition of this misinterpretation was Liddell Hart's *The Real War, 1914–1918* (London: Faber & Faber, 1930).

32. Robert H. Larson, *The British Army and the Theory of Armoured Warfare, 1918–1940* (Newark: University of Delaware Press, 1984), chaps. 2–3.

33. The Imperial German Army, in contrast, pursued operational and tactical offense while on the strategic defensive on the Eastern Front in World War I, an approach that defeated tsarist Russia. Norman Stone, *The Eastern Front, 1914–1917* (New York: Scribner, 1976).

34. Bond and Murray, "The British Armed Forces," 98.

35. Lord Cavan, for example, Chief of the Imperial General Staff (CIGS), during the early 1920s opposed officers' publishing books. J. F. C. Fuller, *Memoirs of an Unconventional Soldier* (London: Nicholson & Watson, 1936), 420.

36. Harold R. Winton, *To Change an Army, General Sir John Burnett-Stuart and British Armoured Doctrine, 1927–1938* (Lawrence: University of Kansas Press, 1988).

37. Recent scholarship has emphasized that a military institution's cultural values are often the most crucial factor in innovation but equally also the most difficult to change. Alan R. Millett and Williamson Murray, eds., *Innovation in the Interwar Period* (Washington, D.C.: Office of Net Assessment, DOD, 1994).

38. Some 41,000 troops participated in the 1925 maneuvers, while ten divisions exercised in 1935. Richard Challener, comp., *U.S. Military Intelligence, 1914–1927* (New York: Garland, 1978), 10213-14; Maj. Gen. J. H. MacBrien, "The British Army Maneuvers September 1925," *Canadian Defense Quarterly* 2 (January

1926), 132–150; Basil Liddell Hart, "Army Manoeuvres, 1925," *Journal of the Royal United Services Institute* 70 (1925), 647–655; Lt. Col. A. G. Armstrong, "Army Maneuvers, 1935," *Journal of the Royal United Services Institute* 80 (November 1935), 520.

39. The army diverted few resources toward technological advances in artillery target acquisition, for example. The RAF in comparison developed radar and two first-rate fighters, the Hawker Hurricane and Supermarine Spitfire, and then constructed an air defense system around these planes and radar that enabled the RAF to win the Battle of Britain. Millett and Murray, *Innovation in the Interwar Period*, iii; Bond and Murray, "British Armed Forces," 114.

40. Coordinated infantry and armor brought victory at Cambrai (fall 1917) and Amiens (August 1918). But the other British victories in 1918 were traditional and costly infantry-artillery battles. Basil Liddell Hart, *The Tanks, 1914–1939* (London: Cassell, 1959); Rosen, *Winning the Next War;* Travers, *How the War Was Won;* Shelford Bidwell and Dominick Graham, *Firepower: British Army Weapons and Theories of War, 1904–1945* (London: Allen & Unwin, 1982).

41. The RTC comprised four tank battalions and eight armored car companies, a major force in an army of only 200,000 men. The 1926–1934 EMF maneuvers showed the potential of armored forces and illustrated that the army both possessed innovative officers and was not opposed to reform. It was the interplay of financial constraints and personalities that ultimately led to the disbandment of the EMF in 1934. Barton C. Hacker, "The Military and the Machine: An Analysis of the Controversy over Mechanization in the British Army, 1919–1939," Ph.D. thesis, University of Chicago, 1968, 41–42. On doctrine see War Office, *Mechanized and Armoured Formations, 1929* (London: HMSO, 1929).

42. Studies that have stressed financial constraints and mission orientation in the British failure to develop a tank arm include Maj. L. F. Ellis, *The War in France and Flanders, 1939–1940* (London: HMSO, 1953), 315; Maj. Gen. Iam S. O. Playfair, *The Mediterranean and Middle East* (London: HMSO, 1956) II, 174; Donald C. Watt, *Too Serious a Business* (Berkeley: University of California Press, 1977), 81; Bond, *British Military Policy,* 180–189. See also J. P. Harris, "British Armour and Rearmament in the Late 1930s," *Journal of Strategic Studies* 11, 2 (June 1988); Larson, *Armoured Warfare,* chaps. 3–4.

43. Works that have stressed the officer corps social conservatism and faith in cavalry include Anthony J. Trythall, *Boney Fuller* (New Brunswick, N.J.: Rutgers University Press, 1977); Kenneth Macksey, *Armoured Crusader* (London: Hutchinson, 1967); and Correlli Barnett, *Britain and Her Army, 1509–1970: A Military, Political and Social Survey* (London: Penguin Press, 1970). Recent scholarship has shown that historians have exaggerated the proportion and power of the landed elite in the interwar officer corps and has demonstrated that the interwar prestige of the cavalry declined considerably, and that by no means did all cavalry officers oppose mechanization. Larson, *Armoured Warfare,* 15–32.

44. Larson, *Armoured Warfare,* 115.

45. Ibid., chap. 4.

46. Ibid., 130–132.

47. Ibid., chap. 5.

48. Murray, "Armored Warfare," 30; Bond and Murray, "British Armed Forces," 122.

49. Basil Collier, *The Defence of the United Kingdom* (London: HMSO, 1957), 27–28.

50. On the background to the reintroduction of conscription, see Peter Dennis, *Decision by Default: Peacetime Conscription and British Defense, 1919–1939* (London: Routledge & Kegan Paul, 1972).

51. By the mid-1930s, aside from the royal arsenals, only Vickers Armstrong remained of the more than thirty World War I arms factories. Bond and Murray, "British Armed Forces," 103.

52. The Vickers Medium of 1924 was the best tank of its day but the later Mark I infantry tank was so mechanically unreliable that the army dared not display it at the 1939 Aldershot Military Tattoo. Larson, *Armoured Warfare,* 222; David Fletcher, *The Great Tank Scandal* (London: HMSO, 1989).

53. The 1924 Vickers Medium remained the mainstay of Britain's tank force until 1937. In September 1939 Britain had 60 heavy tanks out of a total of 1,600. Sir James M. Butler, *Grand Strategy* (London: HMSO, 1964) II, 28.

54. Larson, *Armoured Warfare,* 191.

55. Hobart saw what was to come but he ran afoul of his many enemies and was recalled in disgrace in spring 1939. Macksey, *Armoured Crusader,* chaps. 6–7.

56. Bidwell and Graham, *Firepower* 143; P. Mead, *The Eye in the Air: History of Air Observation and Reconnaissance for the Army, 1785–1945* (London: HMSO, 1983), 51ff.

57. Brig. R. G. S. Bidwell, "The Development of British Field Artillery Tactics, 1920–1939: Reform and Reorganization," *Journal of the Royal Artillery* 94 (1967), 13–24.

58. War Office, *Field Service Regulations* II (London: HMSO, 1920); War Office, *Artillery Training—War* (London: 1928), 13–15; Bidwell and Graham, *Firepower,* 150–152.

59. Shelford Bidwell, "Indirect Fire Artillery as a Battle Winner/Loser," in Correlli Barnett, ed., *Old Battles, New Defences: Can We Learn from Military History?* (London: Brassey, 1986), 115–140.

60. War Office, *Mechanized and Armoured Formations* (London: HMSO, 1929).

61. Bidwell and Graham, *Firepower,* 151–153.

62. Liddell Hart blamed artillery indifference for the demise of close support artillery. Basil Liddell Hart, *Memoirs of Captain Liddell Hart* (London: Cassell, 1967) I, 101.

63. Doctrine stated that "certain field guns may be placed in or near the front line." War Office, *Field Service Regulations* (London: HMSO, 1935) II, 14.

64. Bidwell, "Field Artillery Tactics," 16–19.

65. It is worth noting that in September 1939 that the Americans had no self-propelled artillery and that the Germans had a mere thirty-eight self-propelled 15cm heavy infantry guns. Eric Grove, *World War II Tanks: The Axis Powers* (London: Orbis Publishing, [1971]), 7.

66. Bidwell, "Field Artillery Tactics," 20.

67. Bidwell, "Field Artillery Tactics," 21–22.

68. War Office, *Field Service Regulations* II (London: HMSO, 1935), chap. 1, para. 5.

69. Bidwell, "Field Artillery Tactics," 23–24.

70. Murray, "British Military Effectiveness," 111–113.

71. British intelligence exaggerated German military capabilities during 1933–1938 but underrated them during 1938–1939 when German rearmament and expansion finally bore fruit. Wesley K. Wark, *The Ultimate Enemy: British Intelligence and Nazi Germany, 1933–1939* (Ithaca, N.Y., London: Cornell University Press, 1985).

72. Bruce Gudmundsson, *Stormtroop Tactics: Innovation in the German Army, 1914–1918* (New York: Praeger, 1989); Hubert C. Johnson, *Breakthrough: Tactics, Technology, and the Search for Victory on the Western Front in World War I* (Novato, Calif.: Presidio Press, 1994).

73. P[ublic] R[ecord] O[ffice], Kew, CAB[inet] [Papers] 23/97, "Meeting of the Cabinet, 22.2.1939," 306.

74. Bond and Murray, "British Armed Forces," 121.

75. David Pritchard, *The Radar War: Germany's Pioneering Achievement, 1904–45* (Wellingborough: Patrick Stephens, 1989); Tony Devereux, *Messenger God of Battle: Radio, Radar, Sonar: The Story of Electronics in War* (London: Brassey, 1991).

76. W. A. Jacobs, "Air Support for the British Army, 1939–1943," *Military Affairs* XLVI, 4 (December 1982), 175.

77. Norman Gibbs, "British Strategic Doctrine, 1918–1939," in Michael Howard, ed., *The Theory and Practice of War* (Bloomington: Indiana University Press, 1975), 185–212.

78. On Canada's military history, see C. P. Stacey, *The Military Problems of Canada: A Survey of Defence Politics and Strategic Conditions Past and Present* (Toronto: Ryerson Press, 1940); G. F. G. Stanley, *Canada's Soldiers: The Military History of an Unmilitary People* (Toronto: Macmillan, 1974); Desmond Morton, *Canada at War: A Military and Political History* (Toronto: Butterworth's, 1981).

79. On Canada's role in the War of 1812, see Morris Zaslow and W. B. Turner, eds., *The Defended Border: Upper Canada and the War of 1812* (Toronto: Macmillan, 1964); J. Mackay Hitsman, *The Incredible War of 1812: A Military History* (Toronto: University of Toronto Press, 1965); G. F. G. Stanley, *The War of 1812: Land Operations* (Toronto: MacMillan, 1983); Pierre Berton, *The Invasion of Canada, 1812–1813* and *Flames Across the Border, 1813–1814* (Toronto: McClelland & Stewart, 1980–1981).

80. The CEF raised a motor machine gun brigade that became adept at sophisticated indirect-fire barrages. Lt. Col. G. S. Hutchinson, *Machine Guns: Their History and Tactical Employment* (London: Macmillan, 1938), 175–176; William F. Stewart, "Attack Doctrine in the Canadian Corps, 1916–1918," M.A. thesis, University of New Brunswick, 1982.

81. After 8 August 1918 the CEF shattered the German front at Amiens, penetrated the Hindenburg line, took Cambrai, and reached Mons by the armistice. Col. Gerald W. L. Nicholson, *Official History of the Canadian Army in the First World War: The Canadian Expeditionary Force, 1914–1919* (Ottawa: Queen's Printer, 1962); John A. Swettenham, *To Seize Victory* (Toronto: Ryerson Press, 1965) and *Breaking the Hindenburg line* (Ottawa: Canadian War Museum, 1986); D. J. Goodspeed, *The Road Past Vimy: The Canadian Corps, 1914–1918* (Toronto: Macmillan, 1969); Daniel G. Dancocks, *Spearhead to Victory: Canada and the Great War* (Edmonton: Hurtig, 1987).

82. On the Canadian military's drive for economy, see J. Mackay Hitsman, *Military Inspection Services in Canada, 1855–1950* (Ottawa: Department of National Defense, 1962).

83. Defense spending fell 40 percent during 1930–1933. W. A. B. Douglas and Brereton Greenhous, *Out of the Shadows: Canada in the Second World War* (Toronto: Oxford University Press, 1977), 13–14.

84. John English, *The Canadians in Normandy: A Study of Failure in High Command* (Toronto: Praeger, 1991), chap. 1.

85. By 1935 Canada only retained the Dominion Arsenal at Quebec. Col. C. P. Stacey, *Six Years of War: The Army in Canada, Britain, and the Pacific* (Ottawa: Queen's Printer, 1955), 8–9.

86. Mackenzie King consistently opposed increased defense spending. J. W. Pickergill, ed., *The MacKenzie King Record* (Toronto: University of Toronto Press, 1960–1970) 4 vols.; C. P. Stacey, *Canada and the Age of Conflict, A History of*

Canada's External Policies, Vol. II, 1921–1948: The Mackenzie King Era (Toronto: Macmillan, 1981); and J. L. Granatstein, *Canada's War: The Politics of the Mackenzie King Government, 1939–1945* (Toronto: Oxford University Press), 1975.

87. Stephen J. Harris, *Canadian Brass: The Making of a Professional Army, 1860–1939* (Toronto: University of Toronto Press, 1988), chap. 10.

88. In June 1931, for example, the PAM and NPAM stood at only 53 percent and 38 percent, respectively, of authorized strength. Stacey, *Six Years,* 5.

89. The PAM comprised three infantry and two cavalry regiments. During the Depression training declined further. During 1931–1932 only 2,182 troops trained on average for 4 days, and one militia battalion exercised just twice as a unit between the wars. Stanley, *Soldiers,* 339–343; William E. J. Hutchinson, "Test of a Corps Commander: General Guy Granville Simonds, Normandy 1944," M. A. thesis, University of Victoria, 1983, 57.

90. In 1935 the militia possessed two armored cars but no antitank guns, mortars, or Bren guns. Lt. Col. E. L. M. Burns, "The Defence of Canada," *Canadian Defense Quarterly,* 13, 4 (July 1936), 341.

91. In 1924 Canada spent one-sixth of what Britain spent per capita on defense. Hutchinson, "Corps Commander," 56.

92. Defense spending increased 19 percent during 1936–1937, but the Militia's share fell from 61 percent in 1936–1937 to 50 percent in 1938–1939. Stacey, *Arms,* 3–4.

93. During 1935–1939 the strength of the PAM increased 19 percent while reorganization slashed NPAM cavalry regiments and infantry battalions, raised new machine gun battalions and fifty-two artillery batteries, and earmarked eight battalions for mechanization. Stanley, *Soldiers,* 346.

94. For a more positive evaluation of the effectiveness of Canadian military reform in the late 1930s, see Stanley, *Soldiers,* 344–354.

95. The title "mobile force" was misleading because the planned force completely lacked mobility. Stanley, *Soldiers,* 352; Harris, *Brass,* Chap. 8.

96. Dennis Showalter, *Railroads and Rifles: The Influence of Technological Development on German Military Thought and Practice, 1815–66* (Hamden, Conn.: Archon Books, 1975).

97. These new defensive tactics crippled the French spring 1917 offensive and led to the French army mutiny of that year. Timothy Lupfer, *The Dynamics of Doctrine: The Development of German Defensive Doctrine in World War I* (Fort Leavenworth: U.S. Army Staff and Command College, 1981).

98. German gas attacks caused three times as many casualties as did Entente gas attacks. National Archives Records Administration, Washington D.C., Captured German Records Collection Microfilm (hereafter NARA) series T–78, roll 18, frame 151208ff.

99. Lt. Col. Georg Bruchmüller developed accurate massed fire without the ranging fire that warned of an imminent attack. Storm troops were elite attack squads strong in firepower that infiltrated enemy trench lines. These combined tactics restored mobility and surprise to the offensive at Riga in September 1917 and at Cambrai in November 1917. Bruce Gudmundsson, *Stormtroop Tactics: Innovation in the German Army, 1914–1918* (New York: Praeger, 1989); Hubert C. Johnson, *Breakthrough: Tactics, Technology, and the Search for Victory on the Western Front in World War I* (Novato, Calif.: Presidio Press, 1994); David Zabecki, *Steel Wind: Col. Georg Bruchmüller and the Birth of Modern Artillery* (Westport, Conn.: Praeger, 1994).

100. The *Reichswehr* also comprised a 15,000-man navy of obsolete warships banned from possessing planes, submarines, or capital ships over 10,000 tons.

James S. Corum, *The Roots of Blitzkrieg: Hans von Seeckt and German Military Reform* (Lawrence: Kansas University Press, 1992), xiv; Barton Whaley, *Covert German Rearmament, 1919–1939: Deception and Misperception* (Frederick, Md.: University Publications of America, 1984), 7–8.

101. Versailles limited the *Reichswehr* to 102,000 rifles, 1,926 machine guns, 252 mortars, and 288 artillery pieces. It also severely limited munitions stocks. Whaley, *Covert Rearmament,* 136–137.

102. Hans von Gatzke, *Stresemann and the Rearmament of Germany* (Baltimore: Johns Hopkins Press, 1954), 4–11.

103. Krupp acquired the Dutch Blessing company that "bought" 1,500 German howitzers, and Fokker smuggled 220 planes into Holland. In 1927 the *Reichswehr*'s secret stockpiles amounted to 350,000 rifles, 12,000 machine guns, 400 mortars, and 675 howitzers. Whaley, *Covert Rearmament,* 11–13; F. L. Carsten, *The Reichswehr and Politics, 1918–1933* (Oxford: Clarendon Press, 1966), 221; Herbert Schottelius and Gustav-Adolf Caspar, "Die Organisation des Heeres 1933–39," in Militärgeschichtliches Forschungsamt (MGFA), *Handbuch zur deutschen Militärgeschichte, 1648–1939* (Stuttgart: Bernard & Graefe, 1978) VII, 396.

104. Germany built seaplanes and submarines in Sweden and Finland and tested weapons and planes in the Soviet Union. Whaley, *Covert Rearmament,* 11–13, 25–26; Hans Gatzke, "Russo-German Military Collaboration during the Weimar Republic," *American Historical Review* 63 (1958), 565–597; F. L. Carsten, "The Reichswehr and the Red Army, 1920–33," in *Survey: A Journal of Soviet and East European Studies* 44–45 (1962); George H. Stein, "Russo-German Military Collaboration: The Last Phase 1933," *Political Science Quarterly* 77 (1962–1963).

105. Albert Seaton, *The German Army, 1933–1945* (New York: Meridian Books, 1982), 76–90; Corum, *Roots of Blitzkrieg,* 181–182; Whaley, *Covert Rearmament,* 19–23; Jacques Benoist-Mechlin, *Histoire de L'Armée Allemande* (Paris: Editions Albin Michel, 1938) II, 147; Robert M. Citino, *The Evolution of Blitzkrieg Tactics: Germany Defends Itself Against Poland, 1918–1933* (Westport, Conn.: Greenwood Press, 1987), chaps. 1–2. For covert German training in the 1920s, see NARA T–78, roll 202; T–77, 110, 837563ff, Heereswaffen Amt. Wi., "Allgemeine Organisations Fragen," 1923–1932.

106. Such analysis recognized Germany's strategic failures. German officers between the wars came to believe that the army high command had made four strategic errors during the Great War: von Moltke had bungled the Schlieffen Plan in 1914; von Falkenhayn missed great opportunities to knock Russia out of the war with an offensive in the east in 1915 and should never have launched the 1916 Verdun offensive; and that Ludendorf mismanaged the 1918 western offensives. Jehuda L. Wallach, *The Dogma of the Battle of Annihilation: The Theories of Clausewitz and Schlieffen and Their Impact on the German Conduct of Two World Wars* (Westport, Conn.: Greenwood Press, 1986), 211–218; Corum, *Roots of Blitzkrieg,* 2–5; Holger Herwig, "Clio Deceived, Patriotic Self-Censorship in Germany after the Great War," *International Security* (Fall 1987).

107. Gudmundsson, *Stormtroop Tactics,* 21–22, 161–162; Rod Paschall, *The Defeat of Imperial Germany, 1917–18* (Chapel Hill, N.C.: Algonquin, 1989).

108. John Morrow, *German Air Power in World War I* (Lincoln: University of Nebraska Press, 1982); Raymond Fredette, *Sky on Fire: The First Battle of Britain, 1917–18 and the Birth of the RAF* (New York: Holt, Rinehart & Winston, 1966); Corum, *Roots of Blitzkrieg,* 16–17. Richard Hallion, *The Rise of the Fighter Aircraft, 1914–1918* (Annapolis: Nautical and Aviation Publishing, 1984); Bryan Phillpott, *The Encyclopaedia of German Military Aircraft* (London: Bison, 1981), 53–54; Corum, *Roots of Blitzkrieg,* 13–18.

109. Germany produced one tank in World War I, the A7V, of which only twenty saw combat. Peter Chamberlain and Christopher Ellis, *Tanks of World War I* (New York: Arco, 1969), 59–64; B. Fitzsimons, ed., *Tanks and Weapons of World War I* (London: Phoebus, 1972).

110. Opposition, for example, to the introduction of a new U.S. 105mm howitzer in the 1930s centered around the large stocks of 75mm guns still in service. Janice McKenney, "More Bang for the Buck in the Interwar Army: The 105mm Howitzer," *Military Affairs* 42, 2 (April 1978), 80–85. Rheinmetall's purchase of the Swiss Solothurn firm led to development of the Luftwaffe's 7.92mm MG 15 and 2cm *Flak* 30, for example. Whaley, *Covert Rearmament*, 10–11; Terry Gander and Peter Chamberlain, *Small Arms, Artillery and Special Weapons of the Third Reich* (London: Macdonald and Jane's, 1978), 7, 71–72, 127.

111. The 7.5cm *leichte Infanteriegeschütz* 18 entered production in 1929, the infamous 8.8cm *Flak* 18 in 1933, and the 10.5cm *leichte Feldhaubitz* 18 in 1936. Ian Hogg, *German Artillery of World War II*, 18–21, 26–30, 45–47, 57–63, 144–145; Gander and Chamberlain, *Small Arms*, 71–72, 107–112, 170–171, 248–249, 260, 282–284, 287.

112. Much interwar German literature eulogized rather than condemned the Great War struggle. See, for example, Ernst Jünger, *Storm of Steel: From the Diary of a German Storm Troop Officer on the Western Front* (London: Chatto & Windus, 1929).

113. Citino, *Blitzkrieg Tactics,* 182.

114. On German evaluation of foreign military developments, see NARA T-77, rolls 891–892, Reichswehrministerium (RWM), Ausland, 1933–1935; T-77, 898, 5650778-1013 and 902, 5655983-6124, RWM, Ausland III, "Luft-Allgemeines, 1934–1935;" T-77, 904, 5658191-489, RWM Ausland, "Nachrichten über Fremde Luftmächte, 1934;" T-77, 904, 5658490ff, Gen. v. Bötticher, Miltär-Attache, Washington, "Kampf um die Seele des amerikanischen Heeres."

115. Chef der Heeresleitung, Heeresdienstvorschrift 487, *Führung und Gefecht der verbundenen Waffen* (Berlin: Verlag Offene Worte, 1921–1925).

116. NARA T-78, 201, 6144926-5212, Chef der Heeresleitung T.A. Nr 3000/33 T4 and Nr 2200/34 T4, Heeresdienstvorschrift 300, *Truppenführung* (Berlin: Verlag Offene Worte, 1933–1934).

117. Corum, *Roots of Blitzkrieg,* 11.

118. Six of Germany's seven infantry divisions participated in the 1926 fall maneuvers, and elements of all ten divisions joined the 1930 maneuvers. Richard Challenger, comp., *United States Military Intelligence: Weekly Summaries* (New York: Garland, 1978), XXV, 1–13; Citino, *Blitzkrieg Tactics,* 79–93.

119. NARA T-78, 201, 6144910-12, RWM, Wehrmachtsabteilung Inland, "Ausbildungsplan einen Artl.-Abtl. für das Sommerhalbjahr nach der Einzelbesichtigung bis zu den Herbst-übungen," n.d.; T-78, 275, 6224340ff, 6. Artl. Rgt. "Ausbildung," 1922–1935. The first experiments with motorized troops occurred as early as 1921 in the Harz Mountains. An ad hoc motorized division and motorized brigade participated in the 1926–1927 winter games. Citino, *Blitzkrieg Tactics,* 72; Corum, *Roots of Blitzkrieg,* 11–12; Craig, *Politics of the Prussian Army,* 396; *U.S. Military Intelligence* XXIII, 10432–33; XXV, 1–13; Gudmundsson, *Stormtroop Tactics,* 25; Wallach, *Dogma,* 79; Holger Herwig, "The Dynamics of Necessity: German Military Effectiveness in World War I," in Alan R. Millett and Williamson Murray, *Military Effectiveness* (Boston: Allen & Unwin, 1988) I, 101.

120. See, for example, Bundesarchiv-Militärarchiv, Freiburg-im-Breisgau (hereafter BAMA), RH 12–2/200, Gen. Walter Reinhardt, "Erfahrungsbericht," 11 November 1927.

121. For the impact that potential conflict with Poland had on development of

the German military between the wars see Citino, *Blitzkrieg Tactics*. This study, however, neglects the historic roots of blitzkrieg in the Prussian military tradition.

122. Versailles allowed Germany 16,407 cavalry in three small divisions. By 1933 the *Reichswehr* had transformed this force, which the Allies had conceived as useful only for crowd control, into a motorized mobile corps. Edgar Graf v. Matuschka, "Organisation des Reichsheeres," in *Handbuch zur deutschen Militärgeschichte* VI, 322–324; Klaus C. Richter, *Die Feldgrauen Reiter: Die berittenen und bespannten Truppen in Reichswehr und Wehrmacht* (Stuttgart: Motorbuch, 1986), 31–32, 121–124.

123. Citino, *Blitzkrieg Tactics,* 190–196.

124. In 1934, the German military possessed twelve disassembled submarines and sixteen clandestine air squadrons. On covert rearmament see NARA T-77, 2, 713988-991, Waffen Amt, Nr. 1279/33 g.k. Wa. Wi. an V.G.H., vom 7 October 1933; Georg Tessin, *Formationsgeschichte der Wehrmacht, 1933–39* (Boppard am Rhein: Harald Boldt, 1959), 251–252; Whaley, *Covert Rearmament,* 69.

125. On Hitler's foreign policy objectives, see Eberhard Jäckel, transl. Herbert Arnold, *Hitler's Weltanschauung: A Blueprint for Power* (Middletown, Conn.: Wesleyan University Press, 1972).

126. Williamson Murray, *Change in the European Balance of Power, 1938–1939: The Path to Ruin* (Princeton, N.J.: Princeton University Press, 1984), 32.

127. Germany opened an armored school at Kazan in the Soviet Union in 1926 and trained on Soviet-purchased British Vickers medium tanks and covertly produced their own tanks in the late 1920s. Chris Ellis and Hilary Doyle, *Panzerkampfwagen: German Combat Tanks, 1933–1945* (Kings Langley, England: Bellona Publications, 1976), 24–28. In 1928 the *Reichswehr* issued its first armored doctrine based largely on the British *Provisional Instructions for Armoured Vehicles* (London: War Office, 1927). For German analysis of British maneuvers see NARA T-77, 901, 5654541-887, RWM, Ausland, Oberst Geyr v. Schweppenburg, Militär-Attache, London.

128. Germany's first mechanized formations were the 1st Tank Brigade, 1st and 2nd Motor Combat Brigades, and the 3rd Motorized Cavalry Division, which became the Light Division in 1935. Tessin, *Formationsgeschichte,* 54–62.

129. NARA T-79, 30, 000937, Kdo. d. Panzertruppen, "Besichtigungsbemerkungen des Kommandierenden Generals des Kommandos der Panzertruppen im Jahre 1937," Ia Nr. 4300 3770/37, Berlin, 15 November 1937.

130. NARA T–79, 16, 000790ff, Chef des Truppenamts, "England: manöver des Panzerverbandes, 18. bis 21.9.1934," December 1934; T–79, 30, 000983ff, Reichsministerium, Ausland, "England: Die manöver mit motorisierten Truppen, September, 1939."

131. These formations—the 4th and 6th Panzer Brigades, the 1st–4th Light and the 2d, 13th, 20th, and 29th Motorized Infantry Divisions—were concentrated in the XIV–XVI Corps. Tessin, *Formationsgeschichte,* 58–59.

132. The transfer of motorized reconnaissance troops from the panzer arm to the cavalry in 1938 illustrates the important role of the cavalry in mechanization. Tessin, *Formationsgeschichte,* 38–41, 54–62.

133. A semimotorized cavalry corps reinforced with bicycle troops and dummy tanks participated in the fall 1932 Silesian maneuvers. Richter, *Feldgrauen Reiter,* 122–124; Corum, *Roots of Blitzkrieg,* 42.

134. German tank designers, for example, had no understanding of the superior protection sloped armor offered until the 1941 invasion of the Soviet Union. Seaton, *German Army,* 69.

135. In 1938 Germany possessed only 1 percent of global gold and financial reserves. The occupation of Czechoslovakia in March 1939 increased Germany's financial reserves nearly tenfold. Murray, *Balance of Power,* 12–17.

136. Coal was the only raw material that Germany possessed in abundance, but such deposits were located vulnerably close to Germany's frontiers. The German economy was weakest in the petroleum and metals sectors and was especially reliant on Swedish iron ore imports. Murray, *Balance of Power,* 4–16.

137. German defense spending during 1935–1938 was 13 percent of aggregate national expenditure. In France the figure was 7.0 percent and in Britain 5.5 percent. Macgregor Knox, *Mussolini Unleashed* (London: 1982), 294–296.

138. On 2 March 1939 field units were short of the following: rifles 18.5 percent, machine guns 29.0 percent, antitank guns 25.0 percent, light mortars 58.0 percent, medium mortars 53.5 percent, infantry guns 24.0 percent, light field howitzers 20.0 percent, and heavy field howitzers 50.0 percent. Schottelius and Caspar, "Organisation des Heeres," 397; Manfred Messerschmidt, "German Military Effectiveness during the Interwar Period," in Murray and Millett, eds., *Military Effectiveness* II, 227.

139. In June 1938 Germany possessed only four months of petroleum reserves. Murray, *Change,* 8.

140. In 1939 Germany had prototypes of the "Freya" aircraft early-warning, the "Wurzburg" antiaircraft artillery fire-control, and naval tactical (*Seetakt*) radars. David Pritchard, *The Radar War: Germany's Pioneering Achievement, 1904–1945* (Wellingborough, Northants.: P. Stephens, 1989); Tony Devereaux, *Messenger Gods of Battle: Radio, Radar, Sonar: The Story of Electronics in War* (London: Brassey, 1991); Alan Beyerchen, "From Radio to Radar: Interwar Military Adaptation to Technological Change in Germany, the United Kingdom, and the United States," in Williamson Murray and Allan R. Millett, eds., *Military Innovation during the Interwar Period* (Washington, D.C.: Office of Net Assessment, DOD, 1994), 440–450.

141. In March 1936 after expansion to twenty-four divisions, the *Reichswehr* only rated four brigades and six air squadrons as combat ready. Whaley, *Covert Rearmament,* 58–59.

142. In September 1939 less than 5 percent of combat battalions were nondivisional army troops. Tessin, *Formationsgeschichte,* passim.

143. Capt. Robert J. O'Neil, "Doctrine and Training in the German Army 1919–1939," in Michael Howard, ed., *The Theory and Practice of War* (New York: Praeger, 1965), 158–185.

144. Five divisions and 80,000 troops participated in the 1936 maneuvers, while nine divisions and 300,000 troops exercised in the September 1937 Mecklenburg exercises. O'Neil, "Doctrine and Training," 159–160.

145. NARA T-78, 269, 6218073ff, Insp. d. Artillerie, "Artillerie-Rahmen-übung 1938," Az. 35 o 10/38 Ia Rah. Nr. 3430/97 geh. [1938].

146. Halving training time for officer cadets, increasing intake of candidates tenfold, absorbing police officers, commissioning NCOs, and recommissioning Imperial Army officers failed to fill junior officer vacancies. Thus the officer-enlistee ratio of 1:24 in 1933 had widened to 1:26 by September 1939 and reached 1:40 in June 1944. Corum, *Roots of Blitzkrieg,* 76; Wolf Keilig, *Das Deutsche Heer* (Bad Nauheim: Podzun, 1956) 203, 1–24.

147. Some 19,000 German troops, 180 tanks, and 250 planes fought with the Condor Legion in Spain. On German lessons learned in Spain see Wolfgang Kern and Erhard Moritz, "Lehren des faschistischen deutschen Oberkommandos des

Heeres auf der bewaffneten Intervention in Spanien 1936–39," *Militärgeschichte* 15 (1976).

148. Nine Junkers Ju-52 transports ferried 13,523 nationalist rebels from Spanish Morocco to Spain in five weeks. Raymond Proctor, *Hitler's Luftwaffe in the Spanish Civil War* (Westport, Conn.: Greenwood Press, 1983), 30–31, 256–258.

149. Murray, *Change,* 144–146.

150. Georg Tessin, *Zur Geschichte der Ordnungspolizei, 1936–1945* (Coblenz: n.p., 1957), Part II, 10–11.

151. NARA T–79, 14, 000447, Heeresgruppenkdo. 3, "Der Einsatz der 8. Armee in März 1938 zur Wiedervereignung österreichs mit dem deutschen Reich," 18 July 1938. Guderian provided a much more positive view of the campaign in his memoirs. Heinz Guderian, *Panzer Leader* (London: Joseph, 1952), 36–37.

152. On German occupation of the Sudetenland and the rump Czechoslovakia see Hans Umbreit, *Deutsche Militarverwaltungen 1938–39: Die militärische Besetzung der Tschechoslowakei und Polens* (Stuttgart: Deutsche Verlags Anstalt, 1977).

153. Beck also played a crucial role in the formation of Germany's first three mechanized brigades in 1934. Walter Nehring, *Die Geschichte der Deutschen Panzerwaffe, 1916 bis 1945* (Berlin: Propyläen, 1969), 89ff.

154. Interwar German infantry routinely marched 30 miles a day. English, *Infantry,* 69.

155. In 1930 German infantry units received the 7.5cm *lIG* 18 and 3.7cm *Pak* 35/36. The following year the army increased by 50 percent the number of light machine guns in each infantry battalion. Matuschka, "Organisation des Reichsheeres," 320–321.

156. The Treaty of Versailles allowed the *Reichswehr* 208 7.7cm and 86 10.5cm guns plus 38 fortress pieces. On interwar developments in the German artillery arm, see Joachim Engelmann u. Horst Scheibert, *Deutsche Artillerie 1934–45* (Limburg: 1974); Matuschka, "Organisation des Reichsheeres," 325–327.

157. In the summer of 1938 the heaviest German artillery piece was a 21cm gun, of which only twenty-three were in service. Walter Bernhardt, *Die Deutsche Aufrüstung, 1934–1939* (Frankfurt am Main: Bernard & Graefe, 1969), 96–97.

158. Williamson Murray, "The Luftwaffe Experience, 1939–1941," in Benjamin F. Cooling, ed., *Close Air Support* (Washington, D.C.: Office of Air Force History, 1990), 71–114; and "The Luftwaffe Before the Second World War: A Mission, A Strategy?" *Journal of Strategic Studies* (September 1981).

159. *Luftkriegführung* (Berlin: Verlag Offene Worte, 1935), 125–132.

160. Murray, "Luftwaffe Experience," 75–79.

161. This total comprised 6 armored, 4 light mechanized, 4 motorized infantry, 1 cavalry, 3 mountain, and 86 infantry divisions organized in 4 mobilization waves: 35 regular (first wave), 16 reserve (second wave), 21 *Landwehr* (third wave) and 14 recruit (fourth wave). Georg Tessin, *Verbände und Truppen der deutschen Wehrmacht und Waffen SS im zweiten Weltkrieg* (Osnabrück: Biblio, 1960) I, 43–46.

162. NARA T–77, 13, 724018ff, OKH Wi. Rü. Amt., "Rüstungsstand, Bd. I;" T–78, 143, 146, and 149, OKH Heereswaffenamt, "Rüstungsstand"; T–78, 158, 15860913–1871, Der Chef der Heeresrüstung und Befehlshaber des Ersatzheeres, Stab II (Rüst.), "überblick über die Rüstungsstand des Heeres (Munition), 3.1940-5.1941;" T–78, 174, 6113064-509, OKH He.Wa.Amt "Munitionslage (Gen.)," 1939–1943.

163. Richard L. DiNardo, *Mechanized Juggernaut or Military Anachronism?*

Horses and the German Army in World War II (Westport, Conn.: Greenwood Press, 1991).

164. Williamson Murray, "Armored Warfare: The British, French, and German Experiences," in Millett and Murray, eds., *Military Innovation in the Interwar Period*, 20–22.

2

The United States, 1939–1944: The Leviathan Awakens

When war broke out in Europe in September 1939, the U.S. Army was still small, understrength, underequipped, and largely outdated in equipment, organization, and doctrine. Only three of twenty-seven divisions were at all battleworthy and even these remained at half strength. Divisional organization was bulky and unwieldy, the army had only a single armored brigade, lacked antitank capability, and had no clear operating procedures with air power. The belief of the U.S. Army Air Corps (USAAC) that its primary mission was to gain air superiority and then conduct a strategic bombing campaign, ensured the relegation of battlefield interdiction to a secondary, and close air support to a tertiary, role. As a result, it was largely incapable of supporting U.S. ground forces.[1] In sum, in September 1939 the United States was incapable of deploying and supporting its land forces overseas.

The U.S. geostrategic position ensured that the renewal of hostilities in Europe barely perturbed the nation. As in 1914, most Americans believed that the conflicts of squabbling Europeans did not concern them. Indeed, since Japan appeared to be the most likely opponent between the wars, the U.S. military developed War Plan ORANGE, a blueprint for an extended maritime campaign in the Pacific that contemplated opposed amphibious operations.[2] It took the resounding German victory in northwest Europe during the summer of 1940 to shake the United States out of complacency into general military preparation. Even then most Americans remained ignorant of the threat that nazism posed to U.S. strategic interests; racism led many Americans to fear potential Japanese aggression more than actual German aggression.[3] Such racial antagonism intensified after the surprise Japanese attack on Pearl Harbor on 7 December 1941 that brought the United States into World War II and hindered the nation's prosecution of the struggle against Germany after Hitler declared war on the United States in the wake of Pearl Harbor.[4] It took all the skill and statesmanship of Franklin Roosevelt to steer the United States toward military preparation for a war in Europe.

The first substantive expansion of the U.S. Army, therefore, only materialized in late summer of 1940, during which the army expanded to 375,000 and activated a general headquarters (GHQ) to oversee mobilization.[5] On 16 September 1940 a second stage of expansion began with the passage of the Selective Service Bill, the first ever U.S. peacetime conscription, and the absorption of the National Guard into the regular army. This process, completed by November 1941, quintupled the size of the army.[6] Massive and rapid expansion during 1940–1941, however, presented the army with enormous mobilization difficulties. The most serious manpower problem was the need to improve officer quality even while in the middle of meteoric expansion. Lack of funding between the wars had prevented evaluation of command fitness, and rapid expansion in 1940–1941 mandated quantity rather than quality. Inevitably, many unsatisfactory officers not only had to be retained but elevated. That the United States had a large pool of trained reserve officers gave it an advantage over its allies and enemies alike.[7] The pool reduced the strain of rapid expansion and allowed the army to grapple earlier and more vigorously with the necessary but painful task of weeding out those too old, too poorly trained, or too incompetent to command. In fact, the wartime army demonstrated determination to remove officers ill fitted for command. While continual officer shortages during mobilization hampered initial efforts to dismiss inept officers, from 1943, as an officer surplus materialized, the army intensified its efforts to remove unsuitable officers.[8]

The introduction of Selective Service ended army recruitment difficulties, but it created insurmountable training problems. Rapid expansion brought with it staggering instructional tasks as a small and inexperienced teaching staff grappled with training large numbers of civilian recruits in an as yet unproven doctrine for an uncertain mission against an unknown enemy. It was, therefore, hardly surprising that much early war training proved inadequate. The chaos of early war mobilization also brought huge personnel turnover, which ruined logical progression in instruction and delayed the building of divisions. Basic training, advanced officer instruction, and unit tactical drills all went on simultaneously, eroding quality and lengthening the time required to produce combat-ready divisions to well over a year.[9]

The strength of U.S. military training, however, was its offensive orientation. Because traditional doctrine emphasized halting the enemy far from U.S. shores and launching an early counteroffensive, by late 1939 the military had produced War Plan RAINBOW 5, a strategic blueprint for offensive transatlantic operations against Germany and Italy. The creation of RAINBOW 5 allowed U.S. troops to begin offensive-oriented training in 1940, much earlier than their Anglo-Canadian counterparts. It also meant that from 1939 U.S. armed forces regularly practiced amphibious operations and developed a sound understanding of amphibious warfare techniques, even if they lacked specialized forces and landing craft to conduct opposed landings.[10]

Another major army strength was its thorough evaluation and refinement of training during the 1940–1941 period. The outbreak of the European war overrode financial restraints and prompted the army to conduct an ordered and structured program of large-scale peacetime maneuvers. The first of these, conducted in August 1940, revealed manifold shortcomings that ranged from poor training and signals communications to inadequate artillery support. Army observers concluded that most troops required further basic training.[11] More than 350,000 troops joined the September 1941 Louisiana maneuvers, the largest peacetime maneuvers in U.S. history. Lt. Gen. Lesley J. McNair, the Army Ground Forces (AGF) commander, insisted on closely replicating combat conditions and demanded frank honesty in appraising troop performance.[12] The exercise identified serious flaws in preparation, including poor reconnaissance, small-unit tactics, combat intelligence, and communications.[13] The Carolina maneuvers that followed in November 1941 confirmed the findings of previous exercises and led General McNair to conclude that the army had only limited combat capabilities and required extensive retraining before it would be combat ready.[14] Thus in the spring of 1942 the U.S. Army went back to basic training to rectify the deficiencies. The army's willingness to evaluate critically its performance on maneuvers allowed significant enhancement of training quality before the commitment of U.S. ground forces to combat (in North Africa) late in 1942.

As it experienced unprecedented expansion in 1940–1941, the army also underwent simultaneous reorganization as it raised new types of formations, restructured existing units, and modernized its equipment all in the light of German successes. In this period the army formed its first armored divisions. As with the British, however, the Americans initially organized their armored formations poorly: the units were too large, unwieldy, and tank-heavy. Such organization reflected the army's misperception of the nature of the German blitzkrieg victories. The army believed that massed employment of armor operating ahead of the infantry, rather than intimate combination of arms, was the key to the German blitzkrieg success.

Among new ground forces raised during 1940–1941 were paratrooper and glider infantry units. The army had only minimally experimented with airborne troops prior to 1939; so it required the bold German employment of airborne forces in northwest Europe in May 1940 to make the army appreciate their potential. Thereafter, the U.S. Army organized its first parachute battalion in September 1940, but a critical shortage of transports hampered the development of airborne forces.[15] By June 1941 paratroopers still represented only a minute fraction of ground force strength, and the army did not form its first air-landing unit until after the daring German employment of such troops in Crete. In February 1942, the army established its first four parachute regiments and an independent Airborne Command. Finally, in August 1942 the army raised the 82d and 101st Airborne Divisions, the progenitors of an airborne force that by 1945 had grown to five divisions.[16]

The prevailing interwar notion that the bomber would always get through and the reality that no effective means of active antiaircraft defense existed meant that the army also had little antiaircraft artillery in 1939. The effective German tactical air strikes in Western Europe and in North Africa in 1940–1942, however, forced the U.S. Army to move major resources to antiaircraft defense. Driven by the threat of Axis air power, the antiaircraft artillery arm expanded eighteenfold between 1941 and 1943.[17]

In addition to raising new types of units in the years 1940–1941, the army also reorganized existing formations. Experiments by the 2d Infantry Division during 1937–1939 had resulted in a dramatic change in infantry organization. During 1940–1941 infantry divisions underwent "triangularization"—they converted from their large and unwieldy four-brigade "square" structure to a smaller, more flexible, and more mobile triangular pattern that brought U.S. organization in line with European norms.[18] The old organization had reflected the army's commitment to a doctrine of annihilation; but the new, sleeker, and more mobile organization reflected both the principle of economy in U.S. military thought and the increasing popularity of a doctrine that stressed speed and mobility. The reorganization abolished intermediate brigade headquarters and established simpler and more streamlined formations with greater mobility and striking power.

Rearmament also accompanied expansion and reorganization. Drawing on its World War I experience, interwar governments had prepared detailed plans for wartime industrial mobilization. Thus the United States was able to mobilize quickly and efficiently its enormous industrial potential after 1941. But the army not only had to produce large numbers of existing weapons, it also had to develop more modern weapons—several of which did enter service during 1940–1941, including the M3 Grant tank and the first half-track tank destroyers, which increased both firepower and mobility.

Doctrinal development also continued during the same period and culminated in the publication of *Field Service Regulations* (*FM 100-5*), which codified an offensive strategy to annihilate the enemy based upon the maintenance of the initiative.[19] In its offensive orientation *FM 100-5* resembled German doctrine, but in other respects it differed markedly. The limited U.S. combat experience, a military tradition of applying overwhelming material superiority, and an essentially civilian army engendered a more managerial conception of war than did the German approach. U.S. doctrine thus stressed scientific management more and individual action less. Moreover, since historically the United States had never had to rely heavily on raw fighting power, doctrine had stressed organization, planning, and logistics far more than German doctrine, but neglected the operational level of war that lay between tactics and strategy. The absence of an operational dimension to this doctrine hampered U.S. combat performance throughout World War II.[20]

At the outbreak of war on 7 December 1941 the army had grown to 1,636,086 troops and thirty-four divisions, half of which McNair rated as combat ready. The peacetime measures taken in 1940–1941 had done much to promote the rapid expansion and quick achievement of wartime combat readiness. Yet while adequate to defend the country from external threat, the U.S. Army of December 1941 remained unprepared for major offensive action. Most formations were still in training, and massive expansion combined with inexperience increased the time required to mobilize a combat-ready division to well beyond a year.

To become fully operational and develop offensive capability the peacetime army had to restructure for war. In late 1941 the army reorganized itself as a dual structure: the Army Ground Forces (AGF), which included training units, and the Army Service Forces (ASF), which absorbed the replacement system. After its experiences in World War I, the army had abandoned territorial affiliation for its field formations and structured, organized, and equipped its divisions according to a small number of uniform tables of organization and equipment (TO&Es). Thus, marked homogeneity and uniformity characterized the army's wartime organization. This uniformity reflected General McNair's powerful influence on the wartime army's structure. His basic philosophy was to concentrate maximum offensive fighting power. He tirelessly advocated streamlined combat units with minimal "tail" and vigorously promoted the principle of "pooling," the removal and centralization of all nonessential divisional elements, to achieve this end. McNair believed that such rationalization would bring unity in command, economy of force, and operational flexibility.

U.S. mobilization policy also significantly affected the size, character, and combat effectiveness of the wartime army. In 1942, the United States limited its army to ninety divisions in recognition of the need to channel unprecedented resources into air and naval forces as well as the support services to project military power overseas.[21] This limitation in size had significant operational repercussions because it made it difficult for the army to sustain its combat power through the rapid rotation of units out of line for rest, rehabilitation, and replenishment. Instead, the ninety-division ceiling placed the onus of sustaining combat effectiveness on the army's manpower replacement system. To maintain divisions near full combat strength and sustain their combat effectiveness required a constant stream of replacements. Thus the army's replacement system developed to produce large numbers of replacements that could be assigned where needed. This system emphasized flexibility and quantity over quality and prevented a repetition of the chaos that accompanied the replacement provisions during World War I, but at the price of impeding efforts to sustain cohesion, morale, and combat effectiveness.[22] The replacement system was a vicious circle that resulted in unnecessarily heavy casualties: heavy losses brought large numbers of undertrained replacements, which in turn brought higher casualties that brought even more replacements.[23]

Initial army manpower allocation priorities exacerbated the pernicious impact of the replacement system on combat effectiveness. The USAAC, now redesignated the Army Air Force (USAAF), the ASF, and the airborne and special forces received draft selection priority and thus siphoned off the most skilled and talented personnel. The AGF thus received relatively less educated, less skilled, and less physically fit personnel. Within the AGF, disproportionate numbers of the highest rated personnel also went to the technical and mechanized branches, leaving the infantry with lower quality recruits. This mobilization policy eroded infantry quality.[24]

Before it could take the offensive the army required further expansion and reorganization. The development of a powerful, independent tank arm was a vital prerequisite for offensive action. The army formed an independent Armored Force in July 1940 and by December 1941 it had raised five armored divisions that participated in the 1941 maneuvers as a unified tank corps.[25] During 1940–1942 the Armored Force developed a doctrine to govern the organization, training, and mission of armor. This doctrine rejected the British approach of armor specialization and direct tank-to-tank combat within a strategy of attrition. Since armor had the potential to be both highly mobile and strong in firepower it appealed equally to American advocates of attrition and mobility and thus generated less controversy than it did in the British military. The German blitzkrieg victories, though, led to the gradual triumph of an armored doctrine that utilized the tank in a mobile exploitation role rather than in a breakthrough role.

If the mission of armor was exploitation, what weapon should be used to stop enemy armor? It was only after the collapse of France that the army seriously considered the question of stopping the tank. Yet the army's offensive orientation robbed it of any significant antitank capability, and during 1942 it desperately needed both an effective antitank weapon and a suitable doctrine to halt the German blitzkrieg.[26] It developed a new offensive antitank weapon—the tank destroyer, a self-propelled antitank gun that, theoretically, married mobility, speed, and firepower. The Tank Destroyer Center activated at Fort Meade, Maryland, developed doctrine during 1942 that called for large tank destroyer groups to seek out and destroy enemy armor.[27] Although the tank destroyer's speed, mobility, and firepower reflected a compromise between competing doctrines of mobility and annihilation, intense controversy raged over the relative merits of tank destroyers versus towed antitank guns. General McNair's powerful support of the tank destroyer, however, ensured the centralization of divisional antitank battalions into pooled tank destroyer groups in 1942.[28]

The emphasis on tank destroyers and the army's disdain for purely defensive weapons meant that the army devoted few resources to antitank gun development.[29] Thus U.S. infantry lacked antitank capability early in the war and had to rely on the obsolete 37mm M2 gun. Moreover, the army's wartime record of antitank gun procurement was unimpressive. The improved 57mm M1 introduced in 1942, essentially a copy of the British 6-pounder gun, remained the primary antitank gun of U.S. infantry through-out the war. Towed-gun battalions, meanwhile, deployed a 75mm antitank gun, modified from an outdated foreign field gun, that lacked penetration. Poor antitank capability left the infantry vulnerable to the quick local com-bined-arms counterattacks that were integral to German defensive tactics.[30] Deprived of resources for antitank guns, the army nonetheless displayed considerable ingenuity in developing a novel and cheap infantry antitank weapon—the "bazooka" hollow-charge rocket launcher. The bazooka first used in action late in 1942 in Tunisia, where it proved a valuable and cost-effective antitank weapon, and thereafter it saw wide use.[31]

Offensive action by the army also required amphibious capability. The heavy commitment of the U.S. Marine Corps to the Pacific led the army to train four infantry divisions for amphibious assault during 1941–1942 and to organize specialized amphibious engineer brigades.[32] But to undertake offensive action the AGF required extensive logistic support. During early mobilization the buildup of combat arms took precedence over support services. While U.S. forces engaged in bitter defensive fighting in 1942 in the Pacific, inadequate logistic support initially hampered operations. By late 1942, however, the expansion of the ASF had caught up with that of the AGF, and from 1943 the army experienced lavish logistic support.

Another prerequisite for an offensive army was the provision of effec-tive tactical air support. Yet air force resistance and lack of suitable aircraft meant that no workable air-ground system emerged prior to the commit-ment of U.S. troops to combat in the European Theater of Operations (ETO). The 1940–1941 maneuvers demonstrated that command and control difficulties presented many obstacles to effective air-ground coordination.[33] These trials led to the issuance of *Field Manual 31-35* in April 1942 that established Air Support Commands (ASCs) based on the British system developed in the western desert during 1941.[34] Unfortunately *FM 31-35* failed to create a workable ground-air support system. It was cumbersome and flawed in conception and execution. The ASC structure was decentral-ized and thus had air assets dispersed to army corps commanders, who pro-vided close air support at the expense of battlefield interdiction. Most seri-ously, doctrine prevented concentrated employment of air power in support of the ground battle.[35]

A critical shortage of shipping space and General McNair's commit-ment to economy brought a major streamlining of the army during 1942–1943. This rationalization trimmed the manpower and increased the fire-power of the army shipped overseas. Smaller, more compact units were easier to supply, provision, maintain, and replenish. Mobility and maneuverability were also improved. Manpower economy allowed the army both to augment its combat capabilities and to retain an adequate reservoir of replacements. Reorganization increased the army's ability to sustain combat power by trading off less self-sufficiency for more flexible, mobile, and powerful combat formations, but without essentially altering the force structure. Nor was rationalization achieved at the price of reducing support facilities. The result was that when U.S. divisions joined combat in late 1942 they were leaner and meaner formations.

The army streamlined infantry division organization by paring excess manpower and increasing firepower (see Table 2.1). Cutting divisional manpower by 7 percent and transport by 23 percent reduced required shipping space by 15 percent.[36] At the same time, the army increased overall firepower by adding regimental cannon companies, bazookas, and extra machine guns and mortars. These reforms turned the infantry division into a standard, general-purpose combined-arms fighting formation, stripped of all nonessential specialist combat and support units.[37]

U.S. armored divisions underwent parallel reorganization and streamlining. The participation of an armored corps in the 1941 maneuvers led the army to identify many flaws in its armored organization prior to commitment to combat. Thus the tank-heavy, unbalanced, and cumbersome armored divisions of 1940 gradually gave way to streamlined and well-organized armored forces. In 1942, McNair's army review concluded that the Armored Force was the most inefficient arm in its use of manpower and equipment. The halting of the German blitzkrieg in North Africa and in the Soviet Union, moreover, demonstrated that massed armor was not invincible. During 1942–1943 U.S. armored divisions became smaller, less tank-heavy, and better balanced combined-arms formations as the army learned from experience that armored formations required not only better balance but also a genuine combined-arms doctrine.

Table 2.1   Streamlining the U.S. Infantry Division, 1941–1943

	1941	1943	Percentage Change
Total manpower	15,245	14,253	–07
Infantry	10,020	9,354	–07
Artillery	2,656	2,160	–19
Reconnaissance troops	147	155	+05
Engineers	634	647	+02
Machine guns	292	393	+35
Mortars	117	144	+23
Antitank guns	60	57	–05
Artillery	54	68	+26

Source: Greenfield, *Organization,* Table 1, 274–275.

Unfortunately, the army failed to appreciate fully the need for effective interarms cooperation before 1944. The March 1942 armored division, though an improvement on its 1940 predecessor, still remained tank-heavy and short on infantry.[38] The first U.S. combat experience in the ETO resulted in a superior 1943 armored organization, which doubled the existing infantry-tank ratio.[39] Despite progress, however, the 1943 division still lacked infantry.[40] Combat experience in Sicily and Italy led to the introduction of the 1944 armored division, which continued the trends of earlier reorganizations. Between 1940 and 1944, the organization of U.S. armored divisions improved considerably (see Table 2.2). Total manpower fell by 25 percent and tank strength by one-third, while infantry strength rose 26 percent. With all its infantry mounted on half-tracks and its entire artillery self-propelled, the 1944 armored division had become a lean, flexible, and highly mobile formation.

Table 2.2   Reorganization of the U.S. Armored Division, 1942–1944

Date	Manpower	Infantry	Mortars	Guns	MGs	Bazookas	Vehicles
1942	14,620	2,389	390	54	394	—	3,630
1944	10,937	3,003	263	54	869	607	2,653
Percentage change	−25	+26	−24	0	+121	na	−27

Source: Palmer, "Reorganization for Combat," 320–321.

Armored organization also became more flexible because the army evolved the combined-arms armored combat command. Based on combat experience, the army increasingly divided armored divisions into three mixed brigade groups termed combat commands.[41] The net effect of these reorganizations was to create a more effective combined-arms team and to shift the bulk of tank strength from armored divisions to infantry support. The 1944 armored division remained both less flexible and less well balanced a combined-arms team than its German counterpart and lacked its punch, but it was better organized than its Anglo-Canadian equivalent. The U.S. armored division's biggest weakness remained its lack of infantry—it still had only three infantry battalions—and the policy of pooling prevented integration of the tank destroyer and antiaircraft battalions that the Armored Force repeatedly demanded. This lack of punch was offset by the increasing use of the armored division by 1944 not in an attack role but as a lean, mobile, and flexible formation designed to exploit a breakthrough.

A significant, indeed revolutionary, reorganization of the army during 1942–1943 was the introduction of a flexible battalion/group structure for nondivisional troops. The army disbanded existing fixed brigades and regiments of mechanized cavalry, artillery, and combat engineers; made their battalions independent; and reorganized them under newly activated group headquarters.[42] The army also dissolved fixed regiments of service troops and rearranged them into flexible, self-sufficient companies attached to battalion headquarters. These reforms made the composition of field forces more flexible and streamlined units in accordance with the principle of economy. Since the army maintained much of its combat strength in nondivisional units (see Table 2.3) this reform was of major significance.[43] Army reorganization between 1940 and 1943 thus forged a more flexible, sinewy, and powerful fighting force to join combat in the ETO late in 1942.

However, despite retraining, reorganization, and reequipment, the AGF generally failed to forge fully combat-ready divisions prior to commitment to action in the ETO. Given the immense task that confronted the army at the start of the war, it had come a long way—perhaps as far as anyone could have expected. By the fall of 1942 the army was capable of limited offensive action, and it clearly forged its offensive capability more quickly than its Anglo-Canadian allies. Here, the extra two years of peace were of critical importance in allowing the U.S. Army a better planned, organized, and executed expansion. The army's managerial approach also played an important role in facilitating an ordered transition to an offensive-oriented field force.

In keeping with its offensive doctrine and its desire to defeat its enemies far away from the United States, the army sought the earliest possible commitment to the European theater. Having to fight a coalition war with a more fragile and war-weary partner, however, proved fortuitous for it was

Table 2.3 **Expansion of U.S. Army Combat Formations, 1942–1944**

	1 January 42	1 July 42	1 January 43	1 July 43	1 January 44
Infantry	29	33	52	63	67
Cavalry	2	2	1	2	2
Armored	5	8	14	15	16
Airborne	—	—	2	4	4
Other	—	4	5	4	—
Total Divisions	36	45	75	88	89
Heavy Artillery		32	44	61	116
Medium Artillery		53	67	75	112
Light Artillery		57	101	95	87
Antiaircraft		391	547	557	479
Armor		26	41	65	64
Tank Destroyer		80	106	101	78
Total Battalions		639	906	954	924

Source: Stanton, *Order of Battle,* Chart 1, p. 4.

only in the face of adamant British opposition that the Americans abandoned Operation SLEDGEHAMMER, the quixotic plan for a 1942 invasion of France.[44] Thereafter, the United States pinned its hopes on a 1943 invasion, ROUNDUP. In retrospect the compromise that inevitably attends coalition warfare proved beneficial, for, as the Dieppe raid illustrated, a 1942 invasion attempt would surely have ended in disaster. None of the Western Allied armies then possessed significant offensive capability, nor the amphibious assault techniques, landing craft, and logistic support, let alone the aerial and naval mastery, that guaranteed them success in 1944.[45] It must be stressed that the 1942 U.S. Army remained ill prepared to tackle the *Heer* in strength. It did not have the troops, heavy weapons, or the logistic base in the United Kingdom to mount a successful invasion.[46] Determined that U.S. ground forces join combat in the ETO in 1942, President Roosevelt instead committed the II U.S. Corps under overall British command to Operation TORCH, the Allied invasion of French North Africa on 8 November 1942.[47] After landing at Casablanca, Oran, and Algiers, the Allies dashed to capture Tunis before winter and quickly wrap up the campaign. But limited strength, inadequate logistic support, overextended lines of communication, and a rapid German reaction ensured that the campaign dragged on until May 1943.

The deployment of U.S. forces in strength on the periphery where the Germans were weak proved sound strategy. Although it delayed the invasion of France until 1944, the Mediterranean diversion brought the army invaluable combat experience that paid enormous dividends in northwest Europe during 1944–1945. Combat in Tunisia demonstrated that serious deficiencies remained in the preparation of troops, flaws that brought several serious local reverses. These setbacks shocked the army out of complacency and resulted in renewed efforts to enhance combat capabilities. Troop performance was uneven and initially poor, and U.S. forces often advanced recklessly and with little coordination. This allowed the Germans to inflict a number of local defeats on the green troops, the most serious of which occurred at Kasserine Pass in February 1943.[48] This defeat taught the Americans several valuable lessons; in particular, it revealed the weaknesses of unseasoned troops and the heavy price of inferior equipment.[49]

An important element of the army's wartime success was its determination to learn from its combat experience and to refine its doctrine, tactics, and organization in the light of combat lessons.[50] Indeed, General McNair firmly believed that the final arbiter of military effectiveness was combat itself.[51] The application of strength against German weakness made Tunisia a particularly valuable learning environment for U.S. ground forces. Relatively light casualties guaranteed continuity in personnel, which allowed combat lessons to be readily absorbed.[52] Despite uneven troop performance during TORCH, the campaign proved that army doctrine was essentially sound. Combat demonstrated the superiority of the offensive and of operational maneuver; the army concluded that local setbacks had resulted primarily from the misapplication and/or inflexible application of existing doctrine.[53]

Tunisia did, however, expose fundamental flaws in three areas of doctrine: the new armored, tank destroyer, and tactical air support procedures. Armor doctrine that stressed en masse employment of armor echeloned in depth on a narrow front to break through enemy lines and exploit the enemy rear proved unrealistic. Unsuitable terrain and lack of mobile reserves ensured that armor could rarely be employed in this manner in Tunisia. Instead, commanders frequently dispersed armor in an infantry support role to buttress an overextended front and provide effective means of defense against German armored counterattacks. This U.S. II Corps only concentrated its sole armored division late in the campaign, and reckless dash characterized its operations.[54] In addition, mechanized infantry proved slow to follow up and consolidate ground captured by armor.[55]

Operations in Tunisia also revealed that one of the army's most serious organizational and doctrinal problems lay in antitank warfare. Tank destroyers never lived up to expectations in TORCH, largely because they lacked punch and armor protection and thus could not engage German armor on equal terms. Combat in Tunisia also revealed serious flaws in tank destroyer doctrine. The blitzkrieg had engendered an exaggerated fear of the tank in the U.S. military, so tank destroyer doctrine developed around the unrealistic assumption that large numbers of tank destroyers would engage large numbers of unsupported panzers.[56] In reality, the army only once employed tank destroyers en masse in Tunisia, where they suffered prohibitive losses.[57] Indeed, the Germans—unlike the British—rarely attacked with massed armor, but instead with combined-arms battle groups. The U.S. Army in Tunisia typically employed tank destroyers as it did armor—dispersed forward to buttress the infantry in a mobile indirect-fire support role.[58] The army learned to modify the traditional approach of "seek, strike, and destroy" to meet the capabilities and limitations of tank destroyers. Tunisia demonstrated that tank destroyers had to be used en masse and coordinated with other antitank weapons to provide short-range antitank defense from hull-down positions and to maneuver for advantage. Combat also revealed the critical importance of cover, concealment, and camouflage in the effective employment of tank destroyers.[59]

Tunisia also illuminated deficiencies at the operational level. U.S. forces typically attacked on a broad front with all available forces, leaving few reserves echeloned in depth to exploit a successful penetration.[60] Such an approach quickly exhausted offensive strength, but at the same time lack of reserves hampered the rotation of formations out of line for necessary rest and replenishment. Offensive practices, therefore, made it difficult for the Americans to sustain combat power. The campaign also revealed that offensive-oriented training had inculcated an unwise, often reckless, aggressiveness in U.S. troops. The tempo of early offensive operations was too fast: troops often sacrificed time-consuming preparation, reconnaissance, intelligence, and coordination for speed, resulting in unnecessary setbacks and losses. Reconnaissance and patrolling proved particularly poor, but Americans quickly recognized the frequent need to fight to acquire battlefield intelligence.[61]

TORCH also showed that the army had devoted insufficient attention and resources to the German defensive use of mines and booby traps, which proved a far more formidable obstacle than anticipated. Prior to TORCH the army had conceived mine clearing as a specialized engineer task. Tunisia, though, demonstrated that all troops had to be proficient in mine warfare if the pace of offensive action was to be maintained—and the U.S. Army found no antidote for minefields except laborious and time-consuming clearance. Likewise, initial inexperience in laying and marking its own minefields led to numerous casualties among its own troops.[62]

The ASC system for tactical aviation also proved a failure in Tunisia. U.S. air-ground cooperation was so poor that the army and its air force essentially fought separate wars. Only rarely did the missions of XII ASC meet actual army needs, and when most needed, during the defeat at Kasserine, air support was desultory. Tunisia illuminated that not only did serious deficiencies in training exist but that the underlying air-ground support doctrine of *FM 31-35* was faulty. No effective control and coordination existed, and the doctrine dissipated air strength and neglected deep interdiction missions against German airfields. Tactical aviation also experienced grave difficulties in acquiring targets, which resulted in numerous friendly fire incidents. At the root of these failures lay the interwar controversies over the proper uses of air power and the triumph of the strategic bombing theorists.[63] Inadequate air support resulted in frequent hostile air attacks against U.S. ground troops. Yet these same troops provided poor self-protection. Indifferent camouflage and concealment, inadequate dispersion and entrenching, and ill-disciplined antiaircraft fire all contributed to heavier casualties and damage from air attacks.[64]

Nevertheless, the preponderance of doctrine proved fundamentally sound in Tunisia and allowed the U.S. Army to concentrate on correcting the more prevalent tactical, operational, and organizational defects that combat had illuminated. The most significant tactical and operational lesson of TORCH was the need for combined-arms coordination to guarantee victory. Combined-arms training proved inadequate in Tunisia because the AGF had failed to forge a combined-arms army during 1940–1942. Novel weapons systems like armor and tank destroyers, with their concomitant doctrinal controversies, inevitably bred parochialism and militated against interarms cooperation. The magnitude of the army's training tasks during 1940–1942 also meant that the AGF was unable to identify quickly flaws in its combined-arms preparation. The need to perfect basic training first and a lack of resources (prior to 1944 there were not enough independent tank battalions to train with infantry divisions) further delayed interarms training. In evaluating the lessons of Tunisia, the army also failed to recognize fully the need for intimate combined-arms coordination.[65]

The TORCH landings illustrated the need for extensive logistic preparation for a successful amphibious assault. Arranged at short notice and initiated on a logistic shoestring, the Quartermaster and Engineer Corps were ill-prepared for TORCH. Inadequate preparation, combined with inexperience in amphibious assault and troop resupply, resulted in a heavy loss of landing craft and considerable confusion and disorder on the beaches that delayed the buildup ashore.[66] That the chaos was quickly brought under control testified to the improvisational skills and ingenuity of supply troops who unloaded throughout the night, beached landing craft, and pressed pontoon bridges into service as floating supply boats.[67] TORCH was a valuable learning experience which demonstrated the supply service's adaptability as logisticians and engineers recovered quickly from initial disorganization. Nonetheless, supply shortages slowed the Allied advance and the logistic situation remained tight through January 1943, with supplies becoming abundant only in March. The most serious logistic limitation on Allied operations in Tunisia was inadequate fuel supplies during the campaign.[68]

The TORCH landings, like the one at Dieppe before them, also revealed the need for extensive amphibious assault training. The disorganization of the amphibious assault and resultant heavy loss of landing craft might have jeopardized success if there had been determined opposition rather than the halfhearted resistance offered by the Vichy French.[69] The landings revealed the need for well-trained and equipped supply troops, a clear chain of command, efficient loading and unloading operations, and a significant salvage capability—and many of these lessons had to be subsequently relearned in the face of far stronger German opposition.[70]

Tunisia also highlighted many deficiencies in the U.S. infantry. Riflemen failed to maneuver and apply firepower, overrelied on artillery fire, and proved slow in consolidating and bringing up supporting weapons.[71] They also experienced difficulty in generating the firepower needed to obtain objectives, displayed defensive thinking rather than aggressive drive, and often failed to use terrain to their advantage. Units both failed to acquire high ground for observation and frequently plowed through valleys in hilly or mountainous terrain, suffering heavy losses to observed fire from high ground.[72] Early on, infantry personnel also suffered heavily because they advanced too far behind their own artillery barrages and because they frequently consolidated at enemy positions on which the Germans had preregistered their own fire.[73] But perhaps the most serious weakness was the infantry's poor scouting and passive patrolling, which prevented U.S. troops from seizing and maintaining the initiative.[74] The troops often resorted to night operations, but inadequate training and inexperience in such inherently complex operations initially brought frequent failure and a poor standard of proficiency.[75]

The Tunisian campaign also indicated that U.S. airborne forces—in their first wartime combat drop—required more extensive preparation and a fundamental rethinking of their mission. The Allies, however, were too ambitious and reckless in the employment of airborne forces, dropping them on high-risk targets of limited value without adequate reconnaissance, planning, and support. In fact, it was only a combination of good fortune and the training of the U.S. paratroopers that prevented heavier casualties.[76]

U.S. antiaircraft defenses did not prove particularly effective in TORCH either. The threat posed by Axis air power forced the hasty dispatch of undertrained antiaircraft units to Tunisia, and inexperience brought numerous friendly-fire incidents. Moreover, although the army began to recognize for the first time the potential of heavy antiaircraft artillery in a secondary ground role during TORCH, it lacked established procedures for their effective employment.

The artillery proved reasonably effective in Tunisia and confirmed most of the fundamental principles taught by the artillery school at Fort Sill. Artillery spotters laid highly accurate observed fire that often forced the enemy to retire.[77] In fact, many German veterans regarded U.S. artillery as the deadliest fire they had ever encountered.[78] Well-trained gunners, effective communications, and flexibility underpinned this performance. U.S. artillery rarely used predicted fire, except at night to harass and demoralize the enemy.[79] For offensive operations, artillery units fired concentrations and box barrages alongside rolling barrages and employed timed high-explosive fire for devastating airburst effect, especially against antitank guns.[80] Artillery units also used a lethal mix of percussion, timed-fuse, and white-phosphorus rounds, and fired smoke adjacent to a target to negate hostile flanking fire.[81]

TORCH indicated, however, that the fixed regimental structure for corps and army artillery was inflexible.[82] What was most lacking was not quality but quantity: the coordination of artillery fire at division level and the lack of corps artillery limited the effectiveness of fire support.[83] Divisional artillery, though, proved quick to respond and proficient at defensive and counterbattery fire.[84] In fact, the majority of German casualties in Tunisia resulted from Allied defensive-fire missions during Axis counterattacks.[85] Moreover, dispersed deployment of field artillery and the use of deception measures, including dummy battery positions, provided great protection from German counterbattery fire and minimized the loss of guns.[86] But TORCH operations revealed that the army required greater centralization and concentration of artillery as well as more medium and heavy artillery to generate greater firepower. In addition, fire for effect was often hastily called down before proper adjustment onto the target, wasting ammunition and dissipating the effectiveness of the bombardment. The artillery proved effective in Tunisia, but the U.S. Army realized it could be even more efficient.[87]

The army's embryonic replacement system was also found wanting during the Tunisian campaign. Replacement provision was poorly coordinated, and even though it met total replacement needs, infantry shortages developed during winter 1942–1943 due to the War Department's underestimation of both casualty rates and the proportion of casualties suffered by the infantry.[88] In addition, many replacements found themselves siphoned off into unofficial provisional units that proliferated in the face of many unexpected needs. Just as serious was the replacements' quality, which was often unsatisfactory. Many replacements arrived undertrained, and thereafter their morale and discipline dwindled as they languished at rear depots. Replacement provision also proved disorganized and wasteful, with the misassignment of specialists as infantry—and vice versa. As a result of these flaws, a combat unit would experience great difficulties in successfully integrating replacements before they became casualties.[89]

The experience in Tunisia did, however, reveal important strengths. The campaign demonstrated the resilience and recuperative strength of U.S. ground forces. More important, it illuminated a flexibility, originality, and adaptability that the enemy grudgingly recognized. Indeed, as Rommel wrote of them, "the American generals showed themselves to be very advanced in the tactical handling of their forces. . . . The Americans, it is fair to say, profited far more than the British from their experience in Africa."[90]

In fact, the U.S. Army showed the determination to examine its performance in detail both during and immediately after the campaign. This drive to learn lessons allowed the army to correct many of the weaknesses displayed in Tunisia in the year preceding Normandy landings. The army that returned to northwest Europe on 6 June 1944 was far superior to the one that had landed in North Africa eighteen months earlier.

In particular, the defeat at Kasserine Pass brought a major shakeup in air-ground cooperation. The setback starkly illuminated the inadequacy of existing doctrine and led to the scrapping of *FM 31-35* and the appointment of British Air Marshal Coningham as commander of the Allied Northwestern African Tactical Air Force (NATAF). This integration led the Americans to adopt the RAF's combat-proven direct-control system. Coningham assigned NATAF the primary mission of destroying enemy air power in the final months of the Tunisian campaign. It took defeat at Kasserine and exposure to the RAF's western desert air support system to force the USAAF to address realistically the problem of supporting ground forces by direct air attack. A revised air-ground doctrine, *FM 100-20,* grounded in TORCH's combat experience, emerged in July 1943 and governed U.S. close air support operations for the rest of the war. The new doctrine abandoned distribution and subordination in favor of centralization and coequality in status between air and ground forces to restore flexibility.[91]

By the end of the Tunisian campaign, the performance of many U.S. ground units showed discernible improvement. In particular, the infantry learned to reduce losses by closely following creeping barrages, while improved night fighting skills allowed troops to obtain jumping-off positions with fewer casualties and to achieve surprise more often.[92] Troops also made unexpected use of smoke for both offense and defense.[93]

The subsequent conquest of Sicily (Operation HUSKY) during July–August 1943 confirmed the lessons derived from Tunisia. The perceived failure of U.S. arms in North Africa led Gen. Sir Harold Alexander, commander-in-chief of the British 15th Army Group, to assign General Patton's U.S. Seventh Army a secondary role of flank protection for General Montgomery's British Eighth Army in HUSKY.[94] Montgomery's slow progress in the face of stubborn German resistance, however, forced Alexander to give Patton greater operational freedom as the campaign developed. As a result, the Americans beat the British to Messina, demonstrating the growing firepower, mobility, and proficiency of U.S. troops.[95]

HUSKY confirmed again that the army had not yet mastered airborne warfare; U.S. paratroopers made a poor showing in Sicily. Alexander had given Allied airborne forces a major role in HUSKY to drop inland and bar the advance of German reserves while assault troops secured a viable lodgement. But inexperienced transport pilots badly scattered the drop of the U.S. 505th Parachute Regiment on the first day of a HUSKY, and a later drop by the 504th Regiment went disastrously awry. Routed over the invasion fleet, friendly antiaircraft fire savaged and scattered the transports: a day later less than one-quarter of the regiment had been able to assemble.[96] Sicily demonstrated that the Allies still had a lot to learn about the effective employment of airborne forces, the campaign confirming what Tunisia had suggested—that airborne forces had to be employed en masse with well-trained transport and glider crews for less ambitious tactical objectives.

The proficiency of U.S. artillery also improved in Sicily and Italy during 1943–1944 as corps- and army-level operational commands for massed fire finally emerged.[97] Centralized control prevented dispersion of effort and allowed the army to apply rapid and effective massed fire. In addition, in 1943 the army abandoned its fixed field artillery brigade and regimental organizations in favor of a more flexible organization. At the same time, the accuracy of the Americans' gunnery showed improvement as forward observers became adept at adjusting fire.[98]

After the experience in North Africa and Sicily the army had begun to recognize the potential of heavy antiaircraft guns in a ground role, but it was only in May of 1944 that the combined training of heavy antiaircraft gun units with other ground forces was regularized.[99] Heavy antiaircraft units were thus not ready for a secondary indirect-fire role. As an illustration, by late 1943 the Allies had all but gained aerial superiority in the ETO, yet U.S. antiaircraft artillery had absorbed four times as many personnel as the field artillery, leaving the army with large numbers of surplus antiaircraft gunners. Consequently, massive reductions in the antiaircraft establishment followed in 1944, with most of the gunners ending up as infantry replacements. Because of the absence of a new mission once the Axis air threat had diminished, antiaircraft artillery remained an underutilized asset.

Despite the reforms initiated after Kasserine, only limited improvement in U.S. air support materialized in Sicily and Italy. The army still employed tactical aviation in Sicily primarily on air superiority missions. Once this superiority was achieved, the USAAF shifted to close air support and battlefield interdiction. This recipe became standard and was used on a much bigger scale for OVERLORD in Normandy. Nevertheless, USAAF intelligence gathering and photo reconnaissance remained poor, as did the effectiveness of close air support missions (part of the latter problem was that the USAAF lacked an effective dive bomber).[100] More significantly, the two campaigns illustrated that three major obstacles to effective air-ground cooperation remained: the problem of target acquisition; the lack of a direct means of air-ground communication; and the poor aerial recognition skills of U.S. ground troops, which led to numerous attacks on Allied aircraft. Given the propensity for air and ground assets to harm each other and their inability to communicate, close air support remained an unpredictable and dangerous weapon throughout 1943.[101]

Sicily and Italy proved especially instructive in terms of the logistic requirements for an amphibious invasion against a defended coast. Beach organization had clearly improved since the chaos in the TORCH landings (technological innovation aided this improvement as Sicily saw the debut of the DUKW amphibian truck).[102] By the Anzio landings in January 1944, U.S. logistic support for amphibious assault had gained a high degree of efficiency.[103]

With all the Mediterranean experience under its belt, U.S. ground forces made major strides toward becoming a powerful offensive army in the year before D-Day. Americans learned an invaluable lesson regarding the skill and tenacity of the enemy, thus paving the way for a successful second front in the West. In the year preceding D-Day, the army devoted considerable attention to improving combined-arms coordination both among forces fighting in Italy and those stationed in the United Kingdom.[104] The most effective means of promoting combined-arms teamwork was the principle adhered to by the Germans—habitual association of combat arms in genuine combined-arms formations. But the policy of pooling prevented U.S. divisions from easily developing combined-arms expertise. The army remained wedded to pooling throughout 1943 on grounds of economy and both because it anticipated the employment of armor, tank destroyers, and artillery en masse in certain combat situations and because it believed that permanent attachment would prevent training for massed employment.[105] Combat experience demonstrated, however, that pooling undermined combined-arms coordination.[106]

Lack of available army troops also hindered combined-arms training. Because of tactical requirements and matériel shortages, it was only in the fall of 1943 that sufficient independent tank, tank destroyer, and antiaircraft units became available for extensive combined-arms training with divisions. Moreover, after the summer of 1943, a reaction set in against the extreme emphasis on economy and flexibility, and a realization grew that the army had gone too far in pooling to the detriment of building interarms expertise.[107] Even though General McNair still opposed modification of prevailing army organization, from August 1943 the army unofficially began the semipermanent attachment of nondivisional troops to formations preparing for OVERLORD in the United Kingdom.

Increased organizational flexibility from 1943 offset the decrease in operational flexibility accorded by semipermanent attachment of army troops to divisions. From TORCH onward the army started to make increasing use of the regimental combat team (RCT) concept—a combined-arms group of artillery, armor, and engineers built around an infantry regiment—which added greater flexibility to U.S. infantry divisions.[108] As a result of stepped-up training, the retreat from pooling, and greater organizational flexibility, American coordination improved in the year before D-Day. However, serious deficiencies remained, especially among the raw divisions in Britain, as the army's unwillingness to abandon pooling still limited the degree of improvement possible. Despite progress, the U.S. Army officially refused to sanction permanent assignment of army troops to combat divisions.[109]

Renewed discussion about pooling led to broader reevaluation of army troops in general. Mediterranean combat experience had pointed to a pressing need for more heavy artillery and combat engineers and for fewer antiaircraft and tank destroyer units.[110] Reevaluation brought important changes in artillery force structure too as the army increased the proportion of medium and heavy artillery after mid-1943.[111] Growing experience also led to a rethinking of the role and utility of tank destroyers: in light of lessons learned, the army reduced the number of tank destroyer units and shifted back to towed antitank guns.

During 1943–1944 the army for the first time seriously tackled the problem of the continuing decline of manpower quality. Combat experience had revealed that existing manpower allocation policies eroded not only junior officer leadership but morale and cohesion as well, and thus increased casualties.[112] By mid-1943, the army was well aware of the existing manpower policies' adverse effect on combat effectiveness, and from

August 1943 on the transfer of high-quality personnel from service to combat units began.[113] Circumstances, however, circumscribed the AGF's efforts to improve manpower quality. Mobilization was all but complete, and the AGF could not alter the War Department's distribution of manpower to the armed services; it could only reshuffle its existing manpower. The army's commitment to homogeneity and uniformity meant that, unlike the British Army, it raised few special forces during World War II, ensuring only minimal diversion of quality manpower from the AGF.[114] In September 1943, the AGF initiated an infantry program to improve troop quality and morale.[115] Yet this program was only cosmetic; a more substantive effort was the introduction of the Physical Profile Plan in February 1944 to classify manpower according to physical strength. But this occurred too late to radically improve manpower quality before OVER-LORD, even though it did marginally increase the quality of army replacements during the Normandy campaign and freed more high-quality personnel for the AGF.

In 1944, the army reversed its manpower allocation priorities in favor of the combat arms: the army cut back its Specialized Training Program (ASTP), aviation cadets were transferred to the AGF, and antiaircraft gunners were retrained as infantry. In addition, the army redoubled its efforts to get troops to volunteer for the infantry. Although such efforts were insufficient to rectify fully the inequalities caused by manpower policies they did bring a gradual improvement in AGF troop quality during 1944.

From 1943 on the army, like its Allied counterparts, experienced a manpower shortage. But it proved able to shuffle its available manpower to meet its needs. As early as August 1942, the army had begun inducting "limited-service" personnel into rear headquarters and front-line service units, but the army maintained its strength overseas largely by cadreing divisions that remained in the United States.[116] Despite these efforts there was an infantry shortage by early 1944, but the army exhibited vigor, drive, and tenacity in freeing fit combat troops for service overseas.[117]

During 1943–1944 the army and the USAAF also overcame many of the problems that had plagued air-ground cooperation in the Mediterranean. (The army also vigorously improved the aerial recognition skills of its troops.)[118] But solutions to the command, communication, and control (C3) problems eluded the U.S. military before the Normandy campaign. The first effective C3 system emerged in Italy in the spring of 1944 with the forward air controller (FAC) system known as Horsefly. This involved FACs flying in observation planes with direct radio communication to both air and ground units. This was a great leap forward in coordinating air-ground assets and proved very effective in interdicting enemy rear areas. It was less effective in the immediate combat zone, however, and the USAAF was unable to perfect better close-support techniques before OVER-LORD.[119] Nonetheless, by 1944 the USAAF had become more effective at close air support: it had made major strides in overcoming the problems that had bedeviled air-ground coordination in Tunisia and Sicily, but the major change was the virtual neutralization of the *Luftwaffe*, which allowed the USAAF to provide close support rarely hindered by enemy air power. In Sicily and Italy the USAAF tested and developed the methods of control and communication, the doctrine, and the commanders who led the air battle in northwest Europe. Technological advances contributed to the increased effectiveness of U.S. tactical aviation too as the USAAF deployed new fighters—the P-38 Lightning, P-47 Thunderbolt and P-51 Mustang—that doubled efficiently as fighter-bombers.[120] The development of external fuel tanks that greatly extended combat range and increased payloads also contributed directly to the increasing success of U.S. tactical aviation.

With a new generation of high-performance fighter-bombers equipped with drop tanks, close air support became an important, regular, and integral component of ground operations for the first time in Italy during late spring 1944. The burgeoning of U.S. close air support capabilities in 1944, though, was aided by a remarkable coincidence of circumstances: alongside technological advances, the battering taken by Allied heavy bombers over Germany during the winter of 1943–1944 finally softened doctrinal prejudices against close air support.[121]

The use of strategic bombing forces in the direct support of ground forces represented a final development in the application of air power to land warfare. On 15 February 1944, the Allies made their first use of "carpet" bombing tactical targets in the combat zone as 250 bombers dropped 600 tons of bombs on Monte Cassino. One month later 435 bombers dropped 1,000 tons on Cassino. Despite their awesome destructive power, these initial attacks were not very effective: carpet bombing obliterated the monastery of Monte Cassino but allowed the Germans to dig deep into the rubble. The novelty and complexity of this form of attack prevented the Allies from fully mastering carpet bombing prior to OVERLORD.

Flaws still existed in U.S. air-ground coordination on the eve of D-Day, but the alacrity with which military commanders addressed these issues suggested that they were likely to perfect their execution of the land-air battle in northwest Europe. By 1944, close support had become an integral element of U.S. aerial operations, and was becoming integral to the combined-arms team. The increasing effectiveness of tactical air support powerfully reinforced the striking power of U.S. forces as they prepared for OVERLORD.

The final element of the successful Allied air-ground battle that would be waged in northwest Europe was the orchestration of a systematic aerial interdiction campaign. The first Allied attempt at this was in March 1944 in Italy with Operation STRANGLE, a deep interdiction mission to sever German communications.[122] Although it failed to isolate the battlefield,

STRANGLE contributed to the Germans' defeat in Italy by taking away their tactical mobility.[123] In May 1944 STRANGLE gave way to DIADEM, a combined air-ground offensive, which proved more effective because combined attacks forced the Germans to stand and fight, exposing them to heavy attack. So, DIADEM was the precursor of the successful Allied air-ground victory in France in August 1944.

The U.S. air and ground forces that stood poised on 1 June 1944 in Britain for OVERLORD were better prepared to tackle the Germans than their predecessors who had gone ashore in Tunisia, Sicily, and Italy. A key feature of U.S. preparation for OVERLORD during 1943–1944 was its adaptation to German operational procedures. For instance, revised training emphasized the German tactics of reverse-slope defense in depth, and by 1944 the infantry had learned not to consolidate on captured enemy positions but to push well beyond them to offset losses from enemy artillery preregistered on these positions.[124]

To launch the second front the United States had to establish an advanced base in Britain. The first U.S. troops arrived in January 1942, and by D-Day more than 1.5 million Americans had arrived.[125] However, the Mediterranean diversion absorbed most of these forces. The buildup of an invasion force only really began in 1943, and lack of shipping capacity delayed the buildup from hitting high gear until spring 1944. By D-Day nineteen U.S. divisions were in the United Kingdom.[126]

The Supreme Allied Command earmarked the First U.S. Army, which began to assemble in Britain in September 1943, to spearhead the American assault. Central to the U.S. buildup was the army's determination to redeploy rapidly veteran formations from the Mediterranean for OVERLORD. Thus a full half of the divisions seasoned in the Mediterranean returned to England in 1943.[127] Nevertheless, the bulk of the First U.S. Army still comprised green troops, and this inexperience confronted commanders with their most serious problem. For despite the AGF's best endeavors, many troops had arrived in the United Kingdom incompletely trained. To minimize the impact of their inexperience and undertraining, U.S. forces underwent extensive retraining and exercising in the year preceding D-Day.[128]

The failure of U.S. airborne forces in Tunisia and Sicily also led to a rethinking of their role for OVERLORD. The obvious need for concentrated employment in greater numbers ultimately led to the inclusion of both the 82d and 101st Airborne Divisions in the initial invasion and with a less ambitious mission. The OVERLORD plan called for both divisions to be dropped inland and to block the arrival of German reinforcements while the assault troops established a bridgehead. The lessons drawn from previous failure thus resulted in a more modest and sensible tactical employment of airborne forces than the bold use witnessed in Tunisia and Sicily.

Shipping limitations meant that little U.S. medium and heavy artillery arrived in the United Kingdom during 1943, so that in the spring of 1944 there was a buildup of heavy artillery. Even so, the First U.S. Army still lacked heavy artillery on the eve of OVERLORD.[129] (Despite this, the artillery arm remained the most effective army instrument in the ETO on the eve of D-Day.) The U.S. replacement system's emphasis on quantity over quality ensured that the army's replacement situation on the eve of D-Day remained satisfactory, with some 78,000 replacements available in Britain. This large pool allowed U.S. ground forces to fight harder and longer than their Anglo-Canadian allies in northwest Europe. The replacement system erected in Great Britain also benefited from lessons learned in the Mediterranean and, as a result, functioned more effectively.[130]

Integral to OVERLORD preparations was a massive buildup of American logistical support during 1943 as the army learned from Tunisia, Sicily, Salerno, and Anzio the critical importance of excellent supply support for victory. U.S. forces returned to France in June 1944 with a massive support tail. Based on its previous amphibious assaults, the army employed three Engineer Special Brigades in the initial assault to clear the beaches and to establish quickly the necessary infrastructure ashore to keep the ground forces supplied. Shipping shortages, as well as the Mediterranean diversion, inevitably delayed the logistic buildup in the United Kingdom for OVERLORD. Throughout 1943, U.S. forces in Britain remained short on support and service units as well as supply stockpiles. The Quartermaster Corps accomplished a remarkable organizational feat to complete its buildup during the spring of 1944 so that the army had abundant supply stocks by D-Day.[131]

Despite its victories in North Africa, Sicily, and Italy, on the eve of D-Day the First U.S. Army was still not a perfectly honed fighting machine. Shortcomings in training, lack of emphasis on interarms coordination, and manpower and replacement policies all meant that U.S. ground forces had still not reached their full offensive potential. Combat experience in the Mediterranean during 1943 had illustrated serious weaknesses in U.S. infantry who often lacked aggressiveness, frequently abandoned their prescribed doctrine of fire and maneuver, failed to effectively employ their own firepower, and instead relied too much on artillery to smash the opposition.[132] Battle experience also demonstrated poor infantry-armor coordination, which reflected the lack of training in planning and organizing combined-arms operations. Experience repeatedly showed that infantry commanders employed armor ineffectually and failed to take advantage of its mobility and firepower. Armor, on the other hand, had often proved hesitant and reluctant to support infantry. Thus, it was only infrequently that armor and infantry arrived together at the objective.[133] Combat experience in 1943 had also identified weaknesses in army organization, notably in the policy of pooling. Independent battalions of armor and artillery frequently rotated between divisions and, consequently, joined battle without the familiarity needed for good teamwork and effective combined-arms operation.[134]

Despite these deficiencies, the army in the ETO on the eve of D-Day was far superior to the one that had landed in Tunisia eighteen months earlier. It had greater firepower and mobility; it was more flexibly organized and better coordinated, and had improved tactical air support. If one compares the 1939 and 1944 U.S. armies, one sees that its firepower had grown appreciably, its mobility vastly increased, and its proficiency in combined-arms warfare and in air-ground operations had improved. Most important of all, the U.S. Army had demonstrated an ability both to learn quickly from its combat experience and to adapt rapidly by improvising and retraining in the field, even during combat operations. This army identified deficiencies quickly because it exhibited an honest and serious commitment to gather and analyze combat lessons and to identify and rectify problems. It was quick to learn, innovate, and adapt—despite an informal, decentralized learning process.

The learning process by which ground forces adapted during World War II clearly reflected broader American cultural characteristics. The American democratic tradition of individualism, competition, and entrepreneurial spirit encouraged innovation. As soldiers, Americans displayed confidence in their ability to find solutions to problems, and their ill-defined class distinctions meant that the army was receptive to ideas from junior officers and enlisted personnel.[135]

Other factors help to account for the flexibility and adaptability of the army. Doctrine can be refined and perfected during wartime as long as it is not fundamentally flawed. A key factor in the wartime success of the U.S. Army was that it was able to hone its combat skills and reorganize effectively because combat proved much of its prewar doctrine to be essentially sound. The army's managerial approach also contributed to its flexibility and success, with the result that the wartime army produced a number of highly effective divisions.[136]

Circumstances also allowed the army to reorganize, adapt, and innovate effectively. That the United States experienced twenty-seven months of peace after the outbreak of war in Europe was a major advantage that allowed its army to embark on a well-planned, thought out, organized, and executed program of expansion, reorganization, and reequipment. The country's geostrategic position was of course a benefit: since enemy action rarely directly threatened the contiguous United States, the army was able to pursue mobilization, reorganization, and adaptation undisturbed. The size and topography of the United States was also conducive to large-scale maneuvers that allowed the army quickly to discern existing deficiencies.

Examination of the U.S. forces poised for OVERLORD in the United Kingdom at the beginning of June 1944 suggested that they were reasonably well prepared doctrinally, tactically, materially, and mentally for the coming audit of war. U.S. forces had already demonstrated that they possessed the resources, skill, and flexibility to overcome the gruelling and unpredictable test of battle that they would face in Operation OVERLORD.

Notes

1. Tactical U.S. aviation in December 1941 comprised the A-8 and A-12 Curtis Shrike, the Norththrop A-17 and A-18, and the Douglas A-20. Gordon Swanborough and Peter Bowers, *United States Military Aircraft since 1908* (London: Putnam, 1971), 198–200, 215–222, 437–438.

2. Edward S. Miller, *War Plan ORANGE: The U.S. Strategy to Defeat Japan, 1897–1945* (Annapolis: Naval Institute Press, 1991).

3. Eberhard Jäckel, trans. Herbert Arnold, *Hitler's Weltanschauung: A Blueprint for Power* (Middletown, Conn.: Wesleyan University Press, 1972) shows that Hitler's long-term goal was global domination. On American anti-Asian sentiment see John Dower, *War Without Mercy: Race and Power in the Pacific War* (New York: Pantheon Books, 1986).

4. Race hatred in the Pacific Theater fueled atrocities on both sides, intensified and prolonged Japanese resistance, and threatened to divert the United States from the Allied strategy of defeating Germany first. Thus, in the summer of 1943 the majority of U.S. forces remained in the Pacific. Dower, *War without Mercy;* Walter J. Dunn Jr., *Second Front Now—1943!* (Tuscaloosa: University of Alabama Press, 1980).

5. Few significant improvements materialized after September 1939, though by June 1940 the army had grown in size to 257,095 regulars, 226,837 National Guardsmen trained by individual states and exercised for two weeks each summer, and 104,228 trained officers from Reserve Officer Training Corps and citizen military training camps in the Organized Reserve Corps. Kent R. Greenfield et al., *The Organization of Ground Combat Troops* (Washington, D.C.: OCMH, 1947), 2.

6. The army included twenty-seven infantry, four armored, and two cavalry divisions. It absorbed 278,526 National Guard personnel and by July 1941 had inducted 606,915 selectees. Greenfield, *Organization,* 10.

7. In summer 1940, the army and National Guard comprised 13,797 and 21,074 officers, respectively. In addition, there were some 33,000 reserve officers plus 104,228 graduates of the Reserve Officer Training Corps.

8. In May 1943 the army removed a mere four officers but in December 1943 the figure rose to 287. Robert Palmer and William R. Keast, "The Procurement of Officers," in Robert R. Palmer et al., *The Army Ground Forces: The Procurement and Training of Ground Combat Troops* (Washington, D.C.: OCMH, 1948), 48–50, 125–126.

9. Peter Mansoor, "The Development of Combat Effective Divisions in the World War II U.S. Army," M.A. thesis, Ohio State University, 1992, 3; and "Building Blocks of Victory: American Infantry Divisions in the War Against Germany and Italy, 1941–45," Ph.D. thesis, Ohio State University, 1995.

10. Between the wars the tiny U.S. Marine Corps developed a specialized amphibious warfare capability to preserve its organizational independence and held ten annual fleet landing exercises. The participation of the Caribbean Amphibious Force in the 1941 exercises illustrates the early U.S. shift toward offensive training. Allan R. Millett, *Semper Fidelis: The History of the United States Marine Corps*

(New York: Macmillan, 1980) and "Assault from the Sea: The Development of Amphibious Warfare in Great Britain and the United States Between the War," in Millett and Williamson Murray, *Innovation in the Interwar Period* (Washington, D.C.: Office of Net Assessment, DOD, 1995), 102–114.

11. Greenfield, *Organization,* 10–11 and 33–34.

12. McNair wrote, "The truth is sought regardless of whether pleasant or unpleasant, or whether it supports or condemns our present organization and tactics." Letter on "Antitank Defense," General McNair to CGS, 15 May 1941, quoted in Greenfield, *Organization,* 44.

13. Joseph R. Cerami, "Training: The 1941 Louisiana Maneuvers," *Military Review* (October 1987), 34–43.

14. General McNair wrote, "Are these troops ready for war? It is my judgement that, given complete equipment, they certainly could fight effectively. But it is to be added with emphasis that the losses would be unduly heavy, and the results of action against an adversary such as the Germans might not be all that could be desired."

15. The army raised an experimental platoon in June 1940 that made its first drop on 16 August 1940. In June 1941 only twelve transports were available for parachute training, which restricted practice drops to company level. John Weeks, *Assault from the Sky: The History of Airborne Warfare* (Newton Abbott: David & Charles, 1988), 63–64.

16. Airborne divisions were very small infantry divisions of 8,500 personnel and with heavy weapons and transport pared to a minimum. Greenfield, *Organization,* 339–341; Weeks, *Assault from the Sky,* 68–69.

17. Greenfield, *Organization,* 418.

18. Triangularity continued down through the division: each infantry regiment had three battalions, each battalion three rifle companies, each company three rifle platoons, and each platoon three squads. This provided at every level a fire element, a maneuver element, and a reserve. Stanton, *Order of Battle,* 8.

19. "The ultimate objective of all military operations is the destruction of the enemy's armed forces in battle." "Through offensive action a commander exercises his initiative, preserves his freedom of action, and imposes his will on the enemy," *FM 100-5, Field Service Regulations, 1941,* paras. 112 and 115.

20. Martin van Creveld, *Fighting Power: German & US Army Performances, 1939–45* (London: Arms & Armour Press, 1983), chap. 4; Weigley, *Eisenhower's Lieutenants* I, 6–10.

21. Maurice Matloff, "The 90-Division Gamble," in Kent R. Greenfield, ed., *Command Decisions* (Washington, D.C.: OCMH, 1960), 365–381.

22. Robert P. Palmer and William R. Keist, "The Provision of Enlisted Replacements," in Palmer, *Procurement and Training,* 369–428; Lt. Col. Leonard L. Lerwill, *The Personnel Replacement System in the United States Army,* Dept. of the Army (DOA) Pamphlet 20–211, (Washington, D.C.: DOA, 1954), chaps. 5–6.

23. During the war the eighty-nine American divisions raised absorbed 2.67 million replacements, thus on average each division received twice its original establishment in replacements. Palmer, *Procurement and Training,* 177.

24. In 1942 the AGF received 40 percent of manpower but only 34 percent of the highest rated (AGCT classes I–II) and 44 percent of the lowest rated troops (AGCT IV, V). In March 1942 the distribution of U.S. Army manpower by AGCT category was I–II: 34 percent, III: 31 percent, IV–V: 35 percent. In 1943 the respective totals were 30 percent, 33 percent, and 37 percent. During 1943 only 30.0 percent of infantry recruits were rated AGCT I or II, compared to 31.5 percent in the

armored force and artillery, and 34.0 percent among chemical warfare troops. Palmer, *Procurement and Training*, 3–4, 15–18.

25. Greenfield, *Organization*, chap. 3.

26. The army's first towed-gun divisional antitank battalions only came into existence in June 1941. Weeks, *Men Against Tanks*, 91–92.

27. *FM 18–5, The Organization and Tactics of Tank Destroyer Units* (Washington, D.C.: GPO, 16 July 1942).

28. The first U.S. Army tank destroyer, the M3, which mounted a modified 1918-vintage 75mm field gun on an M2 half-track, went into production late in 1941. Christopher Gabel, *Seek, Strike, and Destroy: The Evolution of American Tank Destroyer Doctrine in World War II* (Fort Leavenworth: Combat Studies Institute, U.S. Army Command and General Staff College, 1985), 1.

29. The 75mm M5, for instance, married an antiaircraft gun with a light field howitzer carriage. It was not until 1944 that the United States produced an effective heavy antitank gun in the 90mm T8. Weeks, *Men Against Tanks*, 92–93.

30. Timothy Lupfer, *The Dynamics of Doctrine: The Changes in German Tactical Doctrine during the First World War* (Fort Leavenworth: U.S. Staff and Command College, 1981); Maj. Christopher Wray, *Standing Fast: The Development of German Defensive Doctrine, Prewar to Spring 1943* (Fort Leavenworth: Command and Staff College, 1986).

31. Weeks, *Men Against Tanks*, 95–99.

32. Jester A. Isley and Phillip A. Crowl, *The U.S. Marines and Amphibious War* (Princeton, N.J.: Princeton University Press, 1951), 58–67; Alfred Beck et al., *The Corps of Engineers: The War Against Germany* (Washington, D.C.: USACMH, 1984).

33. Christopher Gabel, "The U.S. Army GHQ Maneuvers of 1941," Ph.D. thesis, Ohio State University, 1981, 65–71, 92–99, 310–313.

34. *FM 31–35, Aviation in Support of Ground Forces* (Washington, D.C.: GPO, April 1942); Riley Sunderland, *Evolution of Command and Control Doctrine for Close Air Support* (Washington, D.C.: Office of Air Force History, 1973).

35. Richard P. Hallion, *Strike from the Sky: A History of Battlefield Air Attack, 1911–45* (Washington, D.C.: Smithsonian Institute Press, 1989), 163–187; Jacobs, "AAF Close Air Support," 38–39; Muller, "Close Air Support," 290–291; Greenfield, *Air-Ground Battle Team*, 32–47; Thomas T. Maycock, "Notes on the Development of AAF Tactical Air Doctrine," *Military Affairs* 14 (1950), 186.

36. Stanton, *Order of Battle*, 10.

37. Palmer, *Procurement and Training*, 300–318.

38. The infantry-to-tank ratio in the 1940 German armored division was five times that of the U.S. division and it too lacked infantry.

39. Stanton, *Order of Battle*, 47–50.

40. McNair hoped to attach independent armored infantry battalions to existing divisions once they went into combat, but the AGF deactivated all but one of these battalions in 1943. Stanton, *Order of Battle*, 268–272.

41. Combat Commands A, B, and R, abbreviated CCA, CCB, CCR. Lt. Col. Waqyne, "Armoured Division's Combat Commands," *Cavalry Journal* 55 (March–April 1946), 43.

42. Stanton, *Orders of Battle*, 5.

43. By June 1944 less than half of army combat troops were organic to combat divisions. Tank destroyer, artillery, mechanized cavalry, transport, antiaircraft, bridging, signals, quartermaster, ordnance, and supply units were all pooled at army level in accordance with the principle of flexibility.

44. Gen. George C. Marshall, the U.S. Army chief of staff, was the most stri-

dent exponent of the direct approach; Gen. Sir Alan Brooke, chief of the Imperial General Staff was the strongest supporter of the peripheral strategy. Weigley, *American Way of War,* 317; David Fraser, *Alanbrooke* (London: Collins, 1982), 242–250.

45. On U.S. logisitic deficiencies in 1942 see Beck, *Engineers Against Germany,* 68–82; Capt. William G. Gessner, "TORCH: Unlearned Logistics Lessons," *Army Logistician* 15 (November–December 1983), 28–32.

46. In June 1942 there were only 4,305 U.S. troops in England. William F. Ross, and Charles F. Romanus, *The Quartermaster Corps: Operations in the War Against Germany* (Washington, D.C.: OCMH, 1965), 18.

47. TORCH was also motivated by the desire to relieve pressure on the Soviets and keep them in the war. Kent R. Greenfield, *American Strategy in World War II: A Reconsideration* (Baltimore: Johns Hopkins University Press, 1963).

48. On 24 December 1942, the Germans savaged the 18th Infantry Regiment on Longstop Hill and mauled the 168th Infantry Regiment at Sidi Bou Zid during 14–15 February 1943. Gregory Blaxland, *The Plain Cook and the Great Showman* (London: W. Kimber, 1977), 140–141 and 157–159; George F. Howe, *Northwest Africa: Seizing the Initiative in the West* (Washington, D.C.: OCMH, 1957), 338–344. Martin Blumenson's *Kasserine Pass* (New York: PBJ Books, 1983) offers a definitive study of the battle in which the Americans lost 235 tanks and 4,000 prisoners.

49. Blumenson, *Kasserine Pass,* 5–7; Richard W. Stewart, "The 'Red Bull' Division: The Training and Initial Engagements of the 34th Infantry Division, 1941–43," *Army History* 25 (Winter 1993), 1–10.

50. Initially, U.S. forces failed to learn well from their earliest combat experience in Tunisia, or so Montgomery thought. Letter from Montgomery to Gen. Sir Alan Brooke, 23 February 1943, in Stephen Brooks, ed., *Montgomery and the Eighth Army* (London: Bodley Head, 1991), 154.

51. From April 1942 on McNair demanded detailed combat reports on the effectiveness of training, equipment, and organization. Greenfield, *Organization,* 273.

52. American ground forces suffered 4 percent casualties in Tunisia. Howe, *Seizing the Initiative,* 675.

53. War Department, *Lessons from the Tunisian Campaign* (Washington, D.C.: GPO, October 1943), 1–2.

54. Ibid., 35–39; Peter C. Hains III, "Tanks in Tunisia," *The Cavalry Journal* 52 (July–August 1943), 13–17; Michael D. Doubler, *Closing with the Enemy: How GIs Fought the War in Europe, 1944–45* (Lawrence: University of Kansas Press, 1994), 16–17.

55. This occurred at Tebourba in December 1942, Ousseltia in February 1943, Kasserine in March, and Maknassy in April. Howe, *Seizing the Initiative,* 311–320, 376–384, 469–474, 543–556.

56. Gabel, *Seek, Strike, and Destroy,* 24–41; Charles M. Bailey, *Faint Praise: American Tanks and Tank Destroyers during World War Two* (Hamden, Conn.: Archon Books, 1983); *Lessons from the Tunisian Campaign,* 56–58.

57. National Archives Record Administration Record Group (NARA RG) 337, entry 29, Maj. Allerton Cushman, "Final Report to Commanding General AGF on Tank Destroyer Ops. in North Africa," 3 May 1943.

58. Gabel, *Seek, Strike, and Destroy,* 24–41; Bailey, *Faint Praise,* 56–60; *Lessons from the Tunisian Campaign,* 56–58; NARA RG 337, file 470.8, entry 40, Gen. Orlando Ward, "Rpt. of Board of Officers on the Subject of Tanks and TDs Employed as Field Artillery," 8 September 1943; AGF ETO, observer report 190, "Tanks and TDs as Reinforcing Artillery," 25 August 1944.

59. *Lessons from the Tunisian Campaign,* 56–60.

60. Ibid., 40–41.

61. Ibid., 53–55.

62. Ibid., 61–62.

63. In Tunisia, close air support was provided by XII Air Support Command flying A-20 attack bombers, Bell P-39 and Spitfire fighters, and B-25 medium bombers. Richard G. Davis, *Tempering the Blade: General Carl Spaatz and American Tactical Air Power in North Africa* (Washington, D.C.: Center for Air Force History, 1989); David Syrett, "The Tunisian Campaign, 1942–43," in Benjamin Cooling, ed., *Case Studies in the Development of Close Air Support,* 161–165; NARA WNRC RG 407, box 5771, file 301-3.01, 1st Infantry Division, "Lessons from Operation TORCH," 25 December 1942, 7–8.

64. *Lessons from the Tunisian Campaign,* 65–70.

65. The campaign study contained only a single paragraph on combined-arms coordination. *Lessons from the Tunisian Campaign,* 6–7.

66. Night landings brought unnecessary confusion, and the *coup de main* attempts on Oran and Algiers ended in disaster. The Eastern Assault Force lost 94 percent of its landing craft. Millett, "Assault from the Sea," 137–138; Beck, *Engineers Against Germany,* 78–81; Mansoor, "Building Blocks," 155–167.

67. Beck, *Engineers Against Germany,* 69–82; Capt. William G. Gessner, "TORCH: Unlearned Logistics Lessons," *Army Logistician* 15 (November–December 1983), 28–32.

68. Ross and Romanus, *Quartermaster Corps,* 38–86, 157–158.

69. Samuel E. Morison, *History of United States Naval Operations in World War II* (Boston: Little, Brown & Co, 1947) II, 123; NARA WNRC RG 407, box 5662, File 301-0.3, 1st Division, "After Action Report," 5 December 1942.

70. Beck, *Engineers Against Germany,* 79–82; Maj. John M. Taylor, "North African Campaign: Logistic Lessons Learned," *Military Review* 63 (October 1983), 46–55; Capt. William G. Gessner, "TORCH: Unlearned Logistics Lessons," *Army Logistician* 15 (November–December 1983), 28–32.

71. *Lessons from the Tunisian Campaign,* 5–6.

72. Ibid., 3–9; NARA WNRC RG 407, box 7326, file 309-0.3, 9th Division, "Rpt. on Ops., Mar–Apr. 1943," 25 August 1943.

73. *Lessons from the Tunisian Campaign,* 6–8.

74. Ibid., 9–12.

75. Ibid., 14.

76. Weeks, *Assault from the Sky,* 50–55.

77. *Lessons from the Tunisian Campaign,* 4–5.

78. Ibid., 17–22.

79. Ibid., 22–23.

80. Ibid., 29–30, 41.

81. The rule of thumb developed in Tunisia was that one-third of artillery employed should fire smoke in the attack. Ibid., 40.

82. The army fielded seven major calibers of artillery in the war and pooled all its heavy artillery at corps level. Light artillery comprised the 75mm air-transportable pack howitzer, the 105mm M2 and M3 howitzers (the mainstay of divisional artillery), and the 105mm M7 self-propelled howitzer used by armored units. Medium artillery comprised the 4.5-inch gun and 155mm M1 howitzer. Heavy artillery consisted of the 155mm "Long Tom" gun, the 155mm M12 self-propelled gun, the 8-inch M2 howitzer, the 8-inch gun used for counterbattery work, and the 240mm "Black Dragon" M1 howitzer. Stanton, *Order of Battle,* 28–32.

83. The artillery arm neglected concentrated corps artillery fire until well into

the war. "The Employment of Corps Artillery," *Military Review* 23, 2 (May 1943), 56–57.

84. Average response time was under five minutes. Col. E. B. Gjelseteen, "Massing the Fire of Division and Corps Artillery," *Field Artillery Journal* 33, 6 (June 1943), 426–429; Howe, *Seizing the Initiative*, 560–562.

85. *Lessons from the Tunisian Campaign,* 29.

86. Ibid., 31–32.

87. Ibid., 25.

88. Up to 31 October 1943 the War Department dispatched 340,616 replacements to the Mediterranean to replace 59,429 battle casualties. Lerwill, *Personnel Replacement System,* 265–275, 419.

89. Mansoor, "Building Blocks," 169–170; Stewart, "The 'Red Bull' Division," 1–10.

90. B. H. Liddell Hart, ed., *The Rommel Papers* (London: Collins, 1953), 523. See also OKH/GenStdH/Op. Abt. (II), Afrika-A I Berichte-Bd. III, 16.1.–18.5.1943, cited in Howe, *Seizing the Initiative,* 674.

91. U.S. War Department, *Field Manual FM 100-20, Command and Employment of Air Power,* 166–191; Jacobs "Tactical Air Doctrine," 35–49; James A. Huston, "Tactical Use of Air Power in World War II: The Army Experience," *Military Affairs* 14 (Winter 1950), 166–191.

92. By May 1943 troops routinely advanced only 100 to 200 yards behind the barrage. *Lessons from the Tunisian Campaign,* 7; NARA WNRC RG 407, box 7326, file 309-0.3, 9th Div., "Rpt. on Ops., Apr–May 1943," 10 September 1943, 12–16.

93. *Lessons from the Tunisian Campaign,* 14–15.

94. Seventh Army comprised 1st, 3d, 9th, and 45th Infantry, 2d Armored, and 82d Airborne Divisions. Samuel Mitchum and Friedrich von Stauffenburg, *The Battle of Sicily: How the Allies Lost Their Chance for Total Victory* (New York: Orion Books, 1991), 12–13; Carlo D'Este, *Bitter Victory: the Battle for Sicily 1943* (New York: Dutton, 1988), 338.

95. That Patton faced mostly demoralized Italian defenders facilitated his rapid advance, while Montgomery had to engage elite German mechanized troops and paratroopers. Mitchum and von Stauffenburg, *Sicily,* 196–213.

96. The paratroopers were scattered over 65 miles and less than a company landed on the drop zone. Mitchum and von Stauffenburg, *Sicily,* 92–93; Weeks, *Assault from the Sky,* 55–62.

97. In Sicily the Seventh U.S. Army's 13th Artillery Brigade eventually comprised 13 battalions. Jonathon Bailey, *Field Artillery and Firepower* (Oxford: The Military Press, 1989), 192.

98. The most serious limitation of U.S. artillery effectiveness in Sicily, as in Tunisia, was constant munitions shortages. War Department, *Lessons from the Sicilian Campaign* (Washington, D.C.: GPO, 1943), 25; *Lessons from the Italian Campaign* (Washington, D.C.: GPO, 1944), 84–85.

99. Greenfield, *Organization,* 423.

100. The A-36 Invader proved unsuccessful in this role in Italy.

101. During 1942–1943 the USAAF was poor at providing photographic and visual reconnaissance. The 11 July 1943 airborne assault on Sicily tragically illustrated poor recognition skills and fire discipline: friendly fire shot down twenty-three transports and damaged a further thirty-seven. Mitchum and Stauffenburg, *Sicily,* 127–130.

102. Ross and Romanus, *Quartermaster Corps,* 75–86.

103. Ibid., 103.

104. Charles Heller and William Stofft, eds., *America's First Battles, 1776–1965* (Lawrence: University Press of Kansas, 1986), 161–165.

105. Greenfield, *Organization,* 411–417.

106. In Tunisia and Italy, pooled independent tank battalions proved much less effective than divisional ones because pooling brought frequent rotation through divisions, thus hampering the development of the familiarity, trust, and confidence crucial to effective combined-arms teamwork. *Lessons from the Italian Campaign,* 22–27; Doubler, *Closing,* 17.

107. Lt. Gen. Jacob Devers, chief of the Armored Force, for one, did not believe that pooling brought either unity of command or economy of force. Greenfield, *Organization,* 271–276.

108. The historical antecedents of the RCT were the U.S. Army sublegions of 1792–1796. A typical RCT included a divisional artillery battalion and engineer, signals, and medical companies. Stanton, *Order of Battle,* 13.

109. Only on 14 June 1944 did the army retreat from pooling and authorize the semipermanent attachment of independent battalions to divisions.

110. From January 1944 the army deactivated, on average, sixteen antiaircraft and two tank destroyer battalions each month. Stanton, *Orders of Battle,* 6–7.

111. The March 1944 Lucas review board led to the activation of additional heavy artillery battalions. Between June 1943 and April 1945 the number of medium and heavy artillery battalions increased by 69 and 211 percent, respectively. Seaton, *Orders of Battle,* 30.

112. Palmer, *Procurement and Training,* 50–51.

113. Ibid., 52.

114. The 1st Special Service Force was a composite U.S.-Canadian special forces brigade. Raiding forces comprised six army Ranger battalions. The army also employed several Office of Strategic Services operational groups on sabotage missions behind enemy lines. Stanton, *Order of Battle,* 14.

115. The infantry program established the Bronze Star medal for "heroic or meritorious achievement or service," introduced the Expert and Combat Infantryman badges, and increased pay. Palmer, *Procurement and Training,* 62–64.

116. After 22 April 1944 the army cadred 22 divisions at home and stripped 91,747 personnel from them before their departure overseas. Bell I. Wiley "The Building and Training of Infantry Divisions," in Palmer, *Procurement and Training,* 472–474.

117. In spring 1944, the army classified some 210,000 troops stationed in the United States as fit for overseas combat service. By fall 1944 almost none remained. Ibid., 80–81.

118. Doubler, *Closing,* 23.

119. Doubler, *Closing,* 24; Greenfield, *Air-Ground Battle Team,* 78–85; *Lessons from the Italian Campaign,* 53–55.

120. The Mustang was a high-performance, long-range escort fighter that combined exceptional performance with good range and endurance as a fighter-bomber. The Thunderbolt was the best fighter-bomber of the three and very rugged.

121. Jacobs, "AAF Tactical Aviation Doctrine," 47–48.

122. The interdiction of German supplies to Tunisia, though highly effective, had emerged extemporaneously.

123. Edward Mark, "A New Look at Operation Strangle," *Military Affairs* 52, 4 (October 1988), 176–184.

124. Doubler, *Closing,* 28.

125. Stanton, *Order of Battle,* 115–116.

126. Ten divisions and nine independent combat battalions arrived in 1943,

and a further eight divisions and twenty-one battalions came during spring of 1944. Seaton, *Order of Battle,* 46–594.

127. The 1st and 9th Infantry, 2d Armored, and 82d Airborne Divisions were redeployed from the Mediterranean. This extensive and rapid redeployment reflected the U.S. Army's skepticism about the strategic value of the Italian campaign. Stanton, *Order of Battle,* 46–188; Greenfield, *American Strategy: A Reconsideration;* Michael E. Howard, *The Continental Commitment: The Dilemmas of British Defence Policy in the Era of the Two World Wars* (London: T. Smith, 1972).

128. Field artillery perfected Serenade procedures for rapid, unarranged massed artillery fire, tank destroyer and heavy antiaircraft battalions retrained in a secondary field artillery role, and the First U.S. Army raised and trained Joint Assault Signal Companies and Naval Shore Fire Control Parties. First U.S. Army *Report* V, 169–170.

129. During April–May 1944 U.S. medium and heavy artillery in the ETO increased by 54 percent. PRO WO 219/282, SHAEF G3, "Heavy Artillery for U.S Forces in the ETO, 15 April 1944," and "Heavy and Super-heavy Field Artillery Situation, 1 June 1944."

130. The replacement system in the Mediterranean experienced severe strain due to the heavy combat in Italy and a serious replacement shortage contributed to halting the Fifth Army's offensive in Italy on 15 November 1943. In February 1944, the U.S. 36th Division possessed less than one-quarter of its authorized rifle strength and only vigorous rationalization brought units up to strength in time for renewed offensive action in the spring. Lerwill, *Personnel Replacement System,* 420–426; Chester G. Starr, *From Salerno to the Alps* (Washington, D.C.: OCMH, 1948), 53, 112–113, 161–169, 179, 202, 243–248.

131. The U.S. Army assembled 352 quartermaster, 41 trucking, and 9 troop transport companies for OVERLORD. Each engineer special brigade was 5,500 men strong and possessed a lift capacity of 3,300 tons. Ross and Romanus, *Quartermaster Corps,* 319–361.

132. Weigley, *Eisenhower's Lieutenants,* 24–28.

133. This difficulty was partly technical because inadequate means of communication existed between armor and infantry. Doubler, *Closing,* 10–11.

134. Ibid., 11.

135. Ibid., 6.

136. John Sloan Brown, *Draftee Division: The 88th Infantry Division in World War II* (Lexington: University Press of Kentucky, 1986); Peter Mansoor, "Building Blocks," passim.

3

Britain, 1939–1944:
Toils and Troubles

If mortal catastrophe should overtake the British nation, historians a thousand years hence will never understand how it was that a victorious nation suffered themselves to cast away all they had gained by measureless sacrifice.

—Winston Churchill

During the first three years of World War II the British Army suffered some of the most disastrous defeats in its history. Repeated defeat profoundly influenced the army's subsequent performance, and it was only slowly and at heavy cost that it improved its combat proficiency. The army proved slow to adapt because its culture and traditions, as well as its interwar neglect, had left it devoid of modern doctrine and without mechanisms to evaluate its performance. At the same time, its disdain for intellectual preparation ensured that the army extracted from its experiences and those of its opponents support for its preconceived notions—that is, that it learned better from its few successes than it did from its more frequent reverses.[1]

In September 1939 the British Army remained small, poorly organized and equipped, unbalanced, undertrained, defense-minded, and vulnerable in spirit. It lacked coherent, realistic doctrine, and was unready for interarms and interservice cooperation. It was so tactically, materially, and mentally unready for war that it was at best capable only of limited defense. The hasty, haphazard, and incremental dispatch of the British Expeditionary Force (BEF) to France during the fall of 1939 left it ill prepared to confront the German Army because it lacked balance and cohesion. Moreover, many of its officers were newly thrust into positions of responsibility for which they had not been trained. Most serious of all, though, is that the BEF went to France with a defensive mentality. Fundamentally, the BEF's condition reflected the aversion of interwar British society to military preparedness and renewed continental warfare.[2]

While Germany overran Poland, the BEF expanded to ten divisions but remained predominantly an infantry force that lacked supporting arms. By spring of 1940, Britain had organized a war economy and production blossomed. But so great were equipment shortages during mobilization that the BEF had only partly reequipped by May 1940 and still lacked communications, transport, and heavy weapons. Its troops remained undertrained and, although the regulars had sufficient discipline and experience to progress in unit training, the Territorial Army troops were still perfecting basics when the Germans attacked. The necessary emphasis on basic training left the BEF little time or resources for collective training, maneuvers, analysis of the German victory in Poland, or retraining. Thus the BEF simply lacked the base of preparedness—in leadership, equipment, and sound doctrine—to become an effective force.

The BEF also lacked armored forces. Reorganization of the 1st Armoured Division delayed its arrival—underequipped and poorly supplied—until after the German onslaught had begun. On 10 May 1940 the BEF had only two operational tank battalions, and its meager mechanized forces lacked balance and cohesion. At the same time, the BEF lacked the antitank weapons needed to stop the panzers that had rampaged through Poland.[3] Nonetheless, the BEF and the *Heer* faced many similar problems: both lacked officers, ordnance, communications, munitions, and transport. But marked differences existed in training, morale, spirit, and deployment. While the *Heer* had trained its troops well, possessed high morale and an aggressive offensive spirit, and, most significantly of all, had concentrated its strength, the BEF dissipated its strength in linear defense.

The German invasion of Norway in April 1940 brought the first clash between British and German ground forces and revealed how ill equipped and unprepared British troops were to fight the Germans. The invasion forced Britain and France to launch a hastily improvised campaign to retain a hold on Norway. Lacking joint-operations experience, the Allies undertook a campaign that required extensive interservice cooperation without an appropriate command mechanism. That the Allies ineptly executed their counterinvasion exacerbated the difficulties British troops faced as Britain haphazardly shipped the 49th Territorial Division, mostly infantry with few supporting arms, to central Norway. Oversupplied but undersupported, the division fought a short, abortive campaign to maintain a toehold in Norway before being withdrawn.[4]

British troops clearly came off worse in their first clash with the Germans. They experienced what later became all too familiar: the demoralizing ease with which enemy infiltration and flanking tactics dislodged British troops from their positions.[5] Troop performance was variable but generally poor. The few regulars committed conducted a skilled delaying withdrawal, but the territorials lacked the leadership, training, and discipline even to defend themselves effectively. In fact, the Norway operation first demonstrated a weakness that plagued the British Army throughout the war: its vulnerable morale, which plummeted with reverses and retreats even though losses were light. The campaign also revealed that British doctrine and training had produced a sluggish, methodical army, as well as a trait of logistic overinsurance. It shipped huge quantities of unnecessary stores to Norway, while the ground forces lacked heavy weapons, communications, and transport.

The army had no time to draw lessons from Norway before the German offensive in Western Europe (10 May 1940) rapidly penetrated the French lines in the Ardennes and forced the BEF to retreat to the Channel coast and be evacuated. The catastrophe was all the more shocking because British and French commanders were confident that their troops could repeat the successful defense of 1914 by pursuing the same simple and conventional strategy: adoption of defense to stop a renewed German offensive through neutral Belgium. Once it was halted, the Allies planned to mobilize their economies and wear Germany down into defeat through a strategy of attrition they had used in World War I. Because they outnumbered the Germans, this confidence seemed well placed.[6]

But the defensive Allied deployment and the concept of armor as a specialized tactical weapon rather than a versatile, self-contained combat system, led them to disperse their armor defensively for infantry support, for reconnaissance, screening, and raiding in the light cavalry tradition, and as a counterattack force in the heavy cavalry tradition to repulse German armored penetrations in direct tank-to-tank combat.[7] Decentralization of armor to less mobile forces robbed the Allied dispositions of sufficient depth and strength to prevent a strategic penetration by massed German mechanized forces, and left Allied forces too dispersed to launch an effective counterstroke.[8] Thus when German armor broke through the weakly held Ardennes and breached the Meuse, their own dispositions prevented the Allies from assembling sufficient strength for their strategic counterattack at Arras on 21 May to succeed.[9] Britain reinforced failure so that ultimately sixteen divisions, virtually its entire field force, were sucked into a lost battle. Desperate improvisation, stubborn defense, and good fortune combined to allow the evacuation of the mainly weaponless remnants of the BEF from Dunkirk.[10]

The troops' performance in France was uneven, though they demonstrated the stoic defense that became a hallmark of the wartime army. The BEF, however, lacked the firepower and mobility to halt the blitzkrieg. The Royal Artillery, though partly reequipped with the excellent 25-pounder field gun, still deployed many obsolescent guns and lacked medium and heavy artillery as well as mobility. Its training for static warfare, its obsolete ordnance, limited communications, defective organization, lack of munitions, and dispersed deployment all crippled artillery effectiveness. British artillery was neither numerous nor mobile enough, nor suitably equipped or trained, to provide the rapid, concentrated fire necessary to halt the German advance.[11]

Nor could tactical aviation stem the German onslaught. The commitment of the Royal Air Force (RAF) to strategic bombing meant that it only grudgingly supported the BEF with the Advanced Air Striking Force (AASF), which comprised ten squadrons of obsolete Fairey Battle and Bristol Blenheim light bombers, tasked to fly close-support and battlefield interdiction missions. Yet Allied fighter forces, while well equipped, were too few and too dispersed to maintain air superiority. The loss of control of the skies, combined with the AASF's lack of specialized training, communications, and a viable doctrine, resulted in the force's decimation without its even slowing the German ground advance.[12]

During 1940–1941 Britain contemplated the lessons of defeat in Norway and France. But the army failed to draw appropriate lessons from these defeats because it was unwilling to evaluate its performance openly and honestly and because it selectively interpreted from its experience that which validated its prevailing preconceptions. The army concluded that German aerial supremacy had brought defeat in Norway and thus blamed lack of interservice cooperation, especially the RAF's hostility to ground support, for failure. At the same time, the army blamed poor troop performance on interwar politicians—who had left the army unprepared for overseas service—and the RAF, Royal Navy, and the French for inept support. Quick to seek scapegoats elsewhere, the army failed to evaluate its own weaknesses objectively.[13]

The lessons of the French campaign were more numerous, but more ambiguous since the speed and scale of defeat provided few clear messages for the army's reconstitution. As a result, the army misinterpreted the lessons of the campaign. Having misused armor in France, it losing 98 percent of the tanks deployed, the army concluded that massed employment of armor had secured German victory. The army failed to comprehend the true nature of German success: the intimate combination of combat arms as part of an aggressive strategic doctrine of deep penetration to disrupt enemy communications and logistics and thus paralyze enemy resistance.

This misperception forged in summer 1940 the "panzer myth," an exaggerated sense of the power and strategic potential of massed armor, which the Royal Armoured Corps (RAC) never entirely dispelled. This myth gained ground in part because it appeared to vindicate both the armored enthusiast and the cavalry views of exponents of armored warfare. The myth supported both the "limited-liability" proponents' call for a small, mechanized elite and the cavalry school approach of massed employment to smash enemy armor. As important, the notion that the Germans had won because their massed armor had annihilated dispersed Allied armor appeared to validate the prevailing British strategic doctrine of attrition. That the supposed lessons of France seemed to vindicate exist-ing strategy made such "lessons" all the more persuasive.[14]

The various arms drew their own lessons from the French campaign. British armor had proved mechanically unreliable, undergunned, and underarmored. The RAC thus demanded more, better armed and armored, and more reliable tanks to be employed en masse to shatter enemy armor in direct engagement. The campaign also revealed that the Royal Artillery lacked the firepower, range, and speed for effective defensive and counter-battery fire. It was likewise concluded that the artillery needed greater fire-power—more and better medium, heavy, and antitank artillery—as well as greater mobility. The campaign highlighted the artillery's defective organi-zation, its lack of reliable field radios, and its sluggishness: the speed of blitzkrieg war simply did not allow for the meticulous fire plans practiced between the wars.[15]

Then there was the infantry performance. That hastily raised, trained, and committed territorials performed poorly was little surprise; but even the performance of regular units varied considerably due to inadequate fire-power, poor manpower quality, and indifferent training. But, at the same time, the most important lesson of the campaign—that ground forces could no longer operate effectively without interarms and interservice coordina-tion—remained poorly understood. The army failed to recognize that the root cause of its failure was the absence of the base of professional prepara-tion required to repulse German attacks. The army was simply too poorly equipped, trained, organized, and integrated to withstand blitzkrieg war-fare. These weaknesses stemmed both from the army's failure to preserve its Great War experience and from crippling interwar financial cutbacks that had left the army mentally and materially unprepared for renewed con-tinental warfare.

While defeat in 1940 was probably unavoidable, what was not was the army's unwillingness to learn honestly from experience as it once again sought scapegoats to explain away defeat in France. It thus concluded that intelligence errors, unreliable Allies, and poor interservice support had brought defeat. Intelligence failures, the army claimed, had left the Allies unable to discern the German strategic focus, the RAF had held back many fighter squadrons that might have tipped the balance in the air war, and the French had collapsed due to a fundamental flaw of national character—a lack of will to fight—as they had in 1917.[16] What the army failed to recog-nize, however, was that although these alleged "failings" may have magni-fied the speed and scale of defeat, better intelligence, stronger-willed Allies, or even every squadron the RAF possessed would not have changed the outcome.

The British army of 1940 lacked mechanisms to derive and dissemi-nate combat lessons. Instead, it focused on the task of salvaging, protecting, and buttressing its battered reputation rather than openly assessing its strengths and weaknesses. At the same time the speed and scale of defeat, the army's lack of combat experience, the disdain for intellectual preparation, and the lukewarm commitment to retraining all slowed the pace of reform early in the war. The BEF's ejection from the continent, though, was a blessing in disguise that dispelled lethargy and complacency and propelled the army into action from which emerged a stronger and more effective "New Model Army."[17] Even though this new army never became as large, powerful, or proficient as the army of 1918, it was sufficient to secure victory. The circumstances of 1940, however, were not conducive to sober assessment followed by rational and planned reform, the continental debacle energizing Britain to rebuild a ground force to resist an anticipated German invasion. The army thus underwent meteoric, if hasty and unbalanced, expansion during summer 1940 as it churned out what it could most easily and quickly produce—defense-oriented infantry.[18] The desperate need of the hour led the army to sacrifice quality for quantity: to reequip the army quickly the War Office kept obsolete weapons in production, prematurely rushed new equipment into service, and shelved longer term projects. Such expedients met the immediate challenge but delayed entry into service of powerful, offensive weapons, thus preventing the British Army from closing the quality gap in armaments for much of the war.[19]

Unparalleled defeat also inevitably accentuated Britain's strategic predisposition toward defense because it suggested that blitzkrieg was a revolutionary and unstoppable new form of mechanized warfare. But the army mistakenly assumed that strategic defense negated offensive defense, and was slow to learn that blitzkrieg did not fundamentally alter the nature of war and that it could be stopped by mobile defense and firepower. It was not until 1942–1943 that the army learned how to counter the blitzkrieg. The new army that emerged in Britain after Dunkirk bore the stamp of Sir Alan Brooke, the chief of the Imperial General Staff, and Sir Brian Paget, the commander, Home Forces. They conducted the first serious pruning of the officer corps, reorganized the army, improved training and small-unit tactics, and toughened the minds and bodies of the soldiers despite major equipment shortages and limited battle experience.[20] The most serious obstacle to effective reconstitution of the army, however, was doctrinal. As the panzer myth spread after Dunkirk, it cemented both the army's adherence to its particular brand of armored warfare and its determination to seek victory in set-piece battles waged in accordance with the principles of a strategy of attrition.[21] The RAC remained wedded to the dogma that the primary task of armor was to seek out and destroy enemy tanks. Not only did the army not reconsider its employment of armor in light of its experiences in France, but the panzer myth cemented prevailing, yet misguided, armored warfare notions.

The army thus tripled its armored force during 1940–1941 and for the first time concentrated most of its tanks in armored divisions. While reorganization marginally increased the proportion of infantry and supporting arms, which had proven inadequate in France, British armored formations remained essentially massed tank forces, not balanced combined-arms teams. The panzer myth hampered realization that integrated and mobile combined-arms forces (i.e., firepower and mobility) was what the army needed to halt the blitzkrieg.

Continued lack of battle experience after Dunkirk was another major obstacle to improved combat effectiveness. While the army rebuilt the Commonwealth bore the brunt of combat: between Dunkirk and the summer of 1942 only four British divisions fought the Germans.[22] That these British forces suffered repeated defeat provided few clear lessons, and the widespread perception among senior officers that few lessons could be learned from setbacks further slowed the pace of reform.

Italy's entry into the war in June 1940 drew the Middle East Command (MEC) into combat and brought Britain's first, albeit ephemeral, victories. The MEC was quite different from the army defeated in France. Dominated by regulars, it had escaped the massive, uncoordinated expansion experienced by the BEF and it contained the army's best division, the 7th Armoured, the only offensively trained and organized formation.[23] Moreover, the MEC possessed a number of able officers. Its commander, Gen. Sir Archibald Wavell, had gained a reputation as a versatile, unorthodox, and innovative commander between the wars.[24] His deputy, Lt. Gen. Richard O'Connor, the commander of the Western Desert Force (WDF) that defended the Egyptian frontier, was equally talented.[25] Between them, Wavell and O'Connor inculcated in their command offensive spirit and daring.[26]

On 9 December 1940, despite marked numerical inferiority and serious equipment shortages, the WDF boldly launched Operation COMPASS, Britain's first offensive of the war.[27] Heavily outnumbered and outgunned, Wavell relied on mobility and speed to mass strength against hesitant Italian defenders. A combination of O'Connor's aggressive leadership, the 7th Armoured's offensive spirit, and a poorly equipped, trained, officered, and deployed Italian army, led the WDF to crush in just three days two Italian corps that were dispersed in fortified camps along the frontier. Thereafter, the fresh 6th Australian Division, aided by combined artillery-aerial-naval bombardment, stormed Bardia and Tobruk during January. Then, as the Australians pursued the Italians along the coast road from Gazala to Benghazi, the 7th Armoured made a daring inland march via Mechili and Msus to cut the Italian retreat. Between 5–7 February near Beda Fomm, the two divisions annihilated the trapped Tenth Italian Army.[28]

Even though the WDF advanced 600 miles and destroyed a force five times as large, its victory was not a result of the adoption of blitzkrieg warfare. Rather, COMPASS comprised a series of limited tactical attacks that met with unexpected success due to a combination of unusual British opportunism and considerable Italian timidity and ineptitude. Although this was a remarkable and much needed achievement, these were tactical—not strategic—victories for British armor, and success largely derived from profound enemy deficiencies rather than British strengths. Lacking a professional officer corps, poorly equipped, with limited mobility and low morale, the Italian formations rapidly disintegrated.[29]

British troops performed better in COMPASS than they had in Norway or France. Wavell orchestrated elaborate deception to achieve total surprise and to inflate Italian perceptions of British strength.[30] Short on artillery and munitions, and with little air support, he utilized naval bombardment to augment available firepower.[31] His foresighted establishment of forward supply dumps provided the logistic base necessary for success. Good interservice cooperation, especially from the Mediterranean Fleet, dynamic leadership, and aggressive troops all aided victory. Attack tactics built around the superiority of the heavy Matilda II tank played an important role in defeating an enemy weak in armor and antitank capability. Just as important, gunners adapted prewar principles to desert circumstances in which terrain, poor visibility, unreliable communications, and fluid warfare made surveying and fire planning difficult. Gunners improvised quick fire plans as, on 9 December, the 4th Indian Division fired the first full Commonwealth divisional artillery barrage of the war to demonstrate that targeted massed fire was possible in mobile operations.[32]

Ironically, though, the startling victories against the Italians hampered army efforts to enhance its combat effectiveness. While the MEC drew important lessons from COMPASS—most notably the need for better radios, that artillery support did not hamper the mobility of armor, and the efficacy of offensive defense—desert troops quickly forgot these lessons.[33] More significant, though, was that victory disguised serious underlying weaknesses, most notably the inadequacy of British tank doctrine. The Matilda II's important role in the success of COMPASS merely reinforced the view that unsupported massed armor was a battle winner. COMPASS thus delayed realization of the need for integrated combined-arms mechanized forces. At the same time, victory gave the army the false impression that it could easily and effectively master maneuver warfare: COMPASS promoted fluid warfare and mobile defense that the army was neither equipped, organized, nor mentally prepared for.[34] Strategically, victory in the desert also appeared to vindicate J. F. C. Fuller's and Liddell Hart's notions of an "indirect approach," a peripheral strategy that would wear the enemy into submission. The success of COMPASS solidified Britain's adherence to a strategy of attrition. As a result, victory against the Italians contributed to defeat by the Germans.

The fruits of success quickly evaporated with the arrival in February

1941 of stiffer opposition—Erwin Rommel's Africa Corps. The War Office's ill-advised diversion of forces to Greece and the arrival of German troops transformed the situation in North Africa as Wavell halted COMPASS, unwisely disbanded O'Connor's command, and dispatched major forces to Greece and Italian East Africa, which denuded British strength in Libya.[35] The Balkan fiasco bore striking similarities to the Norwegian flop. Wavell dispatched three divisions to man the Aliakhmon Line in Greece, but the rapid collapse of Yugoslavia after the German invasion of 6 April 1941 allowed the Germans to outflank the line and force a phased withdrawal.[36] Once again it proved difficult to move troops in the face of enemy-controlled skies, and morale ebbed. During late April the Royal Navy evacuated the majority of Commonwealth troops to Crete, where they fought a short, desperate action to deny the island to the first strategic airborne assault in the history of warfare. The uncertain mission of the Crete garrison; Wavell's heavy commitments elsewhere; the acute shortage of shipping, heavy weapons, and air power; and the depleted state of the garrison prevented the defenders from vigorously fortifying the island. Nevertheless, while the Royal Navy blocked any German seaborne reinforcements, the defenders resisted fiercely and nearly defeated the invaders. But German numbers ultimately prevailed, and the Royal Navy had to undertake at heavy cost another desperate evacuation.[37]

As the Balkan drama played out the Africa Corps arrived in Libya. British intelligence was slow to discover the arrival of German troops and seriously underestimated the speed, aggressiveness, and daring with which Rommel would attack the British western flank in Libya, which had been reduced to a weak and polyglot force of two green divisions commanded by Lt. Gen. Phillip Neame.[38] Woefully short of artillery and armor, Wavell opted for a delaying withdrawal, but with limited mobility the retreat turned into a rout during which the Germans captured Neame and O'Connor on 6 April. Two days later the remnants of the 2nd Armoured Division surrendered at Mechili, and on 11 April Rommel invested, but was unable to take, the port city of Tobruk.[39]

In retrospect, the foremost causes of defeat were that Wavell had overextended himself in COMPASS and the Greek diversion had sapped his strength. The British had also underestimated German offensive potential, and Rommel's speed and daring took them by surprise. Wavell's decision to conduct a delaying withdrawal was also, in retrospect, a mistake, for the retreat became a debacle that forced the British to fall all the way back to the Egyptian frontier.[40]

In the months that followed, Rommel carved up the British in North Africa in large part because of the British Army's inadequate grasp of the mechanics of modern war and its failure to preserve its Great War experience or to develop doctrine between the wars. British operations in the desert in 1941 suffered from poor leadership (the result of new and undertrained commanders), inadequate equipment, and poor organization, tactics, integration, coordination, and cohesion. Defeat also stemmed from Wavell's again resorting to maneuver warfare to compensate for lack of strength and firepower. He tried to outfight the Germans in the fast mobile operations at which they excelled. Failure further reduced British forces and reinforced their dependence on mobile action as armor adherents attempted to put into practice Fuller's and Liddell Hart's ideas about mobile warfare.

Repeated defeat gradually brought disenchantment with mobility, and British forces abandoned mobile defense for static, all-around "box" defenses. Lack of reserves and a desire to replicate German tactical flexibility also led to abandonment of formation integrity and brought reliance on ad hoc task forces. But these innovations barely enhanced British defensive capabilities. Box defenses were often incapable of mutual support and the fragmentation and dispersion of already ill-balanced formations further eroded morale and cohesion. Moreover, still hampered by regimental parochialism, British forces proved poor at providing mutual defensive support.

Serious flaws afflicted British offensive operations too. Troops attacked rashly, often without adequate reconnaissance, and failed to concentrate or coordinate. Wedded to a strategy of attrition, British forces also sought to outfight rather than outmaneuver the enemy. Armor thus tried to smash through German defenses, hoping that cavalry élan could compensate for inferior firepower and desultory fire support as the infantry waited to "follow through" once the armor had secured the objective in accordance with doctrine.[41] The German panzers, though, typically refused combat and repeatedly lured British armor onto well-sited and camouflaged antitank screens that savaged it. Only then did the panzers counterattack to smash the remaining British tanks and often to overrun the British gun line. As a result, British armored regiments regularly suffered horrific losses as poorly supported armor roamed the desert.[42] British antitank guns also usually fought their own separate war with equally tragic results: repeated defeat in detail. Moreover, terrible radio discipline and signals security provided much intelligence to the enemy, directly contributing to British offensive failures.[43]

The most egregious British folly in North Africa, however, was the abandonment of established artillery doctrine as, for a while, the success of blitzkrieg appeared to threaten artillery dominance on the battlefield. This led to the decentralization, dispersion, and forward deployment of field artillery at battery, and even troop, level, which crippled its effectiveness. Decentralization stemmed both from the interwar reaction against massed fire and from the army's lack of antitank capability, which necessitated deployment of field guns in a direct-fire role.[44] The 25-pounder gun thus became the mainstay of British antitank defense in the desert during 1941–1942.[45] Reliance on mobile armored warfare also contributed to the abandonment of sound artillery practices; tank commanders continued to reject the lesson of COMPASS that massed artillery support was possible for maneuvering armored forces.[46]

British field artillery suffered such heavy personnel and equipment turnover through line-of-sight engagements that basic artillery expertise dwindled as gunners lost their skill at target identification and acquisition, as well as counterbattery fire.[47] At the same time, dispersion aggravated the inherent difficulties of desert communication. These developments robbed British troops of suppressive and defensive fire and, when coupled with ammunition shortages, reinforced gunners' reliance on observed fire, the legacy of the interwar reaction against extravagant Great War shell expenditures. As a result, fire planning all but ceased in the desert in 1941 and artillery rarely supported armor because gunners mistakenly believed that indirect fire against tanks was ineffective and wasteful. Poor equipment, in particular the lack of modern medium and heavy guns, exacerbated the effects of the misuse of field artillery and prevented gunners from providing either long-range defensive fire or from suppressing enemy artillery with counterbattery fire.[48]

Poor organization contributed to British difficulties too. Armored divisions still emphasized speed over firepower and so remained poorly structured for an attack role. Despite hundreds of tanks, these formations lacked firepower and supporting arms, especially infantry, and remained poorly integrated. The divisional support group—an infantry battalion and a field artillery regiment—had only an auxiliary role to provide "safe harbor" at night and was incapable of directly supporting the armor in combat.[49]

British forces rarely displayed combined-arms proficiency because regimental parochialism and the absence of holistic doctrine led armor and infantry to fight their own separate wars. Lack of an interarms tradition meant that it took long association—years in fact—for Commonwealth forces to develop combined-arms proficiency. This deficiency bred reliance on improvised combined-arms raiding parties, or "Jock Columns," but these poorly imitated German combined-arms battle groups. Efforts to forge effective combined-arms forces failed in North Africa because British arms lacked the habitual association fundamental to successful German coordination. Only at the lowest level, with ad hoc improvised combined-arms units, did the British develop even limited combined-arms proficiency during 1941–1942, but these forces lacked the firepower for effective defense.[50]

At the same time, Wavell failed to examine soberly British performance as he blamed the loss of Cyrenaica on a lack of tanks. It was true that the quality and quantity of armor was a factor in defeat, but exaggerated faith in the efficacy of massed armor had led commanders to exaggerate the role of armor in the British defeat. Senior officers thus largely failed to identify the flaws in training, leadership, tactics, and doctrine that brought defeat. Instead, Wavell insisted that reinforcement alone could reverse British fortunes.

Political interference also influenced British fortunes. Even though the loss of O'Connor and the diversion to Greece had crippled the MEC, Churchill pressured Wavell to launch an ill-conceived, ill-prepared, and impromptu offensive to relieve Tobruk and defeat Rommel—while simultaneously campaigning in Syria.[51] Wavell's counteroffensive, Operation BATTLEAXE (15–17 June 1941), revealed that the MEC had lost its sharp edge.[52] Concurrent operations denied the British sufficient strength to secure decisive victory, and haste led to the loss of most of the new Crusader tanks prematurely thrown into battle.[53] Wavell conducted a classic attack in accordance with doctrine. He launched a frontal infantry assault on Haifa and Sollum to pin German forces in place while the 7th Armoured Division, in a tactical role, swept into the German rear to seek out and destroy German armor—in accordance with the strategy of attrition—and then relieve Tobruk.

Lack of aerial reconnaissance, though, meant that Wavell had underrated Axis strength and capabilities. At the same time, failures of communication slowed British operations and poor radio security sacrificed the element of surprise and gave Rommel an edge. Inferior British tactical skill and the superiority of German armor then ensured that the offensive broke down with heavy losses. BATTLEAXE was a marginal victory for the British forces but one bought at heavy cost because of flawed doctrine and poor execution.[54] Weak air power also meant that the RAF could not gain air superiority, and lack of air-ground communications ensured that tactical aviation made little contribution to the ground battle. Heated interservice conflicts over the role and mission of air power continued to hamper conduct of the air-ground battle; the RAF remained wedded to strategic bombing and refused to divert resources to tactical missions. Along with the pernicious effects of interservice rivalry, technical and technological obstacles limited the impact of tactical aviation. No ground-air communications system existed, and suitable tactical strike aircraft were lacking both in quantity and quality. The air support for Wavell's offensive to retake Tobruk was so slow and inadequate that the army derided the RAF as the "Royal Absent Force."[55]

That the MEC was slow to learn from experience exacerbated the difficulties it faced. Months passed before it determined the correct reasons for defeat in 1941 and took steps to rectify shortcomings. The absence of clear doctrine and of mechanisms to collect and disseminate combat reports hindered quick and accurate evaluation of its performance. At the same time, the British tried to replicate German success by imitating them without understanding the underlying reasons for the enemy's success. Thus British assessments of the causes of defeat in the desert during 1941 paralleled the earlier misguided evaluations of the operations in Norway and France: the army concluded that the inferiority of British armor had squandered chances for greater success during BATTLEAXE.[56] Yet, the real causes of defeat were both more complex and more fundamental: hasty execution, inadequate doctrine and equipment, and poor coordination, tactics, and air-ground cooperation.[57] Moreover, throughout 1941, the MEC assessed its performance without questioning or reevaluating preconceptions about the efficacy of a strategy of attrition and of massed armor. Wavell had massed his armor, but the slow speed of his infantry tanks limited his mobility and equipment deficiencies hampered his operations. All the same, neither Wavell nor his subordinates questioned the wisdom of throwing ill-supported masses of tanks against enemy armor in direct engagements, despite horrific losses.

Analysis of BATTLEAXE did, however, demonstrate the unsatisfactory nature of air-ground cooperation and led to formation of the Middle East Air Force under Air Marshal Sir Arthur Tedder and interservice examination of the problems of air-ground cooperation. It took the combination of the army's shocking defeats during 1940–1941, Fighter Command's need for a new mission after winning the Battle of Britain, and the arrival of Tedder and Air Vice Marshal Arthur "Mary" Coningham in the western desert for the RAF to take tactical air support seriously.[58] During summer 1941 Coningham created a system with centralized RAF control, initiated joint army-air force exercises, and established a means of communication and control. At the core of these reforms was the attachment of air support control (ASC) organizations to corps and armored divisions connected by a "tentacle" radio link to forward air support links (FASLs) attached to infantry brigades. Ground troops passed requests for air support to the ASC via their tentacle, and the FASLs directed aircraft dispatched by the ASC on the target.[59] At the same time, increased aircraft strength and the introduction of new planes—Beaufighter, Hurricane II, and Kittyhawk fighters as well as Beaufort, Wellington II, and Baltimore medium bombers—increased aerial capabilities.[60] The reorganization of air support during the summer of 1941 was an important first step in the air-ground battle and brought the first substantive improvement in British ground combat capabilities since the start of the war.

The disgraced Wavell's successor, Gen. Claude Auchinleck, was unable to turn the tide in North Africa.[61] His November 1941 CRUSADER offensive, however, was the genesis of the army's future battle-winning operational approach: the set-piece battle of attrition. He also set in motion reforms that later bore fruit as he more closely scrutinized the lessons of BATTLEAXE. Recognizing that troop performance had fallen well below expectations, he demanded retraining. At the same time, British intelligence gathering improved during fall 1941 as the genesis of the RAF photo- and strategic reconnaissance units and survey flight, as well as the army's Long Range Desert Group (LRDG) brought more accurate assessment of enemy

capabilities.[62] Increasing interdiction of Axis supplies by the RAF, Royal
Navy, and the Special Air Service and LRDG on land also allowed
Auchinleck to build superiority on the ground and in the air.[63]

Auchinleck used elaborate deception measures to gain total surprise for
CRUSADER, aided by bad weather and local air superiority.[64] He also
launched a bolder and more sophisticated attack, but one that still conformed to prevailing doctrine. A frontal assault sought to pin the enemy in
place, while massed armor outflanked the German position and searched
out the enemy armor. But when the panzers refused to do battle, Auchinleck
gradually dispersed his armor. The battle degenerated into series of uncoordinated actions in which ill-supported British armor once again shattered
itself against German gun lines or in tank-to-tank engagements in which the
better trained and more experienced panzers invariably prevailed.[65] This
battle witnessed some of the severest and most confused fighting seen in
the desert. Despite the tank losses, Auchinleck boldly (and at great risk)
pressed the offensive, and the arrival of fresh reserves allowed superior
numbers to wear down Axis strength and forced Rommel to abandon his
siege of Tobruk and to retreat to Mersa Brega.

Though a victory, CRUSADER was a messy, protracted, and costly
success. In fact the battle revealed numerous defects in its execution.
Armor had still attacked with negligible support and had consequently suffered crippling losses. British forces had often failed to concentrate or coordinate, which forced them to fight at a disadvantage. Commanders failed to
mass artillery support either in attack or defense, which greatly weakened
available fighting power. The result was repeated defeat in detail and the
overrunning of several Commonwealth brigades. Equipment defects, especially the poor penetration of the 2-pounder gun, the mechanical weakness
of the new Crusader tank, and the vulnerability and short range of the new
American Stuart tank all exacerbated British losses.[66]

Command and control too remained problematic. Desert combat necessitated the extensive use of radios, but few were available and these were
unreliable and of short range. Undependable communications in the heat of
battle occasionally left commanders and formations out of touch, which
delayed the issuing and execution of orders. Moreover, inexperience at
enciphering and lack of cipher personnel brought poor radio security and
discipline, which resulted in frequent use of "veiled" conversations that
were far more revealing than the speakers hoped.[67]

The Western Desert Air Force (WDAF) also began to make its presence felt for the first time during CRUSADER as Coningham tested the
new joint communications system for direct air support. Its reorganization
and the flow of new aircraft allowed the WDAF to average a record 190
sorties daily, and despite inevitable teething problems the new system generally worked well. The pre-CRUSADER attritional battles won a large
measure of local air superiority, but the WDAF lacked the strength to main-

tain air superiority as the newly activated British Eighth Army pursued westward. Air Vice Marshal Coningham established an effective centralized RAF command of all air operations during CRUSADER and attached his headquarters to that of Eighth Army.[68] New aircraft, including Hurricane fighter-bombers and Liberator heavy bombers, increased available strike power and curtailed the battlefield impact of Axis aviation. Technological advances, in particular the invention of the fighter-bomber, which saw its debut during CRUSADER, also made close support more viable as the RAF discovered that fighters armed with bombs, cannon, and rockets, could provide effective tactical support.

The air-ground communications system, though, remained in its infancy, and thus Coningham received few calls for air support during CRUSADER and even fewer could be executed. Although Coningham and Tedder had formulated a basic framework, many problems remained. Inexperience, lack of recognition procedures, problems of desert target identification, and limited aerial reconnaissance capability made it difficult to apply air power effectively and brought many friendly-fire incidents. Response time to a call for air support in 1941—generally three hours— was slow, and the use of medium bombers for direct support missions proved disappointing. A framework had been built for future success, but during 1941 tactical air power remained an unpredictable and largely ineffectual weapon in support of ground forces.[69]

CRUSADER was imperfectly executed with heavy losses, but it was a victory, nonetheless, which suggested that an attritional strategy could still bring victory in the era of blitzkrieg.[70] The operation also saw limited improvement in British defensive skill. German after-action reports noted improved Commonwealth defensive artillery fire that, for the first time, turned back a tentative German armored thrust on 25 November. Moreover, during CRUSADER British troops had not retreated before bold German armored thrusts as they had in BATTLEAXE.[71]

Instructions and exhortations from above had little impact on troops in combat, however, because British forces were slow to learn lessons and reluctant to retrain in the field. The army was slow to learn because it evaluated its performance and the problems that beset it intuitively rather than analytically.[72] What the MEC required, but did not get, was a quiet period to consider lessons, identify weaknesses, formulate doctrine, and then, most importantly, retrain. But the urgent political need for victory pushed each new commander into premature offensives before he had established "the form," as Montgomery called it. The quest for victory thus ironically promoted further defeat, and as a result the MEC learned slowly through costly trial and error.

The parallels between the events of spring 1942 and those of the preceding spring demonstrate the British slowness in learning from experience. Pressed by Churchill, Auchinleck had dissipated his strength and

overreached himself to win CRUSADER. Exhaustion thus halted the
British pursuit at Mersa Brega. At the same time, Japan's entry into the war
led to the transfer of major assets to the Far East, which lifted the choke on
the flow of Axis supplies to North Africa. Auchinleck also withdrew his
depleted armor into deep reserve for rehabilitation and replaced them with
the raw, ill-trained, and incomplete 1st Armoured Division. But he had
underestimated German powers of recuperation, and on 21 January 1942
the renamed Panzer Army Africa launched a spoiling attack that took the
British completely by surprise and forced them into another delaying withdrawal that rattled troop morale. The new commander of Eighth Army,
Gen. Neil Ritchie, misread the situation and Axis pressure forced him to
retire in disorder to the Gazala Line. The parallels to the previous spring
were readily apparent: Auchinleck, like Wavell, had overreached himself
and had paid the price.[73]

Yet after it dug in at Gazala, the Eighth Army failed to make the most
of the lull that lasted until May 1942. British commanders still continued to
blame defeat on defective equipment and demand increased quantities to
reverse their fortunes. Even as the WDAF retrained in a strenuous effort to
improve its operational efficiency, there was no parallel improvement in
army-air cooperation. Auchinleck did recognize that poor coordination had
marred CRUSADER and attempted to improve interarms association by
ordering formations reorganized into combined-arms brigade groups. But
tinkering with organization could not surmount ingrained regimentalism
and bring improved coordination in a few short months. He also recognized
the need for formation integrity and thus limited use of the improvised Jock
Columns that Ritchie had employed to delay and harry the enemy during
the retreat to Gazala.[74]

Because of his inexperience and continued defeats, interservice cooperation deteriorated as Auchinleck was thrust into a highly complex and
demanding position. Mismanagement, poor staff work, and faulty command resulted in renewed defeat at Gazala (26 May–17 June 1942) as
Auchinleck allowed Ritchie to disperse his forces when Rommel attacked
and outflanked the British "box" area defenses of the Gazala Line. This
happened even though Rommel had initially found himself trapped in the
"cauldron" between the British defenses and their armored reserves, as
improved British defensive coordination and the new 6-pounder antitank
gun increased Axis tank losses.[75]

With Rommel thus pinned down, Auchinleck planned a major nighttime counterattack on 5 June, backed for the first time by a heavy artillery
bombardment, to neutralize the enemy antitank screen before committing
his armor to smash the Africa Corps. This sound plan, which took account
of the vulnerability of Auchinleck's armor, disintegrated as the counterattack went disastrously wrong when Ritchie launched three uncoordinated
brigade attacks by three different divisions. Moreover, the demise of desert

fire planning resulted in the bombardment missing its target. At the same time, the infantry break-in failed to reach the enemy gun line, which then inflicted ruin on the British armor as it followed through. Rommel quickly counterattacked and overran much of the 7th Armoured and 5th Indian Divisions in one of the worst reverses suffered by the British in North Africa.[76]

Having learned a bitter lesson from previous defeats, Auchinleck decided to stand firm. But the battle was lost on 13 June when Rommel destroyed the bulk of the remaining British armor and forced the attenuated Eighth Army to retreat to the Egyptian frontier the next day, leaving the raw 2nd South African Division to be besieged in Tobruk. Ritchie again fragmented his depleted and demoralized formations into Jock Columns and dispersed his field artillery in an antitank role to harass and delay pursuing enemy forces as he retreated to Egypt. But these measures further degraded cohesion and fire support and only fueled the growing demoralization of his troops.[77]

On 20 June, Rommel attacked and took Tobruk in the worst debacle that befell British arms in the desert. The port city's fall epitomized what was right with the German Army and what was wrong with the British. Rommel launched an impromptu assault into which he threw everything he had available on the ground and in the air to take advantage of the perceived disorganization of the garrison. Complacency reigned in Tobruk, and sluggishness, rigidity, inexperience, and lack of initiative prevented the garrison from mounting an effective defense. In fact, most of the garrison remained spectators as the Germans broke through the perimeter defenses on a narrow front and stormed the town. The heroism and courage of individual units notwithstanding, the garrison had to surrender and huge quantities of supplies fell into enemy hands.[78]

The fall of Tobruk was Rommel's greatest success, but it proved a Pyrrhic victory because it induced the Axis to abandon their planned assault on Malta and seriously think of reaching the Suez Canal, which in turn led Rommel to overreach. At the same time, the totality of Eighth Army's defeat led to massive British reinforcement of Egypt and Auchinleck's taking command of Eighth Army on 25 June. He abandoned the use of Jock Columns, but his own mobile defense based on mixed brigade-groups proved no more effective, and he was unable to halt the enemy at Mersa Matruh. British troops were still inexperienced at conducting delaying defense, and Auchinleck's endeavors to reorganize and reform the Eighth Army in the middle of battle proved abortive. The British suffered another serious defeat that further demoralized and disorganized the Eighth Army, which then barely beat Rommel back to the El Alamein position. Air-ground coordination dwindled during the retreat too as Auchinleck abandoned the practice of colocating army and air headquarters.[79]

Widespread ignorance of German doctrine and tactics had contributed to British difficulties. British offensive action depended on armor for its striking power, yet its armor was inferior in quality. British forces learned the hard way from the Germans that the best way to defeat armor was through firepower, not poorly coordinated armored maneuver warfare. Troops repeatedly failed to comprehend German defensive doctrine as, time and again, panzers lured British armor into antitank gun screens with devastating results. Doctrinal emphasis on outfighting the enemy, when combined with inferior equipment, and ignorance of enemy doctrine, ensured that it was invariably British armor that was written off.

The defeat at Mersa Matruh brought morale to its nadir.[80] Repeated defeats sapped troop morale as the debacle in the Far East followed defeat in the desert.[81] Fragile morale further hindered army efforts to learn and adapt. Partial collapses of morale occurred at Dunkirk, on Crete (May 1941), and in Singapore (February 1942) evidenced by units retreating on their own, desertion, panic, and collapse of discipline.[82] Morale concerns led the War Office to censor combat reports from the front for fear that honest admission of British weaknesses might destroy fragile morale and engender a total collapse that would lead to the loss of Egypt. Censorship, seen as necessary to maintain current combat effectiveness, however, retarded the speed of adaptation and slowed enhancement of future combat effectiveness.

During 1941–1942 British forces suffered a succession of defeats in North Africa. Poor generalship, organization, and training, as well as inadequate equipment all contributed to defeat, but underlying them was the army's unquestioning reliance on a strategy of attrition and this strategy's vulnerability to blitzkrieg warfare. British forces were twice routed after successful advances, and, despite numerical and material superiority, Britain nearly lost Egypt.[83] British forces in the desert abandoned sound and established military principles as repeated defeat encouraged expediency and unorthodoxy as the only apparent answer to German prowess.[84] Rapid turnover in commanders and troops, as well as inadequate training, clearly played a part in the deterioration in British combat effectiveness in the desert during 1941. But, clearly, lack of coherent modern doctrine consistently taught lay at the root of defeat.

Not only was the MEC slow in drawing appropriate combat lessons, it proved even less adept at disseminating lessons learned. Heavy defensive fighting on the retreat and doctrinal confusion hampered learning and adaptation. What the MEC required was a lull for rest, rehabilitation, and reeducation. The army's reluctance to learn on the battlefield also clearly hampered adaptation in the desert; peacetime training habits proved hard to undo. The MEC tinkered with organization to correct such problems as poor coordination that only revised doctrine and extensive retraining could solve.

North Africa, though, was a proving ground in which disparate elements would survive to be forged into an army that slowly and painfully relearned the basics of modern war. Gradually the Eighth Army discerned desert warfare lessons and slowly improved its combat effectiveness, even though it was not until the First Battle of El Alamein (30 June 1942) that substantive improvement first materialized. Overstretched and exhausted, Rommel's forces tried to hustle the British out of the El Alamein position. There topography compelled the British to hold the narrow front between the sea and the impassable Qattara Depression, and thus brought the first real defensive concentration. The Desert Air Force too was able to provide increased air support because the proximity of its bases to the front allowed it to achieve sortie rates much higher than hitherto possible. Concentrated defensive fire and stepped-up air support increased Axis losses and accelerated the enemy's exhaustion.[85]

While Auchinleck's defense against an attenuated and exhausted enemy succeeded, his three counterattacks launched between 10–26 July against the Ruweisat Ridge all failed. German armor repeatedly drove back the attackers, and on 31 July the battle ended in mutual exhaustion. Once again troop inexperience, rigidity of command, and poor coordination caused the attack to fail. However, the Eighth Army did display improved offensive art: Auchinleck resorted to nighttime infantry attacks buttressed by massed artillery fire and air support under unified RAF command to break into enemy positions. The struggle for the Ruweisat Ridge thus witnessed the first renunciation of massed-armor attacks and the emergence in embryonic form of the British attack doctrine employed during the last two years of the war.[86]

The First Battle of El Alamein put a stop to the run of British disasters and fought an overextended enemy to a standstill. Victory bought Auchinleck time to strengthen the Alamein position and rebuild the Eighth Army. The battle was a costly defensive victory, achieved in part by improved defensive skill as British troops slowly began to discern the solutions to countering blitzkrieg warfare. But the primary cause of British success was that Rommel had overreached himself. The Eighth Army had reached a watershed as it gradually identified errors and misconceptions in prewar doctrine and tactics. The most significant improvement during 1941–1942 was a gradual reversion to traditional artillery practices: defeat led the army back to the Great War tactics of static defense and infantry assault backed by massed artillery fire. Yet, it was only slowly that the MEC relearned that through firepower superiority artillery saved lives.[87]

The real change in British fortunes in North Africa coincided with the fortuitous arrival in August 1942 of Lt. Gen. Bernard Law Montgomery to command the Eighth Army.[88] Montgomery had impressed the War Office with his orderly withdrawal of the 3d Division in France in 1940 and he then energetically prepared Southern Command to repel a German invasion. One of the most widely read senior British commanders, he imposed a badly needed iron grip on the demoralized Eighth Army. His military thought, while rather narrow, was simple and realistic, and his approach minimized prospects of defeat by leaving nothing to chance. He sought victory through the set-piece battle, by overwhelming fire superiority—rather than by skill—to wear the enemy down into defeat by attrition.[89] Montgomery applied in North Africa the fundamental military principles that his extensive professional study and his Great War staff experience told him would bring success.[90]

One of Montgomery's great strengths was that he was one of few senior Allied commanders who had some grasp of the operational level of war that lay between tactics and strategy—the prosecution of a campaign in a single theater of operations. He immediately laid out his operational doctrine upon taking command of the Eighth Army. He forbade the fluid mobile actions and delaying withdrawals in which the Germans had so often defeated the Eighth Army. He had it stand fast, at all costs, at El Alamein and shatter his opponent's strength in a slow, deliberate set-piece battle of attrition before he attacked. He saw the role of armor as being to secure and dig in on vital ground supported by infantry, antitank guns, and air power that would force the enemy to attack and be destroyed. He abandoned the use of armor in "penny packets" for infantry support.[91] He used massed artillery fire to disrupt and prevent enemy deployment of antitank gun lines; and he also emphasized maintaining the initiative and aggressive offensive action, applying the principle of concentration of effort. He demanded better reconnaissance, a skill long neglected by the army, and opposed the rigid, inflexible organization of training at home and the artificial division between individual and collective training. Instead, he demanded extensive and frequent evaluation of recruits along with combined-arms exercising under realistic conditions.[92]

Montgomery also immediately created a mobile reserve, X Corps, to act as a fire brigade and retrained it in the rear in a counterattack role.[93] Since he had come to understand the vital importance of air power and the need for coordinated air-ground operations in France in 1940, he improved coordination with the Desert Air Force. He as quickly abandoned ad hoc brigade groups and Jock Columns and restored divisional integrity. Reorganization, reequipment, and retraining came alongside a major housecleaning of desert commanders.[94] Montgomery's greatest achievement, though, was his resurrection of the Eighth Army's morale. Integral to his military thought was due emphasis on the "human dimension" of war. A consummate master of public relations, he exuded publicly a total confidence that he did not believe privately. His confidence proved infectious and dramatically improved British morale.[95]

The key to Montgomery's operational approach was firepower dominance. As he massed artillery, the Royal Artillery reemerged as the rightful queen of the battlefield. The fruits of centralization materialized during

Montgomery's first battle in North Africa, Alam Haifa (30 August–6 September 1942), where he massed 248 guns. Short on supplies, Rommel launched a spoiling attack against the Eighth Army to blunt its growing strength. Benefiting from advanced warning from Ultra and aerial intelligence, Montgomery renounced maneuver, held well-prepared defensive positions, refused to be enticed out, thus forcing the Germans to attack the British defenses.[96] Employing mutually supporting combined-arms box defenses buttressed with armor deployed in hull-down positions supported by coordinated artillery and antitank fire plans, the Eighth Army repulsed Rommel and inflicted heavy loss. Montgomery, believing Eighth Army still weak and with little offensive capability, then cautiously counterattacked and pushed the enemy forces back almost to their start line before he abandoned the offensive on 7 September. That most of the British counterattacks failed justified his caution. Sound defense had defeated a weak enemy thrust and boosted morale, air support had reached new heights, and good intelligence had allowed concentrated fire support.[97]

The Battle of Alam Haifa thus marked the first occasion on which British ground forces had orchestrated a successful defense through coordination of armor, artillery, and air power. At the same time, the battle witnessed the first wartime triumph of British mass and firepower over German mobility. Montgomery's reluctance to exploit success reflected his determination not to overextend himself by continuing the battle as had occurred during COMPASS and CRUSADER. Such caution became a cornerstone of Montgomery's operational approach thereafter.[98] The battle also provided a number of important lessons for the Eighth Army. The concentrated employment of armor and artillery was a key ingredient in victory; and the reintegration of army and RAF commanders at a joint battle headquarters brought improved air-ground coordination and with it more effective air support.[99]

Nevertheless, serious deficiencies remained. Artillery command and control remained poor.[100] Coordination remained indifferent, and although Montgomery emphasized combined-arms coordination, he adhered to official doctrine and thus made no effort to integrate below the divisional level.[101] He was also indifferent to radio security and underestimated the value of signals intelligence to the enemy.[102]

It was thus not until October 1942 at the Second Battle of El Alamein that the Eighth Army secured a major offensive victory. Montgomery planned an offensive that incorporated many lessons learned in the previous two years of desert fighting. For his offensive, Operation LIGHTFOOT (23–26 October), he intended a double-pincer attack by the XXX Corps with four divisions in the north supported by the heaviest British artillery bombardment since 1918 to break into the Axis defenses.[103] Thereafter, he aimed for the X Corps to push through and halt astride the enemy supply lines and induce the enemy to attack, while infantry steadily "crumbled"

Axis defenses to the north and south. At the same time, the XIII Corps would launch a diversionary attack to the south to draw away Axis reserves from the main attack.[104]

Geography necessitated that the Montgomery make a frontal attack, but the significant numerical superiority Eighth Army possessed made him confident of success. Montgomery employed extensive deception to disguise the intended attack and thus achieve surprise.[105] The deception plan, Operation BERTRAM, successfully disguised the location and timing of the attack and led the enemy to withhold crucial reserves for four days.[106] Montgomery also demanded aggressive reconnaissance and patrolling to provide intelligence about German defenses. Yet, at the same time lacking confidence in his subordinates, Montgomery exercised a close control over the battle.[107] The XXX Corps attacked at night in moonlight on a narrow front supported by heavy close air support and new mechanical mine-clearing devices. Such massed firepower accelerated the attrition of Axis strength, but Montgomery failed to break through enemy defenses echeloned in depth, and after four days he had to assume the defensive and regroup for a renewed thrust. This shift to the defense proved crucial to victory as Rommel expended his strength in repeated counterattacks to regain lost positions.[108]

The British broke into the enemy defenses, but extensive German minefields and limited British mine-clearing capability hampered the attack and delayed the passage of armor waiting to exploit success. Moreover, British armor remained reluctant to advance aggressively, and so the battle degenerated into a slugging match.[109] After eight days of grinding down Rommel's strength, Montgomery launched a hard blow, once again with a nighttime infantry advance supported by massed artillery fire in the south—Operation SUPERCHARGE—at the Italian-German boundary. This attack gained surprise and broke through the Italians, allowing three Commonwealth divisions to advance into the German rear, where torrential rain bogged them down. At the end of his resources, Rommel had to effect a general withdrawal.[110]

While Montgomery's attention to administration guaranteed ample ammunition, success depended as much on the improved effectiveness of fire support as on greater volume. Increased use of radio communications, better organization, and faster planning and execution of massed fire brought improved effectiveness. Montgomery also revived a somewhat crude counterbattery plan, but a shortage of medium guns and the absence of heavy guns greatly curtailed the Eighth Army's counterbattery abilities and ensured poor results.[111] In fact, Axis defensive fire significantly slowed the British advance, and it was ammunition shortages rather than effective neutralization that reduced enemy fire. Nevertheless, the battle witnessed the first massed employment of medium artillery, and after El Alamein artillery regained its premier position among British arms.[112] Centralized artillery allowed the army to halt German mobile counterattacks and then to neutralize and breach German antitank defenses.

That Montgomery attacked on narrow fronts to mass fighting power at the point of main effort was another key ingredient in victory. Concentration increased his strength, and fire superiority at the focal point and maximized the damage inflicted on the enemy. When combined with secrecy, deception efforts, and night assault that brought tactical surprise, these advantages allowed Montgomery to grind down enemy forces whose inferior strength and supply shortages compelled them to stand and fight.[113]

The victory at El Alamein was a turning point for the wartime British Army. Planned and executed in accordance with the strategy of attrition, this battle ensured that the principles employed were never again challenged. Montgomery was victorious both because the army finally learned how to overcome the blitzkrieg challenge and because "friction" and distance had eroded the enemy's ability to employ maneuver warfare. Thus after much hard fighting and heavy losses, the British relearned that firepower still dominated the battlefield.[114] As German mobility dwindled in the face of growing, and ultimately overwhelming, allied numerical superiority on the ground, at sea, and in the air, the *Heer* proved unable to maintain its small offensive mechanized cutting edge.

The Eighth Army drew important lessons from the El Alamein victory. Success underscored the value of tactical deception; indeed, the margin of victory was narrow enough that deception measures were vital for success and thereafter they were integral to Montgomery's operational approach.[115] British coordination, though better, remained clumsy and advances would lose momentum when the armor passed through the infantry. Since the margin of victory was narrow, Montgomery resisted all pressures to pursue the retreating enemy aggressively, and insisted that undertrained British forces not undertake ambitious operations that might bring local reverses and damage anew his army's fragile morale. Caution thus became the hallmark of Montgomery thereafter.[116]

One must not, however, exaggerate Montgomery's impact. His arrival coincided with the fruition of longer term improvements in Eighth Army capabilities. The arrival of desperately needed fresh troops, for instance, greatly aided victory. Organization also slowly improved through 1942 as desert experience led the MEC to reduce its armored formations to a single tank brigade, and to add an infantry brigade and more artillery to produce better balanced and more cohesive divisions. Gradual improvement in both mobility and firepower also aided success. In 1941 the Germans had outclassed the British in every class of ordnance save artillery, but slowly new weapons entered service that closed the quality gap. During fall of 1941 the Bishop, Britain's first self-propelled 25-pounder gun, entered service and troops gained limited mobile antitank capability with the truck-mounted 2-pounder portee. However, Commonwealth troops initially achieved more mobile firepower only at the expense of decreased protection.[117]

It was not until 1942 that the arrival of a new generation of U.S. and British ordnance significantly narrowed the firepower gap. The appearance of effective antitank weapons in the desert—the U.S. M3 Grant tank armed with a sponson-mounted 75mm gun and the British 6-pounder (57mm) gun—finally allowed field artillery to relinquish its antitank role and be centralized at the division level during the summer of 1942 for conventional indirect fire support. The 6-pounder, a light, mobile, low-silhouette, and sturdy antitank gun first provided a genuine antitank capability and helped stop Rommel's panzers in their last desert offensive in 1942. Greater antitank firepower increased German tank losses and speeded the erosion of Axis striking power in North Africa. In addition, the arrival of new 4.5- and 5.5-inch medium howitzers finally gave gunners longer range and greater hitting power that enhanced defensive and counterbattery fire capabilities.[118]

After El Alamein, other new weapons systems entered service that further narrowed the firepower gap. These included the Deacon, a self-propelled 6-pounder gun that was quickly replaced by the American 75mm-gunned M10 tank destroyer, and the Priest self-propelled 25-pounder gun. Increased firepower reduced the widespread misuse of weapons systems, and as a result the firepower balance shifted in favor of the Allies during 1942–1943. Growing numerical and material superiority, combined with a strategy of set-piece attritional battles, allowed Montgomery to grind down Rommel in North Africa as attrition and precarious lines of communications increasingly strangled Axis forces and hampered mobile defense.

The most significant improvement in British combat capabilities during 1942, though, was the more effective application of air power in support of ground operations. With the genesis of viable air-ground communications and of the fighter-bomber during 1942, the RAF developed a ground-support doctrine that emphasized balanced pursuit of the two major missions of tactical air power: close support and direct support.[119] During 1942, the efficacy of tactical aviation steadily improved as technological innovation gave the RAF its first antitank capability with the introduction of a specialized "tank buster," the Hurricane IIID equipped with a 40mm cannon. Growing experience and greater use of both forward airfields and tentacle radio links had cut response time to 35 minutes by the First Battle of El Alamein. Effectiveness further improved as interservice dissension abated with final army acceptance of centralized RAF command of tactical aviation late in 1942.[120]

British ground combat capabilities clearly grew during 1942 as the pace of learning and reform accelerated with mounting experience. But innovation was patchy because the collection and dissemination of combat lessons remained haphazard. Montgomery greatly influenced the lessons-learned process, and under his tutelage the pace of adaptation in the desert accelerated. Unlike his predecessors, Montgomery was determined that the troops understood the lessons of his campaigns.[121] He vigorously and quickly disseminated lessons learned through memoranda, pamphlets, and correspondence.[122] His emphasis on his own immediate postbattle analysis facilitated adaptation and retraining.[123] He first sought to educate his senior commanders, so that they in turn could disseminate his operational approach to the troops.[124] He would then establish firm doctrine on which to base training and would stress retraining in the field. He, more so than other senior commander, understood the vital importance of retraining for victory.[125] Under his direction, the Eighth Army's defensive capabilities clearly improved during fall 1942.

However, Montgomery's character flaws—his egoism, arrogance, tactlessness, and condescension—subsequently hampered his efforts to disseminate desert campaign lessons to the Home Forces, just as these traits aggravated interservice and inter-Allied friction. He so monopolized lessons-learned analysis in the Eighth Army that he restricted the spectrum of adaptation: the troops had to learn the gospel according to "Monty." Montgomery's ascendancy entrenched the army's class-oriented, top-down approach to learning. Like his peers, Montgomery extracted from combat experience only what supported his preconceived notions. Nevertheless, that he possessed a firm grasp of the mechanics of modern war and some understanding of operational art allowed the pace of adaptation to accelerate under his auspices.

By late 1942 the Eighth Army had painfully begun to feel its way toward military proficiency. Under Montgomery's leadership and through the vicissitudes of the desert campaigns, the Eighth Army finally acquired defensive proficiency as well as limited offensive striking power. Most significantly, the Eighth Army reverted to conventional artillery practices, muddled its way through to devise a successful operational approach, the set-piece battle of attrition, and slowly learned to apply air power to aid the ground battle. New weapons narrowed the enemy's firepower edge and attrition wore down German capabilities as growing Allied aerial and maritime mastery slowly choked off Axis resupply to North Africa.

Nonetheless, the Eighth Army found it difficult to adapt its newly successful defensive tactics to the attack when it took the offensive in North Africa during fall 1942. After El Alamein, the British learned to employ massive artillery bombardment to shatter the enemy as firepower dominance became de facto operational doctrine. Yet even after it had developed weapons and tactics that could defeat the blitzkrieg, the army had to learn to employ them offensively to allow more flexible, massed fire, and to combine firepower with dexterity, which required improved command, control, and communications (C3). Greater speed and flexibility proved elusive, though, because the army remained sluggish and methodical in the attack and failed to exploit opportunities quickly. Yet Montgomery, safe in the knowledge that time was on the Allied side, steadfastly focused on final victory and refused to take chances and risk a setback that could destroy his army's still fragile morale. His operational approach aimed to ensure the greatest prospects of success, and in this he was successful: after El Alamein he never lost a battle. Despite growing firepower superiority, Montgomery experienced great difficulty ejecting the Germans from the well-prepared defensive positions they increasingly relied on. Unused to assaulting fortified positions, lacking mine-clearing capability, and unwilling—or unable—to utilize available firepower, the Eighth Army made slow progress through fortified defenses.[126]

Montgomery's determination to prevent Rommel from regaining the initiative as the latter had so devastatingly done in April 1941 and January 1942 also necessitated caution and the maintenance of strong reserves and good logistic support. These considerations conditioned Eighth Army's advance from Tripoli to El Agheila after 5 November and ensured a deliberate, methodical pursuit—and repeated unsuccessful attempts to pin Rommel on the coast road and then outflank him. The Desert Air Force proved unable to slow appreciably the enemy withdrawal amid new, fluid conditions where target identification was difficult. Thus, in late November, the Eighth Army had to halt before the naturally strong Agheila position to build up its logistic support.[127]

On 13 December the newly promoted General Montgomery launched a classic multistage assault on the Agheila position with a powerful, narrow frontal attack in the north along the coast road to pin the enemy down, while the New Zealand Division made a deep flanking penetration to the south. But the Axis forces quickly withdrew behind thick minefields that delayed the British advance, and Montgomery's flanking move lacked the strength to prevent an Axis retreat. Montgomery had maneuvered Rommel out of a strong position without a major fight, but the enemy had again escaped intact.[128]

On 15 January 1943, the Eighth Army assaulted the Axis position at Buerat in a repeat of the Agheila attack. The enemy once again conducted a skillful delaying withdrawal as Eighth Army cautiously pursued, slowed by mines and German rear guards.[129] On 23 January 1943, the Eighth Army took Tripoli and soon after crossed the Tunisian frontier. Montgomery's advance from Egypt to Tunisia had witnessed a dramatic reversal of British fortunes, and reflected a massive administrative achievement, but nowhere had Montgomery met an enemy that would stand and fight.

During its advance to Tunisia over winter 1942–1943, the Eighth Army gradually improved artillery C3 procedures as it refined desert warfare fire techniques. It permanently brigaded its army artillery and established corps-level control. These refinements allowed the Eighth Army to generate massed defensive fire within five minutes.[130] The failure of the German spoiling attack at Medenine on 6 March 1943 illuminated the maturation of the Eighth Army's defensive skills. For the first time, the British laid out a coherent antitank screen to stop enemy armor rather than to protect infantry and artillery positions. This screen, backed by massed defensive artillery fire, stopped the panzers and inflicted heavy losses.[131]

During the spring of 1943, the Eighth Army also developed greater offensive skill, which speeded the defeat of the Axis in North Africa. Montgomery again utilized tactical deception to conceal his frontal assault on the Mareth Line during March. Nevertheless, despite marked superiority, the attack bogged down amid poor weather conditions and strong German defenses in depth. Yet Montgomery adroitly enlarged the subsidiary flanking thrust by the provisional New Zealand Corps into the main advance, a decision that proved crucial to success. The most notable feature of the battle, though, was the effective close support provided by the Desert Air Force, which for the first time so disrupted and disorganized the enemy that the outnumbered New Zealanders broke through the Axis defenses in the Tebaga Gap on 26 March. Moreover, when Eighth Army armor forces encountered an improvised Axis antitank screen, they did not attack it but withdrew to hull-down positions and provided indirect fire, and threw out their own gun line that halted repeated German armored counterattacks. The New Zealanders' threat to the Axis rear forced the enemy to abandon the entire Mareth Line position, even though Montgomery had again reinforced his unexpected success too late to prevent an orderly Axis withdrawal.

Familiar problems still plagued British operations. Artillery fire plans failed to target the full depth of enemy defenses, and troops proved unable to deploy forward antitank guns quickly. Coordination too remained poor because the regimental parochialism that was so ingrained in the service culture proved resistant to reform. As a result, operationally British forces could only breach German defenses in depth via a protracted slogging match. The continued absence of holistic doctrine and of mechanisms to learn combat lessons, as well as the army's lukewarm commitment to retrain in the field, prevented the army from fully applying its burgeoning strength and firepower. During 1943–1944 British forces slowly developed broader military proficiency as they began to draw more accurate lessons from combat and fully grasp the mechanics of modern war. But this process remained haphazard and inchoate as flawed doctrine, in particular, continued to hamper improved combat effectiveness.

The TORCH landings in northwest Africa on 8 November 1942 had seen the combat debut of the British First Army, commanded by Lt. Gen. K. A. N. Anderson, that comprised "new army" units raised by Home Forces during 1940–1942. The divergent development of Home Forces, its inexperience, and its failure to absorb desert warfare lessons meant that the First

Army initially did not perform well in Tunisia. To understand this it is necessary to examine the genesis of the "new army" in the United Kingdom.

The Home Army's force structure changed dramatically during 1940–1942, and as the threat of invasion receded a more balanced force emerged. The poorly equipped infantry force of 1940 gave way to a better trained, supplied, organized, and balanced force strong in armor and artillery. The expansion of these arms reflected the ascendancy of the principle of machines over men that flourished after Dunkirk as ordnance offset the army's numerical weakness.[132] Reequipment progressed and reorganization also marginally increased combat power and greatly strengthened logistic support.[133]

The Royal Artillery, in particular, steadily enhanced its effectiveness after Dunkirk. It remedied its defective organization as field regiments restructured their two twelve-gun batteries into three eight-gun batteries, doubled the number of forward observers, and reintroduced survey parties.[134] This reorganization restored the one-to-one battery-battalion ratio in divisions, thus fostering affiliation and cooperation. From 1941 on, infantry also began to take part in live-fire artillery exercises, and the appearance of workable field radios in large numbers brought improved coordination.[135] Radio allowed a great advance in fire-control methods that were largely the work of General Parham, who used modern communications to cut response time and increase flexibility as gunners devised, in 1941, the ten-minute quick barrage. Moreover, the switch of forward observation officers (FOOs) to armored observation posts (OPs) during 1941–1942 improved their survivability, and in late 1942 gunners added the artillery spotter. These reforms forged an increasingly effective artillery arm capable of rapid, massed fire support.[136]

Nevertheless, tactical deficiencies, which derived from lack of combat experience, limited artillery capabilities in 1941. Indeed, most enhancements remained theoretical because inexperience obscured continued deficiencies. The terrible muddles and command errors witnessed during Exercise BUMPER (September 1941) starkly highlighted the Royal Artillery's tactical weaknesses. Confusion between "in support" and "under command" created major command headaches; and units decentralized artillery in accordance with prevailing desert practices. Gunners continued to neglect fire planning and most fire remained observed, which resulted in several mock concentrations falling on friendly troops. Exercise BUMPER, nonetheless, was a watershed in the wartime development of British artillery. Its revelations led to the brigading of army artillery into Army Groups Royal Artillery (AGRAs) during the fall of 1942. Yet the army could only exploit the potential of new fire control methods by overcoming the command problems exposed by BUMPER. During 1942, restoration of artillery command authority led to a resumption of fire planning, which allowed new quick-survey techniques perfected by the 38th Division to reduce response times for massed fire to six minutes.[137]

Another major advance in artillery effectiveness was the development of the air observation post (Air OP)—artillery officers, in direct communication with gunners, flying in low-level Auster light observation planes that could land and take off on rough terrain near the front to observe and direct fire. Air force opposition to the concept and the long and bitter service rivalry that ensued seriously hampered the development of artillery spotting, however. Prewar trials had taken place, but the first joint RAF-army air OP unit did not see action until TORCH.[138]

That these advances were technical rather than tactical partly explains why the Royal Artillery innovated relatively quickly: technical adaptation generated considerable consensus. Tactical innovation proved more difficult. Continued lack of higher training and the rarity of map exercises involving integrated artillery problems obstructed improved coordination. Likewise, range shoots typically took place in a tactical vacuum and rarely involved counterbattery work. Most significant of all, however, was that these reforms in Home Forces developed independent of the changes in artillery practices that occurred in the western desert.

The new army also required an expanded logistic base to undertake simultaneous offensives in distant theaters. Growing material plentitude, as Britain's war mobilization hit full stride, brought improved supply support. During 1941, the creation of essential services caught up with the meteoric expansion of combat units. The need to fight in multiple theaters greatly increased British logistic requirements, yet from 1942 this tail expanded beyond the reasonable demands required of it. Logistic overinsurance, first witnessed in Norway and France, became pervasive once resources became abundant.[139]

Revitalization of the infantry was also necessary if the army was to take the offensive. After Dunkirk, the War Office revised tactical doctrine to stress small-unit fire and maneuver, which became the basis of battle drill. But these efforts met with only partial success because they failed to address the infantry's two fundamental weaknesses: manpower quality and inadequate firepower. The army only marginally improved infantry quality. Its most substantive reform was a major reduction of infantry battalions during 1941–1943; but the troops were mostly transferred to the expanding armor and artillery branches. Lack of firepower also dogged the infantry throughout the war. Even in 1944 infantry retained the same personal weapons, the .303 Lee-Enfield rifle and the magazine-fed Bren gun, they had started the war with. The Bren, though portable and reliable, could not match the higher and more sustained rates of fire of German belt-fed machine guns. Limited use of machine guns and mortars paralleled at company and battalion level this lack of squad-level firepower. The Vickers

.303 was a sound machine gun with a good rate of fire, but its size and bulk were serious tactical limitations that led to its centralization at battalion level. Thus the gun was rarely on hand for infantry attacks or at the critical moment of enemy counterattack as the "Tommies" consolidated on their objective. Likewise, the 2-inch mortar with its short range and light charge could not generate the firepower of the heavier and more numerous German mortars. All this made it difficult for the infantry to adhere to a tactical doctrine of fire and maneuver; the troops could rarely generate sufficient firepower to suppress enemy fire and maneuver on the battlefield.[140]

Lack of antitank capability also prevented the infantry from fending off enemy armor without strong artillery and air support. The loss of most of its antitank gun inventory in France had forced the army to keep the obsolete 2-pounder gun and the Boys antitank rifle in production and improvise many expedient antitank weapons, most of which proved as dangerous to the user as they were ineffective.[141] Antitank capability improved in 1942 when the 6-pounder (57mm) gun entered service, but rifle companies never had sufficient 6-pounders to protect themselves from German armor, and so infantry continued to rely on the antiquated Boys rifle until 1943.

Another serious problem that confronted Home Forces was the poor quality of training, which manifested itself in Norway and France. The training system had expanded dramatically from a minuscule base early in the war, and lack of modern equipment and experienced instructors affected training badly. The regimental system also produced great diversity in training quality. Inexperience, scarcity of instructors, and massive training demands forged unimaginative and unrealistic training, which in turn bred boredom and apathy among recruits.[142] The obvious need for improvement generated two major wartime innovations—the introduction of battle drill and battle schools. Major General Alexander instigated battle drill during the summer of 1940 that both emphasized fire and maneuver and sought to inculcate individual initiative and flexibility at the small-unit level. Later, Home Forces introduced battle schools designed to replicate combat conditions and instill combined-arms teamwork.[143]

The inception of battle drill clearly improved training quality, and indeed during 1942–1944 Home Forces repeatedly practiced battle drill. However, such drills still lacked realism and failed to address the fundamental problem of British small-unit tactics: the difficulty Bren groups experienced in generating enough firepower to allow rifle groups to maneuver. Moreover, the army's commitment to the maneuver element in battle drill was superficial because these small-unit tactics were inconsistent with the army's de facto operational doctrine of firepower dominance that emerged during 1942. Infantry rarely employed battle drills in combat because such drills were incompatible with the requirements of preplanned artillery barrages.[144]

The problems associated with battle drill multiplied when the War

Office extended such drills to other arms to improve coordination. The contradictions inherent in the extension of battle drill techniques clearly reflected the army's lack of holistic doctrine. Armored battle drill equated armor with the infantry Bren group (the firepower element) and infantry with the maneuver group. The result was the shackling of the tactical mobility of armor. That basic battle-drill techniques were both fundamentally flawed and inconsistent with operational procedures clearly illuminates the muddled nature of British doctrine.[145]

Lack of conformity in training forged disparate quality, safety precautions for live-fire exercises were so extensive that battle schools failed to simulate realistic combat conditions, and amateurism bedeviled training as units often restricted exercises to daytime and good weather. Training thus failed to expose troops to the full range of conditions they would face in combat. As a result, British soldiers acquired fewer skills from training than U.S. and German recruits.[146] Most serious of all was the artificial division of instruction whereby recruits only underwent collective training once they had joined field formations. The failure to integrate basic and collective training was a major weakness that seriously retarded development of coordination and cohesion.[147]

The capabilities of the RAC also increased slowly during 1940–1942. The army's reliance on armor as its primary antitank weapon limited the effectiveness of its armored forces. Britain proved unable to produce a first-rate battle tank capable of engaging German armor on equal terms. In fact, throughout the war the RAC remained the weakest link in the army order of battle. The key cause of inferior quality of armor was not prewar budget restrictions, uncertain national defense policy, or even tardy rearmament, though these were partly to blame. It was the prevailing strategic doctrine of attrition that viewed the role of armor as engaging and neutralizing enemy armor in direct tank-to-tank engagements combined with the army view of armor specialization that led to creation of myriad specialized tanks of limited utility.[148]

The working up of Home Forces also suffered from a paucity of large-scale maneuvers. In comparison with the Germans and Americans, British troops went on exercises less often and less intensively. Circumstances clearly militated against the resumption of maneuvers early in the war. Britain was a small, densely populated island nation subject to air attack, with its maritime communications imperiled by U-boats, and whose coastal areas remained manned against enemy incursion. Britain also had few sparsely populated areas suitable for conducting exercises, a situation exacerbated by the urban-to-rural displacement of civilians during the blitz. Moreover, the army's history of imperial policing had failed to ingrain a tradition of regular maneuvers: Home Forces conducted only three large-scale exercises during 1941–1943. Operation BUMPER of September 1941 tested Home Forces' defensive capabilities; at DRYSHOD (August 1942) troops first practiced large-scale amphibious assault and exploitation drills; and only during SPARTAN (March 1943) did six OVERLORD divisions practice offensive operations. These exercises revealed serious flaws in British military capabilities, especially among armored forces.[149]

In 1942 Britain finally began to prepare for the second front. To return to the continent required an extensive amphibious capability. Yet despite a rich heritage of amphibious operations, financial constraints prevented either the army or navy from developing specialized amphibious forces between the wars. Moreover, the lessons of the Great War, especially the failure of the 1915 Gallipoli campaign, suggested that amphibious operations against a defended locality were prohibitively costly.[150] Thus, in 1939, Britain had neither trained forces nor landing craft to conduct amphibious warfare.[151] The resultant ineptness in joint operations contributed directly to failure in Norway and led to the creation of the Directorate of Combined Operations in 1940. The military gained valuable, if often costly, amphibious warfare experience from the 1940–1942 commando raids that culminated in the Dieppe debacle. This reverse galvanized the army to identify the causes of defeat and to enhance its amphibious assault capability. Study emphasized the recklessness of attacking a well-defended port, the need for special amphibious assault armor and engineers, and constant air and naval fire support.[152] After Dieppe, Britain diverted major resources to amphibious warfare, and Percy Hobart directed his unique talents to create specialized assault armor—the "Funnies."[153] Nonetheless, the military remained inexperienced at amphibious assault on the eve of TORCH. The earmarked troops had little amphibious training, and the invasion flotilla lacked both specialized tank landing craft and operational experience.

Both circumstance and policy thus limited the new army's improvement in combat effectiveness. Reequipping Home Forces proved difficult as Churchill sent the latest and best weapons to North Africa first to stave off defeat and then to reinforce success. Home Forces thus was underequipped on the eve of TORCH. The anticipated improvement in training quality also proved illusory as firepower dominance became de facto operational doctrine in the field and as battle drill quickly turned into an inflexible, regularized drill devoid of battlefield reality.

Between 1940–1942 Home Forces did manage to transform itself from an organization with only marginal defensive capacity into one with limited offensive capability. Given the extent of interwar neglect, exacerbated by the stunning early defeats, the task that confronted Home Forces was enormous. Although it made considerable progress, the problems it faced could not be quickly or easily remedied. Thus, on the eve of TORCH, the combat capabilities of Home Forces remained limited. Most troops remained focused on basic and small-unit training, and combined-arms coordination was poor. More serious was that the army remained mired in controversy over fundamental, unresolved issues regarding doctrine, tactics, force structure, and organization.

That Home Forces was reluctant to learn from the desert experiences slowed the pace of reform. This unwillingness stemmed in part from the widespread belief among senior officers that the desert war was unique and, therefore, that it held few lessons relevant to the European theater.[154] Home Forces thus left the dissemination of desert combat experience to veteran officers, which ensured that any improvement was haphazard, partial, and incomplete. The Home Forces' failure to absorb combat lessons forced the First Army to learn modern warfare the hard way—in combat in Tunisia. Indeed, it was not until Montgomery's success in Sicily that Home Forces began to appreciate the general applicability of lessons learned in the Mediterranean to combat in northwest Europe. The prevalent view of desert warfare as anomalous ensured that on the eve of TORCH the First Army remained less proficient than the Eighth Army. Only in terms of its ability to provide massed fire via the Parham system and aerial spotters, did it possess capability potentially superior to the Eighth Army's.

In November 1942 General Anderson's First Army executed TORCH, the invasion of French North Africa. Inexperience and underpreparation, combined with the lack of strategic direction behind the campaign, ensured that Anderson faced major obstacles. Planned with only three months' notice after the cancellation of BOLERO, the projected 1942 invasion of France, TORCH was the largest amphibious assault of the war to date.[155] Lack of experience in amphibious operations generated considerable confusion and disorder during the landing, and it was fortunate that the Vichy French offered only desultory opposition.[156] TORCH also saw the first, largely unsuccessful, British airborne assault of the war as the First Army dropped parachutists deep in the Axis rear where they suffered heavy losses.[157]

The biggest flaw in TORCH, however, was that the Allies lacked a clear, coherent, and integrated theater strategy to prosecute the war in North Africa, a reality that reflected poor Anglo-American understanding of the operational level of war. Indeed, the TORCH planning banked upon the rapid capture of Tunis by coup de main to wrap up the campaign quickly. Thus the Allies neither planned nor prepared for a protracted campaign. When the Axis forces reacted much more rapidly than the Allies had deemed possible, they defeated the feeble Allied attempt to quickly take Tunis and inflicted a series of local reverses. Lack of cooperation, both in the air and on the ground, between green British and U.S. forces fighting for the first time side by side exacerbated these setbacks.[158]

Poor strategic planning, the hasty implementation of TORCH, and the failure of Home Forces to absorb desert lessons all impinged upon First Army's performance and delayed Allied victory in Tunisia. Many problems that had previously bedeviled British operations resurfaced early on in

Tunisia. Unit performance remained variable and coordination was again poor. Most seriously, initial lack of antitank guns, due to shipping limitations, once again brought the misuse of field artillery in an antitank role. The debut of brigaded army artillery was also inauspicious as Anderson decentralized his army artillery early in the campaign.[159] Moreover, during the dash for Tunis and the winter battles, Anderson allowed Allied formations to fragment and become intermixed, which eroded morale and cohesion.

Most lacking in the early stages of TORCH, though, was effective air support. The Eastern Air Command (EAC) that provided tactical support to the First Army had failed to absorb desert warfare lessons, and so its doctrine was obsolete and its organization cumbersome. It flew obsolete Bisley tactical bombers in daylight when the Desert Air Force had long since abandoned such day missions as suicidal. The EAC relearned this lesson the hard way when German fighters annihilated an entire squadron during December.[160] Initially, EAC also had very limited fighter-bomber capability and misused its fighters to provide defensive umbrellas in contravention of desert practices. Nor did it initially possess centralized control of fighters or of radar, which curtailed its aerial reconnaissance capability. The air OP too made little impact at first because few spotters were available, interservice conflict raged on, and the First Army misused the aircraft as liaison and courier planes.[161] Lacking preparation and infrastructure, especially communications and transport, the EAC experienced major administrative, organizational, and maintenance difficulties.[162]

The First Army, though, enhanced its combat effectiveness more quickly than British forces had hitherto in the western desert. Understanding of the mechanics of modern war was gradually diffused through the army, and recognition of the need to learn from combat experience spread. During February 1943 Anderson reorganized the First Army, restored formation integrity, and created operational reserves. At the same time, the new commander of the 18th Army Group (formed to coordinate the actions of First and Eighth Armies), General Alexander, instigated a coordinated air-ground campaign—which involved alternate limited attacks by one army to draw off enemy reserves while the other launched a major attack—to grind the enemy into defeat. This strategy regained, and then retained, the initiative, kept the enemy off balance, prevented the Germans from massing against danger points, and inexorably wore down Axis strength.[163]

Fire support also improved as Anderson slowly reconcentrated army artillery and began to employ it en masse. The First Army also gradually learned to harness the air OP, and at Bou Arada on 18 January 1943 the 6th Armoured Division fired the first spotter-directed, radio-controlled divisional barrage to halt German counterattacks.[164] This battle also saw the Royal Artillery fire its first UNCLE target—the full, massed fire of brigaded artillery. Late in the campaign the air OP demonstrated its potential as more aircraft became available, as interservice wrangling abated, as the First Army employed them more appropriately, and as the army finally painted aerial recognition symbols on its vehicles.[165] Thus, during February 1943, at Hunts Gap spotter-directed massed fire single-handedly repulsed German counterattacks, confirming another important lesson that the army had been slow to learn—that heavy artillery could be effective against armor. As a result, during late spring gunners finally began to use heavy guns in defensive fire missions to halt German armored counterattacks.[166]

The continued Axis air threat early in the campaign, however, demanded careful camouflage, concealment, and dispersion of artillery, which diluted its effectiveness, as did initial ammunition shortages. From April 1943 on, however, the acquisition of aerial supremacy and abundant ammunition allowed Allied artillery to dominate the battle. The final Allied offensive in Tunisia, Operation VULCAN, saw two divisions advance on a 3,000-yard front behind a massive preliminary bombardment that included the First Army's first major counterbattery program.[167]

The single most significant advance in the Allied prosecution of the war during 1943 was the evolution of a integrated, interservice, and interallied war effort. Originally, Britain and the United States had planned their own separate roles in TORCH and had sought only minimal coordination. But the speed of Axis reinforcement and the local defeats the enemy inflicted throughout the winter dispelled complacency and precipitated greater cooperation between air and ground forces—and between the air forces themselves.[168] The fusion of Air Marshals Tedder and Coningham with the equally talented U.S. airmen "Tooey" Spaatz, James Doolittle, and "Pete" Quesada fostered reform and saw tactical aviation reach new heights of effectiveness.

Coningham's appointment to head Northwest Africa Tactical Air Force (NATAF) on 18 February 1943 finally solved the problems faced by EAC. Horrified at what he found when he took command—the air support arrangements in northwest Africa being no more advanced than those in the western desert during summer 1941—Coningham abandoned the defensive use of fighters and concentrated them for offensive missions that protected ground troops by forcing enemy planes onto the defensive. Likewise, he abandoned attacks on well-defended targets, like armor, for interdiction strikes on more vulnerable "soft-skinned" motor transport.[169]

More importantly still, from February on, the Allies used air power en masse for the first time along with a coherent, multistage plan to gain air superiority and then to support the land battle. Air power became an integral and coherent element of an interallied, interservice theater strategy to destroy Axis forces in Tunisia, rather than an independent strategy. Increased coordination during the spring allowed the Allies to apply their growing strength in the air more effectively. Combined with improved communications and maintenance abilities, serviceability rates steadily climbed and by March the Allies had established a level of air supremacy comparable to that achieved in Libya by the Second Battle of El Alamein.

By April 1943, both the quality and quantity of air support in Tunisia had markedly improved. It assisted ground operations on a scale never before possible: on 6 May 1943 NATAF flew an unprecedented 2,000 sorties. The integration of air power into an overarching joint-services strategy considerably enhanced the overall impact of air power, and from Tunisia onward it became a vital and growing element of Allied striking power in the air-land battle. The integrated strategy and the improved coordination that first emerged in Tunisia enhanced Allied fighting power more than any other single wartime advance.[170]

The final assault launched in Tunisia in April 1943 finally shattered a demoralized enemy for whom supply shortages had compromised mobility and powers of resistance. In late April, the Eighth Army frontally attacked the naturally strong Wadi Akarit line. Around-the-clock air strikes accelerated the exhaustion of the enemy, but Axis forces again were able to withdraw intact. Then, on 6 May, the First Army spearheaded Operation VULCAN, a narrow 3,000-yard frontal attack under a huge air umbrella and with the support of massed artillery fire that cracked the attenuated Axis defenses. By 12 May enemy resistance had ceased.

The British Army derived more lessons from Tunisia as it finally began to recognize the need to collect and disseminate combat experience. The War Office concluded that the campaign demonstrated the general soundness of army training, equipment, leadership, and morale. Yet, at the same time, the army noted an unprecedented number of defects that included poor combined-arms, junior officer, and replacement training; poor fire discipline and use of mortars, and inadequate infantry tactical training. The War Office also concluded that battle drill had instilled rigidity rather than initiative. The campaign also highlighted the deficiencies of Allied armor, notably the inferior quality of British optics and the flammability of the new American Sherman tank.[171]

TORCH confirmed the army's need for greater antitank capability. The accelerating tank gun-versus-armor race left the 6-pounder gun hard-pressed to deal with the new third-generation German Tiger tanks dispatched to Tunisia until the new 17-pounder gun entered service in March 1943. With this weapon Britain finally had a powerful, high-velocity antitank gun capable of destroying enemy armor at typical combat ranges, even though the gun's bulk and retention in reserve limited its tactical effectiveness. Thus 17-pounders were rarely in the right place at the right time to engage panzers.[172] Late in the campaign infantry received the PIAT (Platoon Infantry Anti-Tank), a tube-launched armor-piercing projector, to replace the Boys rifle. Although inaccurate, short in range, and with poor penetration, the PIAT was nevertheless an improvement on the Boys rifle.[173] But because the PIAT left much to be desired, the 17-pounder lacked mobility, and few tank destroyers were available, infantry continued to rely on the 6-pounder for antitank defense.[174]

British fire support became more effective in Tunisia. Improved aerial photoreconnaissance and use of spotters increased artillery accuracy, while the Parham system of rapid-response massed fire brought greater flexibility. The First Army's arrival in Tunisia allowed a gradual fusion of the North African reforms with developments among Home Forces. Tunisia thus first witnessed the massive shell expenditures that became the hallmark of British operations during 1944–1945. Increasingly sophisticated employment of artillery enhanced defensive capabilities too: at Takrouna on 19 April massed defensive artillery fire shattered German counterattacks.[175]

The RAC, however, discerned few lessons in Tunisia because the terrain so hampered the employment of armor that its contribution was negligible. Tunisia's difficult mountains finally began to break down desert practices, as it forced armor and infantry to work together more closely. The campaign also demonstrated the effectiveness of the Churchill infantry tank as a dependable, multipurpose vehicle. Thus the Tunisian campaign first shook the RAC's faith in massed armor as well as its view of armor specialization.

British fortunes changed suddenly in 1943 as Montgomery triumphed in North Africa, the Royal Navy won the Battle of the Atlantic, and RAF Bomber Command took the war to the enemy. Moreover, equipment arrived in plenty, even if quality was still wanting. Increasing mastery of the skies and seas greatly eased the army's struggle for victory, but simultaneously masked the difficulties of projecting military power against continental Europe. It took amphibious operations in the Mediterranean during summer 1943 to illuminate these problems.

In July 1943 the Allies launched Operation HUSKY, a massive amphibious assault on Sicily. A three-week around-the-clock air offensive against the tiny island of Pantelleria, 70 miles southwest of Sicily presaged the assault and first demonstrated the demoralizing effect of sustained air bombardment: the Axis garrison surrendered before landing operations began.[176] The Allies expected that Sicily, defended by poorly equipped and demoralized Italian forces shored up by two hastily improvised German mechanized divisions, would fall quickly, especially as a brutal attritional air war established Allied aerial superiority by the time of the invasion.[177] But the Germans fought a skilled delaying action that inflicted heavy losses, and Montgomery's methodical pace prevented British forces from wresting the initiative from the greatly outnumbered enemy force, which was able to withdraw intact to mainland Italy. It was the more aggressive and faster reacting Americans who smashed through demoralized Italians to beat Montgomery to Messina, an achievement that clearly demonstrated the growing tactical proficiency of U.S. forces.

The Allies also repeated the mistake of overambitious use of airborne forces in HUSKY that they had made in TORCH. The drop of the 1st Air Landing Brigade marked the first major British airborne operation of the war, but inexperience and excessive demands placed on the paratroopers resulted in wide dispersion and heavy losses.[178] Airborne forces gained useful experience but, as with the Germans, inflated expectations of airborne units' capabilities hindered their effectiveness and led the Allies to emphasize strategic missions at the expense of less ambitious tactical missions.[179]

British tactical skill further improved during HUSKY. In particular, British forces more extensively and effectively utilized aerial spotters, including the first spotter-directed naval gunfire against Catania's harbor. After the success of this mission, spotter-directed naval fire became common and brought accurate naval fire support.[180] The September 1943 Salerno landings (Operation AVALANCHE), in southern Italy, gave the British more experience in amphibious assault and demonstrated the efficacy of defensive artillery fire. The caution of Allied forces prevented them from seizing a sizeable lodgement, and enemy reserves contained the invaders in a shallow, vulnerable bridgehead that the Germans vigorously attacked.[181] But spotter-directed artillery and naval fire repeatedly broke up German counterattacks, demoralized the enemy, sapped German strength, and prevented then from overrunning the bridgehead. Likewise during the January 1944 Anzio landings (Operation SHINGLE), the lack of ground observation made spotters vital and they proved crucial in breaking up German counterattacks. In fact, spotter-directed fire became the dominant method of artillery employment in Italy during 1944.[182]

The rugged, highly defensible terrain in Italy that restricted operational maneuver finally led British forces to develop an all-around proficiency. British artillery effectiveness continued to improve in Italy as mass employment became commonplace. Poor observation in mountainous terrain brought aerial spotters into their true element, and the campaign saw the debut of spotter-directed counterflak bombardment that sought to suppress enemy antiaircraft fire prior to airstrikes. The decline of the German air threat in 1944 allowed increased employment and success for spotters, as did the arrival of superior planes. Through trial and error, gunners learned to employ ever larger amounts of artillery to shatter enemy defenses. In the Liri Valley during May–June 1944 commanders called down record levels of massed fire with unprecedented rapidity. By the summer of 1944 the army had achieved the adept handling of massed artillery fire, the belief that "shells save lives" had become an army byword, and gunners, if well supplied, could thwart all German attacks.[183] In fact, artillery handling was the area in which the army most improved its capabilities during the war.

Rugged terrain forced British troops to coordinate more effectively. The inability of armor to advance without infantry support and the gradual taming of the panzers finally eroded British faith in massed armor. Initially, poor coordination brought severe tank losses from enfilading German anti-tank guns and the new close-combat antitank weapons that appeared in increasing numbers during fall 1943. Gradually, through trial and error, British armor and infantry learned to fight together: combined-arms coordination improved, and brigaded army artillery brought down ever larger amounts of fire. It was, therefore, in Italy in 1944 that British forces finally developed a genuine comprehensive military proficiency.

With victories in Tunisia, Sicily, and Italy, British morale began to recover. But it was the intensification of preparations for the invasion of France from mid-1943, the influx of material might, and Montgomery's November 1943 appointment to command of the 21st Army Group, picked to spearhead the Anglo-Canadian landings, that boosted British morale.[184] However, the army group, which comprised the British Second Army and Canadian First Army, benefited little from combat experience in Italy because Home Forces still lacked mechanisms to disseminate combat lessons.

The preparation of British forces for OVERLORD during 1943–1944 occurred against the backdrop of important doctrinal change, as the War Office revised tactical doctrine to incorporate lessons learned in the desert. The most important change was the abandonment of the use of armor to spearhead offensives that had gotten so many British units shattered. In 1944, armor instead performed the secondary function of providing indirect fire support from hull-down flank and rear positions while the infantry, backed by massed artillery fire, resumed the primary attack role.[185] Armored units retrained to these revised tactics during the spring of 1944, but many infantry units apparently failed to appreciate or to practice the new doctrine during the last few months of hectic invasion preparations.

That the upcoming invasion would tax British capabilities and resources gave senior military and political figures much food for thought, and most remained uncertain whether the Allies could triumph in Normandy.[186] Allied successes in North Africa and Sicily were strategic victories that had derived from the ability to apply great strength against an enemy that operated at the end of extended and tenuous lines of communication. But a second front in northwest Europe would require the Allies to project their power against an enemy in unprecedented strength on the strategic defensive. This enemy had the advantage of interior lines and recognized that repelling the invasion presented nazism with its last opportunity to forestall defeat. Given the inexperience and inadequate training of the army in Britain, Montgomery remained gravely concerned about prospects of success. Indeed, he wrote:

> The army in England is not really battle worthy; they are not veteran soldiers, fully versed in the technique of battle. It is all theory, and a good deal of it is unpractical and on the wrong lines. Many of the generals have

never seen a shot fired in this war—most of them in fact; they are not in touch with the "feel of the battle"; they cannot possibly teach their subordinates if they themselves do not know the game. We ought to make more use of our active front to train our generals; corps and divisional generals *must* know the game.[187]

During 1943, the pace of British adaptation to the changing character of the war accelerated as the fortunes of war turned in favor of the Allies. Since the army learned better from its successes than from its failures, the pace of innovation accelerated during 1943 as the strategic initiative passed to the Allies. While eager to identify what they had done right that had brought them victory, the army was much less interested in identifying what had gone wrong.[188] This approach skewed the adaptation because it led the army to enhance its capabilities in areas where it had already attained proficiency—amphibious assault, massed artillery fire, and set-piece battles—but retarded improvement in areas where mastery was lacking, for example, small-unit tactics and coordination. This misguided intellectual approach to lessons-learned analysis ensured that British capabilities improved more quickly once British forces had begun to win victories.

Montgomery also shaped the lessons-learned process and his impact narrowed the spectrum of innovation and adaptation. Nevertheless, he was undoubtedly the man to lead Commonwealth forces in northwest Europe, for he alone could inject confidence and boost morale. On taking command he vigorously tackled the task of fully readying the army for OVERLORD in a few short months.[189] He had neither time nor resources to inculcate desert methods and experience. All he could do was tinker with the army; so he attempted a "quick fix." He would overcome mentally what could not be fixed materially or structurally, and Montgomery's belief in the human dimension of war was never more clearly displayed than here. Human resourcefulness and grit would surmount doctrinal, tactical, organizational, and equipment flaws to guarantee success. He visited every formation to boost morale, and stressed repeatedly that every man must give his all in the forthcoming invasion.[190]

Montgomery strengthened his army group in more tangible ways. Worried about the home army's inexperience, he posted desert veterans to green divisions to disseminate battle experience, even though this inevitably diluted the value of all this combat experience. Just as important, Montgomery imprinted his distinctive operational approach on the OVER-LORD planning and devised a clear "masterplan"—a theater strategy—to govern Allied operations in northwest Europe that emphasized the El Alamein formula for victory: maintaining the initiative and massed employment of overwhelming firepower. Operationally, the weight of shells would blast the British infantry onto their objectives in a replay of the artillery barrages of 1917, albeit enhanced by such technical developments as improved communications and aerial spotters, which greatly improved command and control.[191] Given Allied capabilities, the timing, location, and theater strategy for the second front were crucial to Allied chances of victory. Montgomery's strategy for OVERLORD has generated considerable controversy, but the evidence clearly indicates that his theater strategy coalesced during the spring of 1944 and called for the Second British Army on the eastern flank to capture Caen rapidly and establish a defensive position inland at Falaise.[192] While continual feints would draw the bulk of German forces against the British, U.S. forces, after capturing Cherbourg, would break out in the west, secure the Breton ports, hook toward the Seine, and fan out into the French interior, while the Second Army advanced on the inner flank of this hook.[193]

In fact, Montgomery wrought significant changes to the OVERLORD plan. He insisted upon a broader and more powerful initial assault, a less ambitious tactical role for airborne forces, and a more limited secondary role for Anglo-Canadian forces. He also demanded the early capture of Cherbourg and the Breton ports to guarantee the logistic base for a permanent lodgement. These revisions to the OVERLORD plan appreciably increased Allied chances of victory in Normandy.

British ground forces made much progress in amphibious assault preparation during 1943–1944. Assault formations extensively rehearsed for their missions, and the military vigorously enhanced its amphibious capability. The result was marked innovation as Britain developed specialized assault armor, including amphibious and flamethrowing tanks, armored bulldozers, tracklayers, and ditch fillers, as well as rocket-firing landing craft, to overcome the German Atlantic Wall defenses.[194]

Despite Montgomery's endeavors, deep-rooted problems that defied quick remedy still afflicted British forces on the eve of D-Day. Reequipment, for example, had progressed slowly because the priority accorded to the Mediterranean theater meant that many OVERLORD formations did not reequip until spring of 1944. But the greatest deficiency remained the army's inadequate coordination. By the summer of 1943 Home Forces was well aware of coordination problems as combat experience filtered back from the desert and Tunisia. In the year before D-Day Home Forces energetically addressed the issue. Yet inexperience, regimentalism, and lack of holistic doctrine all hampered efforts to improve coordination, and so only limited progress was made. Regimentalism prevented the army from discarding its "joint-operations" approach—the loose combination of combat arms, rather than intimate coordination—and hindered efforts to improve combined-arms training. There was some progress, most notably between infantry and independent tank brigades, but it was patchy.

The combined-arms preparation that dominated training during 1943–1944 clearly illustrates the detrimental effects of regimentalism: the army's "joint-operations" approach ensured that infantry and armor invariably trained together in conjunction rather than in concert. The army's tradition of imperial policing and its deep-seated regimentalism worked against improved coordination; the traditionalism enshrined in the regimental system led each branch of service to guard jealously its sacred independence. At the same time, the army's coordination difficulties were in part doctrinal because doctrine failed to extend coordination below division level. The armored division, for example, coordinated the firepower provided by the motorized infantry brigade with the maneuverability of the armored brigade. Only slowly, as the war progressed, did training manuals place greater emphasis on combined-arms coordination.[195]

Concern over infantry quality still remained. Political decisions about manpower allocation in part accounted for the limited improvement in infantry quality that had occurred. The infantry remained at the bottom of recruitment priority, given the unprecedented manpower demands of industry, the technical branches, and the other services. The doctrine of machines over men that flourished with the cementing of the British-U.S. alliance drew many men of ability out of the infantry and into the technical and mechanized branches. At the same time the Battles of Britain and of the Atlantic, the bomber offensive, and the amphibious armada drew more high-quality personnel into the Royal Navy and the RAF.

Yet the army itself was also responsible for poor infantry quality: starved from without, the infantry was also robbed from within.[196] In a break with tradition, the wartime army diverted major resources to special forces—volunteer elite units—as repeated defeats tarnished its reputation and promoted the creation of elite forces that appeared to offer good prospects of restoring wounded pride. The proliferation of special forces also reflected Churchill's determination to strike back at nazi-occupied Europe when regular forces were incapable of offensive action. The first British special forces, the independent companies that harassed the German advance in Norway while the Allies evacuated, evolved into the commandos, army and Royal Marine light raiding units. After Dunkirk, Churchill expanded and concentrated these raiding forces into the Directorate of Combined Operations, which represented a major diversion of resources at a time when Britain had few operational divisions. Thereafter, special forces proliferated beyond all reasonable demands, resulting in more than twenty distinct types whose functions often overlapped.[197]

The most significant elite troops were the airborne forces. After the daring German capture of the Belgian fort of Eben Emael and despite the powerful opposition of Air Marshal "Bomber" Harris and chief of the Air Staff, Air Marshal Portal, airborne infantry forces had expanded to two divisions by 1943.[198] But its own obsession with strategic bombing led the RAF to neglect the support of airborne operations, with the result that its glider and transport pilots were initially badly trained. This led to the poor showing in Sicily, where the RAF deposited under 10 percent of the paratroopers on their drop zones. Thus, prior to D-Day, airborne forces had yet to demonstrate their full potential.

By D-Day, special forces amounted to one-quarter of British infantry strength and were a clear drain on infantry quality.[199] Moreover, the achievements of special forces did not justify such large-scale diversion of resources. Commando raids on mainland Europe, though they sustained morale during the dark days of 1940–1942, with a few notable exceptions, had little strategic impact.[200] The most important contribution they did make was in gaining badly needed amphibious warfare experience, which bore fruit with the successful invasions of Sicily, Italy, and Normandy. Moreover, many special forces were not really elite units at all. The army's notion that combined-arms units (like Jock Columns) and interservice forces (like the Long Range Desert Group) constituted elite troops reflected the army's conservatism and reluctance to embrace modern combined-arms warfare.

The drain of quality personnel into special forces exacerbated a growing manpower shortage. At the root of this lack of available manpower lay the bloodletting of the Great War, not just in a demographic sense but especially psychologically. The shackling interwar never again mentality lingered well into the war, and the ghosts of the Somme and Passchendaele haunted even Churchill, who feared that Normandy might become another Gallipoli. This psychological legacy saw the emergence of a limited-conflict mentality that proved impossible to dispel. Even Churchill succumbed; he, like many, had come to believe that a future war would never see great forces massed against one another.[201] He thus repeatedly advocated a peripheral strategy that would first "close the ring" around Nazi Germany and then attack through the "soft underbelly" of Italy and the Balkans. But this approach eschewed the Clausewitzian imperative for a direct battle confrontation, which had become embedded in U.S. military policy and doctrine, and thus engendered serious British-U.S. disagreements over strategy.[202] In addition, this limited conflict mentality fueled the world of elite British miniarmies that siphoned the best soldiers out of the infantry.

Manpower concerns exerted a powerful influence on British planning for, and operations in, northwest Europe. An infantry shortage existed by the fall of 1943 that left few replacements available for OVERLORD.[203] Contrary to Carlo D'Este's claims, the preparation of OVERLORD casualty estimates made Montgomery aware that his army group would be a wasting asset.[204] Precisely when this would occur depended on the government's success in finding extra manpower, the War Office's determination to remuster personnel for the infantry, and on Montgomery's skill in avoiding undue casualties.

Both government efforts to furnish more manpower and army efforts to utilize its existing manpower more effectively failed to alleviate the manpower shortage before D-Day. The army began remustering personnel as infantry in 1943, and though it endeavored to increase the supply of trained infantry drafts—by transfers from the RAF Regiment and from antiaircraft gunners—these required many months of retraining. During the spring of 1944, the army disbanded existing formations and stripped Home Forces to bring divisions up to strength and provide replacements to cover OVERLORD's first three months' projected losses.[205] The United Kingdom in 1944 was thus a nation with a manpower shortage, and the diverse needs of the services and of industry strictly limited army reinforcements. Consequently, manpower concerns solidified the caution inherent in Montgomery's operational approach and firmly established casualty minimization as a cornerstone of British operational art in northwest Europe.[206]

During 1943–1944 the capabilities of British ground forces continued to improve, however variably, and adaptation was by no means universal. The continued lack of holistic doctrine hampered army efforts to enhance combat effectiveness. The army culture disparaged theory and elevated improvisation, obstructing doctrinal development, and thus the army relied more on extemporaneous pragmatism than a formal, explicit doctrine.[207] Dual impulses drove wartime doctrinal development: the War Office and the experiences of senior British commanders. Doctrinal development was thus both top-down and dualistic. This duality forged an army that possessed multiple, and sometimes conflicting, doctrines as the individual styles of senior commanders modified official doctrine.[208] Doctrinal ideas flowed both from the War Office and from senior commanders and it was through the confluence of these ideas that a unique Commonwealth style of warfare emerged.[209] This de facto decentralization of doctrine sometimes resulted in a sharp dichotomy between official doctrine and the reality practiced by individual commands.[210]

Of the senior commanders, Montgomery had the greatest influence on doctrinal development. As commander of South-Eastern District in 1941–1942, he taught his embryonic operational ideas to much of the Home Forces before his approach matured in North Africa.[211] By 1944, Montgomery was intellectually ascendent within the army because of the zeal with which he expressed and disseminated his ideas, his professional reputation, his unrivaled experience, and his excellent relations with senior officers. Once in the ascendent, he nurtured protégés, like Oliver Leese in Italy, who spread the gospel according to Monty.[212]

By spring of 1944 Montgomery's operational thinking had reached its definitive form.[213] His military thought, while somewhat innovative, was grounded in the conservative bedrock of interwar British military thought and his ideas, like most Commonwealth generals, adhered to traditional gunner methods. His intellectual ascendancy and the crystallization of his operational approach effectively narrowed the parameters for innovation in northwest Europe, and ensured that his army group largely failed to absorb lessons from the Italian campaign.

Lack of holistic doctrine hampered army efforts to enhance its offensive capabilities during 1942–1944. Unrealistic expectations generated by the "small conflict" and the "massed armor" mentalities dogged refinement of offensive doctrine. Throughout 1942, attack doctrine had continued to envisage the armored division acting in a cavalry role as a fast, exploitation force designed to employ "soft-spot tactics"—concentrating on an existing gap in the enemy line—rather than fight its way through. Doctrine also continued to overemphasize the hitting power of the armored brigade and underemphasize combined-arms teamwork in exploitation.[214] Fundamentally, such a quixotic doctrine reflected the army's failure to preserve the experience of World War I, its repeated defeat, and its inexperience in armored warfare.

But even after British forces abandoned the offensive spearhead role of armor during late 1943, attack doctrine remained fundamentally flawed. For it still emphasized a ponderous, centralized, deliberate, three-staged attritional battle on a narrow front. Frontal attacks first pinned the enemy in position; then artillery smashed the infantry into enemy positions, where they then consolidated on the objective; and finally armor moved through the gap torn in the enemy line to push into the enemy rear.[215] Whereas British attack doctrine stressed concentration of effort and narrow-front attacks to maximize offensive striking power, it was poorly attuned to German defensive tactics of defense in depth and immediate counterattack to disrupt, contain, and repulse enemy attacks. The slow, deliberate pace of British attacks not only gave the enemy time to recover from the massive preliminary bombardment and respond, but narrow attack fronts often caused terrible traffic congestion and allowed German flanking fire and counterattacks to so cripple attack momentum that follow-up units could not move forward quickly or smoothly. So, British attack doctrine was fundamentally mechanistic, ponderous, deliberate, and controlled; its emphasis on units' consolidating after a break-in before exploiting led to fatal delays that made penetration of enemy defenses unlikely.

The tradition of imperial defense meant that the army failed to stress field training and thus never really committed itself to retraining while in combat theaters.[216] This reluctance to retrain on the battlefield further slowed the pace of innovation, and the army remained poorly structured to reassess its practices and disseminate new ideas. Of the senior British commanders, only Montgomery demonstrated a strong commitment to retraining. However, once he had developed what he considered a battle-winning formula in the desert in 1942, his operational and tactical ideas barely changed thereafter.[217] He was reluctant to address other inadequacies of British arms, for as long as he had good artillery, air power, and administration he believed he would prevail. Montgomery was thus both a boon and a bane to wartime reform: he did stress retraining and learning, but only of his solutions. His ascendancy, therefore, narrowed the areas in which reform occurred. His approach was the product of much more than egoism, however. Britain desperately needed to win: the end was far more important than the means. Victory was what counted. Britain wished to defeat Germany at tolerable cost and to preserve its empire, army, and international standing in the process.

One of Montgomery's major achievements was to sharpen air-ground cooperation prior to OVERLORD. The Home Forces' lack of preparation for the air-ground battle had horrified him when he assumed command of 21st Army Group, so he promoted the effective blueprint for prosecuting the air war in Normandy that the Tunisian campaign had provided. First, Allied air power sought air superiority as an absolute prerequisite for the invasion. Then, during the spring of 1944, it flew deep interdiction strikes to isolate the battlefield. And once the campaign began it provided battlefield interdiction and close support.

A new generation of long-range fighters equipped with drop fuel tanks allowed the Allies to take the fight to the *Luftwaffe* in late 1943 to win the air superiority battle.[218] But German fighters refused to engage as the enemy husbanded its strength for the impending invasion. However, the *Luftwaffe* energetically opposed the Allied heavy bombers that, after the July 1943 introduction of Window (aluminum foil chaff) blinded the entire German defense system radar, inflicted a rising tide of destruction on German cities.[219] German countermeasures soon overcame the Window challenge, though. Tame Sow tactics—night-fighters vectored onto targets by ground-based early-warning stations—inflicted a mounting toll on Allied bombers as they struck deeper into Germany and nearly forced the Allies to suspend the bombing campaign.[220] But the new Allied long-range fighters, when committed to escorting the bombers, were finally able to engage and cripple the *Luftwaffe*'s fighter force over the winter of 1943–1944 and acquire the aerial superiority necessary for an invasion. Just as important, the near crippling of RAF Bomber Command over the skies of Germany overcame the vehement bombing advocates' opposition to the employment of heavy bombers in direct support of the invasion. The full application of available air power in support of OVERLORD gave the Allies an enormous advantage that contributed directly to eventual victory.

The quality of British leadership also troubled Montgomery. The wartime conscripts came from a decidedly unmilitary, even antimilitary, generation. The slaughter in the trenches of the Great War had destroyed the intrinsic trust and faith in officers' abilities that their fathers had shown early in that conflict. The hardships of the Depression had heightened suspicion of and hostility toward authority. These soldiers would have to be led rather than driven, and the army's performance thus rested heavily on the quality of its officer corps. But rapid expansion of the army prevented rigorous weeding out of the unfit, and repeated defeats did little to instill confidence in the army leadership. Moreover, the British Army was overofficered, especially at the higher levels of command.[221] Officer selection and training standards diverged markedly between arms, and the War Office gave heavy weight to class origins in its standards. Only in 1942 did the War Office establish selection boards (along German lines) to provide more rigorous and scientific assessment of aspiring officers. Also, Officer Cadet Training Units of the early war years lacked experienced instructors, and only after 1942 did the War Office reassign veteran officers as instructors—but by then many undertrained officers were serving in the field.

The army also lacked a continental-style general staff. The Army Staff Colleges at Camberley and Quetta, India, trained selected officers for staff positions, but the press of time and numbers meant that the colleges never sought to refine doctrine but simply imparted existing doctrine to an increasing number of Commonwealth staff officers. Unlike in Germany, staff appointments were neither attractive nor prestigious, especially given the army's neglect of operational art and its disdain for intellectual study. The army viewed staff officers with suspicion. Encouraging high-quality, energetic officers to join the staff proved difficult, so the general standard of wartime staff officers never approached German standards.[222]

Question marks thus remained over many of the senior British commanders, few of whom had seen action. Lt. Gen. Miles "Bimbo" Dempsey commanded the British Second Army that was to spearhead the Anglo-Canadian assault. Though a tough, quiet, efficient, and unflappable commander, Dempsey had never led an army in combat.[223] His command comprised I, VIII, XII, and XXX Corps commanded by Lt. Gens. John Crocker, Richard O'Connor, Neil Ritchie, and Gerard Bucknall, respectively. Since the War Office had few veteran commanders to choose from, it was difficult to find qualified corps commanders.[224]

Backed by Churchill, O'Connor received the Home Forces' *corps de chasse*, the VIII Corps. One of the most talented British officers, his capture in North Africa in April 1941 badly set back his career. Even though he escaped in December 1943, his confinement had left him out of touch with military developments. He thus only briefly fought the Germans and had never handled armor.[225] Neil Ritchie, too, survived the disgrace of defeat after mishandling the Eighth Army at Gazala and subsequently proved a competent corps commander, as did Crocker.[226] Montgomery had promoted Bucknall for corps command over Alanbrooke's strong objections.[227] The quality of divisional commanders also varied widely. Maj. Gen. "Pip" Roberts had forged the 11th Armoured Division into an effective formation and was the best British armored commander. Other commanders were less satisfactory, reflecting the limited pool of seasoned senior officers. General Agair of the Guards Armoured Division, for example, was a Grenadier Guardsman with no operational armored warfare experience.[228]

On the eve of D-Day, the British Second Army's assault formations stood poised to launch a meticulously planned invasion for which they had extensively trained and that would take place with mastery of the seas and skies. Allied intelligence had provided a good picture of enemy strength and dispositions, and the War Office had met the gigantic logistic requirements for a successful invasion. It was thus likely that the Allies could secure a bridgehead, the greatest danger coming from a rapid German armored counterattack. Yet the War Office remained uncertain of what would happen after Allied forces had gotten ashore, because they would face the enemy in considerable strength and because their lack of operational-level doctrine left them unclear as to how precisely to effect the breakout battle once ashore. Moreover, not only did the Allies face in Normandy a large German field force operating on interior lines, but serious weaknesses still afflicted all the Allied armies. The British Army had not yet fully shaken off its defensive mentality, its attack doctrine was mechanistic and ponderous, its coordination remained poor, its armor was inferior, its morale brittle, and its manpower limited. British fighting power—the sum of the forces available times their combat effectiveness—was finite. The lack of manpower, in particular, meant caution and careful husbanding of available forces.

In these circumstances, Allied mastery in the air proved decisive in tipping the balance in favor of Allied victory even before D-Day. Air supremacy allowed the Allies to conduct deep interdiction strikes during the spring of 1944 that effectively isolated Normandy. Such a mission was more controversial than in Tunisia, where the length of Axis lines of communication had made them vulnerable to deep interdiction. It was not obvious that effective disruption of France's modern communications network was possible. Indeed, air forces had never undertaken interdiction on the scale and scope necessary to isolate Normandy, and the need to preserve the secrecy of the precise invasion site compelled the Allies to disperse their attacks. Nevertheless, the mission went ahead and massive, repeated air attacks systematically smashed German communications and effectively isolated Normandy by the eve of D-Day. The interdiction campaign had a major, perhaps even decisive, impact on the success of this second front, even before the first shot was ever fired on the Normandy beaches.

The British Army entered World War II markedly inferior to its opponent and without a ground force structured, organized, trained, or equipped for modern continental warfare. It lacked appropriate doctrine, suffered from poor morale and a defensive mentality, and was wholly unprepared for interarms and interservice cooperation. Its tasks of mobilization, expansion, and rearmament early in the war were gargantuan. The consequence of this unpreparedness was a string of serious defeats early in the war, which while providing impetus for reform, simultaneously hampered adaptation. Only slowly, painfully, and at heavy cost did the army relearn the fundamentals of modern war in North Africa and the Mediterranean. Thus it was only in 1943 that Great Britain had turned its attention to the decisive land engagement in France; even then these efforts were mostly direct-ed to the mighty amphibious armada required to get the army into battle.

While the British Army had transformed itself from a force possessing only marginal defensive capability to one with limited offensive capability, the degree of improvement varied tremendously. The British military had made most progress in interservice coordination as repeated defeat forged greater service cooperation, a process cemented by the intimate teamwork required to return the army to the continent. The army, in turn, had ulti-mately mastered a single successful operational approach that relied on existing strengths—artillery, air power, and administration. But the army had not made all the necessary progress in reequipment, retraining, force structure, organization, tactics, and operational art.[229] Morale had improved but it remained fragile, and the least progress had been made in combined-arms coordination and doctrinal development.

The army's relative tardiness in discerning combat lessons slowed the pace of adaptation and thus limited enhancement of combat effectiveness. The failure to preserve lessons learned at such great cost during World War I, as well as the lack of basic professionalism in army culture and of mech-anisms to derive and disseminate combat lessons, all hampered wartime adaptation. As the war progressed, the British learning process improved as senior commanders began to appreciate the need to learn from combat experience. As a result, in the middle of the war the army adopted a more professional and scientific approach to lessons-learned analysis. The army created the Directorate of Tactical Investigation to examine tactical devel-opments and pioneered operational research to examine operational, tacti-cal, and technical questions scientifically. Nevertheless because army cul-ture rewarded loyalty over honesty and because the army leadership was so concerned about troop morale, the derivation and dissemination of accurate combat lessons remained problematic. So, adaptation was haphazard and sporadic rather than general and widespread; and though there was consid-erable change in the wartime army, much of it appears in retrospect mis-guided, even quixotic.

A combination of interwar neglect, inexperience, amateurism, and a lack of honest self-criticism led to a British approach that one could charac-terize as muddling through. Many sincere efforts at reform failed because the army proved both unable and unwilling to assess accurately, and then vigorously address, its underlying problems. Lack of holistic doctrine fueled doctrinal inconsistency, even on occasions schizophrenia, and com-partmentalized military thought and adaptation. By 1944 the army had made limited progress toward a comprehensive, realistic combined-arms doctrine, tinkering with various doctrines, but little substantive improve-ment had materialized. Inadequate doctrine seriously hampered reform and explains why the army experienced such difficulty refining and improving its tactics, training, coordination, organization, and force structure. For without definitive and realistic doctrine, it proved very difficult to structure, organize, equip, and train the army appropriately.

The army's reluctance to open itself to honest, rigorous self-appraisal, partly justified by morale concerns, further slowed the pace of reform. A military institution that is unwilling to examine its problems cannot rectify them. Class concerns also left senior officers reluctant to listen to advice from the rank and file. Therefore, bottom-up innovation, the fastest and most effective method of adaptation, was less widespread in the British Army than in the U.S. and German Armies. Class differences hampered efforts to improve coordination as socially exclusive ex-cavalry armor units disdained cooperation with all except the Guards, the Greenjackets (the Rifle Brigade), and the Royal Horse Artillery, for example.[230] Moreover, hierarchical army culture so elevated senior officers in stature that it vitiated criticism and ensured that any criticism in after-action reports was euphemistic and diluted. Regimentalism too hampered development of combined-arms coordination and uniform training. And deeply ingrained regimental attitudes that were at the core of army culture could not be easily or quickly modified by initiatives from the top.

Armies reflect their societies. The British Army's approach to reform reflected broader characteristics, values, and attitudes of British society. That the army innovated from the top down reflected the influence of class in British society. In the first four years of the war, the army proved slow both to identify and then to disseminate lessons-learned experience, which hobbled its ability to adapt and innovate at more than an incremental pace.

Notes

1. The common British military aphorism "reinforce success, retreat from failure" illuminates this unwillingness to learn from mistakes.

2. The BEF in September 1939 was clearly less well prepared for war than its August 1914 predecessor. See David Fraser, *And We Shall Shock Them: The British Army in the Second World War* (London: Hodder & Stoughton, 1983), chap. 1.

3. The BEF deployed one antitank gun per 180 meters of front. Jonathon B. A. Bailey, *Field Artillery and Firepower* (Oxford: Military Press, 1989), 168.

4. The War Office dispatched only one artillery battery and one tank troop to Norway. On the campaign, see T. K. Derry, *The Campaign in Norway* (London: HMSO, 1952); and Earl F. Ziemke, *The German Northern Theater of Operations, 1940–1945* (Washington, D.C.: Center of Military History, 1989).

5. Lt. Gen. H. R. S. Massy, *Operations in Central Norway* (London: HMSO, 1946), 7–13.

6. For strength comparisons see L. F. Ellis, *The War in France & Flanders* (London: HMSO, 1953), 358–369; and R. H. S. Stolfi, "Equipment for Victory in France in 1940," *History* (1970).

7. On 10 May 1940 the BEF fielded 350 tanks. Ellis, *France & Flanders,* 358–369.

8. Robert Doughty, *The Breaking Point: Sedan and the Fall of France, 1940* (Hamden, Conn.: Archon Books, 1990).

9. Only two infantry battalions and seventy-four tanks participated in the Arras counterattack, which did, however, aid in the extrication of the BEF. Col. H. C. B. Rogers, "Arras 1940," in *Hitler's Panzers* (London: Marshall Cavendish, 1974), 5–11.

10. After Dunkirk six British divisions continued the fight south of the Somme. Basil Karslake, *1940, The Last Act: The Story of the British Forces in France after Dunkirk* (Hamden, Conn: Archon Books, 1979).

11. Bailey, *Firepower,* 167–171.

12. On 14 May alone, the AASF lost forty of seventy-one Fairey Battles during desperate attacks on the German Meuse bridgehead. Richard P. Hallion, *Strike from the Sky: The History of Battlefield Air Attack, 1911–1945* (Washington, D.C.: Smithsonian Institute Press, 1989), 142–145; W. A. Jacobs, "Air Support for the British Army, 1939–43," *Military Affairs* 46, 4 (December 1982), 174–182.

13. The War Office study on Norway contained only one page of lessons and failed to identify any of the major causes of defeat. National Archives of Canada, Record Group 24, 12304, 3/Norway/1 *British Operations in Norway, April–June 1940* (London: War Office, July 1940).

14. Robert H. Larson, *The British Army & the Theory of Armoured Warfare, 1918–40* (Newark: University of Delaware Press, 1984), chap. 8; Norman Gibbs, "British Strategic Doctrine, 1918–1939," in Michael Howard, ed., *The Theory and Practice of War* (London: Cassell, 1965), 185–212.

15. Brig. R. G. S. Bidwell, "The Development of British Field Artillery Tactics, 1940–1943," *Royal Artillery Journal* 95, 1 (March 1968), 2.

16. On poor French morale, see Alistair Horne, *To Lose A Battle* (London: Macmillan, 1969).

17. "New Model Army" drew parallels to the Parliamentary Army created in 1645. Mark Kishlansky, *The Rise of the New Model Army* (Cambridge: Cambridge University Press, 1979).

18. During the summer of 1940 alone the army raised 120 new infantry battalions. Fraser, *Shock Them,* 84.

19. MacCleod G. Ross, *The Business of Tanks* (Ilfracoombe: Arthur H. Stockwell, 1976), 75–77.

20. PRO CAB 44/264, 4; Fraser, *Shock Them,* chaps. 4–5.

21. Larson, *Armored Warfare,* 238.

22. In the same period ten Commonwealth divisions fought in the Mediterranean. H. F. Joslen, *Orders of Battle: United Kingdom & Colonial Formations & Units in the Second World War, 1939–1945* (London: HMSO, 1960) 2 vols., passim.

23. Percy Hobart, an armored warfare pioneer, had trained the 7th Armoured. Kenneth Macksey, *Armoured Crusader: General Sir Percy Hobart* (London: Hutchinson, 1967); Maj. Gen. G. L. Verney, *The Desert Rats* (London: Hutchinson, 1954); Robin Neillands, *The Desert Rats* (London: Weidenfeld & Nicolson, 1991), chaps. 1–4.

24. Wavell was a progressive and perceptive advocate of armor, who possessed broad vision, and who tried to rehabilitate the infantry through realistic training, improved mobility, and modern weaponry. Good biographies of him include Ronald Lewin, *The Chief: Field Marshall Lord Wavell, Commander-in-Chief and Viceroy, 1939–1947* (London: Hutchinson, 1980); Michael Carver, *Wavell and the War in the Middle East 1940–41* (Austin: University of Texas at Austin Press,

1993);. Harold E. Raugh Jr, *Wavell in the Middle East: A Study in Generalship* (London: Brassey's, 1993).

25. John Baynes, *The Forgotten Victor: General Sir Richard O'Connor KT, GCB, DSO, MC* (London: Brassey's, 1989).

26. National Archives Record Administration, Washington D.C., RG 165, 2017-744/20, U.S. Mil. Intel. Div., War Department General Staff, Military Attache Report Egypt, "Training Exercise, Western Desert," 7 December 1940, 4.

27. The WDF comprised the 7th Armoured and 4th Indian Divisions and totalled 31,000 troops, 275 tanks, 120 artillery pieces, and 205 aircraft. The Italians fielded 7 weak divisions, 275 tanks, and 11 artillery batteries. Maj. Gen. I. S. O. Playfair et al., *The Mediterranean and Middle East* (London: HMSO, 1954) I, chap. 14.

28. NARA RG 165, U.S. MID, War Dept General Staff, Military Attache Report BES-134, "British Campaign in the Western Desert," 1 May 1941; PRO WO 169/6-9, WD GHQ MEC, Spring 1941; Playfair, *Mediterranean* I, 274–362; W. G. F. Jackson, *The North African Campaign, 1940–43* (New York: Madson, 1975), chap. 1; Kenneth Macksey, *Beda Fomm* (New York: Ballantine, 1971); John Strawson, *The Battle for North Africa* (New York: Bonanza Books, 1969), chaps. 2–3; Fraser, *Shock Them,* 113–126.

29. At a cost of 1,938 casualties the WDF took 130,000 POWs, 380 tanks, and 845 guns. On the Italian officer corps lack of professionalism, see Macgregor Knox, *Mussolini Unleashed, 1939–1941: Politics and Strategy in Fascist Italy's Last War* (New York: Cambridge University Press, 1982); Field Marshal Lord Michael Carver, *The Apostles of Mobility: The Theory and Practice of Armoured Warfare* (London: Holmes & Meier, 1979), 69–70; Playfair, *Mediterranean* I, 274–362.

30. In December 1940 the Italians estimated British strength in Egypt at sixteen divisions. Hans Otto Behrendt, *Rommel's Intelligence in the Desert Campaign, 1941–43* (London: W. Kimber, 1985), 24–26.

31. The WDAF fielded only one fighter and two bomber squadrons. Raugh, *Wavell,* 123–124; Playfair, *Mediterranean* I, 266–272.

32. The 4th Indian Division massed fire from seventy-two guns in fifteen-minute quick fire plans that used aerial reconnaissance for registration. Playfair, *Mediterranean* I, 267; Bidwell, "Field Artillery Tactics, 1940–42," 82–93.

33. PRO WO 169/9, MEC, *Training Pamphlet* 10 (1941) Pt. III, 640.

34. Bailey, *Firepower,* 171.

35. Playfair, *Mediterranean* II, chap. 5; F. H. Hinsley, *British Intelligence in the Second World War* (London: HMSO, 1978) I, 409; Martin van Creveld, "Prelude to Disaster: The British Decision to Aid Greece, 1940–41," *JCH* 9 (1974), 78–79; Robin Higham, "British Intervention in Greece, 1940–41: the Anatomy of a Grand Deception," *Balkan Studies* 23 (1982), 111.

36. PRO WO 210/72, Lt. Gen. Sir H. M. Wilson, "Rpt. on Ops. in Greece," 5 May 1941; Playfair, *Mediterranean,* II, chap. 5.

37. PRO WO 201/99, MEC, "Report by the Inter-Services Committee on Crete and Ops. in Crete," 2 July 41; Playfair, *Mediterranean* II, Chap. 7; Ian M. G. Stewart, *The Struggle for Crete, 20 May–1 June 1941* (London: Oxford University Press, 1966); Fraser, *Shock Them,* 138–147.

38. PRO WO 169/924, WD MEC GS (I) Feb. 1941, apdx. 25, "German Intentions in Southeast Europe and North Africa," 17 February 1941 and apdx. 37, "Weekly Review of the Military Situation," 24 February 1941; PRO F[oreign] O[ffice] 371/27549, "German Forces in Tripolitania," 20 March 1941.

39. Playfair, *Mediterranean* II, chap. 8.

40. Raugh, *Wavell,* 204–206.

41. War Office, *The Tactical Handling of Armoured Forces* (London: 1941) governed British operations in the desert. For a description of British armored action in North Africa, see Robert Crisp, *Brazen Chariots: An Account of Tank Warfare* (New York: Bantam, 1960).

42. For example, the 23rd Armoured Brigade lost 83 percent of its armor on 22 July 1942 during the First Battle of El Alamein. Bryan Perrett, *Through Mud and Blood: Infantry/Tank Operations in World War Two* (London: Robert Hale, 1975), 108–110.

43. Initially British troops rarely used code words and even when they did they provided but a thin disguise. "Capital of England," for example, barely camouflaged references to London. Behrendt, *Rommel's Intelligence,* chap. 4.

44. Dispersion was also a legacy of the passive air defense techniques introduced in 1940 after the debacle in France to limit the impact of German air power. Bailey, *Firepower,* 178–180.

45. Weeks, *Men Against Tanks: A History of Antitank Warfare* (New York: Mason/Charter, 1975), 87–88.

46. Bailey, *Firepower,* 178–180.

47. During the Battle of Gazala, for example, the Germans overran and destroyed sixty-four guns. Playfair, *Mediterranean* III, chap. 10.

48. The only examples of fire planning were several brigade actions by the XIII Corps during Operation BREVITY. Bailey, *Firepower,* 178–180; Bidwell, "Field Artillery Tactics, 1940–42," 87–88.

49. Only two infantry battalions supported six tank battalions. Joslen, *Orders of Battle.*

50. A Jock Column typically comprised a tank squadron, a 25-pounder battery, an antitank and antiaircraft gun troop, and a motorized infantry company. They were named after Maj. Gen. "Jock" Campbell VC who first used them during CRUSADER. Contemporaries often overstated their value: they were too small and were employed piecemeal too often to do more than harass the enemy. On their usefulness, see Playfair, *Mediterranean* III, 254.

51. Ronald Lewin, *Churchill as Warlord* (New York: Stein and Day, 1982; Scarborough Books, 1982), 76; Fraser, *Shock Them,* 155.

52. Larson, *Armored Warfare,* 239.

53. That Churchill put excessive faith in the impact of his "Tiger Cubs" (the Crusaders) illustrates how pervasive the panzer myth mentality had become. Playfair, *Mediterranean* II, chap. 1.

54. The British suffered 969 casualties during BATTLEAXE and lost 91 tanks. German losses were 585 troops and 12 tanks. PRO WO 201/357, MEC, "Rpt. on the Battle of Capuzzo, 15–17.6.1941," 6 August 1941; Corelli Barnett, *The Desert Generals* (New York: Viking, 1961), 67–75; Jackson, *North Africa,* 155–167; Playfair, *Mediterranean* II, 163–171.

55. The lack of suitable tactical strike aircraft reflected the prevalent prewar notion that only specialized attack planes could provide effective tactical support. The American Brewster Bermuda and Vultee Vengeance purchased during 1940–1941 proved failures. In March 1941, tactical aviation averaged a mere fourteen sorties daily in North Africa. Owen Thetford, *Aircraft of the RAF Since 1918* (London: 1970), 531–532, 562; Bailey, *Firepower,* 183.

56. PRO WO 169/924, WD MEC May 1941, *Rpt. on BATTLEAXE;* Raugh, *Wavell,* 236.

57. PRO WO 169/924, WD MEC May 1941, *Rpt. on BATTLEAXE;* Playfair, *Mediterranean* I, 172–173.

58. Jacobs, "Air Support," 177.

59. PRO WO 169/924, WD MEC Oct. 1941, apdx. 10, Army & RAF Joint Middle East Training Pamphlet 3, *Direct Air Support* (September 1941); Playfair, *Mediterranean* II, 287–296; Vincent Orange, *Coningham: A Biography of Air Marshal Sir Arthur Coningham* (Washington, D.C.: Center for Air Force History, 1992), chap. 7.

60. The aircraft strength of MEAF increased from 549 in June 1941 to 846 in October. Playfair, *Mediterranean* II, 289–290.

61. John Connell [John H. Robertson], *Auchinleck* (London: Cassell, 1959); Philip Warner, *Auchinleck: The Lonely Soldier* (London: Sphere Books, 1982).

62. Playfair, *Mediterranean* III, 3–5, 15.

63. During summer 1941 the Axis lost 20 percent of the supplies dispatched to North Africa. In November this figure jumped to 62 percent but declined to 18 percent in December. Playfair, *Mediterranean* II, chap. 14; III, chap. 4.

64. Playfair, *Mediterranean* III, 38.

65. On 21 November the 6th Royal Tank Regiment lost 75 percent of its armor on a German gun line. Loss ratios in direct tank-to-tank battles during CRUSADER ranged from 3:1 to 6:1 in the Axis's favor. Playfair, *Mediterranean* III, chaps. 2–3.

66. The 22d Armoured Brigade attacked the Italian Ariete Division supported by a single RHA battery, which provided only observed fire. Playfair, *Mediterranean* III, 43–100.

67. Throughout the war, the British underestimated the valuable intelligence the enemy gained from intercepted radio communications. Ibid., 35–37; Behrendt, *Rommel's Intelligence,* chap. 6.

68. Playfair, *Mediterranean* III, 98–99.

69. Extensive Axis use of captured British vehicles further complicated identification, as did the army's reluctance to paint distinctive air recognition signs on vehicles. Playfair, *Mediterranean* III, 35–51.

70. Richard Humble, *CRUSADER: Eighth Army's Forgotten Victory, November 1941–January 1942* (London: Cooper, 1987); John Sandars, *Operation CRUSADER* (London: Altmark Publishing, 1976); Barnett, *Desert Generals,* 90–114; Jackson, *North Africa,* 180–229.

71. Playfair, *Mediterranean* III, 49–50.

72. Bidwell, "British Artillery Tactics, 1940–42," 92.

73. Eighth Army suffered 1,390 casualties and lost seventy-two tanks in the retreat to Gazala. Playfair, *Mediterranean* III, chap. 6.

74. Playfair, *Mediterranean* III, 207–209, 254, 312–314.

75. Axis forces lost 200 tanks on 26 May, their heaviest single day's losses in the desert. Ibid., chap. 10.

76. The 32nd Tank Brigade lost 75 percent of its armor. Ibid., 231–234.

77. Ibid., 236–242.

78. At a cost of 2,490 casualties Rommel took 33,000 prisoners. Ibid., 274.

79. Ibid., 335–336.

80. PRO CAB 106/121, "Morale," 31.

81. In the Far East, marginally more numerous Japanese forces rapidly overran Malaya and Singapore against inadequately trained, badly led, ill-equipped, dispirited, and ill-prepared British forces. Both strategic overstretch and racial prejudice contributed to the debacle. Ivan Simson, *Singapore: Too Little, Too Late* (London: L. Cooper, 1970); Paul Haggie, *Britannia at Bay: The Defence of the British Empire Against Japan 1931–41* (Oxford: Clarendon Press, 1981); S[tanley] W. Kirby, *The Loss of Singapore* (London: HMSO, 1957), and *Singapore: The Chain of Disaster* (London: Cassell, 1971).

82. Poor discipline, high absence-without-leave, and desertion rates signified

bad morale. Morale dropped so alarmingly during 1940–1942 that the War Office set up the Morale Committee to evaluate its causes and offer remedies. PRO WO 106/121, "Morale."

83. Ultra initially proved of limited help to the Allies in North Africa. Only after mid-1942 did it bring frequent interception of Axis resupply convoys and the slow strangulation of German logistics. Ronald Lewin, *Ultra Goes to War* (London: Hutchinson, 1978) and Ralph F. Bennett, *Ultra and the Mediterranean Strategy, 1941–45* (New York: Viking Penguin, 1989).

84. Bailey, *Firepower,* 171.

85. The Desert Air Force averaged 570 sorties daily during July 1942. Playfair, *Mediterranean* III, 335.

86. The battle also saw the first widespread German use of antitank mines, which added another powerful defensive counter to British armor. Playfair, *Mediterranean* III, 346–359.

87. Shelford Bidwell and Dominick Graham, *Firepower: British Army Weapons and Theories of War 1904–1945* (London: Allen & Unwin, 1982), 232–233.

88. Scheduled to serve as Eisenhower's deputy for Operation TORCH, the death of the new British Eighth Army Commander, G. C. Gott, led to Montgomery's being sent to Egypt. Martin Blumenson, *The Battle of the Generals: The Untold Story of the Falaise Pocket* (New York: William Morrow, 1993), chap. 1.

89. PRO CAB 106/703, "Montgomery's Address to Officers of HQ Eighth Army," 13 September 1942; Francis W. de Guingand *Operation Victory* (London: Hodder & Stoughton, 1947), 137–138.

90. He set out his guiding principles in his address to the Middle East Staff College, Haifa, on 21 September 1942. Stephen Brooks, ed., *Montgomery and the Eighth Army: A Selection from the Diaries, Correspondence, and Other Papers of Field Marshal The Viscount Montgomery of Alamein, August 1942–December 1943* (London: The Army Records Society, 1991), 47–61.

91. "Montgomery's Address to the Middle East Staff College, Haifa," 21 September 1942, in Brooks, ed., *Montgomery,* 47–61.

92. Ibid., paras. 15–19, 25.

93. Imperial War Museum, Montgomery Papers (IWM MP) BLM 27/1, "Situation in August 1942," [October 1942], paras. 3–4; PRO CAB 106/703, Montgomery's Address to Officers HQ Eighth Army, 13 August 1942., para. 6.

94. For his views on air power, see PRO WO 219/223, BLM, *Some Notes on the Use of Air Power in Support of Land Operations* (Holland: TFAG, Dec. 1944).

95. Stephen Hart, *Montgomery and "Colossal Cracks": The 21st Army Group in Northwest Europe, 1944–45* (Westport, Conn.: Praeger, 2000), chap. 2.

96. Montgomery received on 17 September a decrypt of the German 15 September attack plan. Hinsley, *British Intelligence in the Second World War* II, 408.

97. The armor loss ratio in the battle, 2:3 (Axis:British), was the lowest yet seen in the desert. Playfair, *Mediterranean* III, 388–397.

98. Hart, *Montgomery,* chap. 2.

99. On 3 September 1942 the Desert Air Force set a new record with 957 sorties. PRO CAB 104/403, "Battle of Munassib: Notes by Cmdr. Eighth Army," 7 September 1942; Nigel Hamilton, *Monty: The Making of a General 1887–1942* (London: H. Hamilton, 1982), 674–711.

100. Bidwell, "Development of Field Artillery Tactics, 1940–42," 89.

101. "Address to the Staff College," paras. 10, 20.

102. IWM MP BLM 28/5, "LIGHTFOOT Army Cmdr. Memo 2," 6 October 1942, para. 17.

103. Field, medium, and heavy artillery fired 102, 133, and 157 rounds per gun, respectively. Playfair, *Mediterranean* IV, 35.

104. Playfair, *Mediterranean* IV, chap. 1.

105. Eighth Army Training Memorandum 1 (31 August 1942); Perrett, *Mud and Blood,* 122–123; Playfair, *Mediterranean* IV, 13–18.

106. IWM MP, BLM 28/4, "LIGHTFOOT Memo 1 by Army Commander," 28 September 1942; BLM 28/5, "LIGHTFOOT Memo 2 by Army Commander," 6 October 1942; Bernard L. Montgomery, *Memoirs* (London: Collins, 1958), 121–122; Charles Cruickshank, *Deception in World War II* (Oxford: University Press, 1979), 26–33.

107. IWM MP BLM 28/5, "LIGHTFOOT Army Cmdr. Memo 2," 6 October 1942, paras 11–12.

108. The Eighth Army outnumbered the Axis 2:1 in troops; 5:2 in armor; 5:4 in aircraft; 3:2 in artillery; and 7:4 in antitank guns. Montgomery employed 24 Matilda Scorpion flail tanks in the attack. IWM, MP BLM 28/3, "LIGHTFOOT: General Plan of Eighth Army," 14 September 1942; Playfair, *Mediterranean* IV, chap. 1.

109. Montgomery, Diary Notes, "Opening of the Battle of El Alamein, 23–24 October 1942," in Brooks, ed., *Montgomery,* 71–75.

110. IWM MP BLM 28/1, "Montgomery Diary Notes, "The Battle of Egypt, 23 October–7 November 1942," para. 2.

111. Montgomery overestimated the efficacy of the counterbattery program, which he believed played a great part in victory. Liddell Hart Centre for Military Archives, Kings College, London (LHCMA) Alanbrooke Papers (AP) 6/2/21, Ltr., Montgomery to Brooke, 10 November 1942.

112. Bidwell, "Field Artillery Tactics, 1940–42," 93.

113. Rommel had an eleven-day supply of fuel and a nine-day supply of ammunition. In October 1942 the Allies sank 44 percent of Axis supplies sent to North Africa. Playfair, *Mediterranean* IV, 25–27.

114. The Eighth Army suffered 13,560 casualties and lost 500 tanks and 111 guns during the Second Battle for El Alamein. Ibid., 79.

115. Although Montgomery relied heavily on strategic deception for OVER-LORD, his emphasis on tactical deception declined as Allied numerical and material superiority grew. Michael Howard, *Strategic Deception in the Second World War* (London: HMSO, 1990).

116. IWM MP BLM 28/5, "LIGHTFOOT: Army Commander Memo 2," 6 October 1942, para. 10.

117. The "portee" mounted the 2-pounder on the back of a truck. It gave increased mobility, but it was so vulnerable that it was withdrawn from service in December 1942. Bailey, *Firepower,* 173.

118. When German armor isolated the the 2d Battalion of the Rifle Brigade during LIGHTFOOT, its 6-pounders destroyed thirty-two tanks. Playfair, *Mediterranean* IV, 56.

119. "Battlefield interdiction" was "direct support" in British parlance. U.S. tactical air support doctrine emphasized the former more than close air support. British doctrine advocated balance between both. Hallion, *Strike,* 149–162.

120. Montgomery, played an important role in the genesis of air-ground coordination because he favored air force control and believed that the massed use of air power in support of the ground battle was a battle winning formula. PRO WO 219/223, BLM, *Some Notes on the Use of Air Power in Support of Land Operations*

(Holland: TFAG, December 1944); Orange, *Coningham,* chaps. 8–9; Jacobs, "Air Support," 178–181.

121. IWM MP BLM 52/3-6, *Some Brief Notes for Senior Officers on the Conduct of Battle* (December 1942).

122. IWM MP BLM 52/3–6, *Some Brief Notes for Senior Officers on the Conduct of Battle* (December 1942) and *Some Notes on High Command in War* (January 1943). He issued his "Main Lessons of the Battle [of Alam Haifa]" on the last day of the battle, 7 September 1942. Brooks, ed., *Montgomery,* 30–33.

123. Brooks, ed., *Montgomery,* 6.

124. Lt. Gen. Sir Brian Horrocks, *A Full Life* (London: Collins, 1960), 126.

125. Montgomery, "Tripoli Tactical Talks," 15–17 February 1943, in Brooks, ed., *Montgomery,* 139–140.

126. *Current Reports on Operations* 10 (London: War Office, 7 August 1943), 3–4.

127. Playfair, *Mediterranean* IV, chap. 4; Montgomery, *Memoirs,* 140.

128. On the Agheila battle, see William G. Stevens, *Bardia to Enfidaville* (Wellington: War History Branch, Department of Internal Affairs, 1962), 57–58; Playfair, *Mediterranean* IV, chap. 9.

129. IWM MP BLM 49/14, letter, Montgomery to Brooke, 12 January 1943; Playfair, *Mediterranean* IV, 229–230.

130. Brig. R. G. S. Bidwell, "The Development of British Field Artillery Tactics, 1940–1943," *Royal Artillery Journal* 95, 1 (Mar. 1968), 1–13.

131. The Germans lost fifty tanks in one of their worse defeats in the desert. Playfair, *Mediterranean* IV, 325–326.

132. Churchill proclaimed on 15 October 1940: "We cannot hope to compete with the enemy in numbers of men, we must therefore rely on an exceptional proportion of armored fighting vehicles." Winston Churchill, *Their Finest Hour* (London: Cassell, 1949), 462.

133. The 1942 mixed division, which traded an infantry brigade for an armored brigade, aimed to enhance coordination, but entrenched regimentalism ensured that the experiment failed. The army's tinkering with organization reflected a misguided effort to rectify more fundamental problems and Montgomery, for one, vehemently opposed the mixed-division concept. IWM MP BLM 49/14, letter, Montgomery to Brooke, 12 January 1943.

134. Brig. R. G. S. Bidwell, "The Development of British Field Artillery Tactics, 1920–1939: Reform and Reorganization," *Journal of the Royal Artillery* 94 (1967), 13–24.

135. Bidwell, "Field Artillery Tactics, 1940–1943," 1–12.

136. Response times for a divisional barrage fell from 12 hours in 1939 to only a few minutes by 1943. Jonathon Bailey, *Field Artillery and Firepower* (Oxford: The Military Press, 1989), 184–186.

137. Bidwell, "Field Artillery Tactics, 1940–43," 2–4.

138. Maj. Gen. H. J. Parham and E. M. G. Belfield, *Unarmed into Battle: The Story of the Air Observation Post* (Winchester: Warren & Son, 1956), chaps. 1–3.

139. Fraser, *Shock Them!* 93; Brian Bond and Williamson Murray, "British Military Effectiveness in the Second World War," in Williamson Murray and Allan R. Millett, eds., *Military Effectiveness* (Boston: Unwin Hyman, 1988) III, 128.

140. David A. Wilson, "The Development of Tank-Infantry Co-Operation Doctrine in the Canadian Army for the Normandy Campaign of 1944," M.A. thesis, University of New Brunswick, 1992, 80–86.

141. Particularly dubious improvisations included the Sticky Bomb (No. 74 Grenade), the Self Igniting Phosphorous Grenade, the Northover Projector, the

29mm Blacker Bombard Spigot Mortar, and the Smith Gun. John Weeks, *Men Against Tanks: A History of Antitank Warfare* (New York: Mason-Charter, 1975), 38–50.

142. PRO CAB 106/1121, *Training,* 32. For discussion of the Royal Artillery's flexible training, see Shelford Bidwell, *Gunners at War: A Tactical Study of the Royal Artillery in the Twentieth Century* (London: Arrow Books, 1972).

143. Gen. Sir William Morgan, "The Revival of Battledrill in World War II," *Army Quarterly* 104 (October 1973), 57; Col. E. M. K. Macgregor, "In Defence of Battledrill," *Canadian Defence Quarterly* 1, 4 (Spring 1942), 29.

144. Creeping barrages demanded that infantry follow at a set pace that could not be maintained while implementing battledrill techniques. Wilson, "Tank-Infantry Co-Operation Doctrine," 83–86.

145. This equation of armor with firepower and infantry with maneuverability directly contradicted the organization of the armored division where infantry provided firepower and armor maneuverability. Wilson, "Tank-Infantry Co-Operation Doctrine," 84–86.

146. After 22 to 42 weeks basic and branch training, recruits had theoretically only gained "a fair grounding" in their duties and only then did they progress to 5 to 6 weeks of section training. For Montgomery's criticism of training, see his "Address to the Middle East Staff College, Haifa, 21 September 1942" in Stephen Brooks, ed., *Montgomery and the Eighth Army* (London: Bodley Head, 1991), 55–61.

147. PRO CAB 106/1121, *Training,* 15–16.

148. David Fletcher, *The Great Tank Scandal* (London: HMSO, 1988).

149. General Paget concluded that the armored corps deployed in SPARTAN had "exerted little or no influence on the course of operations." Poor coordination led to a mapboard "annihilation" of an entire armored brigade. PRO CAB 44/264, 10–25 and 59–60; WO 199/234, *Lessons of Operation SPARTAN.*

150. John Masefield, *Gallipoli* (London: Heinemann, 1916).

151. Britain conducted only four interwar amphibious exercises, and the Royal Marines remained dispersed in small shipborne units and guarding bases. Kenneth J. Clifford, *Amphibious Warfare Development in Britain and America from 1920–1940* (Laurens, N.Y.: Edgewood, 1983); Bernhard Fergusson, *The Watery Maze: The Story of Combined Operations* (New York: Holt, Rinehart & Winston, 1961); Allan R. Millett, "Assault from the Sea, the Development of Amphibious Warfare Between the Wars: the American, British, and Japanese Experiences," in Allan R. Millett & Williamson Murray, eds., *Military Innovation in the Interwar Period* (Washington, D.C.: Office of Net Assessment, DOD, 1994), 67–143; Donald F. Bittner, "Britannia's Sheathed Sword: The Royal Marines and Amphibious Warfare in the Interwar Years—A Passive Response," *Journal of Military History* 55 (July 1991), 345–364.

152. War Office, *Lessons of Dieppe* (London: 1943).

153. These included the Sherman mine-flailing Crab, Churchill engineer AVRE, and Churchill Crocodile flamethrower. Geoffrey W. Futter, *The Funnies: The 79th Armoured Division and Its Specialized Equipment* (Hemel Hempstead; Model & Allied Publications, 1974); Nigel W. Duncan, *The 79th Armoured Division (Hobo's Funnies)* (Windsor: Profile Publications, 1972); David Fletcher, *Vanguard of Victory: The 79th Armoured Division* (London: HMSO, 1984).

154. See Montgomery's complaints on this issue. LHCMA, AP 14/62, letter, Montgomery to Alan Brooke, 23 February 1943.

155. Gregory Blaxland, *The Plain Cook and the Great Showman: The First and Eighth Armies in North Africa* (London: Kimber, 1977), 83.

156. Capt. William Gessner, "TORCH: Unlearned Logistics Lessons." *Army Logistician* 15 (November–December 1983), 28–32.

157. The 2d Parachute Battalion suffered over 60 percent losses during the drop on Depienne on 29 November. Blaxland, *Cook and Showman,* 99–115.

158. The Germans defeated the 6th Royal West Kent Regiment and 6 Commando at Ajred Djebel and Azag Djebel (28–29 November), inflicted a "nasty setback" on the 11th Brigade at Tebourba (29 November–3 December), and mauled the 2d/5th Battalion, Leicestershire Regiment at Thala (21 January). Blaxland, *Plain Cook,* 115–129 and 162–164.

159. For example, the two troops of 99 Medium Battery, RA, still operated 40 miles apart in March 1943. Bidwell, "British Artillery Tactics, 1940–43," 11.

160. Playfair, *Mediterranean* IV, 308.

161. Parham and Belfield, *Unarmed,* chap. 5.

162. Thus it was not before January 1943 that serviceability rates rose to acceptable levels. Playfair, *Mediterranean* IV, 309–310.

163. Ibid. IV, chaps. 13–14.

164. Parham, *Unarmed,* 38; Blaxland, *Cook & Showman,* 152–153.

165. Playfair, *Mediterranean* IV, 312–313.

166. Bidwell, "British Artillery Tactics, 1940–43," 7–8.

167. Some 652 guns fired 368 rounds per gun. John Terraine, "Indirect Fire as a Battle Winner/Loser," in Corelli Barnett et al., eds., *Old Battles and New Defences: Can We Learn from Military History?* (London: Brassey's, 1986), 27–30.

168. Wesley F. Craven and James L. Cate, *The Army Air Forces in WWII* (Chicago: University of Chicago, 1951) II, 153–161; Playfair, *Mediterranean* IV, chap. 11.

169. Playfair, *Mediterranean* IV, 310–311; Vincent Orange, *Coningham: A Biography of Air Marshal Sir Arthur Coningham* (Washington, D.C.: Center for Air Force History, 1992), chaps. 10–11.

170. Playfair, *Mediterranean* IV, 307–313.

171. PRO WO 231/10, Directorate of Military Training, *Lessons from the Tunisian Campaign* (London: War Office, July 1943).

172. The 17-pounder weighed 2.5 tons and required a 3-ton truck to pull it. Its mobility problem was overcome by placing it in an self-propelled mount, the Valentine, which entered production in 1944. In Normandy in 1944 17-pounder guns fired on average only once every three days. Weeks, *Men Against Tanks,* 88–89; Max Hastings, *OVERLORD* (London: 1984), appendix.

173. The War Office concluded on the basis of exercises that the prospects of destroying enemy armor with the PIAT were "slim." PRO WO 291/153, AORG, "The Effectiveness of PIAT Shooting" [1944].

174. It was only after crippling tank losses in North Africa that the War Office finally developed tank destroyers and the first of these, the Archer, joined U.S. M10s in British armored divisions during spring 1944. Weeks, *Men Against Tanks,* 29–50, 74–91.

175. Playfair, *Mediterranean* IV, 404–405.

176. Cate and Craven, *Army Air Forces* III, 428; Solly Zuckerman, *From Apes to Warlords: the Autobiography of Solly Zuckermann* (London: H. Hamilton, 1978), chap. 10; Arthur Tedder, *With Prejudice: The War Memoirs of Lord Tedder GCB* (Boston: Little, Brown, 1966), 440–444.

177. Air Ministry, *The Rise and Fall of the German Air Force* (London: Air Ministry, 1948), 260–261.

178. The brigade suffered 23.5 percent casualties. Samuel W. Mitchum, Jr., and Friedrich von Stauffenberg, *The Battle for Sicily: How the Allies Lost Their*

Chance for Total Victory (New York: Orion Books, 1991), 85; Carlo D'Este, *Bitter Victory: The Battle for Sicily, July–August 1943* (New York: Collins, 1988).

179. Hew Strachan, *European Armies and the Conduct of War* (London: Allen & Unwin, 1983), 180–181.

180. Parham and Belfield, *Unarmed*, 44.

181. Eric Morris, *Salerno: A Military Fiasco* (New York: Stein and Day, 1985).

182. In the first month at Anzio spotters flew 244 sorties, conducted 104 shoots, and directed 90 percent of all naval and 70 percent of ground artillery barrages. Parham and Belfield, *Unarmed*, 54–56; Carlo D'Este, *Fatal Decision: Anzio and the Battle for Rome* (New York: HarperCollins, 1991).

183. "If a cabbage gets in your way, blast it away," was the War Office's lead conclusion from the Tunisian Campaign. War Office, *Lessons Learnt from the Tunisian Campaign* (London: HMSO, July 1943), 1. On 22 January 1944, at Anzio, the 56th Division fired twenty defensive fire missions alone and in the Liri Valley in May it took just 35 minutes for 668 guns to fire 3,500 rounds against a single target. Bailey, *Field Artillery*, 190–192.

184. PRO CAB 106/1121, 31–32.

185. PRO WO 232/41, DTI, *The Tactical Handling of the Armoured Division and Its Component Parts* (London: War Office, November 1943).

186. For the CIGS's fears, see David Fraser, *Alanbrooke* (London: Collins, 1982), 422–423.

187. Emphasis in original. National Archives of Canada, Crerar Papers, vol. 7, letter, Montgomery to Crerar, 9 January 1943.

188. A case in point was an after-action report of a botched attack that was not published on the grounds that nothing could be learned from failure. IWM, Imd. Rpt. 102, "Attack by the Leicesters on 29 Sept. 1944," 5 October 1944.

189. In February 1943 Montgomery wrote: "The Army in England has got to be got ready for battle." Letter, Montgomery to Alan Brooke, in Brooks, ed., *Montgomery*, 136; Stephen Brooks, "Montgomery and the Preparations for OVERLORD," *History Today* (June 1984), 18–32.

190. Montgomery stated on 15 May 1944 that "we shall have to send the soldiers into battle seeing red. We must get them completely on their toes; having absolute faith in the plan; and imbued with infectious optimism and offensive eagerness. Nothing must stop them. If we send them into battle in this way—then we will succeed." PRO CAB 44/264, 176.

191. On his operational concepts, see Bernard L. Montgomery, *High Command in War* (War Office: Army Training Manual, June 1945); IWM MP BLM 156 "Some Notes on the Conduct of War and the Infantry Division in Battle"; BLM 158 "The Armoured Division in Battle"; BLM 160 "Modern Administration in the Field in European Warfare"; BLM 161 "Morale in Battle: Analysis." See also Hart, *Montgomery*, Chaps. 1–4.

192. Carlo D'Este has argued that Montgomery intended an equal British offensive role and that the strategy that did emerge was by default. But Montgomery clearly enunciated a subordinate British role at OVERLORD planning conferences. PRO AIR 37/784, Leigh-Mallory, "Impressions of the Meeting held at St Paul's School"; PRO WO 205/118, TFAG G(Plans), "Appreciation of the Possible Development of Ops. to Secure a Lodgement Area," 8 May 1944; D' Este, *Decision*, 62, 75–79, 82–92, 99–100; Lewin, *Montgomery as Military Commander*, 183; David Irving, *The War Between the Generals* (London: Allen Lane, 1981), 99, 177; Hart, *Montgomery*, chap. 4.

193. Montgomery reiterated this strategy almost daily to his most trusted col-

leagues. See, for example, letter from Montgomery to Grigg, 2 July 1944, quoted in Irving, *Generals,* 223.

194. PRO CAB 44/264, 29–30; Futter, *The Funnies,* passim.

195. Revised doctrine still overemphasized the importance of armor. PRO WO 232/41, *Tactical Employment of the Armoured Division* (London: War Office, 1942); PRO WO 232/41 DTI, War Office, *The Tactical Handling of the Armoured Division and Its Components,* (London: Military Training Pamphlet 41, July 1943).

196. PRO WO 277/19, War Office, *Personnel Selection.*

197. Special forces included Small Scale Raiding Force, Special Boat Section, Special Boat Squadron, Special Air Service, Raiding Forces, Long Range Desert Group, Special Identification Group, Combined Operations Pilotage Parties, Royal Marine Boom Patrol Detachment, Sea Reconnaissance Unit, Special Operations Group, Popski's Private Army (No. 1 Demolition Squadron), Special Raiding Squadron, Royal Marine Force Viper, V Force, Gideon Force, Mission 101, and Special Service Regiment. William Seymour, *British Special Forces* (London: Sidgwick & Jackson, 1985); James D. Ladd, *Commandos and Rangers of World War II* (London: MacDonald & Jane's, 1978); Cecil Hampshire, *On Hazardous Service* (London: Kimber, 1974); C. E. Lucas Phillips, *Cockleshell Heroes* (London: Heinemann, 1956); G. B. Courtney, *SBS in World War Two* (London: Hale, 1983); W. B. Kennedy Shaw, *Long Range Desert Group* (London: Collins, 1945); Philip Warner, *The SAS* (London: Kimber, 1972); Barrie Pitt, *Special Boat Squadron* (London: Century, 1983).

198. That expansion took place at all was largely due to the staunch support of Sir Alan Brooke. Fraser, *Shock Them!* 84–95.

199. Special Forces were the equivalent of six divisions when Britain fielded only eighteen front-line infantry divisions. H. F. Joslen, *Orders of Battle* (London: HMSO, 1960); Seymour, *Special Forces,* 26.

200. The most valuable commando raids were the destruction of the German heavy-water production facilities in Norway that crippled their atomic weapons program, and the March 1942 St. Nazaire raid that prevented the repair of German capital ships on France's Atlantic coast. Sir Brian Paget believed that "the operations undertaken by the Commandos were largely a waste of effort, and could have been better done by a unit of the field army." PRO, CAB 44/264, apdx. 2, 3; Brig. Peter Young DSO MC, *Commando* (New York: Ballantine, 1969).

201. John Terraine "Who Bore the Brunt: What Contribution to Allied Victory did Britain's Armed Forces Really Make?" *World War Two Investigator* 1, 1 (April 1988), 22.

202. Russell Weigley, *The American Way of War* (New York: Macmillan 1973; Bloomington: Indiana University Press, 1977), chap. 14; Fraser, *Alanbrooke,* chaps. 11–18.

203. On the eve of D-Day, 38,000 trained infantry replacements were available in the United Kingdom. PRO WO 216/101, "Infantry Requirements for TFAG."

204. The War Office estimated British losses for the first three months of OVERLORD at 91,034. PRO WO 205/152, "Estimate of Casualties Operation OVERLORD," apdx. C, 12 February 1944.

205. By 1 April draftable infantry in the United Kingdom had shrunk to 11,488. PRO WO 199/1334, DA+QMG Home Forces, "Drafting Home Field Army," 27 February 1944; W0 199/1238, GSO1(SD) HF, "Examination of Drafting Figs. Now Known," 14 February 1944; WO 199/1335, DA+QMF HF, 2 May 1944.

206. Hart, *Montgomery,* chap. 3.

207. Shelford Bidwell, "Indirect Artillery Fire as a Battle Winner/Loser," in Barnett, *Old Battles New Defences,* 138–139.

208. Letter from Montgomery to Lt. Gen A. E. Nye, VCIGS, 21 December 1943, in Brooks, ed., *Montgomery,* 346.

209. John A. English, *The Canadian Army and the Normandy Campaign: A Study in the Failure of High Command* (London: Praeger, 1991), 160.

210. Montgomery's ideas, for instance, differed strikingly from War Office doctrine over armored organization and the infantry-cruiser tank distinction. Letters from Montgomery to Lt. Gen. A. E. Nye, 28.8. and 7.12.1943, and replies 7.10 and 21 December 1943 in Brooks, ed., *Montgomery,* 274–275, 342–346.

211. For expression of his operational policies, see "Address to the Middle East Staff College, Haifa," 21 September 1942; "Diary Notes on Battle of Alam Halfa, 31.08–07.09.1942"; and "Battle of Egypt, 23.10.–7.11.1942," in Brooks, ed., *Montgomery,* 30–33, 47–60, 79–82.

212. English, *Canadians,* 160; Roland Ryder, *Oliver Leese* (London: H. Hamilton, 1987), 47.

213. He summarized the tenets of his approach in his address of 20 March 1944. "Montgomery's Notes for Address to Senior Officers, Second Army, 20 March 1944," quoted in Nigel Hamilton, *Monty: Master of the Battlefield, 1942–1944* (London: H. Hamilton, 1983), 549–550.

214. GHQ Home Forces, *Doctrine for the Tactical Handling of the (New Model) Division and Armoured Division* (London: HMSO, October 1942), 3.

215. Doctrine called for armor to exploit gaps in the enemy defenses created by the infantry break-in. This emphasis on exploitation left armored formations deficient in striking power. Ibid., 1–2.

216. This was evident in that the War Office designed its *Notes from the Theatres of War* and *Current Reports from Overseas* publications primarily for Home Forces.

217. IWM MP BLM 159, *High Command in War* (Germany: TFAG, June 1945).

218. The range of Allied fighters increased from 175 miles in May 1943 (Spitfire) to 600 miles in spring 1944 (P-51 with drop tanks). Williamson Murray, *Luftwaffe* (Baltimore: Nautical & Aviation, 1985), 166–168.

219. Four attacks on Hamburg during July–August 1943 shattered the city and killed 50,000 civilians. Martin Middlebrook, *The Battle of Hamburg: Allied Bomber Forces Against a German City in 1943* (London: Allen Lane, 1980), chap. 15.

220. Loss rates for the 8th USAAF peaked in October 1943 at 26 percent for planes and 37 percent for crews. Murray, *Luftwaffe,* 162–170.

221. The officer-enlistee ratio dropped from 1:15 in 1939 to 1:13 in 1945. Fraser, *Shock Them!* 100–101.

222. Ibid., 102–104.

223. Dempsey remains the least understood senior British wartime commander. An introvert, he shielded himself from public scrutiny throughout his career. Early in the war he rose from brigadier to corps command. LHCMA, LHP 1/230, *London Times* obituary of Dempsey, 7 June 1969; Brian Horrocks, *Corps Commander* (London: Sidgewick & Jackson, 1977), 22–24; Hart, *Montgomery,* chap. 6.

224. The VIII Corps went through five commanders in the year before D-Day. PRO PREM 3/336/2, "Army and Corps Commanders for OVERLORD, January 1944; John Baynes, *The Forgotten Victor: General Sir Richard O'Connor* (London: Brassey's, 1989), 184.

225. D'Este, *Decision,* 61; Baynes, *Forgotten Victor,* 183–184.

226. Michael Craster, "Cunningham, Ritchie and Leese," in John Keegan, ed., *Churchill's Generals* (London: Weidenfeld & Nicolson, 1991), 200–224.

227. LHCMA, AP/5/2/24, 7 April 1944; D'Este, *Decision,* 61; Alistair Horne and Brian Montgomery, *The Lonely Leader: Monty 1944–1945* (London: Macmillan, 1994), 146; Hart, *Montgomery,* Chap. 8.

228. Montgomery rated Agair as unsuited for divisional command, but O'Connor refused to replace him. Baynes, *Forgotten Victor,* 186.

229. British military thinking termed the operational level "grand tactics," which falsely implied that operational art was merely an extension of tactics on a larger scale. Operations involve the control and direction of armies and army groups within a single, discrete combat theater. Trevor Dupuy, *Understanding War: History and Theory of Combat* (New York: Paragon, 1987), 70–71.

230. Graham, *Fire-Power,* 227–228.

4

Canada, 1939–1944:
The Politics of Neglect

The Canadian armed forces in September 1939 possessed very limited military capabilities and, as in the United States and Britain, the Canadian military was neither materially nor mentally prepared for war in Europe. Canada had no well-trained, equipped, organized forces capable of deployment overseas. Its militia had no real doctrine and little recollection of the harsh realities of modern war that Canadian troops had learned on the Western Front during 1914–1918. Protected by the Atlantic both from the immediacy and direct danger of the war and possessing an exaggerated faith in Britain's resilience, most Canadians believed that there would be sufficient time to prepare for war if, or when, it materialized. At the same time, the militia lacked the professionalism to develop military proficiency quickly. It had little practical doctrine and was not structured to obtain, absorb, or disseminate battlefield lessons so that it might learn from experience. In fact, few militia officers recognized the importance of studying, evaluating, and learning from the warfare that engulfed Europe after September 1939. Thus there was little in the interwar Canadian military's experience to suggest that it could readily adapt to meet the challenges that awaited it in World War II.

It took the audit of war to illuminate the army's deficiencies, and the legacy of interwar neglect limited Canadian military effectiveness throughout World War II. In contrast to the Great War, the tardy combat deployment of Canadian ground forces meant that they benefited less from combat experience, not developing genuine military proficiency until late in the war. To have expected military excellence in these circumstances from the wartime Canadian Army was wishful thinking. Its interwar neglect and its inexperience left it initially unable to prepare quickly or effectively for its operational debut. It was also hampered in its efforts to innovate and adapt to combat conditions because much time was lost in relearning basics and developing professionalism to regain military proficiency. Much of Canada's early war military preparation lacked rigor and realism. Nevertheless, once it was committed to combat the Canadian Army, like its Great War predecessor, displayed flexibility and creativity and thus proved able to adapt and to innovate faster than its British counterpart.

Underscoring this confusion was the lack of military, political, or popular consensus about the form of Canada's contribution to the Allied war effort. While most Canadians supported a declaration of war, opinions diverged over the extent of Canada's contribution. Government officials and public commentators alike recognized that Canadians were not prepared to make the same sacrifices as they had during 1914–1918. Moreover, memories of the 1917 conscription controversy—when the narrow passage of the Military Service Bill forced Prime Minister Sir Robert Borden to call a general election—tortured political opinion.[1] Prime Minister W. L. Mackenzie King remained determined to avoid a similar political crisis that he feared might bring down his government.

Thus political as much as military considerations dominated Canada's wartime policies, as Prime Minister King pursued a policy of limited liability in which he opposed the dispatch of an overseas expeditionary force and sought to restrict Canada's contribution to the air and maritime wars. He hoped that machines rather than men could provide Canada's contribution and thus lessen human casualties—and thus head off another conscription crisis. Popular opinion thwarted King, however, because most Canadians expected that Canada's main contribution would once again be an expeditionary force, though this time one led by Canadian commanders, which would again demonstrate Canada's martial prowess. To maintain national unity, King formed an all-volunteer overseas expeditionary force, the Canadian Active Service Force (CASF). Its all-volunteer nature reflected the fact that Canada's territorial interests were not directly threatened and that no public consensus existed on what form Canadian involvement in the war should take.

In keeping with limited liability, the Canadian government initially conceived of the CASF in very modest terms as a mobile force based around a single infantry division. At a later date the government planned to expand the CASF to two divisions. The modest size of the CASF reflected the pervasiveness of the "never again" mentality of the 1930s, which contended that future conflicts would be small wars. Indeed, most interwar Canadian politicians, soldiers, and civilians alike simply could not contemplate Canada's involvement in another major war. Given the prevailing political and social climate, Canada had to start virtually from scratch in September 1939 in raising, training, equipping, and deploying an overseas expeditionary force. Given the inadequacies of the militia at the start of the war, even these apparently modest goals were in fact significant military commitments.

Against the backdrop of limited liability and of military unpreparedness, Canada's early war mobilization was inevitably chaotic. In September

1939 Canada mobilized the 1st Division of the CASF for overseas combat service. There were few quality controls over early war enlistment, and some men clearly volunteered to escape the unemployment of the Great Depression rather than out of patriotism or belief in the threat posed by Nazi Germany to Canadian interests.[2] Interwar neglect meant that it was not possible even to supply all volunteers with basic clothing and equipment, let alone weapons. Confusion reigned about where, when, and how the CASF would be dispatched overseas, thus it was not until November 1939 that the 1st Division left for Britain. Moreover, since the British government pledged to equip the CASF from British stocks there was little impetus to resurrect Canada's arms industry. Nevertheless, given the condition of the Canadian military in September 1939, that Canada was able to deploy a full division overseas in 1939 was in itself a major accomplishment.

The specter of British defeat, which loomed large after Dunkirk, transformed Canada's military policy and compelled its government to abandon limited liability and reverse the priority accorded Canada's air and naval forces since 1937. German victory in the West demanded an expanded CASF to help fill the void in the Allied order of battle caused by the loss of the French Army, the largest Allied ground force contingent. The Canadian government thus ordered the expansion of the CASF to a corps of four divisions. Yet extensive war mobilization had to wait until 21 June 1941 when Canada enacted the National Resources Mobilization Act (NRMA), which introduced limited conscription for home defense. The NRMA, by establishing a national service force for domestic defense, both gave Canada's wartime ground forces a dual character and created political-military problems that plagued Canada throughout the war. Not only did the NRMA hamper efficient Canadian manpower utilization, it was the source of considerable friction between the volunteers and what the CASF considered the less patriotic NRMA conscripts.

Dunkirk radically altered the character of the Canadian Army. From the summer of 1940 on, Canada for the first time took armored warfare seriously as the blitzkrieg apparently demonstrated the potential of armor to win campaigns quickly and cheaply. Given the Canadian government's concern about manpower, it was not surprising that from 1940 on the Canadian Army enthusiastically embraced armored warfare and diverted major resources into armored forces. The Allied defeat in the West also led Canada to rebuild its domestic arms industry as a desperate Britain asked for help to reequip the British Army.[3]

Canadian difficulties in readying the CASF inevitably delayed the deployment of Canadian formations overseas. It was spring 1941 before the original two-division CASF corps had concentrated in Britain. Canada's tardiness, both in abandoning limited liability and in recognizing the potential of armored forces, meant that it was much later before additional formations reached the United Kingdom. The 1st Tank Brigade, 3d Infantry Division, and 5th Armoured Division arrived in 1941; the 4th Armoured Division in 1942, and the 2d Tank Brigade not until 1943. Given Canada's elevated national status and the memories of the heavy loss of Canadian lives during World War I, it was inevitable that Canada would demand to exercise independent command of its ground forces now that it had five divisions overseas. Canada thus formed the Canadian First Army in the United Kingdom on 6 April 1942 and raised a second corps headquarters in 1943. By the summer of 1943, the Canadian Army Overseas (CAO) had reached its definitive force structure of five divisions and two brigades.

As the Canadian Army gradually materialized in the United Kingdom, many factors retarded its activation and working up. Equipment shortages, inadequate early war training, and the lack of established Canadian doctrine all militated against its becoming quickly operational. No army can fight well without effective weapons, yet in 1939 the militia remained utterly ill equipped for modern warfare. It had almost no modern antitank or antiaircraft guns, few Bren guns, and even fewer mortars; it was virtually immobile, and its artillery was largely obsolescent.[4] Reequipping the army for combat encountered numerous obstacles and was protracted: even in June 1944 some Canadian formations still lacked authorized ordnance.

Canada's neglect of its defense industries seriously impeded the reequipping of the CAO and increased Canada's dependence on British, and later U.S., arms.[5] Yet Canada was unable to produce quickly its own weapons.[6] The Canadian government's prewar belief that it could rely on Britain while Canada resurrected its military-industrial complex proved false. In reality the reverse was true. The limits of Anglo-American arms production, coupled with prevailing military realities, meant that early in the war Canada would receive obsolete weaponry from its allies.[7] Moreover, what little ordnance Canada had available, however obsolete, was put at the disposal of Britain in its hour of greatest need in 1940.[8] But once its armaments industry finally got into gear during 1942, Canada then diverted most of its war production to Britain, the Commonwealth, the Soviet Union, and China. In fact, in the last two years of the war no less than 71 percent of Canadian armament production went to other nations.[9]

This reality reflected that political and economic, as much as military, considerations governed the channeling of Canada's war production. The Canadian government adhered to the principle of "material over men," that fully giving of the nation's industrial resources could both offset Canada's limited manpower commitment to the Allied cause, and thus minimize casualties, and simultaneously drag Canada out of the Depression. Such motivations, whatever their merits, had significant military ramifications. Canada's prodigious sale of its armaments left Canadian forces underequipped and delayed both reequipment and the acquisition of combat readiness.[10]

Canadian ground forces might have been more effective had the nation been able to produce its own quality weapons. But inexperience, lack of infrastructure, and its position as a junior partner in a multinational coalition restricted Canada's wartime weapons development. Initial expansion of the armaments industry in 1940–1942 produced British weapons for the British Army, a process that reinforced the anglicization of the Canadian military. Canada retained a small, if precarious, capability as an independent weapons developer by designing hybrid weapons that combined existing Anglo-American equipment and technology. In 1940 Canada developed the Ram tank, which married design features of Anglo-American armor, but the Sherman tank soon superseded it in Allied service. Canada proved more successful in developing self-propelled artillery, where the Sexton, which mounted the British 25-pounder gun on a U.S. chassis, became standard equipment in the self-propelled artillery regiments of Anglo-Canadian armored divisions. Despite this enterprise, the wartime Canadian Army fought largely with British ordnance.

Tardy reequipment seriously hindered acquisition of combat readiness. Reliance on obsolete hand-me-downs and the diversion of war production to other combatants brought lengthy equipment shortages and repeated reequipments, which badly delayed the combat preparation of Canadian formations. Most units earmarked for OVERLORD only acquired the heavy weapons they fought with in Normandy in the year preceeding D-Day. In some cases, like the 4th Armoured Division, formations had not even completed reequipment by 6 June.[11]

Inadequate training also hampered the CAO's combat preparation. Repeated barrack square parading and monotonous, repetitive drill sapped the optimism, enthusiasm, and vigor of many a volunteer. Nor was training intensive: troops spent the majority of their time on duties and fatigues. Moreover, with no battle experience available, training inevitably lacked realism and the dearth of qualified personnel for combat commands led to a lack of quality instructors. Uncertainty over potential theaters of operations, army missions, and force structure hardly helped forge quality training either. Given these realities, Canadian training was slow and patchy at best in the early war years.

In 1942, the army became obsessed with the new battle drill training methods recently introduced in the British Army. Designed to restore the small-unit tactical flexibility that the BEF had lacked in 1940, battle drill's emphasis on assault courses, highly controlled live-fire exercises, and flexible small-unit fire-and-maneuver drills was a welcome change from barrack square drill and improved the ebbing morale of the Canadians in Britain. During 1942–1944 the CAO extensively practiced battle drill. But how an army trains is far more important than for how long. The time devoted to such training would not be rewarded in combat because the tactical doctrine that underlay battle drill was incompatible with the de facto

Commonwealth operational doctrine of firepower dominance that became ascendant from 1942 on. The Canadians had no combat experience under their belt, so they could only follow British practice and hope they were pursuing effective training. But battle drills were, however, mechanical and not very realistic.[12]

The failure of battle drill illustrated that the lack of a distinct Canadian doctrine of war, let alone a comprehensive, holistic one, seriously hampered the CAO's combat preparation. Doctrine is the intellectual substance that binds together an army's organization, equipment, personnel, training, tactics, and that provides the army's basic procedures that allow it to operate effectively. Doctrine is most important at the operational level, and studies undertaken by officers at staff colleges are the foundation of operational doctrine in all armies.[13] But the interwar Canadian military did not have a staff college; it depended for doctrinal development on a very small number of officers who attended the British Royal Staff College at Camberly and returned imbued with prevailing British doctrine. The paucity of trained staff officers left the Canadian staff poorly equipped intellectually to prepare Canada's ground forces for modern war.[14] Thus what passed for Canadian doctrine between 1919–1945 was contemporary British doctrine, doctrine that failed to emphasize an integrated combined-arms and interservice approach to war. Nor did modern British military thought explicitly recognize the existence of an intermediate, operational level of warfare that lay between tactics and strategy. Consequently, wartime Anglo-Canadian forces operated without clearly defined operational doctrine.[15] Wartime Canadian staff officers were woefully undereducated in operational art, a deficiency that directly contributed to the operational difficulties Canadian forces experienced during the war.

The military necessities of the war exacerbated the inadequacy of the Canadian Army staff because the urgent need for more trained staff officers led to curtailment of courses offered at British staff colleges. This simply continued the inadequate grasp of operational art of Canadian Army staff personnel.[16] The lack of seasoned officers forced Canada to elevate those who had not gained a basic knowledge of operational art, and thus the wartime army remained singularly unprepared to handle large independent forces. Without any combat experience to illuminate the deficiencies of operational art, the Canadian Army remained largely ignorant of the weaknesses of its staff, training, and preparation until well into the war.[17] The onset of the war did not give Canada sufficient time to prepare an army practically from scratch or to train a competent staff. So the army's dependence on Britain to become operational led to an unquestioning adherence to British doctrine and a peculiarly British style of war.

As already noted, the Canadian Army's most fundamental problem was its dearth of battle experience. Only 2 percent of the troops slated for OVERLORD had ever seen action—and for most of these this amounted to a single day's combat in the disastrous Dieppe raid of 19 August 1942. Designed as a reconnaissance in force to test the feasibility of a major amphibious assault on a defended enemy coastline, and prompted by Canadian public pressure as well as concern from Canadian commanders over the ebbing morale of their inactive troops, Dieppe saw the combat debut of the 2d Canadian Division. But the plan, reflecting Allied inexperience at amphibious assault and interservice operations, was cumbersome and unrealistic. Two-thirds of the Canadian troops landed became casualties, and nearly half were taken prisoner.[18] The operation was beyond the capabilities of the 2d Canadian Division—or probably of any Allied division at that time. Given the Canadians' limited amphibious assault training and the inadequate naval and air support, the well defended port was simply too tough a nut to crack.[19] Thus, the Canadian pool of battle-experienced personnel, some 2,000 troops, was insufficient to instill cohesion.

The inexperience of the army was reflected in the reluctance of Prime Minister Mackenzie King and Gen. A. G. L. McNaughton, the army commander in chief, to commit Canadian troops to combat. King feared that heavy casualties would force his government to send NRMA conscripts overseas, which could induce a political crisis to threaten his government. Therefore, he sought both to delay and to limit any combat commitment. General McNaughton, on the other hand, though he recognized the army's need to gain experience, vehemently opposed any breaking up of the army, which would sacrifice its ability to operate independently of British command.[20]

The fall of France dealt a severe blow to King's plan. Thereafter, he fought an unavailing rearguard action against both the creation of a large army and the commitment of Canadian forces to major combat. Despite his intentions, however, manpower became a military and a political problem for Canada during the war: its commitment to voluntary enlistment for service overseas imposed significant restrictions on efficient manpower use. Both the government and the military still optimistically believed that Canada could maintain six divisions overseas for five years through voluntary enlistment. But by 1943, the supply of volunteers had largely dried up, plunging the army into manpower problems that forced the government to cap the CAO in 1943 at five divisions, with 226,000 personnel. Thereafter the army struggled to maintain even this establishment.[21]

Canada's response to its manpower shortage was the least satisfactory of those of the Western Allies to the problem of efficient manpower utilization. This reaction reflected the legacy of limited liability, the unpopularity of the war, and the government's perceived inability to take strong and unpopular action. Canadian territory was never directly threatened, so the government felt that it lacked the popular support to compel more extensive military service—yet, in reality, Canada possessed more than sufficient manpower to meet its mobilization needs. Canadian manpower regulation remained lax and inefficient; even the NRMA conscription introduced for home defense failed to meet Canada's wartime manpower needs.

The NRMA restricted liability for compulsory service to single men between ages 18 and 42 and to married men between ages 18 and 31. Even so the government failed to conscript rigorously within this limited manpower pool—of those eligible for compulsory military service only 42 percent actually served in the wartime armed forces. Not only did the government fail to call up many men eligible to serve, but conscription boards rejected as medically unfit a high proportion of those summoned. The Canadian government also pursued a liberal deferment policy on economic, moral, or compassionate grounds. During the war, one in three conscripts received a temporary deferment of service of up to a year; and the government granted no less than 89 percent of deferment requests.[22] Because of the decline in volunteers for overseas service, it became apparent early in the war that at some point the Canadian government might have to send conscript soldiers overseas in contravention of the NRMA. In April 1942 the government sought, and the electorate passed, a national referendum that released the government from the NRMA prohibition against such overseas service "in principle and if unavoidable." Quebec maintained its traditional opposition with a 75-percent vote against the government's move. The government was now theoretically free to dispatch conscripts overseas if militarily necessary, but it kept in mind Quebec's hostility to this. Fearing the political consequences of exercising this power, the Canadian government refrained from sending conscripts overseas until November 1944. Of course, the government's reluctance to exercise its authority exacerbated the army's manpower problems; by 1943, even before Canada committed its army to combat in any strength, the CAO was affected by a shortage.

Greater political will could have allowed the government to avoid Canada's wartime manpower problems. Expansion of conscription age to 45, the inclusion of married men over 31 years, less exacting medical requirements, and a more exacting deferment policy could have produced many more conscripts. The crux of the issue, however, was that neither the Canadian government nor its citizens saw a military need for greater sacrifice. This reality is clearly illustrated in the government's reluctance to address the serious problem of evasion of compulsory military service.[23]

The Canadian Army's failure to utilize its available manpower efficiently merely exacerbated its shortage of personnel. The political decision to create separate overseas and home defense forces obviously had made effective employment difficult. Yet the army's inexperience and its dependence on the British military, which led to the adoption of British organizational establishments, added to its difficulties. Abandonment of its organizational independence meant that there was no independent Canadian effort to trim excess from its establishment, in contrast to what occurred in the

U.S. Army. Canada's demographic profile also hindered efficient manpower utilization. The proportion of French Canadians who volunteered for active service was far below that of English speakers, and throughout the war French Canadians remained a small minority in the army. As a result, the army raised few exclusively French-Canadian units and experienced considerable difficulty maintaining them at full strength.[24]

Canada's long militia tradition also fostered the retention of excess strength in auxiliary defense forces of marginal military value. Throughout the war, Canada's militia tradition was preserved in the form of the part-time Canadian Army Reserve (CAR). Formed from NPAM personnel who did not volunteer for the CASF, the CAR peaked in strength in 1943 with 105,000 personnel organized in twelve brigade groups. The equivalent of the British Home Guard, the CAR was conceived as a trained reserve. In reality, it possessed negligible military capability and further drained manpower and resources from the CASF, while contributing to the excessive duplication of overhead. Moreover, the "great majority" of men who enrolled in the CAR did so simply to avoid conscription.[25] The Canadian Army also kept a disproportionate strength inside Canada during the war. Declaration of war on Japan in December 1941 once again turned attention toward domestic defense. During the spring of 1942 the government expanded its NRMA home defense forces to three divisions. The ease with which the government raised these—in contrast to the difficulty in sending divisions overseas—reflected the degree to which political, rather than military, considerations governed military policy. Mackenzie King's efforts in 1942 to avoid a future conscription crisis centered on a deliberate government publicity campaign to exaggerate the Japanese threat to Canada's west coast backed by an extension of NRMA forces inside Canada. King hoped these efforts would focus public attention on domestic defense and thus forestall pressure to send conscripts abroad.[26] In reality, however, Japan posed no threat to Canada's Pacific coast.[27] The government's deliberate inflation of this threat for domestic political reasons had unfortunate military consequences: it led to excessive retention of troops in Canada, forced by the need to assuage public fears.

It was only in mid-1943, as the Japanese threat receded after U.S. forces recaptured the Aleutian Islands, and as the manpower crunch bit deeper, that the Canadian government trimmed its home defense forces and disbanded the 7th and 8th NRMA Divisions.[28] But these efforts were half-hearted, and a large number of nondivisional combat units remained in Canada. The government was still unable to curb the growth of auxiliary military forces, so that total army manpower in Canada peaked only in 1944—long after the Japanese threat had disappeared.[29]

The army training establishment was also inefficient and excessive. The training system had expanded unchecked during the early war years, but, as recruit intake declined during the middle of the war, efforts to reduce the training establishment met with limited success. Even in November 1944, as one study has estimated, the training establishment remained overstaffed by 40 percent.[30] Such inefficient manpower utilization meant that from late 1942 the CAO had increasing difficulty in maintaining its strength, and by early 1943 there was a shortage of infantry replacements—even though no Canadian troops were engaged in combat. Lack of manpower hampered Canadian operations when the CAO finally entered combat in Sicily and Italy in the late summer of 1943, and combat losses in turn inevitably exacerbated the Canadian infantry shortage. Lack of manpower reinforced the government's political determination to avoid heavy losses, and the avoidance of heavy losses remained a cornerstone of Canadian operations for the remainder of the war.

During the spring of 1944, as the Canadian Army geared up for OVERLORD, it became evident that a significant infantry shortage existed and that the CAO lacked the replacements needed to cover anticipated casualties during the opening months of OVERLORD.[31] On 16 March 1944, the CAO reported to General Montgomery a healthy 7 percent surplus in aggregate replacements over its projected requirements for the first three months of OVERLORD—although the report admitted a serious deficiency of 8,744 infantry replacements, some 37.5 percent of those authorized.[32]

The official Canadian history of World War II has argued that this replacement shortage was solely due to the adoption of flawed British casualty forecast charts that underestimated both total casualties and the proportion of casualties that would be suffered by the infantry. The official history thus shifts responsibility for the Canadian infantry shortage from the Mackenzie King government to the British War Office. Such an interpretation is erroneous. It is true that during the summer of 1942 the Canadian Army discarded its own "wastage" projections and adopted lower British casualty forecast rates because it lacked the experience to calculate its own rates. The War Office based its casualty projections (the "Evett Rates") on Commonwealth forces' experience in North Africa, where mechanized formations predominated and limited artillery firepower and tactical air support kept infantry losses to 63 percent of total casualties.[33] But in the more rugged terrain of Tunisia, Sicily, and Italy, the infantry suffered about 75 percent of total casualties. Thus the War Office adopted new wastage rates in February 1944 that increased the proportion of required infantry replacements, but the CAO, while aware that its existing casualty forecast rates were inadequate for the ETO, failed to revise upward its casualty estimates before D-Day.[34]

Unfortunately, the 16 March 1944 report to Montgomery deliberately camouflaged a far more unsatisfactory replacement situation, for it included as reinforcements large numbers of unavailable personnel. In reality, the CAO possessed only about one-third of the infantry replacements called for by its war establishment. Despite the intended deception the report did not deceive Montgomery, who characterized the Canadian infantry shortage as "most serious."[35] Canadian efforts to rectify its growing manpower shortage prior to D-Day represented too little, too late. A strenuous publicity campaign temporarily increased the number of NRMA conscripts persuaded to volunteer for overseas service, but this still fell far short of providing enough infantry.[36] It was not until March 1944 that the government remustered 2,000 soldiers in other arms as infantry. Nevertheless, King's government still opposed more extensive use of its conscription powers to release further active-service personnel for overseas service. Canada's manpower was drying up, and the NRMA was no longer producing men in sufficient numbers.[37]

Increased efforts reduced the "official" infantry reinforcement deficiency to 3,337 by 31 May 1944.[38] Throughout May, the CAO struggled just to bring formations up to strength and to assemble one month's projected replacements.[39] But even based on its existing, inadequate projection rates, the Canadian First Army remained short of infantry replacements on the eve of D-Day. According to the upwardly revised War Office casualty projections, which increased by 45 percent the required number of infantry replacements, the Canadian infantry shortage was serious.[40] Yet senior Canadian military and political leaders still displayed unwarranted optimism in their handling of manpower problems. On the eve of D-Day, the First Canadian Army still lacked at least half its authorized infantry replacements—far more than the "official" estimate.

The Canadian Army, of course, had a complete lack of operational experience, since Canada had yet to deploy an army in the field. At Dieppe Canadian forces had served under British command as they did in Sicily and Italy. That Canada before 1941 had not seen its commitment to the Allied cause extending beyond one corps meant thatCanadian First Army came into existence only in April 1942. The highest level of Canadian command experience before D-Day was limited to the I Canadian Corps in Italy. (In the fall of 1943 the corps had advanced up the Italian mainland but did not launch its first major offensive until the Liri Valley campaign of May 1944.)[41] The army's operational inexperience raised doubts about its potential.

The Canadian Army's inability to maintain sufficient troop strength in Britain before D-Day exacerbated its lack of operational experience. The dual pressures of public opinion at home and the military need for combat experience forced the Canadian government to press the British for the operational employment of the CAO in 1943. Yet the army's need for battle experience and concentration of force in Britain for OVERLORD were antithetical goals. The Dieppe fiasco gave impetus to the decision to dispatch the 1st Infantry Division and 1st Tank Brigade from Britain to the Mediterranean in April 1943 to gain experience before participating in OVERLORD. This limited and temporary diversion was sound policy, though once Canada made such a commitment additional forces were drawn to the Mediterranean. In October 1943, Mackenzie King again importuned Britain to send the I Canadian Corps with the 5th Armoured Division to Italy to avoid the heavy losses that he suspected the Allies would suffer in Normandy.[42] Once Canada had committed an entire corps in Italy, it proved impossible to withdraw formations for OVERLORD.

The failure to redeploy Canadian divisions from the Mediterranean robbed the Canadian First Army of both the strength to act as a truly independent national force in Normandy and of the experience it required to perform well. In fact, the Canadian First Army's reduction to a single corps put its existence into question. To bolster the army's strength Britain reinforced it with continental contingents of Dutch, Belgian, Czech, and Polish troops who had escaped from occupied Europe. Not only had these forces been raised, organized, and equipped from scratch in Britain, but they lacked the replacements so that they could not be employed in an assault role.[43] The shortage of Canadian forces in Britain, the limitations of the added on continental contingents, and the apparent deficiencies in Canadian preparation wisely led the Allied planners to assign a follow-up role to the Canadian First Army in OVERLORD. It would be deployed to Normandy only after the Allies had established a bridgehead and would then advance northeast toward Le Havre and the Flanders coast. Given the condition of the Canadian forces, this supporting function was clearly appropriate.

From mid-1943 on, Canadian preparation for the second front intensified as formations finally focused on invasion-oriented training.[44] The disaster at Dieppe had stimulated a major review of training and doctrine that exposed many shortcomings of the Canadian forces in Britain. The deficiencies in basic training conducted in Canada, forced the CAO to retrain at British facilities and with British philosophies. As a result the CAO thus became a mirror of the British Army.[45] Lack of equipment, transport, and experienced instructors all hampered Canadian training, while the enforced reliance on the British Army inevitably lengthened the time required to prepare Canadian formations for battle. Considering these realities, it is hardly surprising that the Canadians did not begin offensive training until 1943.[46]

The CAO was to acquire an increasingly British cast. In late summer of 1941 the Canadian Corps joined South-Eastern Command, where General Montgomery appraised Canadian capabilities during the September 1941 Operation BUMPER, the first major wartime maneuver in Britain. Disappointed with the Canadians' performance, Montgomery demanded— and received—the dismissal of two of the three Canadian division commanders.[47] Thereafter, Montgomery imbued the Canadians with his operational approach. Under his tutelage, the Canadian Corps quickly enhanced its combat capabilities, as it demonstrated during Exercise TIGER (April-May 1942) when the Canadians outfought the XII British Corps and took "large numbers of 'prisoners'."[48] Nonetheless, these early exercises revealed that manifest weaknesses remained, including poor intelligence, communications, signals security, reconnaissance, "complete indifference" to air threat, and poor aerial recognition skills.[49]

Growing awareness of training problems led to substantive measures during 1942–1943 to improve training quality by greater standardization and reorganization so as to diminish duplication and inefficiency. Testing of trainees finally began in 1942, and a new standardized syllabus took effect on 12 December 1943. But even under the new syllabus training remained far from intensive.[50] Moreover, in 1943 the Canadians finally began offensive-oriented maneuvers, but inexperience generated manifold problems during these early offensive exercises. Orders were inflexible, units became entangled with each other, march discipline was poor, artillery support inadequate, and tactics unoriginal. At the same time observers evaluated intelligence gathering, signals procedures, and security as unsatisfactory.[51]

That serious deficiencies remained in Canadian training, tactics, and operational art was starkly illuminated during Operation SPARTAN (4–12 March 1943) when the Canadian First Army practiced the breakout operations it was scheduled to conduct on the continent.[52] This debut exercise illuminated the inadequacy of Canadian commanders and troops; Sir Alan Brooke, the chief of the Imperial General Staff, concluded from it that General McNaughton was unfit to command theCanadian First Army in combat.[53] The exercise also illustrated that Canadian formations were still perfecting basics rather than focusing on collective training, and had yet to improve aerial recognition skills and radio discipline.[54] The revelations of SPARTAN led to a return to basics and intensified efforts to correct the obvious deficiencies.[55]

In July 1943, the transfer of the Canadian 3d Infantry Division and 2d Armoured Brigade to British command to train for the D-Day amphibious assault further undermined prospects of independent Canadian operations in northwest Europe. The Canadian First Army was thus reduced to a single corps of two divisions, neither of which were operational. A lack of strong leadership contributed to Canadian problems: the War Office's final ouster of General McNaughton in December 1943 had created a command hiatus at a critical juncture in Canadian preparations. On 20 March 1944 Gen. Harry Crerar returned from Italy, where he had briefly led the I Canadian Corps, to assume command of the Canadian First Army. However, senior British officers had misgivings about Crerar's qualifications for the appointment: despite his time in Italy, Crerar had never commanded the corps in a major operation.[56]

The lack of command experience was a major weakness of theCanadian First Army. The pool of combat-experienced Canadian officers remained small and thinly spread. Indeed, only six of fourteen senior commanders had seen combat and none had experience at their new levels of command.[57] In this, General Crerar was typical. A World War I artillery officer, he had held various staff positions between the wars. A brigadier at the start of World War II, he was promoted to lieutenant general and chief of the general staff in July 1940. He subsequently took command of the I Canadian Corps in the fall of 1943 even though he had never commanded a combat unit. His experience as a corps commander was only for a few months before his elevation to command of the Canadian First Army. This inexperience caused Montgomery serious doubts about his ability to lead this army in northwest Europe.[58] In fact, of the four Allied army commanders slated for OVERLORD, Montgomery had the least faith in Crerar.[59] Lt. Gen. Guy G. Simonds, commander of the II Canadian Corps, was a 1925 Sword of Honor graduate from the Royal Military College, who had served as an artillery major at the outbreak of hostilities in 1939. He received rapid promotion, and served in several staff positions and as a regimental and brigade commander. He also served with the Eighth Army in North Africa, where he had immediately impressed Montgomery. In the summer of 1943, Simonds became Canada's youngest general when he took command of the 1st Canadian Division in Sicily. He also briefly commanded 5th Canadian Armoured Division in Italy before being recalled to lead the II Canadian Corps in January 1944. Simonds was clearly both the most experienced and talented of the senior Canadian commanders.[60]

The three Canadian division commanders, however, all lacked command and combat experience. Maj. Gen. R. F. L. Keller, who had begun his career as a permanent force infantry officer, took command of the 3d Division in September 1943. Maj. Gen. Charles Foulkes had also begun his career as a permanent force infantry officer. After 1939 he received steady promotion and took over the 2d Division in January 1944, even though, like Keller, he had not held an operational command. Maj. Gen. G. Kitching was a Sandhurst graduate who had served with a British infantry regiment, then commanded the Loyal Edmonton Regiment, and the 11th Canadian Infantry Brigade. To his surprise he was promoted to command the 4th Armoured Division shortly before D-Day, even though he had never previously commanded armored forces.[61]

The roots of the uncertain leadership abilities of the senior Canadian commanders lay in the interwar retrenchment of the Canadian military, which meant that Canada entered World War II with an extremely small pool of potential future senior commanders. Because the officer corps expanded two hundredfold in the early war years, there was a constant shortage of qualified officers. Out of necessity even mediocre officers received relatively rapid promotion. Thereafter, the army's continued lack of combat exposure meant that battle-experienced commanders remained a rare commodity. Even in 1944, most senior Canadian command positions were held by men who did not possess the experience normal for such high rank. The Canadian Army entered the northwest European campaign with unproven senior commanders; only Simonds was really experienced enough to perform at a level commensurate with his rank. Further, tardy appointments exacerbated the uphill leadership task that such officers faced: as of 1 January 1944, only one of the five most senior command positions had been permanently filled. None of this augured well for the operational performance of Canadian First Army in Normandy.

From 1939 to 1944 the Canadian Army had made huge strides toward transforming an indifferent militia barely able to defend Canada into an independent army capable of limited offensive action. Despite these strenuous efforts, however, the army had not entirely succeeded in this task by June 1944. The ground it had to cover to catch up to its adversary was truly enormous, and the Canadians' lack of combat experience so hampered these efforts that even five years of preparation proved insufficient to forge a Canadian army of significant offensive capabilities. Indeed, inexperience even misdirected much of the Canadian effort.

Another major concern that remained in 1944 was the quality of the infantry. As early as 1941 there was evidence of serious problems with the Canadian manpower procurement and training system. In theory Canadian recruits went overseas only after completing four months of basic training. But inexperience, excessive decentralization, and inefficiency led to the frequent dispatch of undertrained recruits to Britain. The arrival of so many "raw or nearly raw" recruits forced Canadian Reinforcement Units in Britain to conduct additional basic training before progressing to collective training.[62] This policy produced a multiplication and duplication of the Canadian training establishment on both sides of the Atlantic—uncontrolled expansion that went unchecked until late 1943 when the army half-heartedly tried to cut waste and duplication. Decentralization also caused considerable variety in training.

There was little improvement in training quality before D-Day: instruction in Canada and Britain remained poorly coordinated, recruits continued to arrive in Britain undertrained, and training remained decentralized. In 1944, for example, Canadian recruits still were attending, on average, five training centers prior to departure for Britain.[63] These deficiencies in procurement and training lengthened the time it took the army to produce fully trained troops and exacerbated the difficulties of maintaining troop strength. As a result, in May 1944 the Canadian First Army was still under strength.[64] In fact, it took the replacement shortage in the spring of 1944 to force the Canadian Army to address the poor quality of training in Britain. Prior to D-Day, however, the army made no sustained effort to improve the quality of instruction.[65]

Yet another serious problem on the eve of D-Day was the inadequacy of Canadian combined-arms preparation. In theory, Canadian troops had repeatedly practiced cooperation between armor and infantry. In fact, in the final year before D-Day, some Canadian formations had spent 90 percent of their training time on collective training, but the amount of combined-arms training undertaken varied enormously. The assault formations inevitably neglected combined-arms training as they honed amphibious assault techniques. These units believed that they would be rapidly withdrawn from the bridgehead once they had accomplished their mission and, therefore, had no rationale for combined-arms preparation.[66]

The quality of Canadian combined-arms training left much to be desired because it was conceptually flawed. Lacking the independence and experience to formulate its own doctrine, Canadian combined-arms training scrupulously followed prevailing British doctrine.[67] The result was the Canadians being inculcated with the prevailing British philosophy of "joint operations," the loose combination of arms, rather than the intimate integration that modern warfare demanded. Canadian troops also spent too much training time on the abstract and theoretical; infantry and armor spent little time actually exercising together. Even when they did, the impact of British doctrine was starkly evident: Canadian infantry and armor exercised alongside one another rather than together.[68]

During the last year of preparation for Normandy, Canadian combined-arms training intensified. Unfortunately it suffered from increasing doctrinal confusion. Illustrative of this confusion was the distinction drawn by the II Canadian Corps in November 1943 between tank-infantry and infantry-tank cooperation![69] Such confusion was a result of the significant changes in British attack doctrine brought about by crippling tank losses in North Africa, and the War Office's finally abandoning the offensive spearhead role for armor.[70] There was a reversion to the prewar doctrine in which infantry once again led the attack, with armor providing indirect-fire support from hull-down positions on the flanks and rear.[71] This reversal of doctrine six months before D-Day sowed confusion among Canadian forces, which apparently failed to grasp the import of these doctrinal changes during the hectic last few months of preinvasion activity. Reequipment likewise hampered training.[72] Doctrine change combined with reequipment effectively invalidated much of the Canadians' previous combined-arms preparation. While doctrinal reform reduced Anglo-Canadian tank losses in Normandy, it also destroyed any prospect of effective infantry-armor cooperation. Self-preservation led these armored formations to abandon any pretense of coordination in favor of indirect-fire support designed to blast the infantry onto their objectives.[73]

Armored forces were the weakest link in the Canadian order of battle on the eve of D-Day. Canada had not fielded any operational armored forces in World War I, and in the face of financial stringency no rationale had existed for a militia designed for domestic defense to develop an independent tank force between the wars.[74] In the late 1930s the army had introduced limited mechanization, but equipment and financial constraints, and the assumption that Britain would furnish any required armor, guaranteed that Canada did not develop a tank force prior to World War II. Only after the resounding German victory in the West in 1940 did Canada take armored warfare seriously, and the Canadian Royal Armoured Corps (CRAC) came into existence on 13 August 1940. Established from scratch with 250 World War I–vintage Renault FT-17s legally purchased from a neutral United States as "scrap iron," the CRAC raised its first armored brigade in October 1940.[75] Expanded during the spring of 1941 to become the 5th Armoured Division, the CRAC soon added the 1st Army Tank Brigade for infantry support in accordance with prevailing British armored warfare conceptions. These two formations arrived in Britain in 1942, and after expansion of the CASF to army status in January 1942, the CRAC raised the 4th Armoured Division and the 2d Tank (later Armoured) Brigade, both of which arrived in Britain in 1943.

After the fall of France, both the Canadian government and its army high command became enthusiastic converts to armored warfare. For both military and political leaders, armor appeared a way to guarantee the military independence that befitted Canada's elevated international standing: the army because of its apparent military effectiveness and the government because of armor's potential to save lives. The CRAC consequently underwent unprecedented expansion, and on the eve of D-Day the CAO was the most armored army among the Western Allies.[76] Meteoric expansion, however, failed to disguise serious weaknesses that still afflicted Canadian armored forces in 1944. Equipment deficiencies seriously hindered activation; a motley array of obsolete foreign tanks constituted the CRAC's inventory during its early existence. It was reequipped in 1942 with the new Canadian Ram tank and in 1943 with British armor, before standardizing with the U.S. Sherman tank in 1944.[77] Reequipment was protracted and seriously hindered the tactical and operational readiness of Canadian armored forces for OVERLORD. The 2d Armoured Brigade, for example, designated to spearhead the Canadian amphibious assault on D-Day, had only ten Shermans in January 1944, and trained instead with obsolete British Valentines and Canadian Rams. The brigade reached full strength only in late May 1944, and even then remained short of its quota of upgunned Sherman Fireflies.[78] As an assault formation, the 2d Armoured Brigade received priority over the 4th Armoured Division, whose reequipment and preparation so lagged behind that the division was still rated nonoperational on D-Day. In addition, the Canadians lacked a significant reserve of tanks and tank crews to replace projected battlefield losses. Finally, Canadian armor had failed to exercise extensively and had rarely participated in joint maneuvers.[79]

The CRAC had adopted British armored warfare doctrine and thus embraced the British two-tier structure of infantry support and cruiser tanks as well as the disastrous British emphasis on direct tank-to-tank combat. So the CRAC entered the 1944 Normandy campaign with the same deficiencies that plagued the RAC. British doctrine trained Canadian armor to seek out and destroy enemy armor, even though its tanks were inferior to those of the enemy. Worse yet, the Canadian armored formations assigned to OVERLORD had no combat experience, were less familiar with their equipment, and were less well trained than their RAC counterparts. Training had not prepared Canadian armor to operate in concert with other combat arms because the adoption of British armored warfare doctrine hindered combined-arms preparation. Focused on tank-to-tank combat, Canadian armor for too long paid little attention to coordination with infantry and artillery. Moreover, repeated reequipment delayed the progress of Canadian armor from basic and unit training on to combined-arms preparation. The 3d Division and 2d Armoured Brigade, for example, began to train together only in April 1944.[80] Canadian armored formations remained the weakest element in the Canadian order of battle on the eve of D-Day.

Unlike in the British Army, artillery never became the backbone of the Canadian Army. The major drawback of the wartime Canadian artillery was not quality but quantity. Because field artillery was one of the few areas in which Canada preserved a limited productive capacity between the wars, reequipping the wartime Canadian Royal Artillery (CRA) was easier than for the other combat arms. Canadian ordnance was obsolete in 1939, but the nation quickly produced the excellent British 25-pounder gun, and by 1942 the CRA had been completely reequipped with it.[81] As well, Montgomery quickly converted Canadian gunners to his doctrine of massed fire while under his command in 1941–1942. The CRA therefore rapidly adopted prevailing British gunnery tactics, and by 1944 Canadian First Army fielded its own Army Group, Canadian Royal Artillery (AGCRA). But its weakness was a lack of quantity. Canada deployed for OVERLORD only a fraction of the army artillery fielded by the Royal Artillery—a mere five regiments and no heavy artillery.[82] As a result, the AGCRA had to be brought up to strength with British regiments.[83] Consequently, given the Anglo-Canadian operational approach of firepower dominance, lack of artillery severely compromised the Canadian First Army's ability to operate without British assistance.

A key distinction between the Canadian Army of the two world wars was its exposure to combat. During the Great War Canada had quickly dispatched an expeditionary force to the Western Front where extensive combat exposure allowed it to adapt and to enhance its combat effectiveness. In World War II, however, lack of battle experience meant that many of the Canadian deficiencies went unidentified and uncorrected before the government finally committed its forces to extensive combat in the Mediterranean in mid-1943. When finally committed to combat, Canadian forces performed relatively well and learned quite quickly from their battle experience. Canada committed its 1st Division and 1st Army Tank Brigade to the invasion of Sicily, and both formations performed well; in fact, the

Canadians fought better in Sicily and Italy than they would in Normandy.[84] The 1st Division advanced farther and fought longer in inhospitable terrain than any other Commonwealth formation, while confronting significant operational limitations imposed by both the loss of much of its transport at sea and the lack of artillery and reinforcements.[85] The limitations forced the division to jettison the British doctrine of firepower dominance it had learned and to innovate tactically. Much of the division's initial success was due to uncharacteristic infiltration techniques, active patrolling, and aggressive junior leadership, as well as excellent artillery support.[86]

The 1st Division's performance was due to a combination of its high-quality personnel (it contained more PAM personnel than any other formation), the quality of its training, and the professionalism of its commander, Guy Simonds. In fact in Sicily the Canadians, and Simonds in particular, greatly impressed Montgomery. The 1st Division and 1st Army Tank Brigade were the cream of the crop because they were the most senior, and hence most combat-ready, Canadian formations.[87] Even though Sicily was inevitably a rugged experience, the 1st Division learned quickly under the tutelage of Simonds, who alone among the senior Canadian commanders recognized the need to both analyze combat experience and to retrain in the field during combat. Nevertheless, despite his endeavors, many of the weaknesses that afflicted Canadian operations in Sicily were not quickly or easily remedied.[88] The I Canadian Corps performed nearly as well in Italy. The 1st Division again distinguished itself in house-to-house fighting for Ortona and displayed the same penchant for good artillery support and tactical flexibility that it had shown in Sicily. In fact, it performed better than more experienced British divisions.[89]

That the I Canadian Corps was able to operate under British command contributed to its solid performance because it minimized the limitations imposed by the Canadian lack of operational experience. Under British command, the Canadians got the logistic and artillery support required to fight effectively.[90] Moreover, Canadian forces initially avoided sustained heavy combat, allowing them to adapt to combat conditions and to remedy some weaknesses before major actions. Thus when the I Canadian Corps launched its first big offensive in May 1944 in the Liri Valley, it had ten months of experience under its belt and did not fumble as the Canadian First Army would in Normandy.

At the tactical level, Canadian troops adapted quite quickly once in combat in the Mediterranean. During December 1943, the 1st Division out-fought the elite and battle-hardened 1st German Parachute Division dug in at Ortona.[91] After the enemy repelled an initial attack, the Canadians changed tactics and systematically cleared the town to prevent German reinfiltration. The Canadians quickly learned to advance from house to house using "beehive" charges to blast through walls under the cover of masking mortar fire. To compensate for reduced artillery effectiveness in close-quarter urban combat, Simonds deployed his antitank guns in a direct-fire role, and the division demonstrated "excellent" combined-arms coordination.[92] The Canadian urban warfare techniques developed at Ortona subsequently became standard procedure for Commonwealth forces and ultimately influenced U.S. Army urban warfare tactics.[93]

Among the most serious deficiencies initially displayed by Canadian forces in the Mediterranean was poor tank-infantry cooperation. After sustained but relatively light combat, Canadian combined-arms coordination improved fairly quickly. The 1st Army Tank Brigade, for example, learned to integrate at lower levels.[94] The growing tactical skill of Canadian troops in the Mediterranean clearly reflected Simonds's professional commitment to retraining.[95] On closer examination, though, the performance of the I Canadian Corps in the Mediterranean revealed many of the same operational weaknesses that afflicted the Canadian First Army in Normandy. The 1st Division generally fought well in Sicily, overcoming the stiffest opposition of the campaign at the battles of Agira and Regalbuto, but command and control problems plagued the Canadians.[96]

The success and economy of Canadian participation in Italy intoxicated Canada's government; it thus decided not to withdraw the 1st Division for OVERLORD as originally planned but instead sent additional forces to Italy. This decision, which was based on political rather than military considerations, was an error.[97] Once the I Canadian Corps encountered German forces determined to hold the powerful Gustav Line, the 1st Division bogged down in the winter of 1943–1944, suffered heavy casualties, and lost its offensive edge.[98] The I Canadian Corps experienced as many difficulties with offensive action as the Canadian First Army would in Normandy. In its first major attack, the assault on the Liri Valley in May 1944, Canadian command and control again proved poor and their operations in the race for Rome in early June demonstrated their inexperience in fluid battle conditions.[99]

Unfortunately, Canadian combat experience in the Mediterranean had little impact on Canadian preparation in Britain for OVERLORD. Insufficient time existed for Crerar's command to absorb lessons learned from the Mediterranean because the Canadian offensive in the Liri Valley occurred too late to influence preparations for OVERLORD. Equally serious, amateurism bedeviled the lessons-learned process because senior commanders mistakenly believed that Mediterranean experience offered few lessons pertinent to combat in northwest Europe. Thus there was relatively little experience to challenge existing doctrine, tactics, and training, even though the I Corps experience clearly illuminated the operational inexperience of Canadian troops.

A combination of the inexperience, the dual character of the wartime army, and the need to field an overseas expeditionary force also ensured that the combat "teeth" of the CAO was proportionately much smaller than in the Anglo-American armies.[100] Uncertainty about the size of the field force to be deployed, over theaters of operations, and casualty forecasts all contributed to the uncontrolled expansion of "overhead." Thus only a fraction of the army was in combat formations ready to be deployed in the field. The CAO also suffered from overstaffing and overadministration, and was overprovided with engineering, ordnance, and medical units.[101] The need to maintain the CAO overseas both in Britain and in active theaters inevitably led to duplication; it was only through combat experience that the army became aware of overmanning problems. But because Canadian troops got into combat so late in the war, little rationalization of available manpower materialized prior to the Normandy campaign. Consequently, by 1944 no belligerent required so many support troops to keep one combatant in action as did Canada.[102]

Despite their elaborate service and support tail assigned to OVER-LORD, Canadian troops lacked certain critical areas of support and, consequently, could not operate without British assistance. The First Army's heterogeneous organization had stunted self-sufficiency because the contingents assigned to Crerar's command possessed minimal support services. Moreover, the available Canadian truck transport capacity was wholly inadequate and its tank recovery, repair, and replacement organization underdeveloped. Logistic deficiencies would hamper the Canadian Army's effort to make a decisive contribution to Allied victory in Normandy.[103]

Interservice cooperation is a vital ingredient in military effectiveness. Yet Supreme Headquarters Allied Expeditionary Force (SHAEF) did not earmark Canadian air and sea forces to support Canadian ground forces directly during OVERLORD. A sizable Canadian air contingent formed part of 83d Group, 2d (British) Tactical Air Force, which Canadian ground forces trained with during 1943.[104] But since SHAEF rated the 83d Group as the most combat-ready, it assigned it to support British Second Army, and appointed the all-British, and less proficient, 84th Group to support Canadian ground operations. Canadian tactical aviation did not support Canadian ground forces in Normandy. Due to their inexperience and resultant failure to learn from the combat experience of their allies, Canadian forces were slow to recognize the necessity for close liaison with tactical aviation.[105] Even with the liaison structures established by the War Office, Canadian forces had conducted few exercises with tactical air support before OVERLORD.[106] In addition, Canadian gunners did not begin training with aerial spotters until the late spring of 1944, and so had not gained proficiency with the air OP system prior to OVERLORD.[107]

The Canadian Army's early war experience raised serious concerns about its ability to fight effectively in northwest Europe. While Canadian troops generally exhibited good morale and enthusiasm, such spirit and esprit de corps were not matched by adequate higher leadership, doctrinal and tactical soundness, extensive battle experience, effective organization, quality training, or an adequate grasp of operational art. Significant variations existed in the quality of Canadian preparation. The 3d Division, which had intensively trained for its assault role, was clearly the best prepared Canadian formation. The 2d Division had worked hard to reconstitute itself after Dieppe, but never fully recovered from that setback and thus remained less battleworthy. The 4th Armoured Division's working up had lagged so far behind schedule that the CAO still rated it as nonoperational on the eve of D-Day. Canadian preparation was equally disparate as divisions focused on narrow projected missions, rather than broad combat preparation. The 3d Division's necessary emphasis on amphibious assault training had left it little time for combined-arms exercising with its accompanying armor from the 2d Armoured Brigade. The War Office considered neither of the continental armored contingents, the 1st Polish Division and the Czech Brigade, fully operational on the eve of D-Day. Lacking replacements, these formations were wasting assets whose combat power had to be carefully preserved by avoiding heavy combat.[108]

The Canadian wartime experience also illustrates the inherent obstacles to the efficient utilization of national resources for a war effort lacking overwhelming popular consensus and a direct threat to home territory. The most limiting influences on Canadian military operations in northwest Europe were Canada's growing manpower crisis and Canadian First Army's inability to operate independently of British support. The manpower problem on the eve of D-Day was ill recognized, let alone adequately addressed, and this oversight seriously impeded Canadian combat effectiveness in northwest Europe. Yet the personnel to avoid the manpower crisis did exist; what was lacking was determined political and military will to trim excess and rationalize manpower to mobilize the necessary people. As a result, manpower concerns for Canada shaped operations in northwest Europe as powerfully, if not more so, than for Britain. Minimizing casualties dominated Canadian operations throughout the northwest Europe campaign.

The Canadian Army's preparation for Operation OVERLORD demonstrates that it could not easily or quickly remedy its prewar neglect of the basic elements of the military profession. Such neglect necessitated dependence on Britain, which gave the Canadian Army that landed in Normandy a distinctly British cast. The Canadian military inherited the strengths, and the considerable defects, of the British Army of World War II, experiencing all the problems that beset the British troops in Normandy. Yet the Canadian Army faced its own unique difficulties, which derived from its unparalleled interwar neglect as well as Canada's geostrategic position and sociocultural background. Canada's need to deploy, train, equip, and maintain an army overseas in Great Britain added immensely to the difficulty of forging an effective wartime ground force and bred considerable waste, duplication, and inefficiency. Moreover, as the war progressed, the volunteer character of the CAO precipitated a growing manpower crisis, especially among French-Canadian units. These additional obstacles exacerbated the manifold problems caused by Canada's severe interwar neglect of its military. Canada had gone to war in 1939 without a modern army; by 1944 the nation had acquired one. Its achievements were considerable, but the gap between Canada's and the enemy's abilities was immense. Consequently, the Canadians were unable to compete tactically or operationally with the Germans in Normandy in 1944, and they could not replicate the Canadian triumphs of the Great War.

The Canadian Army on the eve of D-Day was thus a poor imitation of the British Army. Its Commonwealth status and strong cultural, linguistic, economic, and military ties with Britain meant that Canada naturally looked to Britain for the expertise and experience with which to forge its wartime army. Unfortunately, British doctrine and weapon procurement remained in many ways flawed. Canada's neglect of its military between the wars had denied it the expertise necessary to operate during World War II as a truly independent military force, and such inexperience led the Canadian Army to uncritically adopt a Commonwealth style of warfare.

Yet Canadian military preparation in Britain in 1943–1944 in no way demonstrated that the Canadians had mastered the Commonwealth style of warfare as well as their tutors. The CAO had not overcome serious manpower procurement and training problems, and, although it had come a long way from its state in late 1940, equipment and doctrine problems ensured that it was still far from being proficient, especially in combined-arms operations. Canadian commanders and troops remained largely unproven, and Canadian First Army had been stripped of the fighting power beyond the point it could operate effectively as a wholly Canadian force. Finally, the rapid but haphazard wartime proliferation of support and service elements further curtailed Canadian ability to operate independently. In recognition of these circumstances, SHAEF wisely assigned the First Canadian Army the subsidiary role of landing only after the Allies had established a successful bridgehead to operate across northeast France and the Low Countries on the flank of the Allied advance. Such a role acknowledged the limited capabilities of First Canadian Army, and only the audit of war in Normandy would determine how well placed this limited faith would prove.

Notes

1. On Canada's conscription problems, see J. L. Granatstein and J. Mackay Hitsman, *Broken Promises: A History of Conscription in Canada* (Oxford: Oxford University Press, 1977) and F. W. Perry, *The Commonwealth Armies: Manpower and Organisation in Two World Wars* (Manchester: Manchester University Press, 1988), 127–136.

2. Illustrative of the lack of quality control in early war enlistment was the discharge of 453 soldiers before June 1941 as mentally ill, including thirty-six categorized as psychopaths. C. P. Stacey and Barbara M. Wilson, *The Half-Million: The Canadians in Great Britain, 1939–1945* (Toronto: Toronto University Press, 1986), 33.

3. Canadian defense spending quintupled during 1940–1941. C. P. Stacey, *Arms, Men and Governments: The War Policies of Canada, 1939–45* (Ottawa: Queen's Printer, 1970), 32.

4. In the spring of 1939 the Canadian military possessed only sixteen light tanks, twenty-nine Bren guns, twenty-three antitank rifles, four modern antiaircraft guns, four antitank guns, five mortars, and 122 automobiles. Stacey, *Six Years of War: The Army in Canada, Britain and the Pacific* (Ottawa: Queen's Printer, 1955), 20–25.

5. Shortages of 40mm Bofors antiaircraft guns, for example, delayed the formation of light antiaircraft regiments until 1943. Stacey, *Six Years*, 242.

6. Canada was only able to expand production rapidly in 1941 where it had retained a peacetime capacity. Thus in 1941 Canada produced 17,800 Bren guns, 1,300 artillery pieces, and 189,000 motor vehicles. In 1940 Canada began producing British 25-pounder guns, 2-inch mortars, 40mm Bofors guns, and Valentine tanks.

7. In 1940–1941 the United States provided 250 obsolete M17 light tanks, 20,000 Enfield rifles, twenty-five 37mm antitank guns, and sixteen 155mm howitzers. Col. Stanley W. Dziuban, *Military Relations Between the U.S. and Canada, 1939–1945* (Washington, D.C.: Office of the Chief of Military History, DOA, 1959), 91–94.

8. In May 1940 Canada sent 75,000 Ross rifles and 60 million small-arms rounds to Britain. By late 1940 Britain had placed contracts in Canada for 300 tanks, 72,434 vehicles, 3,450 guns, and 100,000 rifles. Stacey, *Arms*, 35–36.

9. Dziuban, *Military Relations*, Table 6, 295.

10. For example, the 2d Armoured Brigade, earmarked to spearhead the D-Day assault had only 6 percent of its authorized armor in January 1944, and only 2 percent of Canadian-built Valentine tanks saw service with Canadian forces. Public Record Office, Kew, London, War Office Papers [PRO WO] 179/ 2839, WD, 2d Cdn. Armoured Brigade, Jan. 1944; Arthur C. Odell, "The Origins, Development, and Utilisation of the 5th Canadian Armoured Division," M.A. thesis, University of Victoria, 1976, 39–40, 54.

11. Canadian gunners, for example, initially trained with obsolete 18-pounders and 4.5-inch howitzers. Light antiaircraft guns, 4.2-inch mortars, and PIATS all remained scarce until 1944. The 4th Armoured Division first test-fired with its M10 tank destroyers in May 1944 and had still not received its full complement of Sherman tanks by D-Day. National Archives of Canada Record Group 24 [NAC RG 24] c2 9797, "Training 1st Division, CASF," 17 October 1939, 1–2; RG 24 13711, IICC, Weekly Progress Report to Canada Week Ending 13.5.1944, WD GS IICC, May 1944, apdx. 12, 1; PRO WO 205/151, Brigadier, Royal Armoured Corps, Twenty-First Army Group [BRAC, TFAG], "Policy of Issue of AFVs," 14 May 1944.

12. On Canadian wartime training, see John English, *The Canadians in Normandy: A Study of Failure in High Command* (London: Praeger, 1991), chap. 5.

13. For a definition of the operational level of war, see Edward Luttwak, "The Operational Level of War," *International Security* 5 (Winter 1980–1981), 61–79.

14. In September 1939 there were only fifty-six Canadian staff officers. William Hutchinson, "Test of a Corps Commander: Lieutenant-General Guy

Granville Simonds, Normandy 1944," M.A. thesis, University of Victoria, 1983, 100.

15. Tactical doctrine involves the teaching of tactics, the conceptual constructs that govern the tactics of an army. The term strategic doctrine is less widely used because the ideas and considerations that govern national strategic decisionmaking are rarely inculcated in officers and troops, but remain the preserve of senior military and political leaders.

16. English, *Canadians,* chap. 3.

17. By contrast, the German *Kriegsakademie* spent at least three years preparing staff officers for high operational command. English, *Canadians,* 100.

18. Some 67 percent of the 4,963 Canadian ground troops committed at Dieppe became casualties, and only 2,211 returned. The worst hit battalion, the Essex Scottish, extricated 10 percent of its committed troops. NAC RG24 c2 12,300, File 3/Dieppe/1 *The Dieppe Raid (Combined Report),* "Ic-Bericht Englische Landung am 19.8.1942 bei Dieppe," LXXXI A.K. Ic Anl. 4 z. G.K. LXXXI A.K. Ia Nr. 640/42 g.Kdos, HQu., 22 August 1942. On the Canadians at Dieppe, see Terence Robertson, *The Shame and the Glory: Dieppe* (Toronto: MacClelland and Stewart, 1962); Lt. Col. T. Murray Hunter, *Canada at Dieppe* (Ottawa: Balmuir, 1982).

19. Some 250 officers served in the Mediterranean under the CANLOAN scheme, and a few veteran officers returned from Italy. PRO CAB 106/1121, 23; Wildred I. Smith, *Code Word CANLOAN* (Toronto: Dundurn Press, 1992).

20. Stacey, *Arms,* 43–44; John Swettenham, *McNaughton* (Toronto: Ryerson Press, 1968–1969) 3 vols., passim.

21. The CAO peaked in strength at 234,500 troops in August 1944 and the entire army at 495,804 in March 1944. Stacey, *Arms,* 45–48; Maj. Gen. E. L. M. Burns, *Manpower in the Canadian Army 1939–1945* (Toronto: Clarke, Irwin & Co., 1956), Table 12.

22. The government classified 34 percent of those called up as medically unfit, deferred another 15 percent, and 2 percent evaded service. Stacey, *Arms,* 415; Burns, *Manpower,* Table 22, 148.

23. The government's unwillingness to tackle draft evasion makes it difficult to assess its scale. In April 1944 the government listed 13.5 percent of those men called for military service as evaders. But it prosecuted only 19 percent of these, and punishments consisted of fines or short imprisonments. Thus most evaders were neither traced nor prosecuted. Stacey, *Arms,* 414–415.

24. In March 1944 French Canadians made up 19 percent of the army and 14 percent of officers. The proportion of male Ottawans who served in the Canadian armed forces in World War II was double that of Quebec. Canada raised from French Canadians one engineer and four infantry battalions, as well as an artillery regiment. Officer shortages prevented the formation of an envisaged French-Canadian brigade, however. Stacey, *Arms,* 421–424.

25. Burns, *Manpower,* 139.

26. Stacey, *Arms,* 44–49.

27. The worst case scenarios envisaged possible Japanese raids in company strength. G. F. G. Stanley, *Canada's Soldiers: The Military History of an Unmilitary People* (Toronto: Macmillan, 1974), 355.

28. In the spring of 1943, 62,768 NRMA, 35,000 CASF, and over 100,000 CAR personnel remained in Canada organized in 3 divisions, 8 brigades, and 42 infantry battalions. Burns, *Manpower,* 133–135.

29. In late 1943, for example, Canada still retained 31 infantry battalions at home and even in November 1944, 125,545 general service and 68,120 NRMA sol-

diers remained in Canada, some 55 percent of the entire Canadian Army. Ibid., 132–135.

30. Ibid., 20, 83–86.

31. The CAO's war establishment called for the maintenance of four months' reinforcements at projected "intense" casualty rates. The most serious shortages were for infantry and French-Canadian replacements. NAC, Crerar Papers Vol. 15, letter, Crerar to CoS CMHQ, 21 May 1944.

32. The CAO's war establishment in January 1944 included 57,592 infantry. In March the CAO had 39,742 replacements available in Britain. Burns, *Manpower,* 74–76.

33. Stacey, *Arms,* 424–25.

34. The revised Evett rates increased the proportion of projected infantry casualties to 70.8 percent. Burns, *Manpower,* 112.

35. Of 23,000 projected infantry replacements, the CAO had only 14,500, 43 percent of which were either serving in ad hoc units or were unfit. Unavailable replacements comprised personnel serving in ad hoc units, replacements adjudged unfit for combat service, and personnel earmarked for remustering but not yet remustered. The practice of dumping "unfit" and "undesirable" personnel into the replacement pool exacerbated Canadian manpower difficulties. Thus under 8,000 infantry replacements were actually available. Stacey, *Arms,* 425–427; Burns, *Manpower,* Table 13, 91.

36. Only 20 percent of conscripts volunteered for active service. Stacey, *Arms,* 429; Burns, *Manpower,* Table 19, 121.

37. Even in 1944 only one-third of men called up were inducted, and the number of NRMA conscripts who converted to active service fell from 18,274 in 1942 to only 6,560 in 1943. Stacey, *Arms,* 429.

38. During April–May 1944 5,656 infantry reached Britain, and in early June a further 2,000. Burns, *Manpower,* 88–89.

39. PRO WO 179/3772, WD, GS HQ Canadian Reinforcement Units, apdx. 8, "Operational Instruction, 16.5.1944."

40. Ibid., 432–433.

41. Gerard W. L. Nicholson, *The Canadians in Italy, 1943–45* (Ottawa: Queen's Printer, 1957), chaps. 6–7; Dominick Graham and Shelford Bidwell, *Tug of War: The Battle for Italy, 1943–45* (New York: St. Martin's Press, 1986), chap. 18.

42. King wrote: "The more of our men participate in the campaign in Italy, the fewer there are likely to be who will be involved in the crossing of the Channel which, as Churchill says, will be a very tough business." J. W. Pickersgill, ed., *The Mackenzie King Record* (Toronto: Toronto University Press) I, 607.

43. The continental contingents consisted of the 1st Polish Armoured Division, the Czech Armoured Brigade, the Prinses Irene (Dutch) Brigade, and the Belgian Brigade. Malcolm A. Bellis, *Twenty-First Army Group Order of Battle* (Crewe: M. A. Bellis, 1991), 57–64.

44. David A. Wilson, "The Development of Tank-Infantry Co-Operation Doctrine in the Canadian Army for the Normandy Campaign of 1944," M.A. thesis, University of New Brunswick, 1992), 44–48.

45. In 1941 the CAO adopted as standard the British prewar training manual. War Office, *Infantry Training: Training and War, 1937* (Ottawa: King's Printer, 1941).

46. See, for example, Exercise TOURIST IV (2 December 1942). NAC RG24 13725, "1st Div. Plan to Defeat Invasion," 1 CID Op. Instruction 25, 15 December 1942.

47. The commanders removed were Maj. Gen. G. R. Pearkes, VC (1st

Division) and Maj. Gen. C. B. Price (3d Division). Stacey and Wilson, *Half-Million,* 16; Reginald H. Roy, *For Most Conspicuous Bravery: A Biography of Major-General George R. Pearkes V.C., Through Two World Wars* (Vancouver: University of British Columbia Press, 1977).

48. NAC RG 24, 13611, HQ FCA, "Notes on Ex. TIGER," 28 May 1942, apdx. 18; WD GS FCA, June 1942, 1; HQ FCA, "Notes on TIGER," 3 June 1942, apdx 19, WD GS FCA, June 1942.

49. During exercise BEAVER IV (1–15 May 1942) in Sussex, for example, the 2d Division ordered its 4th Brigade to concentrate in the middle of known enemy territory, and during BEAVER V (22–24 May 1943) the umpires cheated to prevent the 2d Division from overrunning 1st Division headquarters and thereby bring the exercise to a premature end. NAC RG24 13611, HQ FCA, "Points Arising out of Beaver IV Requiring Consideration and Action by Cmdrs., I Cdn. Corps," 19 May 1942, WD FCA GS, May 1944; "Observations by Cmdr. I Cdn. Corps on Ex. Beaver V," WD GS FCA, June 1942, 4–6.

50. Department of National Defence (DND), *The Standard Syllabus for Basic Training* (Ottawa: 1 November 1943). The stated goal of the new standardized syllabus was "to produce a formidable fighting man." The syllabus prescribed a 37.5-hour training week that with administration, sports, and processing, actually involved 32 hours of training. The evaluations were entitled Tests of Elementary Training (TOETs). On the standardization of TOETs, see NAC RG24 13241, DND, "Manpower for Overseas," Ottawa, 27 November 1943, apdx. 1.

51. The 1st Division's first offensive exercise was PRESENT (19–22 February 1943). NAC RG 24 13725, "Remarks by GOC 1 Cdn. Div. on Ex. PRESENT," 2 March 1943, WD GS 1 CID Mar. 1944, apdx. 2.

52. English, *Canadians,* 144.

53. Other Canadian commanders came out of the audit well, however. Alan Brooke praised Crerar for his leadership of the I Canadian Corps during the exercise. David Fraser, *Alanbrooke* (London: Collins, 1982), 188–189.

54. NAC RG 24 c2 9750, File 2/Air Rec/1, War Office, *Air Recognition Notes 4* (London: HMSO, February 1944). On procedures to deny signals intelligence to the enemy, see War Office, *The Enemy Listens: Some Notes on the Transmission of Radio Waves from Field Wireless Sets* (London: HMSO, November 1942) and *R/T Signals Procedure—1942* (London: HMSO, September 1942).

55. From late 1943 on, for example, Canadian troops vigorously retrained to improve aerial recognition skills. NAC RG24 c2 9750, File 2/Air Rec/1, HQ FCA, "Aircraft Recognition," 19 December 1943.

56. Stacey, *The Victory Campaign: The Operations in North-west Europe, 1944–45* (Ottawa: Queen's Printer, 1960), 29–31.

57. The six veteran senior officers were Generals Crerar and Simonds, Major General Kitching (4th Armoured Division), and Brigs. E. L. Booth, J. C. Jefferson, and R. A. Wyman. Stacey, *Six Years,* 417.

58. Crerar's preferment was largely due to the staunch support of Sir Alan Brooke. Fraser, *Alanbrooke,* 188, 422, 482.

59. English, *Canadians,* 183.

60. An excellent biography of Simonds is Dominick Graham's *The Price of Command* (Toronto: Stoughton, 1993).

61. Reginald Roy, *1944: The Canadians in Normandy* (Ottawa: Macmillan, 1984), 44–45; Maj. Gen. Kitching, *Mud and Green Fields: The Memoirs of Major General Kitching* (Langley, B.C.: Battleline Books, 1986).

62. Stacey, *Six Years,* 243.

63. Recruits arrived at a reception center, progressed to a basic training center,

then to a corps training center, followed by a brigade training group, before finally transferring to a transit camp for shipment overseas. Stacey, *Six Years,* 138–139.

64. PRO WO 179/3772, GS WD, HQ Canadian Reinforcement Units, Operational Instruction 5, 16 May 1944.

65. PRO WO 179/3772, WD Advanced HQ CRU, June 1944, Normandy, 12 June 1944; "Minutes of Brigade Majors Meetings 30 May and 20 June 1944."

66. The 2d Armoured Brigade, for example, exercised with the 3d Division for just three days prior to D-Day. Wilson, "Tank-Infantry Co-Operation Doctrine," 96, 117.

67. This doctrine was articulated in *Army Instructional Manual No. 2: Employment of Army Tanks in Co-Operation with Infantry* (London: HMSO, March 1941).

68. During Operation BRIDOON (October 1943), for example, the 4th Armoured and the 10th Infantry Brigades launched simultaneous but uncoordinated exercises. Wilson, "Tank-Infantry Cooperation Doctrine," 96, 113.

69. NAC RG 24 14139, WD 4th Cdn. Armd. Bde., "Training Instruction 17," 7 November 1943.

70. See War Office, *Tactical Handling of Army Tank Battalions* (London: HMSO, 1939); *The Employment of Army Tanks in Co-Operation with Infantry* (London: HMSO, March 1941); *Handling of an Armoured Division* (London: HMSO, May 1941); *Training in Co-operation—Army Tank Regiments and Infantry* (London: HMSO, 1942); GHQ Home Forces, *The Handling of the Re-organized Armoured Division* (London: HMSO, June 1942); War Office, *Tactical Handling of the Division and Armoured Division* (London: HMSO, Jan. 1943).

71. Hull-down positions utilized terrain so that only the turret was directly visible to the enemy. Wilson, "Tank-Infantry Cooperation Doctrine," 109–110.

72. In 1943–1944, the 2d Armoured Brigade converted from Churchill infantry tanks to U.S. Sherman cruiser tanks, which were less suited for infantry support. Wilson, "Tank-Infantry Cooperation Doctrine," 118.

73. Ibid., 136–137.

74. In September 1939, Canada possessed two armored cars and six militia infantry battalions that had undergone one week of training at the British Tank School at Bovington, Dorset. Wilson, "Tank-Infantry Cooperation Doctrine," 11, 30, 45–46.

75. The American M17 tanks were so obsolete that the United States sold them as "scrap iron" to evade congressional arms exportation restrictions. Odell, "5th Canadian Armoured Division," 29.

76. In 1944 CAO fielded thirty-nine infantry battalions and fourteen armored regiments, a ratio of nearly 3:1. Stacey, *Six Years,* 88.

77. The 5th Division only received its full establishment of Shermans in February 1944. Odell, "5th Canadian Armoured Division," 54–66.

78. The Firefly was an upgunned Sherman that mounted a high-velocity 17-pounder gun hastily converted by the British during the spring of 1944. During May 1944, Canadian units earmarked for OVERLORD received no fewer than 213 Shermans. PRO WO 179/3001, WD, 25th Cdn. Tank Delivery Regiment, May 1944, 8–11.

79. The 4th Armoured Division only began squadron training in August 1943, and regimental training in mid-September, and did not conduct its first divisional exercise until October 1943. The 5th Division's first full maneuvers occurred in exercise SPARTAN, its first involving air support, GRIZZLY and SNAFFLE (August 1943), and its first offensive exercises, ATTACK and DITTO (October 1943). NAC RG 24 13796, WD GS 5 CAD, Aug.–Sept. 1943; Odell, "5th Armoured Division," 61.

80. PRO CAB 44/297, 45.

81. The 3d Division had fully reequipped with 25-pounders by November 1941.

82. In 1944 artillery units constituted 16 percent of the Canadian Army strength, as compared with 30 percent in the British Army. Burns, *Manpower,* Table IV, 22.

83. The AGRCA comprised the 19th Field Regiment, the 3d, 4th, and 7th Medium Regiments, and the 2d Heavy Antiaircraft Regiment, RCA. It was fleshed out by the 191st Field and 1st Heavy Regiments, RA. By comparison, Britain fielded 104 army artillery regiments for OVERLORD. Malcolm Bellis, *21st Army Group,* 45–47.

84. Montgomery characterized their performance as "simply wonderful" and "quite amazing," while Oliver Leese called it "magnificent." NAC RG 24 c2 9841, File 2/Reps Ops/1, Extract of letter from Montgomery to HDG Crerar, 8 August 1943, I CC GS WD, Aug. 1944; RG24 13726 Extract of letter from Leese to Simonds, HQ 1 CID, 8 August 1943, I CID GS WD Aug. 1944.

85. There were no corps troops available, and only a single reinforcement battalion. NAC RG 24 13725, "Order of Battle, 1st Cdn. Div.," 22 May 1943, WD GS 1 CID, May 1944, apdx. 87.

86. NAC RG24 13726, interview with Guy Simonds, CBC [Aug. 1943], I CID GS WD Aug. 1943.

87. The 1st Division included all three PAM infantry battalions—the Royal Canadian Regiment, the 22ᶜ Régiment, and the Princess Patricia's Light Infantry.

88. Simonds's efforts to tighten signals security, for example, were not very successful. Even though he demanded that units change codes daily, many units kept the same prefixes and simply renumbered sequentially. NAC RG 24 13726, WD 1 CID GS, Aug. 1943, "Signals Security," 12 August 1943, apdx.

89. Bidwell and Graham, *Tug of War,* passim; Nicholson, *Canadians in Italy,* chaps. 11–12.

90. During the Liri Valley campaign, for example, 810 guns supported the I Canadian Corps. Jonathon Bailey, *Field Artillery and Firepower* (Oxford: Military Press, 1989), 191–192.

91. The Germans deliberately left weak spots in their defense to channel attackers toward the city center, which had been cleared as a "killing zone" and upon which all heavy weapons were registered. NAC RG24 13727, GS 1 CID, "Ortona," Italy, 16 February 1944, 1–2; Stanley, *Soldiers,* 367–368; Bidwell and Graham, *Tug of War,* 120.

92. NAC RG24 13727, "Tank Cooperation in Street Fighting," apdx. A to "Ortona," GS 1 CID, 16 February 1944, 1.

93. NAC RG24 13727, "Ortona," GS 1 CID, Italy, 16 February 1944; Michael Doubler, *Closing With the Enemy: How GI's Fought the War in Europe, 1944–45* (Lawrence, University of Kansas Press, 1995).

94. Montgomery observed of the Canadians in Sicily that "they are very willing to learn and they learn fast." Letter, Montgomery to Brooke, 27 July 1943, in Stephen Brooks, ed., *Montgomery and the Eighth Army: A Selection from the Diaries, Correspondence and Other Papers of Field Marshal The Viscount Montgomery of Alamein, August 1942–December 1943* (London: Bodley Head, 1991), 254.

95. NAC RG 24 13728, Ex. Instr. BUTTERCUP II, 3 March 1944, apdx. 7, WD GS FCA, March 1944.

96. William A. Douglas and Brereton Greenhous, *Out of the Shadows: Canada in the Second World War* (Toronto: Oxford University Press), 122–129; Samuel W. Mitchum and Friedrich von Stauffenberg, *The Battle for Sicily: How the Allies Lost*

Their Chance for Total Victory (New York: Orion Books, 1991), 153–154, 182–194, 239–240; Stanley, *Soldiers,* 367–368; Bidwell and Graham, *Tug of War,* 120.

97. It would have been wiser to have withdrawn the 1st Division from Italy during the spring of 1944 (replacing it with the green 2d Division) and rebuilt the former in time for the Normandy breakout battles of August 1944.

98. "As a result of our protracted period of static warfare, the div. has . . . become morally and physically soft," Simonds concluded. NAC RG 24 13727, GOC 1 CID, WD GS 1 CID, April 1944, Apdx. 7.

99. Stacey and Wilson, *The Half Million,* 18–22; Bidwell and Graham, *Tug of War,* chap. 18.

100. In November 1944, 53 percent of the Canadian personnel in Italy were classified as combatants, compared to 65 percent in the British army. The U.S. Army—which shared the same geostrategic problems of projecting military power from North America to Europe via an advanced base in Britain—achieved a much higher ratio of combat to service personnel in the ETO. In late 1944 only 40 percent of the CAO's manpower was in combat formations in contrast to 52 percent for the U.S. Army. Average divisional slices for the U.S., British, and Canadian armies in November 1944 were 71,100, 84,300, and 93,150, respectively. Burns, *Manpower,* Tables III–IV, 20–22.

101. Service units comprised 47 percent of the CAO in Italy in November 1944 compared to only 35 percent among British forces. Burns, *Manpower,* 22.

102. A comparison of divisional slices illustrates this point: Canada, 93,150; Great Britain, 84,300; United States, 71,100; Germany, 23,000; Soviet Union, 22,000. John English, *On Infantry* (New York: Praeger, 1981), 138.

103. The Royal Canadian Electrical and Mechanical Engineers deployed only a single recovery company and the Royal Canadian Army Service Corps a mere ten companies, one-seventh the number fielded by the Royal Army Service Corps. Bellis, *Twenty-First Army Group,* 34–50.

104. Sixteen Canadian squadrons (eleven Spitfire, two Mustang, and three Typhoon) were assigned to 2d (British) Tactical Air Force for OVERLORD. Ibid., 1–20.

105. The Canadians only established an Air Support Command system during the summer of 1942. NAC RG 24 13611, HQ FCA, "Prov. Instrs. for the Employment of Canadian Air Support Control," 24 July 1942.

106. The 3d Division conducted none of its preinvasion exercises with tactical aviation, and of 83d Group's 4,777 missions in September 1943, only sixty-six were exercise sorties in conjunction with Canadian forces. Montgomery warned the Canadians in 1942 that "you must make special efforts to gain more practical experience in air co-operation." NAC, Crerar Papers, vol. 2, Letter Keller to Crerar, 22 April 1944; NAC RG 24 13614, "Air Exercises," Periodical Air Int. Sum. (PAIS) 4, 24–30 September 1943, apdx B; PAIS 5, 1–8 October 1943, HQ FCA, 16 October 1943; RG 24 c2 12,300, File 3/Ex. BEAVER/1, "SE. Cmd. Ex. BEAVER Final Conference, 2.1.1942—Remarks by Army Cmdr."

107. NAC RG24 13711, IICC, "Weekly Progress Report to Canada Week Ending 13.5.1944," 15 May 1944, WD GS IICC May 1944, apdx. 12, 1.

108. PRO WO 205/1151, BRAC TFAG, "Policy of Issue of AFVs," 14 May 1944.

5

Germany, 1939–1944: Blitzkrieg Unleashed

Early in World War II, Germany had won a series of military victories that shattered the European balance of power. Central to German success was the *Heer*'s willingness to evaluate its own performance critically and honestly, to absorb combat lessons, and to retrain, reorganize, and reequip to enhance its combat effectiveness. This determination helped Germany acquire a hegemony in Europe despite a weak strategic base and the absence of an economy organized for war.

On 1 September 1939, Germany unleashed fifty-five of its best divisions and most of its armor and aircraft against Poland's forty-division army. While lack of prepared defenses, modern equipment, and communications hampered the Polish defense, Poland's decision to defend its extended western frontier left its army vulnerable to strategic encirclement and annihilation as the Germans executed a double envelopment to destroy the main body of the Polish Army in the bend of the Vistula River. The Poles fought valiantly, but their strategic position was untenable against superior German strength, and resistance ceased after thirty-six days. This campaign saw the first application of blitzkrieg warfare, which combined traditional Prussian *Kesselschlacht* encirclement strategy with revolutionary new mechanized forces.[1] The Germans remained uncertain about the potential of armored forces, and they dispersed much of their armor. Nevertheless armor played a major role in the German victory. Mechanized forces—occasionally supported by punishing tactical air strikes—penetrated deep into the enemy forces' rear to disrupt communications and paralyze the Polish units until German infantry and artillery could arrive to annihilate them. This combination allowed the Germans to overrun Poland rapidly at light cost.[2]

Central to the remarkable early German triumphs was the German military's professional commitment to critical self-appraisal and a refusal to equate victory with excellence in performance. This determination allowed the *Heer* progressively to enhance its combat capabilities. During winter of

1939–1940 the army extensively evaluated its experience in Poland and, despite its stunning victory, was dissatisfied with troop performance.[3] Equally important, the *Heer* did not simply seek to validate existing doctrine but to refine and improve it as it concluded that hasty and excessive expansion had forged an army inferior to the 1914 Imperial Army. Study revealed organizational defects, including the inadequacy of the light mechanized division and the unwieldiness of the motorized division.[4] Reconnaissance, coordination, and camouflage skills had all proven inadequate, and troops had largely failed to adopt defense in depth on the few occasions they had gone on the defense. Undertrained and hastily mobilized reservists had also fought poorly, and even regular infantry had lacked aggressiveness, fared badly in night fighting, and depended too heavily on artillery support to overcome opposition. Even the elite panzer forces had dispersed their armor, coordinated poorly, and displayed poor march discipline.[5]

During the winter of 1939–1940 the *Heer* intensively retrained, reorganized, and reequipped to correct the flaws illuminated in Poland, to raise the standards of reservists and to inculcate offensive-mindedness and speed. After-action reports from Poland confirmed the efficacy of mechanized forces and won over many conservatives, including Erwin Rommel and Gerd von Rundstedt, to the potential of armor. As doubt receded the army fully adopted blitzkrieg warfare; the panzer arm expanded as the *Heer* upgraded its light divisions to full panzer divisions and troops rigorously exercised in the field to improve combined-arms coordination.[6] Analysis also showed the *Luftwaffe*'s significant aid to victory in Poland: it had quickly gained air superiority, then isolated the enemy front from reinforcement and resupply with interdiction attacks on railways and bridges, and materially assisted the German ground advance with bombing, strafing, and dive-bomber attacks. Buoyed by this success, the *Luftwaffe* strengthened its tactical orientation during the winter of 1939–1940 to provide more rapid and intimate ground support.[7]

The *Heer*'s realistic doctrine, broad professionalism, and quality training allowed it to surmount Germany's weak strategic position, which was the biggest obstacle to Hitler's goal of world domination. Germany simply lacked the manpower, industrial base, and raw materials to dominate the world. Only by dividing its enemies and conquering them piecemeal could Germany acquire the continental European hegemony that was a prerequisite in any bid for global domination.[8] Blitzkrieg tactics and operational concepts aimed to dislocate the enemy's command, communication, and control system and thus sought to outmaneuver rather than outfight the enemy. Such an approach allowed the *Heer*, which had only a marginal firepower advantage and which lacked the resources and industrial base for protracted combat, to overwhelm powerful opponents quickly.

Yet significant deficiencies remained, most notably the *Heer*'s limited motorization, inadequate logistic base, and weak artillery capability. Yet the markedly greater deficiencies of Germany's opponents obscured these weaknesses throughout the early war years. At the same time, overexpansion (as Hitler ordered another forty-nine weak infantry divisions raised in the winter of 1939–1940) reduced the *Heer*'s combat effectiveness. Renewed expansion so soon after mobilization outstripped German productive capacity, exacerbated equipment shortages, and seriously delayed activation of new divisions. Optical and signal equipment, motor vehicles, weapons, and munitions all remained in short supply, and these deficiencies seriously delayed the rapid acquisition of combat readiness by German formations.[9]

In April 1940 Germany launched a hastily improvised invasion of Denmark and Norway—Operation *WESERÜBUNG*—to forestall an anticipated Allied occupation of Norway. Hitherto, Scandinavia had barely figured in German strategic thinking, and the *Heer* lacked forces prepared for winter warfare in the Arctic.[10] Operationally, the German occupation of Norway was a great success that secured for the *Wehrmacht* its first victory over Anglo-French forces. Executed in the face of vastly superior British sea power, *WESERÜBUNG* was boldly conceived, well planned, and skillfully executed. Though a minor campaign, this provided important lessons for the protagonists.[11] *WESERÜBUNG* represented the first joint operation that involved all three German armed services, and its success required close interservice cooperation. Germany swiftly air- and sea-lifted six divisions to Norway and successfully resupplied them.[12] Seaborne assaults on eight Norwegian ports supported by paratroop drops, the first combat use of airborne forces, began the campaign. Britain and France reacted by landing forces in northern central Norway to contest the German invasion, yet their counterinvasion failed—only at Narvik in the far north did Anglo-French forces temporarily threaten the German lodgement before they abandoned Norway.[13]

The Norwegian campaign first demonstrated the supremacy of air power over sea power, as air support proved decisive to German victory. While unable to prevent the Allies landing in strength, the *Luftwaffe* kept the Royal Navy at bay, obstructed Allied ground operations, and aided the German ground advance to prevent Anglo-French forces from gaining a firm foothold in Norway. The small-scale German tactical employment of airborne forces to secure vital airfields and allow air-landing of reinforcements also demonstrated the value of airborne forces operating in conditions of air superiority against an unprepared enemy. The campaign revealed the ability of aircraft to reinforce and resupply isolated forces: airlifts sustained the German lodgement at Narvik until the ground advance from the south achieved a linkup.[14]

Despite their lack of preparation for winter and Arctic warfare, German troops adapted quickly to local conditions and innovated tactically to surmount the unfamiliar terrain and conditions. Mountains, deep snow, and winter weather both heavily favored defense and hampered mobility. The campaign confirmed the lessons of Poland regarding the efficacy of armor: the single light tank company shipped to Norway played an important role in German success. Lacking antitank capability, neither Anglo-French nor Norwegian forces could halt the obsolescent Panzer I and II tanks.[15] But, only small combined-arms combat groups built around armor and heavily reinforced in firepower proved able to penetrate Allied blocking positions across narrow valley floors that denied German maneuver. Forced to launch unsubtle frontal attacks, German troops maintained a furious tempo, passing battalions through one another to maintain offensive momentum, and attacking at dawn and dusk to wear down enemy resistance. German troops also repeatedly crossed terrain considered impassable to seize mountain peaks and outflank enemy forces.[16] The Norwegian campaign confirmed the tactical flexibility and adaptability that German forces had shown in Poland.

Once again detailed examination of troop performance followed victory in Scandinavia. The protracted fight for Narvik, in difficult terrain and against a larger force, revealed that the offensive orientation of German training had left troops ill prepared for defense. At the same time, the German assessment of Anglo-French performance in Norway as poor reinforced Hitler's determination to launch a blitzkrieg in the west. The *OKH* concluded that the British lacked fighting spirit, panicked easily, suffered from poor morale, and were ill equipped, tactically inept, and slow to adapt to German outflanking and infiltration tactics.[17]

Yet faults that later contributed to German defeat surfaced in Norway, though they were not prominent enough to affect the course of the campaign. German victory relied heavily on daring, surprise, and the enemy's unreadiness. The campaign also revealed that the *Wehrmacht* lacked a command organization for large-scale joint operations, even though the services had cooperated fairly well in the face of few operational difficulties. Interservice friction did emerge, however, over the proper use of air power. The army demanded close air support, especially during the struggle for Narvik, while the *Luftwaffe* sought to attack naval targets at sea.[18] Moreover, the crippling losses suffered by the *Kriegsmarine* while transporting troops and supplies to Norway revealed how unbalanced German military capabilities were. All the same, the vulnerability of German lines of communication to air and sea attack was a lesson of the campaign that went unrecognized by both sides.

On 10 May 1940 Germany launched Operation SICHELSCHNITT, a massive blitzkrieg invasion of France and the Low Countries. Hitler employed maximum strength—135 of Germany's 156 divisions—in the attack, but German forces were still outnumbered and outgunned.[19] Lacking numerical and material superiority or the resources for a protracted campaign, the operation depended on concentration, speed, and surprise for success. As in Poland, Hitler threw virtually his entire air and ground forces into the attack to overwhelm quickly his enemies before they had time to mobilize their demographic and industrial strength. Concentrated German mechanized forces conducted a daring, rapid, and deep penetration through the wooded, hilly Ardennes to isolate and pin down the entire left wing of the Allied front until the bulk of the *Heer* could arrive and annihilate it. This advance split the Allied front and forced the BEF to fight its way back to the Channel port and be evacuated. Having cut off the BEF, Hitler halted his stretched armored forces before the Channel ports, while the infantry caught up before launching a final attack on Calais and Dunkirk: a delay that allowed the battered BEF to escape from Dunkirk to fight again.[20]

The fall of France was one of the greatest martial achievements in the history of warfare as Germany rapidly overran France at light cost. Bold, swift, and imaginative employment of combined-arms mechanized forces ably supported by *Luftwaffe* tactical aviation secured victory.[21] Similarly daring employment of airborne forces—most notably in the seizure of the reputedly impregnable Belgian fort of Eben Emael—speeded success on the ground. Moreover, the impact of the German winter retraining was manifest in better concentration and coordination, as well as greater confidence and aggressiveness, as enhanced combat effectiveness contributed to the devastating German victory.

These spectacular victories were, however, misleading. Despite its blitzkrieg aura of modernity, the *Heer* was in many ways less modern than its opponents. Germany was among the least motorized societies in Western Europe and outside the elite armored troops, the *Heer* remained a predominantly horse-drawn infantry force.[22] Moreover, even though the Germans used modern communications effectively in their early campaigns, field radios were never common. In addition, because blitzkrieg aimed to overwhelm enemies rapidly, the *Heer* lacked the service support or resources to fight a long and protracted conflict. What the tremendous victory in the West obscured was that late in the campaign "friction" had badly eroded the combat power of German mechanized forces.[23] Thus blitzkrieg only worked so well early in the war due to a unique combination of German organizational and improvisational skill, the flexibility instilled by the *Reichswehr* in the 1920s, and the obvious unpreparedness of Germany's enemies.

During the summer of 1940 the *Heer* reduced its strength, reorganized, and absorbed the lessons of the French campaign. The proven efficacy of armored forces in France led to massive expansion of mechanized forces during the fall of 1940. The *OKH* simultaneously reorganized its panzer formations in light of lessons learned in Poland and France that showed the existing organization to be tank-heavy and lacking infantry, supporting arms, and close integration. Reorganization slashed tank strength but enhanced combined-arms capabilities. The *OKH* also revised training manuals to emphasize greater coordination.[24] The result was better organized, balanced, and coordinated mechanized forces.

During 1940 the *Heer* underwent few major doctrinal, organizational, or equipment changes; its great victories provided little impetus for extensive or radical transformation. Nevertheless, modest reform and reorganization continued, including the expansion of assault gun formations to increase provision of armor for the infantry.[25] The *Heer* also raised junior leadership standards and retrained reservists and recruits to the highest standards. Consequently, by summer 1941 the *Heer* had become exceptionally well trained. At the same time, while the army's overall equipment situation remained unsatisfactory, partial reequipment occurred as uniformity increased and several excellent new weapons entered service.[26]

In February 1941, Hitler reluctantly committed a small motorized force led by an energetic and competent young commander, Erwin Rommel, to shore up his Italian ally since its position in North Africa had disintegrated after a crippling winter 1940–1941 defeat by the British in Libya. Hitler's strategic goals did not encompass North Africa, and Germany lacked forces even remotely prepared for Mediterranean service.[27] Once it was committed events forced Hitler to reinforce German strength in Libya, from which emerged the famous Africa Corps. Unique desert conditions brought new challenges for German troops and denied them many of the advantages they were accustomed to. Rommel's forces operated along extended and tenuous lines of communication, often without air superiority, and with troops untrained and ill equipped for desert warfare. Because Libya contained only one all-weather road, the Via Balbia, and cross-desert tracks were difficult to traverse, poor communications restricted most combat to the narrow coastal plain. At the same time, desert haze, dust clouds, and sandstorms kicked up by hot winds obstructed observation and hampered concealment.[28]

The Africa Corps adapted rapidly to desert conditions during combat and largely without formal retraining. Starved by higher neglect and overextended lines of communication, the troops speedily adapted to the exigencies of terrain and climate to become proficient desert fighters within a few months. Standard German tactics often proved inappropriate in the desert, where armor enjoyed even greater prominence and where fluid maneuver warfare was the norm. Lack of air cover and the difficulties of camouflage forced German troops to learn the need for dispersion. Moreover, though given a defensive mission, doctrine said relatively little about desert defense where reverse slopes were uncommon. Tactically, the Africa Corps quickly learned from experience to eliminate British armor first by offensive defense. Mechanized combined-arms battle groups built around armored wedges (*Panzerkeile*) echeloned in depth learned to retire when they encountered British armor, and lure them onto novel antitank screens reinforced by heavy antiaircraft guns that outranged British armor and routinely shattered British tank regiments before the summer of 1942.[29]

The Africa Corps experimented and retrained during the lull between the battles of the summer and of fall 1941, and by spring 1942 had become a proficient desert force.[30] The superior fieldcraft displayed by the Africa Corps reflected the sophistication of German holistic combined-arms doctrine. German troops reconnoitered aggressively and routinely employed tactical deception to disguise their attacks. In fact, the open terrain so hampered concealment that deception became much more important than in Europe. Lack of firepower and ammunition shortages also meant that it was in the desert the Germans would first employ concentrated artillery support. Almost always understrength, the Africa Corps relied heavily on artillery fire for its offensive and defensive power—even though soft sand reduced shells' effectiveness.[31] Moreover, good aerial reconnaissance and excellent wireless interception provided valuable intelligence that gave the Germans an edge in the desert during 1941–1942.

The Africa Corps assessed British capabilities much more accurately than vice versa. Rommel drew on assessments of British performance in Scandinavia and France as inept, methodical, slow, and inflexible. He concluded that the boldness that led to Wavell's stunning victory over the Italians was atypical and that, therefore, the British remained vulnerable to fast-paced maneuver war.[32] German involvement in North Africa brought extensive exposure to British combat techniques, and, at the same time, German professionalism, flexibility, and ingenuity all directly contributed to the stunning early Axis victories in the desert.

Hitler's ambitious plans to annihilate the Soviet Union (Operation BARBAROSSA) in a racial struggle that would acquire the *Lebensraum* needed to guarantee a thousand-year *Reich* ended the consolidation process begun in 1940. Hitler demanded an even larger army to effect his grandiose strategic designs. During winter of 1940–1941 the *Heer* thus added another sixty-seven divisions to its order of battle. This rapid renewed expansion once again temporarily reduced the *Heer*'s combat efficiency and left the army understrength and without reserves.[33] The envisaged scale and nature of BARBAROSSA wrought important changes to the army's character and organization. Hitler conceived the campaign as an ideological and racial war of extermination against the Soviet Union, Bolsheviks, Slavs, and Jews—the culmination of his genocidal master plan.[34] The scope of the undertaking envisioned thus stretched German resources to the limit as the *Wehrmacht* prepared during the spring of 1941 for the impending campaign.

The most significant change in the character of the *Wehrmacht* was its increasing nazification. Politicization was a double-edged sword that both enhanced and eroded German combat effectiveness, however. Nazi racism inflated German perceptions of their military superiority, which when coupled with the spectacular conquests of 1939–1941, exacerbated the German military's traditional disdain of Soviet/Russian military capabilities. Whereas the *Reichswehr* had soberly assessed the military capabilities of potential opponents, the *Wehrmacht* increasingly embraced ideological and racial rhetoric.[35] The rapid destruction of Poland merely reinforced traditional German contempt for Slavic martial qualities. Thus the BARBAROSSA plan lacked the sober assessment that characterized *Reichswehr* planning. Moreover, the effects of Stalin's military purges—demonstrated by Finland's humiliation of Soviet arms in the 1939–1940 Winter War—suggested easy German successes. (At the same time, however, the Germans ignored contrary evidence provided by Soviet victory over Japan at Khalkin Gol in the Far East during the summer of 1939.)[36] Germany's brilliant blitzkrieg conquests thus bred arrogance, appeared to validate nazi racism, and denigrated Soviet military capabilities.[37] Indeed, the *Wehrmacht* had become so intoxicated with success that it was not unduly alarmed by its lack of information about the force structure, military potential, and staying power of the Soviet Union. Such inadequate intelligence led the Germans seriously to underestimate Soviet military strength and resilience, and also meant they failed to detect the Soviet buildup of reserves deep within the Soviet Union.[38]

The conquest of Yugoslavia and Greece in April 1941, which interrupted BARBAROSSA preparations, marked the epitome of blitzkrieg. Germany launched a hastily prepared invasion with troops drawn from all over the Nazi empire. Yugoslavia's twenty-eight-division army lacked modern equipment and suffered from internal ethnic tensions, and its near encirclement by Axis countries gave the Germans an immense strategic advantage. The Greek Army was much smaller but equally backward. The rapidity with which Germany conquered the Balkans demonstrated that the *Heer* had considerably enhanced its combat effectiveness since Poland and France. Indeed, close ground-air coordination characterized German operations in the Balkans: intimate liaison allowed powerful air support to compensate for the obstacles to artillery support in the Greek mountains.[39] That Germany overwhelmed resistance in the field in three weeks without special preparation reflected the high standard of coordination and training that the *Heer* had reached by spring 1941. Concluding the Balkan campaign was the German airborne conquest of Crete, the first truly strategic employment of airborne forces. But here Germany gained a Pyrrhic victory. German casualties were heavy, and Hitler misinterpreted the lessons of Crete and never again employed airborne forces en masse instead of limiting their future use to less ambitious tactical missions. As a result, after Crete, the *Luftwaffe* gradually transformed its paratroop arm into another elite ground infantry force.[40]

Despite its increase to 208 divisions, in June 1941 the *Heer* was only marginally more powerful than it had been in May 1940. Even though partial reequipment had been carried out, there was little increase in armor, air-craft, or artillery strength. The biggest improvement was increased stan-dardization and a better quality of leadership. But the army remained too large; serious officer shortages persisted, especially in the general staff; units remained understrength and underequipped; many divisions still used captured weapons and motor vehicles; and antitank ammunition were still especially tight due to raw material shortages. At the same time, overexpan-sion had prevented the replacement army from raising its training capacity, so divisions now shared training units and the *Heer* lacked a large pool of replacements.[41]

The German failure to increase production and reequip was a conse-quence of political decisions by Hitler. In retrospect, the year between the fall of France and BARBAROSSA was a lost period. The *Heer* underwent greater psychological changes as it prepared for BARBAROSSA. For the first time, the officer corps systematically inculcated a National Socialist worldview to condition troops for the genocidal struggle ahead.[42] BAR-BAROSSA was to be the largest military operation in history as Germany committed 153 of its 208 divisions and 3.3 million troops for a short, brutal summer blitzkrieg campaign to overwhelm the Soviet Union. But given that country's size, population, industrial potential, and the savage war the eastern army (or *Ostheer*) was to wage, Germany lacked the resources to defeat the Soviet Union in a single summer campaign. Dismissing Soviet military capabilities, Germany abandoned use of the political subversion that had aided the German victory against Russia during World War I and to which Stalin's unpopular regime remained vulnerable. Blinded by racism and overconfidence, Hitler and his generals failed to realize that waging genocide would inevitably intensify Soviet resistance and rally the Soviet peoples behind Stalin's regime.[43]

Germany thus greatly underestimated the size and resilience of the Red Army.[44] In fact, in anticipation of a quick ground victory, Hitler actually scaled back arms and ammunition production for the army during summer of 1941.[45] The war games had recognized the massive frontage and depth of penetration required if BARBAROSSA were to succeed, and the army had addressed, however inadequately, the problems this presented. It expanded signals units to allow long-distance communication, doubled its strategic motor transport reserve, acquired thousands of Polish horse-drawn carts to improve infantry mobility, increased railway troops to convert the Soviet rail net to German track gauge, and, as an interim measure, built 170 locomotives to the Soviet gauge.[46] Such measures considerably expanded German logistic resources, but were inadequate for the immense task out-lined. If the Soviet Union did not quickly collapse, the *Ostheer* would sim-ply lack the logistics base—transport, fuel, and munitions—for victory in a single summer campaign. As well, bridging and radio equipment and prime movers all remained in short supply.[47] To compensate for these deficiencies

Germany would once again resort to a blitzkrieg attack and concentrate massive strength to outmaneuver and quickly overwhelm Soviet resistance. Yet the uncompromising fight the Germans were to wage would leave the Soviet people with no alternative but to fight to the bitter end, and so the Soviet Union simply could not be conquered quickly or easily.

BARBAROSSA initially met with huge success as the *Ostheer* conducted devastating strategic deep penetrations that encircled and eliminated millions of Soviet troops and thousands of planes, guns, and tanks.[48] Yet the vastness of the Russian steppes ultimately swallowed up the blitzkrieg and sapped German strength as losses mounted. Simultaneously, the Soviet Union mobilized its enormous manpower resources and relocated its industry east of the Urals, in preparation for a protracted war.[49] Depleted and exhausted, the Germans pressed on in search of decisive victory in the belief that one more push would bring a Soviet collapse. Forced to fight beyond its tether, with its strength attenuated, and with precarious logistic support, the *Ostheer* suffered heavily and its combat power dwindled.[50]

The Eastern Front, which absorbed the majority of Germany's armed forces throughout World War II, wrought important changes in German doctrine, organization, tactics, and equipment, as the *Ostheer* adapted to novel combat conditions in an ever more desperate and vicious battle for survival. The *Heer* possessed sound defensive doctrine based on defense in depth, but its offensive-oriented training left German troops inexpert at defense. Moreover, the unique features of the Eastern Front—distance, terrain, weather, and overextension—rendered existing doctrine inadequate. German troops initially fared poorly in defensive operations in the east, especially early on during the Soviet winter 1941 counteroffensive. However, German troops quickly improvised modified defensive tactics grounded in the core principles of German defensive doctrine—depth, firepower, mobility, and counterattack—to halt the Soviet forces, and the revised techniques that emerged during 1941–1943 became standard practice on all fronts for the rest of the war.[51]

Hard defensive fighting accompanied the meteoric blitzkrieg advances of summer 1941 as distance, terrain, and weather negated standard elastic defense in depth. Aggressive drives took panzer formations well forward of the slower infantry and often forced them to engage in heavy defensive fighting, generally without prepared positions in depth, against both Soviet forces attempting to evade encirclement and counterattacking relief forces. Panzer divisions lacked infantry or defensive training, and defense negated the mobility that was central to their effectiveness. They were, therefore, not very effective at encirclement operations and often could not fully contain enemy pockets, with the result that many encircled Soviet troops escaped.[52] Moreover, Soviet counterattacks with heavy armor often pressed the panzer forces hard, and they increasingly had to deploy *Luftwaffe* heavy antiaircraft guns in a ground antitank role, the Flak 88 being the only German weapon that could destroy Soviet heavy armor at long range.

The infantry experienced defensive difficulties too. With troop densities often averaging half those in other theaters, the thinly stretched infantry faced frequent Soviet counterattacks. Combat quickly revealed that infantry lacked antitank capability and had no effective counter to Soviet heavy armor. Infantry divisions often had to deploy forward artillery and heavy flak guns in a direct-fire role, even though this brought heavy losses through line-of-sight engagements.[53] Since these heavy weapons were scarce assets and difficult to redeploy quickly, the infantry often had to destroy Soviet armor in close combat with antitank mines, grenades, and Molotov cocktails. Successful destruction in close combat required iron discipline and the separation of Soviet armor from accompanying infantry. If this was not achieved, Soviet armor often overran the thinly stretched German line and inflicted heavy loss.[54]

At first the clumsy, unsophisticated, and ill-coordinated nature of early Soviet counterattacks saved many German units from destruction.[55] But as the advance continued German units became dangerously separated and more depleted, and the Red Army counterattacked frequently. The breadth of the front and paucity of German forces prevented elastic defense in depth, and German troops often had to adopt linear defenses (consisting of widely spaced strongpoints, with few or no reserves) that Soviet counterattacks regularly penetrated.[56] German combat power further waned as troops outdistanced their lines of supply. The terrible Russian roads and the vast distances took a catastrophic toll of German motor transport, and little equipment and few troops were available to replace losses.[57]

Its strategic and logistic situation demanded that the depleted, tired, and overextended *Ostheer* halt in late September 1941; consolidate and construct winter defensive positions and a supply infrastructure; and prepare for a renewed offensive the following summer. However, the *OKH* gambled on a final big push to take Moscow during the fall—Operation TAIFUN—with weakened forces that lacked ammunition and fuel. German strength and mobility plummeted during the fall as troops slogged through the terrible mud and as the Soviet forces threw all available troops, including fresh, well-equipped reserves from the Far East, into the line to halt the enemy at the gates of Moscow.[58] Though exhausted, and despite its unpreparedness for winter combat and facing mounting partisan attacks in the rear that further disrupted supply deliveries, the German Army Group Center resumed the attack in mid-November in winter snow and ebbing morale until this weak offensive ground to a halt in sheer exhaustion on 5 December.[59]

During the winter of 1941–1942 the German defense rarely conformed to established doctrine.[60] Limitations imposed by terrain and weather; by troop, equipment, supply shortages; and by Hitler's orders to stand fast prevented elastic defense in depth. Instead, the Germans adopted expedient defensive techniques dictated by circumstances as, on 6 December, the Soviets counterattacked. The Red Army launched heavy but unsophisticated, ill-coordinated, and dispersed frontal assaults all along the central front in an effort to drive the Germans back from Moscow. The depleted panzer divisions that had spearheaded the German advance were thus embroiled in heavy defensive fighting. Slow to predict the Soviet counteroffensive or to discern its magnitude, the Germans also underestimated their own weaknesses.[61] Inexpert at defense, lacking reserves, and dismissive of Soviet capabilities, the *Ostheer* conducted half measures—piecemeal local withdrawals and small-scale unit rotations—that failed to stem the Soviet drive. Forced back in uncoordinated withdrawals, gaps opened in the German lines through which Soviet forces poured into the German rear.[62] The German front began to disintegrate as the overstretched supply organization unraveled under the combined effects of winter weather and Soviet dislocation of the German rear. Unused to reverses, German generals and troops panicked when confronted with their first major defeat of the war.

The Soviet counteroffensive prompted significant changes in German strategy and brought about modified defensive tactics employed on all fronts for the rest of the war. The Germans faced two strategic options—a major withdrawal to a shorter, defensible winter line (which the generals wanted) or to stand fast and weather the Soviet onslaught, which Hitler chose on 16 December. Hitler was right. A strategic withdrawal in midwinter with limited mobility would have cost the Germans their heavy weapons and might well have turned into a rout like Napoleon's 1812 retreat. Hitler ordered the *Ostheer* to hold and unflinchingly defend "hedgehog" positions. These were centered on dispersed fortified village strongpoints in which beleaguered German forces desperately massed during December 1941 to escape both the winter weather and annihilation.[63] By late December most of the front comprised hedgehog defenses that the Germans fortified as best they could, but doctrine, equipment, and training proved inadequate for winter defensive warfare. Nonetheless, the Germans' holding fast, coupled with winter weather, ultimately halted the Soviet offensive.

That such expediency stopped the Soviet onslaught was as much due to Soviet disorganization and lack of tactical sophistication as to the inherent defensive qualities of hedgehog defenses or the steadfastness of German troops. While holding fast prevented the *Ostheer* from disintegration, it cost the Germans heavily. Badly prepared for winter warfare, the *Ostheer* suffered 228,000 casualties from frostbite alone, and the Soviets isolated and overran some units.[64] Soviet armor posed a great danger because the T-34 tank had good cross-country mobility in winter, while such weather rendered many German weapons unreliable and ineffective.[65]

The *Ostheer* quickly improved its defensive and winter warfare capabilities as well as the strength of its hedgehog defenses through trial and error and rapid dissemination of after-action reports.[66] Troops quickly recognized that village strongpoints had serious limitations: massed defenders were vulnerable to artillery fire, and their defenses lacked depth and conceded control of the ground between positions to the enemy.[67] Thus the troops gradually extended hedgehog defenses beyond village perimeters to improve security, enhance observation, and reduce the gaps in the front through which Soviet forces regularly infiltrated.[68] Experience showed that vigorous, immediate counterattack employing massed firepower was necessary to repel Soviet incursions.

These defensive experiences led the *Heer* during 1942 to develop for the first time mechanisms and procedures for coordinated massed defensive fire plans. Although the strongpoint defense system did not conform exactly to doctrine, its emphasis on depth, firepower, and counterattack demonstrated that it was firmly rooted in traditional German defensive doctrine. By maintaining active and aggressive defense, German hedgehogs, despite their expedient nature, often survived against great odds.[69]

Soviet deficiencies also contributed to the success of hedgehog defense. Initial Soviet operations after 6 December 1941 were fundamentally defensive in nature and aimed to gain room for maneuver in front of Moscow rather than to destroy the enemy. Moreover, hedgehog defense inadvertently exploited flaws in Soviet organization, leadership, and doctrine: the Soviet forces lacked the expertise, firepower, and mobility to encircle and annihilate major German formations.[70] Poor leadership, faulty doctrine, and unsubtle, broad frontal attacks by green, depleted, poorly trained and equipped troops, as well as poor coordination, ammunition shortages, inadequate communications, and limited armored and artillery support, all hampered Red Army operations.[71] Soviet forces rarely exploited penetrations quickly or with determination and usually recoiled when counterattacked. Early success led Stalin to launch a counteroffensive along the entire front between 5 January and late February 1942 that aimed to destroy the *Ostheer*. This all-out offensive was well beyond the weakened Red Army's capabilities as Stalin in turn underestimated German defensive power and the powerful obstacle the weather presented to offensive action. Lack of strength and dispersion of effort across the front meant that Soviet strategy thus spared German forces from annihilation.[72] Without massed artillery, adequate ammunition, or effective coordination, the Red Army failed to defeat the Germans, and it was the Soviet spearheads that were cut off and eradicated during the spring.[73]

Soviet successes forced the *Luftwaffe* to employ airlifts to resupply German forces isolated by the Red Army offensive at Kholm, Demyansk, and Velikie Luki. But the *Luftwaffe* viewed air supply as an emergency task only and thus lacked significant lift capacity. During the winter, it organized a major airlift that sustained resistance at Kholm and Demyansk until German counterattacks relieved both pockets in May 1942.[74] Success was bought, however, at heavy cost in transports and crew, and, as significantly, success inflated *Luftwaffe* perceptions of its aerial resupply capabilities, which rashly led the air force to promise the following winter to resupply the German Sixth Army after it became cut off at Stalingrad.

During the spring and summer of 1942, the *Ostheer* collected and disseminated lessons learned and revised training in the light of its experiences. Units forwarded detailed after-action reports that illuminated serious deficiencies in German equipment, organization, and training.[75] Also, the German success apparently vindicated Hitler's orders to hold fast and his belief that iron will could triumph over a more powerful enemy. Armed with these false notions, Hitler thereafter ordered German troops not to retreat in the face of overwhelming odds, thereby aggravating losses and hastening disaster.

After-action reports starkly illuminated the inadequacy of German antitank doctrine and equipment, and demonstrated the difficulty troops faced in destroying Soviet heavy armor. German antitank guns could only destroy heavy Soviet tanks at short range, so troops learned to deploy them in reverse slope (defilade) positions and to engage enemy armor from the flanks or rear.[76] The Flak 88 could destroy Soviet armor at long range, but the curtailed availability of the gun, its vulnerability (due to its high silhouette), and *Luftwaffe* control of most heavy antiaircraft guns ensured that few guns were available for infantry support. As a result, after-action reports universally clamored for greater antitank capability.[77]

Combat in the fall and spring mud and winter snow demonstrated that the Germans needed greater and more mobile firepower. During 1942, therefore, Hitler accelerated development of new, heavier tanks—the Panther and Tiger—and rushed them into service. In the meantime, factories retrofitted Panzer III and IV tanks with heavier cannon and additional appliqué armor; increased production of assault guns; and mounted heavy cannon on tank chassis to produce light tank destroyers.[78] Through improvised designs that sacrificed armor protection and cross-country performance for maximum firepower, these tank destroyers proved to be effective interim mobile antitank weapons and a valuable stopgap until purpose-built vehicles entered service. Simultaneously, infantry and engineers underwent extensive conditioning for close-combat tank destruction, accompanied by a revised antitank warfare manual.[79]

Weather, climate, and rugged terrain also prevented full German application of combat power and mobility against Soviet forces because the Eastern Front was, physically and psychologically, very different from previous German experience. Climatic extremes, from subzero Arctic temperatures and deep snow in the far north to desertlike summer heat in the south, sapped troops' endurance, while lack of all-weather roads badly hampered movement and resupply operations. At the same time, a series of north–south rivers—Dniester, Bug, Dvina, Dniepr, Don, and Mius—provided natural obstacles from behind which Soviet formations delayed and bled the Germans. And extensive, swampy, primeval forests acted as natural barriers to blitzkrieg. Forests limited observation and reduced artillery effectiveness and provided excellent cover and concealment, thus allowing Soviet forces to harry the invaders.[80] Prior to BARBAROSSA the Germans had had little experience of forest warfare, and such combat was one area in which German doctrine lacked realism. Encirclement operations in forests proved ineffective, and the Germans quickly learned that only meticulous preparation and methodical execution brought success in woodlands. The experience of forest combat gained in the East demonstrated the innate superiority of defense and led to the development of new doctrine.[81]

In the far north, too, German troops also initially fared poorly in Arctic warfare, which contributed to the German failure to sever the Murmansk railroad along which Western Lend Lease aid poured.[82] So, during the winter of 1941–1942, the Finns retrained German troops for winter and arctic warfare.[83] All in all, the size and scale of the Soviet Union and the dispersal of its cities and industry dissipated the effectiveness of blitzkrieg.

Indeed, the *Ostheer* never recovered from the horrendous losses of the 1941 campaign. By April 1942 it had lost one-third of the troops, 40 percent of the antitank guns, half the horses, and 79 percent of the armor that had begun BARBAROSSA.[84] Massive vehicle losses had significantly reduced mobility, while ammunition stocks had fallen to one-third of June 1941 levels.[85] New production and replacements could not offset losses, and infantry, officer, and equipment strengths plummeted. Heavy losses, lack of reinforcement and supplies, and undiminished Soviet resistance also sapped German morale. Attrition had crippled the *Ostheer*'s attack strength and curtailed even its defensive capabilities.[86] In retrospect, the 1941 campaign irreparably shattered the *Ostheer*'s striking power, and Germany could no longer triumph over its enemies because Hitler compounded the folly of invading the Soviet Union by declaring war on the United States in December 1941. All that remained to be decided was how long Germany could withstand its enemies. That Germany fought on for three years in no small measure reflected the German military's ability to adapt to changing combat conditions.

Nevertheless, Hitler decided to embark on curtailed offensive action during summer 1942 on the southern sector of the front to capture the Caucasus and its oil fields, which he hoped would knock the Soviet Union out of the war. In preparation for this offensive Hitler reinforced, rehabilitated, and reorganized the *Ostheer* to rebuild its combat power. Only more troops, equipment, and supplies, and better tactics could offer the Germans even a slim chance of victory. The *Ostheer* disbanded some of its worst shattered formations, combed out rear-area service units, and transferred troops and equipment from the West.[87] Moreover, the *Ostheer* remained on the strategic defensive on the northern and central sectors, where it expediently reduced sixty-nine attenuated infantry divisions from nine to seven rifle battalions to cut manpower shortages, even though this destroyed the formations' triangular structure and reduced their tactical flexibility.[88]

German preparations for a renewed offensive thus transformed the *Ostheer* in the same manner that the 1918 peace offensives had recast the German Imperial Army. The Germans created a small force of elite attack divisions and many more second-rate divisions to hold the rest of the front. Incapable of major offensive action, Army Groups North and Center, nevertheless, gradually eliminated any Soviet force cut off in their rear during the spring and constructed hedgehog defenses during the summer. Troop shortages and limited mobility abridged defense in depth and compromised traditional defensive principles of maneuver and depth.[89] Instead, troops relied on static defenses, minefields, coordinated defensive artillery fire, and fortified village strongpoints for defensive strength, and on firepower and counterattacks by local reserves to hold or regain the front.[90] Reserves learned through experience that immediate, aggressive counterattacks at the base of Soviet penetrations usually halted such breakthroughs.[91] During 1942 the *Ostheer* gradually abandoned the delaying withdrawal and maneuver within the defensive zone advocated by doctrine as fixed defenses, firepower, and immediate counterattack became the core of German defensive tactics.

Troops required greater firepower to hold the front because attacking Soviet forces were still powerful when German forces counterattacked immediately. To increase striking power, German commanders deployed forward assault guns and tank destroyers to buttress counterattack reserves. Nevertheless, throughout the summer of 1942, Soviet probing attacks repeatedly punctured Army Group Center's front and wore down its defensive strength as winter approached. During late spring of 1942, the army generated extra manpower to restore German strength in the East and rehabilitated the infantry arm. It expanded the use of Soviet prisoners of war as auxiliaries, again combed out the rear-area echelons, extended the use of alarm units, and stepped up the recruitment of European volunteers for the "Crusade against Bolshevism," as Hitler bullied his Axis partners to strengthen their forces on the Eastern Front.[92] These expedients temporarily alleviated immediate German manpower needs and numerically restored the *Ostheer*'s strength, but its quality and offensive power was considerably lower than in the previous summer. Despite efforts to mobilize anti-Soviet and anticommunist sentiment, nazi racism prevented Germany from fully tapping the well of anti-Soviet and anti-Russian sentiment that alone could have provided Germany with the manpower to defeat the Soviets.[93] Finally, tough enemy resistance also forced the Germans to grudgingly revise their estimates of Soviet capabilities.[94]

The *Ostheer* rebuilt its strength in southern Russia to launch a narrow-front offensive—code named BLAU—to achieve a knockout blow as Hitler once again gambled the army's long-term combat endurance against the chance for a rapid blitzkrieg victory. Strategically, Hitler shifted from the destruction of enemy armed forces to victory through economic means by seizing the Caucasus oil fields.[95] Yet BLAU ended any possibility that Germany could fight the Soviets to an attritional stalemate in the East, the offensive lacking a strategic goal capable of winning the war. Capture of the Caucasus could neither cripple the Soviet war economy nor quickly erode Soviet military capabilities.[96] The advance also greatly extended an already overstretched and thinly held front, left the Red Army intact, and exposed the German flank to counterattack.

German offensive preparations for BLAU were inadequate because the *Ostheer* hastily refitted formations, often in the front line. Lack of troops, in particular, forced the Germans to rely on poorly trained, equipped, and officered Axis troops to hold the northern shield for BLAU.[97] Initially the offensive achieved good results as German forces advanced to Stalingrad and struck deep into the Caucasus. Yet such success was largely due to a shift in Soviet strategy from inflexibly holding fast to a delaying withdrawal that preserved their forces. During the fall of 1942, the Soviets sucked the Germans into a protracted struggle for Stalingrad that sapped German strength while the Soviets massed reserves. By early September, Hitler had conceded that BLAU could not win the war and ordered a bolstering of defensive strength by a return to pre-1917 rigid, linear defense.[98] Hitler thus advocated an attritional defense that massed German strength in opposition to Soviet attacks. Although such defensive strategy temporarily blunted Soviet attacks and held on to territory, it did so at a high price. Hitler also finally sanctioned construction of a major fortification line, the Eastern Wall.[99] These reforms temporarily improved Axis defenses, but the increasing emphasis on immediate counterattack, rather than husbanding strength until friction had worn down Soviet strength, raised the cost of defensive success.

To free the personnel to build and man the Eastern Wall the army reorganized the replacement army, and decentralized training functions to occupied territories so that instructors and recruits could perform garrison duties while training. This measure freed several hundred thousand troops to build and man defenses in the East with only a minor disruption in training.[100] At the same time, increasing organizational diversity and divergent formation quality led the army to introduce a new monthly reporting system in December 1942 in which commanders subjectively evaluated their units' combat worthiness. These candid assessments allowed the high command to gauge unit capabilities accurately.[101]

On 19 November 1942, Soviet forces counterattacked and overran the poorly equipped Romanian forces northwest and southeast of Stalingrad to encircle Colonel-General Friedrich von Paulus's Sixth Army. Isolated on poor defensive ground without prepared defenses, possessing depleted and undersupplied forces, and forbidden to break out, the Sixth Army was doomed unless it was relieved. Yet the Germans were unable to build a defense along the Chir River from which to launch a relief effort, largely because the Red Army had learned from its own mistakes the previous winter, when dispersion of effort had denied decisive success, and now focused on annihilating the Sixth Army. The Germans had to abandon the relief of Stalingrad, and desperately fought to prevent envelopment of their entire southern front between mid-December and February before the front stabilized south of Kursk in March 1943.

That the *Ostheer* was much better trained, equipped, and prepared for its second winter campaign prevented the Red Army from overrunning the German southern front.[102] Improved winter preparation brought defensive successes in the northern and central sectors too, where the Germans conducted a forward linear defense based on a continuous front. Units had greater winter mobility with sleds, reserves trained on skies, and armor received extrawide winter tracks.[103] Nonetheless, the front remained thinly manned, and vulnerable salients protruded at Rhzev, Demyansk, Velikie Luki, and Schlüsselburg that the Soviets repeatedly assaulted over winter 1942–1943. Yet improved German defenses and defensive capabilities denied decisive Soviet success. Although the Soviet forces restored a tenuous land connection with besieged Leningrad at Schlüsselburg and encircled two German divisions at Velikie Luki, they narrowly failed to sever the Rhzev and Demyansk salients. Nevertheless, the Soviets drew the Germans into lengthy attritional battles that expended German reserves, and ultimately during the spring of 1943 the Germans abandoned the Rhzev and Demyansk salients to build a new southern front.[104]

The collapse of the Italians and Hungarians on the Don River south of Voronezh in January 1943 threatened a new encirclement of the entire southern wing, a crisis that forced Hitler to allow Field Marshal Erich von Manstein temporary freedom to conduct mobile defensive warfare.[105] During January–February 1943, Manstein conducted fluid and economical defensive operations as he withdrew from the Caucasus, slowed the Soviet advance with delaying mobile defensive actions, parried Soviet efforts to outflank the German line with mobile reserves, and built up a counterattack force. Dwindling mobility, though, prevented Manstein from conducting a classic mobile defense and forced his infantry to fight a linear defense while mechanized reserves acted as mobile fire brigades to counter Soviet penetrations. Although he used mobility and the terrain to maximum advantage to blunt the Soviet offensive, German defenses lacked tactical depth, and only a combination of maneuver and stubborn positional defense provided artificial depth.[106] These attritional tactics wore down Red Army strength while preserving German fighting power, and as Soviet supply lines lengthened Red Army pressure eased and Manstein finally was able to drive five panzer divisions into the enemy's flank southeast of Kharkov on 22 February 1943 and rout several Soviet armies. This victory, the last major German tactical success in the East, bought the time needed to rebuild a continuous defensive front in the south, roughly on the line the Germans had occupied the previous spring.

As the initiative began to shift toward the Soviets the *Ostheer* buttressed its defensive capabilities. Commanders and troops innovated to minimize casualties and reduce the psychological strain of combat. Since the aggressiveness and skill of the reserves was critical to maintaining the front, formations gathered their best commanders and troops in mobile reserves, powerfully reinforced in firepower, and retrained them for their counterattack role. Increased ideological indoctrination inculcated a sense of superiority in German troops about their weapons, cohesion, and training to strengthen resolve as units conducted live-fire exercises in the field and practiced hand-to-hand combat to condition the troops for brutal close combat.[107]

During 1942 doctrinal controversy raged over the defensive role of armor. Prewar doctrine had stressed its counterattack role, and the panzer arm opposed the dispersion of tanks for infantry support that had contributed to enemy defeats in 1939–1941. German infantry often could not withstand Soviet armored attacks, and immediate counterattack required armor to repel enemy penetrations. So experience demonstrated that infantry required a force of armor for counterattacks, especially because larger armored reserves often could not arrive before Soviet forces had consolidated their penetrations. In practice, the *Ostheer* progressively reinforced its infantry with assault guns and tank destroyers, even though dispersion sacrificed concentrated reserves and surrendered the initiative to the enemy.[108]

But German efforts to construct a ground force with staying power represented too little, too late. The German military's emphasis on the tactical and operational levels of war engendered a concomitant neglect of logistical and intelligence functions. During 1941–1942 German tactical and technical innovation failed to outweigh strategic, logistic, and intelligence failures. At the same time, the unique political structure of Nazi Germany produced numerous problems detrimental to military organization. The structure bred interservice rivalry and empire building that led to inefficient manpower utilization, duplication in research, development, procurement, and production; and diverted significant resources into unrealistic projects. Moreover, Germany often directed technical innovation toward novel weaponry of marginal utility, thus failing to realize the full potential of its extensive technical creativity.[109]

Because the *Heer* continually adapted and innovated throughout 1939–1942, the army of 1942 was quite different in organization, tactics, equip-

ment, training, and character from that of 1939. Its determination to examine its combat performance thoroughly, honestly, and critically and then to
retrain and to innovate at every stage contributed directly to the devastating
German military victories of the early war years. The most significant
change was the evolution of German defensive doctrine on the Eastern
Front, where distance and troop and equipment shortages precluded
defense in depth and forced the *Ostheer* to rely on linear defense and
immediate counterattack. Initially viewed as temporary expedients, by
1943 these defensive techniques had become standard as the *Heer* revised
doctrine to maximize dwindling combat power by honing its doctrinal
edge.

German adaptation and innovation was typically decentralized and
emerged largely from the bottom up. This decentralization meant that the
Heer adapted relatively swiftly and proved able to surmount many of the
challenges it encountered in battle. Indeed, the hedgehog defense of winter
1941–1942 probably saved the *Ostheer* from collapse. Improvisations
retained at their core the four basic principles of German defensive doctrine: depth, maneuver, counterattack, and firepower. German forces
employed fortified villages, heavy weapons echeloned in depth, and alarm
units to create artificial depth. Yet Hitler's orders to hold fast, declining
mobility, and loss of air superiority increasingly restricted German operational maneuver. Denied room to maneuver, the *Heer* resorted to firepower
and immediate counterattack to hold the front, and these principles became
the core of German defensive tactics for the rest of the war. Immediate
counterattack, in particular, frequently proved decisive in restoring German
positions in the East. Defensive tactics, therefore, increasingly stressed
speed over mass. The *Ostheer* inculcated in its troops the need for immediate and constant counterattack in response to the progressive dwindling of
German combat strength and mobility, which both hampered conduct of
elastic defense and mandated increased reliance on static defense, firepower, and counterattack. Such tactical and operational innovation temporarily
kept Germany's enemies at bay during 1942–1943.

As the war turned against the Axis and the strategic initiative passed to
the Allies, the pace and scale of German innovation accelerated as the *Heer*
shored up its shrinking combat power. During 1939–1942 the *Heer* had
largely adapted ad hoc in reaction to unforeseen challenges, but, as it shifted to defense during 1943–1944, adaptation became more systematic and
widespread. The result was a transformation in the character of the *Heer*
that led to a marked, if ephemeral, restoration of its combat power during
the spring of 1944.

The pace of adaptation accelerated during 1943–1944 as Soviet formations first halted the German advance at the gates of Stalingrad and then
slowly began to push back.[110] Indeed, the destruction of the Sixth Army at
Stalingrad and the recoiling of the southern sector of the Eastern Front dur-

ing the spring of 1943 finally shocked the Germans out of their complacency and forced them to revise their estimates of Soviet capabilities. The respite of spring of 1943, which followed Manstein's stunning counteroffensive that threw back the Soviet spearheads in the south and regained Kharkov, allowed the *Ostheer* to examine the lessons of the 1942 campaign.

Study revealed that doctrine had to be revised both because defense in depth was rarely possible and doctrine provided little guidance for forest and swamp fighting or for hedgehog defenses.[111] During 1943, the *OKH* thus revised combat practices to reflect battlefield reality and to maximize its dwindling combat power by honing its doctrinal edge. It informally adopted as standard the expedient defensive techniques of linear defense, holding fast, and immediate counterattack developed in the East. While the *Heer* continued to adhere in principle to the *Truppenführung* and to pay lip service to elastic defense in depth, in the field troops increasingly modified basic defensive practices as informal doctrinal adaptation percolated up at the front, at the local level.[112] Central to this process were the divisional field replacement battalions that acclimated new recruits to local fighting conditions, taught recent battle experiences, and honed combat techniques. Frequent and extensive dissemination of unit after-action reports spread these defensive adaptations along the entire Eastern Front during 1943 as the *Heer* absorbed the most effective adaptations into revised training and doctrinal manuals.[113]

During 1943 the *OKH* also endeavored to enhance its artillery arm. The *Heer*'s mobile offensive orientation early in the war had worked against massed, centralized employment and dictated that the regiment remain the primary fire unit. But the desperate defensive fighting on the thinly manned Eastern Front during 1941–1942 restored artillery as the backbone of German defense, and artillery once again became the most effective means available to counter enemy mobility and maneuver warfare, both in the East and in North Africa. During 1943, the army thus raised its first artillery division to provide massed defensive fire support and greater counteroffensive punch. Despite its efforts, the *Heer* was unable to enhance substantially its artillery capabilities. The artillery division experiment proved unsuccessful because the formation was too large and unwieldy, and mounting equipment shortages forced its disbandment in spring 1944.[114] Indeed, heavy losses of guns and towing tractors prevented the consolidation of artillery into larger formations and steadily degraded mobility.[115] The loss of air superiority also lessened German artillery effectiveness because gunners were denied aerial observation, which reduced their accuracy. The mounting Allied air threat forced gunners adopt elaborate camouflage, redeploy their guns frequently, and to limit barrages. At the same time, growing ammunition shortages curtailed the massed fire required to stop enemy penetrations.

To offset this decline in artillery support, the *Heer* increased its use of *Nebelwerfer* rocket launchers and heavy mortars. These weapons, which were more cheaply and easily produced than artillery, were also more mobile, consumed less ammunition, were harder to detect, and hence were less vulnerable to air attack. The rocket launcher branch grew out of the army's small prewar chemical warfare arm, and during 1941–1943 the Germans developed heavy, multibarreled launchers that could quickly produce massed fire.[116] At the same time, the Germans quickly recognized the lethality of the Soviet 120mm mortar and in 1942 rapidly produced a copy. The appearance of these indirect-fire weapons in combat in 1943 enhanced German infantry firepower.

The most significant shift in German defense practices during 1943–1944, though, was the increasing reliance on fortifications and linear defense as mobility waned. The Western Allies first encountered extensive German fortified defenses in Tunisia in the winter of 1942–1943. Reacting rapidly to the Allied landings in northwestern Africa on 8 November 1942, Germany occupied Vichy France and immediately sent troops to Tunisia to prevent the loss of Panzer Army Africa, forestall an Italian collapse, and keep the Mediterranean closed to Allied shipping. By dint of great improvisation, the Axis forces built up their strength in Tunisia far faster than the Allies had deemed possible, efficiently employing airlift and shipping to build a new front.[117] This rapid buildup foiled the weak Allied drive to capture Tunis before winter. Within two months the Axis forces, redesignated the Fifth Panzer Army, had expanded to five divisions and, after thwarting the Allied attempt to take Tunis, drove the leading Allied troops back from the Tunisian plain into the mountains in some of the last major German tactical successes of the war.

Over the winter of 1942–1943, the Germans built fortifications in depth in the Tunisian mountains. During the spring of 1943, the Allies experienced great difficulty in prevailing against these echeloned defenses, which were covered by deep minefields and numerous boobytraps.[118] But the Germans' decision to defend Tunisia was a mistake strategically, for their position in North Africa, given the precarious supply lines from Europe, was untenable. Over the winter, Allied air power slowly exerted itself as it began to operate in strength from forward air bases in northwestern Africa and as air-ground cooperation improved. The Allies slowly gained air superiority during the spring of 1943 and inflicted mounting losses on Axis resupply operations, sapping enemy strength and strangling their ground forces.[119]

Rommel's Panzer Army Africa still proved as formidable in defeat as in victory as it conducted a skilled delaying withdrawal into Tunisia while preserving its strength. Rommel evaded Montgomery's attempt to trap his army at El Agheila on 14 December and linked up with General von Arnim's Fifth Panzer Army. In February 1943, the Germans launched a spoiling attack at Kasserine Pass that hammered the inexperienced Americans in their only serious reverse in the ETO.[120] But Allied air power for the first time played an important role in disrupting and blunting the German attack, and during March Allied air and sea attacks—accurately informed by Ultra—ended Axis sea transport.[121] Forced to rely entirely on resupply by air, the Axis position in Tunisia became hopeless, the *Luftwaffe* transport arm just enduring another drubbing in this fruitless effort. On 8 May 1943, and with their backs against the sea and out of supplies, the Axis forces capitulated. Although the German occupation of Tunisia had closed the Mediterranean for a further six months, the severe losses sustained by the *Luftwaffe* and the elimination of Panzer Army Africa outweighed any strategic advantage gained from this delay. Forced to fight at great disadvantage, for no worthwhile strategic goal, German air power, in particular, suffered heavy losses.[122]

The lessons of the Tunisian campaign for the Germans were mixed. On the one hand, Tunisia provided misguided lessons as the U.S. rout at Kasserine reinforced prevailing nazi stereotypes of the "Amis" as an incompetent, amilitary, mongrel race. A more positive outcome, however, was enhancement of Axis antitank capability as the Germans quickly recognized the potential of the new U.S. Bazooka antitank rocket launcher encountered in Tunisia. The Germans soon produced a superior copy, the *Panzerschreck* that entered service late in 1943 and which gave German infantry potent antitank capability.[123]

During 1943, however, the *Heer* gradually lost its ability to pursue mobile defense, using mechanized forces to outmaneuver and destroy Allied forces as they had with stunning success at Kharkov and Kasserine Pass. As the firepower balance shifted to the Allies and they gained air superiority, German mobile defense became less successful and more costly. Final German mobilization for total war in response to the defeats at Stalingrad and in North Africa brought a dramatic, if unbalanced, increase in war production.[124] At the same time, the *Heer* underwent sweeping reorganization as, on 17 February 1943, Hitler recalled the disgraced Heinz Guderian and appointed him inspector general of armored forces to revitalize the panzer arm. The new command combined armor, tank destroyers, reconnaissance units, mechanized and motorized infantry, and their affiliate training and replacement units into a new, elite panzer army within the *Heer* that answered to Hitler alone.[125]

Increased production and reorganization allowed Guderian painstakingly to rebuild a strategic armored reserve in the East during spring 1943. But Hitler threw away this reserve in the ill-advised ZITADELLE offensive at Kursk in June 1943. After the failure of the previous summer, Hitler embarked on a major, but less ambitious, offensive with maximum concentration of armored strength on the narrowest of fronts to pinch off the Kursk salient that protruded deep into German lines and to sap Soviet strength. German strategy thus reverted to attrition as the *Ostheer* sought to encircle and annihilate Soviet forces in a replay of the great encirclement victories of 1941. The Germans assembled a mighty concentration of armor, including new Panther and Tiger tanks and Elephant tank destroyers, but ZITADELLE failed because the operation was poorly conceived and repeated postponement lost the element of surprise.[126] The Germans attacked powerful Soviet forces entrenched in prepared positions in depth and with numerous reserves at hand. The Red Army also demonstrated growing appreciation of German doctrine and tactics and adopted effective countermeasures, including it own version of defense in depth.[127] Even though losses were heavy on both sides the *Ostheer* could not absorb losses as readily as the Soviet forces, and the panzer divisions, laboriously rebuilt by Guderian, were burned out anew.

The failure of ZITADELLE marked the permanent passing of the strategic initiative in the East to the Soviet side; and from then on the Red Army steadily pushed back the Germans. Faced with shrinking strength and mobility, the *Ostheer* increasingly resorted to fortified positional defense. But the Soviet steamroller shattered the Eastern Wall, hastily erected along the Dnieper River, during the fall of 1943.

Attrition and the inability of motor vehicle production to keep pace with losses prevented substantial expansion of the panzer arm. Thus there were never sufficient armored reserves to counter every enemy break-through. In fact, the last time the Germans did mount an effective mobile defense to inflict heavy losses on an enemy at minimal cost to themselves was during the defense of Sicily in July 1943. On Sicily two hastily raised German mechanized divisions fought a skilled delaying withdrawal, to buy time for a German buildup in Italy, before retiring intact to the mainland.[128] For mobile defense to work, however, the Germans had at least to contest Allied air supremacy and retain logistic integrity. But the loss of air supremacy increasingly threatened German theater logistics, and the German ability to conduct mobile defense dwindled accordingly.

Total mobilization ensured that German firepower grew steadily during 1943–1944 as new weapons entered service and as production blossomed. The superlative lightweight MG 42 machine gun, that could produce much higher and sustained rates of fire than Allied machine guns, entered service and quickly became the mainstay of squad firepower. Germany also introduced new automatic weapons, including the world's first genuine assault rifle.[129] Antitank capability increased too as antitank gun production blossomed and as a potent new 88mm gun entered service late in 1943. With a low silhouette and high accuracy, this gun could penetrate the armor of any Allied tank at long range.[130] During 1943 the *Panzerfaust* rocket-propelled grenade launcher joined the *Panzerschreck* to give German infantrymen the close-combat antitank capability they had previously lacked. At the same time, production of assault guns increased dramatically and new well-armed and armored tank destroyers entered service. As a result, German infantrymen became much less vulnerable to armored attack than they had been in the East during 1941–1942.

Central to the rapid and marked increase in German firepower was the German willingness to exploit and replicate the technological achievements of its opponents. The Germans adopted the sloped armor and large-caliber overhanging gun of Soviet tanks in the Panther tank and armored tank destroyers. They also copied the Soviet 120mm heavy mortar and *Katyusha* rocket launcher, as well as the U.S. Bazooka. The need for increased production to offset mounting losses inexorably eroded the German advantage in weaponry, however. The services simplified and fixed existing weapons to increase production, and as a result Germany was less able to keep abreast of the technology race as production increasingly sacrificed quality for mass production.[131] Thus, from 1943, the Allies steadily narrowed, but never entirely eliminated, the qualitative edge that the Germans had enjoyed early in the war.

During 1943 the *Luftwaffe* also reoriented itself toward the defensive and sought to enhance its ground support capabilities. Early in the war it had cooperated reasonably well with the army when faced with ineffectual opposition, despite limited assets, the absence of specialized ground attack aircraft, and a cumbersome system of air-ground coordination. But constant combat in multiple theaters steadily wore down its strength thereafter. In 1943, though, the *Luftwaffe* enhanced its ground support capabilities with the introduction of new specialized tactical aircraft—Focke-Wulf FW 190 fighter-bombers, Henschel HS 129B2 ground attack aircraft, and modified Junkers Ju 87 *Stuka* "tank busters"—that became the mainstay of tactical aviation.[132] Concentration of ground attack and tank-busting aircraft under the VIII Air Corps during the spring of 1943 had allowed German tactical aviation to achieve its greatest wartime successes as it smashed Soviet tank spearheads at Kharkov during von Manstein's counteroffensive and at Belgorod and Bryansk in July.

These successes led the *Luftwaffe* to amalgamate its dive bomber and ground attack squadrons into a united ground attack arm in September 1943.[133] More flexible and massed employment temporarily allowed tactical aviation to disrupt dangerous Soviet armored penetrations and thus be a substitute for the army's lack of reserves, a change of emphasis in ground attack operations that temporarily bolstered German defensive capabilities in the East.[134] But ceaseless action as Soviet forces assumed the offensive across the entire front in the wake of ZITADELLE steadily eroded the *Luftwaffe*'s ground attack units. Moreover, the *Luftwaffe*'s shift in priority to defend the Reich in 1943 meant that it could not maintain ground attack strength: diverting fighters to defend Germany left ground attack units exposed and increased their losses. As a result, by 1944 these units could achieve only local tactical successes.

As the Red Army assumed the offensive and German mobility waned, German forces increasingly suffered encirclement. At first, unused to encirclement, German troops often panicked and fought poorly when surrounded.[135] With experience, German troops learned that discipline, concentration, aerial resupply, and rapid countermeasures often allowed them to fight their way out of encirclement. Nonetheless, the *Luftwaffe*'s transport fleet suffered grievously in resupplying forces trapped at Stalingrad and in Tunisia.[136] The result was much diminished lift capacity that the switch in productive priority to fighters exacerbated. Nevertheless, air resupply did help German forces to break out of the Cherkassy and Kamenets-Podolsk pockets in February–March 1944, but these marked the last significant triumphs of air resupply because constant action eroded transport strength.[137] By summer of 1944, the *Luftwaffe* was a broken arm that could no longer provide any significant support to the ground battle.

By fall of 1943 the *Heer* had reached its nadir. Constant attrition in the East left it badly understrength, underequipped, and increasingly immobile.[138] Moreover, throughout 1942–1943 the *OKH* had robbed Peter to pay Paul as it repeatedly raided nonactive theaters to replenish units on the Eastern Front. Late in 1943 the *OKH* vigorously tackled the problem of waning ground combat strength as the *Heer* underwent its most extensive wartime restructuring and rationalization to restore its combat power. Between November 1943 and May 1944, *Wehrmacht* divisions adopted new 1944 TO&Es that substituted firepower for manpower to create lean formations that possessed a high teeth-to-tail ratio.[139] This rationalization was made possible by the full mobilization of German resources for total war. On 27 November 1943 Hitler issued his Basic Order 22 to raise an additional 1 million combat troops through rationalization, which, in the short term, restored German combat power.[140] During the spring of 1944 average divisional strengths increased by 15 percent, reversing a steady three-year decline. At the same time infantry divisions received potent new weapons—tank destroyers, *Panzerschreck* rocket launchers, light antiaircraft guns, and heavy mortars—which increased infantry firepower.[141]

On paper the *Heer* rapidly restored its combat power during the spring of 1944; average division manpower shortages fell from their November 1943 peak of 28 percent to only 3 percent by June 1944.[142] Yet the *Heer* bolstered its combat power at the expense of its staying power, as it had consistently done since 1933, by further weakening its strained logistic base. The army found extra manpower by trimming already meager service branches, further reducing service provision. At the same time, it counteracted dwindling mobility by increased reliance on horses and bicycles. These expedients, however, reduced divisional self-sufficiency and increased formation dependence on higher echelon service support, which left formations more vulnerable to destruction when theater logistics collapsed, as they did in both the East and West during the summer of 1944.

That the *Heer* shifted to strategic defense with relative ease reflected the basic soundness of German doctrine and the growing defensive orientation of German arms production. During 1943–1944 the *Heer* demonstrated that it had become as quick, agile, and skilled at defense as in attack. German doctrinal emphasis on speed, individual initiative, and decisiveness buttressed defensive strength as much as it did offensive striking power. Another element that held the *Heer* together was the harsh, even draconian, discipline that maintained German cohesion and order beyond what could reasonably have been expected late in the war as defeat loomed ever nearer.[143]

The army also modified its replacement system during the winter of 1943–1944 to bolster combat strength. Although the system produced quality replacements, it was inflexible and could not match the mounting combat losses. The army high command increased its flexibility by raising combat march battalions that combined new recruits and veteran convalescents into fully equipped battalions, which could be directly inserted at the front without having to be integrated into divisional field replacement battalions. The result was greater flexibility with little discernible reduction in cohesion among replacements.[144]

In November 1943 Hitler shifted Germany's strategic focus from the East to the West, where the repulse of an imminent second front could at least postpone final defeat. Hitler embarked on a massive resurrection of the fighting power of the army in the West, the *Westheer.* By late 1943, repeated raids on its resources to bolster the Eastern Front had so weakened the *Westheer* that it was unable to repel a major Allied landing.[145] And, because the Germans recognized that the Allies were not yet ready to strike, there was only a modest bolstering of defenses in the West before late 1943.[146]

During the fall of 1943, the *Westheer* had extremely limited combat power: only nineteen of fifty-four divisions were fully battleworthy, and these were all weak coastal defense formations of negligible mobility or offensive power.[147] All divisions were understrength and made up mainly of second-rate garrison troops, convalescents, and foreign volunteers who were largely equipped with obsolete captured weapons.[148] The *Westheer* had almost no operational reserves and few modern tanks. Clearly, if the Allies could have come in 1943 the Germans could not have stopped them.[149]

Between fall of 1943 and June 1944, Hitler resurrected the *Westheer*'s fighting power to contest the Allied invasion of France. After 3 November 1943, when he issued his Directive 51, the *Westheer*'s combat power increased dramatically. Young recruits and experienced veterans flowed west alongside the *Reich*'s latest and most powerful weapons. Meanwhile reorganization, reequipment, rationalization, and retraining rebuilt the *Westheer*'s combat power. But several flaws marred these efforts, just as they had all previous efforts to restore German fighting power. Directive 51 failed to establish an adequate logistic base to underpin the *Westheer*'s transformation in manpower and firepower; nor could it solve the *Wehrmacht*'s most debilitating weakness as it approached its sixth year of war—its shrinking mobility.[150] Finally, Hitler's overexpansion of the *Westheer* failed to maximize its combat potential.

The army first restored troop strength in the West, with the unprecedented influx of new recruits and transferred veterans virtually restoring divisions to full strength by D-Day.[151] One of the *Westheer*'s most serious deficiencies had been poor manpower quality as the Eastern Front progressively siphoned off the best officers, noncommissioned officers (NCOs), and troops and left it markedly underofficered.[152] Most officers stationed in the West were either reservists who had last fought in the Great War or convalescents. After Directive 51 officer strength in the West greatly increased as veteran officers were transferred, with the result that by D-Day officer shortages in combat units in France had all but disappeared.[153]

Central to the *Westheer*'s reconstitution was its marked "easternization" as thousands of decorated Eastern Front veterans (*Ostkämpfer*) arrived.[154] This process enhanced the *Westheer*'s combat potential by providing the experience and motivation that it lacked. The *Ostkämpfer*, brutalized by the vicious struggle for existence in the East, represented the most indoctrinated and motivated nazi soldiers. They provided the glue that held together garrison troops and inexperienced recruits alike in Normandy.[155] Between November 1943 and June 1944, the influx of *Ostkämpfer* greatly improved the *Westheer*'s manpower quality, and by June 1944, in terms of manpower, the *Westheer* was the best German army in the field. It was up to strength and Eastern Front veterans dominated its officer corps. This offset the *Westheer*'s inexperience and its reliance on young recruits and elderly reservists.

Yet the most serious personnel problem the *Westheer* faced was not the increasing German reliance on young, old, or foreign personnel that Anglo-American historians frequently stress, but a mounting dearth of veteran NCOs. Historians have exaggerated both the extent of German reliance on supposedly inferior-quality ethnic Germans from outside Germany (*Volksdeutsch*) and Soviet army volunteers (*Osttruppen*), and the detrimental effects of this reliance.[156] In reality, the *Heer* maintained a strict ceiling on *Volksdeutsch* in combat units, so that they remained a minor proportion of German manpower. Moreover, the *Volksdeutsch* generally fought well.[157] Likewise, the Germans strictly circumscribed their employment of eastern volunteers for they had few illusions about the combat value of the seventy "East" battalions stationed in the West.[158] The Germans employed them to guard unlikely landing points, hence freeing tens of thousands of regular troops to man more likely invasion sectors.[159] In fact, the *Westheer* remained the most "racially pure" field force in 1944: under the strain of war and despite nazi dogma, the *Wehrmacht* in general had become a multiethnic and multinational war machine by 1944.[160] The growing shortage of junior officers and NCOs, which increased the time required to work up units to operational readiness, was the more serious problem.[161]

The *Westheer* also retrained during spring 1944 to reverse the softening of and decline in troop proficiency occasioned by four years of comfortable occupation duty and neglect. Thus, as far as fortification work, garrison duty, and equipment and fuel shortages allowed, the *Westheer* trained. The troops studied Allied combat techniques, tactics, and amphibious assault doctrine, for which the army widely disseminated combat analyses of Salerno and Anzio. Soldiers practiced close-combat tank destruction with the new antitank weapons. The troops also sharpened their camouflage, night fighting, sniping, and infiltration techniques to minimize the inevitable Allied materiel and aerial superiority they would face.[162] These programs represented serious, professional, and realistic preparation based on broad combat experience; only their tardy establishment, serious resource deficiencies, and lack of time diminished their impact. This intensive retraining realistically simulated combat conditions, using live-fire exercises and incorporated recent combat lessons to keep instruction current with battlefield developments. Indeed, the maintenance of close affiliation between field and training units facilitated updating of instruction as frequent transfer of personnel from field to replacement units maintained continuity. This retraining program helped resurrect German combat power in the West during the spring of 1944.

That German training was still of high quality even in 1944, was one of the key strengths of the *Heer.* The training was distinctive in its intellectual approach because it taught that individual initiative could be decisive to battlefield victory. Despite the stereotyped image portrayed by Anglo-American propaganda of rigidly obedient German soldiers, the German troop leadership manual stressed individual initiative and operational flexibility. Soldiers at all levels were taught to act independently and to use initiative.

One of the least recognized, but most significant, aspects of German preparation for the second front was increased ideological indoctrination closely related to the incorporation of Eastern Front veterans. As Germany assumed the defensive, the *Wehrmacht* increased ideological indoctrination to offset growing manpower and materiel shortages. Indoctrination during the blitzkrieg years had been haphazard, ill coordinated, and informal. Only after the setbacks of 1943 did the *Heer* begin systematic indoctrination with the 22 December 1943 creation of National Socialist leadership officers to oversee "martial schooling." The *OKH* carefully selected these officers for their combination of nazi fanaticism, proven battlefield heroism, and military experience. Inevitably, most leadership officers were decorated *Ostkämpfer.*[163]

As veteran *Ostkämpfer*, especially junior officers and NCOs, arrived in large numbers in 1944, they undertook extensive, though still largely informal and uncoordinated, ideological indoctrination.[164] They seized every available moment to strengthen their troops spiritually: they lectured and debated at roll call, while traveling, during meal breaks, on the parade ground, and in the barracks.[165] This indoctrination expounded on typical National Socialist themes: to reinforce combat resolve, it promised new wonder vengeance weapons, hammered home German racial and martial superiority, and dwelt on Allied "terror bombing" of civilians. Lectures also dwelt on the consequences of defeat and stressed the racial, and thus the military, inferiority of the Allies. Such schooling sought to mold a stereotypical, professional National Socialist fighter; and it portrayed combat as an embodiment of racial struggle, the Führer as divine, and National Socialism as religion.[166]

Indoctrination forged a *Westheer* that, like the *Ostheer*, though to a lesser degree, possessed a grotesquely distorted mindset. German troops understood that the second front would be the decisive battle of the war, and most remained convinced of their racial superiority and that this superiority would bring them victory. It must be emphasized that despite the evidence to the contrary, most German soldiers still believed in final victory and their faith in Hitler and the nazi leadership remained intact. Ideological indoctrination thus clearly reinforced German fighting power, cohesion, and tenacity. When combined with reequipment and expansion, indoctrination boosted German morale in the West to its zenith by D-Day.

The *Westheer* also reequipped with the *Reich*'s latest and most potent weapons during spring 1944 as it received large numbers of Panther and Tiger tanks, new low-silhouetted tank destroyers, the lethal 88mm antitank gun, and powerful infantry antitank weapons. The *Westheer* thus entered the Normandy campaign with superior quality armor as well as an edge in infantry firepower and antitank capability. These advantages help to explain the German ability to conduct a tenacious defense despite being greatly outnumbered and suffering enormous losses.

The *Westheer* also upgraded the coastal divisions that Field Marshal Rommel had assigned to delay and disrupt the assault while mobile reserves moved up to counterattack. In the fall of 1943, however, these formations lacked the troops, firepower, and mobility needed to impede an invasion.[167] Rommel thus sought to strengthen the coastal defenses sufficiently to retard and break up an Allied landing while armored reserves were redeployed to eliminate any lodgement. After Directive 51 coastal divisions were expanded, reorganized, reequipped, retrained, and given better quality personnel, greater firepower, and improved mobility.[168]

To repulse an invasion, the *Westheer* required a powerful strategic mechanized reserve. Only massed armored counterattacks could throw the Allies back into the sea. But no such reserve existed in the fall of 1943, and in forming one the *Westheer* encountered its most serious obstacle yet—the army's dwindling mobility. By the spring of 1944, the *Heer* faced a serious automobile shortage as losses outstripped production. Its truck pool shrank at a rate of 2 percent per month; and the decline in artillery tractors was even sharper.[169] The progressive demotorization of the *Heer* undermined its ability to conduct mobile defense, hampering the creation of a strategic reserve in the West. The *Westheer* was neither able to motorize fully its reserves or create a sizable strategic transport reserve to supply troops in combat if Allied interdiction attacks disrupted French rail communications.

On the eve of D-Day, the *Westheer*'s mechanized divisions remained woefully deficient in trucks and tractors (see Table 5.1). This limited mobility created a heavy dependence on rail transportation for troop movement and resupply operations, leaving the *Westheer* vulnerable to aerial interdiction aimed at German communications and logistics. Initially, senior German commanders had remained unconcerned about such logistic weakness in the West. They did anticipate that Allied air attacks on communications would accompany the invasion, but they believed that the excess capacity and high connectivity of the French rail system would easily allow successful supply. Only if air and sabotage attacks totally paralyzed the rail net—a scenario considered improbable—would the Germans face serious resupply difficulties.[170]

Rebuilding offensive strength required major enhancement of formation mobility, absorbing most of the new automobiles sent to the West in the spring of 1944.[171] But the diversion of new automobile production to the mobile reserves prevented the Quartermaster General West from assembling a sizable strategic truck transport reserve to supply German forces in combat. Only belatedly, as Allied air attacks progressively smashed the

Table 5.1   Percentage of Authorized Trucks and Tractors Operational, German Strategic Reserve, 1 June 1944

Division	Trucks	Tractors
21st	93	185
2d	81	73
Lehr	77	73
12th SS	65	33
116th	64	12
11th	26	15
1st SS	25	12
2d SS	27	12
9th	14	15
17th SS	11	15
Average	48	45

Sources: NARA T-78, 616, 623–624, 717–719, Gen. Insp. der Pztrpn., "Zustandberichten," June 1944.

French rail net during spring 1944, was the transport reserve expanded.[172] But lack of trucks meant the quartermaster general was unable to amass an operational reserve exceeding 4,000 tons capacity (see Table 5.2). As the Allied interdiction campaign systemicatically destroyed the French rail network, it forced German supply operations onto the road during late spring of 1944, eroding the serviceability rate of the strategic transport reserve before D-Day.[173] By 6 June 1944 the German transportation situation in the West was serious. Only with close interservice cooperation and strenuous efforts to repair the French railroads could the Germans have hoped to adequately resupply the forces on the invasion front. Given the progressive paralyzation of the French rail network, if the Germans could not quickly defeat the Allies on the beaches, they could not attain victory in Normandy. This was the most debilitating deficiency the *Westheer* faced in its effort to defeat the Allies.[174]

Table 5.2   Expansion of the German Strategic Transport Reserve, Spring 1944
(in metric tons)

Date	Capacity	Operational	Percentage
1 January 1944	9,137	7,073	71.5
1 February 1944	8,856	7,225	80.5
1 March 1944	9,309	8,005	86
1 April 1944	10,185	8,379	82
1 June 1944	9,000[a]	5,850	65

Sources: NARA T-314, 11, 7014858-015007, "Transportraum in der Hand der OB West," Ob. West Qu. 1 Br.B.Nr. 01800/44 g.Kdos, 8 April 1944, 02250/44 g.Kdos, 8 May 1944.
Note: a. Approximately.

The *Westheer* also lacked the ammunition and fuel to prevail if it did not defeat the Allies on the beaches. The pressing needs of other theaters had steadily depleted local stocks, a situation exacerbated by the massive winter 1943–1944 retraining program. On 6 June, the priority fortresses had about 30 days' worth of stockpiled ammunition, the coastal defenses about 14 days', and there was an equal amount in inland dumps.[175] Fuel shortages, especially gasoline, were even greater. Allied air attacks on the German synthetic oil refineries and on the Romanian oil fields had already cut production below consumption levels and forced the *Westheer* to ration use of fuel on 3 June 1944.[176] Only with stringent rationing, especially of fuel for training, was the *Westheer* able to amass by D-Day a 7-10-day stockpile for its strategic reserves, clearly insufficient for a lengthy campaign.[177] After the first two weeks of combat, ammunition and fuel would have to come directly from the Reich, this in the face of the progressive destruction of the French rail net. The collapse of rail movement in the

West and the inadequate capacity and dwindling serviceability of the strategic truck transport reserve presented the Germans with grave distribution problems on the eve of D-Day.

Allied air attacks also impeded stockpiling and forced German quartermasters to decentralize reserve stocks to the field armies during the late spring. Although this measure temporarily alleviated supply difficulties, in the long term it served only to aggravate German resupply problems. Thus by D-Day, the Allied air interdiction campaign had already tipped the military balance toward the Allies. On 6 June 1944 over 1,700 trains, carrying thousands of troops, hundreds of tanks and guns, and tens of thousands of tons of materiel, were struggling toward their destinations.[178] The interdiction campaign had already seriously compromised the German ability both to redeploy forces to Normandy and to supply such forces once committed. The question remained whether German logisticians could improvise and adapt to overcome these serious, and increasingly debilitating, deficiencies.[179]

During the spring of 1944, the *Westheer* had made remarkable progress toward becoming a powerful counterinvasion force, but by D-Day this process was still incomplete. In no small part the *Westheer*'s lack of readiness resulted from Hitler's insistence on overexpanding the *Westheer,* dissipating resources, accentuating shortages, and exacerbating logistical difficulties. Nevertheless, the defeats of 1942–1943 had reinforced the *Heer*'s determination to assess honestly its combat performance. Rigorous examination of its performance, followed by rapid and widespread dissemination of lessons learned, allowed the *Heer* to enhance its defensive strength during 1943–1944. And the greatest enhancement occurred in the neglected *Westheer.* Yet nazi racial prejudices hampered retraining because German perceptions of the Americans as a mongrel race incapable of military prowess blinded the Germans to mounting evidence of improved U.S. combat effectiveness since Tunisia. At the same time, the nazi view of the British as Anglo-Saxon brethren ensured that an exaggerated sense of British capabilities—that were not borne out by experience—continued to prevail.

The *Westheer* underwent a profound metamorphosis during the spring of 1944. Instead of widening the gap between Allied and German capabilities, as the OVERLORD planners had hoped postponement of an invasion attempt until 1944 would, the gap closed. In seven months the *Westheer* had gained a limited counterinvasion capability: it substantially strengthened its coastal defenses and the forces defending them, and it built up a strong strategic reserve.

Despite these measures, lack of supplies and the destruction of the French rail system, which forced the Germans to depend on an utterly inadequate trucking capacity, meant that it was unlikely that the *Westheer* could fight a protracted campaign unless it substantially improved its logistic situation. Victory was only possible—as Rommel clearly understood—if the Germans defeated the Allies on the beaches. But such an outcome was unlikely. Even though the *Westheer* possessed the raw strength to repel an invasion, its defensive posture inevitably gave the Allies the initiative and ensured that the initial stages of the invasion would pit Allied strength against German weakness. In fact, the Germans required four preconditions to prevail on the second front: that intelligence sources provided some forewarning of the time and location of the invasion; that the *Kriegsmarine* and *Luftwaffe* at least contested Allied supremacy at sea and in the air; that powerful, armored reserves were available nearby to launch immediate, heavy counterattacks before the Allies could consolidate their lodgement; and, finally, that the Germans could restore and maintain rail communications to the battle zone.

To achieve these preconditions and defeat the invasion Hitler appointed Field Marshal Rommel as commander in chief of Army Group B in northern France on 31 December 1943. While a superb tactician and operational commander, Rommel had no better grasp of the strategic or logistic dimensions of war than the other German generals. He was a bold, hard-driving, and, by nature, offensive-minded professional, and this emphasis quickly surfaced in the anti-invasion strategy that he orchestrated.[180] However, there was little boldness left in a Rommel who recognized that German chances for victory were slim. His strategy to defeat the enemy on the beaches was the only one with real prospect of success. Hitler veered toward Rommel's plan, but he never fully backed it in the face of the opposition of the commander in chief in the West, Field Marshal von Rundstedt, and of Geyr von Schweppenburg, the commander of Armored Group West. Rommel energized German morale as much as Montgomery did across the Channel, but he was unable to deploy the ground troops to his satisfaction. Nevertheless, he innovated defensively, developing the use of foreshore obstacles and of "Rommel's asparagus," stakes driven into the ground to obstruct airborne landings, to further delay and disrupt an invasion.[181]

Yet Rommel lacked the authority to mount an integrated interservice defense of the West, and the German inability to present an effective joint-service defense was the greatest flaw in their anti-invasion preparations. Neither the *Luftwaffe* nor the *Kriegsmarine* could effectively assist in repelling an invasion. The Allied air forces had shattered a *Luftwaffe,* already badly weakened by the attritional battles of 1943, in the skies over Germany during the spring of 1944 as it tried to defend German cities, industry, and civilians. Moreover, the shift in production priority to fighters meant that the German Third Air Fleet in France had negligible ground attack and airlift capabilities. Only a major redeployment westward of anti-aircraft batteries—despite the need to protect German civilians from bombing attacks—allowed the *Luftwaffe* to even begin to mitigate the growing impact of Allied air attacks on German communications.[182] As seriously, the *Luftwaffe*'s meager long-range reconnaissance force was unable to supply intelligence about the location and timing of the invasion. It was only in mine-sowing operations that the *Luftwaffe* marginally impeded Allied invasion preparations.

The substantial *Luftwaffe* ground organization also could not offer much support in the land battle. Its paratroop formations would conduct a stubborn defense in Normandy, enhancing their reputation as an effective elite, but they lacked a counteroffensive capability. The most significant *Luftwaffe* innovation in support of the impending ground battle was the reluctant consolidation of its mobile antiaircraft units in the West into the III Flak Corps in the spring of 1944, intended for a dual air-ground defense role. However, the retraining of the corps had barely begun by D-Day and, despite claims to the contrary, it never lived up to expectations in Normandy. Finally, in the absence of air reconnaissance, the *Luftwaffe* depended upon its extensive network of radar stations and air direction centers in France to provide at least some warning of invasion. But these were highly vulnerable to air attack, and most were put out of commission in the days before 6 June, rendering the German defenders blind.[183]

Nor could the *Kriegsmarine,* with its surface forces in the West reduced to small escort and patrol vessels, offer much challenge to the Allied invasion fleet.[184] The best anti-invasion assets available were fast E-boats that could harry invasion shipping with hit-and-run tactics, but these were only capable of local tactical successes. Instead, the *Kriegsmarine* High Command pinned its hopes on forty-nine U-boats that it earmarked for anti-invasion operations. Yet this force was utterly inadequate for the task, and the shallow, narrow, and congested waters of the English Channel posed serious limitations to U-boat operations.[185] So, the most significant contribution the *Kriegsmarine* made to the defense in the West before D-Day was to mine the Channel, which compelled the Allies to divert considerable naval assets to mine countermeasures. The *Kriegsmarine* also hoped that its numerous heavy coastal batteries could drive off an invasion fleet, but wartime experience had repeatedly proven that such passive defenses could not succeed in the absence of air superiority.[186]

The *Westheer* significantly and rapidly enhanced its capabilities in the six months prior to D-Day. However, misguided decisions by Hitler concerning the scale of expansion slowed the German buildup, dissipated German strength, and exacerbated dwindling mobility. Yet the gradual modification and honing of German doctrine, tactics, and training during 1943–1944 was as central to the resurrection of German combat power in the West. The basic soundness of German doctrine, rooted in realistic, detailed analysis of both Germany's and her enemy's combat experiences in World War I, meant that the *Heer* had only to adjust and refine as experience and changing conditions required. The pace of innovation and adaptation accelerated during 1943–1944 as the *Heer* shifted its focus to defense and sought to enhance its counteroffensive capabilities. It progressively reorganized its mechanized forces into sleeker, harder hitting, and better integrated combined-arms formations. Indeed, the *Heer* as a whole became leaner and deadlier as rationalization and reequipment brought increased firepower to offset decreased manpower.

But by the summer of 1944 maneuver warfare was a luxury the *Heer* could no longer afford. Blitzkrieg had defeated unprepared, undertrained, and ill-equipped opponents, but by 1944 firepower once again dominated the battlefield. As Germany shifted to defense, the *Heer* increasingly relied on static fortifications, firepower, and immediate counterattack for its defensive successes. But since both the offensive power and military proficiency of its opponents had grown considerably with experience, Germany found itself increasingly outnumbered and outgunned. Victories became fewer and the price of success much greater. Inexorably attrition sapped the *Heer*'s qualitative edge, and no degree of adaptation and innovation could offset growing manpower and equipment losses. Even though German combat prowess, skill, professionalism, and the army's ability to adapt prolonged the fight and exacted a high price, the law of numbers dictated that Germany would ultimately be defeated. The culmination of this struggle, the decisive battles that finally shattered the *Heer,* occurred during the summer of 1944 on the Eastern Front, in Italy, and in Normandy.

Notes

1. Larry H. Addington, *The Blitzkrieg Era and the German General Staff, 1865–1941* (New Brunswick, N.J.: Rutgers University Press, 1971), 3–42.

2. Heinz Guderian's XIX Motorized Corps advanced 260 miles in 10 days with minimal losses (4 percent casualties) to overrun Polish reserves before they could mobilize. The Germans suffered 40,389 casualties, lost 217 tanks, and had 400 aircraft destroyed. Robert M. Kennedy, *The German Campaign in Poland 1939* (Washington, D.C.: OCMH, 1956), 51–133; Robert Jars, *La Campagne de Pologne (Septembre 1939)* (Paris: Payot, 1949), 200–217; Heinz Guderian, transl. Basil Liddell Hart, *Panzer Leader* (New York: Ballantine Books, 1957), 46–63. Gerhart Hass, *Deutschland im zweiten Weltkrieg* (Cologne: Pahl-Rugenstein, 1974) I, 163–186.

3. Günther Blumentritt, *Rundstedt: the Soldier and the Man* (London: Odhams, 1952), 53–54; Guderian, *Panzer Leader,* 67.

4. National Archives Record Administration (hereafter NARA) [series] T-315, [roll] 436, 000480, 2 Lei. Div., "Erfahrungen bei den Operationen im Osten," Ia Nr. 393/39, 19 October 1939; Williamson Murray, "German Response to Victory in Poland: A Case Study in Professionalism," *Armed Forces and Society* 7, 2 (Winter 1981), 285–298.

5. NARA T-314, 550, 000295ff, "XV A.K., "Erfahrungen auf taktischen Gebiet," 3 October 1939; T-314, 550, 000222ff, XV A.K., "Der Feldzug in Polen," KTB XV A.K. Okt. 1939; T-312, 37, 7545415ff, "Erfahrungen beim Marsch motorisierter Verbände während des Feldzuges in Polen," Anl. 1 zu Erfahrungsbericht d. XV A.K.; T-315, 436, 000462, OKH/GenStdH O. Qu. I/Ausb.

Abt. (Ia), "Taktisches Erfahrungen im polnischen Feldzug," 15 October 1939; Kennedy, *Poland*, 132–135; *Kampferlebnisse auf Polen* (Berlin: Offene Worte, 1940), passim.

6. NARA T-78, 202, 61457776-81, OKH GenStdH/Ausb. Abt. (Ia), "Ausbildung des Feldheeres," Nr. 400/39 geh., 13 October 1939.

7. Kennedy, *Poland*, 134–135; Williamson Murray, "Close Air Support: The German Experience," in Benjamin F. Cooling, *Case Studies in the Development of Close Air Support* (Washington, D.C.: Office of Air Force History, 1990).

8. For Hitler's long-range strategic goals, see Erhard Jäckel, *Hitler's Weltanschauung* (Stuttgart: Deutsche Verlags Anstalt, 1969). In fact, German armament programs were not due to reach fruition until 1944. Wilhelm Deist, *The Wehrmacht and German Rearmament* (Toronto: University of Toronto Press, 1981).

9. Average divisional weapons strengths fell between September 1939 and May 1940 by 23 percent (machine guns), 25 percent (antitank guns), 2 percent (mortars), and 26 percent (artillery), while available 105mm shells increased by only 6 percent. NARA T-78, 158, 15860913-1871, Chef d. Heeresrüstung u. Bef. d. Ersatzheeres, Stab II (Rüst.), "Überblick über die Rüstungsstand des Heeres (Munition), 3.1940–5.1941;" T-78, 174, 6113064-509, OKH He. Wa. Amt "Munitionslage (Gen/Qu.), 1940;" Burkhardt Müller-Hillebrand, *Das Heer, 1933–1945* (Darmstadt: E.S. Mittler, 1954) II, 30–55.

10. Samuel W. Mitchum, Jr., *Hitler's Legions: The German Army Order of Battle, World War II* (New York: Stein and Day, 1985), passim.

11. On the campaign see Earl Ziemke, *The German Northern Theater of Operations, 1940–1945* (Washington, D.C.: GPO, 1959; CMH, 1989), chaps. 1–6; T. K. Derry, *The Campaign in Norway* (London: HMSO, 1952); Walter Hubatsch, *Die deutschen Besatzung von Dänemark und Norwegen 1940* (Göttingen: Musterschmidt, 1952); Hans-Martin Ottmer, *Weserübung: der deutsche Angriff auf Danemark und Norwegen im April 1940* (Munich: Oldenburg, 1974).

12. Up to 15 June 391 ships delivered 107,581 troops, 20,339 vehicles, and 109,400 tons of supplies; while 582 *Luftwaffe* transports delivered 9,280 troops and 2,376 tons of supplies. NARA T-312, 982, 9173440ff, Verbindungsstab Marine B Nr. 130 "Seetransportübersicht nach dem Stande von 22.3.40," Gruppe XXI KTB I, Anl. 54 u. 56; Gen. Kdo d. X Fl. Korps, "Weisungen für den Transportchef (Land) u. (See) für die Weserübung," Ia Nr. 10056-57/40; Hubatsch, *deutschen Besatzung*, 129–134, 378, 415; *Rise and Fall of the German Air Force* (London: Air Ministry, 1948; New York: St. Martin's, 1983), 57–64; Ziemke, *Northern Theater*, 33, 55–56.

13. Donald G. F. W. MacIntyre, *Narvik* (New York: Norton, 1960); Alex Buchner, *Narvik: die Kämpfe der Gruppe Dietl im Fruhjahr 1940* (Neckargemünd: K. Vowinckel, 1958); Ernst Haffner, *Kampf um Narvik: Erlebnisberichte* (Heidelberg: Esprint, 1982).

14. Ziemke, *Northern Theater*, 109; *Rise and Fall of the German Air Force*, 59–64.

15. In Norway the Germans employed a single tank company equipped with Panzer I and II tanks. The Norwegians claimed the destruction of seven German tanks but Anglo-French claims are unknown. NARA T-312, 982, 9173609, "Operationsbefehl für die Besetzung Norwegens Nr. 1," Anl. zum KTB, Gruppe XXI, Ia Nr. 20/40; David Thompson, "From Neutrality to NATO: The Norwegian Armed Forces and Defense Policy, 1905–55" (Ph.D. diss., Ohio State University, 1996), 252–253.

16. OKW, *Kampf um Norwegen: Berichte und Bilder vom Kriege Gegen England* (Berlin: Zeitgeschichte Verlag, 1940); Thompson, "Neutrality to NATO," 254–259.

17. Höh. Kdo. XXXI, "Bericht über die Besetzung Dänemarks am 9. u. 10.

April 1940;" 198. Inf. Div., Ia, "Bericht über die Besetzung der dänischen Inseln am 9–10.4.1940,"; 3 Geb. Div., Ib, "Bericht über die Erfahrungen auf dem Gebiet der Versorgung während des Einsatzes in Norwegen," 7 July 1940; Thompson, "Neutrality to NATO," 256–258.

18. Murray, *Luftwaffe,* 38; Ziemke, *Northern Theater,* 109.

19 . Germany only possessed numerical superiority in aircraft. Müller-Hillebrand, *Das Heer* II, 45–49; Alistair Horne, *To Lose a Battle: France 1940* (London: Macmillan, 1969), 218–220; J. F. Ellis, *The War in France and Flanders, 1939–40* (London: HMSO, 1953), 34–35.

20. Historians have often blamed Göring and his bombastic assertion that the *Luftwaffe* could destroy the BEF for the latter's escape from Dunkirk. Yet Hitler's halt order was in accord with the German strategic plan and the classic tenets of *Kesselschlacht.* Telford Taylor, *March of Conquest: The German Victories in the West, 1940* (New York: Simon and Shuster, 1958), 255–263.

21. Average German response time for tactical air attacks was twenty-five minutes. Gen. Paul Deichmann, *German Air Force Operations in Support of the Army,* USAF Historical Studies 13 (Maxwell Air Force Base, Ala.: U.S. Air Force Historical Division, Research Studies Institute, Air University, 1962), 155–156; Murray, *Luftwaffe,* 38–43.

22. Richard L. DiNardo, *Mechanized Juggernaut or Military Anachronism: Horses and the German Army in World War II* (Westport, Conn.: Greenwood Press, 1991); R. L. DiNardo and Austin Bay, "Horse-Drawn Transport in the German Army," *Journal of Contemporary History* 23 (1988), 129–142.

23. Germany lost 753 tanks, 29 percent of its inventory. Guderian, *Panzer Leader,* 75; Maier, *Das deutsche Reich* II, 294.

24. For revised training, see NARA T-78, 169, 6144286-326, OKH GenStdH./Ausb. Abt. Pruf. Nr. 3463, *Richtlinien für Führung u. Einsatz der Panzer Division vom 3.12.1940.*

25. The *Sturmgeschütz,* for example, was a turretless assault gun with a low-silhouette that mounted a limited traverse gun in the hull that was cheap and easy to build. The number of batteries increased from three in May 1940 to thirty-eight in June 1941.

26. New weapons included the quadruple 2cm antiaircraft gun, the 5cm *Pak* 38 antitank gun, and the 15cm *Nebelwerfer* six-barreled rocket launcher. Müller-Hillebrand, *Das Heer* II, 171–173.

27. German vehicles first arrived in North Africa painted gray, and a lack of yellow paint meant they initially had to be camouflaged with sand stuck on with gasoline. James Lucas, *Panzer Army Africa* (London: MacDonald and Jane's, 1977), 18–19; Martin van Creveld, *Hitler's Strategy 1940–1941: The Balkan Clue* (London: Cambridge University Press, 1973); Maj. Gen. Alfred Toppe et al., *German Experiences in Desert Warfare During WWII* (Washington, D.C.: Department of the Navy, U.S. Marine Corps, Fleet Marine Force Publication 12-96-I, 1990), 4–5.

28. Toppe, *Desert Warfare,* 16–22, 56–57.

29. Hans-Otto Behrendt, *Rommel's Intelligence in the Desert Campaign 1941–1943* (London: William Kimber, 1985), 43–44, 65–69, 80.

30. Lucas, *Panzer Army,* 25–26.

31. Toppe, *Desert Warfare,* 65–66.

32. Behrendt, *Rommel's Intelligence,* 47–54; Toppe, *Desert Warfare,* 80–81.

33. Müller-Hillebrand, *Das Heer* II, 76–81, 161–179.

34. On *BARBAROSSA* as a race war, see Franz Halder, *Kriegstagebuch* (Stuttgart: W. Kohlhammer, 1962–1964) II, 335–338; Henry Picker, *Hitler's*

Tischgespräche im Führerhauptquartier, 1941–42 (Stuttgart: Seewald, 1963), 270; Christian Streit, "The German Army and the Politics of Genocide," in G. Hirschfeld, ed., *The Policies of Genocide: Jews and Soviet Prisoners of War in Nazi Germany* (London: Allen & Unwin, 1986), 1–14; Alfred Streim, *Die Behandlung sowjetischer Kriegsgefangener im "Fall Barbarossa": eine Dokumentation* (Heidelberg: Müller, Juristischer Verlag, 1981).

35. This sense of superiority led the Germans to neglect battlefield intelligence. Recent scholarship on the Eastern Front, for example, has shown that Soviet deception efforts successfully disguised the focus and timing of every major Red Army offensive. David Glantz, *Soviet Military Deception in the Second World War* (London: F. Cass, 1989); Glantz and Jonathan House, *When Titans Clashed: How the Red Army Stopped Hitler* (Lawrence: University Press of Kansas, 1995).

36. An authoritative account of this clash is provided by Alvin D. Coox, *Nomonhan: Japan Against Russia, 1939* (Palo Alto, Calif.: Stanford University Press, 1985).

37. E. Moritz, Die Einschätzung der Roten Armee durch den faschistischen deutschen Generalstab von 1935 bis 1941," *Zeitschrift für Militärgeschichte* 1969 Nr. 2, 154–170; O. Groehler, "Zur Einschätzung der Roten Armee durch die faschichten Wehrmacht im ersten Halbjahr 1941," *Zeitschrift für Militärgeschichte* 1968 Nr. 6, 724–738.

38. Louis Rotundo, "The Creation of Soviet Reserves and the 1941 Campaign," *Military Affairs* 50, 1 (January 1986), 23ff; David Glantz, "Soviet Mobilization in Peace and War, 1924–1942," *Journal of Soviet Studies* 5 (September 1992), 9–31.

39. J. B. A. Bailey, *Field Artillery and Firepower* (Oxford: The Military Press, 1989), 183.

40. John Weeks, *Assault from the Sky: The History of Airborne Warfare* (New York: David & Charles, 1988), 30–39.

41. Total recruits in training had only increased by 10,000 over the September 1939 figure of 540,000. Müller-Hillebrand, *Das Heer* II, 102–106.

42. Omer Bartov, *Hitler's Army: Soldiers, Nazis, and War in the Third Reich* (New York: Oxford University Press, 1992); *The Eastern Front 1941–1945 and the Barbarization of Warfare* (New York: St. Martin's, 1988); Hannes Heer and Klaus Naumann, *Vernichtungskrieg: Verbrechen der Wehrmacht 1941–45* (Hamburg: Hamburger Edition, 1995); Jürgen Förster, "Zur Rolle der Wehrmacht im Krieg gegen die Sowjetunion 1941," *Aus Politik und Zeitgeschichte* 45, 8 (November 1980), 3–15; and "New Wine in Old Skins? The Wehrmacht and the War of 'Weltanschauungen,' 1941," in Wilhelm Deist, ed., *The German Military in the Age of Total War* (Leamington Spa: Berg, 1985), 304–322; and "The German Army and the Ideological War Against the Soviet Union," in Hirschfeld, ed., *The Policies of Genocide*, 15–29.

43. Alexander Dallin, *Deutsche Herrschaft in Russland 1941–45: Eine Studie über Besatzungspolitik* (Dusseldorf: Atheneum Droste, 1958), 70ff; Norbert Müller, ed., *Deutsche Besatzungspolitik in der USSR 1941–1944: Dokumente* (Cologne: Pahl-Rugenstein, 1980).

44. The *OKH* understated Soviet divisional strength by one-third (213 estimated versus 314 actual). Halder, *KTB* II, 461; III, 190; Walter S. Dunn, Jr., *Hitler's Nemesis: The Red Army, 1930–1945* (Westport, Conn.: Praeger, 1994), 30–32.

45. The *OKW* cut production during spring 1941 by 85 percent for medium mortars, 92 percent for light infantry guns, and 96 percent for light howitzers. Further reductions in August 1941 reduced light-howitzer production to 1 percent of 1940 levels. Müller-Hillebrand, *Das Heer* II, 92.

46. Müller-Hillebrand *Das Heer* II, 101–102; Seaton, *German Army,* 172–175.

47. The number of heavy motorized artillery batteries in service had declined from 365 to 318. Müller-Hillebrand, *Das Heer* II, 124–125, 158–159.

48. Up to 20 December 1941 the *Ostheer* captured 3,350,639 prisoners of war, 214,062 rifles, 29,003 machine guns, 4,439 mortars, 4,164 antitank and 1,927 anti-aircraft guns, and 19,605 artillery pieces. *KTB/OKW* I, 1106–1107.

49. Dunn, *Nemesis,* 35–40; S. F. Liebermann, "The Evacuation of Industry in the Soviet Union during World War II," *Soviet Studies* 35 (1983), 90–102.

50. In 1941 Germany suffered 750,000 casualties on the Eastern Front and lost 35,159 trucks, 2,469 prime movers, 3,906 antitank guns, 2,097 artillery pieces, and 3,370 tanks. *KTB/OKW* I, 1104–1119.

51. Timothy A. Wray, *Standing Fast: The Development of German Defensive Doctrine on the Russian Front during World War II: Prewar to March 1943* (Fort Leavenworth: U.S. Army Command and General Staff College, 1987).

52. Edgar Röhricht, *Probleme der Kesselschlacht* (Karlsruhe: Kondor, 1958), 30; Halder, *KTB* VI, 181, 209; VII, 64; Wolfang Werthern, *Geschichte der 16 Panzer Division 1939–45* (Bad Nauheim: Podzun, 1958), 53–67; Guderian, *Panzer Leader,* 158–167.

53. USAHD MS D-050, Lt. Gen. Werner Prellberg, "Employment of Flak in an Army Defense Zone" (Germany: 1947), 14; MS D-253, Lt. Gen. Erich Schneider, "Antitank Defense in the East" (Germany: 1947), 9–12; Eugen Beinhauser, ed., *Artillerie im Osten* (Berlin: W. Limpert, 1944), 44–49, 55–58, 230–239.

54. Paul Carrell, *Hitler Moves East* (Boston: Little Brown, 1968), 76–78; Sydnor, *Soldiers of Destruction: The SS Death's Head Division 1933–1945* (Princeton, N.J.: Princeton University Press, 1977; 1990), 192; Maximilian Fretter-Pico, *Missbrauchte Infanterie: deutsche Infanterie-divisionen in osteuropäischen Grossraum 1941 bis 1945* (Frankfurt: Bernard & Graefe, 1957), 21–26.

55. On Soviet unreadiness, see Amnon Stella, "Red Army Doctrine and Training on the Eve of the Second World War," *Soviet Studies* 27 (April 1975); Dunn, *Nemesis,* chap. 2.

56. Wray, *Standing Fast,* 40–42; Halder, *KTB* VII, 44, 52; *KTB/OKW* I, 1045; Sydnor, *Soldiers of Destruction,* 175–178; Erich von Manstein, *Lost Victories* (Chicago: H. Regency Co., 1958), 199–201.

57. By 1 November only 15 percent of the automobiles committed to *BAR-BAROSSA* were still serviceable. Alan S. Milward, *The Germany Economy at War* (New York: Oxford University Press, 1965), 39–45; Halder, *KTB* VII, 49; Martin van Creveld, *Supplying War* (London: Cambridge University Press, 1977), 142–180.

58. By 15 November, the *Ostheer* was 20 percent understrength and its fighting power had dwindled by 40 percent. Burkhardt Müller-Hillebrand, *German Tank Maintenance in WWII* (Washington, D.C.: CMH, 1954); Halder, *KTB* III, 286; *KTB/OKW* I, 1074; Klaus Reinhardt, *Moscow—The Turning Point: The Failure of Hitler's Strategy in the Winter of 1941–42* (Oxford: Berg, 1992), 106–107; Halder, *KTB* III, 222; Werner Haupt, *Heeresgruppe Mitte, 1941/43* (Dorheim: Podzun, 1968); Alfred W. Turney, *Disaster at Moscow: Von Bock's Campaign, 1941–42* (Albuquerque: University of New Mexico Press, 1970); C. Wagener, *Moskau 1941: Der Angriff auf die russische Hauptstadt* (Bad Nauheim: Podzun, 1966).

59. On the partisan threat see Matthew Cooper, *The Phantom War: The German Struggle Against Soviet Partisans, 1941–1944* (London: MacDonald and Janes, 1979); Erich Hesse, *Die sowjetrussische Partisankrieg 1941 bis 1944 im Speigel deutsche Kampfanweisungen und Befehle* (Göttingen: Musterschmidt, 1969).

60. *Truppenführung* (Berlin: Offene Worte, 1935); OKH/GenStdH/ Ausb. Abt. (II), H. Dv. 91, *Der Stellungskrieg* (Berlin: Offene Worte, 1939; 1940); and H.Dv. 89/1, *Die Ständige Front: Teil I: Die Abwehr in Ständiger Front* (Berlin: Offene Worte, 1940).

61. *KTB/OKW* I, 1075–1076.

62. Halder, *KTB* VII, 212–215; Guderian, *Panzer Leader,* 262; Franz Kurowski, trans. Joseph G. Walsh, *Deadlock Before Moscow: Army Group Center, 1942–43* (West Chester, Pa.: Schiffer Publishing, 1992), 19–206; Reinhardt, *Moscow,* 291–345.

63. Even by Russian standards the 1941–1942 winter was very harsh, and the German supply system's inability to deliver winter clothing and equipment led the German troops to suffer terribly from frostbite. Wray, *Standing Fast,* 71–75; Allen F. Chew, *Fighting in the Russian Winter: Three Case Studies* (Fort Leavenworth: Combat Studies Institute, USACGSC, 1981); DOA Pamphlet 20–291, *Effects of Climate on Combat in European Russia* (Washington, D.C.: GPO, 1952), 3–4.

64. Tessin, *Verbände* I, 61; Reinhardt, *Moscow,* 369; USAHD MS P-062, Alfred Toppe, "Frostbite Problems in the German Army During WWII," (Germany: 1951), apdx. 8.

65. NARA T-78, 202, 6145569-81, Gen. Kdo. XX A.K, "Erfahrungen im Winterfeldzug," Ia Nr. 2644/42; T-78, 202, 6145541-42," 5 Pz. Div., Erfahrungsbericht über den Winterkrieg 1941–42 in Russland," Abt. Ia. Nr. 427/42, 20 March 1942.

66. NARA T-312, 184, 7730344-45, Hptm. Haderecker, Kdr. I/IR. 20 (mot), "Erfahrungsbericht, Stützpunktsystem oder H.K.L.," 17 August 1942; T-312, 184, 7730340-41, 10 Inf. Div. (mot) Ia, "Stützpunktartige Verteidigung oder durch-laufende Verteidigungsystem," Anl. zu AOK 4 Ia Nr. 4885/42 g. Kdos, v. 20 August 1942.

67. NARA T-312, 184, 7730353ff, 331 Inf. Div, "Erfahrungsbericht—Widerstand-linie-Stützpunkte," 25 August 1942.

68. USAHD MS D-298, Paul Schulz, "Positional Warfare in Winter 1941–42," (Germany: 1947), 4–12.

69. The encircled hedgehog at Sukhinintsi, defended by a regiment of the 216th Division held off two Soviet divisions for over a month until relieved. Fretter-Pico, *Missbrauchte Infanterie,* 66–67.

70. Wray, *Standing Fast,* 90.

71. The entire Soviet front before Moscow had only 46 serviceable tanks on 6 December. The Soviet High Command subsequently committed 1 million troops, 8,000 guns and mortars, 720 tanks, and 1,370 planes, 40 percent of the Red Army. Reinhardt, *Moscow,* 281–283, 318–320.

72. More limited objectives coupled with greater concentration could have brought decisive operational success in one sector. John Erickson, *The Road to Stalingrad* (London: Weidenfeld & Nicholson, 1975), 298.

73. Soviet artillery munitions were so tight that consumption averaged only one to two rounds per gun per day during January. Red Army forces annihilated included the second Shock, twenty-ninth, thirtieth, and thirty-third Armies and the I Guards Cavalry Corps. Reinhardt, *Moscow,* 350–355; H. Grossmann, *Rshew: Eckpfeiler der Ostfront* (Bad Nauheim: Podzun, 1962).

74. The Kholm garrison was cut off for 103 days until relieved. At Demyansk, the *Luftwaffe* delivered an average of 302 tons daily to resupply the 96,000 encir-cled troops. Lt. Gen. Hermann Plocher, *The German Air Force versus Russia, 1942* (Maxwell Air Force Base, Ala.: U.S. Air Force Historical Division, Air University, 1966; New York: Arno Press, 1968), 74–85, 97–98, 149–150.

75. NARA T-78, 202, 6145525-61, 5 Pz. Div., "Erfahrungsbericht über d.

Winterkrieg in Russland," Ia Nr. 427/42 geh., Div. Gef. Std., 20 May 1942; 6145562-611, G.K. XX A.K., "Erfahrungen im Winterfeldzug," Ia Nr. 26442/42 geh. K. Gef. Std., 16 May 1942; 6145611-26, G.K. IX A.K., "Erfahrungsbericht aus dem Winterkrieg," Ia Nr. 416/42 geh., K. Gef. Std., 19 April 1942; 6145679-700, 78 Inf. Div., "Erfahrungsbericht Kampfführung im Winter," Ia Nr. 243/42 geh., Div. Gef. Std., 9 May 1942; 6146768-77, Heeresgruppe Mitte, "Winter-Erfahrungen im Osten," Ia Nr. 1149/42 geh. HQu. 12 February 1942.

76. NARA T-78, 202, 6145769ff, OKH/GenStdH Ausb. Abt. (II) Nr. 1550/42, "Zusammenstellung von Ostfahrungen über Bekampfung von Panzerkampfwagen und Angaben über Panzerabwehrwaffen und Munition," 19 May 1942.

77. Denigration of Soviet capabilities ensured that the *OKW* did not increase armament production until January 1942. For examples of this denigration see DA Pamphlet 20–230 (Colonel General Erhard Raus), *Russian Combat Methods in World War II* (Washington, D.C.: Department of the Army 1950), 3–7; USAHD MS D-036, Col. Gen. Lothar Rendulic, "Fighting Qualities of the Russian Soldier," in Donald Detweiler, ed., *World War II German Military Studies* (New York: Garland, 1979) Vol. XIX.

78. USAHD MS P-034, Müller-Hillebrand, "German Tank Production & Losses" (Germany: 1951), apdx.; Tessin, *Verbände* I, 179; Richard M. Ogorkiewicz, *Armour: The Development of Mechanized Forces & Their Equipment* (London: Atlantic Books, 1960), 215–217; Guderian, *Panzer Leader,* 276–283.

79. NARA T-312, 1660, 00941ff, Armee-Pi.-Führer AOK 2, *Merkblatt für Panzervernichtungstrupps,* 10 February 1942; T-312, 1283, 000199; OKH GenStdH/ Ausb. Abt. Kampferfahrungen. Panzerabwehr, Nr. 15550/42, d. 19 May 1942.

80. *Terrain Factors in the Russian Campaign* CMH Pub 104–5 (Washington, D.C.: CMH, 1982), 28–29.

81. Ibid., 31–34; USAHD MS P-060n "Small Unit Tactics—Fighting in Russian Forests and Swamps" (Germany: 1952), 1–50.

82. The route of the ill-trained *SS Kampfgruppe Nord* at Salla in July 1941 is a case in point. German mountain troops were trained for alpine (downhill), not cross-country, skiing and had no experience of tundra conditions. USAHD MS P-060m, Lt. Col. Klaus Brockelmann and Hans Roschmann, "Small Unit Tactics—Fighting in Taiga & Tundra" (Germany: 1952).

83. USAHD MS P-106, Lt. Gen. Lothar Rendulic, "Warfare in the Arctic Zones of Europe" (Germany: 1951), 1–15.

84. By 1 February 1942 the *Ostheer* had suffered 917,985 casualties and lost 66,432 rifles, 4,262 antitank guns, 24,247 machine guns, 5,890 mortars, 1,942 howitzers, 1,419 infantry guns, and 4,241 AFVs. It remained 12 percent (625,000 troops) understrength, and on 1 April 1942 had only 140 operational tanks. Officer losses were very heavy, the number of army first lieutenants having plummeted from 12,055 to 7,276. Reinhardt, *Moscow,* 366–370; Hennicke, "Zu den Menschenverlusten der faschistischen deutschen Wehrmacht im zweiten Weltkrieg (Dokumente)," *Zeitschrift für Militärgeschichte* 1967 Nr. 2, 195–208.

85. By 1 February 1942 the *Ostheer* had lost 101,529 vehicles and 179,132 horses. Reinhardt, *Moscow,* 365–368. On munitions consumption, see *KTB/OKW* I, 1110–1111.

86. On 1 April 1942, of 162 divisions in the east only eight were fully fit and forty-seven partially fit for offensive operations. Reinhardt, *Moscow,* 370.

87. Tessin, *Verbände* I, 61.

88. Some eighty-four divisions combined reconnaissance and antitank battalions into a single mobile battalion that constituted the sole divisional mobile reserve. Tessin, *Verbände* I, 152; Müller-Hillebrand, *Das Heer* III, 63.

89. Troop densities of twenty combatants per kilometer were common. NARA T-312, 838, 9003278ff, Gen. Kdo. I A.K., "Korpsbefehl 194," Ia Nr. 1819/42 g. Kdos, 8 July 1942.

90. NARA T-312, 838, 9003278, "Bericht zur Frontriese des Hptm. Muschner in der Zeit vom 31.7–7.8.42 in den Bereich des AOK 2," 9 August 1942.

91. NARA T-312, 838, 9003301-02, 21 Inf. Div., "Erfahrungen über den Kampf an festen Fronten," Ia Nr. 835/42 g. Kdos, 27 November 1942; 9003267-68, AOK 18 Ia Nr. 19140/42, 16 December 1942.

92. By August 1942 thirty-six Axis divisions stood in the East. The *Heer* raised a Spanish volunteer division, and Walloon, French, and Croat regiments, while the *Waffen SS* raised the "Germanic" 5th SS Motorized Division *Wiking.* NARA T-312, 1660, 000747-48, OKH/GenStdH Org. Abt., "Grundlegender Befehl 1: Hebung der Gefechtsstärke," (II) Nr. 9900/42 g. Kdos, 8 October 1942; NARA T-312, 1660, 000726, OKH/GenStdH Op. Abt (I), "Grundlegender Befehl 5," Nr. 11548/42, 29 October 1942; Carlos C. Jurado, *Foreign Volunteers of the Wehrmacht, 1941–45* (London: Osprey, 1983), 3–12; Martin Windrow, *The Waffen-SS* (London: Osprey, 1982), 8–13; Peter Abbott and Nigel Thomas, *Germany's Eastern Front Allies,* 15–24. Franz von Adonya-Naredy, *Ungarns Armee im Zweiten Weltkrieg* (Neckargemünd: Kurt Vowinckel, 1971), 83–86.

93. During the fall of 1941, the *Ostheer* raised Baltic and Ukrainian rear area auxiliary police and security battalions; Cossack cavalry squadrons and "hundreds." And in 1942 the Turkestan, Azerbaijani, North Caucasian, Georgian, Armenian, and Volga-Tartar Legions. Jurado, *Foreign Volunteers of the Wehrmacht 1941–45;* Peter Abbott and Nigel Thomas, *Partisan Warfare 1941–45* (London: Osprey, 1983); Joachim Hoffmann, *Die Ostlegionen 1941–1943* (Freiburg: Rombach & Co., 1976).

94. USAHD MS C-058, General Max Simon, "Experience Gained in Combat with Russian Infantry," in Detweiler, ed., *German Military Studies,* Vol. XIX.

95. H. R. Trevor-Roper, ed., *Blitzkrieg to Defeat: Hitler's War Directives, 1939–45* (New York: Holt, Rinehart, and Winston, 1964), 116–121.

96. In 1941 the Caucasus provided 85 percent of Soviet petroleum products, but both frantic expansion of production in the Urals and Lend-Lease supplies had already appreciably reduced such dependence by summer 1942. Albert Seaton, *Russo-German War* (New York: Praeger, 1970), 266–267.

97. The Germans reinforced their Axis allies with liaison staffs and special mobile "intervention" units. NARA T-312, 189, 7736226-27, ObKdo. d. HG. B, "Eingreifgruppen an Standigen Fronten," Ia Nr. 2889/42, 6 September 1942; Tessin, *Verbände* I, 107.

98. NARA T-312, 189, 7736339-49, Der Führer, OKH/GenStdH Op Abt. (I) Nr. 11154/42, geh., 8 September 1942.

99. The Eastern Wall stretched along the Narva and Dneipr Rivers. NARA T-312, 189, 7736611, OberKdo. HG. Mitte, "Stützpunktbau," Ia/Gen.d.Pi. Nr. 310/42, 18 September 1942.

100. The replacement army ultimately deployed twenty-six reserve divisions for occupation duties. AHA/Ia VII Nr. 4200/42 g. Kdos, 1 September 1942; Tessin, *Verbände* I, 131–132; Victor Madej, *German Army Order of Battle: The Replacement Army* (Allentown, Pa.: Game Publishing, 1984).

101. Commanders rated their formations as category I (fully fit for offense); II (partly fit for offense); III (fit for defense); or IV (partly fit for defense). Later category V (unfit for any duty) was added. NARA T-312, 1660, 000694-95, AOK 2 Ia Nr 1412/42. 1 December 1942.

102. Der Führer, OKH/GenStdH/Op. Abt. (I) Nr 42017/42, "Operationsbefehl 1," 14 October 1942, *KTB/OKW* II, 1301–1304.

103. The *Ostheer* now had five ski battalions and most divisions possessed at

least one ski-mobile company. NARA T-312, 1660, 000736-38, AOK 2, "Vorbereitungen für Gliederung und Umrustung zum Winterkrieg," Ia Nr 2448/42 g. Kdos, 19 October 1942.

104. Earl Ziemke, *Stalingrad to Berlin: The German Defeat in the East, 1943–1945* (Washington, D.C.: CMH, 1968), 112–113; Werner Haupt, *Heeresgruppe Nord* (Bad Nauheim: Podzun, 1967), 149–154; Kurowski, *Deadlock Before Moscow,* 207–367.

105. Manstein, *Lost Victories,* 383–384.

106. Wray, *Standing Fast,* 160–162.

107. Bartov, *Hitler's Army,* 81–82; Ian Kershaw, "How Effective was Nazi Propaganda?" in D. Welch, ed., *Nazi Propaganda: The Power, the Limitations* (London: Barnes and Noble, 1983), 180–205; David Welch, "Propaganda and Indoctrination in the Third Reich: Success or Failure?" *European History Quarterly* 17, 4 (1987), 403ff.

108. The new tank-infantry manual stridently argued for concentrated armored employment. NARA T-78, 202, 6146516-521, Panzertruppenschule Wunsdorf, "*Merkblatt über Zusammenwirken zwischen Panzern und Infanterie in der Verteidigung für die mit Durchführung des Panzereinsatzes verantwortlichen Truppenführer* (February 1943); Franz Kurowski and Gottfried Tornau, *Sturmartillerie 1939–45* (Stuttgart: Motorbuch, 1977), 158–207.

109. An example of duplication was the army–*Waffen SS* fight over spin- versus fin-stabilized rockets. The latter produced its own fin-stabilized copy of the Soviet *Katyusha* rocket, the 8cm *Raketen-Vielfachwerfer* (or "Himmler Organ"—as opposed to the "Stalin Organ," which was a captured *Katyusha* rocket) in opposition to the *Heer*'s spin-stabilized *Nebelwerfer.* Bizarre German weapons projects included wind guns, vortices projectors, sound reflectors, antitank grenade-launching flare pistols, and a rifle that fired around corners. Highly innovative weapons of marginal utility include the V1 and V2 rockets, the 100-ton "Mouse" tank; the 15cm "*Hochdruckpumpe,*" a smooth-bore, multibarreled, long-range gun; the 7.5cm "*Rückstossfreie* "*Kanone* 43 recoilless gun with lethal backblast; the "*Rammtiger*"; and the *Wasserful* supersonic antiaircraft missile. Terry Gander and Peter Chamberlain, *Small Arms, Artillery, and Special Weapons of the Third Reich* (London: McDonald and Jane, 1978); Alan F. Beyerchen, "From Radio to Radar: Interwar Military Adaptation to Technological Change in Germany, the United Kingdom, and the United States," in Alan R. Millett and Williamson Murray, eds., *Innovation and Adaptation in the Inter War* (Washington, D.C.: Office of Net Assessment, 1994), 433–492.

110. Wray, *Standing Fast,* 166–177.

111. Ibid., 166–168.

112. Ibid., 173–177.

113. The *Ostheer* produced thousands of combat reports during the war. For a sampling see NARA T-312, 556, 8166882ff, AOK 16, "Erfahrungsberichte, 9.9.41–4.4.42"; 582, 8199888ff, AOK 16, "Erfahrungen u. Ausbildung," 17.6–10.12.42"; 671, 8305653, AOK 17, "Erfahrungs- u. Gefechtsberichte, 29.6. 41–16.1.42"; 685, 8320698, "AOK 17, "Gefechts- u. Erfahrungsberichte, 10–28.2.42"; 695, AOK 17, "Gefechts- u. Erfahrungsberichte, 13.2.–19.7.42"; AOK 17 Gefechts- u. Erfahrungsberichte, 1.7.–9.10.43."

114. Paul Wolfgang, *Geschichte der 18 Panzer Division 1940–43 mit Geschichte der 18. Artillerie Division 1943–44* (Reutlingen: Preussischer Verlag, 1995); Joachim Engelmann, *German Artillery in WWII* (Pitglen, Pa.: Schiffer, 1995), 7; Eugen Beinhauer, ed., *Artillerie im Osten* (Berlin: W. Limpert, 1944).

115. NARA T-78, 428, 6393155-76, OKH GenStdH Org. Abt.,

"Zahlenmassige Entwicklung des Heeres," Nr. 1/18340/44 g.Kdos. [1944]; Engelmann, *German Artillery,* 109–112.

116. Hitler wisely refrained from employing chemical weapons and thus the "smoke troops" (the cover designation for these units) became conventional mortar units. In late 1941 the six-barreled 15cm *Nebelwerfer* 41 entered service, in 1942 the heavy 21cm *Nebelwerfer* 42, and in 1943 the superheavy 30cm *Nebelwerfer* 43. Joachim Emde, *Die Nebelwerfer: Entwicklung u. Einsatz d. Werfertruppe im 2. Weltkrieg* (Friedberg: Podzun-Pallas, 1979), 112–138.

117. Within fifteen days the Germans had 15,000 troops in Tunisia. I. S. O. Playfair, *The Mediterranean & Middle East* IV (London: HMSO, 1966), 172–184.

118. USAHD C-098, Maj. Gen. Jürgen von Arnim, "Recollections of Tunisia," (Germany: 1951), 6–36; D-001 Gen. Gustav von Värst, "Operations of the Fifth Panzer Army in Tunisia" (Germany: 1947), 4–11; Gregory Blaxland, *The Plain Cook & the Great Showman* (London: W. Kimber, 1977), chaps. 7–9; Charles Messenger, *The Tunisian Campaign* (Shepperton: Ian Allen, 1982), chaps. 3–6; Toppe, *Desert Warfare,* 65–66.

119. John Strawson, *The Battle for North Africa* (New York: Scribner's Sons, 1969), 172–174; Williamson Murray, *Luftwaffe* (Baltimore: Nautical & Aviation, 1985), 154–155.

120. Martin Blumenson's *Kasserine Pass* (New York: Tower, 1966) remains the best study of this defeat. See also Charles Whiting, *Kasserine: First Blood* (New York: Military Heritage Press, 1984), and Ward Rutherford, *Kasserine: Baptism of Fire* (London: Macdonald & Co., 1970).

121. Ralph Bennett, *ULTRA and Mediterranean Strategy* (New York: William Morrow, 1989), chap. 8.

122. The *Luftwaffe* lost 2,422 aircraft in the Mediterranean during the Tunisian campaign, 40 percent of its November 1942 strength, including 62 percent of its fighters. Murray, *Luftwaffe,* 158–159.

123. The 8.8cm *RPzB* 43 "Tank Terror" fired a 3.25kg rocket to 150 meters. The improved RPzB 54 superseded it in 1944. Gander & Chamberlain, *Small Arms,* 332.

124. Germany achieved massive production increases at the expense of reduced production of replacement parts, thus diminishing serviceability rates. Wolfgang Schumann et al., *Deutschland im zweiten Weltkrieg* (Cologne: Pahl-Rugenstein, 1985) IV, 468; Burckhardt Müller-Hillebrand, *German Tank Maintenance in WWII* (Washington, D.C.: GPO, 1982), 3–4.

125. The artillery, however, retained control of *Sturmgeschütz* assault guns. Albert Seaton, *The German Army, 1933–45* (New York: Meridian Books, 1982), 201–202.

126. The Germans committed 50 divisions, 25 percent of those in the East as well as 46 percent of their armor on a sector that amounted to 13 percent of the length of the front. E. Klink, *Das Gesetz des Handelns, "Zitadelle" 1943* (Stuttgart: Deutsche Verlags-Austalt, 1966); Leopold Urba, *Kursk: die Letzte deutsche Panzer-Offensive in Russland* (Rastatt: Möwig, 1986); Joachim Engelmann, *Zitadelle: die grosste Panzerschlacht im Osten 1943* (Friedberg: Podzun-Pallas, 1980).

127. Forward-deployed antitank units, closer coordination, and greatly increased fire support inflicted heavy casualties on the Germans. David Glantz, *From the Don to the Dnepr: Soviet Offensive Operations, December 1942–August 1943* (London: F. Cass, 1991), chap. 7; David Glantz and Jonathan House, *When Titans Clashed* (Lawrence: University of Kansas Press, 1995), chap. 11; Ivan Parotkin, *Kursk* (Moscow: Progress, 1974), 161–162; Walter S. Dunn, Jr., *Hitler's Nemesis: The Red Army, 1930–1945* (Westport, Conn.: Praeger, 1994), 20–21;

David Glantz, *Soviet Defensive Tactics at Kursk, July 1943* (Fort Leavenworth: CSI, U.S. Army Command and General Staff College, 1986), 12–66.

128. Samuel W. Mitchum and Friedrich von Stauffenberg, *The Battle for Sicily: How the Allies Lost Their Chance for Total Victory* (New York: Orion Books, 1991); D'Este, *Bitter Victory;* Albert N. Garland and Howard Smyth, *Sicily and the Surrender of Italy* (Washington, D.C.: GPO, 1965); C. J. C. Molony et al., *The Mediterranean and the Middle East* (London: HMSO, 1973) Vol V.

129. Gander and Chamberlain, *Small Arms,* 49–55.

130. The 8.8cm *Pak* 43 was undoubtedly the deadliest antitank gun of the war and it was fortunate for the Allies that the gun was never common. PRO WO 205/1165, "Survey of Casualties Among Armoured Units" (1945) 15–16.

131. Gander and Chamberlain, *Small Arms,* 9.

132. Richard Hallion, *Strike from the Sky: The History of Battlefield Air Attack, 1911–1945* (Washington, D.C.: Smithsonian Institute Press, 1989), chap. 4.

133. Roger Edwards, *Panzer: An Evolution in Warfare, 1939–1945* (London: Arms & Armour Press, 1989), 120–121.

134. Edwards, *Panzer,* 120–129; Christopher Calhoon, *German Air Anti-armor Operations on the Eastern Front: Lessons for Tomorrow's Army* (Carlisle Barracks, Pa.: U.S. Army War College, 1987).

135. Wray, *Standing Fast,* chap. 3.

136. Up to May 1943 the Germans averaged 173 transport missions daily carrying 1,247 troops and 195 tons of supplies. The *Luftwaffe* lost 5,926 transports during the war, including 1,149 in 1942 and 1,969 in 1943. Maj. Gen. Fritz Morzik, USAF Historical Study 167, *German Air Force Airlift Operations* (U.S. Air Force Historical Division Research Studies Institute, Air University, 1961; New York:, Arno Press, 1968), 301; CMH 104–15, *Operations of Encircled Forces: German Experiences in Russia* (Washington, D.C.: CMH, 1982; 1988), 65–66.

137. *Operations of Encircled Forces,* 15–51; Morzik, *German Airlift Operations,* 219–225, 242–260.

138. The *Feldheer* was 28 percent understrength and the *Ostheer* 20 percent understrength. Infantry and mechanized divisions averaged 73 percent and 78 percent, respectively, of establishment strength. Keilig, *Deutsche Heer* Pt. 204, 1943, 8–9.

139. The new 1944 infantry division cut manpower by 27 percent but increased firepower by 10 percent. NARA T-312, 516, 8115042, AOK 15, "Inf Div 44," Ia Nr. 3115 /44 g. Kdos, [1944]; James F. Dunnigan, ed., *The Russian Front: Germany's War in the East 1941–45* (London: Arms & Armour Press, 1978), 107–133.

140. Der Führer, OKW/WFSt/Org. Abt., "Grundlegender Befehl 22," Nr. 007436/43 g. Kdos., 27 November 1943. By 20 September 1944 this measure had released 732,930 personnel for combat duty. "Ergebnis der Personneleinsparungen Gemäss Führerbefehl v. 27.11.1943," WFSt/Org. (I), 1826/44 g.K, 7 June 1944; Der Chef. d. Generalstabes des Heeres, "Zahlenmassige Ergebnisse der durchgeführten Personaleinsparungen," Org. Abt. Nr. 2555/44 g. Kdos, H. Qu., OKH, 6. October 1944.

141. The new antitank battalion contained a company of 12 towed or 14 self-propelled antitank guns, a battery of 10 assault guns, and a company of 12 light or 9 medium antiaircraft guns. The infantry received 108 *Panzerschreck* rocket launchers. NARA T-313,516, 8115042, "Grundgliederung I.D. n.a," Ia Nr. 3115/g. Kdos, [1944].

142. Martin van Creveld, *Fighting Power: German & US Army Performances, 1939–45* (London: Arms & Armour Press, 1983), table 6.10.

143. During the war less than .1 percent of the *Wehrmacht* deserted. Mutiny, that is collective disobedience, was even rarer—only 442 soldiers were tried for mutiny during the war. If convicted, however, punishments were draconian. Up to mid-1944 11,664 death sentences had been handed down. Jürgen Förster, "New Wines in Old Skins: The Wehrmacht and the War of Weltanschauungen," in Deist, *The German Military in the Age of Total War,* 304–335; Otto Hennicke, "Auszüge aus der Wehrmachtkriminalstatistik," *Vierteljahrhefter fur Zeitgeschichte* 1985, 438–445.

144. Tessin, *Verbände* I, 125–126; Madej, *Replacement Army,* 3–4.

145. NARA T-311, 27, 7032458ff, OB West, "Beurteilung der Lage OB West," 28 October 1943; T-311, 15, 7016267-73, OB West, "grundlegender Befehl des OB West 32," 28 October 1943.

146. Alan Wilt, *Hitler's Atlantic Wall* (Ames: University of Iowa Press, 1975), chap. 5; Hans Wegemüller, *Die Abwehr der Invasion: Die Konzeption des Oberbefehlshaber West 1940–44* (Freiburg in Breisgau: Rombach, 1979).

147. NARA T-311, 27, 7032325ff, OB West, "Die Kräfte in der Kustenverteidigung im Westen, Oktober 1943."

148. Imperial War Museum, Captured Enemy Documents Collection (hereafter IWM EDS) AL 1645, OB West, "Austauch Osttruppen gegen deutsche," 25 September 1943; NARA T-312, 27, 7533775, AOK 1, "Kriegsgleiderungs-mässige Eingliedeung v. Ost Btlen. in bodenständige Div.," 9 October 1943.

149. The *Westheer* had only 150 modern Panzer IV tanks, and its operational armored reserve consisted of two battalions of obsolete French tanks captured in 1940. Its only fully battleworthy mobile reserve was an artillery regiment equipped with Soviet guns. NARA T-78, 623, Gen-Insp. d. Pztr., "Panzerlage Westen, Stand: 1.6.1943;" T-78, 410, 6378303-308, HG D., "Artillerie im Westen," Anl. zu HG D Abt. Ia Nr. 6787/43 geh.

150. On 1 July 1943 the *Westheer* was short 10,140 trucks. NARA T-78, 614, 000601, "Kraftfahrzeuge (ungepanzert) im Westen, Stand 5.9.1943," Anl. 6 zu OKH GenStdH/Gen.Qu.1/Nr. 5800/43 g. Kdos, v. 6 September 1943.

151. On 1 April 1944, the forty-two army combat divisions in the West were short only 296 German personnel. NARA T-77, 1421, 000237-38, OKW WFSt/Op.(H)/ West, "Fehlstellen der Divisionen im Bereich Ob. West: Stand 1.4.1944," Nr. 004662/44 g. Kdos, F.H.Qu., 3 May 1944.

152. The army's officer-enlistee ratio had widened from 1:30 in June 1940 to 1:44 by October 1943. NARA T-314, 1604, 001032, "Personelle Zusammensetzung. A: Offiziere," Beilage zu Anlage zu Gen. Kdo. LXXXIV A.K. Ia. Nr. 1808/43 g. Kdos., v. 4.10.1943."

153. By April 1944, the Seventh Army's officer-enlistee ratio had dropped to 1:31.5, well below the *Feldheer* average of 1:42.5. Keilig, *Deutsche Heer* III, 204, 1944, 1–4.

154. In October 1943 only 23.5 percent of army officers in Normandy were Eastern Front veterans, but by April 1944 60 percent of Seventh Army officers were *Ostkämpfer.* NARA T-314, 1604, 001032, "Personelle Zusammensetzung. A: Offiziere," Beilage zu Anlage zu Gen. Kdo. LXXXIV A.K." Ia. Nr. 1808/43 g. Kdos., 4 October 1943; T-312, 1566, 000695, TKB d. Abt. IIa/IIb z. KTB d. Führ.abt. AOK 7, 1 January–31 March 1944.

155. For discussion of the ideological indoctrination of the *Ostheer* and its resultant brutalization, see Omer Bartov, *The Eastern Front, 1941–45, German Troops and the Barbarisation of Warfare* (New York: St. Martin's Press, 1988); and *Hitler's Army: Soldiers, Nazis, and War in the Third Reich* (New York: Oxford University Press, 1991); Christian Streit, *Keine Kamerade: die Wehrmacht und die*

Sowjetskriegsgefangenen, 1941–1945 (Stuttgart: Deutsch-Anstalt Verlag, 1978); Hannes Heer and Klaus Naumann, *Vernichtungskrieg: Verbrechen der Wehrmacht, 1941–1944* (Hamburg: Hamburger Edition, 1995).

156. Contemporary POW reports that appeared to confirm the unreliability of *Volksdeutsch* and *Osttruppen* shaped this view. In reality, more *Volksdeutsch* appeared in Allied POW camps than actually fought in the West: German soldiers lied about their ethnicity to avoid anticipated mistreatment or to secure preferential treatment. PRO WO 241/1, Department of Army Psychiatry, "The German Deserter: A Psychological Profile."

157. The 243d Division assessed the conduct of its *Volksdeutsch* in Normandy as "good." USAHD MS D-382, Lt. Col. E. Mauer, "243d Infantry Division, March–June 1944" (Garmisch: 1947), 9.

158. For example the 441st East Battalion near Caen was rated as unfit for any combat service and was thus relegated to Atlantic Wall construction work. It nevertheless launched several counterattacks on the Allied airborne bridgehead after D-Day. NARA T-311, 278, 001410, "Kriegsgliederung, 716th Division, Stand: 1 Juni 1944"; T-78, 413, 6281269-70, Gen. d. Freiw. Verbände "Schematisches Gliederung d. Landeseigene Verbände," 602/44 g. Kdos, 17 March 1944.

159. Two battalions, for example, defended the 30-mile stretch of Norman coastline between Coutances and Granville. Kurt Mehner, ed., *Die Geheimen Tagesberichte der deutschen Wehrmachtführung im Zweiten Weltkrieg, 1939–1945* (Osnabrück: Biblio, 1984) X, apdx.

160. On D-Day *Volksdeutsch* and *Osttruppen* constituted 5 percent of the *Westheer*'s manpower. In contrast, on 1 May 1944 Axis troops alone made up 31 percent of the *Ostheer*'s personnel. *KTB/OKW* III, 1484, IV, 273; Glantz, *When Titans Clashed,* 304.

161. This NCO shortage was most pronounced in the *Waffen SS*. On 1 June 1944 the 12th SS Panzer Division, for example, lacked 48 percent of its authorized noncommissioned officers. Craig W. Luther, *Blood and Honor: The History of the 12th SS Panzer Division "Hitler Youth" 1943–1945* (San Jose, Calif.: Bender, 1987), 58.

162. NARA T-84, 302, 000001-000150, 3d Battalion, 1053rd Grenadier Regiment, "Militärische Ausbildung, 27.3.-26.7.1944"; 000151-190, 8th Fallschirmjäger Regiment, "Unterrichts-Themen fur Gruppen- u. Zugführer, 10–18.5.1944" ; 000191-00220, 352d Inf. Div., "Ausbildungs Anordnung, 10.1943-29.4.1944."

163. Ironically, it was the *Heer,* not the SS, that pushed for greater and more systematic indoctrination. Each division had a leadership officer, and these officers were informally appointed down to battalion, even company, level. PRO WO 208/3201 MIRS, "The National Socialist Indoctrination Officer in the German Armed Forces"; R. L. Quinett, "Hitler's Political Officers: The National Socialist Leadership Officers," Ph.D. diss., University of Oklahoma, 1979.

164. NARA T-354, 156, 3800397-98, 12 SS Pz. Div. IIa, "Die Weltanschauliche Schulung in die SS Pz. Div. HJ," 22 November 43; NARA T-84, 302, 000026-027, 3rd Bn., 1053d Grenadier Regiment, "Nationalpolitischer Unterricht für die Zeit v. 19–25.6.1944," 17 June 1944; T-84, 161, 1628589-90, 712. Inf. Div. NS Führung, "NS Führungshinweise 5," Div. Gef. Std. July 1944; 1628464-65, 171 Res. Div. Abt. Ic, "Wehrgeistige Führung d. Truppe," 7 August 1944.

165. Lt. Col. Günther Keil, commander of the 919th Grenadier Regiment, the last German formation to surrender on the Cotentin Peninsula, took every opportunity to motivate ideologically his troops. USAHD MS C-018, Lt. Col. Günther Keil, "Grenadier Regiment 919, Kampfgruppe Keil" (Germany: 1948), 35.

166. Bartov, *Hitler's Army*, 33.

167. NARA T-311, 27, 7032325ff, OB West, "Die Kräfte in der Kustenverteidigung im Westen, Oktober 1943."

168. NARA T-78, 317, 6271440-44, OB West, "Vorbereitung für den Kampf," Ia. Nr. 673/43 g. Kdos., Chef, 18. November 1943; T-314, 1604, 000731, "Hebung der Kampfkraft der Infanterie," Oberltnt. Rohrbach, 709th I.D. Abt. Ia. Nr. 1427/43 g. Kdos., d. 29 July 1943; T-312, 521, 8121995, 15 AOK, "Übersicht d. Küstendivisionen mit panzerbrechenden Waffen," 14 March 1944; T-314, 1604, 001167, G.K. LXXXIV A.K. "Neugliederung und Umbewaffnung der Art.," Nr. 1958/43 g. Kdos., d. 11 November 1943; T-314, 1604, 001281-84, Gen. Kdo. LXXXIV A.K., "Aufstellung von Pz.-jäger Kompanien," Nr. 2127/43 g. Kdos, d. 14 December 1943.

169. From January–April 1944 truck losses exceeded production by three to one, and the number of tractors in service fell 21 percent. NARA T-78, 168, n.f., OKH Gen. Qu., "Waffenstillstand Juni 1944," Blatt Nr. G 401-07.

170. Spring 1944 war games suggested that the *Westheer* required 40,000 tons of transport capacity to repel an invasion, a figure well below the capacity of the French rail net. PRO WO 233/30, DMI, Prof. Solly Zuckermann, *Report by SHAEF on the Effects of the OVERLORD Air Plan to Destroy Enemy Rail Communications* (November 1944), 34; USAHD MS B-827, Eckstein, "Activities of the Quartermaster General West Before and During the Invasion" (Germany: 1946), 21–24, 33–36.

171. The number of trucks and prime movers assigned to mechanized divisions increased from 2,774 and 398, respectively, to 9,668 and 755. NARA T-78, 623, 718, and 719, Gen.Insp. d. Pztrpn., Zustandberichte, January–May 1944.

172. Military rail traffic had dropped to 30 percent of January 1944 levels by D-Day. PRO WO 233/30, *Effects of the OVERLORD Air Plan*, 9–10.

173. Supplies transported by the strategic truck transport reserve increased from 252 tons on 1 January 1944 to 1,732 tons by 1 May 1944. NARA T-311, 14, 7014653 and 7015142, Beilung für d. KTB OQu West, January–May 1944.

174. On 1 June 1944 the *Westheer* still lacked 11,447 trucks and 1,760 prime movers. NARA T-78, 726, 6076170, "Kraftfahrzeuge (ungepanzert) Heer: Westen," OKH Gen. Qu., 5. August 1944.

175. NARA T-311, 27, 7033361-64, Anl. 26 zu "Kampfanweisung für die Festung Hoek v. H." [spring 1944]; 312, 517, 8116447, AOK 15 OQu., "Munitionswesen," Anl. 1 zu AOK 15/OQu/Qu.1 Nr. 1500/44 g. Kdos, 4 June 1944; T-311, 24, 7028940, "Mun. Bevorratung im Westen," GenStdH/Gen. Qu./Gr. Mun. I Az. 2359 Nr. I/011 901/44 geh. Kdos., 25 May 1944.

176. Total fuel stocks in the West increased fractionally from 74.157 million liters on 1 January 1944 to 81.1 million liters on 1 May. NARA T-311, 14, 7014621-24, Anl. 6 zu Ob. West/O.Qu. West/Qu.1 Nr. 0700/44 g. Kdos., v. 12 February 1944; T-311, 014, 7015022-23, Anl. 6 zu Ob. West/ O.Qu.West/Qu.1/Betr. Stoff Nr. 02290/44 g. Kdos. 8 May 1944; T-311, 29, 7183272, OB West, "Betreibstoff Einschränkung," Ia.Qu. West.1 Nr. 027921/44 g. Kdos., v. 3 June 1944.

177. Russell A. Hart, "Feeding Mars: The Role of Logistics in the German Defeat in Normandy, June–August 1944, *War in History* 3, 4 (Fall 1996), 418–435.

178. These carried 3.233 million gallons of fuel, some 15 percent of total stocks in the West. NARA T-311, 1, 7000664, "Vortragnotiz," Anl. zum KTB. Ob. Kdo. HG. B Vers. Abt. Ib, 3 June 1944.

179. PRO AIR 40/1669, RAF Bombing Analysis Unit, "The Effect of the OVERLORD Air Plan to Disrupt Enemy Rail Communications"; PRO WO 205/172, "Pre-invasion Bombing Campaign"; Wesley Frank Craven and James Lea Cate, *The Army Air Forces in World War II* (Chicago: University of Chicago Press,

1951) Vol. III; Sir Charles Webster and Noble Frankland, *The Strategic Air Offensive Against Germany, 1939–1945* (London: HMSO, 1961) III; Walt W. Rostow, *Pre-Invasion Bombing Strategy: General Eisenhower's Decision of 25 March, 1944* (Austin: University of Texas Press, 1981); and Maj. O. Jaggi, "Normandie 1944: Auswirkung der allierten Luftüberlegenheit auf die deutsche Abwehr," *Allegemeine schweizerische Militärzeitschrift* 124 H5 (1958), 333–361.

180. His avoidance of the slaughter on the Western Front in World War I profoundly shaped his military thought. He naturally inclined to take the enemy in the flank and shunned the *Materialschlacht*. Biographies of Rommel invariably offer a sympathetic and inflated portrait. Desmond Young, *Rommel: The Desert Fox* (New York: Harper & Row, 1950); Ronald Lewin, *Rommel as Military Commander* (New York: Ballantine, 1970); David Irving, *The Trail of the Fox* (New York: E.P. Dutton, 1977).

181. NARA MMB RG 331, SHAEF/12NX/INT, "German Coastal Defenses in the West: Part VII: Underwater Obstacles," 7 August 1944, 2; Basil Liddell Hart, ed., *The Rommel Papers* (London: Collins, 1953), 458–459, 470–471.

182. Between December 1943 and May 1944, the number of Luftwaffe anti-aircraft batteries in the West increased from 555 to 756, and the number of flak guns from 28,026 to 33,345. H. A. Koch, *Die Geschichte der Deutschen Flakartillerie* (Bad Nauheim: Podzun, 1954), 422.

183. Paul Ingouf, *La Bataille de Cherbourg* (Bayeux: Editions Heimdal, 1979), 16–23.

184. In the West the *Kriegsmarine* deployed 5 destroyers, 6 torpedo boats, 29 E-boats, 310 mine warfare vessels, 102 patrol craft, and 42 artillery barges. Theodore Krancke, "Invasionsabwehrmassnehmen der Kriegsmarine in Kanalgebiet 1944," *Marine Rundschau* LXVI (June 1969), 171–172.

185. Only thirty-five U-boats were operational on D-Day, and a mere nine possessed snorkels. J. F. Ellis, *Victory in the West* (London: HMSO, 1968) I, 519.

186. On 6 June 1944 the *Kriegsmarine* fielded 111 coast artillery batteries in the West. Wilhelm von Harnier, *Artillerie im Küstenkampf* (Munich: J. F. Lehmann, 1969), 85–169.

PART 2

Normandy 1944

6

A Campaign Overview

At first light, on 6 June 1944, Allied forces began landing at five beaches along a 20-mile front on the coast of Normandy between the eastern Cotentin Peninsula to the west and Le Havre Bay to the east. On the left flank of the invasion Anglo-Canadian forces belonging to Gen. Bernard Law Montgomery's 21st Army Group landed on three beaches, designated Gold, Juno, and Sword, in front of the city of Caen. Montgomery's troops quickly established themselves ashore in the face of moderate resistance but were unable to capture their ambitious D-Day objective, the important port town of Caen. On Montgomery's right, to the west, troops of General Omar Bradley's U.S. First Army landed on Omaha Beach astride the bluffs of the Calvados coast and at Utah Beach at the southeastern tip of the Cotentin Peninsula. At Utah, U.S. troops soon established themselves ashore in the face of light opposition, but at Omaha the outcome hung in the balance for many hours in the face of determined German resistance before troops of the 1st and 29th U.S. Infantry Divisions established a shallow and tenuous lodgement. On the flanks of the bridgehead the Allies dropped three parachute divisions. The British 6th Airborne Division landed east of the Orne River to gain a buffer zone that would protect the left wing of the lodgement from flanking counterattacks. The U.S. 82d and 101st Airborne Divisions dropped behind Utah Beach astride the Merderet River to protect the right flank of the bridgehead. Though badly scattered, Allied airborne forces added depth to the lodgement and managed to disrupt and foil the weak German counterthrusts aimed at repelling the Allied landings. By the end of D-Day, even though few realized it at the time, the Allies had secured a permanent footing in France.

After D-Day, however, the British advance quickly stalled as powerful enemy armored reserves massed at Caen in an effort to drive the Anglo-Canadians back into the sea. In the process, these Allied forces suffered a number of local reverses, the Canadians especially so. The most serious of these occurred on 7 June as the Canadian 3d Division pushed boldly inland toward its D-Day objective of the Carpiquet airfield, despite the known movement of powerful German armored reserves toward Caen.[1] The Canadian spearhead was ambushed and outfought by the vanguard of the 12th SS Panzer Division *Hitlerjugend* and thrown back in confusion. Further local Canadian reverses followed as German armor conducted an aggressive defense, probing for weak spots in the Allied lines that they might subsequently exploit in a planned, general counteroffensive. On 8 June SS troops defeated the Royal Winnipeg Rifles and retook Putot.[2] Three days later, the Canadian 6th Armoured Regiment and the Queen's Own Rifles of Canada launched a hasty and ill-conceived right-flanking movement through Le Mesnil Patry to seize the high ground south of Cheux. But a lightning German counterattack decimated this force and threw the Canadians back to their start line in disarray.

In front of Caen too, Montgomery's assault divisions found themselves embroiled in bitter fighting against the expected German armored counterattacks that sought to split the Allied bridgehead and drive the enemy back into the sea. A combination of tenacious British defense and Allied domination of the seas and the skies, however, effectively stalled the counteroffensive planned by the I SS Panzer Corps before it had ever really got started. In the aftermath of these abortive initial offensive efforts, the Germans assumed the strategic defensive across the entire front on 10 June and thus effectively surrendered the initiative to the Allies. Rommel hoped that this situation would only be temporary as he awaited the arrival of fresh armored forces—in particular the II SS Panzer Corps from the Eastern Front—with which he hoped to launch a well-planned and organized strategic counteroffensive intended to divide the Allied bridgehead. While Montgomery's forces beat off these aggressive initial German counterthrusts, Anglo-Canadian forces were unable to advance in the face of this massed armor and the 21st Army Group in turn had temporarily to assume the defensive in mid-June because its assault forces had exhausted themselves in ten days of continuous, heavy combat. The struggle for Caen bogged down into a grim, bitter and protracted battle of attrition that lasted for six weeks.

After firmly establishing themselves ashore at Utah Beach on D-Day, the troops of Gen. Lawton "Lightning" Joe Collins's U.S. VII Corps struck north and west to quickly seize the strategically important port of Cherbourg at the northern tip of the Cotentin Peninsula, and thus guarantee the logistic base for a permanent lodgement. Stiff enemy resistance around Montebourg and on the Quineville Ridge, however, slowed the U.S. advance. General Collins's forces also pushed slowly west and south to gain ground for operational maneuver, and after a stiff fight took the important communications center of Carentan on 12 June, facilitating the permanent connection of the two U.S. bridgeheads the following day.

In the meantime, Maj. Gen. Leonard T. Gerow's U.S. V Corps continued a slow, but inexorable advance on St. Lô from Omaha Beach in the face of diminishing enemy opposition from the chewed-up German 352d Infantry Division. On 7 June, U.S. and British forces linked up west of Bayeux and then pushed south to cross the barrier of the Aure River by 9 June. However, by the time that the U.S. 29th Infantry Division assaulted across the next water obstacle, the Elle River on 12 June, the powerful German 3d Parachute Division had arrived from Brittany to slow the U.S. advance on St. Lô to a crawl.[3] With priority accorded to Collins's advance on Cherbourg, Gerow's depleted and tired forces could launch only weak and poorly supported attacks that were easily beaten off by the German paratroopers, and the V Corps offensive came to a halt in sheer exhaustion two miles short of St. Lô in mid-June.

Back on the Cotentin Peninsula, where there was stiff and undiminished resistance, General Collins abandoned the original campaign plan that called for a direct advance on Cherbourg. Instead he shifted the weight of the offensive westward, and on 15 June the Americans struck west to cut the Cotentin Peninsula and isolate Cherbourg from the main body of German forces. With U.S. offensive strength now concentrated and with the German defense attenuated by two weeks of bitter fighting, the renewed drive rapidly crumbled a German front already badly weakened by previous broad-front attacks. The seasoned U.S. 9th Infantry and 82d Airborne Divisions spearheaded the offensive and advanced boldly and aggressively to break the backs of the German defenses south of Valognes. Collins's troops then dashed westward to Barneville on 17 June to cut the peninsula and isolate Cherbourg.[4]

During the last two weeks of June, the Americans directed most of their strength and resources to the campaign to capture Cherbourg and its vital port facilities. Isolated from reinforcement and resupply, the German position in the northern Cotentin was ultimately untenable, but the Germans conducted a delaying withdrawal back to the outer city defenses, seeking to buy time to build a new front in the southern Cotentin and destroy Cherbourg's port facilities. The final U.S. combined-arms assault on the city began in earnest on 22 June, and, despite stubborn resistance, Cherbourg was in U.S. hands by 29 June. All resistance in the northern half of the Cotentin Peninsula ceased by 1 July. The Allies had gained their first port in France, but German demolitions ensured that it would be weeks before the first supplies could be off-loaded at Cherbourg.

Back on the Anglo-Canadian front, after a week of consolidation, replenishment, and preparation, General Montgomery launched his first major offensive in Normandy on 26 June, designated EPSOM. He began an ambitious operation designed to penetrate the strong enemy defenses west of Caen, cross the significant obstacles posed by the Orne and Odon Rivers, and gain the high ground southwest of the city, thereby outflanking Caen and rendering its defense untenable. Montgomery employed his *corps de chasse,* the VIII Corps, his best, but as yet unbloodied, troops to head the offensive. With strong air, naval, and artillery support he hoped to smash through the powerful German defenses and capture the city. However, misfortune dogged the offensive from the beginning. The neighboring XXX Corps failed to take the commanding Rauray Ridge on the flank of the intended assault during the night of 25–26 June, and much of the planned air support failed to materialize due to poor weather. Both these failures badly hindered the entire attack. Nevertheless, concentration and massive fire support allowed the VIII Corps to penetrate the thin German linear defenses of the 12th SS Panzer Division and establish a bridgehead across the Odon River. Thereafter, the 11th Armoured Division advanced through the bridgehead to seize the vital height of Hill 112 beyond. By 28 June Montgomery had torn a 6-mile gap in the German defenses, captured the dominating high ground that overlooked Caen, and rendered a heavy blow to German hopes to retain Caen indefinitely.

But Montgomery's very success attracted German reserves from other sectors of the front that vigorously engaged the flanks of the penetration and pinned British forces in place, hampering the movement forward of the follow-up forces tasked with consolidating the ground won. The British advance also coincided with the arrival of the fresh 9th and 10th SS Panzer Divisions of the II SS Panzer Corps from the Eastern Front. As German reserves dangerously massed to counterattack the narrow British corridor and the slim Odon bridgehead, the cautious Lt. Gen. Miles "Bimbo" Dempsey, commander of the British Second Army, abandoned Hill 112, withdrew to a shorter, more defensible line and dug in. Between 29 June and 2 July, the VIII Corps repulsed a series of heavy but poorly coordinated German counterblows in some of the toughest fighting of the Normandy campaign.[5]

These attacks were part of the long-awaited German strategic counteroffensive. After corralling the Allied forces in a shallow lodgement during June, and although he could not prevent the fall of Cherbourg, Rommel eagerly awaited the arrival of the fresh II SS Panzer Corps with which he hoped to regain operational maneuver and return to the offensive. On 28 June, elements of five SS armored divisions led the major counteroffensive that was to throw the Allies back into the sea. The SS troops hurled themselves against the newly established British bridgehead over the Odon River in an effort to break through to the coast and split the Allied lodgement. Despite strong armored and artillery support, at least by German standards, the SS troops made little headway in the face of Allied defensive firepower and an inadequate German logistic situation. The operation petered out on 2 July after heavy losses.

The failure of this counterblow confirmed that the Allied lodgement had become permanent, and in its aftermath Hitler announced a new strategy for the Western Front. The German forces would conduct an unyielding defense to pen the Allies into a narrow lodgement through a savage battle of attrition that exploited the defensive advantages of the terrain and interior lines to deny the enemy the room and favorable terrain needed to conduct mobile operations. This decision locked the Germans into an attritional battle, in range of the Allied fleet, that they could not ultimately win.

The heavy losses sustained during EPSOM as well as the need to rebuild supplies and organize air support meant that it was not until 8 July that Montgomery could resume the offensive toward Caen with a rare multicorps attack on the city. This was CHARNWOOD, an all-out drive for Caen, the D-Day objective that Rommel had denied him for over a month. Montgomery relied heavily on air power to shatter enemy resistance, and the operation saw the first use of heavy bombers in support of ground operations in Normandy. The Caen bombing raid was, however, as controversial as it was ineffective: it caused heavy French civilian losses, inflicted negligible damage on the enemy, and, with the resultant devastation of the city, produced mounds of rubble that slowed the Allied ground advance. Moreover, delay in launching the ground attack in the aftermath of the bombing allowed the enemy to recover. The raid, therefore, failed to live up to the excessive hopes that it could blast the German defenses into oblivion.[6]

Nonetheless, as in EPSOM, Anglo-Canadian forces initially met with success as they launched concentric attacks on the beleaguered and greatly outnumbered German defenders. Inexorably, superior numbers and firepower drove the enemy back, and the now-seasoned British 3d Division outfought and mauled the green 16th *Luftwaffe* Field Division that had entered the line only three days before. After two days of heavy fighting, Rommel conceded defeat in this attritional battle that he could not sustain, Anglo-Canadian forces finally fought their way into northern Caen on 9 July, four weeks behind schedule, and the Germans effected a planned general withdrawal behind the Orne River. Northern Caen was now in Allied hands, but the southern half and the strategic heights to the south, which barred the way to the excellent tank country of the Falaise Plain beyond, remained firmly in enemy hands. Moreover, the German retreat behind the Orne gave them a shorter, more defensible front. The prospects for further successful Anglo-Canadian advances without inordinate casualties faded.

Meanwhile on the U.S. sector, after a few days' rest, recuperation, and reshuffling, the First Army struck south in strength toward St. Lô on 3 July. In highly defensible terrain that consisted of low-lying marshes and thick *bocage* hedgerows, the Americans made slow progress, and the next three weeks consisted of bitter and costly close-range combat in which U.S. units inexorably, if slowly, ground toward St. Lô in grim attritional warfare. Despite reinforcement by Collins's VII Corps and fresh divisions from Britain, the U.S. First Army still struggled to advance in the thick bocage that greatly aided defense. Maj. Gen. Troy H. Middleton's VIII

Corps attacked south from the base of the Cotentin Peninsula with three divisions, and in five days captured the important communications center of La Haye-du-Puits against stiff resistance. But determined enemy opposition ultimately halted the offensive along the Ay and Sèves rivers on 15 July after heavy U.S. losses.[7]

Simultaneously, Collins's VII Corps struck south from Carentan on 3 July with the fresh, yet green, 83d Division. Its attack toward Périers in poor weather and difficult marshy terrain made little progress. Even after the veteran U.S. 4th Division joined the attack on 5 July, the VII Corps inched forward; even battle-tested troops found it hard going in the dense *bocage* south of Carentan.[8] Though it beat off several vigorous enemy regimental counterattacks during 10–12 July, the depleted VII Corps too had to go over to the defense on 15 July.

On 7 July Maj. Gen. Charles H. Corlett's newly arrived U.S. XIX Corps had also struck south toward St. Lô with three divisions and achieved greater success. The 9th and 30th Infantry Divisions established bridgeheads across both the Taute-Vire Canal and the Vire River, and quickly captured St. Jean-de-Daye and its road net.[9] The 29th Infantry Division likewise overran the strongly entrenched German 9th Parachute Regiment and stormed the strategic Martinville Ridge that dominated the northeastern approaches to St. Lô on 11 July.[10] That same day the U.S. 2d Division captured Hill 192, heavily defended by the German 3d Parachute Division, at the eastern end of the Martinville Ridge, a key position in the German defense of St. Lô because it dominated all approaches to this Norman town. The 2d Division then advanced across the St. Lô–Bayeux highway to attack St. Lô from the east.[11] Thereafter, the U.S. XIX Corps slowly, but steadily, advanced until it cut the Périers–St. Lô highway on 20 July to deny the Germans a key communications link with St. Lô.[12] East of the Vire River the newly arrived U.S. 35th Infantry Division joined the 29th Division in its drive on St. Lô from the northeast. With the German defense weakened by the loss of high ground, the 35th Division stormed the final height north of St. Lô, Hill 122, on 18 July, to render the defense of the city untenable, and the next day the Germans abandoned the city.[13]

In the meantime, on the British front, as U.S. forces rested and prepared to resume offensive action in the aftermath of the fall of St. Lô, on 18 July General Montgomery launched another major offensive, GOODWOOD, south of Caen. Striking out of the airborne bridgehead—the area east of the Orne River captured by the British 6th Airborne Division on D-Day—Montgomery sought to push southeast to gain more ground for operational maneuver and to attract German reserves to the Caen front in accordance with previously agreed Allied theater strategy. Carpet bombing and artillery fire smashed the British armor through the German forward lines to extend the bridgehead to the foot of the high ground south of Caen.

At the same time Gen. Guy Simonds's newly operational Canadian II

Corps launched a subsidiary operation, ATLANTIC, to support the right wing of the main British drive by capturing German-held Caen south of the Orne River and then seizing the Verrières Ridge, the dominating high ground due south of the city.[14] This operation witnessed the first Canadian multidivision corps-level operation in northwest Europe. Simonds launched the Canadian 3d Infantry Division on an advance to the southwest along the eastern bank of the Orne from the British airborne bridgehead to capture the Caen suburbs of Colombelles and Vaucelles. With the 3d Division having loosened the German grip on the south bank of the Orne, the unseasoned Canadian 2d Infantry Division then struck across the Orne with the intention of mopping up enemy resistance in southern Caen, and then storming the Verrières Ridge to the south.[15]

But after great initial success on both the British and Canadian fronts, the Germans reacted swiftly and these Allied formation suffered serious setbacks. Local German reserves conducted an effective delaying withdrawal though a deep defensive belt that slowed, deflected, and disrupted the British armored advance and delayed the follow-up forces.[16] As dusk fell on 18 July and Allied tactical aviation returned to its bases, vigorous and well-coordinated German combined-arms counterattacks drove the British armor back from the foot of the Bourguébus Ridge with further heavy losses.[17] Dempsey doggedly attacked for two more days, even though the advance had lost its momentum, until Montgomery halted the operation on 21 July. Nowhere had British forces established a solid foothold on the Bourguébus Ridge that commanded the Falaise Plain below.

Similar reverses afflicted the Canadians in their subsidiary Operation ATLANTIC. The Canadian 2d Division experienced hard going in its first operation since its 1942 decimation at Dieppe. Its tricky mission in ATLANTIC—an opposed daylight assault crossing of the Orne—went awry. By midafternoon, on 18 July, the division's assault had ground to a halt in disorder as its follow-up battalions got tangled with the attack battalions as the former tried to pass through, and as Canadian artillery fire repeatedly hit its own troops.[18] When the 2d Division resumed the attack the following day, misfortune continued to dog it. Its green assault companies were again badly hit by their own artillery, and stalled short of Fleury. Throughout the day, its infantry slowly advanced but failed to reach their objectives.[19] To salvage the situation Simonds committed the reinforced Canadian 6th Infantry Brigade, without armor support, on 20 July to storm Verrières Ridge.[20] During the morning, the brigade consolidated on a forward slope along the ridge line but halted short of Verrières.

Late on 20 July the brigade suffered a serious reverse when the 1st SS Panzer Regiment counterattacked in torrential rain that negated Allied artillery and air support. The SS armor caught Canadian antitank guns and armor moving up and picked these off. The panzers quickly overran and dispersed two battalions of the brigade at Trotéval Farm.[21] The 2d Division hastily threw forward another unsupported infantry battalion in a vain effort to restore the situation. But the SS troops also outflanked this battalion and drove it back.[22] The following day a renewed German counterattack broke into the Essex Scottish positions, and only a combined-arms counterattack stabilized the Canadian center. ATLANTIC, like Montgomery's GOODWOOD offensive, came to an ignominious end as it failed to achieve its objectives and brought heavy losses. Indeed, the Germans achieved their greatest defensive successes of the campaign during GOODWOOD-ATLANTIC as they savaged Anglo-Canadian armor driving south toward Falaise.

Despite the failure of GOODWOOD-ATLANTIC, Montgomery undertook further limited attacks aimed at holding German reserves on the Caen front, while U.S. forces prepared and launched another major offensive south of St. Lô, Operation COBRA, on 25 July.[23] Simonds's Canadian II Corps launched the first of these holding attacks on 25 July, a renewed assault, SPRING, on the Verrières Ridge. The two Canadian divisions reinforced by British armor and artillery attempted to storm the ridge on a 4-mile front at night to nullify German observation from the ridge and so reduce the defensive advantage enjoyed by the enemy. Thereafter, British armor was to drive south to Cintheaux in a classic exploitation role.[24] Against still powerful and well-entrenched veteran German troops in highly defensible terrain, the weak probe rapidly ground to the halt after severe losses—and after Dieppe the most costly single-day of combat for the Canadians during World War II. Although it was achieved at heavy cost, Montgomery had succeeded to a degree in holding much of the German armor near Caen.

After a brief rest, the U.S. First Army vigorously prepared for its largest operation to date, COBRA, that was begun on 25 July. COBRA was originally intended as a limited breakthrough operation designed to advance U.S. forces out of the bocage into more open ground south of St. Lô, allowing both operational maneuver and resumption of mobile warfare. To prevail against intact and strong German defenses and to facilitate their advance, the Americans now relied heavily on a massive attack by heavy bombers to pave the way for the ground advance on a much narrower frontage than hitherto conducted.

The carpet bombing crippled German communications and so stunned, disorganized, and demoralized the German defenders of the elite Panzer *Lehr* Division that even its seasoned troops could not resist the VII Corps concentrated attack as the Americans advanced 2 miles into the German defenses on 25 July.[25] The U.S. forces rapidly exploited the initial penetration and reinforced success faster than the Germans could redeploy reserves. Increasing logistic deficiencies for the first time crippled the Germans' defense.[26] On 26 July, the U.S. VII Corps gained 8,000 yards as mounting fuel and ammunition shortages badly hampered enemy counter-measures. Under the pressure of this rapid exploitation the stretched German front began to collapse. As U.S. armor passed through out into the open, supporting attacks on the flanks pinned German troops in place, while dislocated communications slowed the Germans' appreciation of, and reaction to, the scale of the crisis.[27]

On 27 July the U.S. First Army achieved a decisive breakthrough. As the enemy abandoned Lessay and Périers to release troops to shore up the disintegrating front, the VII Corps penetrated 12 miles into the German defenses until halted by fierce resistance 2 miles short of Coutances. The same day, General Corlett's neighboring XIX Corps thrust out of St. Lô to seize the dominating heights south of the city and prevent the German II Parachute Corps from disengaging to move west and patch the disintegrating German front. Corlett's flanking attack also sucked into battle the first German armored reinforcements—the 2d and 116th Panzer Divisions—that had been withdrawn from the British sector and that were tasked with stabilizing the western flank. The arrival of fresh armored reserves precipitated the heaviest fighting experienced during COBRA as the panzers counterattacked westward through the thick remnant of bocage hedgerow southeast of St. Lô in an abortive effort to seal off the U.S. breakthrough.[28]

On 18 July, the U.S. VIII Corps loosed the 4th and 6th Armored Divisions south from Lessay to reach Coutances and link up with VII Corps pincer. At this juncture, Gen. Paul Hausser, the commander of the German Seventh Army, made a serious tactical error. He ordered the LXXXIV Corps to fight its way southeast to regain a continuous front and seal off the U.S. penetration, instead of retiring unopposed due south to reestablish a defensive position south of Coutances. The retiring German forces thus ran into the U.S. spearheads advancing southeast of Coutances and were encircled in the Roncey picket.[29]

With the German front torn open, the U.S. First Army expanded COBRA on 29 July into a larger operation. What had begun as a limited offensive became a strategic breakout. The VII and VIII Corps renewed their drive to the south, and the next day the U.S. 6th Armored Division crossed the Sienne River, while the 4th Armored took Avranches and seized a bridgehead across the Sée River. On 31 July, the U.S. 4th Armored Division secured a bridgehead over the Sélune River, gateway to Brittany, at Pontaubault. Once the armor was out in the open, U.S. mobility came into play. On 31 July the 2d Armored Division took the communications hub of Villedieu-les-Puits, while on the eastern flank the XIX and V Corps pushed southeast to tie down German reserves attempting to counterattack the exposed U.S. left flank. Thus by the end of July, though few yet realized it, the Americans had decisively shattered the German front in Normandy and effectively won the battle for France.

After the Americans' success, Miles Dempsey's British Second Army

launched its own impromptu breakout bid on 28 July, Operation BLUE-
COAT, with a drive on Mont Pinçon and the important communications
hub of Vire. Even though the British faced a weakly held German front in
the thick bocage around Caumont, the operation failed ignominiously.
Montgomery had intended the operation to maintain pressure on the
Germans and prevent the transfer of additional enemy armor against the
Americans. But, once again, BLUECOAT was Dempsey's brainchild and
he again hoped to achieve a decisive breakout to mirror the U.S. triumph.
Montgomery, though he remained skeptical, had bowed to Dempsey
because he needed to initiate a quick offensive to prevent the transfer of
German reserves to the U.S. front, even though he realized that the buildup
for the attack was insufficient to guarantee victory. BLUECOAT was the
only offensive in Normandy where Montgomery attacked prematurely to
assist the U.S. breakthrough.[30]

For BLUECOAT Dempsey had hastily recalled the 11th and Guards
Armoured Divisions from their post-GOODWOOD refit. But the need to
prevent the transfer of enemy armor forced him to launch the operation pre-
cipitately three days ahead of schedule and before the British VIII Corps
had fully assembled. The offensive saw simultaneous attacks by the VIII
and XXX Corps, with three armored and three infantry divisions.[31]
Dempsey thus committed massive strength against greatly thinned German
defenses. But the premature start ensured that BLUECOAT lacked the massive artillery support that habitually accompanied British offensives.
Moreover, although the German defense was weak and had almost no
armor, the front had been static since mid-June and the Germans had established defenses in depth in the thick bocage. Dempsey committed most of
the available British armor, but he did so in one of the sectors least suited
for offensive armored operations. The result was a steady, if unspectacular
advance that failed to take advantage of the opportunities that existed to
split apart a German front that was slowly disintegrating under the pressure
of the U.S. breakthrough on the western flank.

On 1 August, General Bradley's U.S. 12th Army Group became operational and assumed command of the U.S. First Army and Gen. George
Patton's newly activated Third Army. U.S. forces were now able to conduct
the fast-paced maneuver war that the peacetime army had trained and prepared for. While the First Army advanced southeast and occupied Mortain
on 3 August, Patton's forces conducted a spectacular and rapid armored
advance into Brittany as the 4th Armored Division took Rennes and Vannes
to isolate the Breton peninsula and the 6th Armored Division raced deep
into the peninsula to seize Pontivy. Nonetheless, most of the German forces
in Brittany were still able to retire in time into the fortified ports of Brest,
St. Malo, and Lorient, where they prepared to offer protracted resistance
against a thinly spread U.S. Army.

During the first week of August, U.S. forces for the first time assumed the defense to thwart a major German counteroffensive that aimed to seal off the American penetration and to isolate the Third Army. The rapid advance into Brittany had thinned the central sector of the U.S. front, a weakness the enemy sought to exploit. On 2 August 1944 Hitler condemned the *Westheer* to total defeat when he ordered the new commander of Army Group B, Field Marshal Hans von Kluge, to launch Operation LÜTTICH, a powerful armored counteroffensive to retake Avranches and contain the U.S. breakout from Normandy. The Germans committed six attenuated mechanized divisions.[32] Von Kluge chose Hans von Funck, a daring and experienced armored commander, and his XLVII Panzer Corps headquarters to lead the attack.

On 5 August the Americans first detected a German buildup around Mortain as eleventh-hour Ultra intelligence gave warning of the enemy attack and allowed the First Army last-minute efforts to bolster its defenses and to take up good defensive positions against the onslaught.[33] Despite reinforcements, U.S. troops were still thin on the ground, occupied unprepared positions, remained inexperienced at coordinating defensively, and lacked the antitank capability to repel concentrated enemy armored attacks. On the night of 6–7 August, von Funck struck west in strength toward Mortain and Avranches, without a preliminary barrage, down the narrow corridor between the Sée and Sélune Rivers on a 10,000-yard front with five divisions and obtained tactical surprise.[34] Nonetheless, his troops were too depleted and tried to achieve strategic success, and von Funck attacked prematurely, before his forces were ready.[35]

The U.S. 30th Infantry Division conducted a determined defense, especially at Hill 317 where an isolated battalion thwarted all German efforts to push through Mortain toward Avranches.[36] This stubborn combined-arms defense disrupted the enemy advance, and the immediate commitment of the 4th Infantry Division from reserve allowed the Americans to slow the German drive. Thereafter, the commitment of U.S. reserves, aided by punishing Allied tactical air strikes, soon halted the offensive.[37] Bradley then launched a concentrated counterattack northeast between Mortain and Barenton with the recalled 35th Infantry Division that took the enemy in the flank.[38] The German forces were understrength, operating along tenuous supply lines, and were subject to heavy, repeated air and artillery attack that disrupted their push.[39] Indeed, the imbalance of forces was simply too great to allow a restablization of the front and logistically, LÜTTICH was doomed. Funck had neither the firepower, the infantry, nor the supplies to recapture and hold Avranches.[40]

For the first time, the defeat of the German counterattack at Mortain presented the Allies with strategic opportunities to encircle and destroy the German forces in Normandy, either in the Argentan-Falaise area or through a larger envelopment along the Seine. But U.S. forces fanned out of Normandy heading east, south, and west, dissipating their strength in the process. AS these forces advanced deep into enemy territory, they became too spread out and left their logistic support behind. Bradley also made the cardinal error of dividing his forces as he directed the U.S. V Corps to the Seine and his other corps to Argentan to meet the advancing Canadians. Divided and increasingly strung out, neither prong proved strong enough to defeat decisively the enemy. Fearful that his depleted, tired, overextended, and undersupplied spearheads would be overrun if they tried to prevent the German retreat, Bradley halted the advance toward Argentan on 13 August and did not resume it for five days. When he did, his forces still proved too weak to close firmly the door from the south to the Falaise pocket at Argentan, or to push quickly north up both banks of the Seine after the U.S. V Corps had established a bridgehead across the river on 19 August.

In the meantime, the front became fluid in the second week of August as the Germans began a phased strategic withdrawal in reaction to the U.S. breakout on the western flank. But tired, demoralized, and depleted British forces had failed to pursue the enemy aggressively and were largely content to follow up after German withdrawals.[41] As troops sensed that victory was at hand, British pressure slackened across the entire front during mid-August.[42] As a result, it was not until 16 August that Montgomery launched Operation KITTEN, the long planned Anglo-Canadian advance to the Seine.

Consequently, the burden of carrying the war to the enemy fell to Gen. Harry Crerar's newly activated Canadian First Army, which assumed operational control on 31 July of II Corps and the three Canadian divisions now ashore.[43] Prospects for Canadian success appeared greater than ever during late July as Panzer Group West dramatically thinned its defenses on the Caen front to shore up its west flank and to mask the U.S. breakout from Avranches.[44] So "Monty" asked Crerar to renew holding attacks south of Caen to prevent further German withdrawals to the Americans' sector. Given the major German westward redeployment, such holding attacks seemed much more likely to succeed now that the backbone had been removed from the German defense.

In early August it fell to the inexperienced Canadian 2d Division and the raw Canadian 4th Armoured Division to launch a series of battalion attacks designed to pin German reserves on the Caen sector. On 1 August the Calgary Highlanders thrice struck for Tilly–la Campagne but were halted each time by withering enemy fire.[45] During the night of 1–2 August, the Lincoln and Welland Regiment launched a silent Canadian night attack that also proved abortive.[46] This series of attacks concluded on 5 August with three abortive battalion assaults on Verrières, May, and Tilly–la Campagne. These failed attacks brought to an end the second phase of Canadian operations in Normandy.[47]

Given the deployment of the Canadian forces and the depleted state of most British formations, it naturally fell to the Canadians to assume the offensive mantle of 21st Army Group. On 8 August the Canadian First Army launched its first major offensive, Operation TOTALIZE, with the objective of capturing Falaise and thus completing the encirclement of the German forces in Normandy. The operation, planned by Guy Simonds, witnessed the first systematic Canadian effort to overcome the German defense in depth that had stalled all previous Canadian offensives.[48] The operation's name implied that it would be a total effort on the part of the Canadian II Corps. Thus early on 8 August massed Canadian armor and infantry stormed Verrières Ridge.[49] Where infantry and armor coordinated effectively they quickly took their objectives with minimal casualties. Indeed, the first stage of TOTALIZE had proven remarkably successful.

In its later stages the offensive went wrong, however. Simonds had planned an early afternoon carpet bombing attack to smash the rearward German defenses and their counterattack reserves and to presage the second phase of the offensive. The delay that proceeded the bombing gave the enemy time to recover and unfortunate "short" bombing disrupted the continued advance.[50] Moreover, severe congestion in the rear caused by passing four divisions through a narrow corridor and exacerbated by the short bombing slowed the Canadian advance.[51]

The slowness of the Canadian advance on 8 August led to a daring dash forward the following day by a combined-arms force of the 4th Armoured Division to occupy the important heights, designated Hill 195. Unfortunately, this enterprise ended in disaster as the inexperienced Canadian troops got lost and occupied Hill 140, far to the southeast where German armor surrounded, counterattacked, and annihilated the force.[52] Nevertheless, during the night of 9–10 August the Argyll and Sutherland Highlanders boldly seized Hill 195 with a silent night attack. Crerar, believing the enemy defenses broken and with the high ground taken, unleashed the tanks of his two armored divisions to exploit forward on 10 August with terrible consequences. The German antitank defenses mauled the inexperienced Canadian and Polish armor.[53] To regain the momentum of the advance, Simonds threw the veteran and now rested Canadian 3d Infantry Division into the battle late on 10 August. It attacked Quesnay Wood but was outfought by the SS defenders who ambushed the two Canadian lead battalions at dusk and threw them back in disarray.[54] This failure brought TOTALIZE to a precipitate end on 11 August. The offensive had gained 9 miles, but neither had the Canadians reached Falaise nor had they shattered the attenuated German defenses.

The Canadian failure to reach Falaise during TOTALIZE occurred while the COBRA breakout was rapidly forming a pocket around the German Seventh Army and the newly redesignated Fifth Panzer Army, the former Panzer Group West. On 11 August, Montgomery ordered Crerar to attack again toward Falaise, link up with the U.S. forces advancing toward Argentan, and complete the encirclement of the German forces in

Normandy. Simonds rapidly put together a plan for a new offensive to seize Falaise, called TRACTABLE, which he launched on 14 August.

Simonds employed a revised version of the TOTALIZE plan that this time took place in daylight, using smokescreens to give the cover that darkness had afforded TOTALIZE. Simonds employed two Canadian divisions, the 4th Armoured and 3d Infantry, on a narrow frontage. To maintain surprise, Simonds again avoided a long preliminary barrage that would warn the Germans of an impending attack. Moreover, a combined-arms brigade group built around armor led each divisional advance as Simonds reverted to the discredited pre-1943 British attack doctrine in which massed armor spearheaded the break-in battle.[55] Despite the final fall of Falaise on 16 August, the Germans offered desperate resistance as they sought to hold open a narrow corridor to allow their retreating forces to escape encirclement. Thus TRACTABLE failed in its objective to complete the encirclement of the enemy in the Falaise pocket.

As the German forces retired eastward it became imperative for the Canadian First Army to renew its attempt to close the pocket. Lacking the time to organize a new offensive, Crerar ordered his divisions to continue the attack southeast until they met the U.S. forces advancing northeast beyond Argentan. On 17 August, the tired Polish 1st and Canadian 4th Armoured Divisions aided by the Canadian 3d Infantry Division again struck southeast and fought their way forward until they linked up with U.S. troops at Chambois on 19 August to finally seal the Falaise pocket.[56] But Crerar's troops could not seal the pocket tightly, and over the next three days, tens of thousands of German troops fought their way out of the pocket during some of the most ferocious combat of the campaign.

During late August, the Germans achieved their most significant defensive success of the campaign as they extricated virtually all their surviving personnel and a surprising amount of equipment from behind the Seine amid a general strategic withdrawal.[57] After the breakout from Falaise, the specter of a much larger encirclement on the Seine threatened the annihilation of all the German forces west of the river. The dwindling mobility, catastrophic supply situation, and increasing demoralization of German forces, presented the Allies with a genuine strategic opportunity to annihilate the enemy against the Seine. But in late August, the Germans pulled off their greatest success of the campaign as they extricated from west of the Seine virtually all their remaining forces in Normandy in a remarkable feat of organization and improvisation. The retreat beyond the Seine, completed by the end of August, not only effectively ended the Normandy campaign but also had important consequences. The preservation of the core of the German forces deployed in Normandy allowed Hitler to flesh out a new *Westheer* in the fall with which he would launch the December 1944 Ardennes counteroffensive. In fact, without success on the Seine in late August, Hitler could not have attacked in the West in 1944 at all.

Notes

1. Both Ultra intercepts and theater intelligence provided ample warning of the advance of *Kampfgruppe Meyer,* the reinforced 25th SS *Panzergrenadier* Regiment, into the Caen area during the night of 6–7 June. The Canadian dash was probably the result of Montgomery's exhortation to drive boldly inland to seize a sizeable bridgehead.

2. The Winnipegs suffered 256 casualties, the Canadian Scottish 125. NAC RG 24 15233, WD GS Royal Winnipeg Rifles, 8 June 1944; Craig Luther, *Blood and Honor: The History of the 12th SS Panzer Division "Hitlerjügend"* (San Jose, Calif.: Bender, 1987), 157–160; Stacey, *Victory,* 135–136; English, *Canadians,* 209.

3. USAHD MS B-541, Lt. Gen. Richard Schimpf, "3d Parachute Division (Jan–Aug 1944)" (Germany: 1947), 16–17; Joseph Balkoski, *Beyond the Bridgehead* (Harrisburg, Penn.: Stackpole, 1989), 190; Gordon Harrison, *Cross Channel Attack* (Washington, D.C.: OCMH, 1951), 371–376.

4. The Americans' doctrinal emphasis on destroying the enemy in battle often blinded them to German logistic weaknesses and the fact that outmaneuvering the enemy could disrupt German supplies and speed German defeat at lower cost. Joseph L. Collins, *Lightning Jose: An Autobiography* (Baton Rouge: Louisiana State University 1979), 206–216; Harrison, *Attack,* 404–416.

5. Max Hasting, *OVERLORD: D-Day & the Battle of Normandy* (London: Joseph, 1984), 166–180; Carlo D'Este, *Decision in Normandy: The Unwritten Story of Montgomery & the Allied Campaign* (London: Collins, 1983), chap. 14; L. F. Ellis, *Victory in the West* (London: HMSO, 1960) I, 274–286. Alexander McKee, *Caen: Anvil of Victory* (London: Souvenir Press/Pan Books, 1964), chap. 12; Henry Maule, *Caen: The Brutal Battle and Breakout from Normandy* (London: David & Charles, 1976' 1988), 38–42, John Keegan, *Six Armies in Normandy* (London: Jonathan Cape 1983: New York: Penguin, 1984), 170–181.

6. Some 443 bombers dropped 2,276 tons of bombs on Caen. PRO WO 233/28, "Attack by Bomber Command on Targets at Villers-Bocage and Caen, 30 June and 7 July, 1944"; WO 106/4348, 2 ORS Rpt. 5, "Heavy Bombing in Op. CHARNWOOD"; NARA T-311, 420, KTB PzGr West, 8–9 July 1944.

7. FUSA, *Report* I, 81–82; Elbridge Colby, *the First Army in Europe, 1943–45* (Washington, D.C.: 91st Congress, 1st Session, DOC. 91–25, 1969), 44–46; USAHD MS A-983, Lt. Gen. Paul Mahlmann, "353d Division (24 Jul–14 Sep. 1944)," 3–4; B-418, Gen. Dietrich von Choltitz, "LXXXIV Corps (18 Jun–15 Jul. 1944)," 22–24; Martin Blumenson, *Breakout and Pursuit* (Washington, D.C.: OCMH, 1961), 53–77, 123–138; Dieter Choltitz, *Soldat unter Soldaten* (Konstanz: Europa, 1951), 187; *A History of the 90th Division in WWII* (Baton Rouge, La.: Army and Navy Publishing), 11–15.

8. FUSA, *Report* V, 198; Blumenson, *Breakout,* 78–88; Michael Doubler, *Busting the Bocage* (Fort Leavenworth: Combat Studies Institution, 1988), 49–50; Collins, *Lightning Joe,* 228–229; *Thunderbolt Across Europe: History of the 83d Infantry Division, 1942–45* (Munich: F. Brackman, n.d.), 29–33.

9. Colby, *First Army,* 50–51.

10. *St. Lo,* 51–58; Blumenson, *Breakout,* 153–157.

11. *St. Lo,* 58–68.

12. Blumenson, *Breakout,* 90–144; *St. Lô,* 9–14; Robert L. Hewitt, *Workhorse of the Western Front: The Story of the 30th Infantry Division* (Washington, D.C.: Infantry Journal Press, 1946), 26ff; Beck, *Engineers,* 371–374.

13. Colby, *First Army,* 49–50; Blumenson, *Breakout,* 159–174.

14. This kidney-shaped ridge rises to a height of 88 meters.

15. NAC RG 24 13711, IICC Ops. Instr. 2, 16 July 1944.

16. The British believed the German defenses to be only 3 miles deep, when in fact they were 10 miles deep. PRO WO 232/21, DTI, "Operational Research Report—Operation GOODWOOD"; N. Heywood, "GOODWOOD," *Household Brigade Magazine* (Winter 1956–1957) 171–177.

17. The British Second Army had 213 tanks disabled on 18 July, its highest single day's loss of the war. PRO WO 205/112, TFAG RAC, "Statement of Tank Losses to 20 July," 21 July 1944, apdx. A.; John Sweet, *Mounting the Threat: the Battle for the Bourguébus Ridge, 18–21 July 1944* (San Rafael, Calif.: Presidio Press, 1977), 111–115.

18. NAC RG 24 13750, WD GS 2 CID, 18–19 July 1944.

19. NAC RG 24 13750, WD GS 2 CID, 19 July 1944.

20. NAC RG 24 14116, WD GS 6 CIB, 20 July 1944.

21. The SSR had 208 casualties. NAC RG 24 14116, WD GS 6 CIB, 20 July 1944.

22. Officers and military police had to force the fleeing Essex Scottish back into the line at gunpoint. The battalion's 210 casualties and 50 percent loss of its Bren guns illuminates the extent of the rout. Roy, *1944,* 95.

23. Montgomery, *Normandy to the Baltic,* 85.

24. For SPRING planning see NAC RG 24 13750, WD GS IICC, 22–24 July 1944; IICC Ops. Instr. 3, WD GS July 1944, apdx. 35.

25. Collins, *Lightning Joe,* 241–242; Blumenson, *Breakout,* 241–246; Wesley F. Craven and James L. Cate, *The Army Air Forces in WWII* (Chicago: University of Chicago, 1951), III, 236–237.

26. Russell A. Hart, "Feeding Mars: Logistics and the German Defeat in Normandy, June–August 1944," *War in History* 3, 4 (Fall 1996), 418–435.

27. Blumenson, *Breakout,* 249–263.

28. Ibid., 264–275.

29. The German force comprised elements of the 2d SS Panzer, 17th SS Panzergrenadier, 77th, 91st, 243d, and 353d Infantry Divisions, and 6th Parachute Regiment. Blumenson, *Breakout,* 275–290; Dieter Choltitz, *Soldat unter Soldaten* (Koustanz: Europa, 1951), 208–209.

30. Maj. J. J. How's *Normandy: The British Breakout* (London: W. Kimber, 1981) presents an inflated assessment of BLUECOAT. For a more balanced view, see LHCMA LHP 1/341/4A, Comments of Maj. G. T. Armitage, MBE, appended to letter from Brig. James Hackett to Liddell Hart, 31 October 1955, 4.

31. The British order of battle for BLUECOAT was XXX Corps—43d Wessex Division, 50th Northumbrian Division, 7th Armoured Division; VIII Corps—15th Scottish Division, 11th Armoured Division, 6th Guards Tank Brigade; Reserve—Guards Armoured Division.

32. The XLVII Panzer Corps on 7 August fielded 248 tanks, 164 howitzers, 59 antitank guns, and 40 assault guns. PRO DEFE 3/116, Ultra Decrypt XL 5600, 11 August 1944.

33. A myth of the battle for Mortain is that Ultra forewarned Bradley and allowed him to set a trap. In reality, Ultra provided Bradley with only a few hours' advanced warning, and front-line units as little as twenty minutes. Blumenson, *Breakout,* 419–475; Ralph Bennett, *Ultra in the West: The Normandy Campaign* (New York: Scribner, 1980), 113–115; Frances W. Winterbotham *The Ultra Secret* (New York: Harper & Row, 1974), 148–150; Alwyn Featherstone, *Saving the Breakout: The 30th Division Stand at Mortain, August 7–13, 1944* (Novato, Calif.: Presidio Press, 1993), 69–74.

34. The attack force comprised the 17th SS Panzergrenadier and 1st SS, 2d, 2d

SS, and 116th Panzer Divisions. USAHD B-179, Lt. Gen. Paul Hausser, "Attack Toward Avranches" (Germany: 1947); Blumenson, *Breakout,* 457–465.

35. Only one of the attack divisions, the 116th Panzer Division, was at all fresh and still strong. PRO DEFE 3/116, Ultra Decrypt XL 5600, 11 August 1944; USAHD MS ETHINT 17, Lt. Gen. Gerhard Graf von Schwerin, "116th Panzer Division in Normandy" (Luxembourg: 1945), 21.

36. Ultra gave Bradley only four hours' warning of the German attack and front-line troops as little as twenty minutes' notice. Ralph Bennett, *Ultra in the West* (London: Hutchinson, 1979), 119; Carlo D'Este, *Decision: The Unwritten Story of Montgomery and the Allied Campaign* (London: Collins, 1983), 415–419; Omar Bradley, *A General's Story* (New York: Holt, 1951), 291.

37. Postbattle analysis confirmed 9 German tanks, 11 armored personnel carriers, 1 armored car, and 6 trucks destroyed by air attack. PRO WO 106/4348, ORS Rpt. 4, "Air Attacks on Enemy Tanks and Motor Transport in the Mortain Area, August 1944," table II.

38. Featherstone, *Saving the Breakout,* 69–74; Hewitt, *Workhorse,* 48–78; Blumenson, *Breakout,* 465–475; Lloyd J. Karamales, et al., *U.S. Antitank Defense at Mortain, France (August 1944)* (McLean Va.: Science Applications International Corporation [SAIC], 1990), 48–55, 67–78; Robert A. Miller, *August 1944* (New York: Warner Books, 1988), 69–71.

39. Another myth about the battle for Mortain is that tactical aviation halted the German offensive. John Golley, *Day of the Typhoon: Flying with the RAF Tank-busters in Normandy* (Wellingborough: Patrick Stephens, 1986), 123–134; Hallion, *Strike,* 216–217. For more realistic assessment of the role of fighter-bombers at Mortain see FUSA, *Report* I, 5; TUSAG, *Report* V, 36; Milton Schulman, *Defeat in the West* (London: Ballantine, 1968), 148; Cate and Craven, *AAF* III, 248–249.

40. The Germans might have recaptured Avranches if they had struck farther south where there were few U.S. troops, but clearly they could not have held the town for long.

41. Hart, *Montgomery,* 33–34.

42. By mid-August morale problems were evident in nine of sixteen divisions, and only the depleted British 6th Airborne Division attacked aggressively out of the Orne bridgehead but ran into intact defenses. PRO WO 106/4466, 6th Abn. Div., "Rpt. on Ops., 6.6–29.8.44," 19–26; LHCMA LHP/15/15 (CWP)/130, "Notes of Discussion with Horrocks," 14 May 1946.

43. The Canadian First Army headquarters finally became operational on 23 July in the Orne bridgehead, even though initially it had only Crocker's British I Corps under command. The Canadian 4th Armoured Division arrived in late July. NAC RG 24 13622, WD GS FCA, 31 July 1944.

44. Between 17 July and 1 August five panzer divisions (2d, 9th SS, 10th SS, 21st, and 116th) and three infantry divisions (84th, 326th, 363d) were transferred from Caen to the U.S. sector. NARA T-313, 410, KTB PzGr West, July 1944.

45. NAC RG 24 13751, GS 2 CID Sitreps 1–2 August 1944.

46. This was the first action by the 4th Armoured Division in Normandy. NAC RG 24 13625, G. (Ops) FCA, "Minutes of Morning Joint Conference," 2 August 1944, WD GS FCA Aug. 1944.

47. Between 18 July and 5 August, II Canadian Corps launched twelve abortive battalion assaults against the Verrières Ridge at a cost of more than 2,000 casualties. From 1–6 August the Canadians took only twenty-four prisoners. PRO WO 219/1449, "Daily Enemy POW Reports."

48. NAC RG 24 13711, WD GS IICC, 30 July 1944; IICC Op. Instr. 4, 5 August 1944.

49. The three Kangaroo-mounted battalions suffered only sixty-three casualties, while the four foot battalions lost 260. Stacey, *Victory,* 220.

50. Crerar's command suffered 315 casualties and lost 4 guns, 55 vehicles, and 3 days' munitions stocks due to short bombing. The North Shore Regiment alone suffered over 100 casualties, and one of its companies was so disrupted that it could not participate in TOTALIZE. NAC RG 24 13625, "Bombing of own Troops by 8 USAAF, 8.8.1944," WD GS FAC, August 1944.

51. NAC RG 24 18789, WD GS 4 CAD, 8–9 August 1944.

52. Worthington Force, Commanded by Lt. Col. D. G. Worthington, comprised B and C Companies, 27th Canadian Armoured Regiment, plus two rifle companies of the Algonquin Regiment. The force suffered 240 casualties and lost forty-seven tanks. Stacey, *Victory Campaign,* 288.

53. NAC RG 24 13625, "Minutes of Morning Joint Conference," 11 August 1944, WD GS FCA, August 1944, para. 6.

54. Stacey, *Victory,* 230–231.

55. The 3d Division column on the right comprised the 2d Armoured Brigade, 7th Reconnaissance Regt., 9th Infantry Brigade (Kangaroos), and 7th Brigade on foot. The left column under command of the 4th Division consisted of the 4th Armoured Brigade, 8th Infantry Brigade (Kangaroos), and 10th Infantry Brigade on foot. Charles P. Stacey, *The Victory Campaign* (Ottawa: The Queen's Printer, 1960), 239–240.

56. Northeast of the mouth of the pocket, a Polish force occupied the heights that dominated the only German escape routes through Vimoutiers. It was almost overrun as it enfiladed the fleeing German forces.

57. Montgomery, like most Allied officers, saw only a hazy distinction between the operational and strategic levels of war. Bernard L. Montgomery, *Memoirs* (London: Collins, 1958), 87.

U.S. troops wading ashore on the Cotentin Coastline of Normandy, 6 June 1944

A U.S. howitzer shells German forces retreating through the south of Carentan, 11 July 1944

Corporal Charles H. Johnson of the 783d Military Police Battalion waves on a truck convoy near Alençon, France, 5 September 1944

Field Marshal Erwin Rommel, depicted in more successful times commanding Axis forces in North Africa in 1942

A German police general, dressed in a Home Guard uniform, who committed suicide in Leipzig on 19 April 1945 while clutching a portrait of his beloved Führer

Adolf Hitler poses before the Eiffel Tower in the aftermath of the stunning German defeat of France during the summer of 1940

A V-1 rocket plunging toward the ground in southern England captured on film by a civilian air spotter, summer 1944

Troops of the 28th U.S. Infantry Division triumphantly march down the Champs Élysées, Paris, 29 August 1944

Field Marshal Walther Model arrives in the west on 18 August 1944 to replace the disgraced Field Marshal Walter von Kluge as commander of Army Group B

General Anton Dostler, a former commander of German occupation forces in France, is tied to a post prior to his execution by firing squad in the Aversa Stockade, Italy, 1 December 1945. He had been convicted of war crimes committed by occupation forces under his command in both France and Italy.

Field Marshal Wilhelm Keitel signs the Instrument of Surrender in Berlin on 7 May 1945

The winning U.S. team reassembles after the end of the war: Seated from left to right are generals: William S. Simpson, George S. Patton, Jr., Carl Spaatz, Dwight D. Eisenhower, Omar Bradley, Courtney Hodges, and Leonard T. Gerow. Standing are Ralph F. Stearley, Hoyt S. Vandenberg, Walter Bedell Smith, Otto P. Weyland, and Richard E. Nugent.

7

The United States:
The Leviathan Triumphant

The U.S. Army made the major, and possibly decisive, contribution to Allied victory in Normandy. The Americans demonstrated that they had significantly enhanced their capabilities since their first faltering combat in Tunisia, and during the campaign the army mastered both maneuver warfare and the air-ground battle. In fact, the Americans broke through the German front twice: on 16–17 June at St. Saveur-le-Vicomte to cut the Cotentin Peninsula, isolate Cherbourg, and hasten the city's fall; and in late July during Operation COBRA to burst out of Normandy and collapse the German defense of France. Not only did the Americans possess the manpower and material reserves to absorb the heavy losses of the bitter fighting during June and July that ground down German resistance and sapped Anglo-Canadian offensive strength, but U.S. forces also clearly enhanced their combat capabilities during the campaign. Initial combat revealed that significant deficiencies still plagued the U.S. Army, as a result of which it experienced great difficulty progressing in the Norman bocage hedgerow terrain. Yet the army overcame its initial difficulties and sluggish progress and adapted and retrained in the field to fight more effectively. Such adaptation and innovation emerged largely from the bottom up and encompassed operational and tactical adaptation, as well as technical innovation. It brought improved interarms and interservice coordination, which paved the way for a U.S. breakout from Normandy in late July 1944.[1] The army's determination to learn from experience and to enhance its combat performance was central both to the triumph of U.S. arms and to Allied victory in Normandy.[2]

The Americans experienced contrasting fates on their two D-Day assault beaches. At Utah, on the eastern flank of the Cotentin Peninsula, they suffered light casualties and established a solid beachhead; at Omaha Beach, on the western Calvados coast, they came close to defeat. Success at Utah Beach was due to the accuracy of the preliminary bombardment and the paucity of the German defense.[3] At Omaha a combination of difficult

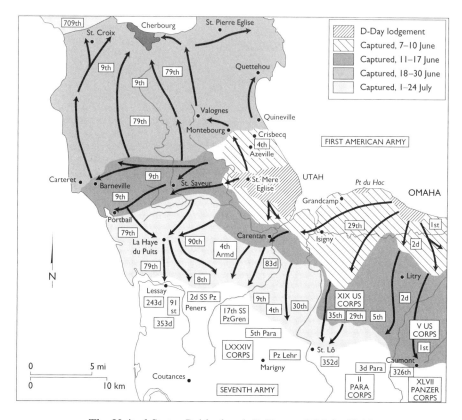

The United States Bridgehead, D-Day to 26 July 1944

terrain, the failure of the preliminary bombardment, the loss of most assault armor at sea, the inherent defensive strength of the draws and bluffs behind the beach, and a stronger German defense brought the landing close to failure.[4] Ultimately, sheer numbers, toughness, and heroism, backed by murderous short-range naval gunfire, overwhelmed the defenders.[5]

The Americans also used airborne forces extensively to support their amphibious assault. Having learned from experience in the Mediterranean, the U.S. First Army dropped the 82d and 101st Airborne Divisions inland behind Utah Beach and astride the Merderet River to protect landing troops until they had established themselves ashore. The drops were widely scattered, reflecting the inherent hazard of airborne operations. Dispersion, however, also proved beneficial because it obscured the focal points and objectives of the drop, and thus hindered German countermeasures and allowed the paratroopers both to dislocate German communications and prevent a major counterattack against Utah Beach.[6]

U.S. troops prevailed on D-Day due to months of meticulous preparation that generated the joint-service coordination necessary for a successful amphibious assault against strong opposition. Massive fire support, mastery of the seas and skies, numerical superiority, and the achievement of surprise all materially aided success. Powerful air and naval fire support directed by aerial observers and naval fire control parties ashore suppressed enemy defenses, and accurate destroyer fire from close inshore provided crucial support to the beleaguered troops at Omaha.[7] The innovative use of tank and artillery fire from landing craft, for which new procedures and extensive rehearsal was necessary, also helped to suppress enemy fire during the approach after the preliminary bombardment had lifted.[8] Finally, good combined-arms coordination learned through intensive preparation and rehearsal greatly assisted success, while the expanded engineer special brigades rapidly cleared and organized beaches for large-scale unloading operations.[9]

But after D-Day signs of flaws in U.S. preparation surfaced. Gen. "Lightning" Joe Collins's VII Corps made slow progress north from Utah Beach toward Cherbourg as a combination of tenacious enemy resistance and the breadth of the offensive temporarily checked the 4th Division's advance on Montebourg.[10] Nor could Collins's troops make much headway west or south due to poor coordination and drive in the green 90th Division and as German reserves in the Cotentin redeployed to block the U.S. advance.[11]

The advance of Maj. Gen. Leonard T. Gerow's V Corps on St. Lô from Omaha Beach was likewise slow. After D-Day, the 1st and 29th Divisions battered the German 352d Division, and when Isigny fell on 9 June few enemy troops barred the way to St. Lô.[12] Yet, the American advance remained methodical, cautious, and slow, largely due to prudent recognition of German tactical skill. Recklessness, for example, led to the defeat of a battalion of the 115th Infantry Regiment on 9 June as Gerow ordered the regiment to advance rapidly through the flooded Aure valley toward St. Lô. After the battalion outdistanced its flanking units, retiring German troops ambushed the battalion from the rear and dispersed it with heavy losses.[13]

The slow advance allowed German reserves to come up and prevent the fall of St. Lô. By 12 June, when the U.S. 29th Division assaulted across the Elle River, the German 3d Parachute Division had moved into line.[14] Moreover, poor U.S. tactics nearly defeated the crossing attempt. Failure to comprehend German defensive doctrine rendered the heavy preliminary barrage ineffective as the Americans had hit only the thinly held enemy outpost line, rather than the German main line of resistance (MLR) or enemy reserves dispersed in depth. In addition, poor radio discipline and indifferent radio security warned the Germans of the attack. These lapses enabled the Germans to hit the U.S. infantry in their jump-off positions with a furious barrage that stopped the attack dead. Only an impromptu, surprise dusk assault by the 116th Infantry Regiment secured a narrow bridgehead.[15]

Thereafter, ammunition shortages and mounting losses curtailed Gerow's drive on St. Lô as Collins's VII Corps received priority to capture Cherbourg. When the V Corps resumed its advance on 16 June, it did so with considerably restricted fire support that prevented it from overpowering the enemy. Again, poor American tactics and coordination helped the defenders stop the attack dead, while vigorous enemy counterattacks again ambushed elements of the 115th Regiment and threw it back in confusion.[16] The advance of the V Corps ground to a halt at Hill 108, 2 miles short of St. Lô. Too weak to take the town, the V Corps assumed the defensive on 18 June.

Skilled and tenacious German resistance combined with U.S. operational, logistical, and tactical deficiencies had slowed progress. Operationally, U.S. doctrinal emphasis on broad-front attacks slowed the advance because such attacks dissipated available resources and firepower, increased losses, and, in the short term at least, denied the Americans substantial progress and decisive success.[17] Logistical shortages also slowed the U.S. drive in the first weeks of the invasion as supply deliveries fell well behind schedule (see Table 7.1). Planning estimates proved too optimistic and at the same time, the First Army experienced unexpectedly high ammunition consumption as bogged-down troops relied heavily on fire support to advance in the bocage.[18] Slow unloading, high consumption, and unofficial unit hoarding, kept stockpiles ashore low and necessitated the introduction of rationing on 15 June. Lack of ammunition prevented the First Army from fully employing its firepower early in the campaign.[19]

Troops and commanders quickly became aware that flaws in tactics, training, and equipment had hampered troop performance and slowed the U.S. advance. In the meantime, as the First Army sought to identify and to

Table 7.1   **Percentage of Planned U.S. Supplies Delivered, Summer 1944**

	7 June	9 June	10 June	11 June	13 June	15 June	17 June	30 June	31 July
Percentage Delivered	21	31	38	47	60	71	76	81	93

Sources: FUSA, *Report* I, 78; V, 147; Roland G. Ruppenthal, *Logistical Support of the Armies* (Washington, D.C.: OCMH, 1953) I, 390, 401, 416–421, 457; Steve R. Waddell, *U.S. Army Logistics: The Normandy Campaign, 1944* (Westport, Conn.: Greenwood Press, 1994), 55–67.

correct these defects, it revised its operational plan, improvised logistically, and utilized air and sea power extensively to maintain the pace of the advance and bring about the fall of Cherbourg, despite the operational and tactical flaws that hampered progress in the bocage.

Senior U.S. commanders also displayed operational flexibility. The slowness of the advance on Cherbourg as the Germans stubbornly fought before Montebourg led Collins to jettison the original invasion plan that, couched in traditional doctrinal tenets, called for a direct advance on Cherbourg.[20] Instead, on 15 June Collins struck west to cut the peninsula and isolate Cherbourg from the main body of German forces. At the same time, since supplies were insufficient to sustain offensive action across the entire front, Gen. Omar Bradley, U.S. First Army commander, halted the V Corps advance on St. Lô to focus on taking Cherbourg.

Quartermasters also improvised to speed the flow of supplies and reduce munitions shortages that handicapped the U.S. drive. From 12 June, supply troops unloaded around the clock, beached landing craft to allow faster unloading, and quickly assembled the prefabricated Mulberry artificial port to accelerate cargo discharge rates. As a result, during the second week of the invasion, the supply situation ashore improved considerably (Table 7.1).[21] An improved logistic position allowed Collins's drive on Cherbourg to move into top gear in the second week of the invasion. By 15 June, the VII Corps had enlarged its bridgehead sufficiently to concentrate its strength for the push west across the peninsula. This renewed drive rapidly penetrated a German defense already attenuated by previous broadfront attacks. Spearheaded by the experienced 9th Infantry and 82d Airborne Divisions, which advanced aggressively and boldly without regard for their flanks, Collins's troops severed the Cotentin peninsula on 17 June, isolated Cherbourg from reinforcement and resupply, and thus hastened its fall.[22]

The Americans also employed air and sea power to good effect in support of the advance on Cherbourg. In accordance with doctrine, the IX Tactical Air Command (TAC) interdicted enemy reinforcements and supplies moving into the Cotentin, inflicted heavy loss on German motor transport, slowed the arrival of reinforcements, and exacerbated German supply shortages.[23] The U.S. buildup in the Cotentin far outstripped the enemy's (see Table 7.2). To compensate for munitions shortages ashore, the U.S. First Army also widely employed naval bombardment, which suppressed German defensive fire, demoralized the defenders, and played an important role in the fall of the strong German defensive line along the Montebourg-Quineville ridge during 13–15 June. Naval gunfire, though slighted in official U.S. Army reports, was a crucial ingredient of success and more feared by the Germans than air attacks.[24]

Table 7.2   Buildup of U.S. and German Strength in the Cotentin Peninsula, June 1944 (Number of battalions)

	Infantry		Artillery		Armor		Total		Ratio
	U.S.	Ger.	U.S.	Ger.	U.S.	Ger.	U.S.	Ger.	U.S.:Ger.
6 June	30	14	14	5	3	1	47	20	2:1
8 June	42	18	18	6	3	1	63	24	3:1
10 June	45	26	19	9	3	2	67	37	2:1
12 June	48	31	25	10	3	2	76	43	2:1
14 June	60	38	31	11	3	3	94	52	2:1
16 June	60	38	33	11	3	3	96	52	2:1
18 June	60	40	37	11	3	3	100	54	2:1

Sources: Stanton, *Order of Battle;* NARA T-78, 142, "Gefechtsbericht KG. Hoffmann"; T-78, 418, 6386950, OKH GenStdH Org. Abt. (I) "Heerestrupen auf d. Halbinsel Cherbourg," Nr. I/17 633/44 G.Kdos., v. 22 June 1944; USAHD MS C-018, Lt. Col. Günther Keil, "919th Gren. Regt., KG. Keil (June 1944)," (Germany: 1948); PRO DEFE 3/175, Ultra Decrypt KV 8956, "Strength Return, Battle Group Schlieben, 17.6.1944," 20 June 1944.

On 22 June Collins launched a final three-division attack on Cherbourg. Even though previous offensives had badly weakened and demoralized the defenders, Cherbourg remained a hard nut to crack.[25] Its landward defenses consisted of a network of reinforced field positions anchored by two modern forts and supported by powerful coastal artillery and antiaircraft defenses.[26] Moreover, Collins's troops lacked specialized equipment and training to reduce fortresses, and ammunition shortages limited available fire support. To compensate for these deficiencies, powerful naval gunfire directed by spotter planes and the heaviest aerial attack yet seen in the campaign backed the final assault.[27] In addition, for the first time, an intensive counterflak program preceded the aerial bombardment to neutralize the strong enemy antiaircraft defenses. The artillery barrage followed immediately, which allowed the infantry to close and breach the thin, German defense lines on a broad front.[28] Nevertheless, although their situation was hopeless, the Germans fought fiercely and final resistance only ceased on 1 July.[29] Indeed, the outer breakwater forts that guarded the harbor entrance resisted conventional artillery fire and could only be silenced by air and naval bombardment combined with direct fire from medium guns at point-blank range.[30] The Americans finally captured Cherbourg, but they did so well behind schedule and after the enemy had left the port in ruins. The enemy had fought stubbornly and with skill, but broad-front attacks had also dissipated U.S. strength, ammunition shortages had limited fire support, and inexperience at tackling fortifications had all delayed the city's capture.

The slow drive on Cherbourg and St. Lô led U.S. commanders to evaluate their performance, identify flaws, and devise solutions. The commanders quickly realized that projected rates of advance were too optimistic: progress had proved slow and costly. This in part reflected German skill and tenacity and the powerful defensive advantage of the bocage terrain, but it also reflected flaws in U.S. Army combat preparation. Slow progress demonstrated that planners had seriously underestimated the debilitating and constricting effect of the bocage terrain on operations. The bocage's tall, thick hedgerows, sunken lanes, and small fields presented both advantages and drawbacks to the attacker. While it canceled the superior range of German armor and antitank guns, it reinforced the natural superiority of defense and aggravated the negative consequences of the U.S. infantry's lack of firepower.[31]

Inevitably focused on getting ashore, Allied planners had barely considered the problems of conducting the battle inland. Indeed, the U.S. First Army had not specifically prepared troops to fight in the hedgerow terrain.[32] Thus, the formidable barrier that the bocage presented surprised officers and troops alike. Commanders soon realized that standard attack methods were ineffective in the bocage because the terrain forced troops to launch frontal assaults to batter the enemy into defeat, and the thick vegetation and compartmented terrain hampered unit deployment and maneuver, negating standard fire-and-maneuver techniques. Hedgerow fighting also demanded excellent combined-arms coordination if the attacker was to prevail. Yet evidence of poor coordination among the unseasoned formations quickly mounted.[33]

Lack of infantry firepower also slowed the advance. The effectiveness of the most powerful squad weapon, the Browning automatic rifle (BAR), a light and easily handled automatic rifle of World War I design, was restricted by its limited twenty-round magazine capacity and low sustained rate of fire. The hedgerow terrain hampered the forward deployment of the belt-fed, .30- and .50-caliber machine guns with which U.S. infantry traditionally reinforced its firepower.[34] As a result, the infantry lacked sufficient firepower to acquire the fire superiority that doctrine demanded. Troops often responded with one or another extreme: extravagant, wild fire to suppress superior enemy firepower or reluctance to fire so as not to present a target.[35]

Lacking firepower, the infantry simply could not gain fire superiority or battlefield dominance without heavy indirect-fire support. The close combat that the bocage necessitated, however, hampered bringing indirect fire to bear and made observation and adjustment of fire difficult.[36] The bocage also aggravated inherent problems of command and control: assault units often got lost or disoriented, and attacks often became canalized on frontages much smaller than doctrine advocated. So, the army's doctrine, training, and equipment had left it ill prepared for fighting in such conditions.[37]

The U.S. forces' inexperience exacerbated the inherent problems of hedgerow fighting because bocage combat put a premium on small-unit leadership and initiative. Troops would rely heavily on their commanders, and green units often failed to move under fire and or to press the advantage. Commanders were forced to lead by example, which brought high officer losses. Many units lost what drive they did possess when their officers became casualties.[38]

Poor infantry quality also contributed to the slow advance. The difficulties of operating in the bocage underscored the infantry's lack of aggressiveness that derived from inadequate firepower and poor manpower selection and replacement policies. Infantrymen were hesitant and often failed to maneuver to bring greater firepower to bear, but instead went to ground and, lacking faith in the efficacy of their own firepower, relied on indirect fire to neutralize the enemy.[39]

Initially U.S. tactics also addressed German defensive practices inadequately. Because they applied their advantage in indirect fire artillery poorly, the Americans generally prevailed in the bocage only if they had marked numerical superiority and overwhelming firepower. Initially, attack methods dealt badly with German defensive techniques because the U.S. Army had yet to develop responses to the problems of enemy defense in depth first encountered in Sicily and Italy. The Germans lightly manned their forward outpost line and kept most of their strength back in their MLR and as mobile reserves even farther back to counterattack any penetration of the MLR once forward troops had identified the composition, axis, and objective of the main enemy attack. These defensive tactics aggravated U.S. offensive difficulties: initially U.S. artillery only targeted the lightly held enemy outpost line, dissipating the powerful fire support available, wasting scarce ammunition, and inflicting minimal damage on the dispersed defenders.[40]

The bocage so negated the firepower and mobility of armor that it severely constrained armored operations. The tall, thick hedgerows and narrow sunken lanes restricted maneuver, reduced visibility and fire, and left U.S. tanks vulnerable to close-combat destruction. U.S. armor initially attacked en masse in columns along roads and tracks as doctrine prescribed, but suffered heavily at the hands of German antitank guns, mines, and rocket-propelled antitank missiles. Armor quickly learned to move across country, but the bocage so restricted such movement that it seriously obstructed any offensive employment of armor. The terrain denied armor its central role in the combined-arms advance and relegated it to a secondary role.[41]

Poor tank-infantry coordination further hampered combined-arms operations in the hedgerows. Many rookie units had undergone limited combined-arms training and so remained inexperienced at coordinating tanks and infantry.[42] Even veteran formations found coordination difficult because the terrain rendered existing combined-arms doctrine inadequate. Tanks and infantry could not communicate properly, often misunderstood their respective roles and capabilities, and thus rarely operated together effectively. Poor coordination brought setbacks and increased losses and slowed the advance on St. Lô in mid-June.[43]

Renewed logistic difficulties also hampered U.S. progress in the bocage. No sooner had the supply situation improved in the second week of OVERLORD, when the worst Channel storm (18-20 June) in fifty years hit and wrecked hundreds of ships, landing craft, and the U.S. Mulberry artificial port. The storm set back the U.S. buildup by weeks, made worse a growing ammunition shortage ashore, and forced the introduction of tighter rationing that prevented the First Army from using its firepower superiority to full effect for the rest of June.[44]

Commanders quickly sought to identify and fix the problems that had slowed the advance.[45] The organizational flexibility of the U.S. Army, the willingness to examine and learn from combat experiences, and ingenuity meant that the problems that confronted them were quickly overcome as troops adapted in the field during combat. In fact, the determination of both troops and commanders to retrain in the field was a key strength that consistently allowed them to enhance their combat effectiveness. Little in doctrine, training, or combat experience had prepared them for hedgerow fighting, but the troops quickly realized that they had to restore tactical mobility, deploy more firepower, and coordinate mobility and firepower and bring it to bear in a concerted combined-arms assault.[46]

The U.S. soldiers soon realized that they needed more firepower to gain ground in the bocage with tolerable casualties. They demanded more automatic weapons, grenade launchers, bazookas, and mortars. When the First Army could not meet these unexpected demands from available stocks, it redistributed weapons from nondivisional and noncombat units.[47] Troops also improvised in the field to generate more firepower. Infantry adeptly "acquired" extra submachine guns, BARs, and bazookas; modified semiautomatic carbines to make them fully automatic; and pressed captured machine guns and mortars into service.[48] Ordnance personnel also modified several weapons in the field to enhance their effectiveness. The poor mobility of light antiaircraft guns, the towed .50-caliber quad-mounted M51 machine gun in particular, resulted in several field expedients. Workshops mounted the M45 quad-gun turret on an M2 half-track to improvise a self-propelled variant, the M16B.[49] This proved a highly successful expedient, which became a standard design. Field improvisation and innovation allowed infantrymen to augment their own firepower during the campaign.[50]

U.S. forces also learned to deploy more indirect-fire support and to use it more effectively. In Normandy, the First Army pioneered the use of heavy antiaircraft guns in a field artillery role where they proved effective at long-range harassing and interdiction fire.[51] The First Army also employed tank destroyers as assault guns to provide extra indirect-fire support for the infantry, and pressed into service captured artillery pieces.[52] Gunners also both made increasing use of deadly white phosphorus (WP), or "Willie Peter" as the troops termed it, which combusted with oxygen and burned anything it touched. Gunners also often quickly brought down unplanned massed fire by using quick-fire procedures practiced in Britain.[53]

Continued improvisation by quartermasters offset the ammunition shortages caused by the June storm. Logisticians employed emergency airlifts to overcome critical shortages in the immediate aftermath of the storm, while ordnance personnel even used captured ammunition.[54] As a result, the First Army was able to sustain unprecedented levels of fire support in the final battle for St. Lô during mid-July (see Table 7.3).[55]

Table 7.3   Weekly U.S. Fire Support (Rounds per Gun)

Weapon	10 June	17 June	24 June	1 July	8 July	15 July	22 July	29 July	5 August
105mm Howitzer	42	63	35	29	55	80	26	20	26
155mm Howitzer	17	37	24	18	41	53	12	18	15
155mm Gun	10	18	16	13	27	31	12	8	11
4.5" Gun	—	13	27	24	29	33	9	20	15
8" Howitzer	—	—	12	6	15	20	3	4	4
8" Gun	—	—	—	—	21	10	.3	1	—
240mm Howitzer	—	—	—	—	16	5	—	7	—

Source: FUSA, *Report* V, 185–186; VI, 70–71.

The Americans also innovated to allow armor to operate more effectively in the bocage. Units had used armored bulldozers to plough through the hedges, but few 'dozers were available.[56] Other units blasted gaps in the hedges with explosives but, while effective, this method was laborious and exorbitant in demolitions.[57] By early July, improvised hedgecutter tanks had emerged that allowed armor to plough through the thick hedges. These improvisations culminated in the Rhinoceros hedgecutter, whose employment in late July helped restore armored mobility.[58]

The U.S. First Army also addressed the problem of poor tank-infantry communication that disrupted coordination. Since infantry and tank radios rarely operated on the same frequency, armored units improvised "deck phones" by attaching infantry field radios inside the tank and on the outside rear to improve communication.[59] Infantry units also acquired armor radios (and vice versa), and tank-infantry teams developed new universal signals to overcome the confusion caused by different infantry and armored visual signals.[60]

General Bradley also revised operational procedures that hampered coordination. Combat had revealed that independent battalions "pooled" at army level lacked cohesion and coordinated poorly.[61] During the campaign, the First Army gradually retreated from pooling and unofficially sanctioned permanent attachment of pooled units to corps and divisions.[62] Although operational necessity initially forced the frequent transfer of pooled units between formations, during July growing association between divisions and pooled units brought improved coordination.[63]

The First Army also tackled the problems of artillery observation and control in the bocage. To compensate for the frequent loss of forward observers, the First Army made greater use of aerial artillery spotters, whose mere appearance often suppressed German artillery because of the enemy's fear of accurate counterbattery fire directed by the spotter.[64] Spotter planes proved the most effective means of observation among the hedgerows and were especially effective in locating enemy troop locations and guns.[65] U.S. forces increasingly used spotter aircraft to aid materially their advance through the hedgerows.

Attack procedures also gradually became more sophisticated and better attuned to German defensive techniques as U.S. troops learned through trial and error to train their fire on the entire German defensive system. By the COBRA offensive of 25 July, planners had developed complex fire plans that targeted the full depth of enemy defenses.[66]

Despite deficiencies that had slowed their advance, the U.S. military still achieved greater success than its British and Canadian allies during June. The U.S. Army captured Cherbourg, bagged large numbers of prisoners, and inflicted heavy losses on the enemy. Although poorer quality German troops and more pronounced German supply difficulties on the western flank contributed to these successes, the Americans also clearly fought harder and longer than their allies. Since the Germans had rarely inflicted serious defeat on the Americans, U.S. troops sometimes lacked the respect that the British had for the enemy. At the same time, their manpower and material reserves and their doctrinal emphasis on continuous, direct, and vigorous offensive action led U.S. troops to engage and destroy the enemy in combat.[67] This more aggressive approach did mean that occasionally operations ended in disaster, but it also meant that U.S. troops vigorously exploited opportunities when they arose.[68] Thus doctrine kept the Americans pushing forward long and hard. The consequence of these contrasting British and American approaches was that although the Anglo-Canadian forces on several occasions pushed the enemy defense close to breaking point, only the Americans shattered the German defenses.[69]

Despite initial efforts to adapt to hedgerow warfare, reinforcement by Collins's VII Corps, and fresh divisions from Britain, the U.S. First Army still struggled to advance in the bocage when it renewed its offensive toward St. Lô on 3 July. Maj. Gen. Troy H. Middleton's VIII Corps struck south from the base of the Cotentin Peninsula with three divisions, and in five days enveloped and took the important communications center of La Haye-du-Puits despite fierce opposition. But continued poor U.S. coordination and determined German opposition halted his offensive at the Ay and Sèves Rivers on 15 July after heavy losses.[70]

Simultaneously, the U.S. VII Corps struck south from Carentan on 3 July with the rested, yet inexperienced, 83d Division. Its attack toward Périers in poor weather and difficult marshy terrain disintegrated amid indifferent coordination.[71] Even after the veteran 4th Infantry Division joined the attack on 5 July, the VII Corps gained only 700 yards in four days because even experienced troops found it difficult progressing in the dense bocage south of Carentan.[72] The Germans defended skillfully and counterattacked repeatedly and vigorously to sap U.S. strength. Even though it repulsed several enemy regiment-sized counterattacks between 10–12 July, the VII Corps had to abandon its offensive on 15 July. During the first week of the renewed attack, U.S. formations continued to struggle to gain ground against determined resistance without massive numerical and firepower superiority.

In the second week of July, however, a combination of new "bocage busting" techniques, which brought greater tactical success at lower cost, and sustained offensive action wore down enemy resistance and speeded the advance on St. Lô. The lull in fighting on the southern front in late June gave units a respite to examine their performance, identify flaws, and devise and rehearse solutions. Throughout the First Army widespread experimentation and improvisation allowed the infantry to bring greater firepower to bear and to coordinate more effectively in the bocage.

The result was improved combat performance that speeded the fall of St. Lô. On 7 July, Maj. Gen. Charles H. Corlett's newly arrived XIX Corps attacked south toward St. Lô with three divisions. Enhanced fire support, better tactics, and improved coordination allowed the 9th and 30th Divisions to storm both the Taute-Vire Canal and Vire River and rapidly capture St. Jean-de-Daye.[73] Corlett made rare use of tactical deception with a crossing feint, and organized a coordinated assault that employed dozer tanks and that was backed by an elaborate fire plan that included dive bombing, tank destroyers in an indirect fire role, and extensive use of white phosphorous. Thereafter the corps slowly, but inexorably, gained ground until it cut the Périers-St. Lô highway on 20 July to deny the Germans a key communications link with St. Lô.[74]

During early July the 29th Division also perfected new bocage-busting techniques. It organized combined-arms assault groups, heavily reinforced in firepower, around a Sherman hedgecutter mounting a rear deck phone.[75] The division employed this new close-assault, combined-arms tactical organization on 11 July to renew its drive on St. Lô. With only light casualties, its attack overran the strongly entrenched German 9th Parachute Regiment and stormed the strategic Martinville Ridge that dominated the northeastern approaches to St. Lô.[76]

The new tactics and organization also helped the U.S. 2d Division to capture Hill 192 at the eastern end of the Martinville Ridge that same day. The hill, which dominated all approaches to the Norman capital, was a key position in the German defense of St. Lô and was strongly held by the German 3d Parachute Division. The U.S. 2d Division organized integrated assault teams and intensively retrained in combined-arms tactics. As a result, on 11–12 July, the division stormed Hill 192 and advanced across the St. Lô-Bayeux highway to attack St. Lô from the east.[77]

Improved combined-arms coordination and hedgerow tactics cut losses in all three attacks, and, once these methods had proven successful, they were quickly adopted and adapted throughout the First Army. It took time, familiarity, and retraining to develop and refine bocage-busting techniques. New, untested divisions were retrained in the field in these methods before entering combat, and throughout July the First Army rotated formations out of line to rest and to retrain.[78] East of the Vire the newly arrived U.S. 35th Infantry Division joined the 29th Infantry Division in its drive on St. Lô. The loss of high ground weakened the German defense, allowing the 35th Division to storm the final height north of St. Lô, Hill 122, on 18 July, and compelling the Germans to abandon the city the next day.[79]

During June and July the army exhibited serious, professional concern in identifying and rectifying the flaws that had slowed its advance. It sought technical and tactical solutions to its problems and tackled them with urgency, intelligence, and creativity. As a result, by late July offensive coordination had already improved in many formations.[80] Enhanced tactics and coordination had speeded the fall of St. Lô and put the U.S. First Army in a position to launch a full-scale breakthrough attempt, Operation COBRA.

Operational flexibility again characterized U.S. planning for COBRA. Despite the fall of St. Lô, the First Army still labored under major difficulties, including dwindling infantry strength and growing ammunition shortages, which conditioned planning for COBRA.[81] Firepower enhancement and the unexpectedly heavy ammunition expenditures of bocage fighting had created serious shortages, which a major depot fire on 12 July and heavy expenditures during the final battle for St. Lô had only made worse. The shortages forced wider and more stringent ammunition rationing, which meant that the First Army could not rely on its own firepower to smash through the enemy during COBRA.[82]

By mid-July, the First Army also faced a growing infantry shortage because its forces had suffered heavy casualties in sustained combat. Vigorous opposition, the defensive advantages of the hedgerow terrain, and inexperience and poor coordination had combined to bring unexpectedly heavy infantry losses during grim attritional warfare. Allied planners had seriously underestimated the extent to which the campaign would be an infantry slog, and as a result infantry losses had greatly exceeded available replacements.[83] Riflemen suffered such casualties in the bocage that individuals' survival times averaged mere days.[84] Such turnover eroded combat effectiveness, and as a result, many infantry units had become badly depleted by mid-July.[85] From a relative perspective, though, the U.S. infantry position remained healthier than was the case for its allies and its enemy: since the First Army's large replacement pool allowed it to sustain its striking power for longer than either its allies or the enemy could.[86]

At the same time, drawbacks of the U.S. replacement system increased casualties and lowered combat effectiveness. The system met First Army numerical needs, with the exception of infantry (see Table 7.4), but the poor quality of replacements both increased casualties and the incidence of combat exhaustion, thus undermining infantry performance. Assignment by individual, lack of territorial or unit affinity between field and replacement units, and direct induction into combat units engendered no esprit de corps and poor morale among replacements. The system thus failed to sustain the cohesion of field units that had to absorb many replacements. The weaknesses of the replacement system only aggravated the extremely high turnover among riflemen during June and July, thus eroding infantry combat effectiveness.[87]

The key advantage of the replacement system, though, was that it could replace battle losses more flexibly and far faster than the enemy could. Despite its serious flaws, the system suited the U.S. strategy of applying continuous, massive force. As a result, the U.S. Army could replenish units in the front line without having to withdraw them, which, given the ninety-division ceiling, would have been difficult to achieve. The mere replacement of numbers, however, could not immediately restore unit fighting power, because such qualitative factors as cohesion and morale were as important as numbers.[88]

Lack of infantry and munitions meant that the First Army could not rely on raw fighting power to smash through enemy defenses south of St. Lô and thrust into Brittany. Although the fall of St. Lô had finally brought the First Army into more open terrain west of the city and inflicted heavy

Table 7.4   Cumulative U.S. Casualties and Replacements, June–July 1944

Date	Losses	Replacements	Net
12 June	14,146	3,500	−10,646
14 June	16,354	11,000	−5,354
15 June	17,890	14,750	−3,140
17 June	22,969	23,000	+31
19 June	25,625	29,000	+3,375
21 June	28,088	33,500	+5,412
22 June	28,761	33,750	+4,989
25 June	33,326	34,000	+674
27 June	35,321	36,000	−679
28 June	35,704	37,250	+1,546
29 June	36,229	39,500	+3,271
30 June	38,378	41,250	+2,872
1 July	38,882	39,500	+618
3 July	35,295	41,750	+2,455
7 July	43,464	42,750	−714
9 July	46,427	45,350	−1,077
13 July	57,146	54,650	−2,496
15 July	62,144	63,000	+856

Sources: PRO WO 219/938-939, "Casualties OVERLORD"; WO 219/1538-39, TFAG, "Casualty Reports."

casualties on the Germans, the enemy defenses remained intact. Indeed, despite heavy losses, the Germans had steadily reinforced their strength on the St. Lô front and still held strong positions on high ground south of the city.[89]

Once again U.S. operational flexibility played a major role in the success of COBRA. Short on infantry and ammunition and facing intact defenses, the First Army recognized that it could not break through with the conventional broad-front attacks advocated by doctrine. It had learned from the grueling fight for St. Lô that it had to launch a highly concentrated offensive to penetrate the enemy front. General Bradley thus devised an original plan that could succeed despite prevailing attack doctrine, ammunition shortages, and shrinking infantry strength.

The COBRA plan was innovative in several key respects. To provide the firepower it lacked, the U.S. First Army relied heavily on carpet bombing to smash a hole in the German front, on a narrow-front offensive to penetrate the German line, and on mobility and speed to outmaneuver, rather than outfight, the enemy and achieve a breakthrough. The First Army thus planned COBRA as a concentrated break-in attack by three infantry divisions on a narrow front, supported by intense air and artillery attack, to secure the flanks while three mechanized divisions punched through to the rear, swung southwest, captured Coutances and cut off the German LXXXIV Corps on the Atlantic coast.[90]

After the fall of St. Lô, the First Army prepared frantically for COBRA. It depleted its reserves to bring formations up to strength in personnel and equipment (see Table 7.5), though cohesion and offensive drive inevitably suffered from the absorption of large numbers of undertrained replacements.[91] General Bradley also rigorously removed officers who had failed the test of war.[92] As formations rotated out of the line for rest and rehabilitation, they established divisional training centers where subunits intensively retrained and exercised alongside independent tank battalions to improve coordination.[93] Armored divisions also retrained during mid-July, in preparation for their breakout role, to attain maximum speed during the advance.

Table 7.5   U.S. Ordnance Shortages, 31 July 1944

Weapon	Reserves	Losses	Net
Rifle	12,115	7,103	+5,012
Carbine	5,420	3,800	+1,620
BAR	490	1,784	−1,294
SMG	2,790	1,689	+1,101
MG	2,245	2,158	+87
ATG	23	86	−63
Artillery	75	83	−8
TD	54	30	+24
Tank	404	637	−234

Sources: FUSA, *Report* I, 99; V, 203; VI, 101–111.

Its previous slow progress meant that the First Army had conceived COBRA as a limited breakthrough operation that would propel it beyond the confines of the bocage into territory better suited for mobile warfare along the line Coutances-Caumont. The planning and execution of COBRA, therefore, starkly illuminated the lack of U.S. operational-level doctrine. COBRA was a multidivision attack on a narrow front, and due to the pessimism surrounding prospects of a breakout—few U.S. commanders dared hope that COBRA would destroy the German defense of Normandy—the operation lacked a definite strategic goal or a clear operational dimension. The subsequent breakout of August was thus an extemporized affair.[94]

The carpet bombing that opened COBRA was the largest and most effective air attack on ground forces yet seen in the war. A comprehensive counterflak program adjusted by aerial spotters suppressed enemy antiaircraft fire and allowed the bombing to achieve good concentration.[95] Allied aircraft dropped over 5,000 tons of bombs, WP, and a new weapon, napalm (jellied gasoline), on 6 square miles, although once again there was short bombing, which reflected the inherent hazard of this novel ground weapon.[96] Faulty planning, sloppy execution, and bad luck dogged the COBRA aerial bombardment, but the damage inflicted on the Germans was heavier and more effective than even Eisenhower had dared hope.[97] The attendant artillery fire plan engaged the entire depth of the German defenses: the U.S. First Army had learned to target the entire enemy defense zone, including the reserves dispersed in depth, and fired smoke both to mask the ground advance and to confuse German flanking fire. Simultaneously, heavy and accurate counterbattery fire effectively suppressed the German artillery.[98] To augment its firepower and compensate for shell shortages, the First Army used tank destroyers and heavy antiaircraft guns for indirect-fire support. Combined artillery-air attacks suppressed all long-range German batteries and impeded German countermeasures.[99]

The carpet bombing crippled German communications and so stunned, disorganized, and demoralized the Panzer *Lehr* Division that even its seasoned troops could not resist the concentrated attack by the VII Corps as the Americans advanced 2 miles into the German defenses on 25 July.[100] But it was American speed and mobility that turned this break-in into a breakout. Short on infantry and ammunition, the First Army achieved a breakout because it outmaneuvered, rather than outfought, the enemy. The U.S. troops exploited their penetration faster than the enemy could react as supply shortages badly hindered German countermeasures.[101] On 26 July, the VII Corps gained 8,000 yards as fuel and ammunition shortages badly impeded enemy countermeasures. Under the pressure of this rapid exploitation the stretched German front began to give way. As U.S. armor passed through and out into the open, supporting flanking attacks pinned German troops in place as dislocated communications slowed enemy appreciation of, and reaction to, the scale of the crisis.[102]

The U.S. forces achieved a major breakout on 27 July. As the Germans fell back in an effort to retain a coherent front, the U.S. VII Corps fought its way forward to the outskirts of Coutances. Simultaneously the XIX Corps captured the high ground south of St. Lô and drew into battle the first German reinforcements, the 2d and 116th Panzer Divisions, dispatched from the Caen front. These developments precipitated the most intense fighting seen during COBRA as the panzers repeatedly attacked westward through the bocage southeast of St. Lô in a desperate attempts to restabilize the front.[103]

The following day, the 4th and 6th Armored Divisions of VIII Corps captured Lessay and linked up with the spearhead of the VII Corps. At this moment, General Hausser, commanding the German Seventh Army, erred when he instructed his LXXXIV Corps to fight its way out toward the southeast, rather than retiring unopposed due south. This decision ensured that the retiring forces ran into the U.S. vanguard advancing southeast of Coutances and were isolated in a pocket astride Roncey.[104]

With the German front ripped apart, the U.S. First Army expanded COBRA. The VII and VIII Corps continued their push south and the next day seized bridgeheads across the Sienne and Sèe Rivers. On 31 July, the 4th Armored Division crossed the Sèlune River at Pontaubault, and was thus poised to attack into Brittany.

The most intensive and effective U.S. tactical air attacks yet seen accompanied the COBRA ground operations. Indeed, COBRA witnessed the largest and most effective application of tactical air power up to that point in the history of air warfare.[105] A major development was the increasing shift in tactical air support from the battlefield interdiction that doctrine advocated to close support as Elwood "Pete" Quesada's IX TAC came to the aid of Bradley's struggling ground forces.[106] Quesada extended and refined the Horsefly system of air-ground coordination developed during the late spring of 1944 in Italy to provide "armored column cover."[107] He organized continuous air cover for armored formations and innovated technically to create effective means of coordination via tank-mounted air support parties fitted with very high-frequency (VHF) radios attached to armored divisions. These innovations forged excellent coordination between tactical aviation and mechanized forces during the breakout.[108]

The development of armored cover represented the greatest advance in the U.S. conduct of the air-ground battle in Normandy.[109] Tactical air power seriously hampered German countermeasures, redeployments, and resupply operations. Moreover, the novel daylight drop of delayed-fuse bombs that detonated after dark and the use of radar- and radio-controlled blind night bombing disrupted German nighttime movement.[110] As German columns retired southward all along the front they suffered heavy air attack. On 29 July in the Roncey pocket air force, artillery, and armor smashed German units as the U.S. 2d Armored Division repelled numerous enemy efforts to break out. The air strikes by the IX TAC on the pocket proved to be the most damaging Allied tactical air strikes yet launched in the European Theater of Operations (ETO).[111]

From COBRA on, U.S. fighter-bombers widely provided armored cover for armored spearheads.[112] Such cover for the armor improved intelligence available to ground forces, which allowed them to bypass resistance more easily. It also facilitated the ground advance because this cover provided rapid-response air attacks when armored forces met opposition.[113] The provision of this cover clearly aided the rapid advance of U.S. armored forces across France during August 1944.[114]

Bradley also employed his armor en masse and in depth during COBRA in accordance with proven doctrine. Once the armor was out in the open, American mobility came into play. On 31 July the 2d Armored took the communications hub of Villedieu-les-Puits, while on the eastern flank the XIX and V Corps pushed southeast to tie down German reserves. What had begun on 25 July in pessimism had ended a week later in a breakout.[115]

A combination of factors had brought success. Operationally, U.S. performance during COBRA was excellent: the infantry divisions had executed a fast break-in, and armored forces performed a textbook rapid exploitation. The most devastating carpet bombing of enemy ground forces, a more sophisticated and powerful artillery fire plan, and the strongest tactical air support of the war to date paved the way for the ground advance. Technical innovation—the First Army using for the first time both the Rhinoceros hedgecutter and armored column cover during COBRA—also contributed to success.[116] When coupled with waning German strength and increasing German logistic shortages, the result was a breakout.

On 1 August, General Bradley's 12th U.S. Army Group became operational and took over the First Army and Gen. George Patton's newly activated Third Army. U.S. forces were now able to conduct the fast-paced maneuver war that the peacetime army had trained for. While the First Army advanced southeast and occupied Mortain on 3 August, Patton's armored divisions fanned out into Brittany: the 4th Armored Division took Rennes and Vannes to isolate Brittany, and the 6th Armored Division raced deep into the peninsula to seize Pontivy. Nonetheless, most of the enemy was still able to retire into the ports of Brest, St. Malo, and Lorient. During the breakout U.S. forces for the first time went on the defense to thwart a major German counteroffensive that aimed to seal off the U.S. penetration and isolate the Third Army. The advance by the Americans had left their center thin, which the enemy tried to exploit. On 5 August, the Americans first detected a German buildup around Mortain. Eleventh-hour Ultra intelligence warned of an enemy attack and allowed the First Army at the last minute to shore up its defenses and to take good defensive positions for the onslaught.[117]

On 6 August, the Germans struck west in strength at Mortain toward Avranches on a 10,000-yard front with five divisions.[118] Despite reinforcement, U.S. forces were still thin on the ground and occupied unprepared positions. Moreover, the troops still had little experience in coordinating defensively, and the infantry lacked the antitank capability to repel concentrated enemy armored attacks. Though the enemy offensive demonstrated the weakness of towed U.S. antitank guns as the German push overran the 823d Tank Destroyer Battalion at Juvigny-Le Mesnil-Tove, the stubborn combined-arms defense of the 30th Division slowed and disrupted the enemy advance.[119]

The availability of the 4th Division in close reserve allowed the Americans to react immediately. Bradley recalled the 35th Division and counterattacked northeast between Mortain and Barenton. The understrength German forces, operating with tenuous supply lines, suffered repeated artillery and air attacks.[120] This combined-arms, air-ground defense halted the Germans well short of Avranches. In retrospect, the decisive factors in U.S. success were the stubborn combined-arms defense by the 30th Division, and the material and logistic weaknesses of the enemy strike force, against the background of a rapidly deteriorating German strategic position.[121] At the same time, the IX TAC flew deep interdiction and air superiority missions and inflicted heavy casualties on enemy forces retreating westward, steadily draining away German mobility as once again the cumulative logistic effects of interdiction attacks exceeded direct destruction of enemy equipment and vehicles. With the enemy forced to retreat in broad daylight, tactical air strikes inflicted very heavy damage.[122]

The thwarting of the Mortain counteroffensive presented Allied forces with opportunities to envelop and annihilate the German armies in Normandy, either between Argentan and Falaise or along the Seine River. Yet the Allies' failure to understand and conduct war at the operational level left them without a strategic blueprint to exploit success, which meant that they failed to capitalize on these opportunities. The improvised theater strategy that thus emerged in August allowed the enemy to evade annihilation in Normandy.[123] The unusual caution displayed by Bradley in the second week of August clearly reflected the lack of U.S. operational-level doctrine. As U.S. forces raced eastward to meet Montgomery's troops pushing south from Caen toward Falaise they became strung out and, again, short on supplies. Bradley believed his forces had become overextended and feared that continuing the advance beyond Argentan would both lead to friendly-fire casualties and a successful German breakout. A deteriorating supply situation, with fuel and ammunition stocks dropping sharply as the advance outran its logistic support, contributed to Bradley's caution.[124] Dwindling intelligence in the fluid conditions of August led Bradley to believe that the majority of the enemy had already slipped out of the pocket forming at Falaise. He planned instead to catch the Germans in a bigger trap along the Seine.[125] In reality, however, the enemy was still in the bag, and a U.S. push to Falaise would likely have produced a German catastrophe. But Bradley halted the advance on 13 August and did not resume it for five days, thus removing possibilities for complete victory in Normandy. Forced to improvise, Eisenhower and Bradley failed to see clearly and grasp firmly the opportunity that had presented itself.[126]

Instead, Bradley divided his forces and directed V Corps to the Seine, which left neither prong strong enough to defeat the enemy. The Americans had too little strength either to firmly close the door to the Falaise pocket at Argentan, or to thrust north along the Seine after the V Corps had stormed across the river at Mantes-Gassicourt on 19 August. By going for a classic double encirclement the Allies got neither.

During the breakout U.S. forces continued to innovate technically to augment their firepower. The 2d Armored Division made the first use by U.S. forces in the ETO of rocket artillery with tank-mounted T34 launchers.[127] Troops also relied heavily on mobile firepower during the pursuit. Self-propelled 155mm howitzers provided invaluable support for armored combat commands and improvised self-propelled light antiaircraft weapons, employed extensively for the first time in a ground support role, demonstrated their effectiveness.[128]

In sum, intimate interservice coordination and growing mastery of the combined-arms air-land battle brought success in Normandy. And the U.S. military did not simply bludgeon the enemy into defeat as conventional interpretation suggests.[129] U.S. troops fought under many limitations—poor coordination, inadequate infantry firepower, lack of preparation for bocage warfare, an inefficient replacement system, flawed attack doctrine, ammunition shortages, and tactics poorly suited to German defensive methods— that limited their combat effectiveness. Central to U.S. success, therefore, was the professional commitment by commanders and troops alike to evaluate honestly their combat performance, identify deficiencies, perfect new tactics and procedures, improvise new equipment, and retrain intensively in the field. As a result, U.S. forces enhanced their combat effectiveness during the campaign.

The most significant improvement occurred in interarms and interservice coordination. By August 1944, U.S. military coordination was superior to that of the Germans in their heyday in 1940 as the U.S. mastered the air-ground battle. American air power ably supported the ground battle in Normandy as fighter-bombers proved more accurate and deadly than heavy artillery. Moreover, the deep interdiction mission that tactical strike aircraft initially focused on exacerbated the already severe logistic difficulties the Germans faced on the American sector of the front and contributed directly to the ultimate German collapse (see Table 7.6).

Table 7.6   Allied Fighter-Bomber Sortie Claims in Normandy

Force	Sorties Flown	Claims Armor	Vehicles	Claims per Sortie
2d (British) TAF	9,896	257	3,340	0.36
IX (U.S.) TAC	2,891	134	2,520	0.92
Total	12,787	391	6,251	N/A

Sources: Hallion, *Strike from the Sky,* 227.

The greater territory overrun by the First Army allowed more U.S. squadrons to operate from airstrips on the Continent, which reduced response times and increased sortie ratios. Aircraft were also of high quality, the Republic P-47 Thunderbolt, in particular, proving a robust and flexible tactical strike aircraft that could absorb heavy punishment.[130] The U.S. Army Air Force (USAAF) also developed radar-guided vectoring onto targets, which allowed U.S. aircraft to conduct blind bombing strikes in poor visibility, as they did, for instance, during COBRA.[131] Use of radar brought greater flexibility to air support missions. The use of carpet bombing in direct support of American ground forces, though, brought mixed results. Used only once during COBRA, carpet bombing, despite heavy friendly-fire casualties, had a devastating, if ephemeral, demoralizing effect on veteran German troops. However, the resultant cratering of the terrain hampered movement on both sides.[132] The use of strategic bombers in COBRA, though playing a central role in the U.S. success, revealed that strategic bombing remained a novel, unpredictable, and dangerous instrument of ground warfare in summer 1944.

U.S. forces became more sophisticated in employing air power in support of the ground battle in other ways. Early in the campaign, technical advances in photoreconnaissance resulted in the fastest photo-processing and delivery service of the war. Photographs processed at airfields in the United Kingdom were passed to units in Normandy via a VHF facsimile radio channel, which allowed much faster intelligence dissemination. The detailed, rapid intelligence that this service provided facilitated the U.S. advance in August.[133] Air superiority and growing sophistication in the application of air power made a ground victory easier.

During the Normandy campaign U.S. forces perfected air-ground coordination, and by the end of the campaign the Americans had become adept practioners of the air-land battle. It had taken just three years for the USAAF to perfect this system. The testimony was that the Allied success in Normandy was the first genuine air-land battle victory of the war.

At the same time, U.S. Army quartermasters overcame many obstacles to keep the troops adequately, if not abundantly, supplied. Massive gasoline deliveries, in particular, kept fuel-hungry units mobile throughout the campaign.[134] The rationing of ammunition, which resulted from unanticipated expenditures in the hedgerows, was the only significant logistic deficiency experienced during the campaign.[135] Yet the American determination to devise new procedures to fight more effectively in the bocage, flexibility of commanders, army mobility, and growing skill in air-ground battle ensured that ammunition shortages did not significantly slow progress.

The U.S. Army thus mastered combined-arms warfare. The army's ability to learn on the battlefield, and to identify and implement lessons learned to enhance its effectiveness, was central to its success. The army innovated and adapted successfully because its peacetime doctrine, though flawed, was fundamentally sound.[136] The commitment of U.S. ground forces to combat in the ETO within a year of entering the war, in a peripheral theater that minimized German and maximized Allied strengths, allowed the U.S. Army to evaluate its doctrine, tactics, organization, and equipment and to revise procedures, reorganize, retrain, and reequip. Moreover, with sizable manpower and equipment reserves, the U.S. Army could afford to—and did—fight aggressively in Normandy.

The army's determination to learn on the battlefield during ongoing combat operations was critically important to victory. The ninety-division limit meant that few formations could be withdrawn from the front line at any given time, and thus the army had to retrain in the combat zone. British commanders who had observed U.S. forces both in earlier campaigns and in Normandy recognized that the Americans had enhanced their combat capabilities considerably since Tunisia. Prescient observers grudgingly conceded that U.S. combat effectiveness was superior to their own, and one British corps commander privately confided that "having seen a good deal of them recently, I think there is a lot to learn from them. Their cooperation is excellent."[137] However, prejudice and ignorance ensured that most British commanders continued to underestimate U.S. military capabilities.[138]

American adaptation and innovation occurred relatively rapidly and all across the spectrum of military effectiveness. Tactical and technical ingenuity, as well as operational flexibility characterized U.S. forces in Normandy. The U.S. Army was able, with experience, consistently to enhance its combat proficiency. Both the quality of basic training and of retraining in the field showed significant improvement by 1944 in comparison to earlier years. The result was that U.S. forces were able both to surmount virtually all the obstacles that confronted them in Normandy and, ultimately, to vanquish the enemy.

Notes

1. Michael Doubler, *Busting the Bocage: American Combined Arms Operations in France, 6 June–31 July 1944* (Fort Leavenworth: CSI, U.S. Army Command and General Staff College, 1988), 61–66; and *Closing with the Enemy: How G.I.s Fought the War in Europe, 1944–45* (Lawrence: Kansas University Press, 1994), 63–68.

2. FUSA, *Report on Ops., 1 August 1943–31 July 1944* (Paris: FUSA, [1944]) 14 vols.; FUSA, *Report on Ops., 1 August 1944–9 May 1945* (Germany: FUSA, 1945); TUSA, *Report on Ops.* (Germany: 1945); Elbridge Colby, *The First Army in Europe* (Washington, D.C.: GPO, 1969); Russell F. Weigley, *Eisenhower's Lieutenants: The Campaigns in France and Germany, 1944–1945* (Bloomington: Indiana University Press, 1981) Vol. I; Martin Blumenson, *Breakout and Pursuit* (Washington, D.C.: OCMH, 1961); Gordon Harrison, *Cross Channel Attack* (Washington, D.C.: OCMH, 1951; New York: BDD Books, 1993); *Omaha Beachhead* (Washington, D.C.: War Department Historical Division [hereafter WDHD], 1945); *Utah Beach to Cherbourg* (Washington, D.C.: WDHD, 1947); *St. Lô (7–19 July 1944)* (Washington, D.C.: WDHD, 1946; CMH, 1984).

3. "Dislokation 709 Inf. Div., 5.6.1944," in Kurt Mehner, *Die Geheimen Tagesberichte der deutschen Wehrmachtführung im Zweiten Weltkrieg, 1939–1945* (Osnabrück: Biblio, 1984), Bd. X, apdx.

4. Harrison, *Attack*, 305–328; Weigley, *Lieutenants*, 131–134; Joseph H. Ewing, *29 Let's Go* (Washington, D.C.: Infantry Journal Press, 1948); General Board U.S. Forces in the European Theater (hereafter GBUSFET) Rpt. 52, "Armored Special Equipment," 18–19.

5. NARA T-78, 142, "Gefechtsbericht 352 Inf. Div. Juni 44"; USAHD MS B-432, Lt. Col. Fritz Ziegelmann, "352d Infantry Division (5 Dec 1943–6 Jun 1944)," (Germany: 1947), 30–42; Harrison, *Attack,* 330–331; Edwin P. Hoyt, *The GI's War: American Soldiers in Europe During WWII* (New York: McGraw-Hill, 1988; Da Capo Press, 1988), 328–401; Stephen Ambrose, *D-Day, June 6, 1944: The Climactic Battle of World War II* (New York: Simon & Shuster, 1994), 254–485; Samuel E. Morison, *History of U.S. Naval Operations in WWII* (Boston: Little, Brown & Co., 1957) XI, 104–106, 143–148.

6. A third of the 101st Division landed over 8 miles from its drop zones and it lost 60 percent of its equipment. GBUSFET Rpt. 16, "Organization, Equipment, and Tactical Employment of the Airborne Division," 2–3; Harrison, *Attack,* 278–300; *Utah Beach,* 8–22; Leonard Rapport and Arthur Norwood, Jr., *Rendezvous with Destiny* (Washington D.C.: Infantry Journal Press, 1948); James Gavin, *On to Berlin: Battles of an Airborne Commander, 1943–46* (New York: Viking, l978); Samuel A. Marshall, *Night Drop: The American Airborne Invasion of Normandy* (Boston: Little, Brown & Co, 1962); Lawrence Critchell, *Four Stars of Hell* (New York: 1947), 52–54; Ambrose, *D-Day,* 196–239; James L. Cate and Wesley F. Craven, eds., *The Army Air Forces in WWII* (Chicago: University of Chicago Press, 1951), III, 187–189; USAHD MS B-839, Col. Frhr. v. d. Heydte, "6th Parachute Regiment (1 May–20 Aug 1944)" (Germany: 1947), 14–18.

7. Warships fired over 7,000 rounds against Omaha. FUSA, *Report* IV, 219ff; V, 177; GBUSFET Rpt. 61, "Study of Field Artillery Operations," 12–13; Harrison, *Attack,* 301–302, 322–326; Craven and Cate, *AAF* III, 190–194; Morison, *Naval Operations,* 104–106, 143–148.

8. FUSA, *Report* I, 118.

9. Alfred Beck et al., *The Corps of Engineers: The War Against Germany* (Washington, D.C.: OCMH, 1985); Harrison, *Attack,* 315–317.

10. The 4th Division attacked on a 7-mile front, gaining 3 miles on 7 June, but failed to capture the St. Marcouf naval battery that disrupted unloading operations on Utah Beach until 11 June. Though a daring commander, Collins's nickname derived not from swift combat maneuver but from his earlier command of the 25th ("Tropic Lightning") Division in the Pacific. Joseph L. Collins, *Lightning Joe: An Autobiography* (Baton Rouge: Louisiana State University, 1979), 205–207; Harrison, *Attack,* 341–348, 386–396.

11. The 90th Division could not advance westward during 9–11 June without help from the 82d Division, suffered heavy losses, abandoned Pont L'Abbé (12 June) and Gourbesville (14 June) when counterattacked, and earned itself the reputation of being a problem division. John Colby, *War From the Ground Up: The 90th Division in World War II* (Austin, Tex.: Nortex Press, 1991); *A History of the 90th Division in WWII* (Baton Rouge, La.: Army and Navy Publishing, 1946), 6–10; Weigley, *Lieutenants,* 145–147; *Utah Beach,* 129; Harrison, *Attack,* 351–356, 401–404.

12. The battered 352d Division defended a 30-mile front with 2,500 combatants. Faulty intelligence that suggested a German counterattack on Carentan on 9–10 June contributed to the Americans' hesitation. USAHD MS B-435, Lt. Col. Ziegelmann, "352d Division (7 Jun.–10 Jul. 1944)" (Germany: 1947), 1–12; Harrison, *Attack,* 336–341.

13. A hasty and piecemeal attack by the U.S. 175th Regiment across the Vire River brought setback on 12 June as the Germans ambushed and decimated a battalion and captured the regimental commander. Joseph Balkoski, *Beyond the Bridgehead* (Harrisburg, Pa.: Stackpole Books, 1989), 179–189, 196–203; Harrison, *Attack,* 367–368.

14. USAHD MS B-541, Lt. Gen. Richard Schimpf, "3d Parachute Division (Jan–Aug 1944)," (Germany: 1947), 16–17; Balkoski, *Bridgehead,* 190; Harrison, *Attack,* 371–376.

15. U.S. units' radio security was very bad and the codes transparent. The call sign for the V Corps was "V for Victor"! Balkoski, *Bridgehead,* 189–194; Harrison, *Attack,* 375–376.

16. Harrison, *Attack,* 380–384.

17. Broad-front attacks implemented the U.S. Army concept of the principles of concentration of effort and economy of force enshrined in *FM 100-5.* Maximum U.S. effort along the entire front, however, inflicted intolerable losses on the enemy and hastened the German collapse in the Cotentin. The German 91st Division, for example, suffered over 4,000 casualties in the first five days of the invasion and by mid-June could only muster 2,000 combatants. *FM 100-5, Field Service Regulations* (Washington, D.C.: GPO, 1941), 11–12; NARA T-311, 26, Lt. Col. Heilmann, Ic Ob. West, "Meldung über die Fährte zur 7 Armee vom 15-16.6.1944," 18 June 1944; Trevor N. Dupuy, *Understanding War: History and Theory of Combat* (London: Leo Cooper, 1992), 142; Charles Whiting, *Bradley* (New York: Ballantine Books, 1971), 23.

18. U.S. field artillery expenditures increased 50 percent during the second week. Heavy consumption resulted from efforts to compensate for poor observation, overcome the defensive advantages of the terrain, and sustain the morale of attacking infantry. FUSA, *Report* V, 185–186; GBUSFET Rpt. 58, "Ammunition Supply for Field Artillery," 14–15.

19. Between 15–17 June the First Army rationed field artillery to fifty rounds per gun and medium guns to forty rounds. FUSA, *Report* V, 185–186; GBUSFET 58, "Ammunition Supply for Field Artillery," 14.

20. FUSA, *Report* II, 7–90; Collins, *Lightning Joe,* 202–212.

21. Waddell, *Logistics,* 53–60; Ruppenthal, *Logistic Support* I, 389–426.

22. Collins, *Lightning Joe,* 206–216; Harrison, *Attack,* 404–416.

23. The IX TAC clearly hampered German resupply efforts in the Cotentin more effectively than the RAF did on the Caen front. The IX TAC's focus on interdiction, greater number and superior quality of strike aircraft, and greater availability of airfields on the Continent all added to its effectiveness. Moreover, German supply routes in the Cotentin were few and thus more vulnerable to attack. *FM 100-20 Command and Employment of Air Power* (Washington, D.C.: GPO, July 1943), 10–12; NARA, MMB, SHAEF/56/GX/1/INT, "Weekly Bridge Reports, May–July 1944"; USAHD MS A-865, Maj. Gen. R. von Gersdorff, "German Troop Movements (6 Jun–10 Aug. 1944)," (Germany: 1946), 1–3; Cate and Craven, *AAF* III, 198–99.

24. Morison, *Naval Operations,* 157–169; Basil Liddell Hart, ed., *The Rommel Papers* (London: Collins, 1953), 476–477; GBUSFET 58, "Ammunition Supply for Field Artillery," 14.

25. The garrison consisted of the battered 709th Division and a regiment of the 243d Division. By 24 June the former had lost 85 percent of its infantry. NARA T-78, 142, "Gefechtsbericht Kampfgruppe Hoffmann;" USAHD MS C-019, "Kampfgruppe Keil," 98–106.

26. The garrison comprised 25,000 troops, a few obsolete French tanks, and dozens of heavy flak guns. NARA T-78, 418, 6386950, OKH/GenStdH Org. Abt(I), "Heerestruppen auf der Halbinsel Cherbourg," Nr. I/17 633/44 g. Kdos, 22 June 1944; PRO DEFE 3/175, Ultra Decrypt KV 8956, "Strength Return, Battle Group Schlieben, 17 June 1944," 20 June 1944; PRO WO 219/1892, "Enemy Flak in the Neptune Area"; PRO WO 171/286, "Flak in Neptune Area" [early June 1944].

27. The air program involved 1,169 aircraft. Rear Adm. Morton "Mort" L. Deyo's Task Force 129 (3 battleships, 4 cruisers, and 11 destroyers) engaged German batteries on 25 June. Craven and Cate, *AAF* III, 199–201; Morison, *Naval Operations,* 195–212; Harrison, *Attack,* 428–429; Raymond Lefevre, *La Libération de Cherbourg* (Cherbourg: Commerciale Cherbourgeoise, 1946), 13–21; GBUSFET Rpt. 66, "Study of Organic Field Artillery Air Observation," 12.

28. Collins, *Lightning Joe,* 218–219; Harrison, *Attack,* 426–449.

29. USAHD MS C-019, "Kampfgruppe Keil," 104–119; Paul Carell, *Invasion—They're Coming* (London: Bantam, 1962), chap. 3.

30. FUSA, *Report* V, 182; Morison, *Naval Operations* XI, 213–215.

31. Arthur Davies, "Geographical Factors in the Invasion and Battle for Normandy," *Geographical Review* 36 (October 1946), 613–631.

32. Only in May did the Allies consider operations in the bocage. On 7 May SHAEF stated that "it is difficult to judge whether such terrain favors the defending or attacking infantry." PRO WO 205/118, "Appreciation of Possible Development of Operations to Secure a Lodgement Area—Operation OVERLORD," 7 May 1944, 4.

33. Poor coordination was evident in the 29th, 83d, and 90th Divisions. FUSA, *Report* I, 117–122; U.S. Army Ground Forces Observer Board, ETO (hereafter USAGFOB) Rpt. 157, "Notes on Interviews with Various Infantry Commanders in Normandy, 5–10 Aug. 1944," 5; Richard S. Faulkner, "Learning the Hard Way: The Coordination Between Infantry Divisions and Separate Tank Battalions During the Breakout from Normandy," *Armor* 99 (July–August 1990), 24–29.

34. GBUSFET Rpt. 15, "Organization, Equipment, and Employment of the Infantry Division," 8; USAGFOB Rpt. 195, "Lessons from the Present Campaign, 4th and 9th Divisions," 28 August 1944.

35. Doubler, *Busting,* 23–26.

36. The bocage, for example, seriously hampered deployment of the towed guns of infantry cannon companies. GBUSFET Rpt. 15, "Employment of the Infantry Division," 5–6.

37. Doubler, *Busting,* 25–27.

38. Officer casualties in three infantry divisions up to 31 July averaged 79.5 percent. Samuel A. Stouffer et al., *Studies in Social Psychology in WWII* (Princeton, N.J.: Princeton University Press, 1949) II, 8ff.

39. Doubler, *Busting,* 22–23.

40. The 29th Division's 12 June assault across the Elle River exemplifies the inadequacy of U.S. Army attack doctrine. Doubler, *Busting,* 22–23; Harrison, *Attack,* 366–375.

41. Doubler, *Busting,* 23, 27–29.

42. Preinvasion combined-arms training had focused on infantry-artillery cooperation. GBUSFET Rpt. 15, "Employment of the Infantry Division," 13.

43. Poor coordination, for example, brought defeat at Villers-Fossard on 20 June. Harrison, *Attack,* 381–384.

44. During 20–22 June only 8 percent of scheduled supplies arrived, and a further 140,000 tons were delayed or destroyed. Not until early July did cargo discharges return to prestorm levels. Consequently the First Army restricted artillery fire to thirty rounds per gun between 22–24 June. FUSA, *Report* V, 183–186; VIII, 183; Waddell, *Logistics,* 60–68; Ruppenthal, *Logistic Support,* 416–421, 427–474; Harrison, *Attack,* 423–426; GBUSFET Rpt. 130, "Supply and Maintenance on the European Continent," 10–17; GBUSFET Rpt. 100, "Ammunition Supply and Operations, European Campaign," 7–9.

45. As early as 9 June, the First Army had begun to grapple with these problems. Doubler, *Busting,* 30.

46. Ibid., 30.

47. From 3 July, the First Army redistributed all mortars from independent tank, artillery, and tank destroyer battalions, and on 24 July stripped all grenade launchers from noncombat units. NARA WNRC, RG 407, V Corps G4, Daily Journal, 3 July 1944 and 24 July 1944.

48. Many rifle companies formed assault sections equipped with bazookas. GBUSFET Rpt. 15, "Employment of the Infantry Division," 8; Henry Grader Spencer, "Hedgerow Fighting: Baptism in the Hedgerows," *Infantry Journal* 55 (October 1944), 10; James D. Sams, "Ordnance Improvisation in the Combat Zone," *Military Affairs* 28 (May 1948), 35; Balkoski, *Bridgehead,* 84; Waddell, *Logistics,* 76–78; Blumenson, *Breakout,* 205; Beck, *Engineers,* 369.

49. Workshops improvised 320 M16Bs during the campaign. FUSA, *Report* V, 261.

50. The 29th Division in particular had "an amazing knack for acquiring extra, unofficial weapons." Balkoski, *Bridgehead,* 84.

51. FUSA, *Report* V, 177–179, 272–273.

52. Captured German light field howitzers expended 30,000 rounds during the campaign. FUSA, *Report on Operations, 23 February–8 May 1945* (hereafter FUSA, *Report*), anx. IV, 21; GBUSFET Rpt. 60, "Organization, Equipment, and Tactical Employment of Tank Destroyer Units," 2–3, 13–14; GBUSFET Rpt. 100, "Ammunition Supply," apdx. 7.

53. The number of WP rounds fired increased from 5,091 during 11–17 June to 7,477 during 9–15 July. Such was its popularity that stocks ashore were perpetually low, and on 15 July the U.S. First Army had only 3,060 155mm WP rounds ashore. FUSA *Report* V, 182–186; Leo P. Brophy, Wyndham D. Miles, and Rexmond C. Cochrane, *The Technical Services: The Chemical Warfare Service: from Laboratory to Field* (Washington, D.C.: GPO, 1959), 197; Waddell, *Logistics,* table 4–3, 84; GBUSFET Rpt. 58, "Ammunition Supply," 18.

54. From 20 to 22, June the First Army airlifted 1,500 tons of munitions to Normandy and a total of 6,620 tons by 31 July. Airlift remained, however, a novel and limited means of resupply. During the campaign, the First Army fired 7,000 French 155mm rounds and 300,000 German 81mm mortar shells. FUSA, *Report* I, 80; GBUSFET Rpt. 58, "Ammunition Supply," 14; GBUSFET Rpt.100, "Ammunition Supply," apdx. 7; GBUSFET Rpt. 130, "Supply & Maintenance," 102–103; Ruppenthal, *Logistic Support,* 448.

55. During the week of 9–15 July the First Army averaged 69,974 artillery rounds fired daily, compared with only 7,965 rounds per day up to 10 June. As a result, stockpiles ashore fell by one-third and the First Army had to extend rationing. FUSA, *Report* V, 185–186; VI, 70–71.

56. On 1 June the First Army had only 105 of its authorized 390 'dozer tanks. GBUSFET Rpt. 52, "Armored Special Equipment," 14–16.

57. Doubler, *Busting,* 31–32; Blumenson, *Breakout,* 206.

58. FUSA, *Report* I, 122; Doubler, *Busting,* 30–35; Bradley, *Soldier's Story,* 342; Eisenhower, *Crusade in Europe,* 269.

59. In an infantry company attack supported by a tank platoon only three radios operated on the same frequency, James Butler, "Individual Tank-Infantry Communications," *Armored Cavalry Journal* 56 (July–August 1947), 43–45.

60. GBUSFET 50, "Organization, Equipment, and Tactical Employment of Separate Tank Battalions," 4–7; Doubler, *Busting,* 35–36.

61. GBUSFET Rpt. 60, "Tank Destroyer Units," 15–16.

62. Seven pooled battalions each fought continuously in northwest Europe with the same division: the 745th and 746th Tank Battalions (1st and 9th Divisions); the 612th, 630th, and 644th Tank Destroyer Battalions (2d, 1st, 8th Divisions); and the 376th and 445th Antiaircraft Auto-Weapons Battalions (9th and 8th Divisions). Shelby Stanton, *World War II Order of Battle* (New York: Galahad, 1984), 77–79, 89–91.

63. The 746th Tank Battalion, for example, served with three divisions between 12 June–16 July. Faulkner, "Learning the Hard Way," 25.

64. GBUSFET Rpt. 20, "Liaison Aircraft with Ground Force Units," 6–7.

65. FUSA, *Report* V, 180–181; GBUSFET Rpt. 20, "Liaison Aircraft," 6.

66. Normandy. FUSA, *Report* 2, anx. 4, 16–17.

67. Russell F. Weigley, *The American Way of War: A History of U.S. Military Strategy and Policy* (New York: MacMillan, 1973; Bloomington: Indiana University Press, 1977), 312–359.

68. The St. Marcouf repulse (7–9 June), the Aure Valley ambush, and the Sèves "island" debacle (23 July) were all partly due to haste.

69. By early July, senior U.S. Army commanders had come to believe that the British were not pulling their weight. Eisenhower on 7 July criticized Montgomery because he had not attempted "a major full dress attack on the left flank supported by everything we could bring to bear." Liddell Hart Centre for Military Archives (LHCMA), King's College, London, Alanbrooke Papers AP14/27, fol. 7.

70. FUSA, *Report* I, 81–82; Colby, *First Army,* 44–46; USAHD MS A-983, Genltnt. Paul Mahlmann, "353d Division (24 Jul–14 Sep. 1944)," 3–4; B-418, Gen. Dietrich von Choltitz, "LXXXIV Corps (18 Jun–15 Jul. 1944)," 22–24; Blumenson, *Breakout,* 53–77, 123–128; Dieter Choltitz, *Soldat unter Soldaten* (Konstanz: Europa, 1951), 187; *A History of the 90th Division in WWII* (Baton Rouge, La.: Army and Navy Publishing), 11–15.

71. The division, supported by the 746th Tank Battalion, gained 1,600 yards at a cost of 2,800 casualties and "heavy" tank losses. FUSA, *Report* V, 198; Blumenson, *Breakout,* 78–88; Doubler, *Busting,* 49–50; Collins, *Lightning Joe,* 228–229; *Thunderbolt Across Europe: History of the 83d Infantry Division, 1942–45* (Munich: F. Brackman, n.d.), 29–33.

72. Blumenson, *Breakout,* 86.

73. Colby, *First Army,* 50–51.

74. Blumenson, *Breakout,* 90–144; *St. Lô,* 9–14; Robert L. Hewitt, *Workhorse of the Western Front: The Story of the 30th Infantry Division* (Washington, D.C.: Infantry Journal Press, 1946), 26ff; Beck, *Engineers,* 371–374.

75. Doubler, *Busting,* 39–43.

76. *St. Lô,* 51–58; Blumenson, *Breakout,* 153–57.

77. *St. Lô,* 58–68.

78. Balkoski, *Bridgehead,* chap. 5; Doubler, *Busting,* 48–49.

79. Colby, *First Army,* 49–50; Blumenson, *Breakout,* 159–174.

80. Improved coordination was apparent in the 2d, 29th, 30th, 83d, and 90th Divisions. Faulkner, "Learning the Hard Way," 24–29.

81. The capture of St. Lô had cost the First Army 40,000 casualties. And the U.S. forces had not quite reached the more open terrain (the line Caumont—St. Lô—Coutances) required for a breakthrough attempt. Prior to COBRA, the U.S. First Army launched several hasty limited attacks to obtain a better start line. The decimation of a battalion of the 90th Division during the Sèves "island" disaster of 22–23 July illustrated the danger of excessive haste when combined with inadequate resources.

82. The fire at Depot 101 destroyed 1,500 tons of munitions and led to a major shortage of 81mm mortar rounds that forced tight rationing on 15 July. On 25 July

the First Army rationed fire support for COBRA to a mere three to fifteen rounds per gun. Field artillery expenditures between 23–29 July averaged twenty rounds per gun, one-quarter of previous rates. FUSA, *Report* V, 185–186; VI, 71; Lida Mayo, *The Ordnance Department: On Beachhead and Battlefront* (Washington, D.C.: GPO, 1968), 251; Waddell, *Logistics,* 83–86; GBUSFET Rpt. 58, "Ammunition Supply," 15–16.

83. By 31 July, U.S. casualties had passed 100,000 and the 29th Division alone had suffered 9,939 casualties. Many rifle companies were down to less than half their strength. The ETO U.S. Army had furnished infantry replacements calculating that they would make up 70.3 percent of casualties, whereas, in actuality, up to 31 July they amounted to 85 percent. As a result, the First Army had to make an emergency request for 25,000 additional infantry replacements.

84. Up to 31 July, casualties among rifle companies in three infantry divisions were 79.5 percent for officers and 73.5 percent for other ranks. In the 29th Division three days in the line earned a rifleman the title of an "old" soldier. Stouffer, *Studies* II, 8ff; Balkoski, *Bridgehead,* 220.

85. On 17 July, for example, the 3d Battalion, 115th Infantry Regiment was down to 20 percent of its strength. Balkoski, *Bridgehead,* 262.

86. Only the elite U.S. airborne forces lacked replacements. FUSA, *Report* IV, 22–23.

87. New replacements were more likely to become casualties, and as a result units with many raw replacements suffered disproportionate losses. Despite the drawbacks of the replacement system, U.S. infantry remained cohesive throughout the campaign. Up to 24 July military police had apprehended only 228 stragglers. FUSA, *Report* V, 81; Blumenson, *Breakout,* 198–204.

88. A replacement system on German lines would have prevented the continuous flow of replacements to the front and forced the army to raise many more than the ninety divisions it did in order to rotate divisions out of line for rest and rehabilitation. Balkoski, *Bridgehead,* 227–228.

89. Between 27 June and 25 July, the number of German infantry battalions assigned to LXXXIV Corps more than doubled and armored strength nearly tripled. The conventional view that sustained attrition had crippled German resistance simply does not fit the evidence. The loss of St. Lô, however, did ensure that the German defenses were thinner and the troops were concentrated more forward than doctrine advocated. NARA T-314, 1604, "Meldung LXXXIV A.K. v. 27.6.1944."

90. FUSA, *Report* I, 96–99; V, 199–200; Colby, *First Army,* 56–62; Collins, *Lightning Joe,* 232–236; Blumenson, *Breakout,* 187–188, 197–223.

91. Despite heavy losses, most formations remained near full strength throughout the campaign. The 1st Division, for example, was short only 260 grenade launchers, 19 bazookas, and 3 mortars on 31 July. NARA WNRC, RG 407, 1st Division, "Rpt. on Activities, G4 Section, July 1944," 4 August 1944, 2–3; Blumenson, *Breakout,* 210.

92. Up to 1 August the U.S. First Army discharged, transferred, or reassigned 126 officers, including 8 colonels, 5 lieutenant colonels, and 4 majors. Including battle casualties, the First Army replaced no fewer than 27 colonels and 52 lieutenant colonels during the campaign. FUSA, *Report* V, 69–70.

93. FUSA, *Report* V, 198–199; Balkoski, *Bridgehead,* 231–233; Faulkner, "Learning the Hard Way," 26.

94. General Collins subsequently denied that COBRA was intended only as a breakthrough operation. Collins, *Lightning Joe,* 236; Maj. Cole C. Kingseed, "The Falaise-Argentan Encirclement: Operationally Brilliant, Tactically Flawed," *Military Review* (December 1984), 2–11.

95. FUSA, *Report* V, 182.

96. Some 3,300 planes, including 1,800 heavy and 396 medium bombers and 559 fighter-bombers, plus 500 fighters, participated, making it the largest air operation in support of ground forces up to that time. The short bombing on 24–25 July caused 757 casualties and killed Lt. Gen. Lesley J. McNair, the Army Ground Forces commander. Craven and Cate, *AAF*, III, 231–234; Blumenson, *Breakout*, 222–223, 229, 234–236; Bradley, *Story*, 341.

97. Forward concentration exacerbated German losses from the bombing. John J. Sullivan, "The Botched Air Support of Operation COBRA," *Parameters* 18 (March 1988), 97–110; USAHD MS A-902, Lt. Gen. Fritz Bayerlein, "Pz. Lehr Division (24–25 Jul 1944)," 1–4; ETHINT-69, Bayerlein, "Pz. Lehr Division at the Start of Operation COBRA (24–25 Jul 1944)" (Germany: 1945), 1–2.

98. The abortive attack of 24 July actually aided COBRA because it caused the German artillery to open up and reveal its location, which greatly aided the CB program the next day. Blumenson, *Breakout*, 238–239.

99. Between 25–30 July the First Army expended 136,147 artillery rounds. FUSA, *Report* V, 183; GBUSFET Rpt. 61, "Field Artillery Operations," 19–20.

100. Collins, *Lightning Joe*, 241–242; Blumenson, *Breakout*, 241–246; Cate and Craven, *AAF* III, 236–237.

101. Russell A. Hart, "Feeding Mars: Logistics and the German Defeat in Normandy, June–August 1944," *War in History* 3, 4 (Fall 1996), 418–435.

102. Blumenson, *Breakout*, 249–263.

103. Ibid., 264–275.

104. The German force comprised elements of the 2d SS Panzer, 17th SS Panzergrenadier, 77th, 91st, 243d, and 353d Infantry Divisions, and the 6th Parachute Regiment. Blumenson, *Breakout*, 275–290; Choltitz, *Soldat unter Soldaten*, 208–209.

105. During 25–31 July, the IX TAC flew 9,840 missions. Cate and Craven, *AAF* III, 242.

106. Although *FM 100–20* declared that close air support was only a tertiary priority of air power, by mid-July such missions had risen to 70 percent of all IX TAC missions. *FM 100–20, Air Power*, 1–2; Blumenson, *Breakout*, 207; Thomas Hughes, *OVERLORD: General Pete Quesada and the Triumph of Tactical Air Power in World War II* (New York: Free Press, 1995), chaps. 5–8.

107. The 1st Armored Division first used the Horsefly system in Italy during June 1944. GBUSFET 20, "Liaison Aircraft," 14–19.

108. Air support parties were later redesignated TALOs (Tactical Air Liaison Officers). Lewis H. Brereton, *The Brereton Diaries: The War in the Air* (New York: Morrow, 1946), 311; Bradley, *Story*, 337–338.

109. FUSA, *Report* V, 200–201; XIX TAC Report, TUSA, Report on Operations, 1.8.1944–9.5.1945 I, Annex 3, 2; USAHD MS B-723, Maj. Gen. Rudolf Fhr. von Gersdorff, "Breakthrough to Avranches" (Germany: 1947), 1–38.

110. Blumenson, *Breakout*, 208.

111. U.S. forces destroyed 66 tanks, 11 artillery pieces, and 204 motor vehicles, and took 4,000 prisoners. Collins, *Lightning Joe*, 245; Blumenson, *Breakout*, 278–281. USAHD MS B-839, Heydte, "6th Parachute Regiment," 78–80.

112. On 25 July the IX TAC flew seventy-two squadron armored column cover missions. Cate and Craven, *AAF* III, 238–242.

113. By late August response times of three minutes were possible. Cate and Craven, *AAF* III, 197; GBUSFET Rpt. 54, "The Tactical Air Force in the ETO," 2–3.

114. The simplicity of the system for covering armor contributed to its effectiveness. Hallion, *Strike from the Sky: The History of Battlefield Air Attack, 1911–45* (Washington, D.C.: Smithsonian Institution Press, 1988), 199–203; AAF

Evaluation Board in the ETO, *The Effectiveness of Third Phase Tactical Air Ops. in the European Theater, 5 May 1944–8 May 1945* (Dayton, Oh.: Wright Field, 1958); Cate and Craven, *AAF* III, 239–240.

115. Colby, *First Army,* 62–67.

116. "Rhinos" helped U.S. forces advance through the thinning bocage territory southeast of St. Lô. FUSA, *Report* V, 200–201; Blumenson, *Breakout,* 207; Bradley, *Story,* 342.

117. A myth of the battle for Mortain is that Ultra forewarned Bradley and allowed him to set a trap. In reality, Ultra provided Bradley with only a few hours of advance warning, and front-line units as few as twenty minutes. Blumenson, *Breakout,* 419–475; Ralph Bennett, *Ultra in the West: The Normandy Campaign* (New York: Scribner, 1980), 113–115; Frances W. Winterbotham *The Ultra Secret* (New York: Harper & Row, 1974), 148–150; Alwyn Featherstone, *Saving the Breakout: the 30th Division Stand at Mortain, August 7–12, 1944* (Novato, Calif.: Presidio Press, 1993), 69–74.

118. The attack force comprised the 17th SS Panzergrenadier and 1st SS, 2d, 2d SS, and 116th Panzer Divisions. USAHD B-179, Lt. Gen. Paul Hausser, "Attack Toward Avranches" (Germany: 1947); Blumenson, *Breakout,* 457–465.

119. Featherstone, *Saving the Breakout,* 69–74; Hewitt, *Workhorse,* 48–78; Blumenson, *Breakout,* 465–475; Lloyd J. Karamales et al., *U.S. Antitank Defense at Mortain, France (Aug. 1944)* (McLean, Va.: SAIC, 1990), 48–55, 67–78; Robert A. Miller, *August 1944* (New York: Warner Books, 1988), 69–71.

120. Another myth about the Battle for Mortain is that tactical aviation halted the German offensive. John Golley, *Day of the Typhoon: Flying with the RAF Tank-busters in Normandy* (Wellingborough: Patrick Stephens, 1986), 123–134; Hallion, *Strike,* 216–217. For a more realistic assessment of the role of fighter-bombers at Mortain, see FUSA, *Report* I, 5; TUSAG, *Report* V, 36; Milton Schulman, *Defeat in the West* (London: Ballantine, 1968), 148; Cate and Craven, *AAF* III, 248–249.

121. Featherstone, *Saving,* 57–119; Hewitt, *Workhorse,* 54–57.

122. During August, the XIX TAC alone flew 12,292 fighter-bomber sorties and claimed 4,058 motor vehicles, 466 armored fighting vehicles, 246 locomotives, and 181 river craft. Historical Evaluation Research Organization (HERO), *Interdiction from Falaise to Westwall, 14 August–14 September 1944* (Fairfax, Va.: HERO, n.d.), 167–168.

123. Carlo D'Este, *Decision in Normandy: The Unwritten Story of Montgomery and the Allied Campaign* (London: Collins, 1983), 405; Whiting, *Bradley,* 26–31.

124. Waddell, *Logistics,* 141; Ruppenthal, *Logistic Support,* 474–543.

125. The value of Ultra intelligence increased in August as the collapse of German ground communications forced formations to rely more heavily on radio communication. PRO DEFE 3/162–75, Ultra Decrypts, June–August 1944.

126. Blumenson, *Breakout,* 479–589; Dennis D. Dowd, "The Battle of the Falaise Pocket: Differing Interpretations," M.A. thesis, Creighton University, 1982; Cate and Craven, *AAF* III, 257.

127. The T34 consisted of sixty 4.5-inch launchers mounted on a Sherman tank. They were not a great success due to their short range, significant blast, and the quality of German counterbattery fire. Rockets thus continued to play little role in the U.S. arsenal. GBUSFET Rpt. 52, "Armored Special Equipment," 41.

128. FUSA, *Report* 2, Anx. VI, 72–73; GBUSFET Rpt. 17, "Types of Divisions, Post War Army," 12.

129. John Ellis, *Brute Force: Allied Strategy and Tactics in WWII* (New York: Viking, 1990); Weigley, *Lieutenants,* passim.

130. Cate and Craven, *AAF* III, 240.

131. Hallion, *Strike from the Sky,* 196–199.

132. USAHD MS ETHINT-69, Bayerlein, "Panzer Lehr Division," 1–2.

133. National Archives of Canada (NAC) RG 24 v. 9823, File 2/Ops Disp/1, DTI, Battle Study 4, "The Influence on the Battle of Improved Signals Facilities" [1945], 10; GBUSFET Rpt. 19, "Utilization of Tactical Air Force Recon. Units of the AAF to Secure Information for Ground Forces in the ETO," 5–10.

134. William F. Ross and Charles F. Romanus, *The Quartermaster Corps: Operations in the War Against Germany* (Washington, D.C.: OCMH, 1985), 485–543, 647–653; GBUSFET Rpt. 108, "Service Operations of the QMC"; GBUS-FET Rpt. 109, "Quartermaster Supply Operations."

135. Waddell's recent study exaggerates the flaws of the U.S. Army supply system and erroneously claims that it came close to failing. With the exception of munitions, logisticians kept U.S. forces remarkably well supplied throughout the campaign. See, for example, NARA RG 407, 1st Division, "Report on Activities, G4 Section, July 1944," 4 August 1944, 2–3.

136. Doubler, *Closing,* 2.

137. Letter, Richard O'Connor to Lady O'Connor, 18 August 1944, quoted in Richard Baynes, *Forgotten Victor: General Sir Richard O'Connor* (London: Brassey, 1989), 224.

138. Montgomery's support of Bradley's stop order of 12 August reflected his underestimation of American fighting skill and mobility. Brian Holden Reid, "Tensions in the Supreme Command: Anti-Americanism in the British Army, 1939–45," in *American Studies: Essays in Honour of Marcus Cunliffe* (New York: St. Martin's, 1991).

8

Britain: Montgomery's Best Batsmen Fail

The troops have not the spirit essential to victory, our morale frightens me.

—Brig. James Hargest, observer in the XXX Corps, Normandy, Summer 1944[1]

If Tommy was a bit more of a soldier, he could push us anywhere he wanted to.

—*Panzergrenadier,* 21st Panzer Division, Caen, Normandy, 17 July 1944[2]

When one goes deeply into the Normandy operations, it is disturbing and depressing to find how bad our performance was.

—Basil Liddell Hart, private correspondence, 1952[3]

The eventual totality of Allied victory in Normandy has obscured the British Army's lackluster performance in the campaign.[4] British troops proved less flexible, adaptable, and effective than their U.S. counterparts and were unable to overcome enemy defenses. At the same time, mounting losses sapped morale and led to a deterioration in performance as the campaign progressed. British operations remained wedded to a methodical and mechanistic attack doctrine built around the battalion assault and massive coordinated fire plans. But British infantry still lacked firepower, confidence, and independence, and thus rarely reconnoitered aggressively or attempted to outflank the enemy. While the infantry proved stoic in the face of frontal assaults, they remained vulnerable to enemy infiltration and flanking attacks, giving the Germans local successes out of all proportion to the meager resources committed. Infantrymen panicked easily and were often "mortared off" or "shelled" out of their positions, and so had to retake the same objectives repeatedly.[5]

The continued variable performance of British formations was as striking. While elite units, like the 6th Airborne Division and the commandos, and a few well-trained and well-led divisions (the 11th Armoured in particular) fought well, the aggregate was unimpressive because the diversion of quality personnel into elite units underlay the mediocre performance of many regular formations. Performance in Normandy paralleled previous campaigns: the troops performed reasonably well in defense, but they experienced difficulty on the attack.[6] Moreover, the army found it difficult to sustain its combat power as the campaign progressed because operational rigidity and poor coordination denied decisive success. British forces would break into German positions during major operations, but were generally unable to break through German defenses. Moreover, as the campaign progressed and casualties mounted, both the conception and execution of British attacks deteriorated. The evidence thus indicates that British troops were incapable of executing a successful breakout from Normandy.

British problems were most starkly revealed at the moment of the Americans' triumph in late July. After the COBRA breakout, Miles Dempsey, commander of the British Second Army, launched his own breakout bid, BLUECOAT, a drive on Mont Pinçon and the town of Vire, which failed ignominiously. Because of this failure and waning British strength, Montgomery was unable to shut the door of the Falaise pocket in mid-August, or to trap the Germans against the Seine—failures that allowed the *Westheer* to escape from Normandy, reform during the fall, and launch the Ardennes counteroffensive of December 1944.[7]

The army's culture and traditions, the baneful legacies of the Great War, and the resultant interwar neglect continued to impede British performance in Normandy. The amateurism and class consciousness that pervaded the army hampered British efforts to solve the problems the troops faced. The army's social stratification and the gulf between the officer corps, dominated by the middle and upper classes, and the rank and file retarded development of initiative and independence among noncommissioned officers (NCOs). Class consciousness affected British performance in Normandy more than might otherwise have been the case because of the campaign's heavy officer losses. The traditional rigid subordination of British NCOs worked against their taking control of units whose officers became casualties.[8] British attacks often stalled when officers were incapacitated, and many units lost their fighting edge as officer casualties mounted. Class concerns also made army leadership less than receptive to ideas from the troops, and so the army continued to adapt largely from the top down.[9]

The traditionalism enshrined in the British regimental system also continued to retard development of the interarms and interservice coordination that modern war demanded. Emphasis on former glories led each branch of service to guard jealously its sacred independence. The wartime army, therefore, never developed a holistic combined-arms doctrine; its approach remained that of "joint ops," the loose cooperation of independent arms

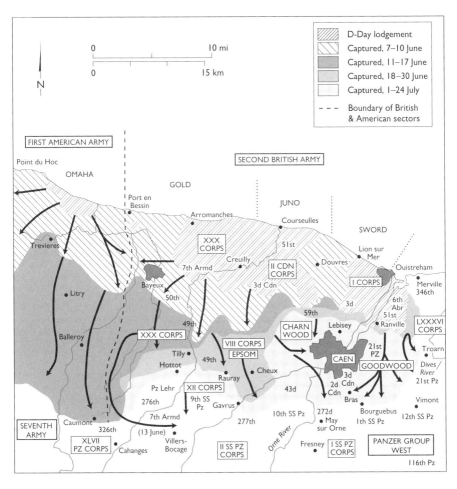

The Anglo-Canadian Bridgehead, D-Day to 24 July 1944

working alongside one another. Thus in Normandy, as before, different arms continued to fight their own wars.[10] Armor-infantry coordination remained poor; and only the Royal Artillery, because of its traditional support role, took combined-arms operations seriously.[11] At the same time, regimentalism bred decentralized training that brought great variation in training quality and performance by formations.

Britain's most serious historical problem, however, was the absence of a great military tradition as a land power. The less martial nature of British society, accentuated by interwar pacifism, meant that Britain fielded an essentially civilian army, in which indoctrination, propaganda, and training failed to promote military professionalism. The army's culture, structure, doctrine, and organization forged a ground force that was predictably slow to adapt.

British forces firmly established themselves ashore on D-Day, thanks to pronounced numerical and material superiority, months of meticulous preparation, and, in no small measure, absorption of lessons from previous amphibious assaults. In particular, the drop of the 6th Airborne Division in a tactical role east of the Orne River to protect the vulnerable left flank of the landing from armored counterattack showed that the War Office had learned from its overambitious use of airborne forces in TORCH and HUSKY and of the danger posed by panzer counterthrusts encountered in Sicily and at Salerno and Anzio.[12] Montgomery did fail to capture his D-Day goal of Caen; but the expectation that it could be taken quickly was unrealistic, despite his uncharacteristic demand that the assault troops push boldly inland.[13]

Despite this exhortation to audacity, after D-Day the British advance quickly stalled as powerful German armored reserves converged on Caen to drive the Anglo-Canadians back into the sea. Montgomery beat off these counterthrusts, but he was unable to advance in the face of the German armor, and the struggle for Caen bogged down into a grim six-week battle of attrition.

That OVERLORD planners had gravely underestimated the terrain's defensive advantages contributed to Montgomery's difficulties.[14] East of Bayeux the bocage hedgerows petered out into the Campagne de Caen, a plain stretching from Tilly to Troan that wrapped Caen inside a tight village grid pattern that provided a powerful, natural defense system in depth with excellent fields of interlocking fire. Topography thus forced Montgomery to assault Caen frontally, and placed the onus of combat squarely on the infantry as he waged a bloody battle of attrition that bled the British infantry dry.

This unforeseen reality reflected a fundamental flaw in the OVER-LORD plan, which was oriented toward two objectives: how to get ashore in sufficient force on D-Day to establish a viable lodgement, and how to exploit a breakout. Indeed, the British force structure—with its full motorization and large numbers of fast cruiser tanks—clearly was geared toward an exploitation role. Yet the plan barely addressed the most difficult task the Allies faced: how to convert a lodgement into a breakout. That British forces had barely planned, let alone prepared, for the breakout battle added greatly to the problems they faced, and helps to explain why they became bogged down before Caen for nearly two months.[15]

Montgomery's task was all the more formidable because he faced the best German formations in the West. Although the overall quality of enemy forces encountered was lower than in North Africa and Italy, Montgomery engaged an unprecedented number of German elite units because Hitler and his generals believed that Caen was the linchpin of the outcome in the West. Thus, there soon gathered a heavy concentration of German armor facing the British forces.[16] While the Canadians struggled with the formidable 12th SS Panzer Division, *Hitlerjugend,* the British fought their old desert rival, the 21st Panzer Division rebuilt around Africa Corps veterans, and the new Panzer *Lehr* Division formed from veteran instructors (and the best equipped division in the *Heer*).[17] As a result, until the U.S. Army breakout from Normandy in late July, the British sector attracted the greater proportion of German forces, including nearly all the elite units and most of the armor (see Table 8.1).[18] At the same time, the restricted size of the Allied bridgehead gave the Germans a relatively short front that allowed them to develop powerful defenses in depth that presented Montgomery with the strongest opposition he had ever encountered.

Table 8.1   **Allied Estimates of German Armor in U.S. and British Sectors, June–July 1944**

Date	U.S Zone	British Zone	Total	Ratio
15 June	70	520	590	12:88
30 June	140	725	865	26:74
10 July	190	610	800	16:84
20 July	190	560	750	25:75
25 July	190	645	835	23:77

Source: John Ellis, *Brute Force: Allied Strategy and Tactics in the Second World War* (New York: Viking, 1990), 377.

Manpower and morale concerns also profoundly affected Montgomery's conduct of the campaign. He refused to take risks that might result in heavy losses or a major setback, for his command was a wasting asset with finite manpower and fragile morale. Above all else, Montgomery feared that a major setback would tarnish his aura of invincibility, upon which the army's confidence and morale rested heavily.[19]

Because of planning flaws, the defensive advantages of the terrain, strong enemy defenses, and morale and manpower concerns, British forces were stuck before Caen for six weeks, during which the infantry suffered severe losses. Casualties among riflemen exceeded preinvasion estimates by more than 25 percent. That the War Office had to add a new "double intense" level to the Evett Rates, their casualty forecast charts, demonstrated how unprepared the British were for the campaign's bloodshed.[20] Moreover, as Montgomery had feared, heavy losses resulted in morale and discipline problems with the infantry. The esprit de corps of the 6th Battalion, the Duke of Wellington's Regiment, 49th Division, for example, sank so low that Montgomery had to disband the battalion in late June. Sinking morale was evident in mounting rates of absence without leave and self-inflicted wounds that were evidently much higher than in the U.S. forces.[21]

The most serious morale and discipline problems materialized among the veteran desert divisions. After their triumphs in the Mediterranean, these formations expected rest and rehabilitation. But the army's inexperience necessitated their reemployment in northwest Europe, which generated much "ill feeling" and "considerable unrest" in the divisions in Britain during the spring of 1944.[22] Once ashore in Normandy these formations proved unable, or unwilling, to adapt to theater combat conditions, as the debacle of the 7th Armoured Division at Villers-Bocage on 13 June demonstrated. Its spearhead advanced without adequate reconnaissance, as if it were still in the open desert, and was duly ambushed and all but annihilated by the lone Tiger tank of Lt. Michael Wittman, the leading German tank ace, in one of the most spectacular single-tank actions of the war.[23] Likewise, the "stickiness" of the 51st Division led Montgomery to brand the formation "not battleworthy" in mid-July.[24]

Limited firepower added to the difficulties that British forces faced. British troops remained less well equipped than the enemy, in every category except indirect-fire artillery. The British had no equivalent to either the German dual-purpose Flak 88, the heavy antiaircraft gun with a formidable antitank capability, or to the *Nebelwerfer,* the multibarreled, rocket-propelled German mortar, which caused many casualties in Normandy. The infantry most keenly felt this lack of firepower as they returned to France with the same squad weapons—the .303 Lee-Enfield rifle and the Bren gun—which they had carried at Dunkirk in 1940. The infantry also still lacked antitank capability, the PIAT proving unwieldy, inaccurate, and lacking in penetration.[25]

Because armor rarely effectively supported the infantry, the lack of a first-rate Allied battle tank only exacerbated the problems caused by limited infantry firepower. Armor was clearly the weakest link in the British order of battle. Flaws in British tank design, procurement, and production ensured that the majority of the tanks the Royal Armoured Corps (RAC) employed in Normandy were variants of the U.S. Sherman provided to Britain after being rejected for overseas combat duty by the U.S. Army.[26] The drawback of these "reject" Shermans was their extreme inflammability, which earned them the sardonic soubriquet "Ronson," after the British cigarette lighter that purportedly "lit every time."[27] Even the upgunned (17-pounder) Sherman Firefly proved a disappointment once combat revealed that it had serious defects. Its 17-pounder (76.2mm) gun made the regular Sherman turret too cramped, and retention of standard Sherman optics meant crews could not take advantage of the gun's superior range. Moreover, tardy conversion meant that crews had little time to familiarize themselves with the tank before joining action. The Firefly also remained in too short supply to have a significant effect on the campaign.[28] Finally, its long overhanging gun was so distinctive that German armor quickly learned to pick off Fireflies first, and so commanders were reluctant to risk them in combat. Thus they rarely engaged, let alone destroyed, German armor.[29]

The absence of a quality battle tank capable of engaging enemy armor on equal terms, the defensive advantages of the terrain, and enhanced German antitank capability all brought heavy British tank losses.[30] Inferior-quality tanks and heavy losses profoundly affected the performance of British armored units in Normandy: hesitancy, caution, and timidity exhibited by British armor reflected a serious crisis of confidence, most clearly shown in the "Tiger tank phobia" that gripped crews in Normandy. The phobia had two dimensions: first, tankers tended to identify all German tanks as Tigers, even though few fought in Normandy, and, second, British armor was unwilling to engage Tigers.[31] This was, after all, hardly surprising when experience has established sending five tanks to knock out a Tiger and expecting only one to return. Such stark reality led to unorthodox improvisations. Crews stacked sandbags or welded spare track sections onto the hull to increase protection. Several regiments even reversed their Shermans into battle to gain the advantage of the extra protection of the engine "up front" and five forward gears with which to make a quick getaway.[32] Fear of incineration also led British Sherman crews to abandon tanks immediately when they were hit, which allowed dozens of serviceable tanks to fall into enemy hands, where they were quickly employed against their former owners. Indeed, in late July 1944 the 21st Panzer Division fielded an entire company of captured Shermans.[33] All told, despite the courage of the crews, British armor made little contribution to Allied victory in Normandy.

Inadequate equipment also left British forces unable to undertake effective battlefield reconnaissance. Even after the RAC absorbed the Reconnaissance Corps in early 1944 in an effort to strengthen reconnaissance capabilities, reconnaissance regiments remained badly equipped and organized to gain battlefield intelligence and lacked the armor and mechanized infantry needed to fight for information the way the the Germans did. Instead, British forces relied heavily on aerial reconnaissance and Ultra intercepts, which provided considerable intelligence.[34]

Limited direct firepower necessitated the troops' coordinating closely to maximize available fire, and since coordination was often absent troops relied heavily on indirect-fire support.[35] The Royal Artillery proved the most effective arm of service in Normandy as the gunners provided rapid, massed fire support. The largest component of the army by summer 1944 (see Table 8.2), gunners could bring down a divisional barrage in five minutes and a corps barrage in eight minutes, an impressive feat. Backed by naval gun fire, British artillery fire nullified the striking power of even the elite panzer divisions, halted every German counterattack that threatened more than local success, and steadily sapped German strength.[36]

Table 8.2   Composition of British Second Army, 30 June 1944

Arm	Troops	Percent
Artillery	114,000	17
Infantry	108,000	16
Engineer	84,000	13
Armor	43,000	7
Signals	32,000	5
Service	280,000	42

Source: PRO CAB 106/1121, 25.

British offensive employment of artillery, however, contributed directly to the difficulties troops faced in breaking through enemy defenses. Artillery fire plans were so complex that they became unimaginative and inflexible as gunners invariably laid down a creeping barrage along the intended axis of advance, which allowed the Germans to gauge rapidly the direction and axis of attacks and to mass their meager reserves astride and along the flanks of the advance.[37] This prescriptive use of artillery multiplied the difficulties the British faced translating a break-in into a breakout. Moreover, the predictability of fire support allowed the Germans to adopt effective countermeasures, such as adopting extreme dispersion by thinly manning their forward positions in exchange for defense in depth to minimize losses. Moreover, barrages were rarely deep enough to shatter the entire German defense, which likewise contributed to the British inability to break out.[38]

The deficiencies of other arms and weapon systems also bred excessive reliance on artillery fire. Instead of complementing the offensive power of the other arms, the Royal Artillery acted as a substitute for their weakness-

es. The infantry invariably went to ground and called down massive fire
when they met anything more than token resistance and thus failed to utilize their own firepower and mobility to gain and hold ground.[39]
Dependence on rigid fire plans also mandated set-piece battalion assaults in
which the infantry jettisoned battle drill techniques of fire and maneuver
taught in training, instead advancing rapidly behind a creeping barrage.[40]
Armor, too, tended to withdraw and call down fire support when encounter-
ing any real opposition.[41] The "shells save lives" philosophy led the British
to shatter enemy defenses by sheer weight of shell, but created a dependence on firepower-based attrition that made British operations inflexible
and exorbitant in ammunition expenditures that caused major logistic
headaches.[42] While artillery was clearly a major factor in Allied victory in
Normandy, dependence on fire support ensured that fire possibilities and
logistic considerations, rather than terrain or the tactical situation, came to
dominate planning.[43]

The logistic requirements of firepower domination ensured that Anglo-
Canadian forces could not quickly or frequently attack, and often dictated
that only a single corps could attack at one time. Such requirements also
entailed that attacks would occur on narrow fronts to maximize the damage
inflicted and to penetrate enemy defenses. Firepower domination thus
unbalanced British operational art and retarded development of combined-
arms coordination. Even though firepower paved the way for victory,
infantry and armor still had to take and hold ground. The reliance on domination by firepower was symptomatic of a wider phenomenon, the
"machines over men" philosophy, a belief that technological advances
could allow ordnance to win wars and minimize the bloody infantry fire-
fights that had destroyed a generation in the Great War. But combat in
Normandy soon showed that machines could not compensate for the lack of
quality infantry, and that they could not hold the ground the infantry captured.

The difficulties British infantry encountered were also the result of
low-caliber manpower. The unprecedented demands of the other services
and the technical branches, as well as the proliferation of special forces,
drew off quality personnel from the infantry. Poor performance also
stemmed in part from training. In 1944 British infantry remained less well
trained than the enemy because instruction failed to instill flexibility and
initiative or to inculcate understanding of enemy doctrine and tactics.

The army's inability to rectify defects partly hinged on leadership: only
leadership had the potential to transcend the army's structural rigidity. Unit
performance in Normandy thus rested disproportionately on commanders.
At the senior level, Montgomery came out of the audit of war reasonably
well. His insistence on fighting a slow, deliberate, no-risk, set-piece attritional battle that both optimized British strengths and German weaknesses
was sound. Even though he was overcautious at times and squandered

opportunities that could have reduced losses in the long run, generally his philosophy was correct. He also overcontrolled the battle and was reluctant to share the reins of command because he had limited faith in his subordinates. His deputy, Lt. Gen. Miles Dempsey, the commander of the Second Army, was inexperienced in the use of air power, was less aware than Montgomery of the limitations of British troops, and desired a more ambitious British role. Montgomery allowed Dempsey little initiative and frequently bypassed him entirely, but Dempsey tried to carve out a role for himself in Normandy.[44] He became much more frustrated than Montgomery with the stagnation before Caen, and sought a breakout through his ambitious GOODWOOD and BLUECOAT plans. His perspective was also more immediate than his superior's, and that caused him to lose sight of Montgomery's master plan in mid-July and led him to seek fame and glory for British arms through a breakout.[45]

The other senior commanders emerged less well from the audit of war. The wide variations in divisional performance in part reflected the spectrum of the commanders' abilities, and the flurry of dismissals during the campaign exemplified that "deadwood" remained in the senior leadership.[46] But the real leadership problem began at brigade and regimental level and got worse lower down the ranks. Junior officers generally proved unable to transcend their methodical training to display the necessary skills of initiative and leadership required for battlefield success.[47]

As a consequence of these deficiencies and the character of the campaign, not only did British forces prove unable to break out from Normandy, but mounting losses, dwindling morale, and lack of infantry replacements sapped British striking power as the campaign progressed. Examination of the four major British offensives in Normandy—EPSOM, CHARNWOOD, GOODWOOD, and BLUECOAT—illuminates both the difficulties British forces faced and the deterioration of troop performance.

On 26 June, Montgomery launched Operation EPSOM, a major offensive intended to force the Orne and Odon Rivers, seize the heights southwest of Caen, and loosen the German hold on the city. To achieve this goal, Montgomery committed his best-trained, yet inexperienced troops, under the VIII Corps. With strong air, naval, and artillery support he hoped to smash the strong German defenses and capture Caen. Yet bad luck bedeviled EPSOM: unseasonal bad weather postponed the operation for three days and ultimately forced Montgomery to attack without the planned air bombardment. Equally seriously, the neighboring XXX Corps failed to take the commanding Rauray Ridge on the flank of the intended assault during the night of 25–26 June, thus spoiling the entire attack.

Operationally, EPSOM was the best executed British assault in Normandy as the VIII Corps with three fresh divisions—15th Scottish, 43d Wessex, and 11th Armoured—executed a textbook attack.[48] Infantry spearheaded the advance on a 4-mile front behind a formidable 700-gun barrage. Such massed firepower allowed the infantry to penetrate the thin German defenses lines, held by the attenuated but still formidable 12th SS Panzer Division, and establish a bridgehead across the Odon River. Thereafter, the 11th Armoured Division "followed through" to seize the vital height of Hill 112 beyond. Though Montgomery had torn a hole in the enemy defenses by 28 June, excessive caution prevented British forces from making further significant gains. Moreover, as German reserves assembled with the obvious intent of nipping off the tenuous bridgehead across the Odon, the cautious General Dempsey relinquished Hill 112 and assumed good defensive positions. Here, the VIII Corps turned back repeated German counterthrusts through 2 July.[49]

At best EPSOM proved a partial success. Montgomery had penetrated the enemy front but, despite marked numerical and material superiority, had not broken through, and neither gained the high ground above the Odon nor rendered Caen indefensible. At the same time the VIII Corps had suffered heavy losses.[50] While the tenacity and skill of the enemy contributed in no small part to British difficulties, flawed British attack doctrine denied the troops decisive success. The rolling barrage gave away both the location of the British main effort and the axis of the advance, and thus allowed the Germans to redeploy their meager reserves quickly to impede the advance.[51] At the same time, the narrow attack frontage left the armored follow-through vulnerable to German flanking fire from the Rauray Ridge and created terrible traffic congestion, especially at Cheux, as units tried to advance down the narrow corridor simultaneously. The failure to take the ridge left the entire western flank of the advance badly exposed to enfilading fire from higher ground that increased the casualty toll.

Montgomery called off EPSOM to conserve manpower and, to protect morale, exaggerated its success in drawing German armor. Although only a partial success, in retrospect, EPSOM was the pinnacle of British achievement in Normandy. At the same time, the operation was a proving ground for British commanders and troops, most of whom were participating in their first action.[52] EPSOM clearly demonstrated the inexperience of British troops and the weakness of their training as poor coordination and a failure to comprehend German defensive tactics marred the operation. Soldiers of the Scottish Division, in particular, suffered heavily when the enemy surprised and ambushed them from a classic reverse-slope position. Moreover, the depth of German defenses repeatedly took the British by surprise.[53]

The heavy losses sustained during EPSOM, as well as the need to rebuild supplies and organize air support, meant that it was not until 8 July that Montgomery resumed the offensive with an unusual multicorps attack on Caen, Operation CHARNWOOD. Montgomery used air power to smash German opposition, and CHARNWOOD witnessed the first use of carpet bombing in support of the land campaign. The Caen raid was, however, as counterproductive as it was ineffective. To prevent bombing short, RAF Bomber Command confined the target zone to the city proper even though the German defenses were outside the city. The result was heavy French civilian losses, negligible damage to the enemy, and devastation that slowed the British ground advance. Moreover, due to the complexity of orchestrating the bombing attack, a five-hour delay occurred between the bombing and the ground assault, allowing the enemy to recover. The raid did make a significant, though unintended, contribution to the fall of Caen, however. Stray bombs destroyed several bridges and sharply reduced the Germans' ability to supply their forces in the northern part of the city.[54]

As in EPSOM, Anglo-Canadian forces initially met with success as they launched concentric attacks on the beleaguered and greatly outnumbered German defenders. Inexorably superior numbers and firepower drove the enemy back. Moreover, the by now seasoned British 3d Division outfought and mauled the green 16th *Luftwaffe* Field Division that had entered the line only three days before. After two days of heavy fighting Montgomery's formations finally fought their way into northern Caen on 9 July, four weeks behind schedule.

Nevertheless, southern Caen and the strategic heights to its south that barred the way to the Falaise Plain remained in enemy hands. That the Germans now held a shorter, more defensible front behind the Orne River backed by excellent observation from high ground made further Anglo-Canadian advances problematic. Only with greater firepower could Montgomery progress at a tolerable cost in lives and materiel. The need for massive fire support and the stockpiling of sufficient supplies to guarantee success meant that it was not until 18 July that Montgomery launched his next major attack, Operation GOODWOOD, out of the Orne bridgehead, the ground east of the Orne captured by airborne forces on D-Day. Three major tactical problems confronted such an attack, however: the difficulty of achieving surprise, the constricted size of the bridgehead that limited employment of massed artillery, and the resulting reliance on aerial bombardment that the first two difficulties engendered.

The GOODWOOD plan was Miles Dempsey's, and he convinced a skeptical Montgomery that he could win the ground that Montgomery desperately needed to placate the air marshals and the Americans, while keeping infantry losses low and "writing down" German strength by having armor spearhead a deep penetration operation toward Falaise.[55] By nature, Montgomery opposed deep penetrations as too risky and he privately maintained grave doubts about the possibility of an armored breakthrough to Falaise.[56] Nonetheless, he adopted Dempsey's ambitious plan to achieve his own less grandiose goal to tie down and write off German reserves.[57]

A new attack was necessary to continue to hold German reserves at Caen while the Americans prepared for their COBRA breakout bid, and the Orne bridgehead offered the best prospects to both gain ground and to write off enemy reserves. Moreover, given the mounting infantry shortage, the massed employment of armor appeared the only way to minimize infantry losses.[58] At the same time, Montgomery had to "talk up" the operation to gain the needed air support and as part of his continuing campaign to hold the Germans at Caen. Much of the controversy surrounding GOODWOOD stems from the fact that Montgomery publicly adopted Dempsey's plan, while privately maintaining grave doubts; and to gain the necessary air support, he exaggerated GOODWOOD's objectives to Eisenhower and the air marshals, all of whom he deliberately misled into believing he was about to launch a full-scale breakout.[59]

In the event, GOODWOOD was ill conceived and executed; the concentration of the attack force in the narrow Orne bridgehead cost Dempsey the element of surprise and restricted the deployment of forces. The offensive followed the typical pattern of British operations in Normandy. Carpet bombing and artillery fire smashed the British armor through the German forward lines to extend the bridgehead to the foot of the high ground south of Caen. But, after great initial success, the Germans reacted swiftly. Local reserves conducted a delaying withdrawal though a deep defensive belt that slowed the British advance, while fortified village strongpoints within the defensive zone deflected and disrupted the armored advance and delayed the follow-up forces.[60] Moreover, as with EPSOM, the constricted corridor created enormous traffic congestion that threw off the entire timetable of the advance.[61] When British armor finally approached the commanding Bourguébus Ridge late on 18 July, it arrived already depleted and with little infantry and no artillery support.[62] It then encountered a German gun line of heavy antitank and antiaircraft guns emplaced on the high ground that repelled piecemeal British armored attacks and inflicted heavy losses.[63] As evening approached and Allied tactical aviation left the battlefield, robust and well-coordinated German combined-arms counterattacks threw the British armor back with further heavy losses.[64] Dempsey attacked for two more days, even though the offensive had lost its momentum, until Montgomery intervened to halt the operation on 21 July. Nowhere had British forces established a firm presence on the Bourguébus Ridge.

Flawed doctrine, as much as poor planning, was at the root of GOODWOOD's failure, continued poor coordination denying the British forces greater success. Critics of GOODWOOD miss the fact that the operation was consonant with prevailing doctrine about the employment of armored forces.[65] And since this doctrine failed to coordinate armor and infantry, the plan naturally separated the two arms.[66] However inadequately, Dempsey addressed the sluggishness of his troops in exploiting success, and admonished his armor to bypass opposition, leave it to be mopped up by the infantry, and gain maximum ground as quickly as possible. The British also sorely felt their lack of armored personnel carriers, but Dempsey countermanded the efforts of the commander of the VIII Corps, Richard O'Connor, to employ ammunition carriers as improvised armored personnel carriers.[67]

The aerial bombardment, the largest Allied carpet bombing in support of ground forces yet witnessed in the war, was clearly the most successful aspect of GOODWOOD.[68] Drawing on the lessons of CHARNWOOD, this bombardment was more effective. For the first time, night bombers dropped delayed-action high-explosive bombs along the flanks of the planned advance to disrupt German counterattacks, while day bombers attacked at first light with fragmentation bombs to limit the cratering that had badly delayed the CHARNWOOD ground advance. Nonetheless, this action did not live up to expectations, because the shallowness of the bomb area once again limited the material damage and left the German reserves deployed in depth virtually unscathed.[69]

The unsupported employment of massed armor against intact defenses brought severe tank losses during GOODWOOD: more than one third of the entire British tank strength in Normandy was disabled.[70] Dempsey had allowed armor to spearhead the operation because he mistakenly believed that plenty of replacements tanks were available. Not only were far fewer available than he imagined, but he had overlooked a growing shortage of replacement crews. GOODWOOD caused a tank shortage that lasted for the rest of the campaign.[71] Nor did GOODWOOD minimize infantry losses as Dempsey had intended; the diversionary attacks launched in support of it caused too many casualties.[72] The operation also failed miserably to "write down" enemy armor as Montgomery had intended. In fact the armored advance barely hurt the enemy, and the offensive did not stop two panzer divisions from being transferred to the U.S. sector.[73] Even though GOOD-WOOD did acquire badly needed room in the bridgehead and temporarily tied some German reserves to the Caen area, these achievements were bought at a price that British forces could not afford to repeat.

Yet GOODWOOD did make an important, if unintended, contribution to the success of COBRA. The heavy defensive combat around Caen during GOODWOOD forced the Germans to focus their resupply efforts in the British sector, so that few supplies reached the U.S. sector in the crucial days before COBRA. The result was a serious deterioration in the German logistic position before COBRA that facilitated the U.S. breakout.[74]

Forced to lick his wounds, it was not until 28 July that Montgomery permitted Dempsey to launch an impromptu offensive, BLUECOAT, against the weakly held German front amid the thick bocage around Caumont. Montgomery intended the operation to maintain pressure on the Germans and prevent the transfer of enemy armor against the Americans.

But, again, BLUECOAT was Dempsey's brainchild, and he again hoped to achieve a decisive breakout. Montgomery, in spite of lingering skepticism, bowed to Dempsey because he needed a quick offensive to forestall the transfer of German reserves to the U.S. front, regardless of the fact that the buildup for the attack was insufficient to ensure victory. BLUECOAT was the only operation in Normandy in which Montgomery compromised on his master plan and launched a premature offensive to assist the U.S. break-through.[75]

For BLUECOAT, Dempsey hastily recalled the 11th and Guards Armoured Divisions from their post-GOODWOOD refitting. The offensive saw simultaneous attacks by the VIII and XXX Corps, with three armored and three infantry divisions.[76] Dempsey deployed an unprecedented concentration of armor and infantry against a single German infantry division. The need to prevent the transfer of enemy armor forced him to launch the operation three days ahead of schedule, and the premature start ensured that the fire support that normally accompanied British offensives was lacking. Even though the German defense was weak and had almost no armor, the front had been static since mid-June and the Germans had entrenched themselves in depth amid the thick bocage. But here Dempsey committed most of the available British armor—in one of the sectors least suited for offensive armored operations. Also, because speed was so important Demspey launched the attack before the VIII Corps had fully assembled.

Historians have generally viewed BLUECOAT as a great success, and, indeed, Dempsey's forces breached the German lines and brought to battle German armor that was being transferred to the U.S. sector. As a holding attack (as conceived by Montgomery), BLUECOAT was a success. As a major breakout bid, as sought by Dempsey, it was a dismal failure. For the immense British numerical superiority (estimated at thirty to one by one scholar) should have produced greater success.[77] But Dempsey had to rush the attack, making it an untidy and unsubtle frontal assault. Moreover, failure to take flanking high ground at Amaye seriously hampered progress just as it had in EPSOM.[78] Caution and sluggishness also prevented British forces from ripping open a weak, depleted, barely coherent German front that was ripe for shattering. On 30 July, the British captured a bridgehead over the Souleuvre River on the undefended boundary between the German Seventh Army and Panzer Group West, and for the next week the two German commands remained detached along this boundary, leaving a 2-mile gap that was not exploited. By the time the British realized the weakness of the enemy and advanced, German reserves had closed the gap.[79]

The position of the Allies' own boundary line also hindered a rapid British advance southwest toward the important communications hub of Vire, which the British could have captured on 2 August with little opposition, but did not because the town was in the U.S. zone.[80] The failure to seize Vire was a serious blunder that aided the enemy's retreat from Mortain. Taking Vire would have severed the enemy's lateral communications lines and seriously compromised the German retreat.[81]

Uneven performance on a unit-to-unit basis also undermined success. While the VIII Corps advanced steadily, the 7th and Guards Armoured Divisions of the XXX Corps soon lagged. This left the 11th Armoured Division's flanks and spearhead dangerously exposed as resistance stiffened on 1 August with the arrival of German armor from Caen. On 6 August, German counterblows came against the apex of the 11th Armoured salient that were barely beaten off. It was fortunate that the German armor was anxious to push westward against the Americans, and so only limited counterattacks were launched.

The XXX Corps performed so poorly during BLUECOAT that Dempsey sacked its commander, Gen. Bucknall, and replaced him with Brian Horrocks.[82] Overwhelming evidence that the 7th Armoured Division was "sticky" led to a major purge of officers among the "Desert Rats."[83] At the same time, the sluggishness of the Guards Armoured Division demonstrated that it had not fully recovered from GOODWOOD.[84]

But BLUECOAT was notable because it saw both improved coordination as well as tactical adaptation among a number of British formations. General O'Connor had recognized during earlier operations both how poorly British forces coordinated and the need for teamwork for success in the bocage. In the few days available prior to BLUECOAT, he reorganized the 11th Armoured Division into two balanced combined-arms brigade groups. Immediate tactical success rewarded those British formations that exhibited improved coordination during BLUECOAT. The 6th Guards Tank Brigade, in particular, coordinated closely with the 15th Scottish Division, which led to the quick capture of Hill 309. These two formations also innovated tactically and employed embryonic converging flanking attacks in the clearance of Lutain Wood, tactics that they would refine and use with increasing effectiveness thereafter.[85]

The front became fluid in the second week of August as the Germans fell back in response to the U.S. breakout. But tired, demoralized, and depleted British forces failed to pursue the enemy aggressively and were largely content to follow up after German withdrawals.[86] The major problem that Montgomery faced during August was that British forces experienced what Clausewitz termed "relaxation of effort" as the troops sensed that victory was at hand. Thus in mid-August British pressure slackened across the entire front.[87] Montgomery, therefore, did not launch Operation KITTEN, the long-planned advance to the Seine, until 16 August.

By August a mounting infantry shortage was affecting British performance (see Table 8.3).[88] Since the War Office had pared Home Forces to the bone during the spring and troops remustered as infantry were still training, during August 1944 Montgomery had to disband the 59th Division

Table 8.3   **British Casualties and Replacements in Normandy, June 1944**

DATE	Casualties		Replacements		Shortage	
	Total	Infantry[a]	Total	Infantry	Total	Infantry[a]
7 June	6,999	6,150	1,900	0	−5,099	−6,150
9 June	9,366	8,250	5,488	2,631	−3,878	−5,600
11 June	11,556	10,150	9,957	5,019	−1,599	−5,150
15 June	13,121	11,550	19,092	10,316	+261	−1,225
17 June	14,593	12,850	21,151	12,170	+6,558	−675
21 June	16,387	14,425	23,758	13,456	+7,371	−975
23 June	17,492	15,400	25,098	14,350	+7,606	−1,050
25 June	18,514	16,350	26,703	15,105	+8,189	−1,250
27 June	21,016	18,500	28,754	16,849	+7,738	−1,650
29 June	22,460	19,775	29,566	17,661	+7,106	−2,100
1 July	24,402	23,250	30,631	18,665	+6,229	−4,600

Sources: PRO WO 171/ 139, WD, TFAG, A Section, June–August 1944; WO 219/1538, TFAG, "Casualty Reports (Sitreps)," Summer 1944; WO 219/1531, TFAG, "Casualty and POW Reports," Summer 1944; WO 219/939, SHAEF G1, "Daily Casualty Reports," Summer 1944.

a. Figures are estimated.

and reduce the 50th Division to cadre strength.[89] The manpower shortage clearly ate away at British drive and vigor during August, but the regimental system hampered War Office efforts to transfer personnel and alleviate shortages. It was fortunate for Montgomery that losses declined as his forces raced across France in the late summer.[90]

Waning British drive contributed to the Allied failure to destroy the Germans in the Falaise pocket in mid-August—that had been a unique opportunity for the Allies to deal a knockout blow to the *Westheer.*[91] Some of the blame for failure lay at Montgomery's door. War weariness, combined with the methodical pace of operations, ensured that Anglo-Canadian forces did not pressure the enemy strongly as the U.S. advance swept northeast and began to push the Germans into a pocket between Argentan and Falaise. This lack of pressure allowed the enemy to conduct an orderly withdrawal from the still open pocket until 19 August, when the Canadians finally closed it—but tens of thousands of German troops escaped in the interim.

Montgomery feared that his tired and depleted forces would suffer heavy losses and a possible setback if he tried to stop the desperate but determined enemy from escaping. Instead he, like Eisenhower, looked toward a larger envelopment along the Seine River. At the same time, Montgomery's continued underestimation of American speed and mobility hampered Bradley's efforts to close the pocket from the south. Montgomery's refusal to alter the army group boundary to allow the Americans to advance past Argentan and close the pocket from the south forced Eisenhower to halt Patton's advance on 13 August for five crucial days, during which many German troops escaped.[92] Thereafter, lack of operational-level doctrine prevented the Allies from encircling the enemy on the Seine. In late August, the Germans extricated virtually all of their surviving personnel and a surprising amount of equipment beyond the Seine.[93] The Normandy campaign thus ended for the British Army, like the rest of the campaign, with a partial success.

The British Army's performance in Normandy was unspectacular, with Montgomery's troops nowhere decisively defeating the enemy. However, British political-military objectives did not require a rapid defeat of the enemy. Given the weaknesses that afflicted British forces, Montgomery coaxed about the best possible performance from the troops that he could. The army's inexperience, its character as a civilian conscript force built around a small professional cadre whose peacetime preparation had been soft, its unremarkable training, its barely adequate equipment, its fragile morale, and its growing manpower shortage all limited its capabilities. That Montgomery was aware of these limitations and developed an appropriate theater strategy in which his army group acted as a foil that lured German reserves away from the stronger Americans to Caen was an important ingredient in Allied victory in Normandy.[94]

The army's continued slowness to adapt in the field contributed to its unimpressive performance in Normandy. Nevertheless, the pace of adaptation clearly accelerated during the later stages of the war, and in Normandy British ground forces enhanced their capabilities in three major areas: combined-arms coordination, fire support, and air-ground cooperation. British forces achieved some improvement in combined-arms coordination, but it remained sporadic.[95] The 11th Armoured Division proved the best led and most adaptable British armored formation, and by late July had reorganized into balanced mixed brigade groups. But coordination in the overexposed 7th Armoured and green Guards Armoured Divisions remained poor: it was only in late August that they too adopted a brigade group structure. Improved coordination also gradually emerged between independent tank brigades and infantry formations as growing association, familiarity, and experience bred closer cooperation. However, operational reliance on firepower as well as deeply ingrained regimental parochialism worked against improved tank-infantry cooperation, and effective coordination still remained the exception rather than the norm during the campaign.

The Royal Artillery continued to enhance its effectiveness and lethality in Normandy as it had steadily done since 1940. In particular, aerial spotters directed ever greater amounts of artillery fire, culminating on 17 July with the first spotter-directed bombardment by three separate concentrations of brigaded artillery.[96] The neutralization of the *Luftwaffe* allowed spotters to operate around the clock and thus achieve their full potential. Spotter-directed fire suppressed enemy fire and constantly harassed enemy operations.[97] Spotters flew continually over the Falaise pocket to deliver accurate, rapid fire even with the close proximity of Allied forces.[98] At the same time, increased use of mobile forward artillery observers with armored formations in Normandy reduced both strike times and friendly-fire accidents.[99] Forward observers proved especially useful during the German retreat from the Falaise pocket, where armored spearheads directed fighter-bombers against the retreating enemy to harry and hinder German movement to an unprecedented degree.[100]

The efficacy of tactical air strikes against the Falaise pocket demonstrated that it was with air-ground cooperation that British forces most enhanced their capabilities during the campaign, reflecting the broad trend since 1942 of improved interservice coordination. Initially, lack of space in the bridgehead had forced most squadrons to continue flying from distant bases in England, but from late July fighter-bombers began to fly in strength from continental airfields, and thereafter tactical air strikes inflicted mounting damage on German forces.[101] Sortie rates steadily climbed, and on 7 August 1944 Typhoons of Second Tactical Air Force (TAF) flew 294 missions to help stop the German drive on Avranches and daily sortie rates peaked at 1,200 during the battle for the Falaise gap.[102] The tactical use of radar also reached new levels of refinement in Normandy and allowed increased accuracy and improved capability in bad weather. All told, fighter-bombers proved more damaging than heavy bombers in Normandy, and the most notable achievement of Second TAF in Normandy—the incapacitation of Field Marshal Rommel on 17 July—was achieved by British fighter-bombers.[103]

Nevertheless the effectiveness of the RAF in Normandy, despite the enormous contribution to victory, remained mixed. Pilot claims notwithstanding, the physical damage inflicted by tactical air strikes was limited. Rather, tactical strikes disrupted and dispersed enemy forces, hampered their movement, exacerbated logistic difficulties, inflicted a steady toll on soft-skinned vehicles, and slowly throttled the German supply effort.[104] Yet the Second TAF was unable to assist Anglo-Canadian ground operations as effectively as the USAAF was aiding U.S. forces. Alongside space restrictions that limited tactical operations early on in the campaign, the Hawker Typhoon—mainstay of RAF tactical aviation—proved less versatile, robust, or accurate a strike aircraft than the U.S. P-47 or P-51. In particular, the 3-inch armor-piercing rockets the Typhoon carried were inaccurate, lacked punch, and were not effective against armor.[105] The Second TAF enhanced its effectiveness during the campaign, but it had yet to develop the potency displayed by U.S. tactical aviation.

The use of bombers in support of ground operations also had mixed results. To the dismay of the air power enthusiasts, strategic and tactical bombing failed to neutralize the well dug-in German defenders on the beaches on D-Day. The bombardment destroyed only a fraction of the defenses, although the bombardment stunned many of the defenders for long enough to allow the assault troops to get ashore.[106] The carpet bombing attacks conducted by RAF Bomber Command in support of Montgomery's CHARNWOOD, GOODWOOD, and BLUECOAT offensives achieved mixed results. The 7 July Caen raid was least effective because inexperience resulted in Bomber Command's demolishing much of the city while inflicting negligible damage on the German defenses.[107] The GOODWOOD bombing proved better as air and ground forces drew appropriate lessons from CHARNWOOD. The inability to mass artillery in the narrow Orne River bridgehead made the success of GOODWOOD too dependent on the efficacy of the bombing. Scheduled only two hours in advance of the ground attack, the bombing stunned and demoralized the forward enemy defenders, but Allied ground troops failed to follow up quickly enough because cratering and the constricted startline hindered the ground advance.[108] During BLUECOAT a smaller bomber force, the paucity of German defenders, and the defensive advantages of the bocage limited the damage inflicted—and the resultant cratering again slowed the ground advance.[109]

Nonetheless, the gradual emergence during 1942–1944 of an integrated, interservice war effort witnessed the most significant improvement in British military capabilities during the war. Clearly, also, the logistic preparations for the campaign were a massive achievement that owed much to the lessons of Norway, Dunkirk, Dieppe, North Africa, Sicily, and Italy. In fact, for the first time in the history of warfare, the Allies in Normandy overturned the traditional supremacy of land communications over maritime communications as aerial interdiction slowed German logistics and as technological innovations—the landing ship tank, embryonic roll-on roll-off ferries, the artificial Mulberry harbors, and the Pluto fuel pipeline—speeded the Allied buildup.[110]

Nevertheless, innovation remained limited, and significant operational and tactical problems that fundamentally stemmed from flawed doctrine continued to plague British operations in Normandy. The army's failure to absorb the lessons of the Great War, the defeats of 1939–1942, and the desperate quest for victory had forged a distinct British operational approach: minutely planned, precise fire plans created tightly controlled set-piece attritional battles in which echeloned British forces attacked the enemy at his strongest to maximize the damage inflicted.

While British attack doctrine played to inherent strengths—logistics, administration, and fire support—this approach had significant flaws. Attrition mandated narrow attack frontages to maximize firepower, facilitate massed fire support, and maximize enemy losses, but limited maneuver.[111] Echeloning often prematurely disclosed British intentions, and attack frontages were so narrow that German flanking fire often fatally disrupted echeloned forces following through the hole punched in the German line, as happened at EPSOM and GOODWOOD.[112] Even though narrow attack frontages allowed echeloned troops to penetrate forward enemy defenses, the narrowness of the penetration restricted maneuver and supply, enabled enemy local reserves to concentrate their counterblows, and left the advance vulnerable to the spoiling counterattacks at which the Germans excelled.[113]

But the most significant drawback of British attack doctrine was that only a fraction of available forces actually engaged the enemy at any one time: concentration meant that usually only one corps fought at any given moment and echeloned deployment meant that only spearheads engaged the enemy. The failure to bring its full fighting power to bear denied British forces decisive success and led contemporaries, both British and U.S., to misinterpret this dissipation of strength as a lack of determination.[114]

Although Normandy was rather disappointing operationally, the imperative driving British operations was to win the war at tolerable cost. The psychological legacies of the Great Wars slaughter in the trenches and the growing manpower concerns cemented casualty minimalization as a cornerstone of British operations.[115] Steady progress with bearable losses was thus more important than excellence in performance or decisive success.[116] Given this goal, Montgomery was the right man to lead British forces. Few wartime personalities have generated as much controversy as he did, and the animus or adulation generated has often distorted evaluation of his performance.[117] But despite his character flaws, Montgomery was the commander most capable of shepherding Anglo-Canadian forces through to victory in northwest Europe. His caution was sensible: he understood, more so than any other British commander, that the army remained a fragile instrument, whose morale had only recently been restored and that lacked manpower reserves. He was thus determined to avoid a serious setback that might demoralize his troops.

Britain's manpower shortage and war weariness, manifested in casualty minimalization, dominated British operations in Normandy. The easiest way to curtail losses was to limit the forces committed and mass strength on a narrow front. After his failure to take Caen quickly, Montgomery withheld his forces from bloody, piecemeal frontal attacks on the city and at EPSOM tried to outflank Caen. In CHARNWOOD he pressed hard from three sides to squeeze the Germans out of Caen, but thereafter wisely refrained from frontally assaulting an enemy well dug in behind the Orne River.[118] Manpower concerns clearly limited British offensive action; although he desired more room for maneuver, airfields, and supply depots, Montgomery was unwilling to suffer heavy losses to reach Falaise. Manpower concerns also led Montgomery to adopt Dempsey's GOODWOOD plan, regardless of skepticism about its prospects for success and to go against a deep conviction to never employ an all-armored corps, because Dempsey promised low infantry losses through reliance on armor and because it would tie down enemy reserves.[119] Casualty minimalization led Montgomery to call off both EPSOM and GOODWOOD when losses mounted, whereas the Americans slogged on toward St. Lô and bled the enemy dry.

During lulls in the fighting, Montgomery maintained the initiative with individual battalion assaults. Such attacks minimized aggregate casualties but they concentrated losses in the attack battalions, writing them off. Deliberate application of limited strength reduced prospects of success, increased losses, and demoralized attack battalions. Even though Montgomery retained the initiative throughout the campaign, his concern to limit losses contributed to the British inability to break out. The operational repercussions of casualty minimalization was that British forces failed to take advantage of opportunities that presented themselves that might have shortened the war and cut losses in the long run.[120]

Montgomery, the master of public relations, persuaded the British people, politicians, press, and soldiery, as well as the Allies, that British troops were of high quality, even when he knew they were not.[121] He recognized that confidence in command instilled and maintained troop morale—hence his obsession with nurturing his image as an undefeated military genius was more than just ego.[122] He believed that a setback might destroy his image of invincibility and with it sap his troops' morale. He was acutely aware of the pernicious effects of heavy losses and recognized that soldiers of democratic, mass civilian armies were less resilient than those of totalitarian or ideologically motivated regimes and so he strove to avoid undue casualties.[123]

Indeed, unlike the Germans, the civilian British conscripts often never recovered from a single tactical drubbing, as in the case of 3d/4th Battalion, County of London Yeomanry Regiment on 13 June at Villers-Bocage.[124] Montgomery knew that his troops could perform well, but only if they were nurtured and husbanded. Casualty minimalization recognized that Britain had limited manpower reserves; that Allied demographic and industrial strength would inevitably prevail; and that Britain's postwar international standing required the preservation of its army. The shackling psychological legacy of World War I also clearly promoted casualty minimization because most senior officers had experienced the slaughter in the trenches of the Western Front, many as infantry officers. The British infantry was not to be used as cannon fodder, even though, inevitably, it was still to bear the burden of both combat and casualties.

As it was, despite all of Montgomery's efforts to preserve combat power and morale, both waned alarmingly as the campaign progressed—until the German collapse in August 1944 boosted morale and gave the British a breathing spell to replenish formations. By late July, despite his efforts, morale had sunk as absence and desertion rates shot up.[125] Given superior German fieldcraft, the defensive advantages of the terrain, and flawed British attack doctrine, the more aggressive British offensive action in Normandy that Dempsey desired might have permanently crippled British fighting power. To avoid this, Montgomery set out to create a sustained, satisfactory performance from British ground forces that (relying on Allied numerical superiority) would bring victory at tolerable cost and preserve the army.[126] Thus he never desired nor sought the best and most effective army attainable. Montgomery understood that a satisfactory performance was all that was realistically possible and all that was necessary for victory.

Contemporary and postwar criticisms leveled at Montgomery were largely inevitable consequences of his operational approach. Highly controlled set-piece battles prevented simultaneous attacks. Moreover, although his focus on administration provided excellent logistic support that sustained British fighting power as long as possible, he attacked less frequently, for shorter periods, and more cautiously than the Americans and thus let opportunities pass. But he did recognize the critical importance of logistics for victory far more clearly than his adversaries, even Rommel. Moreover, Montgomery understood the vital importance of air power to Allied victory and he rated it so highly that he was reluctant to attack without it.[127]

Even though he was frequently criticized by contemporaries and by historians since for his caution, British objectives and the growing manpower crisis made Montgomery's caution generally both appropriate and sensible.[128] Indeed, the worst defeats Anglo-Canadian forces suffered occurred when troops displayed dash and boldness.[129] It is thus apparent that the slow, methodical, controlled battle was appropriate to the capabilities of British forces.

Firepower attrition was the concomitant to concentration in Montgomery's operational approach as massive firepower smashed the infantry through to its objectives.[130] But this approach was a two-edged sword. It was appropriate in light of British morale and manpower concerns, as well as political-military objectives, but it had significant drawbacks. The increasing scale of fire support ultimately became self-defeating because the devastation it caused so hindered the advance that British forces could not exploit the fire support's effect.[131] Carpet bombing reduced built-up areas like Caen and Falaise to rubble, impeded movement, slowed the tempo of the advance, and gave the Germans time to move up reserves, counterattack, and rebuild a continuous front.[132] The planning complexities of bombing also meant that the early bombardments preceded the ground attack by several hours, alerting the enemy to an impending attack. The lethal effect was limited and not in proportion to the resources expended, but the moral effect was significant. It could temporarily stun even veteran defenders, as it did to the Panzer *Lehr* Division during COBRA, so that attacking troops, if following close behind the bombardment, could penetrate the German front at tolerable cost.[133]

Montgomery's operational approach, while crude, was effective: it invariably got infantry onto their objectives with bearable losses. But neither Montgomery nor his subordinates speedily got to grips with the great depth of German defenses in Normandy. British awareness of German defensive doctrine remained poor, and the Germans' light manning of their forward line made British shell expenditures out of all proportion to the results achieved. Massed fire smashed the lightly defended enemy lines and carried the advancing infantry thorough to the German main line of resistance, but then lifted. British commanders also failed to appreciate the enemy's adoption of dispersed defense in depth, or to develop fire plans that attacked the full depth of enemy defenses—nor did they solve the problem of deploying a mass of guns forward in the early phases of battle. Firepower dominance was self-reinforcing and created a dependence that increasingly alarmed Montgomery.[134]

The imperatives driving British operations thus forged highly managed battles. Indeed, Montgomery dominated planning and left his army commanders, Crerar and Dempsey, little room for initiative, and they in turn kept an equally firm grip on their corps commanders.[135] This rigid control denied subordinates the opportunity to display initiative or flexibility.

Although the flaws that afflicted British forces in Normandy had all been demonstrated and identified before the campaign, circumstances in part explain the army's inability to rectify them. The wartime army could not quickly or easily overcome its interwar neglect, especially as battle experience was simultaneously refining and redefining enemy doctrine, training, and tactics. However, the army's unwillingness to evaluate its performance critically and honestly obstructed its efforts to adapt throughout the war. British forces in northwest Europe learned principally from recent operations through after-action reports, the most important of which being the diverse immediate reports series. Quickly produced after the event, they ranged from the tactical and operational to the technical.[136]

Generally, however, after-action reports contained little critical evaluation and were reluctant to acknowledge or to identify deficiencies, let alone demonstrated a desire to correct them. This reluctance to learn stood in marked contrast to the honest, critical self-evaluation that was the hallmark of the wartime German and U.S. Armies. But British commanders and troops often equated success in battle with excellence in performance, and the army found it difficult to escape its emphasis on loyalty above honesty. Troops and commanders remained reluctant to criticize individuals or organizations, and when they did offer criticism it was muted, diluted, and euphemistic.[137]

This unwillingness to acknowledge deficiencies lay at the core of the unspectacular British performance in Normandy. Silence dominated the reports coming back from Normandy and rendered more difficult the adjustments that combat realities demanded. While the Americans enhanced their capabilities during the campaign and, in particular, surmounted the debilitating effect of the bocage on offensive operations, British adaptation occurred more slowly and was less focused, thus ultimately proving less effective.[138]

At the same time, the imperatives that drove British operations, casualty and ammunition conservation and morale preservation, negatively influenced the lessons-learned process.[139] Montgomery influenced the process in northwest Europe in two major areas. Alarmed at the extravagant ammunition expenditure early in the campaign, he censored reports that sanctioned massive artillery support.[140] He also censored reports critical of British performance because he viewed frank admission and discussion of weaknesses incompatible with morale maintenance. He quashed, for example, reports that identified the marked inferiority of Allied tanks.[141] As he censored lessons-learned material to protect his army group from a possible deterioration of its combat effectiveness, Montgomery impeded his command from enhancing its capabilities.

The history of countermortar groups illuminates the army's slowness in learning from experience. Since most British casualties in North Africa had resulted from German mortar fire, formations organized countermortar groups designed to observe enemy mortar fire, locate those mortars, and call down fire to eliminate them. This system proved effective in the Mediterranean and saved many lives. Yet units withdrawn from the Mediterranean for OVERLORD disbanded their countermortar groups to preserve manpower. British formations landed in Normandy without a countermortar organization, with the result that German mortars inflicted 70 percent of total casualties during June and July. Even though divisions gradually improvised countermortar groups during the campaign, it was not until August that Montgomery officially authorized their reformation.[142]

A complex array of factors explains the relative slowness of British forces to adapt in Normandy. British military culture was innately conservative and displayed hostility toward theory and intellectual preparation.[143] Throughout the war, it relied more on extemporaneous pragmatism than on formally expressed doctrine.[144] Doctrinal development was thus dualistic and schizophrenic: the doctrine of individual senior commanders often diverged from official War Office doctrine.[145] Lack of appropriate and holistic doctrine hampered the army's efforts to enhance its combat effectiveness at all levels. Moreover, against a backdrop of soft interwar preparation, the army lacked mechanisms to evaluate and disseminate combat lessons, preventing it from deriving appropriate lessons from its early

World War II experience. The army's unwillingness to question or rethink basic doctrinal tenets, such as its adherence to strategic defense and the offensive primacy of massed armor, further exacerbated this deficiency.

At the same time, problems associated with rapid and massive wartime expansion as well as lack of combat experience further slowed the collection, assimilation, and dissemination of combat experience. The setbacks of 1939–1942 then promoted a desperate search for a solution—a system that would secure victory. This quest ultimately produced Montgomery and his operational approach, which he grounded in recognized British strengths—artillery, infantry on the defense, air power, administration, logistics, and the advantage of time. While Montgomery firmly believed in the need to learn from combat experience, his "recipe" for victory, once established, drove the army to emphasize and to enhance those elements that were integral to the system. Thus, irresistibly, the need for victory to expunge the taint of defeat led the army to enhance its effectiveness in areas in which it had already possessed aptitude and that were largely defensive in orientation, at the expense of improvements in offensive warfare, be they in armored doctrine or coordination.

Montgomery's approach to battle, while progressive in its professionalism and its use of air power, remained grounded in the conservative bedrock of interwar British military thought and in Great War artillery techniques. His formula for victory narrowed and limited the spectrum of innovation and reform. Moreover, an erroneous presumption that pertinent lessons could only be drawn from success bedeviled British lessons-learned analysis. This reluctance to learn from defeat skewed the lessons-learned process and ensured that the army enhanced its effectiveness in areas in which it had already demonstrated expertise (artillery and administration) but was slow to adapt in areas where it lacked expertise (coordination and maneuver warfare). This failing particularly slowed the process of adaptation early in the war when victories were few and far between, and so adaptation was generally slow, ill focused, and disparate.[146]

When a more professional and scientific approach to lessons learned gradually materialized in the middle of World War II, the pace of change accelerated. However, the British Army never achieved the flexibility displayed by the U.S. Army as Montgomery's ascendancy increasingly shaped the learning process. His desire to preserve morale, cut extravagant ammunition consumption, and minimize losses, as well as his quest for a sustained satisfactory performance led him to censor after-action reports, thus further narrowing the breadth of effective adaptation. Finally, the mounting manpower crunch acted as a brake on organizational and tactical innovation: manpower was simply not available for experimentation, as the history of countermortar groups illustrates.

As a result, even though there was improvement in the army's operational and tactical expertise during the Normandy campaign, it was, as it had been throughout the war, incremental. The army's disdain for intellectual development and theory still prevented it from substantially rethinking doctrine and tactics. Nor did it intensively retrain in the field or display determination to remove inadequate officers. Moreover, British forces concentrated much of their strength forward in the line when on the defensive; a policy that made field training more difficult.[147] The British learning process—the manner in which the army gathered, evaluated, and disseminated combat lessons—also remained more centralized than in the U.S. and German Armies. Not only did after-action reports often lack critical appraisal, but suppression of negative information further got in the way of army efforts to enhance its effectiveness.

Dissemination of after-action reports apparently had little impact on the process of innovation in the field. In fact, most adaptation occurred on a unit-by-unit basis based on individual units' experiences. But the lack of effective feedback to provide accurate and honest lessons-learned information meant that adaptation remained slow, idiosyncratic, and piecemeal. Even though the Second Army perpetually fell short of its specific goals and British forces were slow to adapt, the general shape of Montgomery's theater strategy—to pin down the Germans at Caen—went broadly to plan. This illustrated that his master plan was well attuned to strategic, military, and geographic realities. The Americans had massed in western Britain; the Allies knew through Ultra that the Germans viewed the British as the greater threat; and geography both entailed that the Germans would defend Caen vigorously and that their reinforcements would arrive mainly from the southeast. His strategy also recognized the limits of British capabilities as well as the burgeoning American strength, although he failed to appreciate the growing U.S. military proficiency. Moreover, Montgomery's insistence on the early capture of Cherbourg proved vital to Allied victory in northwest Europe. His strategy realistically utilized the sustainable capabilities of Anglo-Canadian forces, even if he had to mislead his superiors to get what he wanted. His master plan displayed an unrivaled grasp of strategic and logistic realities that contributed directly to Allied victory in Normandy. It allowed for a sustained, if unspectacular, performance from British ground forces that, in retrospect, proved sufficient to guarantee victory, as Montgomery had maintained all along. He fought his battles in a way most likely to fulfill British political-military objectives and at a tolerable cost. His arrogance, tactlessness, condescension, and deceit made him many enemies and obscured his achievements, but Montgomery played an important role in Allied victory in northwest Europe.

Notes

1. Public Record Office, Kew, London, Cabinet Papers 106/1060 (hereafter PRO CAB) Brig. James Hargest, "Notes," Normandy [summer 1944].

2. National Archives of Canada, Ottawa, Record Group (hereafter NAC RG)

24 13711, II Cdn. Corps Int.[elligence] Sum.[mary] 17 (27 July 44), Pt. II, 4–5.

3. Liddell Hart Centre for Military Archives, King's College, London, Liddell Hart Papers 1/292/100 (hereafter LHCMA LHP) Letter, Basil Liddell Hart to C. S. Forester, 18 February 1952.

4. Recent works that stress poor Allied performance include Carlo D'Este, *Decision in Normandy* (New York: Collins & Son, 1983); Max Hastings, *OVER-LORD: D-Day and the Battle for Normandy, 1944* (London: Michael Joseph, 1984); John Ellis, *Brute Force: Allied Strategy and Tactics in WWII* (New York: Penguin Viking, 1990); and John English, *The Canadian Army in Normandy: A Study in Failure of High Command* (New York: Praeger, 1991).

5. PRO WO 231/8, *Lessons of the Italian Campaign* (London: War Office: 1944), 78; PRO WO 171/258, I Corps Int. Sum. 26 (July 1944), "Panzer Lehr Division Combat Report," apdx. A; PRO CAB 106/1060, Brigadier Hargest, "Battle Notes on Recent Operations up to D+10."

6. LHCMA LHP 10/1944/12, Basil Liddell Hart, "Method of Attack Is Our Problem."

7. Without the British-Canadian failures in Normandy, it is unlikely that Hitler could have counterattacked in the West at all in 1944. On German success on the Seine and Allied failures in September, see RAF Museum, Hendon, Bombing Analysis Unit Rpt. 44, "The German Retreat Across the Seine August 1944," [1945]; Michel Dufresne, "Le Succèss allemand sur la Seine (Août 1944)," *Revue Historique des Armées* 176 (September 1989), 48–60 and Robert Kershaw, *It Never Snows in September* (Ramsbury: Crowood Press, 1990).

8. PRO WO 232/21, DTI, Lt. Col. A. E. Warhurst GSO1(L), "Notes on the Fighting in Normandy," para. 2; WO 231/8, *Lessons From the Italian Campaign,* 78; CAB 106/1060, Hargest, "Reports on Recent Actions up to D+10."

9. The U.S. military demonstrated greater willingness to garner lessons from its enlisted ranks. Michael Doubler, *Closing with the Enemy: How GIs Fought the War in Europe* (Lawrence: University of Kansas Press, 1995), chap. 9.

10. The constant controversy over whether attached units were "under command" or "in support" exemplified the lack of combined-arms doctrine. PRO CAB 106/ 1060, Hargest, "Diary Notes," 17 June 1944.

11. Shelford Bidwell, *Gunners at War: A Tactical Study of the Royal Artillery in the Twentieth Century* (London: Arrow Books, 1972).

12. German studies confirmed the considerable improvement in Allied airborne operations in 1944. PRO WO 208/3193, SHAEF Special Tactical Studies, Translations of Captured German Documents, "Experiences from Allied Air Landings," 8 November 1944.

13. Montgomery confided that "I would even risk the total loss of the armoured brigade groups to carry out these tactics." His boldness did not predicate an intended major British offensive role, as Carlo D'Este has contended, but reflected Montgomery's awareness of the need to secure quickly a viable lodgement. PRO PREM 3/339/1, Letter, Montgomery to Bradley and Dempsey, 14 April 1944; D'Este, *Decision,* chap. 6.

14. Supreme Headquarters Allied Expeditionary Force (SHAEF) poorly assessed the topography in its invasion planning. For the effect of terrain in the campaign, see Arthur Davies, "Geographical Factors in the Invasion and Battle of Normandy," *Geographical Review* 36 (October 1946), 613–631.

15. SHAEF assumed that the Germans would conduct a delaying withdrawal to the Seine and make a stand there. It thus tardily addressed executing a breakout battle just prior to D-Day. H. P. Willmott, *June 1944* (London: Blanchard Press, 1984), 85–87.

16. On 15 June, the I SS Panzer Corps deployed 210 tanks on a 20-mile front. PRO DEFE 3/175, Ultra Decrypt KV 8884, 20 June 1944.

17. It was the only panzer division that was fully mechanized and contained many "extras." NARA T-78, 623, "Panzer Lehr Division, "Zustandbericht u. Kriegsgliederung, Stand: 1.6.1944."

18. The most balanced assessment of the fanaticism of the *Hitlerjugend* Division is Craig H. Luther, *Blood and Honor: The History of the 12th SS Panzer Division "Hitler Youth" 1943–45* (San Jose, Calif.: R. James Bender, 1987). Less valuable is Hubert Meyer's *Kriegsgeschichte der 12. SS Panzer Division "Hitlerjugend"* (Osnabrück: Munin, 1982). On the Panzer *Lehr* see Helmut Rutgen, *Die Geschichte der Panzer-Lehr-Division im Westen* (Stuttgart: Motorbuch, 1979); and Franz Kurowski, *Die Panzer Lehr Division* (Bad Nauheim: Podzun, 1964).

19. H. M. D. Parker, *Manpower: A Study of Wartime Policy and Administration* (London: HMSO, 1957), 226–228; Stephen Hart, *Montgomery and Colossal Cracks: The 21st Army Group in Northwest Europe, 1944–45* (Westport, Conn.: Praeger, 2000).

20. PRO WO 205/152, TFAG, "Estimate of Casualties-Operation OVER-LORD," 12 February 1944.

21. Provost marshals constantly complained about the reluctance of commanders to report those absent without leave (AWOL). Brigadier Hargest was amazed on a trip to Cherbourg, in early July, at how few stragglers there were in the U.S. rear compared to the British situation. PRO WO 171/167, TFAG Provost Marshal, War Diary, Sept. 1944; WO 277/16, "Morale"; CAB 106/1060, Hargest Diary [July 1944].

22. The 50th Division alone had over 1,000 AWOLs in May 1944. PRO CAB 106/1060, Hargest, Diary Notes, 21 June 1944; WO 163/162, Morale Committee, "Morale of the Army, Feb–Apr. 1944"; Michael Carver, *Out of Step: The Memoir of Field Marshal Lord Carver* (London: Hutchinson, 1989), 166–167; D. Rissik, *The DLI at War* (Durham: DLI Association, 1953), 23; Maj. E. W. Clay, *The Path of the 50th* (Aldershot: Gale & Polden, 1950), 228.

23. On the 7th Armoured's problems in Normandy, see Robin Neillands, *The Desert Rats* (London: Weidenfeld & Nicolson, 1991), chap. 12; PRO WO 232/21, DTI, "Rpt. on Ops. 1, 7th and 11th Armd. Divs." [June 1944], 9–10. On Villers–Bocage see Eric Lefevre, *Panzers in Normandy: Then and Now* (London: Battle of Britain Prints, 1984), 162–180; D'Este, *Decision,* chap. 11; J. F. Ellis, *Victory in the West* (London: HMSO, 1966), 252–255; Hastings, *OVERLORD,* 153–166.

24. PRO 106/1092, 15 July 1944; J. B. Salmud, *The History of the 51st Highland Division, 1939–1945* (Edinburgh: William Blackwood, 1953), 144–149.

25. Trials demonstrated that the chances of destroying enemy armor with the PIAT were "slim." The greatest achievement of a PIAT in Normandy was the disablement of a German armed trawler in the Caen Canal on D-Day. PRO WO 291/153, Army O[perational] R[esearch] G[roup] Rpt. 164, "The Effectiveness of PIAT Shooting"; CAB 44/244, 221.

26. Some 1,976 M4A1, M4A3, and M4A5 Shermans made up 57 percent of Montgomery's armor. PRO WO 205/636, TFAG, "AFV States, June 1944." On British tank procurement problems, see David Fletcher, *The Great Tank Scandal: British Armour in WWII* (London: HMSO, 1989).

27. The Germans derisively dubbed the British Shermans "Tommy cookers." The War Office suppressed knowledge of their inflammability, claiming that crews' fears "were greatly exaggerated." The evidence from Normandy showed otherwise: over 80 percent of Shermans penetrated burned. PRO WO 205/ 1165, Capt. H. B. Wright and R. D. Harkness, RAMC, Medical Research Council Team, 2 ORS, "A

Survey of Casualties Amongst Armoured Units in Northwest Europe," January 1946, 58; WO 106/4398, 2 ORS, "Analysis of Sherman Tank Casualties, 6.6-10.7.1944," 15 August 1944; R. P. Hunnicutt, *Sherman: A History of the American Medium Tank* (San Rafael, Calif.: Taurus Enterprises, 1978); G. M. Ross, *The Business of Tanks* (Ilfracombe: A. H. Stockwell, 1976), 153; John Sandars, *The Sherman Tank in British Service, 1942–1945* (London: Osprey, 1982).

28. Although the number of Fireflies available in Normandy increased from 84 on 11 June to 232 on 30 July, they never exceeded 70 percent of establishment. PRO WO 205/637, "Daily AFV States, Second Army, June–July 1944."

29. This unwillingness to commit Fireflies is reflected in contrasting loss rates. Up to 23 June the enemy had disabled 32 percent of regular Shermans landed, but only 19 percent of Fireflies. In many tank squadrons a single kill merited the distinction of "ace." PRO WO 205/1165, "A Survey of Tank Casualties"; WO 106/4398, "Analysis of Sherman Tank Casualties, 6.6–10.7. 1944"; WO 205/404, Lt. Col. A. H. Pepys DSO, GSO(L) 7th Armd. Div., Imd. Rpt. IN 24, "Points for Discussion with Formation Commanders," 19 June 1944; W. Steel Brownlie, *The Proud Trooper: The History of the Ayrshire Yeomanry* (London: Collins, 1964), 33.

30. Up to 20 July the RAC lost 1,276 tanks disabled, 41 percent of those deployed. PRO WO 205/112, TFAG, "Statement of Tank Losses," 21 July 1944, apdx. A.

31. Less than 150 Tigers fought in Normandy, and up to 7 August only eight destroyed Tigers had fallen into Allied hands. NARA T-78, 624, Gen.Insp. d. Pztr. "Im Western Vorhandenen deutschen Panzerlage, 10.6.1944"; Lefevre, *Panzers in Normandy,* 34–42, 114–119, 162–190; PRO WO 106/4398, 2 ORS Rpt. 17, "Analysis of German Tank Losses In France, 6.6–31.8.1944," [Sept 1944], 202; on British concerns about Tiger tank phobia see PRO WO 205/5b, letter, de Guingand to Montgomery, 26 June 1944; CAB 106/1060, Hargest, "Notes—Tanks," 17 June 1944.

32. John Sandars, *British Guards Armoured Division 1941–45* (London: Osprey, 1979), 12; Andrew Graham, *The Sharpshooters at War* (London: Sharpshooters Regimental Association, 1964), 66; Brownlie, *Proud Trooper,* 33.

33. Statistically Shermans were four times as likely to burn as Churchills. The Germans captured over thirty Allied tanks in Normandy. PRO WO 171/376, G. Branch, Guards Armd. Div., Int. Sum. 6: II, (June 1944), 5; WO 232/21, Lt. Col. L. G. Coleman, AIF, DTI, "Rpt. on Ops. 1: 7th and 11th Armd. Divs.," June 1944, para. G; WO 205/1165, "A Survey," 43–45, 57–59; WO 171/637, WD 31st Tank Brigade. Workshop REME, "Rpts. on Churchill Battle Casualties," 5 July 1944, apdx. Y; NARA T-311, 20, 7022667ff, Anlagenband I Ic Tagesmeldung, OB West, July–August 1944; LHCMA LHP 9/24/103, "Interrogation Report—General Feutchinger," 2.

34. Historians have exaggerated the impact of Ultra in Normandy. Until the breakout in August, the Germans relied mainly on land lines and so passed little useful intelligence via their enciphered Enigma radio messages. Ultra also only regularly decoded high-level messages, and the time required to decrypt and pass on intelligence further limited its value. PRO, WO 232/ 76, DTI, "Battle Study: The Infantry Divisional Recce Regiment"; DEFE 3/48-65, 112–128, and 161–179, Ultra Decrypts, June–August 1944.

35. PRO CAB 106/1060, Hargest, "Battle Notes on Recent Ops. up to D+10."

36. The Panzer *Lehr* Division suffered 100 casualties a day from artillery fire. PRO WO 171/258, I Corps Int. Sum. 26 (July 1944), "Combat Report Panzer Lehr Division."

37. PRO WO 232/21, DTI, Lt.Col. A. E. Warhurst GSO1(L), "Notes on the Fighting in Normandy," para. 2.

38. During GOODWOOD (18–20 July) the German defenses were 10 miles deep. Lt. A. G. Heywood, "GOODWOOD," *Household Brigade Magazine* (Winter 1956–1957), 171–177.

39. Training manuals promoted profligate expenditure of ammunition. One manual asserted that "if a cabbage gets in your way put down a thousand tons of shell." PRO W0 231/11, Directorate of Military Training, *Artillery Notes and Lessons Learnt* (London: War Office: September 1943), 1.

40. PRO WO 171/393, 1 Abn. Div. "Rpt. on MARKET-GARDEN," October 1944, 45.

41. PRO WO 232/21, "Rpt. on Ops. 1," 19 July 1944, 13.

42. A case in point was the 26 June assault on Cristot when the British fired 25,500 shells to kill seventeen defenders. Hastings, *OVERLORD,* 247.

43. Hart, *Montgomery,* chap. 4.

44. Montgomery wrote that "Dempsey and his staff do not know a very great deal *yet* about how to wield air power; and D. himself has slipped up once or twice in the matter." (emphasis in original) Imperial War Museum Alanbrooke Papers (hereafter IWM AP) 14/27, M508, Letter, Montgomery to CIGS "On Present Ops." 7 July 1944, 6; See also Hart, *Montgomery,* chap. 6.

45. On Dempsey's ambitions see LHCMA LHP 1/341/4A, Letter, Basil Liddell Hart to Brig. James Hackett, "Armitage on Bluecoat: Dispelling the Myths"; D'Este, *Decision,* 253–254; Hart, *Montgomery,* chap. 6.

46. Dismissals included Bucknall (XXX Corps), Erskine (7th Armoured Division), and Bullen-Smith (51st Division). LHCMA LHP 10/1946/2 Basil Liddell Hart, "Verdict on the Generals," 25 January 1946; John Keegan, ed., *Churchill's Generals* (London: Grove Weidenfeld & Nicolson, 1991).

47. Williamson Murray, "British Military Effectiveness in World War II," in Allan Millett and W. Murray, eds., *Military Effectiveness* III, 123–125.

48. In accordance with revised attack doctrine outlined in *The Tactical Handling of the Armoured Division* (London: War Office: November 1943).

49. Hastings, *OVERLORD,* 166–180; D'Este, *Decision,* chap 14.; Ellis, *Victory* I, 274–286; Alexander McKee, *Caen: Anvil of Victory* (London: Souvenir Press, 1964: Pan Books, 1964), chap. 12; Henry Maule, *Caen: The Brutal Battle and Breakout from Normandy* (London: David & Charles, 1976; 1988), 38–42; John Keegan, *Six Armies in Normandy* (London: Jonathan Cape, 1982: New York: Penguin, 1984), 170–181.

50. The VIII Corps suffered 4,020 casualties, 2,590 in the 15th Division alone, including 784 missing.

51. Meyer, *Kriegsgechichte,* 178–214.

52. Gen. Richard O'Connor (VIII Corps) learned more quickly than the other corps commanders. Air Marshal Leigh-Mallory regarded him as "a tower of strength." PRO AIR 37/1784, Leigh Mallory Diary, 20 June 1944.

53. McKee, *Anvil,* 172–173; Maule, *Caen,* 38–42; Hastings, *OVERLORD,* 170; John Baynes, *The Forgotten Victor: General Sir Richard O'Connor KT, GCB, DSO, MC* (London: Brassey, 1989), 192.

54. Some 443 bombers dropped 2,276 tons of bombs on Caen. PRO WO 233/28, "Attack by Bomber Command on Targets at Villers-Bocage and Caen, 30 June and 7 July, 1944;" WO 106/4348, 2 ORS Rpt. 5, "Heavy Bombing in Op. CHARNWOOD"; NARA T-311, 420, KTB PzGr West, 8–9 July 1944.

55. PRO WO 171/196, Second Army, Op. Instr. 2 "GOODWOOD," 13 July 1944; LHCMA LHP/1/230/16, "Dempsey's Notes on Goodwood," 21 February 1952, pt. 3; Hart, *Montgomery,* chap. 6.

56. Hart, *Montgomery,* chap. 6.

57. O'Connor had persuaded Montgomery in June that the Orne bridgehead

was unsuited for offensive action. Nigel Hamilton, *Monty: Master of the Battlefield 1942–1944* (London: H. Hamilton, 1983), 732; Baynes, *Forgotten Victor,* 187–188.

58. On 17 July Montgomery had 5,714 infantry replacements left. PRO WO 219/1538, TFAG, "Casualty Report (Sitrep) 43," 19 July 1944.

59. That Eisenhower believed Montgomery was about to launch a major breakout bid indicates that he completely misunderstood "Monty's" theater strategy. Alan Brooke wrote of Eisenhower on 27 July that "Ike knows nothing about strategy and is quite unsuited to the post of Supreme Commander," a conclusion reinforced by Eisenhower's preference for Alexander as land forces commander and his demand for a "fulldress attack on the left flank." Alanbrooke Diary, 27 July 1944, quoted in D'Este, *Decision,* 398; G. Sixsmith, *Eisenhower as Military Commander* (New York: Stein & Day, 1973; Da Capo, n.d.), 119, 147–150; PRO AIR 37/784, Leigh Mallory Diary, 18–21 July 1944; Air Marshal Arthur Tedder, *With Prejudice: The War Memoirs of Marshall of the RAF, Lord Tedder, GCB* (London: Cassell, 1966), 537.

60. The British believed the German defenses to be only 3 miles deep, when in fact they were 10 miles deep. PRO WO 232/21, DTI, "Operational Research Report—Operation GOODWOOD"; Heywood, "GOODWOOD," 171–177.

61. Inadequate mine clearance, which Dempsey kept to a minimum prior to 18 July in an abortive effort to maintain surprise, added to the delay and the congestion. PRO WO 232/21, Op. Research Rpt. "Op. GOODWOOD."

62. British inability to deploy forward artillery to maintain continuous indirect-fire support was a particular weakness. The guns remained stuck in the traffic jam debouching from the Orne bridgehead, and thus the armored spearhead was out of field artillery range.

63. Accounts of GOODWOOD exaggerate the tank-busting success of the III Flak Corps. In fact, it was army 88mm heavy antitank guns that did most of the damage. Janusz Piekelwicz, *Die 88mm Flak in Erdkampf-Einsatz* (Stuttgart: Motorbuch, 1976); Koch, *Flak: die Geschichte d. deutschen Flakartillerie, 1939–45* (Bad Nauheim: Podzun, 1954); PRO WO 232/21, DTI, "Notes on the Fighting in Normandy Obtained During an Interview with Lt. Col. J. A. Eadie DSO," para. 3.

64. The Second Army had 213 tanks disabled on 18 July, its highest single days loss of the war. PRO WO 205/112, TFAG RAC, "Statement of Tank Losses to 20 July," 21 July 1944, apdx. A.; John Sweet, *Mounting the Threat: The Battle for the Bourguebus Ridge, 18–21 July 1944* (San Rafael, Calif.: Presidio Press, 1977), 111–115.

65. The only inconsistency was the armored spearhead role, which was a reversion to the pre-1943 doctrine discredited in North Africa. David A. Wilson, "The Development of Tank-Infantry Co-Operation Doctrine in the Canadian Army For the Normandy Campaign," M. A. Dalhousie University, 1970, 112.

66. Dempsey's subordinates had reservations, and General Erskine (7th Armoured Division) temporized and blamed the congestion for his failure to get forward on 18 July. Bryan Perrett, *Through Mud and Blood: Infantry-Tank Operations in WWII* (London: Hale, 1975), 187.

67. Dempsey's outlook was generally conservative. Baynes, *Forgotten Victor,* 205; Hart, *Montgomery,* 148.

68. Some 1,599 heavy and 482 medium bombers dropped 7,700 tons of bombs. Sweet, *Mounting the Threat,* 46.

69. Postbattle analysis confirmed only three antitank guns that had been destroyed by the bombing. PRO WO 106/4348, 2 ORS, Rpt. 6, "Bombing in Op. GOODWOOD," 7; WO 232/21, DTI, "Op. Research Rpt. Op. GOODWOOD."

70. The Second Army lost 482 tanks disabled during GOODWOOD, 36 per-

cent of its entire inventory. These figures exclude losses sustained in diversionary operations between 16–18 July. PRO WO 205/965, "Rpt. on the Battle of Noyers, 16–18 July"; Sweet, *Mounting the Threat,* 111–115; Ellis, *Victory in the West* I, 348; Ellis, *Brute Force,* 379.

71. On 17 July Montgomery had 50 serviceable replacement tanks in Normandy, all of which he committed on 19 July. On 30 July Sherman equipped regiments averaged only 59 percent of authorized strength, as opposed to 86 percent on 8 July. PRO WO 205/637, "AFV States, 30 July 1944"; WO 205/638, "AFV-RA Equipment States (ARG)," August 1944; WO 205/637, "Daily AFV States: Second Army Summaries," July 1944; WO 205/631, WD Armd. Replacement Grp. IV, July 1944; WO 171/196, "Notes on RAC Conference at VIII Corps," 29 July 1944; WO 205/360, TFAG Ops.(B), "RAC Reinforcements," 7 August 1944.

72. Diversionary attacks by the XII and XXX Corps (GREENLINE on Evrecy and POMEGRANATE on Noyers) between 15–17 cost 3,532 casualties. Total British-Canadian casualties between 18–22 July were 6,102, 14 percent of the total to date. PRO CAB 106/1101, "Casualties OVERLORD."

73. Historians have accepted grossly inflated regimental claims of heavy damage inflicted (109 enemy tanks alone on 18 July). Yet the Second Army only officially claimed 20 tank kills during GOODWOOD, and the I SS Panzer Corps actually lost 27 tanks. NARA T-311, 420, KTB PzGr. West, 18–21 July 1944; PRO WO 285/8, "Enemy Tank Casualties," n.d., table I; David Fraser, *We Shall Shock Them* (London: Stodder & Houghton, 1983), 334.

74. See the author's "Feeding Mars: Logistics and the German Defeat in Normandy, June–August 1944," *War in History* 3, 4 (Fall 1996), 418–435.

75. Maj. J. J. How's *Normandy: The British Breakout* (London: W. Kimber, 1981) presents an inflated assessment of BLUECOAT. For a more balanced view, see LHCMA LHP 1/341/4A, Comments of Maj. G. T. Armitage, MBE, appended to a letter from Brig. James Hackett to Liddell Hart, 31 October 1955, 4.

76. The British order of battle for BLUECOAT was XXX Corps—43d Wessex Division, 50th Northumbrian Division, 7th Armoured Division; VIII Corps—15th Scottish Division, 11th Armoured Division, 6th Guards Tank Brigade; Reserve—Guards Armoured Division.

77. LHCMA LHP 1/292, letter, Liddell Hart to C. S. Forrester, 18 January 1952.

78. IWM Lt. Gen G. C. Bucknall Papers, letter from Bucknall to Col. M. Browne, 17 August 1944.

79. How, *British Breakout,* chaps. 3–8.

80. Ibid., 60–70.

81. Ibid., 92–93, 218–219.

82. That Montgomery expected great things from the daring and energetic Horrocks was shown by the fact that Montgomery gave the XXX Corps, not the VIII Corps, the spearhead role in the drive to the Seine.

83. All told, Montgomery removed or transferred 100 officers, including two brigadiers. Carver, *Out of Step,* 196.

84. The Guards commander, Allan Adair, "was not really a flyer." LHCMA Richard O'Connor Papers 5/4/103, "Notes on Ryan's *A Bridge Too Far.*"

85. O'Connor said of the brigade that "no tank unit has ever been handled with greater dash and determination." Perrett, *Through Mud and Blood,* 192, 229; Sandars, *Guards Armoured Division,* 11, 18.

86. Hart, *Montgomery,* 54–56.

87. By mid-August morale problems were evident in nine of sixteen divisions, and only the depleted 6th Airborne Division attacked aggressively out of the Orne

bridgehead but faced intact defenses. PRO WO 106/4466, 6th Abn. Div., "Rpt. on Ops., 6.6–29.8.44," 19–26; LHCMA LHP/15/15 (CWP)/130, "Notes of Discussion with Horrocks," 14 May 1946.

88. Historians have understated the seriousness of the British manpower shortage, and the official history barely mentions it. Ellis, *Victory in the West* I, 131–133; D'Este, *Decision,* 258–259; Hart, "Montgomery," chap. 3.

89. Despite these measures, shortages grew and many battalions had to disband at least one company. D'Este's claim that untapped infantry remained in Britain is not supported by the evidence. Draftable infantry in Home Forces fell from 18,128 on 15 March to 2,654 by 7 August. D'Este, *Decision,* 268–270; PRO CAB 78/21, War Cabinet Meeting, 20 May 1944; WO 171/219, Second Army GS, "Reorganization of Infantry Brigades," 2 August 1944, apdx. C; WO 199/1334, Memo DA+QMG H[ome] F[orces], "Drafting Home Field Army," 27 February 1944; WO 199/1238, GSO1(SD) HF, "Examination of Drafting Figures Now Known," 14 February 1944; WO 199/1335, Memo, DA+QMG HF, 2 May 1944; WO 166/14174, letter commander in chief Home Forces to undersecretary for state, "Reorganization of the Army in the U.K.," 7 August 1944, 3.

90. Only under great pressure late in the war did transfer rates increase. By 4 September casualties had fallen 17 percent below preinvasion estimates.

91. On the Allied failure at Falaise, see Dennis D. Dowd, "The Battle of the Falaise Gap: Differing Interpretations," M.A. thesis Creighton University, 1982; Martin Blumenson, *The Battles of the Generals: The Untold Story of the Falaise Pocket—the Campaign that Should have Won WWII* (New York: Morrow, 1993); "Battle of the Falaise Pocket," *After the Battle* 8 (May 1975).

92. D'Este, *Decision,* 428; Blumenson, *Generals,* chaps. 15–16.

93. Montgomery, like most Allied officers, distinguished vaguely between the operational and strategic levels of war. Montgomery, *Memoirs,* 87.

94. For Montgomery's theater strategy, see PRO CAB 44/264, Second British Army Outline Plan, 21 February 1944 and Second Army, Op. Order 1, 21 April 1944, 116ff.

95. Forces coordinated well to capture their D-Day objectives after months of meticulous rehearsal, but after that infantry and armor generally returned to their separate wars. PRO CAB 106/1060, Brig. Hargest, "Diary Notes," 17 June 1944.

96. Maj. Gen. H. J. Parham and E. M. G. Belfield, *Unarmed into Battle: The Story of the Air Observation Post* (Winchester: Warren & Son, 1956), 78.

97. 10th SS Pz. Div., "Lessons from the Normandy Front," quoted in Parham, *Unarmed,* 78.

98. One Auster directed twelve shoots in a single day. Parham, *Unarmed,* 80.

99. Richard Hallion, *Strike from the Sky: A History of Battlefield Air Attack* (Washington, D.C.: Smithsonian Institute Press, 1989), 199–203.

100. PRO WO 291/1331, 2 ORS Rpt. 125, "Enemy Casualties in Vehicles and Equipment during the Retreat from Normandy to the Seine."

101. The first continental RAF airstrip became operational on 9 June, and thirty-one were in use by late July.

102. PRO WO 291/1331, 2 ORS TFAG Rpt. 4, "Air Attacks on Enemy Tanks and Motor Transport in the Mortain Area, August 1944," table 2; Hallion, *Strike,* 219.

103. Christopher F. Shores, *2nd TAF* (Reading: Osprey, 1970); Sir Basil Embry, *Mission Completed* (London: Methuen, 1957); Humphrey Wynn and Susan Young, *Prelude to Overlord* (Novato, Calif.: Presidio Press, 1983); Andrew J. Brookes, *Photoreconnaissance* (London: Ian Allen, 1975).

104. Pilots grossly overestimated the damage that they inflicted. Pilots

claimed 136 tank kills at Mortain, but postbattle analysis confirmed only twelve. PRO WO 291/1331, 2 ORS Rpt.4, Table 2; Hallion, *Strike from the Sky,* 217; RAF Museum, Hendon, RAF Bombing Analysis Unit Rpt. 44, "The German Retreat Behind the Seine, August 1944" [1945].

105. Postcampaign analysis attributed only 4 percent of destroyed armor to rockets. Despite numerous strikes the Second TAF claimed only two tank kills on the first day of GOODWOOD. PRO AIR 37/61, 2d TAF Rpt. 36, "The Operational Accuracy of 2d TAF Fighter-Bomber and RP Aircraft"; WO 291/1331, 2d TAF/2 ORS Joint Rpt. 3, "Rocket Firing Typhoons in Close Support of Military Ops."; Christopher Shores, *Ground Attack Aircraft of World War II* (London: MacDonald & Janes, 1977); Ian Gooderson, "Allied Fighter-Bombers Versus German Armor in North-West Europe 1944–1945: Myths and Realities," *Journal of Strategic Studies* 14 (June 1991), 210–231; Alfred Price, "The 3-inch Rocket: How Effective Was It Against the German Tanks in Normandy?" *Royal Air Force Quarterly* (Summer 1975), 127–131. John Golley's, *The Day of the Typhoon: With the RAF Tankbusters in Normandy* (Cambridge: P. Stephens, 1986) inflates the Typhoon's contribution to the ground battle.

106. PRO CAB 44/264, "Report of the Joint Technical Warfare Committee on the Fire Support in the Neptune Phase of Op. OVERLORD," 17 April 1946, 358–360.

107. Postbattle analysis found only a single enemy gun destroyed by the bombing. PRO WO 233/28, "Attack by Bomber Command on Targets at Villers-Bocage and Caen, 30 June and 7 July, 1944"; WO 106/4348, "Heavy Bombing in Support of the Army," 21–22.

108. Aircraft dropped 10,800 tons of bombs in 4,500 missions. PRO AIR 37/762, "Preliminary Analysis of Air Operations—GOODWOOD, July 1944."

109. PRO WO 291/262, AORG. Rpt. 282, "Study of Casualties and Damage to Personnel and Equipment Caused by some Air and Artillery Bombardments in European Ops."

110. Kenneth Macksey, *For Want of a Nail: The Impact on War of Logistics and Communications* (London: Brassey's U.K., 1989), 132–134.

111. Only Crocker (who had come up through the ranks) of the senior British commanders advocated and employed broader divisional attack frontages with two brigades up front. He also adopted defense in depth. NAC Crerar Papers 2, 1-0-7, Crocker, "Ops. RAWLINSON & BYNG," 27 July 1944, 1–4; PRO WO 171/ 258, "I Corps Operational Policy," 22 July 1944, apdx. T.

112. Anglo-American concepts of concentration were antithetical. To the Americans it meant the application of maximum force; to the British it meant concentration of maximum strength. In other words, the simultaneous application of all possible force versus the selective application of all possible force. Thus the Americans deployed greater strength forward, attacking on a broader front with less logistical buildup. LHCMA AP 14/1, letter, Alanbrooke to Montgomery, 28 July 1944.

113. Overmechanization contributed to the congestion in British offensives. Leese wrote of this problem in Italy: "We clog our advance by using too much transport. . . . I am doing my best to cut it down." IWM BLM 97/22, letter, Leese to Montgomery, 11 June 1944, 3.

114. This was both Liddell Hart's and Tedder's view. Tedder, one of Montgomery's fiercest critics, dismissed Dempsey's attacks on Caen as "company exercises." LHCMA LHP, 1/292, letter, Basil Liddell Hart to C.S. Forrester, 18 February 1952.

115. Hart, *Montgomery,* chap. 3.

116. Montgomery wrote that "we have got to try and do this business with the smallest possible casualties." PRO WO 285/002, letter, Montgomery to Lt. Gen. Ronald M. Weeks (Deputy CIGS), 19 March 1944.

117. Michael Howard, "How Will History Judge Montgomery's Generalship?" *The Times,* 25 March 1976.

118. The bloody failure of the diversionary attacks launched in support of GOODWOOD validated Montgomery's restraint.

119. Montgomery wrote, "The Faubourg de Vaucelles lying on the south side of the [River] Orne opposite Caen will be secured and a bridgehead thus gained, if this is can be done without undue losses; I am not prepared to have *heavy* casualties to obtain this bridgehead over the Orne, as we will have plenty elsewhere." (emphasis in original) LHCMA AP/14/27, fol. 12.

120. Nevertheless, casualty minimalization was sensible and appropriate given British political-military objectives. Hart, *Montgomery,* 62–67.

121. Michael Howard, "Montgomery and the Price of Victory," *Sunday Times* 16. October 1983, 42.

122. Hart, *Montgomery,* chap. 2.

123. Nigel Hamilton, *Monty: The Man Behind the Legend* (London: Sphere Books, 1975), 96.

124. Graham, *Sharpshooters at War,* 99.

125. The extent of the AWOL problem is hard to gauge because units were reluctant to report AWOLs, but the evidence suggests that it was serious. By August morale problems existed in nine of sixteen British divisions. PRO WO 171/167, WD, TFAG Provost Marshall, September 1944; Hart, *Montgomery,* 31–32.

126. Hart, *Montgomery,* 35–41.

127. For Montgomery's ideas on air power, see his *Some Notes on the Use of Air Power in Support of Land Operations* (Holland: TFAG, December 1944).

128. For criticisms of his caution see Ellis, *Brute Force,* 375–380; Thompson, *Montgomery,* 173–174; Martin Blumenson, "The Most Overrated General of World War Two." *Armor* (May–June 1962), 9.

129. For example, the defeat of the Desert Rats at Villers-Bocage on 13 June.

130. Up to 15 July, the Second Army fired on average 45,926 25-pounder rounds daily, some sixty-two rounds per gun. IWM Eassie Papers, "The Administration of 2nd Army in the NW Europe Campaign."

131. Hart, *Montgomery,* 93–95.

132. Indeed, the Germans quickly learned to reoccupy bombed areas to disrupt and delay a ground advance. In the rubble of Falaise sixty SS troops held the British and Canadians at bay for three days. Meyer, *Kriegsgeschichte,* 329–335.

133. PRO CAB 106/1021, MORU Rpt. 3 "The Effects of Bombardment: The Present State of Knowledge" (March 1946); CAB 106/1033, AORG Rpt. 292, "Comparison of British and American Areas in Normandy in Terms of Fire Support and its Effects;" WO 291/262, AORG. Rpt. 282, "Study of Casualties and Damage to Personnel and Equipment Caused by some Air and Artillery Bombardments in European Ops."

134. Only O'Connor of the British corps commanders displayed a firm grasp of German defensive doctrine. One corps once fired twenty VICTOR (corps) barrages in one day. Hart, "Montgomery," 276–278; PRO WO 205/404, "R.A. Notes on Recent Ops.," 25 June 1944.

135. Montgomery's professional judgement, though ruthless, was generally accurate and fair. Nevertheless, he truly only respected one officer—Alan Brooke. The British corps commanders were I Corps—John Tredinick Crocker; VIII Corps—Richard ("Dick") Nugent O'Connor; XII Corps—Neil Methuen Ritchie;

XXX Corps—Gerard Corfield Bucknall (from 4 August, Brian Gwynne "Jorrocks" Horrocks). Hamilton, *Monty,* 95; Bernard L. Montgomery *The Path to Leadership* (London: Collins: 1961), 123–127.

136. Liaison officers wrote eighty-six immediate reports during 1944–1945, of which the 21st Army Group disseminated (some in censored form) fifty-nine. Hart, "Montgomery," 173.

137. For an examination of the self-appraisal and flexibility of the German army, see Williamson Murray, "The German Response to Victory in Poland: A Case Study in Professionalism," *Armed Forces and Society* 7, 2 (Winter 1981), 285–298. War Office euphemisms prevalent in Normandy after-action reports include "the attack failed to live up to expectations" (the attack failed); "the troops experienced difficulty getting forward" (the troops would not advance); "the troops filtered back" (retreated without orders); and "the scheduled armored support was not available at the last minute" (armor refused to engage the enemy).

138. Capt. Michael Doubler, *Busting the Bocage: American Combined Arms Operations in France, 6 June–31 July 1944* (Fort Leavenworth: CSI, U.S. Army Command and General Staff College, Combat Studies Institute, 1988).

139. Hart, "Montgomery," 71–72.

140. Montgomery's staff, for example, banned Lt. Col. Jackson's Imd. Rpt. 92, "Action of Guards Group Making the Breakout from a Bridgehead over the Meuse-Escaut Canal, 17.9.1944," of 5 October 1944 because it advocated profligate artillery support. Hart, "Montgomery," 172–174.

141. For censored reports, see PRO WO 205/404, Lt. Col. A. H. Pepys DSO GSO1(L) 7th Armd. Div., IR 24, "Points for Discussion with Fmtn. Cmdrs.," 19 June 1944. De Guingand, Montgomery's chief of staff, called Bucknall's (XXX Corps) adverse comments on the Sherman Firefly "a very bad show" and a similar evaluation by Bowring as "somewhat dangerous," and feared that "if the sentiments expressed therein get down to the troops they may have a great effect upon their fighting." Weeks, the deputy CGIS, labeled Guards Armoured Division complaints about their tanks "defeatism." Montgomery disseminated J. R. Bowring's IR 12, "Impressions of Fighting in Normandy," 17 June 1944, only after deleting "the German Tiger and Panther is an infinitely superior tank to the Cromwell or the Sherman," on all copies except those sent to the RAC on the grounds that "it may seem unwise to publish it at the present time." PRO WO205/5b, letter, De Guingand to Montgomery, 24 June 1944, 2–4; letter, Montgomery to De Guingand, 24 June 1944; WO 205/5c, letter, Weeks to De Guingand, 26 June 44, para. 4; Hart, *Montgomery,* 173.

142. PRO WO 205/404, 51st Division, "Imd. Rpt.2, "Organization of Counter-Mortar Group," 15 June 1944; WO 1771/219, HQ Second British Army General Staff, "Counter-Mortar Organization," 14 August 1944.

143. On the army's unreceptivity to criticism see Brig. J. P. Kiszely, "Originality" in Brian Holden Reid, *Science,* 35–42.

144. Corelli Barnett, et al., *Old Battles, New Defences: Can We Learn from Military History?* (London, Brassey's, 1985), 138–139; J. Mackenzie and Brian Holden Reid, *British Army and the Operational Level of War* (London: Tri Service Press, 1988), 10; Hew Strachan, "The British Way in Warfare," in David Chandler, ed., *The Oxford Illustrated History of the British Army* (Oxford: Oxford University Press, 1994), 417–434.

145. The War Office disseminated official doctrine in the form of Army Training Instructions and Memoranda as well as some ninety Military Training Pamphlets. IWM, *Military Training Pamphlets* 2–90 (London: War Office, 1938–1945).

146. The marginalia by G (Ops) Branch at Army Group on GSOI(L), 49th Infantry Division, Imd. Rpt. IN 102, "Attack by the Leicesters on 29 Sept. 1944" of 5 October 1944 is highly illuminating: "This does not seem worth publication if so many mistakes were made!"

147. PRO WO 171/258, "Operational Policy," WD I Corps, 22 July 1944, Apdx.T.

9

Canada: Learning the Hard Way

The British Soldier appears slower to adapt himself to a new situation than does the Canadian.[1]

The lack of combat experience and a growing manpower shortage both hampered and stimulated the Canadian Army's ability to adapt during the Normandy campaign. All told, however, the Canadian Army in Normandy failed to replicate the martial achievements of its Great War predecessor. The war in Normandy was a learning process that validated some aspects of Canadian preparation but condemned others. Inexperience bred misjudgment and overconfidence that cost the Canadians heavily when facing some of Germany's best troops early in the campaign. Canadian forces proved sluggish in attack and never achieved the speed, flexibility, or versatility that characterized U.S. operations in Normandy.

The worsening manpower crisis undermined Canadian combat effectiveness late in the campaign and engendered a philosophy of casualty minimization that dominated operational planning. This constraint often led the Canadian First Army to commit strength that was inadequate for its operational goals. However, manpower conservation also promoted innovation because troops and commanders alike sought new tactics and equipment that would reduce losses. But despite efforts to minimize casualties, unexpectedly heavy losses—the result of a combination of Canadian offensive inexperience and German defensive skill—depleted units and sapped their drive at the very moment in late August 1944 when Canadian forces finally embarked on the exploitation mission for which they had long trained. The Canadians thus proved unable to pursue aggressively the retreating Germans in August–September 1944. The loss of offensive thrust that the manpower crisis brought about did, however, mask the growing skill that Canadian forces were developing late in the campaign as they adapted ever quicker to battlefield conditions. All ranks showed ingenuity as they sought

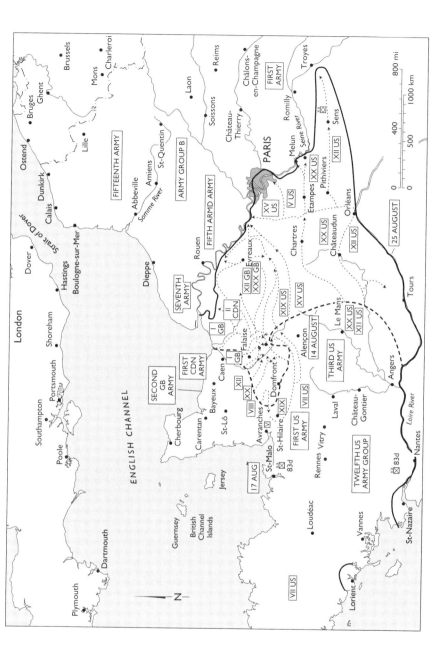

Northwestern France Exploitation, 14–25 August 1944

Table 9.1   **War Establishment of the Canadian First Army in Northwest Europe, Summer 1944**

Formation	Officers	Men	Total
2d Infantry Division	924	17,452	18,376
3d Infantry Division	925	17,449	18,374
4th Armoured Division	750	14,069	14,819
2d Armoured Brigade	188	3,632	3,820
Combat Formations	2,787	52,602	55,389
Corps Troops	499	7,327	7,826
Army Troops	1,332	17,678	19,000
GHQ Troops	1,970	19,115	20,085
1st Parachute Battalion	32	601	633
Grand Total	6,620	97,323	103,943

Source: PRO War Office 179/2574, "Composition of the CAO," WD GS Canadian GHQ, November 1944.

more efficient organization, better tactics, and superior equipment to enhance their combat effectiveness and to prevail on the battlefield.

The Canadian Army experienced its most extensive and costly combat in Normandy. Canadian operations in the campaign fall into three distinct phases: the meticulously rehearsed D-Day amphibious assault; the June-July struggle to execute limited break-in battles; and the August efforts to effect a breakthrough and fulfill the exploitation role that the Canadians had prepared for in Britain.

In Normandy, there was a strong correlation between battlefield success and the orientation of Canadian preinvasion training. Canadian forces performed well in the carefully rehearsed amphibious assault, but experienced considerable difficulties mastering both the limited break-in battle and the all-out breakthrough battle, missions that Canadian forces had neither anticipated nor prepared for before D-Day.

With marked numerical and material superiority, and lengthy amphibious assault training, the Canadian 3d Infantry Division and the Canadian 2d Armoured Brigade established themselves ashore with little difficulty on D-Day. Landing on Juno beach, Canadian assault troops secured a 4-mile-deep lodgement. The 3d Division had trained long and hard for its amphibious assault to restore Canadian honor stained at Dieppe, and the extensive preparation paid off.[2] Effective combined-arms coordination characterized Canadian operations on D-Day, reflecting the spirit of cooperation imbued for the well-rehearsed amphibious assault.[3] The D-Day performance demonstrated that the army could create effective coordination but only after months of rigorous preparation geared toward a narrow, specific mission.[4]

After D-Day, however, Canadian infantry and armor quickly reverted to the practices taught during four years of training in Britain and thus returned to fighting their own individual wars. Coordination remained poor for much of the campaign, and the repeated failure of Canadian combined-operations in Normandy ultimately reflected flawed doctrine as much as inadequate training. Once ashore the 3d Division and 2d Armoured Brigade struggled through June and into July to execute limited break-in battles, and as a result suffered a series of setbacks.[5]

The first of these occurred on 7 June as the 3d Division thrust boldly inland toward its D-Day objective of Carpiquet airfield near Caen, despite the known movement of powerful German armored reserves toward Caen.[6] The Canadian spearhead, built around the North Nova Scotia Highlanders and the 27th Armoured Regiment, was a balanced combined-arms team that conformed to those employed during exercises conducted in Britain.[7] This force thrust south across the assembly area of *Kampfgruppe Meyer,* the spearhead of the 12th SS Panzer Division *Hitlerjugend.* The enemy vanguard was inferior in strength, but it went directly into the attack and took the strung-out Canadian force in the flank. The well-trained and disciplined SS troops, aided by superior armor, soundly defeated the Canadian force. Even after the Canadians had initially held them off, the SS troops infiltrated into the Canadian positions and forced a withdrawal into a defensive box. It took fire from every available artillery piece, as well as a critical German fuel situation, to halt the SS drive for the coast. In the process there were heavy Canadian casualties.[8]

This reverse was the first indication in Normandy that serious flaws remained in Canadian attack doctrine, for the setback was the result of a combination of flawed doctrine and inexperience. Poor Canadian reconnaissance and superb German fire discipline allowed the SS troops to ambush the Canadians at close range. Lack of experience also had led Canadian troops to ignore battlefield conditions while they followed fixed procedures learned in training. Such shortcomings, when coupled with the limited availability of artillery support, allowed an improvised, but well-coordinated and well-executed German counterthrust to succeed as the Canadians were caught off balance and defeated in detail.[9]

The Canadians displayed the weaknesses on 7 June that were to dog them throughout the campaign: a ponderous approach to battle, poor coordination, and amateurish reliance on courage, self-confidence, and good luck rather than sound staff work and planning. Canadian command and control was inadequate, and emphasis on the controlled battle, which these deficiencies promoted, robbed Canadians of both the flexibility to respond quickly to unanticipated and unplanned eventualities and of a "fingertip" feel for the battle.[10] Such command rigidity prevented rapid reinforcement of the 9th Infantry Brigade while it was under attack.

Further reverses followed in the days ahead that confirmed serious weaknesses in Canadian doctrine. The following day, 8 June, the 2d Battalion of the 26th SS *Panzergrenadier* Regiment, outfought the Royal Winnipeg Rifles to retake Putot. With only numerical parity, the SS troops again infiltrated and outflanked the Winnipegs to encircle their three forward companies. The Canadians made a hasty withdrawal under cover of smoke but lost heavily in the process.[11]

The failure of the Le Mesnil-Patry operation on 11 June starkly illuminated the Canadian difficulty in prevailing without lengthy preparation and overwhelming fire support. The 6th Armoured Regiment and the Queens Own Rifles of Canada launched a hastily planned and poorly prepared right-flanking movement through Le Mesnil-Patry to take the high ground south of Cheux. However, the operation was "a complete and costly failure."[12] Once again inexperience and a desire to minimize losses led the 3d Division to commit insufficient resources to the mission. The spearhead, B Squadron, 6th Armoured Regiment, supported by D Company, Queen's Rifles, pushed into Le Mesnil-Patry where the 2d Battalion of 12th SS Panzer Regiment counterattacked and overran them.[13] The failure was again the result of the commitment of inadequate strength, poor coordination, and the recurrent tendency of Canadian units to become dispersed once committed. Le Mesnil–Patry also confirmed the stark reality that both Canadian armor and infantry lacked the firepower necessary to halt concentrated enemy armored counterattacks.[14]

By 11 June, the Canadian 3d Infantry Division had sustained 2,831 casualties and had lost its cutting edge in the face of the resistance of the more powerful, better trained, and fanatical *Hitlerjugend* troops. The division, therefore, went over to the defensive and did not return to the offensive until July. The division used this opportunity to rest, refit, and absorb replacements. But, despite its shift to defense, the division made little effort to evaluate its performance during its operational debut or to withdraw units for retraining.[15]

A combination of bad weather, the constricted size of the bridgehead, and Montgomery's lack of faith in General Crerar delayed the arrival of Canadian First Army headquarters until late July.[16] Thus when the 3d Division returned to the offensive west of Caen in early July it remained under command of the British I Corps tasked with capturing Caen. This headquarters ordered the 3d Division to capture Carpiquet airfield as a preliminary to a full-scale assault on Caen. The Canadians had recognized from their June operations that they required heavier fire support to penetrate German defenses organized in depth. Thus the I Corps postponed the attack (WINDSOR) scheduled for 30 June to strengthen it.[17] The powerfully reinforced Canadian 8th Brigade finally launched WINDSOR on 4 July with heavy fire support. The Canadians brought massive strength and firepower to bear on a small German defending force, and achieved an attack ratio of 20:1.[18] Moreover, for the first time in Normandy, Canadian troops also carried out a diversionary attack on the left toward Gruchy to confuse the enemy and divide German reserves.

Despite overwhelming superiority and the use of tactical deception, the Canadian attack failed to capture the airfield.[19] The failure of WINDSOR not only illustrated the marked superiority of the defense in Normandy, but also the problems that beset Canadian offensive actions. The attack failed due to superb SS defensive tactics combined with flawed Canadian attack doctrine, tactics, and fieldcraft. Increased Canadian radio traffic and poor wireless discipline, along with with aggressive German battle patrolling, warned the Germans on 2 July of an impending attack.[20] Anticipating the attack, the Germans massed their meager mobile reserves at Carpiquet, and disrupted the attack before it went in. As Allied artillery began its rolling barrage, German guns and mortars hit likely Canadian assembly areas, inflicting numerous casualties and disorganizing Canadian assault troops. The Germans then accurately laid fire behind the Canadian rolling barrage, suggesting that Allied artillery had fallen short, further demoralizing and disrupting the Canadian attack.[21] German tactical skill, therefore, depleted and badly disrupted the Canadian assault battalions before they even engaged the defenders.

Flawed Canadian attack doctrine also contributed to the failure of WINDSOR. The attack lacked coordination. In accordance with prevailing British doctrine, two Canadian infantry battalions spearheaded the attack while armor provided fire support from the flanks and rear. After the initial attack faltered, the 3d Division committed additional infantry and armor piecemeal, but the armor provided direct support only grudgingly, tardily, and sparingly.[22] Poor coordination meant that the 3d Division failed to utilize fully the resources available, and because neither the Canadian infantry nor armor possessed the firepower to suppress German defenses on its own, poor coordination resulted in both arms suffering defeat in detail. Again, despite massive superiority, the Canadians had failed to gain ground against the entrenched and tenacious SS soldiers.[23]

On 8 July Montgomery launched Operation CHARNWOOD, a major push for Caen, the D-Day objective that Rommel had denied him for over a month. During that time, the Germans had developed a well-organized and mutually supporting system of defense in depth. To breach these defenses, the Allies reluctantly employed heavy bombers to shatter German resistance in Caen.[24] The bombing took place on the evening of 7 July, 6 hours before the ground attack, and the bomb line was placed 6,000 yards beyond the Allied front line to safeguard the assault troops. However, this placement largely negated the bombing's stunning effect.[25] While inflicting negligible damage on the enemy, the bombing did hurt German, and raise Anglo-Canadian, morale; it also destroyed all but one of the Orne bridges still in German hands, crippling German supply efforts and rendering the German defense of northern Caen untenable.[26]

CHARNWOOD was an unsophisticated frontal attack by three infantry divisions to overwhelm the German defenders and capture northern Caen,[27] with the Canadian 3d Division on the extreme right flank attacking southwest to occupy northwestern Caen. CHARNWOOD did see Canadian efforts to adapt to combat conditions in Normandy. During June Canadian forces gradually recognized that German defensive artillery fire had disrupted and impeded their operations, so Canadian gunners learned the need for more extensive and effective counterbattery fire and, consequently, for CHARNWOOD they launched a larger and extended program of suppressive fire on known German batteries during the night of 7–8 July.[28] Then, on 8 July thirty-one days after its debacle of 7 June, the 9th Infantry Brigade finally captured Buron northwest of Caen, using the heaviest artillery concentrations yet seen in support of Canadian operations. Hit by overwhelming artillery, the already weakened and exhausted *Hitlerjugend* Division was unable to withstand the attack of three Anglo-Canadian divisions.[29]

CHARNWOOD evidenced growing skill by elements of the Canadian 3d Division, but improved proficiency was by no means discernible across the board. Even against eroded resistance the Highland Light Infantry of Canada suffered heavily as it struggled throughout 8 July to take Buron in its first major action of the campaign.[30] Once again poor coordination retarded Canadian progress and brought heavy casualties. Nevertheless, Canadian defensive skill showed signs of improvement as the 3d Division learned from its June experiences to rush forward antitank guns and armor and to organize a coordinated combined-arms defense once an objective had been captured. On 8 July, such a combined-arms defense repulsed two enemy armored counterattacks and inflicted heavy loss, creating the preconditions for final Anglo-Canadian occupation of northern Caen on 9 July as the enemy retired behind the Orne.[31]

The latter stages of CHARNWOOD revealed Canadian weaknesses in urban warfare as they relied heavily on artillery fire to smash enemy resistance. Fighting for northern Caen quickly revealed that prolonged artillery bombardment had little effect on built-up areas; thus, it was fortunate that the Canadians faced only enemy rearguards. Canadian commanders subsequently concluded on the basis of CHARNWOOD that street fighting training had been taught as too much of a drill and that Canadian troops lacked the flexibility and direct-fire support to prevail against a determined enemy in urban warfare.[32]

The tenor of Canadian operations changed on 11 July when Gen. Guy Simonds's Canadian II Corps became operational and assumed command of the 3d Division and the arriving 2d Division on a 8,000-yard front that included northern Caen.[33] Simonds, the most gifted and innovative senior wartime Canadian commander, enunciated a clear, holistic, flexible, and original operational policy for his command that emphasized infiltration, preparation, narrow attack frontages, coordination, good reconnaissance, and massed artillery support.[34] His operational approach reflected his (by Canadian standards) extensive combat experience and accurate appreciation of German defensive techniques. Simonds emphasized that contingency planning against German counterattacks must form an integral aspect of all operational planning.[35] The operations of the Canadian II Corps in July, though, demonstrated that Simonds had an uphill struggle to inculcate this approach in his few short months as corps commander. His troops typically remained wedded to the British methods and procedures absorbed during the previous four years.

On 18 July the Canadian II Corps launched its first attack in Normandy, ATLANTIC, the Canadian element of GOODWOOD, which was Montgomery's push south from the Orne bridgehead. The II Canadian Corps was to support the right wing of the main British drive by capturing German-held Caen south of the Orne River and then seizing the Verrières Ridge, the commanding high ground to the south.[36] ATLANTIC represented the first Canadian multidivisional corps-level operation in northwest Europe. Simonds's plan called for the 3d Division to advance southwest along the eastern bank of the Orne from the British airborne bridgehead to capture the Caen suburbs of Colombelles and Vaucelles. Having loosened the German grip on the south bank of the Orne, the green 2d Division was to strike across the Orne, mop up southern Caen, and storm Verrières Ridge.[37] Simonds's plan was more sophisticated than earlier Canadian operations: for the first time the staff integrated tactical air support to engage enemy defenses and reserves moving up.[38]

Despite a more refined plan, ATLANTIC met with only partial success. This was as much due to the inexperience of the 2d Division and II Corps headquarters as enemy resistance. The 3d Division attacked down the eastern bank of the Orne front, made steady progress and obtained its objectives. The 2d Division, however, experienced much greater difficulty in its first operational employment since its 1942 disaster at Dieppe. Its mission in ATLANTIC was also more difficult in that it had to conduct an opposed crossing of the Orne. By midafternoon on 18 July, the division's attack had stalled in confusion as its follow-up battalions got mixed in with its attack battalions and as Canadian artillery fire repeatedly hit its own troops.[39]

Ineptitude continued to afflict the 2d Division when it renewed its offensive the next day. Its unseasoned assault companies advanced beyond their start line, were again badly hit by their own artillery, and stalled short of Fleury. Throughout the day, the infantry proved unable to occupy its objectives.[40] On 20 July Simonds committed the reinforced 6th Brigade, without armor support, to storm Verrières Ridge.[41] During the morning the Queen's Own Cameron Highlanders took St. André, the South Saskatchewan Regiment consolidated on a forward slope along the ridge line, and the Fusiliers Mont Royal took Beauvoir farm but halted short of Verrières.

The brigade received a drubbing late on 20 July when the 1st SS Panzer Regiment counterattacked in heavy rain that prevented the usual Allied defensive artillery and air support. The SS armor caught Canadian antitank guns and armor moving up and picked these off. Without antitank support, the South Saskatchewan Regiment and the Fusiliers Mont Royal at Trotéval farm were quickly overrun and dispersed by the panzers.[42] The Canadian 2d Division hastily threw the Essex Scottish Battalion forward, also unsupported, to restore the situation. But the SS troops encircled half the battalion and drove the remainder back in disorder.[43] Another German counterthrust the next day penetrated the Essex Scottish positions and only a well-orchestrated counterattack restored the Canadian center.

Although ATLANTIC pushed the Germans back from their strong defensive position along the Orne, it failed to gain the heights south of Caen that dominated movement across the river—and Canadian forces again suffered heavy losses.[44] For the 2d Division, ATLANTIC proved to be an ignominious return to battle, which left three of its battalions badly mauled. The difficult task given the raw division was beyond its capacity in its debut operation. Canadian intelligence had also underestimated the strength and depth of the German defenses.[45] Inexperienced Canadian troops had coordinated poorly and failed to bring firepower to bear, while poor weather had curtailed artillery and air support. Most seriously, the Canadians had again underestimated German capabilities.[46] After the failure of GOODWOOD/ATLANTIC Montgomery undertook further limited attacks aimed at holding German reserves at Caen while U.S. forces launched the Operation COBRA breakout bid on 25 July.[47] Simonds's corps launched the first of these holding attacks on 25 July, a renewed assault on Verrières Ridge, called SPRING. The two Canadian divisions reinforced by British firepower attempted to storm the ridge on a 4-mile front. To obviate German observation from the ridge, Simonds launched his initial break-in at night to seize Verrières, May, and Tilly astride the ridge. Thereafter, British armor was to drive south to Cintheaux in a classic exploitation role.[48]

SPRING marked further Canadian efforts at adapting to overcome the German defenses: Simonds, for the first time, seriously endeavored to camouflage his attack to preserve surprise. Supporting artillery fired timed concentrations, instead of the standard creeping barrage, to disguise the time, location, and axis of advance.[49] SPRING witnessed other innovations too. Artificial moonlight, created by bouncing searchlights off low cloud cover, aided the night attack on 24–25 July.[50] With two divisions massed on a narrow front, backed by enormous fire support and innovative tactics, Simonds expected excellent results.[51]

SPRING was, however, a complex operation that depended on careful coordination. Moreover, the operation went ahead without the support of heavy bombers which were fully committed to COBRA. Intelligence errors again flawed the planning: the Canadians underestimated the strength and depth of the German defense, the availability of mobile reserves, and the impact of topographical features.[52] These errors had serious consequences, given the formidable array of German forces. Despite careful, innovative planning and extensive preparation, SPRING quickly degenerated into a debacle. The searchlights employed to facilitate the night attack silhouetted the Canadians for the Germans, resulting in heavy casualties, and left the startline unsecured. Moreover, Canadian infantry and armor found it impossible to overcome the doctrine taught in training and to coordinate effectively. The North Nova Scotia Highlanders' unsupported attack on Tilly stalled in the face of withering defensive fire that forced them to retire to their startline. In addition, German antitank guns thrice drove off the armor sent forward to support the Canadian infantry as poor coordination stalled the 3d Division's attack.[53]

In the center, German fieldcraft played a major role in disrupting the 2d Division's advance on Verrières. The Canadians failed to detect German tanks cunningly disguised as haystacks, and lack of effective infantry anti-tank capability prevented the Royal Highland Light Infantry from neutralizing these tanks.[54] Nevertheless, the Highlanders ultimately managed to gain Verrières, and Canadian tanks and antitank guns rushed forward just in time to help the battalion ward off two heavy counterattacks.[55] Thereafter, the Royal Regiment of Canada made an unsupported advance through Verrières toward Rocquancourt and ran into a classic German rear-slope position set up in depth that destroyed the Royal Regiment's lead company.[56]

Because German possession of the high ground on the far right allowed them to observe the entire Canadian front, the Calgary Highlanders launched a night attack on the village of May. Intense German machine gun and mortar fire stalled the Highlanders occupying only part of the village. The follow-up battalion, the Black Watch of Canada, launched a conventional, unsupported "square" battalion assault (two companies up, two companies back) in broad daylight against an intact, alerted, well-camouflaged, and entrenched up-slope defense. Murderous enemy fire immediately pinned down the battalion and neutralized its forward observation officers so that it could not call down fire support. The result was a massacre—and besides Dieppe, the most costly single Canadian battalion action of the war.[57]

German counterattacks likewise threw the Calgary Highlanders out of May and back to their startline. The 2d Division threw the Regiment de Maisonneuve into another unsupported advance late on 25 July to stabilize the situation.[58] But after personally assessing the situation late on 25 July, Simonds abandoned the operation. After Dieppe, SPRING was the most costly single day's action for Canada in World War II.[59]

In retrospect, the Germans had clearly once again anticipated the attack, despite Simonds's efforts to camouflage it, and intelligence failures had led to a serious underestimation of German strength.[60] The Canadian attack plan was too ambitious for the forces employed. Inexperience, poor coordination, and flawed attack doctrine dictated that the Canadians would fail to utilize the strength at their disposal. Moreover, the Canadian artillery program had neglected "counterflak" operations—the suppression of enemy antiaircraft fire—which rendered the preliminary air operations ineffective.[61]

Combined-arms teamwork remained poor, and the assault degenerated into seven uncoordinated battalion attacks that were defeated in turn and in detail. Nowhere did the Canadians gain a significant toehold on the high ground south of Caen nor did they inflict significant damage on the enemy.[62] SPRING also failed to draw German reserves into the line.[63] By any objective criterion SPRING was a dismal failure, and, in reality, a less ambitious and better coordinated attack by veteran troops could have forced German reserves into line and kept them there. SPRING was such a debacle that it stimulated an immediate post mortem and a board of inquiry.[64] Despite German strength, Simonds maintained that it was possible to capture Verrières Ridge without inordinate losses and he ascribed failure to faulty tactics.[65] The post mortem identified multiple causes for failure. It concluded that the Canadian 3d Division and 2d Armoured Brigade, which had been in the line since D-Day and had suffered tremendous casualties, were burned out and required extensive refitting.[66] It also concluded that the inexperience of the 2d Division played a key role in the operation's failure.[67] Simonds singled out Gen. Charles Foulkes, its commander, for particular blame.[68]

Despite failure, SPRING nevertheless demonstrated Simonds's determination to devise means to surmount the German defenses. The operation witnessed for the first time in northwest Europe the abandonment of the immense World War I fire plans that smashed a way for Anglo-Canadian forces into German defenses for about a mile. Simonds abandoned a preliminary barrage and instead employed timed concentrations in greater depth than before to deal with German antitank guns and left it to the armor to get the infantry up. He also had medium bombers drop delayed-action bombs to disrupt German reserves moving up to counterattack.[69] This imaginative plan failed, however, due to formidable German defensive strength and the difficulty in getting Canadian troops to overcome the old doctrine and to coordinate on the battlefield.[70]

On 31 July, Gen. Harry Crerar's Canadian First Army finally assumed operational control of the II Corps and the three Canadian divisions now in Normandy.[71] For the first time in the nation's history, an independent Canadian higher command controlled Canadian troops in combat. However, the First Army labored under severe difficulties. Its headquarters was inexperienced, and the abilities of General Crerar gravely concerned General Montgomery, who considered him unfit for command.[72] Moreover, in early August the First Army was incapable of major offensive action because most of its services and its tactical air support remained in Britain.[73] This lack of readiness, in particular the lack of air support, constrained Canadian operations in August. The arrival of the 4th Armoured Division in late July did strengthen the Canadian First Army, though, and allowed the 3d Division to withdraw for rest and refitting after 55 days in the line.[74]

In late July, Panzer Group West denuded its defenses south of Caen to build a new western flank facing the U.S. troops advancing from Avranches.[75] To prevent further enemy redeployments to the U.S. sector, Montgomery ordered the Canadians to launch a series of holding attacks south of Caen. Given the dramatically thinned German defenses, such limited attacks appeared more likely to succeed.

In early August the inexperienced 2d Division and green 4th Armoured Division executed a succession of battalion assaults intended to hold German reserves on the Caen front. On 1 August, the Calgary Highlanders struck three times for Tilly-la-Campagne but were halted each time by heavy enemy fire.[76] In these operations, Canadian troops continued to innovate to minimize casualties and to overcome enemy defenses. During the night of 1–2 August, the Lincoln and Welland Regiment launched the first silent Canadian night attack in northwest Europe, but this too stalled before it had really started.[77] This series of attacks concluded on 5 August with three abortive battalion assaults on Verrières, May, and Tilly by the Black Watch of Canada, the Regiment Maissonneuve, and the Argyll and Sutherland Highlanders.

These abortive assaults on 5 August concluded the intermediate stage of Canadian operations in Normandy. From 7 June on, the Canadians had launched with mixed success a series of limited, break-in battles, which had largely failed in the face of strong German defenses situated in depth in good defensive terrain. Between 18 July and 5 August, the Canadian II Corps launched twelve abortive battalion assaults against the Verrières Ridge at a cost of more than 2,000 casualties.[78] Canadian troops had not performed well in these operations due to inexperience, flawed doctrine, and lack of specific preparation for this role.[79] British attack doctrine had proven inflexible and cumbersome, and failed to stress the combined-arms coordination that was essential for victory. Poor coordination had led to repeated defeat in detail. Canadian training had lacked realism and failed to instill flexibility. Tactically, not only had Canadian troops rarely employed deception measures, but poor radio discipline and predictable artillery fire programs repeatedly compromised surprise in the attack. Canadian forces had also not managed to utilize fully available tactical air support.

When the Canadian First Army became operational in early August, it too was confronted with a situation very different from that for which it had trained. It had practiced exploiting a breakout against a badly weakened German defense, but had encountered intact enemy defenses. Before it could conduct its exploitation mission, the First Army had to execute a breakthrough battle for which it had not been trained. Moreover, logistic constraints aggravated Canadian operational difficulties. The Canadians had limited transport capacity, which prolonged the buildup time required for major operations, with the result that ammunition shortages restricted artillery support for Crerar's two major August offensives.[80]

On 8 August the Canadians launched a major new offensive to shatter the German defenses southeast of Caen. The operation, named TOTALIZE, and planned by Guy Simonds, was the first Canadian effort to devise a comprehensive operational plan to overcome the German defense in depth, which had previously stalled all Canadian offensives.[81] The operation's name implied that it would be a total effort on the part of the II Corps. Simonds sought to achieve surprise through the timing of the attack and the methods employed. To compensate for the inability of Canadian artillery to keep up with the advance and maintain fire support, Simonds substituted the use of air power. He arranged a novel, but complex, nighttime bombing attack, followed by a nighttime break-in. To get the infantry forward quickly and with fewer losses, Simonds mounted them in improvised armored personnel carriers converted from surplus U.S. M7 Priest 105mm self-propelled guns, officially designated Kangaroos, but more popularly known as "unfrocked priests" or "holy rollers."[82] To maintain surprise, Simonds forbade a preliminary artillery bombardment or stepped-up counterbattery fire before TOTALIZE to reduce indications of an imminent assault. Only after the attack began, did 312 guns fire on counterbattery targets and 408 guns lay down a rolling barrage to a depth of 3.5 miles. Behind the barrage, the two infantry divisions supported by two armored brigades organized into combined-arms task forces were to break in to the enemy positions and pierce the German main line of resistance (MLR).[83]

Simonds also addressed the Canadian difficulty in translating a break-in into a breakout. For the first time the planning for TOTALIZE took full account of the depth of German defenses.[84] Once through the forward German line, Simonds arranged for a second strategic bombing attack, 12 hours after the first, to smash the second German line of resistance and flanking positions. Thereafter, two armored divisions, the Canadian 4th and the fresh Polish 1st, would follow through and penetrate the most rearward German defense line.

TOTALIZE was thus an innovative plan that grappled with the problems that had bedeviled earlier Canadian operations. Both the nighttime attack by heavy bombers and the use of improvised armored personnel carriers were new. Given the drastic thinning of the German defenses south of Caen, Simonds had high expectations of success.[85] TOTALIZE began at

11 P.M. on 7 August with precision bombing on the flanks of the axis of advance.[86] Simonds employed radio beams, Bofors guns firing tracers, artificial moonlight from searchlights, and green marker shells to guide the armored armada forward in the dark. Although the Germans had expected an attack, its timing took them by surprise and the Kangaroos got the Canadian infantry into German lines before the Germans had recovered from the bombing and barrage. Early on 8 August Canadian tanks and infantry stormed Verrières Ridge.[87] Good coordination allowed the spearheads to take rapidly their objectives with minimal casualties. The first stage of TOTALIZE had proven remarkably successful.

The second phase, however, went awry. In the early afternoon of 8 August, 492 heavy bombers of the Eighth USAAF dropped 1,488 tons of bombs on German rearward positions; however, twenty-four planes bombed short, hitting Canadian and Polish troops.[88] The Canadian 4th and Polish 1st Armoured Divisions advanced in a textbook exploitation operation. However, congestion in the rear caused by passing four divisions through a narrow corridor and made worse by the short bombing slowed the advance. Despite Simonds's exhortation that the armored formations press on during darkness, they "harbored" for the night in accordance with prescribed doctrine.[89]

The tardy Canadian advance on 8 August brought a bold push on 9 August by a combined-arms force of the 4th Armoured Division, which ended in disaster.[90] The inexperienced Canadian troops lost their way, and the Germans isolated and overran them on Hill 140. During the night of 9–10 August, the Argyll and Sutherland Highlanders boldly seized the strategic Hill 195 in a silent night attack. Believing the enemy defenses broken and with the high ground taken, the armored divisions unleashed their tanks to exploit forward on 10 August with terrible consequences. German armor and antitank guns savaged the inexperienced Canadian and Polish armor, which lost 142 tanks, the First Army's highest single day's tank losses of the war.[91] To regain the momentum of the advance, Simonds threw the veteran and now rested 3d Division into the battle late on 10 August. It launched a coordinated attack on Quesnay Wood, defended by a SS battle group. The struggle for the wood demonstrated the superiority of German forest fighting techniques. The SS troops held their fire until Canadian forces were deep in the wood and then ambushed them at dusk, forcing both lead battalions to withdraw.[92] This setback brought TOTALIZE to a premature conclusion on 11 August.

The offensive had gained 9 miles, largely due to the innovative use of Kangaroo armored personnel carriers and nighttime bombing, but failed to reach Falaise or shatter the attenuated German defenses. But TOTALIZE once again illustrated Canadian tactical and operational ingenuity. It involved novel tactics, equipment, and devices, including several RAF-crewed visual control post tanks as mobile observation posts for the bombing.[93] However, Canadian troops had very little time to prepare for the operation, and this clearly limited the effectiveness of these innovations. But TOTALIZE did demonstrate the 2d Division's developing combat skill.[94] Its patrol efficiency, in particular, had increased markedly, reflecting its gradual transformation into a seasoned formation.[95]

Two flaws had crippled TOTALIZE in spite of its innovations. First, the entire operation was wedded to the nighttime bombing attack. This proved problematic because the initial Canadian break-in met with unexpected success and rapidly smashed through the considerably thinned German defense. The scheduled second strategic bombing attack forced the Canadian spearheads to halt for many hours, a respite that surrendered the initiative and gave the Germans time to marshal their meager reserves and counterattack as the bombing began. So most German troops, especially the armored reserves, evaded the second bombardment. The second flaw of the TOTALIZE plan was its reliance for the breakout on two green armored divisions that were participating in their first major attack. Neither formation performed well during TOTALIZE. As was wholly typical of unseasoned formations in Normandy, they coordinated poorly and stopped to eliminate pockets of resistance rather than bypass them.[96]

Moreover, despite Simonds's efforts the Canadians were unable to disguise their preparations. On 7 August the Germans recognized that the Canadians were about to strike for Falaise.[97] The rapidity with which the Canadian II Corps organized and launched the operation also meant that Canadian troops went in tired and ill prepared, limiting the effectiveness of the new equipment and techniques.[98] Finally, the First Army simply lacked sufficient strength to smash through to Argentan and link up with the Americans.[99]

Nonetheless, TOTALIZE clearly showed the value of the Kangaroo vehicle, and thereafter it became integral equipment in all future Canadian operations. The operation also illustrated the potential of large-scale night operations because the night attack allowed the Canadians to take vital ground with relatively few losses. The Canadians also learned from TOTALIZE the need for tactical aviation to strike beyond the range of field artillery in support of the advance.[100]

While the Canadians were failing before Falaise, U.S. troops began to encircle the German forces defending Normandy. To link up with the U.S. spearheads sweeping northeast toward Argentan, General Montgomery on 11 August ordered Crerar to renew his thrust on Falaise, link up with Patton's troops, and encircle the German forces in Normandy. Simonds hastily devised a new offensive, TRACTABLE, which was executed on 14 August.

Simonds once again innovated to overcome the German defenses. He employed a revised version of the TOTALIZE plan, which incorporated its

successful innovations—nighttime bombing, Kangaroos, and no preliminary bombardment. However, the attack took place in daylight, using
smokescreens to provide the protection that darkness had given TOTAL-
IZE. Simonds committed the 3d Infantry and 4th Armoured Divisions on
the narrowest of frontages. To maintain surprise, Simonds again avoided a
long preliminary barrage that would warn the Germans of an attack.
Moreover, Simonds returned to the defunct pre-1943 British offensive doctrine, concentrating his armor in combined-arms brigade groups to spearhead each divisional assault.[101]

However, Simonds augmented the armor with two Kangaroo-borne
infantry brigades and a new weapon—the Wasp, a carrier-mounted
flamethrower. Once again he had developed an imaginative plan and he
admonished his tank commanders to attack with daring and speed and to
press the attack at night. The TRACTABLE plan represented further innovation to achieve victory by maintaining surprise and instilling speed into
the Canadian advance. Given the greatly thinned enemy defenses and the
heavy concentration of Canadian strength on a narrow front, TRACTABLE
appeared to have good prospects of shattering the German defenses, outflanking Falaise, and completing the encirclement of the German forces in
Normandy.

Shortly before H-Hour seventy-three medium bombers of 2d TAF
attacked German defenses astride the Laison Valley, the main axis of
advance. Soon after H-Hour, the heavies of RAF Bomber Command struck
German positions along the right flank of the intended advance to disrupt
German counterattacks.[102] In addition, supporting artillery provided a
flanking smokescreen and a frontal barrage that combined both smoke and
high-explosive shells.[103] German artillery fire, the smoke, and widespread
disorganization occasioned by the loss of direction during the advance
behind the smokescreen, combined to disorient and disperse the Canadian
columns. At the same time, the Laison River proved a major tank obstacle
that slowed and further disrupted the advance.

Terrible misfortune also dogged TRACTABLE. Late on 13 August, the
enemy captured a Canadian officer who carried the plan of attack, and the
Germans redeployed their meager reserves to meet the impending
onslaught. This misfortune cost the Canadians additional losses and
delayed the fall of Falaise for more than a day.[104] Then Bomber Command
bombed short on Canadian positions, causing casualties and considerable
disruption and confusion.[105] Despite the German redeployment, Canadian
attacks on 14 August overran the German 85th Infantry Division.[106] On 15
August, however, the Germans halted the Canadians just short of Falaise,
and it was not until 17 August that the Canadians captured the town.
TRACTABLE had failed to complete the encirclement of the enemy in
Normandy.[107]

Canadian troops demonstrated during TRACTABLE that they had not yet mastered the complex tactics of advancing under cover of smoke. Yet they had coordinated more effectively than earlier and demonstrated improved proficiency in the use of the Kangaroos. Moreover, the Wasp flamethrower carrier proved highly effective during its operational debut.[108] The capture of the attack plan and the accidental short bombing, however, were the primary reasons for the failure of the operation.

As the German forces conducted a major strategic withdrawal to evade encirclement, the Canadian First Army redoubled its efforts to close the pocket. Without time to plan a new operation, Crerar simply ordered all formations to attack southeast until they linked up with U.S. forces then pushing northeast beyond Argentan. Thus on 17 August, Crerar's formations again struck southeast until they met up with U.S. troops at Chambois two days later to seal the Falaise pocket.[109] But Crerar was unable to establish a solid barrier against the retreating German forces. Between 19–21 August, tens of thousands of German troops escaped from the pocket during repeated, hard-fought breakout attempts.

The battle of the Falaise pocket witnessed the hardest fighting the Canadians had yet encountered as the enemy fought to escape encirclement. By August a growing infantry shortage undermined Canadian combat effectiveness. With only one division in action during June available replacements covered losses, but by mid-July infantry casualties were 80 percent above forecast.[110] By early August, when the infantry deficit reached 1,900, Crerar acknowledged that the replacement situation had become the most serious problem confronting the Canadians.[111] The heavy losses suffered during TOTALIZE and TRACTABLE increased the shortage: on 15 August Canadian formations were short 2,644 riflemen.[112] Manpower shortages thus sapped Canadian offensive drive at the moment when it was put in the unique position of "bagging" the remnants of two German armies in Normandy. Ordered to close the Falaise pocket from the north, the Canadians were too weakened to stem the flood of desperate and determined Germans bent on escaping. The fighting that engulfed the Canadians at the mouth of the Falaise pocket was among the fiercest of the campaign and left Canadian divisions severely depleted.[113] By 2 September the infantry deficiency had reached 4,318, 19 percent of establishment.[114] Because of growing shortages of both infantry and armor the Canadians could not, and did not, play a major role in the exploitation operations of late August and early September.[115]

The Canadian Army remained complacent about its manpower shortage early in the campaign. After the modest remustering of March 1944, it was not until 12 August that renewed remustering began and 4 September before crash retraining began.[116] In the meantime, Crerar had to place in the line cooks, clerks, and others from noncombat units who possessed limited infantry training. The failure of Canadian senior leadership to perceive the scale of the manpower crisis and to enact promptly measures to find more infantry hamstrung Canadian offensive actions during the late summer and the fall of 1944. Lack of infantry not only hampered Canadian operations but obscured the gradual development of military proficiency that the Canadian First Army had gained through often costly trial and error during the Normandy campaign.

The Canadian First Army thus failed to emulate the martial achievements of its World War I forebear. During the early war years the Canadian Army had struggled to recover from its sustained interwar neglect; inexperience and neglect forced it into dependence on British doctrine, tactics, organization, and equipment. Inexperience, especially in the higher command, meant that Canadian troops and commanders were to make many mistakes. Troops initially did not display tactical and operational proficiency as many of the flaws illuminated in training reappeared on the battlefield. In addition, a growing manpower shortage impeded Canadian operations. Commanders were reluctant to take risks that might have brought them greater glory in Normandy, but that might also have incurred heavy casualties. Even so, inexperience brought disproportionate casualties among Canadian units that ended up facing some of the best German troops in the strongest defensive positions in Normandy.[117] The combination of inexperience, inadequate training, unsound doctrine, unsatisfactory commanders, and command friction could only contribute to repeated failure.

The capabilities of Canadian formations at the onset of the Normandy campaign were also far from uniform. The 3d Infantry Division was the most battleworthy Canadian formation, though its combined-arms preparation was inadequate. But the 2d Infantry Division and 4th Armoured Division, which had trained for an exploitation role, were even worse prepared for combined-arms operations.[118] Indeed, the 4th Armoured Division remained nonoperational on D-Day, and it took intensive effort during June and July to ready it for combat.[119] What was striking about the readying of the 4th Division, though, was a new determination to absorb lessons learned from the early battles in Normandy.[120] Before deploying to France, the division formed its own countermortar organization, enhanced tank-infantry cooperation, and honed aerial recognition skills.[121] Nevertheless, the division still performed poorly in its early operations. Inexperience and indifferent integration led to a series of poorly supported frontal armored attacks that were shattered by German antitank defenses during TOTALIZE and TRACTABLE.[122]

Combat readiness also varied among the arms, and clearly the weakest link in the Canadian order of battle in Normandy was its armored forces. The army's belated adoption of armor meant that the tank forces remained underprepared even in June 1944. Equipment shortages, repeated reequipment, limited combined-arms training, and shortages of replacement tanks and crews all undermined the performance of Canadian armor in

Normandy. The Germans handled the 2d Armoured Brigade roughly in its early Normandy operations.[123] Its morale suffered accordingly, and "Tiger tank phobia" rapidly gripped the brigade.

From mid-June on, the Canadians experienced mounting difficulty replacing tank losses.[124] This situation progressively worsened, and by 12 August available replacements had become "very low."[125] During August Canadian armored units therefore dropped well below strength, and by 2 September the First Army's armor deficiency exceeded 40 percent.[126] This tank shortage affected Canadian combat effectiveness as continual high losses among units that had been in the field for two months brought morale of tank crews to their nadir by mid-August. Therefore, because of inadequate equipment and combined-arms preparation, as well as growing shortages of crews and vehicles, Canadian armor made little contribution to Allied victory in Normandy.

The Canadian performance in Normandy rested heavily on leadership provided by its senior commanders. Yet Canadian leadership was often found wanting, and a combination of casualties, promotions, and transfers during the campaign removed most of the senior officers who had commanded on D-Day.[127] The performance of the senior commanders in Normandy varied considerably. General Crerar proved a competent, if unspectacular, army commander. His skill lay in the political and administrative spheres, and he wisely left most detailed operational planning to his corps commander, General Simonds. Nonetheless, Crerar's operational approach was sound and, in many ways, paralleled Montgomery's. Both men exhibited great concern to avoid unnecessary losses.[128] Thus casualty control as much as quest for victory provided the impetus for Canadian tactical innovation in Normandy, and thus the purpose behind the novel methods used in TOTALIZE and TRACTABLE was to penetrate the strong German defenses at minimal cost.[129] Crerar also mirrored Montgomery in his concern in maintaining troop morale. As a career gunner he was as wedded to firepower doctrine as his superior, yet Crerar was not simply an old-fashioned gunner.[130] In Normandy, he emphasized the value of tactical surprise as an alternative to bombardment, an emphasis that bore fruit with the success achieved during TOTALIZE.[131] This emphasis led to the development of a more sophisticated Canadian operational approach during the fall of 1944 that combined flexible artillery tactics with tactical surprise. The Canadian operational approach first employed during TOTALIZE and refined in subsequent operations became the basis of Anglo-Canadian operations in 1945. Crerar also showed great enthusiasm for the use of aerial bombardment, which proved pivotal in both TOTALIZE and TRACTABLE. Though no military genius, Crerar performed competently in Normandy.

If the wartime Canadian Army possessed a military genius it was Guy

Simonds. He emerged from Normandy with a reputation as a daring, innovative officer and proved to be the most professional and gifted senior
Canadian commander. Under his leadership Canadian forces innovated
technically: they developed the first improvised Commonwealth armored
personnel carrier, the Kangaroo, and refined use of the Wasp flamethrower
vehicle. Simonds also displayed tactical and operational creativity.
Operationally, his abandonment of a preliminary artillery barrage brought
tactical surprise at TOTALIZE, but left the German defenses intact. His
strategic bombing attack on the second day of the operation was another
innovation, though one that tied the Canadian advance to a rigid plan that
ultimately undid the operation.

Simonds did "overcontrol" the battle and interfere with the freedom of
subordinates, as did all the senior Anglo-Canadian commanders, because he
had limited faith in his inexperienced subordinates, because of his lack of
success in instilling verve, speed, and flexibility among his subordinates
and their troops, and because he desired to minimize casualties.[132] At division and brigade level Canadian commanders proved less effective. For
example, General Keller's command capabilities earned him the title of
"Killer" Keller; likewise, General Foulkes, commander of the 2d Division,
failed to impress Simonds.

Generally, once committed to combat in Normandy, the Canadians
adapted faster than British troops. Initially all three Canadian divisions had
performed poorly, but they adapted fairly quickly. The 3d Division first
demonstrated improved defensive skill during CHARNWOOD as it finally
began to integrate infantry and armor and to coordinate a combined-arms
defense.[133] But constant combat and heavy losses sapped the division's
effectiveness in July. The 2d Division likewise suffered heavily during its
July battles and did not display improved proficiency until TOTALIZE.
The 4th Armoured Division, which only saw major action during August,
had not had time to become proficient before the end of the campaign.

The most significant Canadian innovation in Normandy was the gradual rejection of conventional British doctrine of firepower dominance.
Instead, the Canadians developed more sophisticated artillery programs
that relied less on predicted fire and creeping barrages and that employed
timed concentrations that made increasing use of smoke and air-burst high-
explosive shells.[134] Greater operational flexibility allowed the Canadians to
achieve surprise during TOTALIZE, the only occasion when Anglo-
Canadian forces obtained it during the campaign.

Moreover, by August, Canadian forces had begun to bring more firepower to bear in the attack. The Wasp armored flamethrower, in particular,
proved a powerful offensive weapon and became an integral element of all
subsequent Canadian offensive operations.[135] Despite manpower constraints, the Canadians also innovated organizationally. Formations established countermortar organizations during the campaign, and in August the

First Army formed both a rocket launcher battery equipped with captured *Nebelwerfer* launchers and the Kangaroo-equipped 1st Carrier Squadron.[136]

Initially, Canadian forces made poor use of the powerful tactical air support available in Normandy. Canadian training for the air-ground battle was inadequate prior to D-Day, and the tactical air support allocated to support Crerar's command only became operational on the Continent on 1 August. Thus there was no harnessing of the potential of tactical aviation either offensively or defensively as part of a combined-arms air-ground team or to ward off German counterattacks. It was only during August that improved air-ground coordination slowly emerged.[137]

The growing infantry shortage, though, both undermined Canadian combat effectiveness and obscured the gradual improvement in Canadian combat capabilities that occurred late in the campaign. The manpower crisis clearly acted as a brake on Canadian innovation in Normandy. Moreover, the army's continued failure to institutionalize the collection, evaluation, and dissemination of combat lessons hampered Canadian innovation. Before D-Day, the Canadian Army Overseas (CAO) had completed postcampaign analyses of Dieppe and Sicily, but had not studied its early operations in Italy.[138] This lack of postcombat evaluation seriously hampered the First Army's ability to absorb lessons learned in the Mediterranean. Only in the spring of 1944 did the CAO recognize the need for more continuous and systematic utilization of combat lessons.[139] And shortly before D-Day, Crerar did demand the completion of comprehensive combat reports in northwest Europe.[140] However, few formations actually prepared them, and even then only irregularly.[141]

This lack of systematic, coordinated collection of after-action reports hindered Canadian adaptation in Normandy. Of the senior Canadian commanders only Simonds exhibited real determination to learn from combat and to conduct retraining in the field.[142] That Canadian forces were locked in heavy combat throughout the campaign, however, prevented the withdrawal of units for retraining in the rear. So there was little drive, even from Simonds, to retrain during combat.[143] Consequently adaptation and innovation occurred only unit by unit.[144]

In conclusion, Canadian forces did not excel in the 1944 Normandy campaign—indeed, as early as 12 June the Germans had concluded that the battleworthiness of the Canadians was poor.[145] Inexperience, inadequate and misguided training, poor coordination, sluggish attack doctrine, poor understanding of enemy fighting methods, and inadequate preparation for the air-ground battle resulted in setbacks and repeated partial success. Nevertheless, Canadian troops adapted relatively quickly to combat conditions in Normandy and demonstrated improved proficiency during the later stages of the campaign. However, Canadian forces had yet to master fully combined-arms coordination, offensive warfare, or the air-ground battle by the end of the Normandy campaign.

Notes

1. National Archives of Canada, Ottawa, Record Group (hereafter NAC RG) 24 [Vol.] 9841 File 2/Reps Ops/1, Lt. Col. J. F. C. Pangmann, Carlton and York Regiment, "Notes: Cdn. Ops.—Italy, Sept. 1943–Jan. 1944," 1.

2. The Canadians encountered 2,500 German troops on D-Day. Public Record Office (hereafter PRO), Kew, Cabinet Papers (CAB) 44/297 "716th Division, Dispositions, 6.6.1944," apdx. J; "Lage 716th Division, Stand 5.6.1944," in Kurt Mehner, ed., *Die Geheimen Tagesberichte der deutschen Wehrmachtfuhrung im Zweiten Weltkrieg, 1939–1945* (Osnabrück: Biblio, 1984), apdx; U. S. Army Historical Division Manuscript Collection (hereafter USAHD MS) B-621, Lt. Gen. Wilhelm Richter, "716th Division (1943–28 Jun 1944)" (Germany: 1947), 24–38.

3. NAC RG 24 13766, Maj. Gen. R. F. L. Keller, "Comments on Op. OVER-LORD," 21 June 1944, War Diary General Staff 3d Cdn. Inf. Div. (hereafter WD GS 3 CID), June 1944; David A. Wilson, "The Development of Tank-Infantry Cooperation in the Canadian Army for the Normandy Campaign," M.A. thesis, University of New Brunswick, 1992, 138–148.

4. The Canadians suffered 1,094 casualties on D-Day, 8 percent of those landed. On the assault see C. P. Stacey, *The Victory Campaign* (Ottawa: Queen's Printer, 1960), chap. 5; Reginald Roy, *1944: The Canadians in Normandy* (Toronto: Macmillan, 1984), chap. 1; John English, *The Canadians in Normandy: A Study in Failure in High Command* (Toronto: Praeger, 1991), chap. 9.

5. The division had expected to be quickly withdrawn after it had established a bridgehead. This misconception reflected the fundamental flaw in the OVER-LORD plan—its failure to address how exactly the Allies would translate a successful lodgement into a subsequent breakout. PRO WO 205/ 118, TFAG G(Plans), "Appreciation of the Possible Development of Ops. to Secure a Lodgement Area," 8 May 1944.

6. Both Ultra intercepts and theater intelligence provided ample warning of the advance of *Kampfgruppe Meyer,* the reinforced 25th SS *Panzergrenadier* Regiment, into the Caen area during the night of 6–7 June. The Canadian dash was probably the result of Montgomery's exhortation to drive boldly inland to seize a sizeable bridgehead even at the cost of heavy losses.

7. The force consisted of a 27th Armoured Regiment recon. troop (M5 Stuarts), a carrier-mounted North Nova Scotia Highlander company, a medium machine gun platoon, an M10 tank destroyer troop, two engineer assault sections, four towed 6-pounder antitank guns, and three North Nova Scotia Highlander companies riding on the Shermans of the Sherbrooke Fusiliers. NAC RG 24 13766, WD GS 3 CID, 7 June 1944; Wilson, "Tank-Infantry Cooperation," 150–154.

8. The German force comprised 3 Panzergrenadier and 2 tank companies. The Canadians suffered 302 casualties, including 128 captured, and 28 tanks destroyed; the Germans 88 casualties and 9 tanks disabled. NAC RG 24 13766, WD GS 3 CID, 7 June 1944; 14152, WD GS 9th Cdn. Inf. Bde (hereafter 9 CIB), 7 June 1944; 14115, WD GS 2d Cdn. Armd. Bde (hereafter 2 CAB), 7–8 June 1944; Hubert Meyer, *Kriegsgeschichte der 12.SS Panzer-division "Hitlerjugend"* (Osnabrück: Munin, 1982) I, 76–84; Wilson, "Tank-Infantry Cooperation," 150–154; Stacey, *Victory,* 126–133.

9. Stacey, *Victory,* 133.

10. Brigadier Cunningham (9th Brigade), for example, remained unaware of the loss of Authie for more than three hours. NAC RG 24 13766, WD GS 3 CID, Jun. 1944, apdx. Q.

11. The Winnipegs suffered 256 casualties, the Canadian Scottish 125. NAC

RG 24 15233, WD GS Royal Winnipeg Rifles, 8 June 1944; Craig Luther, *Blood and Honor: The History of the 12th SS Panzer Division "Hitlerjugend"* (San Jose, Calif.: Bender, 1987), 157–160; Stacey, *Victory,* 135–136; English, *Canadians,* 209.

12. Stacey, *Victory,* 140.

13. B Squadron, 6th Armoured Regiment lost 15 of its 17 tanks and suffered 80 casualties. D Company, Queen's Own Rifles of Canada suffered 99 casualties, a 77 percent loss rate. NAC RG 24 14213, WD GS 6 CAR, 10–12 June 1944; 15168, WD GS QOROC, 10–12 June 1944; Stacey, *Victory,* 140.

14. Stacey, *Victory,* 139–140.

15. The division produced a report on 21 June evaluating its D-Day landing. A major obstacle to retraining was the Anglo-Canadian habit of keeping units forward in the line. NAC RG 24 13766, Maj. Gen. R. F. L. Keller, "Comments on Op. OVERLORD," 21 June 1944, WD GS 3 CID, June 1944.

16. Scheduled to become operational on 20 June, Crerar's headquarters did not do so until 23 July. Montgomery also speeded up the arrival of the 2d Division (it began arriving on 7 July) and phased back the 4th Armoured Division both to gain more infantry and to concentrate two Canadian divisions under what he considered the more competent command of General Simonds's Canadian II Corps, which moved to France in late June. NAC RG 24 13710, WD GS II Cdn. Corps (hereafter IICC), June 1944; 13750, WD GS 2 CID, 7–8 July 1944.

17. NAC RG 24 13766, 3 CID Op. Instr. 3, 29 June 1944.

18. The village and airfield was defended by 250 SS troops, 5 tanks and 6 heavy flak guns. NAC RG 24 13766, 3 CID Int. Sum. 17, 4 July 1944; Meyer, *Kriegsgeschichte* I, 238–239.

19. The Canadians employed in the attack four infantry battalions, three machine gun companies, an armored regiment, and squadrons of Crocodile flamethrowing tanks, flails, and AVREs supported by the fire of twenty-one artillery regiments plus naval gunfire. The Canadians gained only Carpiquet village and suffered 377 casualties, the Germans 155. Roy, *1944,* 45–50; Stacey, *Victory,* 152–155; Meyer, *Kriegsgeschichte* I, 248.

20. Meyer, *Kriegsgeschichte* I, 240–241.

21. The 12th SS Artillery Regiment fired 220 rounds, and the 83d Rocket Launcher Regiment fired two half-salvos. Meyer, *Kriegsgeschichte* I, 241.

22. It took four hours for armor to respond to the Royal Winnipeg Rifles' call for tank support.

23. Improved coordination in itself would not have substantially improved Canadian tactical effectiveness because both infantry and armor lacked firepower. Better integration could have reduced the impact of these deficiencies but could not surmount them.

24. NAC RG 24 13766, "Air Support. Op. CHARNWOOD," WD A+Q 3 CID, Jul. 1944, apdx. 16.

25. General Montgomery later alleged that weather forecasts forced an evening bombing operation, but historians have disputed this explanation. Some 467 bombers dropped 2,562 tons of bombs, and French civilian losses exceeded 400. Montgomery, *Normandy to the Baltic* (London: Hutchinson, 1947), 73; Stacey, *Victory,* 158–160.

26. Since the Orne bridges were well outside the bomb area this benefit was the lucky result of wayward bombing. PRO WO 171/131, TFAG, Int. Sum. 11 July 1944; Stacey, *Victory,* 157–160.

27. PRO WO 171/258, I Corps Op. Order 3, 5 July 1944.

28. NAC RG 24 14319, WD 2 Army Group, Canadian Royal Artillery, July 1944.

29. Meyer, *Kriegsgeschichte* I, 246–268.

30. The battalion suffered 262 casualties, its worst losses in northwest Europe. Allan T. Snowie, *Bloody Buron: the Battle for Buron, Caen 8 July 1944* (Erin, Ontario: Boston Mills Press, 1984).

31. The Canadians claimed twenty enemy tanks destroyed. Stacey, *Victory,* 161. The 3d Division casualties totaled 1,194. Stacey, *Victory,* 163.

32. This experience clearly illuminates that Canadian expertise in urban warfare gained in Italy was not disseminated to Canadian forces preparing for OVER-LORD in Britain. Wilson, "Tank-Infantry Cooperation Doctrine," 78–81.

33. NAC RG 24 13711, WD GS IICC, 11 July 1944.

34. Simonds received universal acclaim from senior British commanders. Montgomery considered him the equal of any British corps commander. Liddell Hart Centre for Military Archives Alanbrooke papers (hereafter LHCMA AP), AP/14/27, M508, letter, Montgomery to CIGS, "On Present Ops.," 7 July 1944, fol. 6; AP/14/28, M511, letter, Montgomery to CIGS, 14 July 1944; NAC RG 24 CP 7, "Operational Policy—II Cdn. Corps," 17 February 1944.

35. NAC RG 24 10799, "Simonds' Draft of Lessons," 1 July 1944.

36. This kidney-shaped ridge rises to a height of 88 meters.

37. NAC RG 24 13711, IICC Ops. Instr. 2, 16 July 1944.

38. On 18 July 83 Group flew a record 1,320 sorties, dropped 199 tons of bombs, and claimed 11 tanks destroyed. NAC RG 24 13711, IICC Int. Sum. 14 (24 July 1944); 13712, "Air Programme for ATLANTIC," 18 July 1944, WD GS II CC Jul. 1944, apdx. 32.

39. NAC RG 24 13750, WD GS 2 CID, 18–19 July 1944.

40. NAC RG 24 13750, WD GS 2 CID, 19 July 1944.

41. NAC RG 24 14116, WD GS 6 CIB, 20 July 1944.

42. The SSR had 208 casualties. NAC RG 24 14116, WD GS 6 CIB, 20 July 1944.

43. Officers and military police had to force the fleeing Essex Scottish back into the line at gunpoint. The battalion's 210 casualties and 50 percent loss of Bren guns illuminates the extent of the rout. Roy, *1944,* 95.

44. Total Canadian casualties were 1,965. NAC RG 24 13711, IICC Int. Sum. 12, 22.7.1944.

45. Canadian intelligence correctly appraised that the German front line was thinly held by the 16th Luftwaffe Field and 272d Infantry Divisions, but failed to identify the 1st SS Panzer Regiment with its nearly 100 tanks in reserve south of Caen. NAC RG24 13711, IICC Int. Sum. 10, 20 July 1944.

46. Roy, *1944,* 79–96; Stacey, *Victory,* 166–180.

47. Montgomery, *Normandy to the Baltic,* 85.

48. For SPRING planning see NAC RG 24 13711, WD GS IICC, 22–24 July 1944; IICC Ops. Instr. 3, WD GS July 1944, apdx. 35.

49. Col. G. W. L. Nicholson, *Gunners of Canada: A History of the Royal Regiment of Canada* (Toronto: McClelland & Stewart, 1972) II, 301–302; PRO WO 241/5, A. L. Pemberton, *The Development of Artillery Tactics and Equipment,* (War Office: HMSO, 1949), 235–237.

50. The 1st Tank Brigade equipped with CDL (Canal Defence Light) tanks for this very task had not yet left England. Geoffrey W. Futter, *The Funnies: The 79th Armoured Division and Its Specialised Equipment* (Hemel Hempstead: Bellona Books, 1974), 84–86.

51. For a discussion of SPRING see Roy, *1944,* chap. 4; English, *Canadians,* 240–250; Stacey, *Victory,* 183–195.

52. The Canadians both failed to note the arrival of the 2d and 9th SS Panzer

Divisions and to appreciate the extent of mine workings that the Germans utilized to infiltrate the Canadian rear. NARA T-313, 420, KTB PzGr. West, 21–25 July 1944; NAC RG 24 13711, IICC Int. Sums. 13-14, 23–24 July 1944; Stacey, *Victory,* 185.

53. B Squadron, the Fort Garry Horse, lost eleven tanks and the North Nova Scotia Highlanders suffered 139 casualties. NAC RG 24 14234, WD 10 CAR, 25 July 1944; 15122, WD NNSH, 25–26 July 1944.

54. The infantry advance was only supported by one troop of 17-pounder anti-tank guns, which forced back some German armor.

55. Stacey, *Victory,* 190–191.

56. Only eighteen survivors of C Company, Royal Regiment of Canada, made it back to their own lines.

57. The two lead companies took 307 casualties, and only twenty-four survivors escaped back to their own lines. The battalion, in fact, took heavier casualties than the Newfoundland Regiment had suffered during the first day of the Somme on 1 July 1916. Reginald Roy, "Black Day for the Black Watch," *Canadian Defence Quarterly* 3 (Winter 1982–1983), 34–42.

58. Pockets of Canadians still holding out in front prevented artillery fire support. Foulkes had thrown good in after bad and was prepared to commit the entire 6th Brigade if necessary to reach his objectives.

59. Accurate loss figures for SPRING are impossible to determine because reporting channels became so clogged that many casualties suffered on 25 July were only reported on following days. The official 25 July total was 1,202, but the real total was nearer 1,500. Stacey, *Victory,* 194.

60. As early as 22 July, Panzer Group West had reinforced its positions south of Caen in expectation of a renewed attack. NARA T-313, 420, KTB 5. Pz. AOK, 22 July 1944. For intelligence gaps, see PRO WO 171/131, TFAG Int. Sum. 149, 25 July 1944.

61. Only 25 percent of the planes bombed their targets. A second attack on the morning of 25 July, which targeted suspected German reserves, brought no assistance to the already stalled ground attack. Stacey, *Victory,* 188–189.

62. During SPRING II Canadian Corps claimed only eleven armored fighting vehicle kills and did not take a single prisoner. PRO WO 171/454, 7th Armd. Div. Int. Sum. 47, 27 July 1944; PRO WO 219/1449, "Daily POW Reports."

63. The official Canadian history claims that SPRING helped purchase a 48-hour delay in the transfer of German reserves to the U.S. sector during COBRA. The 9th SS Panzer Division did replace the exhausted 272d Division, but the latter in turn relieved the 21st Panzer Division. Neither the 2d nor 116th Panzer Divisions were drawn into line, and both formations were redeployed against the Americans on 27 July.

64. NAC RG 24 12745 "Op. SPRING"; William E. J. Hutchinson, "Test of a Corps Commander: General Guy Granville Simonds, Normandy 1944," M.A. thesis, University of Victoria, 1983, 183.

65. NAC RG 24 12745, "Attack by RHC—Op. SPRING," letter, Simonds to chief of staff CMHQ, 31 January 1946.

66. The 3d Division had suffered over 5,000 casualties by 25 July and lost much of its original cadre. The numerous undertrained replacements it absorbed needed time to acclimate, gain experience, and forge esprit de corps. The Canadian Scottish Regiment had suffered 100 percent turnover and remained 34 percent understrength on 27 July, and the incidence of battle fatigue had tripled in July. Simonds's dissatisfaction with the division's performance led to the removal of a brigadier and two battalion commanders. NAC RG 24 Crerar Papers (hereafter CP) 7, letter, Simonds to Dempsey, 27 July 1944; English, *Canadians,* 250–252; Stacey,

Victory, 191; Terry Copp and Robert Vogel, *Maple Leaf Route: Falaise* (Alma, Ontario: Maple Leaf, 1983), 34.

67. Simonds singled out General Foulkes and Brigadier Megill (6th Brigade) for poor tactical planning and for failure to coordinate with the neighboring British XII Corps to suppress German flanking fire from the high ground west of the Orne. Hutchinson, "Corps Commander," 180–182.

68. Simonds had concluded by late July that Foulkes was unfit for divisional command. But, protected by Crerar's patronage and lack of a suitable replacement, Foulkes not only stayed but went on to command the Canadian I Corps in Italy in November 1944 and ironically became commander in chief of the Canadian Army before Simonds. Hutchinson, "Corps Commander," 175–182; Major General Kitching, *Mud and Green Fields* (Langley: Battleline, 1986), 206.

69. NAC RG 24 13711, "Air Program Op. SPRING," 23 July 1944, WD GS IICC, July 1944, apdx. 32.

70. LHCMA, Liddell Hart papers LHP/1/153, letter, Michael Carver to Basil Liddell Hart, 8 May 1952.

71. Canadian First Army headquarters finally became operational on 23 July in the Orne bridgehead, although initially it had only Crocker's British I Corps under command. The Canadian 4th Armoured Division arrived in late July. NAC RG 24 13622, WD GS FCA, 31 July 1944.

72. Montgomery wrote of Crerar on 7 July: "I fear very much that Harry Crerar will be quite unfit to command an Army; I am keeping him out of it as long as I can . . . he is definitely not a commander. He commanded 1 C[anadian] C[orps] for 2 years, and when it went to Italy the corps HQ proved to be quite untrained." "When I hand over a sector to Crerar I will certainly teach him his stuff, and I shall give him tasks within his capabilities. And I shall watch over him carefully." Crerar disappointed Monty as soon as he took command: Monty wrote "Harry Crerar has started off his career as an Army com[man]d[er] by thoroughly upsetting everyone; he had a row with Crocker the first day . . . the basic cause was Harry; I fear he thinks he is a great soldier, and he was determined to show it the very moment he took over command at 1200 hrs 23 July. He made his first mistake at 1205 hrs; and his second after lunch." LHCMA AP 14/27, letter, Montgomery to CIGS, 7 July 1944; AP 14/28, letter, Montgomery to CIGS, 14 July1 1944. See also Hart, *Colossal Cracks,* chap. 7.

73. The 84th Group of the RAF only became fully operational on the Continent on 12 August. Stacey, *Victory,* 202.

74. During SPRING Simonds concluded that the "deterioration of its fighting efficiency was quite out of proportion to actual losses." NAC RG 24 13711, WD GS IICC, 29 July 1944; 13766, WD GS 3 CID, 31 July 1944.

75. Between 17 July and 1 August five panzer (2d, 9th SS, 10th SS, 21st, 116th) and three infantry divisions (84th, 326th, 363d) were transferred from Caen to the U.S. sector. NARA T-313, 420, KTB PzGr West, July 1944.

76. NAC RG 24 13751, G2 2 CID Sitreps 1–2 August 1944.

77. This was the first action by the 4th Armoured Division in Normandy. NAC RG 24 13625, G. (Ops) FCA "Minutes of Morning Joint Conference," 2 August 1944, WD GS FCA Aug. 1944.

78. Between 1 and 6 August the Canadians took only twenty-four prisoners. PRO WO 219/ 1449, "Daily Enemy POW Reports."

79. The Germans rated the Canadians poorly, noting that they were "not particularly well trained." NAC RG24 13712, IICC Int. Sum. 29, translation of 1056th Grenadier Regiment, "Erfahrungsbericht," 4 August 1944, apdx. C.

80. Ammunition shortages delayed the start of TOTALIZE. Short bombing on 8 August destroyed large quantities of ammunition and forced the rationing of medium artillery to 25 rounds per gun daily on 10 August, one-third of that available to British artillery then under command. PRO CAB 44/266, 449–451, 475.

81. NAC RG 24 13711, WD GS IICC, 30 July 1944; IICC Op. Instr. 4, 5 August 1944.

82. During July 1944 the 12th, 13th, 14th and 19th Field Regiments, Royal Canadian Artillery, were reequipped with towed 25-pounders, freeing 96 Priests for conversion to armored personnel carriers.

83. The Canadian II Corps stockpiled 9,000 tons of munitions for TOTALIZE. PRO CAB 44/266, 451.

84. NAC RG 24 13751, 2 CID Int. Sum. 8, 6 August 1944.

85. The recently formed 89th Division, rushed from Norway, replaced the 1st and 9th SS Panzer Divisions that had fought the Canadians during ATLANTIC and SPRING. The Germans on 8 August fielded ninety-three tanks, forty-seven tank destroyers and assault guns, and twenty-nine antitank guns. Force ratios were infantry 3:1, armor 7:1, and artillery 10:1.

86. Some 1,020 bombers dropped 3,462 tons of ordnance for a loss of ten aircraft. Stacey, *Victory,* 218.

87. The three Kangaroo-mounted battalions suffered only sixty-three casualties, while the four foot battalions lost 260. Stacey, *Victory,* 220.

88. Crerar's command suffered 315 casualties and lost four guns, fifty-five vehicles, and 3 days of ammunition stocks due to short bombing. The North Shore Regiment alone suffered over a hundred casualties, and one of its companies was so disrupted that it could not participate in TOTALIZE. NAC RG 24 13625, "Bombing of Own Troops by 8 USAAF, 8.8.1944," WD GS FCA, August 1944.

89. NAC RG 24 13789, WD GS 4 CAD, 8–9 August 1944.

90. Worthington Force, commanded by Lt. Col. D. G. Worthington, comprised B and C Companies, 27th Canadian Armoured Regiment, plus two rifle companies of the Algonquin Regiment. The force suffered 240 casualties and lost forty-seven tanks. Stacey, *Victory Campaign,* 228.

91. NAC RG 24 13625, "Minutes of Morning Joint Conference," 11 August 1944, WD GS FCA, August 1944, para. 6.

92. Stacey, *Victory,* 230–231.

93. NAC RG 24 13625, "Minutes of a Special Conference," 3 August 1944, WD GS FCA August 1944, para. 10.

94. General Foulkes, "Statement in the Field," 9 August 1944, WD GS 2 CID, August 1944, apdx. 6.

95. NAC RG 24 13751, WD GS 2 CID, 3 August 1944.

96. Russell F. Weigley, *Eisenhower's Lieutenants: The Battle for France and Germany, 1944–45* (Bloomington: Indiana University Press) I, 204.

97. So weak were the German defenses that they had to resort to desperate, if cunning, ruses. On 9 August, the I SS Panzer Corps successfully employed a propaganda company to broadcast recordings of German tanks moving up to dissuade the Canadian advance. PRO DEFE 3/118, Ultra Decrypt XL 6060, 13 August 1944; Stacey, *Victory,* 220.

98. During 5–6 August, assault units practiced embussing and debussing from Kangaroos plus deep-penetration operations at night. PRO WO 106/5446, *BAOR Battlefield Tour Operation TOTALIZE* (1947), 61ff.

99. Carlo D'Este has argued that the Canadians might have succeeded in closing the Falaise pocket if Montgomery had reinforced the operation with additional

British troops, and he has hypothesized that Montgomery did not do this to avoid offending Canadian pride. Yet, the real reason was the war weariness that beset British forces in August 1944. D'Este, *Decison,* 427.

100. PRO WO 106/5446, "Study of the Night Advance and Capture of Cramesnil by 144RAC & 7ASH," *BAOR Battlefield Tour Operation TOTALIZE* (1947), 46.

101. The 3d Division column on the right comprised the 2d Armoured Brigade, 7th Reconnaissance Regiment, 9th Infantry Brigade (Kangaroos), and 7th Brigade on foot. The left column under command of the 4th Division consisted of the 4th Armoured Brigade, 8th Infantry Brigade (Kangaroos), and 10th Infantry Brigade on foot. Stacey, *Victory,* 239–240.

102. NAC RG 24 13624, FCA Op. Instr. 14, WD GS FCA, August 1944, apdx. A.

103. Stacey, *Victory,* 238.

104. These included deployment of an additional antitank battery north of the Laison. It was fortunate for the Canadians that German reserves were so meager. Stacey, *Victory,* 238; NAC RG 24 13751, letter, Simonds, "To Be Read By All Officers," 23 August 1944, WD GS IICC Aug. 1944, apdx. 35.

105. Of 769 heavy bombers, which dropped 3,723 tons of ordnance, seventy-seven bombed short causing 397 Canadian casualties. Worst hit was the Royal Regiment of Canada and the 12th Field Regiment, Royal Canadian Artillery. Stacey, *Victory,* 243.

106. Crerar's command took over 1,000 prisoners on 14 August alone.

107. For discussion of Operation TRACTABLE, see Roy, *1944,* 231–280; Stacey, *Victory,* 232–256. The Canadian First Army took 2,442 prisoners during 14–16 August. PRO WO 219/1449, "Daily Enemy POW Returns, 16–18.8.1944."

108. Training on Wasps began during April 1944, but unhappy with the cramped British two-man vehicle, the Canadians redesigned the vehicle for a three-man crew by mounting the tanks externally. NAC RG 24 13625, "Minutes of Morning Joint Conference," 17 August 1944, WD GS FCA, August 1944, 2; 13634, "WASP flamethrower: Notes on Employment," WD GS FCA, 8 February1945, apdx. 29; 9804, File 2/Instrns Army/1/2, "Flame Trg. for Inf. Carrier Pls.," HQ FCA 24 March 1944.

109. A Polish force occupied the heights northeast of the mouth of the pocket that dominated the only German escape routes through Vimoutiers. It was almost overrun as it enfiladed the fleeing German forces.

110. Forecast infantry losses to 10 July were 2,282, while actual losses were 4,105. In fact, Canadian infantrymen stood a greater chance of becoming casualties in Normandy than on the Western Front during the Great War. Replacements available ashore fell from 3,263 on 10 June to 1,146 on 17 July. PRO WO 219/1538, "TFAG Casualty Reports, June–July 1944"; C. P. Stacey, *Arms, Men, and Governments: The War Policies of Canada, 1939–1945* (Ottawa: The Queen's Printer, 1970), 435; English, *Canadians,* 204.

111. On 4 August, five Canadian infantry battalions were over 15 percent understrength and two were more than 25 percent understrength. Stacey, *Arms,* 432–434.

112. With an establishment rifle strength of 11,000, this represented a 25 per-cent deficiency. By 17 August, 76 percent of Canadian losses were infantry against a projected 48 percent. W. Denis and Shelagh Whitaker, *The Battle for the River Scheldt* (London: Souvenir Press, 1985), 216; Stacey, *Victory,* 284.

113. On 26 August, the 2d Division was 1,910 men understrength and its two French-Canadian battalions were 577 men short. Worst hit was the South

Saskatchewan Regiment, which fielded only 12 percent of its authorized riflemen. Jeffrey Williams, *The Long Left Flank: The Hard Fought Way to the Reich, 1944–45* (Toronto: Stoddart, 1988), 30–31.

114. The Canadian First Army had a war establishment of 20,599 infantry. NAC Stuart Papers, DND War Reinforcement File 1/Manpower/2/3, "Strength of Infantry Battalions, 5.8–7.10.1944," 13 October 1944.

115. Lack of transportation also hindered Canadian exploitation operations. Crerar even had to employ tank transporters on supply runs to meet an average daily supply need of 3,221 tons. PRO CAB 44/266, 456–458.

116. The CAO remustered 1,311 troops in April 1944, 564 in May, and 3,515 in August. NAC RG 24 9840, File 2/Reinf Inf/1 "Conversion Training for Remustered Personnel," CMHQ, 9 August 1944, fol. 44; Stacey, *Arms,* 437–438.

117. The Canadian 3d and 2d Divisions suffered the heaviest casualties of any Commonwealth formations in Normandy. Given its short time in combat the Canadian 4th Armoured Division also suffered heavily. By 21 August Canadian losses exceeded 18,000. Copp and Vogel, *Maple Leaf Route: Falaise,* 138.

118. The 2d Division, for example, had never exercised with an armored brigade. Copp and Vogel, *Maple Leaf Route: Falaise,* 45.

119. NAC RG 24 13788, WD GS 4 CAD, June–July 1944.

120. NAC RG 24 13788, 12th Manitoba Dragoons, "Lessons Learned Whilst Acting in an Infantry Role, Caen, 14–15 July 1944," 27 July 1944.

121. NAC RG 24 13788, RCA 4 CAD, "CB and C-M Procedures," 21 June 1944; "Employment of 4 CAD C-M Staff," 21 June 1944, WD GS 4 CAD Jul. 1944, "Interchange of Officers within the Div.," 12 July 1944, apdx. 10; GHQ 4 CAD "Rfts. and Left Out of Battle Policy and Trg. of Personnel," 11 July 1944, apdx. 7; HQ 4 CAD "Schedule Div. Study Week," 1 July 1944, apdx. 2; HQ 4 CAD, "Engagement of Friendly Aircraft," 7 July 1944, apdx. 5.

122. The division joined action on 1 August 1944 and suffered particularly heavily during TOTALIZE. NAC RG 24 13624, "Minutes of Morning Joint Conference," 11 August 1944, WD GS FCA, August 1944.

123. The Germans savaged the brigade on 7 June and again on 10 June at Le Mesnil-Patry. By 11 June it was down to 45 percent of strength. PRO WO 205/636, TFAG, "AFV State," 11 June 1944.

124. Canadian workshops also proved less efficient in repairing armor. PRO WO 179/3001, WD 25th Cdn. Tank Delivery Regt., June 1944, fol. 2-3; PRO, WO 205/631, "Report by Col T. D. Murray, Cdr. 2 ARG," 24 November 1944.

125. NAC RG 24 13624, "Minutes of Morning Joint Conference," 12 August 1944, WD G. Ops. FCA, August 1944.

126. On 17 August, the two Canadian tank brigades fielded only 164 runners. The resumption of mobile operations in late August forced frequent relocation of workshops and disrupted repair activities. By early September, The First Army was short 331 of its authorized 838 tanks. PRO WO 205/151, BRAC TFAG, "Allotment of A Vehicles for Period 2–7 Sept. 1944," 2 September 1944.

127. In Normandy one divisional, eight brigade, four regimental, and twenty-one battalion commands changed hands. Stacey, *Victory,* 275.

128. This was Crerar's first directive as army commander. NAC RG 24 CP, FCA Tactical Directive, 22 July 1944.

129. NAC RG 24 CP 2 1-0-6, "Crerar's Report to Ralston, 1.9.1944," fol. 16.

130. Crerar's formative military experiences was as an artillery staff officer during World War I.

131. Canadian troops achieved surprise in subsequent major attacks. Crerar wrote: "I advocate . . . obtaining maximum surprise by eliminating prolonged pre-

liminary bombardment prior to the initiation of movement." NAC RG 24 CP 16 D265 "Address to Senior Officers, FCA on Veritable," 22 January 1945, WD January 1945, apdx. 2. On the parallels between Crerar and Montgomery see Hart, *Montgomery,* chap. 7.

132. Hart, *Montgomery,* chap. 7.

133. Copp and Vogel, *Maple Leaf Route: Falaise,* 44.

134. The Canadians extensively used airburst high-explosive ammunition during the bombardment of Tilly on 2 August. Stacey, *Victory,* 206.

135. NAC RG 24 13625, "Minutes of the Morning Joint Conference," 17 August 1944, WD G. (Ops.) FCA, August 1944, 2.

136. NAC RG 24 13751, "Use of Enemy Equipment," 14 August 1944, WD GS 2 CID, apdx. 12.

137. Canadian air observation post resources also proved inadequate, and thus Crerar formed three new squadrons during the campaign. NAC RG 24 9750, File 2/Air Reports/1, Director of Air Monthly Liaison Letter 10 (23 May–22 June 1944), 1.

138. The Canadian I Corps operational reports date from 22 March 1944, but the first comprehensive evaluation from Italy was of the Liri Valley campaign (May–June 1944). NAC RG 24 13686, ICC Stdg. Op. Instr. 12, WD GS March 1944; 12305, File 3/ Reports/3, "Rpts. on Ops.," 25 July 1945, 1.

139. CMHQ dusted off guidelines for "Reports on Operations, 1918," as the basis of new instructions for Canadian troops. NAC RG 24 12305, File 3/ Reports/3, fol. 1–13.

140. NAC RG 24 13621, FCA, "Op. Standing Orders," June 1944, Sect. 4; 12305 File 3/Reports/3, D.D. Hist. "Rpts. on Ops.," 25 July 1945, fol. 27–29.

141. The 3d Division's first combat report appeared on 3 July and the first by II Corps on 21 July. Only from March 1945 on did the CAO systematically collect combat lessons. NAC RG 24 12305, File 3/Reports/3, letter, CoS CMHQ to HQ FCA, 10 May 1945, fol. 34; D.D. Hist, "Report on Ops." 25 July 1945.

142. Simonds had ordered the 1st Division studies on Sicily and Ortona and wanted weekly and daily operational studies in northwest Europe. He demanded that "when opportunities occur, it is of great importance that troops should derive the utmost benefit from periods out of contact," and emphasized three goals to be sought during periods out of combat: morale enhancement, rehabilitation, and retraining. NAC RG 24 12305, File 3/Reports /3, fol. 14; 13712, GOC IICC, "To All Formation Cmdrs., II Cdn. Corps," MHQ IICC, 30 July 1944, WD GS IICC July 1944, apdx. 41.

143. The fact that the Canadian kept most of their strength forward in the line in accordance with British operational policy prevented formations withdrawing subunits for field training.

144. The Canadian First Army issued irregular operational reports from 7 August on, but these were brief factual summaries rather than detailed lessons learned. The seven reports issued averaged only eight pages. NAC RG 24 12305, CMHQ Files 3/Reps/1 Army and 3/Reports/3.

145. Von Rundstedt's chief intelligence officer stated that the "Militärische Wert der Kanad. infanterie ist mittelmassig." NARA T-311, 26, 7030892, "Meldung über die Fahrt zur 7 Armee am 11–12 June 1944, Anl. zu KTB, TKB des Ic Ob. West, 12 June 1944.

10

Germany: The Defeat of the *Westheer*

The *Westheer* tenaciously resisted in Normandy despite being greatly out-numbered and outgunned. It remained cohesive and only cracked in August after having sustained severe losses. This protracted defense reflected the realism of German doctrine and training, the pronounced defensive advantages of the terrain, and the limitations of Allied combat effectiveness. It also reflected German military professionalism as the *Westheer* adapted and innovated during the campaign to enhance its firepower, sustain its strength, and minimize the effects of massive Allied superiority. Such adaptation clearly prolonged German resistance.

Yet while the German performance was impressive, the campaign demonstrated that the Nazi war machine was not invincible or its soldiers supermen. The campaign illuminated the steady decline of German combat capabilities as attrition ground down the Nazi war machine and as its most striking weaknesses—poor strategy, logistics, intelligence, and interservice cooperation—increasingly compromised the German defense. Profession-alism, ideological indoctrination, quality training, excellent weaponry, and extensive combat experience forged a powerful, cohesive, and disciplined army, but these strengths ultimately were not enough to overcome marked numerical and material inferiority. German combat excellence postponed defeat, but the law of numbers prevailed. At the same time, distorting nazi racial-ideological prejudices that denigrated American fighting qualities, the poor interservice coordination that nazism promoted, and the German military's neglect of logistics and intelligence increasingly hampered German operations.[1] That the *Westheer* fought on for as long as it did against growing odds in the face of mounting logistic problems and dwindling intelligence testifies to its fighting prowess but underscores how devastating was German neglect of logistics and intelligence.

The *Westheer* fought in Normandy under several major disadvantages. Most significantly, Allied mastery of the air for the first time overturned the traditional supremacy of land communications over maritime communica-

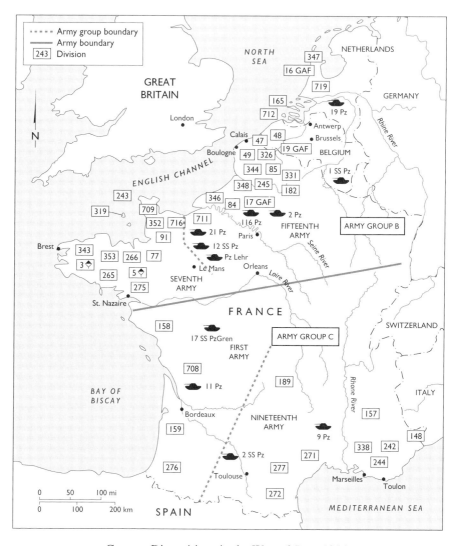

German Dispositions in the West, 6 June 1944

tions. Allied aerial interdiction so hampered German movement that the Allied buildup in Normandy exceeded the German. Thus German forces became steadily outnumbered and came to lack the logistic base for offensive operations. Allied air superiority hindered German operations to an unprecedented degree, disrupting supply operations and badly delaying the arrival of reinforcements and replacements. That the Germans also fought within range of the Allied fleet ensured that naval gunfire halted every major German counterattack and inflicted heavy losses.

Nonetheless, German troops fought in Normandy with advantages they had not often enjoyed. That the Germans defended a short front, in a terrain that strongly favored defense, allowed Rommel to create defenses in depth, strongly backed by artillery and armor.[2] These advantages, coupled with realistic tactics and quality weapons and training, consistently allowed the Germans to inflict greater losses on the enemy than they themselves suffered, despite growing numerical and material inferiority (see Table 10.1).

Table 10.1   Comparative Casualties in Normandy, 1944

Date Ending	German	Allied	Exchange Ratio
11 July	87,000	85,000	0.98
25 July	117,000	124,000	1.06
07 August	144,000	158,000	1.10
13 August	158,000	184,000	1.16

Sources: PRO WO 219/1531,"Casualties"; Dieter Ose, *Entscheidung im Westen 1944: der Oberbefelshaber West und die Abwehr der allierten Invasion* (Stuttgart: Deutsche Verlags-Anstalt, 1982), 132.

Despite these advantages, and the greater firepower German formations deployed, the *Westheer* proved unable, given the constraints it operated under, to conduct major offensive action. Above all else, the diminution of German striking power reflected the greatly improved defensive abilities of its opponents: the blitzkrieg tactics that had triumphed over neglected and unprepared militaries during 1939–1941 no longer prevailed. Indeed, in Normandy, Allied firepower combined with sea and air power halted every major German attack and inexorably sapped German strength.

Nevertheless, the *Westheer* still fought remarkably well, considering its losses, and its overall professionalism meant that it rarely made serious tactical blunders despite the inevitable decline in standards after five years of war. In Normandy, the individual German soldier remained more resourceful and resilient than his Allied counterpart. Severe discipline, nazi ideology, effective propaganda, realistic training that stressed individual initiative, extensive combat experience, and broad professionalism continued to maintain a cohesive and disciplined army. Moreover, numerical inferiority often motivates the outnumbered to greater exertion, and in Normandy German commanders repeatedly asked their troops to do the unreasonable. Time and again weak German forces made determined stands that held off much larger Allied forces, and, just as frequently, tired and depleted German troops skillfully pressed local counterattacks to regain lost positions. It is apparent that the *Westheer* endured serious manpower, equipment, and supply shortages before collapsing in August—absorbing more punishment than the Allied armies could have sustained if the tables had been turned.[3]

On D-Day the Germans failed to throw the Allies back into the sea. Rommel had clearly understood that if the Allies gained the advantage of surprise, it was unlikely that he could prevent their getting ashore in strength somewhere.[4] He saw the task of the Atlantic Wall and its defenders as disrupting and containing an invasion while panzer reserves moved up to drive the Allies back into the sea. The German defense proved weakest in opposing the Utah Beach landings in the eastern Cotentin Peninsula largely because the Germans had thinly manned the sector in the belief that extensive inundation barred a seaborne assault.[5] The Germans came closest to defeating the landing at Omaha Beach on the western Calvados. Here, poor weather, the swamping of most of U.S. amphibious armor, and the defensive strength of the terrain behind Omaha Beach—coastal bluffs bisected by draws—all contributed to the attackers' difficulties. Rommel had also reinforced the defenses here during late spring with the 352d Infantry Division, a redeployment the Allies had not fully recognized.[6]

Most of the German difficulties on D-Day stemmed from the bad weather. The absence of many senior commanders and disruption of communications by aerial and naval bombardment seriously obstructed German countermeasures.[7] Moreover, Allied domination of the skies prevented the *Luftwaffe* from making its influence felt. Immediately after D-Day, the I SS Panzer Corps tried to drive the Anglo-Canadians back into the sea. After these efforts failed, the Germans shifted to defense on 10 June to contain the Allies in a narrow bridgehead, as they had done at Anzio, while they rushed the II SS Panzer Corps to France from the Eastern Front for a counteroffensive to smash the bridgehead. In the interim, the Germans stubbornly defended before Caen and St. Lô to deny the Allies both control of these communications centers and of ground for maneuver.

The defensive advantages of the terrain, the realism and effectiveness of German defensive tactics, and the refinement of defensive techniques in light of Normandy's combat conditions allowed the Germans to conduct a protracted defense despite being greatly outnumbered and outgunned. Both the bocage terrain of low sunken roads, dense hedgerows, and small compartmentalized fields in western Normandy and the Campagne de Caen, the open rolling plain that stretched from Tilly to Troan strongly favored defense.[8] The Germans also employed sophisticated defensive tactics refined through two world wars. They quickly appreciated the defensive advantages of the bocage in the U.S. sector, in particular. Troops dug deep into the banks of its hedgerows for protection against indirect fire, and widely used mines, booby traps, and demolitions to slow the U.S. advance and to exact a heavy price for every yard relinquished while reinforcements moved up.[9]

German troops endeavored to conduct defense in depth that aimed to disrupt the coordination and momentum of enemy attacks. But initially both practice and circumstance led the Germans to employ Eastern Front defensive techniques that emphasized linear defense, forward concentration, firepower, and immediate counterattack. When the German Seventh Army went over to the defense on 10 June and sought to confine the Allied forces in a narrow bridgehead, lack of troops and the absence of prepared defenses inland initially forced it to adopt a linear defense. But Allied artillery, aircraft, and naval gunfire inflicted heavy losses on forward concentrated defenders during June and German losses steadily mounted.[10] Thus, as reserves arrived in mid-June, German troops quickly returned to defense in depth to minimize casualties and buttress defensive strength. The relative shortness of the front allowed the Germans in late June to erect defenses in depth in the southern Cotentin, in the thick bocage south of Caumont, and before Caen.[11]

While German defenses in Normandy varied in detail according to topography and local conditions, after mid-June they conformed closely to doctrine. Troops erected defensive zones that consisted of an outpost line, a forward defensive position, and the MLR.[12] Troops, strongly reinforced with firepower, lightly held the forward belt as the defenders of the outpost line held their positions only as long as it took to gain intelligence about the size, composition, and objectives of an attacker. The Germans held the forward battle zone more strongly. This zone comprised mutually supporting company defense positions, reinforced with firepower, sited in depth, and often built around village strongpoints in Eastern Front style. The forward battle zone's task was to disrupt, disorganize, and retard an attack, and hence its defenses were made up of an elaborate network of dugouts, machine gun posts, and antitank gun positions that provided interlocking direct fire. At the same time, the Germans triangulated indirect fire onto fire zones within the forward position. The Germans held their main strength in the MLR, in the rear of which they stationed mobile local reserves, strongly reinforced in firepower, to counterattack rapidly any penetration of the MLR.

Despite the popular image of nazi fanatics defending to the last round, German Army troops, if less so the *Waffen SS,* rarely made senseless sacrifices.[13] When the MLR became untenable, doctrine instructed troops to retire to previously prepared rear positions, reorganize, link up with local reserves, and counterattack rapidly to regain the MLR. As a result, in Normandy, when a position in the MLR was lost and reserves were available, local counterattacks usually materialized within the hour. Skillful counterstrokes in which German troops sought to infiltrate and outflank the enemy often allowed defenders to regain the MLR at tolerable cost. German counterattacks habitually used all available strength and fire-and-maneuver techniques to pry the enemy out of their positions. The combination of maximum effort and skillful small-unit fire-and-maneuver tactics often retook lost positions at light cost.

Topography, tactical skill, firepower available to German infantry, and flaws in Allied attack doctrine meant that the traditional three-to-one advantage required for offensive success rarely proved sufficient in Normandy. Only when they possessed marked numerical and material superiority could the Allies progress with tolerable losses.[14] The firepower possessed by German infantry bolstered its staying power. The Germans had learned from the Great War the advantages of heavy infantry firepower, and throughout World War II they maintained an edge in small-unit firepower. The superlative MG 42, the best general-purpose machine gun of the war, equipped most German rifle squads in Normandy and generated the majority of squad firepower. The Germans also widely used rapid-fire submachine guns that, though inaccurate, bolstered troop morale. Since the German rifle squad existed to service its machine gun, as long as this remained operational, the squad could sustain heavy losses but remain effective. This helps to explain why German infantry continued to resist even after suffering loss rates that would have rendered Allied infantry ineffective.

Central to the tactical superiority of German soldiers was the realism and quality of German training, which stressed individual initiative and independence. Allied propaganda has left a popular image of German soldiers as dull, blindly obedient automatons, but the reality was very different. The initiative and independence of German junior officers and NCOs was central to German combat effectiveness. Time and again in Normandy, junior officers and NCOs took the initiative to counterattack or to rally wavering troops and patch up the front. Nowhere was this emphasis on individual initiative more clearly illustrated in Normandy than in the breakout from the Falaise pocket and in the retreat behind the Seine in late August. In the face of the collapse of command and control, individual officers and NCOs rallied and reorganized troops into heterogeneous battle groups to break out from an encirclement.

At the same time, German training preached a holistic combined-arms doctrine where the sum of the whole was greater than that of its parts. The *Heer* trained long, hard, and realistically, and thus even half-trained recruits often offered stiff resistance.[15] Even though the high standards of training earlier in the war had inevitably slipped by 1944, recruits still underwent more rigorous, more uniform, and more realistic basic training than their Allied counterparts. Thereafter field training sought to correct remaining deficiencies. Thus, while green or undertrained German units did make tactical errors in Normandy, and while *Waffen SS* troops sometimes operated as if fanaticism could compensate for inadequate firepower, intelligence, and tactical skill, German forces rarely made serious tactical errors.

The quality of replacements also maintained German fighting power and resilience in Normandy. In theory, at least, the replacement system maintained strict territorial and unit affiliation between field formations and their corresponding replacement and training units in Germany, or, increasingly by 1944, in occupied territories. Thus from induction to arrival in a combat theater, German replacements maintained their unit affiliation. On the completion of basic training, troops joined "march" units and headed for the front under the command of veterans. At the front, divisional field replacement battalions assimilated the replacements through field training.[16]

The German replacement system thus maintained replacement cohesion and morale, but sacrificed flexibility and speed for quality. Field replacement battalions gave formations a short-term ability to offset battle casualties, yet the system depended on the speedy dispatch of trained replacements from the Reich. But by 1944 strict affiliation had begun to break down under the strain of five years of war as Germany reached the bottom of its manpower barrel. The German system was also inflexible because field replacement battalions in combat rapidly became depleted, while those unengaged held trained replacements that could not easily be tapped.[17] At the same time, it was difficult to modify the flow of reinforcements to meet combat losses because training units in Germany could not respond rapidly to the manpower needs of combat divisions. As a result, sustained heavy combat rapidly burned out German divisions in Normandy and lack of reserves forced formations to stay in the line until they had virtually lost all fighting power.[18]

That the Germans offered a protracted defense was also due to their refinement of defensive techniques in light of combat conditions in Normandy. The Allies' air superiority and their pronounced firepower advantage rendered standard German defense in depth less effective in Normandy than it had been in the East or in North Africa. In particular, forward concentration and immediate counterattack brought heavy German losses from Allied artillery.[19] Moreover, Allied firepower and the devastating effect of carpet bombing ensured that even standard defense in depth could neither stop the Allies from gaining ground nor prevent heavy losses.

So, the Germans gradually refined their defensive techniques to counter overwhelming Allied aerial supremacy and firepower. Formations gradually adopted extreme dispersion as troops deepened their defensive zones and further scattered their manpower. Where time, resources, and combat conditions allowed, the Germans erected additional defenses behind the MLR and withdrew troops into these rearward positions. These defensive tactical adaptations emerged in the classic bottom-up, top-down decentralized pattern of German innovation as adaptation emerged ad hoc unit by unit during June. After collection and analysis of after-action reports, the German command published guidelines in early July for dispersed deep defense advocating that only one-third of available troops should hold the MLR and that the remainder should man additional positions to the rear.[20] Extended defense in depth curtailed German losses (see Table 10.1) and contributed directly to the defeat of Montgomery's GOODWOOD offensive (18–20 July).[21] Extreme dispersion reduced German losses from artillery and aerial bombardment and at the same time made it even harder for Allied forces to penetrate German defenses.

The Germans also adapted to offset Allied numerical and material superiority as well as growing fighting power and combat proficiency. So powerful did Allied artillery become in Normandy that German troops soon learned that only instant counterattack, before Allied troops could consolidate and register fire, could retake objectives.[22] In Normandy, platoon-strength local counterattacks often materialized within fifteen minutes of the loss of an objective, and in company and battalion strength within the hour.[23]

German troops also adapted to minimize the impact of Allied command of the air, which caused them unprecedented difficulties. Troops learned through trial and error the need for strict radio discipline and to locate radio equipment away from command headquarters to minimize attacks on command and control facilities. Initial failure to adopt countermeasures had led to the neutralization of the headquarters of Panzer Group West by air attack on 10 June.[24] Thereafter, the Germans adopted elaborate security measures to safeguard command and control facilities.[25]

By 1944, coordinated defensive artillery fire had become the backbone of the German defense on the thinly held Eastern Front, where troop densities were often half those attained in Normandy. Although the Germans established a heavy concentration of artillery in Normandy, Allied air power and German supply shortages rendered this artillery ineffectual and it was rarely able to help the German defense.[26] Air attacks dictated that guns had to be relocated often and adopt elaborate camouflage and concealment.[27] This threat forced the Germans to abandon massed fire and resort to "shoot-and-scoot" tactics, random "sprinkling fire" or "roving fire" involving individual guns.[28] At the same time ammunition shortages prevented the heavy barrages needed to repel Allied attacks. Massed fire was thus rare, and gunners increasingly abandoned counterbattery fire entirely.[29] Moreover, poor ground observation, lack of air observation or recent aerial photoreconnaissance, and inadequate communications all hampered

German artillery operations. German gunners were rarely able to provide effective fire support.[30]

In the absence of strong artillery support German troops relied heavily on mortars, which they used to great effect, for fire support in Normandy.[31] The Germans had more and larger caliber mortars than the Allies, and because mortars were more mobile and more easily concealed they were less vulnerable to air attack than artillery. The Germans also made increasing use of the *Nebelwerfer*, the mobile, multibarreled rocket launcher. Opposite the British sector, the Germans soon established the heaviest concentration of *Nebelwerfer* batteries yet seen in the war.[32] These weapons could bring down such rapid massed fire that Allied troops came to dread their "stonks"—and the characteristic, and demoralizing, wail of the projectiles in flight—which often single-handedly stopped Anglo-Canadian assaults.[33] Yet the weapon's short range, ravenous ammunition consumption, and telltale dust cloud on firing (which made them vulnerable to detection and neutralization) were significant tactical limitations. With Allied domination of the skies, the launcher batteries suffered heavy losses.[34]

Since Allied offensive striking power had increased so much, German infantry often could not hold the line without strong fire support. To compensate for inadequate artillery support, the Germans increasingly deployed forward armor, assault guns, and tank destroyers to support the infantry, even in the forward outpost line. Although this forward concentration shored up the German defense, it increased equipment losses.[35] Allied air attacks also inflicted a steady toll on German soft-skinned vehicles—some seventy-five trucks a day on average in June. The Germans adopted numerous passive countermeasures—creating "flak avenues," maintained wide distances between vehicles in convoys, and relegated supply runs to nighttime—yet such measures could only marginally reduce loss rates. The heavy German motor vehicle losses from a combination of air attacks and increased accident rates that accompanied nocturnal supply operations reduced German mobility and proved to be the most debilitating problem. The Germans resorted to all kinds of improvisations and expedients to offset dwindling mobility, pressing captured vehicles into service, rounding up horses and carts, making extensive use of bicycles, and even stealing vehicles.[36]

German troops skillfully employed tactical deception to inflate their own strength and to confuse the enemy. Aware of the Allied propensity to bombard forward slopes, troops often constructed dummy forward-slope positions to attract Allied fire while remaining protected in reverse-slope positions.[37] The Germans were also experts in camouflaging heavy weapons and in ambushing the enemy.

Organizational improvisation was commonplace in the *Heer*, as its myriad tables of organization and equipment attested. Most German forma-tions possessed some ad hoc unit or units improvised from their own resources and designed to increase firepower, mobility, and combat strength.[38] All formations raised alarm units of troops combed from supply and service units to prop up waning infantry strength.[39] German troops often used captured enemy equipment to increase firepower, especially armor. The Germans employed dozens of tanks captured from Allied forces during the campaign, and after Montgomery's abortive GOODWOOD operation (18-20 July) the 21st Panzer Division fielded an entire company equipped with captured British Shermans.[40]

To offset heavy losses, German forces reorganized both to maximize their remaining combat strength and to minimize losses. Grievous losses among unit leaders thrust many junior officers and NCOs into command. To compensate for the resultant inexperience in such positions, formations reduced the size of tactical units, since smaller units were easier to com-mand and also suffered fewer losses. Many formations thus reduced and reorganized companies into two platoons each of three sections plus a rein-forced company assault section for counterattacks. Commanders also pared down front-line strength and equipment to minimize losses and to establish unit reserves to replace losses.[41] Since training inculcated independence and initiative in the NCOs, when they ended up commanding platoons, or even companies as officer losses climbed, German combat effectiveness dropped off less markedly than in Allied units when officer casualties mounted.

Indoctrination and propaganda contributed directly to the *Westheer*'s cohesion, fighting power, and tenacity. Propaganda persuaded many German soldiers that the Allies would not take prisoners, while officers often deliberately kept their troops ignorant of the true situation at the front and dealt severely with signs of defeatism or antinazi sentiment.[42] At the same time, rhetoric about powerful new "vengeance weapons" buttressed German morale and resolve. Indeed, many German soldiers believed propa-ganda claims that the V-1 rocket offensive launched on 14 June would force the Allies into a negotiated settlement that would allow Germany to contin-ue the struggle against the Soviet Union.[43] "Eastern hardness" inculcated through indoctrination helped troops surmount the terrible conditions in which they fought.

In fact, the evidence demonstrates that the picture portrayed by Anglo-American literature of a German soldiery increasingly disillusioned with Hitler and nazism is distorted. Many German prisoners of war expressed disillusionment on capture, and even more claimed to be antinazis after the war. Contemporary prisoner interrogations, however, concluded that most German troops remained ideologically committed to National Socialism, that they rarely blamed Hitler for Axis defeats, and that they still had faith in ultimate victory.[44] Nazi propaganda clearly reinforced the will of

German troops to continue an increasingly hopeless conflict, and indoctrination was one element of military effectiveness in which Nazi Germany maintained a marked edge over the Western Allies throughout the war. However, the *Westheer* embarked on indoctrination too late to erase fully the softening of the troops occasioned by comfortable occupation duty and higher neglect—and so the *Westheer* retained a dual identity that manifested itself as friction between *Ostkämpfer* and garrison troops.[45]

Historians have also sanitized the Normandy campaign. While atrocities never reached the depths of extermination that characterized the war in the East, Normandy saw bitter, often brutal, combat. Although historians have focused on a small number of well-documented atrocities committed in Normandy by the SS, at the time the Allies repeatedly alleged numerous war crimes committed by the regular German Army as well.[46] Likewise, Anglo-American historians have focused on egregious SS massacres of French civilians, such as at Oradour,[47] but army units regularly participated in antipartisan sweeps and routinely did not take prisoners.[48] Indeed, the *Westheer* viewed anti-*maquis* sweeps as excellent experience for new or refitting divisions. At the front, exchanges of atrocities had begun on D-Day between German troops and Allied airborne forces, but the most extensive and sustained exchanges occurred between the 12th SS Panzer Division *Hitlerjugend* and the 3d Canadian Division before Caen. A vicious circle of atrocity and reprisal began on 7 June when the *Kampfgruppe Meyer* executed Canadian soldiers captured during the battle group's abortive drive to the coast, and in the weeks that followed SS troops committed dozens of atrocities.[49]

One of the most significant deficiencies of the *Heer* was its poor, and declining, intelligence-gathering capability. The army's offensive orientation early in the war and the traditional Prussian disdain of staff functions brought about the neglect of intelligence. Early in the war air superiority had allowed the *Luftwaffe* to provided considerable tactical intelligence to advancing ground forces. But the demise of the *Luftwaffe* all but ended photoreconnaissance intelligence by 1944, and left the *Westheer* blind. It had to rely instead on tactical intelligence sources—signals intelligence (SIGINT), prisoner interrogation, patrolling, and captured documents. Of these, only in patrolling did the Germans exhibit any expertise. German SIGINT was not sophisticated, nor were its operators well trained or equipped. But the continued poor Allied signals discipline and security meant that SIGINT remained the largest source of tactical intelligence for German forces in northwest Europe.[50] Given these intelligence deficiencies, constant active patrols were necessary to identify enemy capabilities and intentions. The Germans thus extensively used fighting patrols.[51] Nevertheless, intelligence gathering remained a serious weakness that constricted German efforts to predict and counter Allied initiatives.

After corralling the Allied forces in a shallow lodgement during June, and though they could not prevent the fall of Cherbourg, the arriving II SS Panzer Corps launched a major counteroffensive on 28 June to throw the Allies back into the sea. The SS troops hurled themselves against the newly established British bridgehead over the Odon River in an effort to break through to the coast and split the British-U.S. lodgement. Despite strong tank support, the Germans made little headway, and the operation petered out on 2 July after heavy losses. The failure of this counterblow illustrated that the Allied foothold had become permanent.

The attack failed primarily because the Germans lacked the logistical base for major offensive action. Panzer Group West simply did not possess sufficient ammunition and fuel for more than a couple of days of sustained offensive action.[52] Moreover, the Germans attacked prematurely with troops who had just dashed across Europe and who had not yet fully assembled or reconnoitered the ground, let alone had time to become acclimated to combat in Normandy. Thus only a portion of the corps' strength could be brought to bear and artillery support was inadequate. The SS troops' unfamiliarity with combat conditions in the West also contributed to failure as the corps launched a classic Eastern Front firepower "blitz" operation on too wide a front and without sufficient artillery support. The intensity of Allied defensive artillery and naval fire shook the SS troops and halted the counterattack dead.[53]

After this failure Hitler announced a new strategy: an unyielding defense to pen the Allies into a narrow bridgehead and thereby deny them the room and favorable terrain needed to conduct mobile operations. He hoped to hold the Allies in a narrow area through a savage battle of attrition that exploited the defensive advantages of the terrain and of German interior lines. This decision locked the Germans into a battle of attrition within range of the guns of the Allied fleet, a battle that they could not win. But the other strategic alternative presented by the generals—to retire inland out of the range of those guns—would have surrendered the most defensible terrain, doubled the length of the front, greatly weakened the German defense, and brought about a precipitate German collapse in Normandy.

Despite the new strategy, so pronounced had Allied material superiority become and so unsatisfactory was the German supply situation that the Germans could not stop the Allies from gaining ground despite defenses in depth. On 8 July Montgomery launched a multicorps offensive, CHARNWOOD, to capture Caen. Assailed by three Anglo-Canadian divisions from three sides and unable to supply his forces because of the destruction all but one of the Caen bridges during the 7 July air raid, Rommel finally abandoned northern Caen and withdrew the attenuated *Hitlerjugend* division behind the Orne River. This withdrawal gave the Germans a shorter, more defensible, line in excellent defensive terrain and the Verrières Ridge, the commanding high ground south of Caen, provided excellent observation.

In the week following CHARNWOOD, Panzer Group West deepened and strengthened its defenses south of Caen to create a powerful dispersed defensive belt in depth that consisted of no fewer than five zones. Thus during Montgomery's GOODWOOD offensive (18–20 July) Anglo-Canadian forces encountered the deepest and strongest German defensive system established in Normandy (see Table 10.2).[54]

During GOODWOOD, the Germans orchestrated their greatest defensive success of the campaign as they savaged British armor driving south toward Falaise. A combination of clumsy British execution and skilled German defense in depth defeated GOODWOOD. Allied carpet bombing shattered the forward defenses and incapacitated many defenders, allowing British forces to penetrate rapidly the enemy front, but poor British coordination and methodical execution, combined with skilled German defense, prevented the British from exploiting any success. The belt of fortified village strongpoints, held in company strength and built into the defensive zone in Eastern Front style, beyond the bombing zone slowed and disrupted the poorly integrated and armor-heavy British advance. At the same time, local German reserves utilized mobility and firepower in hit-and-run counterattacks that disrupted and scattered the British drive. The local reserves conducted a classic delaying withdrawal while maneuvering through the depth of the defensive zone to buy time while armored reserves assembled for larger counterattacks.[55] Concurrently, well-sited and expertly camouflaged German antitank guns inflicted a heavy toll of British armor.[56] After local reserves had delayed and disrupted the British advance and denied the enemy the Bourguébus Ridge, the Germans launched well-coordinated counterblows down the Verrières Ridge.[57] Caught down the slope, the poorly supported British armor was picked off.[58]

The defeat of GOODWOOD was a major German defensive success. The British may have gained ground, but German armor took few losses while British armor suffered heavily.[59] Indeed, Panzer Group West dealt a drubbing that Montgomery's army group could not afford to take again. But finally, in late July, after seven weeks of heavy combat, the German defense of Normandy collapsed as the U.S. COBRA offensive, initiated on 25 July, broke through the German front. Historians have traditionally interpreted the German collapse as the inevitable consequence of sustained attrition. After constant battering by Allied firepower, conventional wisdom maintains, the Germans were simply too weak to stop the U.S. breakthrough (see Table 10.3). Historians have also argued that the Germans neglected the St. Lô sector. But the Germans clearly had to conduct a vigorous defense at Caen because a breakout into the excellent tank country of the Falaise Plain would have unraveled the German defense, whereas the Germans still had room to retire to a rearward river line on the U.S. sector.

Table 10.2 German Forces, Caen Front, 18 July 1944

Formation	Infantry Battalions	Artillery Batteries	Antitank	Armor	Armored Fighting Vehicles	AA	Nebelwerfer	Artillery
711th Division	1	8	7	—	—	—	—	??
346th Division	8	10	7	—	14	—	—	??
16th German Air Force Division	7	8	8	—	16	—	—	??
21st Panzer Division	5	8	11	64	—	8	—	??
503d Heavy Tank Battalion	—	—	—	40	—	—	—	—
12th SS Panzer Division	2	1	??	31	—	—	—	??
Corps Troops	—	14	54	—	—	—	—	??
LXXXVI Corps	23	49	87	135	30	8	—	100
272d Division	7	12	19	—	—	—	—	42
1st SS Panzer Division	7	9	20	115	35	14	—	45
Corps Troops	—	6	2	16	—	—	—	7
I SS Panzer Corps	14	27	41	131	35	14	—	94
III Flak Corps	—	—	—	—	—	90	—	—
7th–9th Mortar Brigades	—	—	—	—	—	—	272	—
Panzer Group West	37	76	128	266	65	112	272	194

Sources: NARA T-313, 420, 000935ff; PzGr. West, KTB, 15–20 July 1944; Eric Lefevre, *Panzers in Normandy* (London: Battle of Britain Prints, 1984).

Table 10.3   Replacements as a Percentage of Casualties, Normandy, Summer 1944

Date	Casualties	Replacements	Percentage	Understrength
11 July	87,000	5,210	6	82,000
17 July	100,000	8,395	8	91,000
23 July	113,000	10,078	9	103,000
25 July	117,000	12,000	10	105,000
27 July	127,247	14,564	12	122,000
6 August	144,265	19,914	14	124,000
13 August	158,437	30,069	19	128,000

Source: Ose, *Entscheidung im Westen,* 132.

This interpretation does not stand up to close scrutiny, for the Germans had continually reinforced their strength on the St. Lô sector from late June (see Tables 10.4 and 10.5), and the German defenses south of the city on the eve of COBRA were only marginally weaker than those south of Caen (see Table 10.6).[60] Despite heavy losses, the German forces were not so attenuated that they were incapable of halting a U.S. breakout. In fact, the German Seventh Army had halted all previous attacks, and the heavy U.S. losses and ammunition expenditures experienced during the capture of St. Lô in mid-July forced Bradley to launch COBRA short on infantry and with rationed fire support.

Table 10.4   Reinforcement of LXXXIV Corps, St. Lô Sector, June–July 1944

| | Infantry | | Guns | |
Date	Battalions	Antitank	Artillery	Armor
27 June	27	129	177	64
10 July	?	120	206	?
23 July	58	133	343	189
25 July	58	172	296	357

Sources: NARA T-314, 1604, 00204-06, AOK 7, "Gliederung u. Kampfstärken LXXXIV A.K." Ia Nr. 3454/44 g. Kdos, 27 June 1944; 00387-88, LXXXIV A.K., "Artillerie Gliederung Stand: 21.7.1944."

Despite heavy losses, German formations remained stronger than either Allied intelligence estimates or the German casualty replacement statistics in Table 10.3 suggest. On the eve of COBRA, Allied intelligence estimated that German forces in Normandy were 30 percent understrength, whereas Army Group B reported a deficiency of 103,000 personnel, about 18 percent. But this German figure both overstated permanent losses and understated the influx of replacements.[61] In reality, about three times more

Table 10.5   German Forces, St. Lô Front, 25 July 1944

LXXXIV Corps	Infantry Battalions	Artillery Batteries	Guns Antitank	Guns Artillery	Armor	AFVs
243d Infantry Division	5	16	19	46	—	3
Division Group König	10	10	17	35	—	—
2 SS Panzer Division	6	12	28	37	103	25
17 SS PG. Division	7	8	10	23	—	10
5 Para. Division	4	6	??	28	—	—
Panzer *Lehr* Division	12	14	34	44	40	?
275th Division	5	10	??	50	—	—
353th Division	6	9	13	33	—	8
Corps troops	3	3	22	12	—	11
1041st Antitank Battalion	—	—	27	—	—	—
657th Antitank Battalion	—	—	16	—	—	—
902d Assault Gun Brigade	—	—	—	—	—	18
TOTAL	58	86	176	296	143	75

Sources: PRO DEFE 3/62, Ultra Decrypt XL 3709, "84th Corps Antitank Return, 25.7.1944," 27 July 1944; DEFE 3/114, Decrypt XL 5161, "84th Corps Tank Return, 25.7.1944," 8 August 1944; NARA T-314, 1604, 001388, LXXXIV A.K., "Takt. Gliederung d. Artillerie," Stand: 21 July 1944; 001373-76, LXXXIV Korps, "Wochenmeldung," Kps. Gef.Std., 23 July 1944.

Table 10.6   Comparison of Density of German Defenses, Caen Front (18 July) and St. Lô Front (25 July) (per mile)

Infantry Frontage	Battalions	Guns Artillery	Antitank	Armor
Caen - 15 miles	2.5	14	8.5	21
St. Lô - 23 miles	2.5	13	7.5	15.5

Sources: See Tables 10.2 and 10.5.

replacements had arrived than the official statistics indicated.[62] Front-line personnel shortages were also much less than statistics suggest because of the three ways the *Westheer* responded to attrition to offset crippling casualties and to sustain combat power. First, the Germans withdrew the cadres of the most depleted subunits for complete rebuilding, while transferring their remaining combat troops to other units. Second, they disbanded or consolidated severely depleted units.[63] Third, combat units absorbed infantry-trained service troops and formed service personnel into infantry alarm units.[64] In such fashion the Germans minimized the impact of attrition on their fighting power—and their forces in Normandy were on average about 14 percent understrength on the eve of COBRA, half the figure estimated by Allied intelligence.[65]

Likewise, despite heavy equipment losses, the German war economy was able to dispatch sufficient replacements to cover most combat losses (see Table 10.7).[66] But Allied air attacks so delayed the arrival of replacement personnel and equipment that front-line units became seriously depleted.[67]

Table 10.7   **Equipment Committed and Destroyed, and Replacements Dispatched, June–July 1944**

Weapon	June				July			
	Committed	Lost	Replacements	Net	Committed	Lost	Replacements	Net
Armor	963	164	224	+60	1,347	406	515	+99
Assault guns	157	32	27	−5	337	75	95	+20
Tank destroyers	???	41	29	−12	?	97	44	−45
Heavy antitank guns	428	114	?	?	?	234	97	−137

Sources: NARA T-311, 1, 000829, HG. B, "Waffenlage Stand: 1.7.1944," Ib/WuG Anl. 2 zu Tgb. Nr. 04281/44 geh.; T-78, 726, 6076096-98, OKH GenQu., "Kraftfahrzeuge (gepanzert), Heer: Westen d. 1.10.1944."

If the German defense was not too weak to prevent a U.S. breakthrough, why did the COBRA offensive succeed? Improved U.S. capabilities resulted in a better conceived and executed offensive, but, equally important, a deteriorating German supply situation contributed directly to the Seventh Army's failure to halt the offensive. Thus the German defeat in Normandy was fundamentally a logistic defeat, for the *Westheer* proved unable to reinforce and resupply a field force of sufficient size to contain the Allies in their lodgement. Despite their endeavors, German quartermasters were unable to keep their forces sufficiently supplied to maintain an effective defense.

On D-Day the German logistic position in France was precarious. Ammunition stockpiles were sufficient for about a month of sustained combat, but most reserves were at inland dumps.[68] The German fuel situation was even worse: the *Westheer* had only seven to ten days' worth of fuel available for its strategic reserves. Moreover, Allied air attacks had crippled the French railway and forced the German supply operation onto the roads, thereby further depleting German fuel stocks. So distribution was a serious problem even before D-Day, and the *Westheer* had introduced stringent rationing to preserve its dwindling supply.[69]

When the Germans failed to defeat the Allies on the beaches, they could only fight a protracted defense in the West if adequate supplies of fuel and munitions were forthcoming from the Reich.[70] Given fuel and transport shortages, planned German troop redeployments to Normandy grossly exceeded the available trucking capacity and the German ability to supply these formations once they were committed to combat.[71] The Germans thus established priorities in getting troops to Normandy to cordon off the Allies in as small a bridgehead as possible. Once the troops had arrived, the Germans tried as best they could to supply the forces committed.

Allied air attacks hampered German supply operations so much that the Quartermaster General West could deliver only a fraction of the supplies consumed at the front.[72] For the Germans there never were sufficient supplies to sustain offensive action.[73] Their gasoline situation rapidly became critical because they depleted their entire strategic fuel (gasoline) reserve by 13 June, and the German forces could hardly deal with the destruction of the main German fuel depot at Gennevilles (outside Paris) on 22 June.[74] Thereafter only stringent rationing, diversion of fuel from other field commands, and daily deliveries from Germany kept German forces in Normandy mobile.[75]

Within the first week of the invasion, the Germans had realized that only a dramatic improvement in their supply situation could allow a protracted defense of Normandy. German quartermaster units had to improvise to speed the flow of supplies even as they sought to restore limited rail communications to Normandy. In the first week of the invasion, the Germans could not run a single supply train into Normandy across the Seine and Loire. Thereafter, they abandoned their uncoordinated and scattered rail repair operations and focused on opening—and keeping open—two major rail arteries into Normandy, the Paris-Versailles-Dreux-Vieux-Surdon line from the east and the Tours-Le Mans-Alençon-Sees-Vieux-Surdon line from the south, lines that served the major German supply depots in the Le Mans-Alençon area. Frantic work reopened these two lines during the second week of the invasion.[76]

In late June the German logistical situation in Normandy improved as rail movement into Normandy recommenced, large-scale transport got under way, and combat units collected supplies from rear depots.[77] In late June, the Germans began ferrying operations across the Seine that, during July, delivered a major proportion of the supplies to reach Normandy.[78] With the reopening of rail communications, the flow of supplies to central Normandy increased steadily in July. But the major German problem remained the shipment of these supplies from railheads and loading docks to the front as Allied air attacks inflicted a heavy toll on German motor transport.[79] Only by acquiring supplies on their own could combat units compensate for the quartermaster service's dwindling ability to get stocks from the rear to the front.[80]

During July the logistic situation of the Germans on their eastern flank, where Panzer Group West opposed the British and Canadians, slowly improved as rail movement was restored to Dreux and Verneuil and as ferrying operations across the Seine increased the flow of supplies into eastern Normandy. Allied air forces were unable to neutralize the Seine ferrying operations because the boats were much harder to hit than bridges or rail lines, and they operated mainly at night. But on the Germans' western flank, where the Seventh Army opposed the Americans at St. Lô, there was no parallel improvement in logistics during July; to the contrary, the decline continued: ferrying was far less significant, supply distances greater, and communications lines less developed. But it was the German forces' inability to sustain rail deliveries across the Loire River that directly contributed to the collapse of the St. Lô front in late July.

The catalyst for an ultimately fatal decline in the Seventh Army's supply situation on the U.S. sector was the renewed destruction of the railway bridge and marshaling yards at Tours on 15 July. After they had reopened in mid-June, the Tours bridges had become the supply lifeline for the Seventh Army.[81] At the same time that bombing reclosed the Tours supply artery, growing truck losses reduced the supply service's ability to resupply the Seventh Army by road. The few lateral roads in western Normandy and the greater distances involved made resupplying the Seventh Army more difficult than supplying Panzer Group West on the eastern flank, and thus a smaller proportion of supplies dispatched to the Seventh Army made it to the front. During July, the Seventh Army became increasingly dependent on daily rail and ferry deliveries of fuel to keep it mobile and upon its own truck columns to transship supplies from railheads and ports.[82]

The destruction of the Tours artery undermined the Seventh Army's logistic position because the Quartermaster General West could not compensate for the interruption to rail delivery of fuel by increased road delivery. German fuel stocks on the St. Lô front thus dwindled at the very moment that U.S. forces launched COBRA on 25 July.[83] After frenetic work, the Germans had reopened the Tours rail bridge on 23 July, too late to resupply the Seventh Army before the U.S. attack. In the meantime, replenishing Panzer Group West after its GOODWOOD expenditures meant that the Quartermaster General West was only able to dispatch gasoline by road to the Seventh Army on one day between 18 and 25 July.[84] As a result, on the eve of COBRA German fuel stocks on the St. Lô sector had sunk perilously low: At average consumption rates, the LXXXIV Corps had less than two days' supply left.[85]

The closure of the Tours rail route also had an important, if indirect, impact on the Seventh Army's ammunition supplies. To decrease turn-around time, the Quartermaster General West on 17 July abandoned deliveries to the Seventh Army's largest and most forward ammunition dump Michel at St. Sever, 10 miles behind the front and instead delivered stocks to Martha, 10 miles farther away near Domfront. This quadrupled the distance that units on the St. Lô front had to travel to collect ammunition and thus further strained the German fuel situation. At the same time, sustained combat that led to the fall of St. Lô on 19 July depleted front-line ammunition stocks.[86] On the eve of COBRA, German forces lacked the munitions to halt a major, concerted U.S. offensive.

For the first time in the campaign, during COBRA supply shortages crippled the German defense and prevented them from cordoning off the COBRA break-in on 25–26 July as they had all previous Allied offensives. Supply shortages explain why the elite, and still powerful, 2d SS Panzer Division *Das Reich,* failed to make its presence felt on the COBRA battlefield. By 26 July, LXXXIV Corps had expended all ammunition for the 88mm flak guns that formed the backbone of its antitank defense, while gasoline shortages "significantly prohibited" German countermeasures and forced *Das Reich* to abandon two companies of Panther tanks, an eloquent testimony to the scale of the fuel crisis.[87]

To restore the situation Field Marshal von Kluge rushed the XLVII Panzer Corps (2d and 116th Panzer Divisions) from the British front to take the U.S. breakthrough in the flank and nip off the penetration as German troops had often done on the Eastern Front.[88] But not only did the Germans underestimate the speed, strength, and proficiency of the Americans, but a flanking push south from St. Lô by the U.S. XIX Corps disrupted the planned German counterattack against the exposed U.S. forces' left flank. This push siphoned off part of XLVII Panzer Corps strength and forced the corps to counterattack hastily amid the thick bocage that extended southeast of St. Lô. But the bocage and increasing supply shortages frustrated the German counterattack: the panzer forces experienced the same offensive difficulties in the hedgerows that had earlier bedeviled U.S. operations.[89] The panzers became separated from their supporting *panzergrenadiers* and were unable to hold the ground taken. All that the XLVII Panzer Corps could achieve was to build a defensive front facing west and await promised reinforcements.

As the shattered Germans recoiled, Allied fighter-bombers hastened the diminishing mobility of the enemy.[90] Once the Americans had broken out, growing logistic difficulties and dwindling mobility unraveled the German defense. During early August, U.S. forces overran the forward German supply depots, destroying any lingering chance that the Germans might shore up the front. In retrospect, the fortuitous destruction of the rail bridge and marshaling yards at Tours ten days prior to COBRA contributed directly, if unintentionally, to the success of the operation.

Hitler's insistence on 2 August that Army Group B launch Operation

LÜTTICH, a counteroffensive to recapture Avranches and seal off the American breakout, ensured total German defeat in Normandy. The Germans hastily scraped together a respectable armored strike force with elements of six, much depleted, mechanized divisions, and built up supplies for a few days of sustained offensive action, though only at the cost of denuding the rest of the front.[91] Von Kluge chose Hans von Funck's experienced XLVII Panzer Corps to spearhead the offensive. On the night of 6–7 August von Funck attacked without a preliminary barrage down the narrow corridor between the Sée and Sélune rivers toward Mortain and Avranches and obtained tactical surprise. Nonetheless, his troops were too few and too tired, and von Funck had attacked prematurely before his forces had fully assembled, rested, or reconnoitered.[92]

Forewarned at the last minute by Ultra, the U.S. 30th Division conducted a resolute defense, especially at Hill 317 where an isolated battalion defied all German efforts to punch through Mortain.[93] Thereafter, the rapid arrival of U.S. reserves quickly stalled the offensive as Allied fighter-bombers disrupted the German drive through the bocage once the skies cleared on 7 August.[94] Indeed, the imbalance of forces was simply too great to allow a restabilization of the front and, logistically, LÜTTICH was doomed. Von Funck had neither the firepower, the infantry, nor the supplies to recapture and hold Avranches.[95]

With U.S. forces advancing deep into the enemy rear, the only feasible German strategy was to fall back on the Seine. Given the dire supply position and the deteriorating mobility of German forces, heavy losses were inevitable. Despite earlier isolated incidents, widespread demoralization and disintegration only surfaced after LÜTTICH failed.[96] The counterattack thrust the Germans further into the noose of a pocket forming in the Argentan-Falaise area, which the Allies finally closed on 19 August. Precisely how many German troops became encircled in the Falaise pocket and how many broke out remain a matter of controversy.[97] Yet, most estimates have both inflated the number of German troops encircled and understated the number that broke out.[98] The mouth of the pocket saw some of the bitterest fighting of the campaign, and it was here that the Germans lost most heavily.[99] Nevertheless, the quality of training, experience of breakout operations in the East, and their flair for improvisation allowed the Germans to extricate a surprising number of troops and amount of equipment from the Falaise pocket despite the disintegration of command and control.[100] Junior officers and NCOs assembled stragglers into combat groups and led them in repeated breakout attempts. Moreover, experience in relief operations in the East propped up German resolve and morale: many of the encircled troops remained confident that relief efforts, spearheaded by the II SS Panzer Corps, would rescue them. Only when the relief effort stalled on 20 August did resolve waver and then collapse, though resistance inside the pocket continued until 22 August.

After the breakout from Falaise, the specter of a much larger encirclement on the Seine loomed. The sharply reduced mobility, catastrophic supply situation, and mounting demoralization of German forces presented the Allies with a strategic opportunity to annihilate the enemy against the Seine River. But, in late August, the Germans pulled off their greatest success of the campaign as they extricated virtually all of their remaining forces in Normandy across the Seine in a remarkable feat of organization and improvisation. The retreat east to beyond the Seine, which ended the Normandy campaign, had important consequences. The salvaging of vital staffs, specialists, and veteran cadres allowed Hitler to flesh out a new *Westheer* in the fall with which he launched the December 1944 Ardennes counteroffensive. In fact, success on the Seine was crucial to Hitler's ability to resume the offensive in the West during mid-December 1944.

A number of factors explain why the Germans were able to salvage so much of their army. They retreated skillfully, despite grave handicaps, after 21 August in a full-scale, staged withdrawal behind the Seine.[101] At the same time, the Allies were unable to interdict effectively this retrograde movement. Allied air attacks had destroyed every bridge across the Seine north of Paris by D-Day and, despite herculean efforts by engineers, air attacks demolished bridges faster than the Germans could rebuild them.[102] Increased use of ferrying and of pontoon bridges greatly increased traffic across the Seine from late June, but these ferries could not accomplish a rapid mass evacuation.[103]

Changing strategic priorities, increasing demands for air support, and the weather all prevented Allied air forces from impeding the German retreat. The Allies radically revised their interdiction plan after 9 August to slow the German retreat. Even though the Seine bridges remained a high priority, Allied aircraft increased attacks on targets east of Paris and also the Touques and Risle River bridges west of the Seine.[104] But the planes had barely resumed large-scale attacks on the Seine bridges on 18 August when SHAEF decided instead to try and capture them intact. Tactical aviation turned to transportation targets, a shift that relaxed pressure on German communications. The U.S. breakout also vastly increased the number of targets and inevitably dissipated Allied air power as aircraft supported ground operations across the entire front from Brittany and along the Loire to Paris.[105] Moreover, the punishing strikes against the Falaise pocket during 16–21 August focused the attention of Allied air power and curtailed attacks on the Seine bridges. Finally, unseasonably bad weather for late August also aided the Germans, grounding all Allied daylight air missions on 21 and 23 August.[106]

The failure of Montgomery's tired and weakened forces to pursue aggressively the retreating enemy also aided the German escape. The Germans used over sixty crossing points over the Seine and employed every conceivable means of crossing, including ferries, barges, rafts, yachts, and rowboats, as well as pontoon and boat bridges at night. The German experience in large-scale river-crossing operations in the East aided these efforts, while the strong antiaircraft defenses erected along the Seine to protect the crossings reduced the effect of Allied air attacks.[107]

When forced to retreat in daylight toward the Seine the Germans suffered heavy losses from air attacks, and the catastrophic fuel situation forced the Germans to abandon motor vehicles and heavy equipment in droves.[108] Yet the Germans managed to pull out virtually every soldier and most of the equipment that made it as far as the Seine.[109] Though badly battered and bruised, the *Westheer* escaped to fight another day.

Despite the emphasis of British and American historians on the confused chain of command in the West, German command fragmentation had little impact on the campaign. Rommel was never able to assert control over the Normandy battle the way he had in North Africa, and the campaign offered few opportunities for his famed creative generalship. He had concluded by 11 June that the Allies had established a permanent lodgement and that Germany was doomed.[110] His greatest achievement was his intuitive orchestration of the defense in depth south of Caen that shattered Montgomery's GOODWOOD offensive. Although he despised defense, Rommel adopted those logical defensive counters to his own offensive successes.[111] But, like the other generals, Rommel neglected the U.S. sector during July.[112] His being incapacitated by an Allied strafing attack on 17 July (ironically at St. Foy de Montgoméry) once again salvaged his reputation from the disgrace of defeat. Neither Hans von Kluge nor the iron-hard Walther Model could alter the outcome in the West.

An increase in communications difficulties obstructed the German defense of Normandy. The occupation forces relied heavily on land lines that were vulnerable to sabotage, and by 1944 mobile field radios were in short supply. Increasingly effective Allied radio interception and direction finding brought repeated air attacks on German communications and heavy loss of signals equipment. The paralysis of German communications under the impact of Allied air mastery contributed directly to the Germans' inability to coordinate coherent and rapid countermeasures on D-Day and thereafter. As the campaign progressed German command and control problems grew. Paralysis of communications played a role in the German failure to halt COBRA, and by mid-August German command and control verged on total collapse.

The unbalanced nature of German military capabilities contributed directly to their defeat in France. The impotence of the *Luftwaffe* and the *Kriegsmarine* left the *Heer* to shoulder the burden of thwarting the invasion. The *Luftwaffe* diverted many aircraft from the defense of the *Reich* in an effort to impact the battle raging in Normandy, but to little avail.[113] Though it made determined, and often near suicidal, efforts to aid the German defense, it could not contest Allied air superiority and suffered grievous losses.[114] So overwhelming was Allied aerial mastery that rarely did German aircraft reach the battle zone, and even more infrequently could attacks be pressed home. Moreover, the German lack of ground attack aircraft forced fighter planes to carry the burden of close support as improvised fighter-bombers, which placed them at even greater tactical disadvantage. As a result, German battlefield air support was all but neutralized. The *Luftwaffe*'s only impact was regular night bombing runs and the dropping of magnetic mines in the Seine Bay, which proved a nuisance and forced the Allies to maintain continuous mine sweeping. Apart from that, nocturnal raids inflicted minimal damage, only rarely—on the eve of GOODWOOD and TOTALIZE—did German air attacks disrupt Allied offensive action. The *Luftwaffe* also occasionally resupplied ground forces, but lack of lift capacity meant it could only minimally contribute to the resupply effort.[115] After the breakout, *Luftflotte* III made a determined effort to destroy the Pontaubault bridge, gateway to Brittany, and thus stem the U.S. advance, but failed.[116]

The *Luftwaffe* also diverted large numbers of flak guns to Normandy in an effort to protect ground forces and lines of communication from air attacks. Heavy flak concentrations partly ameliorated the damage caused by Allied bombing and strafing and inflicted a steady toll on Allied planes, but such passive defenses alone could not protect German forces, rear installations, and communications.[117] Heavy flak made an important, though often exaggerated, contribution to the ground defense. As the war turned against the Germans, heavy flak saw increasing service in an anti-tank role. Historians have often viewed the III Flak Corps as a lethal tank-busting force on the Caen front in Normandy: *Luftwaffe* heavy flak did occasionally inflict crippling losses on Allied armor, but this was the exception rather than the rule.[118] In reality, the III Flak Corps had barely begun its training for joint air-ground operations and the *Luftwaffe* High Command (*OKL*) remained loath to dissipate vital flak assets in support of the army. Its assistance to the army was grudging, halfhearted, and spasmodic, and it simply lacked the resources to combine both missions effectively.[119]

The *Kriegsmarine*'s efforts to obstruct OVERLORD were as ineffectual because Allied air and naval superiority thwarted all German surface action. Only fast E-boats achieved even minor tactical successes.[120] At the same time, Allied bombers systematically destroyed the port, dock, and repair facilities required to keep German warships operational.[121] The German U-boat challenge proved equally ineffectual in the shallow, constricted waters of the English Channel.[122] In frustration, the *Kriegsmarine* turned to its "small combat units" as frogmen, human torpedoes, and midget submarines repeatedly sortied against the eastern flank of the Allied bridgehead, but with little success and prohibitive losses.[123] Nor could naval coastal artillery have more than a minimal impact on the naval or ground battles.[124] The *Kriegsmarine* thus failed to interfere with either the invasion or the steady buildup of Allied strength ashore.[125]

The interservice coordination that had accompanied Germany's early war victories was absent in Normandy. As Germany's fortunes receded, interservice strains multiplied and the early war veneer of close cooperation cracked. Indeed, so impotent had the German navy and air force become that the *Heer* fought the campaign virtually alone against an enemy that demonstrated an unprecedented degree of interservice coordination. The inability to orchestrate an effective, integrated interservice defense was a major cause of the Germans' defeat.

In conclusion, the *Westheer* fought tenaciously against overwhelming odds for seven weeks before its defense of Normandy collapsed. Thereafter, despite enormous losses, it extricated one-third of the troops and one-tenth of the materiel that it had committed in Normandy. In the adverse circumstances that it faced, saving even this much was an achievement. The Normandy campaign demonstrated the *Heer*'s resilience, combat prowess, powers of recuperation, and ability to adapt. Yet, improved organization, better manpower utilization, more potent weapons in unprecedented numbers, and honed defensive techniques failed to avert disastrous German defeats in France, the Soviet Union, and Italy during the summer of 1944. These multiple, simultaneous defeats shattered the *Heer,* and Germany's imminent defeat became irrevocable.

The defeat of the *Westheer* illuminates the reality that it was the progressive decline of the strategic base of the German war effort, and the mounting Allied ability to conduct an integrated interservice and interarms onslaught, that was decisive in the defeat of Nazi Germany. The increasing application of Allied air power against German communications and productive capacity, coupled with mounting attrition, progressively robbed the *Heer* of the mobility, the ordnance, and the veteran cadres that had been instrumental both to German victory during 1939–1941 and in the avoidance of irreversible defeat prior to summer 1944. Robbed of its mobility, the *Heer* suffered comprehensive and decisive defeat during summer 1944.

Nonetheless, continual German adaptation and innovation were able to postpone the inevitable. German forces continued to adapt to changing combat conditions in Normandy as they had throughout the war, and innovation remained broad based, decentralized, and fairly rapid. Refinement of defensive doctrine with the adoption of extreme dispersion was the most significant German innovation of the campaign. The gradual adoption of dispersed defense in depth curtailed losses and exacerbated Allied offensive difficulties and thus prolonged the German defense. At the same time, continued organizational reform and deployment of new weapons increased German firepower and buttressed defensive strength. But finally, during late July, the Americans outfought and outmaneuvered the enemy to break out from Normandy. Despite the adoption of numerous expedients the *Heer* could not overcome its most significant deficiencies: its loss of mobility, its weak logistic base, its poor intelligence capability, and its lack of interservice coordination. At the same time, nazi racial dogma continued to warp German perceptions of the combat capabilities of their opponents. Despite growing evidence to the contrary, most German commanders continued to perceive the more racially pure "Anglo-Saxon" British as better soldiers than the mongrel Americans whose racial purity was so diluted that they could not be proficient soldiers.[126] Nazi racism thus led the Germans to underestimate American fighting qualities and their ability to adapt. Only after the COBRA breakout did the German military sharply revise its estimation of U.S. capabilities.

By then, of course, it was too late. By late summer of 1944, staggering manpower and equipment losses had torn the heart out of the *Heer* and reduced it to positional defense. The edge in raw fighting power that German formations had possessed throughout the war had now diminished to the point where quality could only delay the triumph of the law of numbers.[127] That the war lasted another nine months is a testament to the cohesion, discipline, professionalism, and adaptability of the *Heer.* Equally, though, it testified to the brutality, racism, fanaticism, and myopia of the German military.

Notes

1. Martin van Creveld, *Supply War: Logistics from Wallenstein to Patton* (Cambridge: Cambridge University Press, 1977), chaps. 5–6; Military Intelligence Division, U.S. War Department, *German Military Intelligence* (Frederick, Md.: University Publications of America, 1984).

2. In July 1944 divisional frontages in Normandy averaged 7 km, compared to 12 km in Italy and 17 km in the East. "Vergleich d. Feldheeres 1917 mit dem Feldheer 1944," GenStdH Org.Abt. (I) Nr.I/18211/44 g. Kdos, H,Qu. v. 20 July 1944 in Wolfgang Keilig, *Das Deutsche Heer* (Bad Nauheim: Podzun, 1956) II, 201/1944, 1.

3. On cohesion and ideology within the *Heer,* see Morris Janowitz and Edward Shils, "Cohesion and Disintegration in the Wehrmacht in WWII," *The Public Opinion Quarterly* (Summer 1948), 280–315; Omer Bartov, "Indoctrination and Motivation in the Wehrmacht: The Importance of the Unquantifiable" *Journal of Strategic Studies* (March 1986), 16–34; and his *Hitler's Army: Soldiers, Nazis, and War in the Third Reich* (New York: Oxford University Press, 1990).

4. In fact, the breadth of the bridgehead was more important than the depth for a viable lodgement, a fact that both Montgomery clearly recognized in his broadening of the invasion frontage in spring 1944 and Rommel perceived with his heavy attacks on the airborne bridgehead east of the Orne to roll up the Allied flank.

5. Only a single battalion defended the coastal crust supported by another battalion inland and an Eastern battalion of limited combat value. "Lagekarte 709. Inf. Div., Stand 6.6.1944," in Kurt Mehner, ed., *Die Geheimen Tagesberichte der deutschen Wehrmachtführung im Zweiten Weltkrieg, 1939–1945* (Osnabrück: Biblio, 1984), apdx.

6. Historians have contended that the superior quality of the 352d Division were central to U.S. difficulties at Omaha Beach. Yet, the forward-deployed 716th Division bore the brunt of the battle. USAHD MS B-432, Ziegelmann, "The 352d Division on D-Day" (Germany: 1946), 16–18; MS B-621, Richter, "716th Division" (Germany: 1947), 21–25; *Omaha Beachhead (6–13 June 1944)* (Washington, D.C.: GPO, 1966), 110–116.

7. Rommel took advantage of the bad weather to travel to Germany, General Feutchinger (21st Panzer Division) to be with his mistress, Gens. Sepp Dietrich and Wolfgang Pickert (III Flak Corps) as well as Cols. Hans von Templehoff (Rommel's operations officer) and Wilhelm Meyer-Detring (OB West operations officer) to take leave, while Adm. Theodore Kranke was at a birthday party in his honor. Many senior Seventh Army officers, including its chief Dollmann, and Generals Falley (91st Division), Hellmich (243d Division), and Schlieben (709th Division) were en route to a map exercise at Rennes.

8. Arthur Davies, "Geographical Factors in the Normandy Campaign," *Geographical Review* 36 (October 1946), 613–631.

9. In the U.S. sector the Germans destroyed eighteen of ninety-four major bridges. FUSA, *Report on Operations* (Paris: FUSA, 1944) V, 224.

10. The Panzer *Lehr* Division lost on average 100 men a day, mainly to Allied artillery. PRO WO 171/258, I Corps Int[elligence] Sum[mary] 26, July 1944, "Combat Report, Panzer Lehr Division," apdx. A.

11. The southern Cotentin positions were known as the Mahlmann Line.

12. The outpost line was typically sited 400 meters from enemy lines, the advanced position at about 1,500–2,000 meters, and the MLR at 5,000 meters.

13. The SS worldview of hardness promoted iron discipline, aggressiveness, and uncompromising refusal to accept defeat, which sometimes overrode tactical sense and brought heavy losses, as witnessed by the suicidal attack of the 12th SS Armored Engineer Battalion on Norrey on 10 June. Hubert Meyer, *Kriegsgeschichte der 12.SS-Panzerdivision "Hitlerjugend"* (Osnabrück: Munin Verlag, 1982), 109–110; Craig W. H. Luther, *Blood and Honor: The History of the 12th SS Panzer Division "Hitler Youth" 1943–45* (San Jose, Calif.: Bender, 1987), 47–48.

14. National Archives of Canada Record Group (NAC RG) 24 Vol. 12712, II Cdn. Corps Int. Sum. 32, Pt. II., 11 August 1944.

15. Every effort was made to make training realistic. Decorated veterans were routinely cycled through instructor positions, and this reward proved one of most effective inducements for battlefield heroism. Paratroop recruits and Labor Service troops conducted a tenacious defense during the battle for Cherbourg, for example. Paul Ingouf, *La Bataille de Cherbourg* (Bayeux: Editions Heimdal, 1979), chaps. 6–9.

16. The field replacement battalion was in effect a large and powerful infantry battalion that constituted the division emergency reserve.

17. Throughout the Normandy campaign, some 15,000 replacements stood idle in uncommitted replacement battalions stationed in the West.

18. By 28 August the 353d Division, for example, could muster only 1,023 combatants. NARA T-314, 1594, 000975, LXXXI A.K., "Gliederung d. 353. Inf. Div.," 28 August 1944.

19. Most German losses in Normandy occurred during counterattacks. The 12th SS Armored Engineer Battalion, for example, suffered 280 casualties during its abortive 10 June attack on Norrey. Meyer, *Kriegsgeschichte,* 109–110.

20. NAC RG 24 13712, II Canadian Corps Int. Sum. 37, Pt. II, Panzer Group West, "Observations," 19 August 1944.

21. During July, as the Germans adopted dispersed defense in depth, average daily losses fell from 2,500 to 2,250 despite steadily mounting Allied strength.

22. NAC RG 24 12712, II CC Int. Sum. 37, Pt. II, 19 August 1944, Panzer Group West Ia, "Directions for Conducting Battles," Gef. Std., 6 July 1944, apdx.

23. War Office, *Current Reports from Overseas* 34 (London: 1944), 11–12; John A. English, *On Infantry* (New York: Praeger, 1981; 1984), 144.

24. Located by Allied interception of its radio transmissions, naval gunfire blasted it and wrecked its communications. It had to be withdrawn and rehabilitated, and it resumed operations in Normandy only in July.

25. Paul Carell (pseud.) [Paul Karl Schmidt], *Invasion—They're Coming!* (New York: Bantam, 1964), 160–161.

26. The ineffectiveness of German artillery in Normandy has led historians mistakenly to conclude that the Germans did not employ much army artillery in Normandy. In fact, at least twenty-eight army artillery battalions fought in the campaign. NARA T-312, 1565, 0001122, AOK 7 Stoart/Ia, "Befehl für Einsatz v. Heeres-Art. Abteilungen," 3193/44 g. Kdos, AHQu., 18 June 1944.

27. So skillful was German camouflage that Allies experienced great difficulty in locating and neutralizing German guns. Up to 24 June, neither the 12th SS Panzer Division nor the Panzer *Lehr* Division had lost an artillery piece. NARA T-313, 420, 000420, "Besprechung am 24.6.1944," Anl. 13 zu KTB Pz.Gr. West Ia Nr. 3487/44 geh.

28. "Shoot-and-scoot" tactics involved short full-battery barrages followed by displacement to new positions. Sprinkling fire was random battery firing to hinder detection, and roving fire was continuous fire from a single detached gun.

29. That the U.S. First Army lost only four medium guns up to 31 July illuminates the demise of German long-range counterbattery fire. FUSA, *Report* V, 180; VI, 108.

30. On the relatively few occasions when artillery provided effective fire support, as it did, for example, before Montebourg in mid-June, it slowed the Allied advance. The heaviest fire provided was on 3 July against the British airborne bridgehead when 1,826 barrels fired 4,500 rounds. Carell, *Invasion,* 182–185; USAHD MS B-845, Lt. Gen. Wilhelm von Schlieben, "709th Infantry Division, Dec. 1943–30 June 1944" (Germany: 1946), 157; NAC RG 24 13712, IICC Int. Sum 37 Pt. II, 19 August 1944, PzGr. West, "Conduct During Enemy Attack," 2 August 1944, apdx.; NARA T-313, 420, 8713539, PzGr. West, Tagesmeldung, 3 July 1944.

31. Mortars inflicted 70 percent of Allied casualties in Normandy. Particularly deadly was the 120mm heavy mortar, which, fortunately for the Allies, remained rare in Normandy.

32. The 7th, 8th, and 9th Launcher Brigades deployed 316 *Nebelwerfers* and included two of only five heavy regiments in existence. Joachim Emde, *Die Nebelwerfer: Entwicklung u. Einsatz d. Werfertruppe im 2. Weltkrieg* (Friedberg: Podzun-Pallas, 1979), 152–155; Georg Tessin, *Verbände u. Truppen der Wehrmacht u. Waffen SS im zweiten Weltkrieg* (Osnabrück: Biblio Verlag, 1979) I, 213–214.

33. The British and Americans, respectively, dubbed the *Nebelwerfers* "moaning minnies" and "screaming meemies."

34. On 18 July alone the 9th Launcher Brigade lost 52 *Nebelwerfers*. NARA T-311, 1, 7000812, HG. B Tagesmeldung 18.7.1944, Ib/BrB.Nr. 01068/44 geh., 20 July 1944.

35. Carell, *Invasion,* 154–160.

36. The LVIII Panzer Corps sent raiding parties to Paris to "acquire" vehicles, and on 14 August alone rounded up six motorcycles, seven cars, and ten trucks. NARA T-314, 497, 000353-54, LVIII Pz. Korps Qu. KTB, 14 August 1944.

37. NAC RG 24 12712, I CC Int. Sum. 37, Pt. II, 19 August 1944, Chef. PzGr. West, "Conduct During Enemy Attack," Gef. Std. 2 August 1944, apdx.

38. The 711th Division had a self-propelled artillery platoon, and a battery of 170mm guns, while in July the 21st Panzer Division improvised an assault pioneer platoon with six mortar-equipped half-tracks—the deadly *"Stuka zu Fuss."* USAHD MS B-403, Lt. Gen. Joseph Reichert, "711th Division, 1.4.1943–24.7.1944" (Germany: 1946), 12; NAC RG 24 13711, IICC Int. Sum. 17, 27 July 1944. On interpreting German tables of organization and equipment see the author's, "Understanding German WWII Divisional Tables of Organization and Equipment," *World War II Historical Journal* 38 (1994), 11–18.

39. The 266th Division in Brittany, for example, raised an alarm battalion that freed one of its infantry battalions for service in Normandy. NARA T-315, 1841, 000034, 266 Inf. Div. Ia Nr. 2162/44 geh., 1 July 1944.

40. NARA T-311, 26, 7030786-865, Anl. zu KTB, TKB des Ic Ob. West, June 1944; T-311, 28, 7035069, Anl. zu KTB Ob. West Ia, 3 August 1944; T-311, 1, 70000698, TKB HG B Abt. Qu. Ib, 19 June 1944; T-311, 20, 7022667ff, Anl. Ic zu Tagesmeldung Ob. West July–August 1944; PRO WO 171 286, VIII Corps Int. Sum. 7, 2 July 1944; NAC RG 24 13712, IICC Int. Sum. 40, 23 August 1944.

41. NAC RG 24 13712, IICC Int. Sum. 32, Pt. II, 11 August 1944.

42. Prisoner interrogations demonstrate that many German soldiers believed that they would not be taken prisoner right up to the moment of capture. Many officers kept their troops ignorant of the fact that they had been surrounded in the Falaise pocket, for example.

43. Allied intelligence concluded on 15 July that "[there] is no indication that the fighting spirit of the Germans being seriously impaired." Washington National Records Center (hereafter WNRC), Suitland, Md., RG331, SHAEF G2 Weekly Int. Sum. 17, 15 July 1944. For propaganda disseminated to the *Westheer,* see NARA T-84, 302, 000001-220, III/1053. Grenadier Regiment, "Militärische Ausbildung," 27 March–26 July 1944; 8. FsJag. Rgt., "Unterrichts Themen für Gruppen- u. Zugführer, 10–18.5.1944"; 352. Inf. Div., "Ausbildungs Anordnung," October 1943–29 April 1944.

44. Even most of those who claimed to be antinazis, Allied psychiatrists concluded, were lying. PRO WO 219/4716, Lt. Col. H. V. Dicks, Directorate of Army Psychiatry, "The German Deserter: A Psychological Study," October 1944. On the unreliability of postwar German claims concerning antinazi activity, see Donald McKale, *Rewriting History: The Original and Revised WWII Diaries of Curt Prüfer, Nazi Diplomat* (Kent, Oh.: Kent State University, 1988). A fervent Nazi, Prüfer rewrote his diaries after the war to portray himself as opposed to nazism.

45. German memoirs of Normandy stress how veteran officers and NCOs often forced reluctant troops to fight on. Friction compelled von Rundstedt to issue orders admonishing the veterans not to insult garrison troops. Joseph Balkoski, *Beyond the Bridgehead* (Harrisburg, Pa.: Stackpole Books, 1989), 66.

46. Allied protests to the International Red Cross alleged war crimes committed by the 752d and 997th Infantry Regiments, for example. Alfred M. de Zayas, *The Wehrmacht War Crimes Bureau, 1939–1945* (Lincoln: University of Nebraska Press, 1989), 116–18.

47. James Lucas, *Das Reich: The Military Role of the 2nd SS Division* (London: Arms & Armour Press, 1991), 127–130; Max Hastings, *Das Reich: The March of the 2nd SS Panzer Division Through France* (New York: Holt, Rinehart, and Winston, 1981); Philip Beck, *Oradour* (London: Leo Cooper, 1979).

48. On 11 June, near Toulouse, Battalion Schreiber killed 325 *maquisards* and took no prisoners, while the 11th Panzer Division's "heavy combat" on 22 June at Mouleydier cost four wounded versus 125 *maquisards* killed and none captured.

NARA T-314, 1496, 000374, LVIII Panzer Korps, "Verluste der Terroristen vom 4.5 bis 15.6.1944"; T-314, 1496, 000327ff, LVIII Panzer Korps, Tagesmeldung, 22 June 1944.

49. The Germans also regularly violated the Geneva Convention by employing ambulances to carry military supplies and using hospitals to store weapons. PRO WO 171/30, XII Corps Int. Sum. 38, 14 August 1944.

50. NAC RG 24 13712, IICC Int. Sum. 46, Pt. II, 2 September 1944, 2–4.

51. NAC RG 24 12712, IICC Int. Sum. 37, Pt. II, 19 August 1844, PzGr. West Ia, "Directions for Conducting Battles," 6 July 1944, Gef.Std., apdx.

52. German planners estimated that they required 20,000 tons of supplies for a counteroffensive and daily delivery of at least 4,500 tons, yet the Seventh Army's available truck transport capacity was only 1,300 tons. NARA T-313, 1566, AOK 7, "Beurteilung d. Versorgunslage d. 7. Armee," AHQu. 21 June 1944; T-311, 1, 70009707, TKB Abt. Qu. 1b Ob. West, 19 June 1944.

53. The 9th SS Panzer Division and the attached Battle Group Weidinger (2d SS Panzer Division) suffered 1,781 casualties and lost thirty-two tanks and assault guns, plus nineteen antitank and infantry guns. NARA T-354, 147, 3789052, 9. SS-Panzer-Division "Hohenstauffen," "Zusammendfassung der Ausfälle der 9.SS-P.D. bis 1.7.1944 (einschl.)," Abt.Ia/Nr. 2400/44 geh., Div.Gef. Std., 2 July 1944.

54. British intelligence estimated that the VIII Corps would meet only 120 German tanks, whereas in reality the Germans had 300 tanks and assault guns east of the Orne. PRO WO 285/3, Second Army Int. Sum. 43, 17 July 1944; NARA T-313, 420, Tagesmeldungen PzGr West, 15–20 July 1944; Robert J. Sauer, "Germany's I SS Panzer Corps: Defensive Armored Operations in France, June–September 1944," Ph.D. diss., Boston College, 1992.

55. The 21st Panzer Division's 200th Assault Gun Battalion equipped with Marder I tank destroyers, in particular, effectively harried the British advance. Hans von Luck, *Panzer Commander* (New York: Praeger, 1989), 159.

56. It was the eighteen surviving 88mm antitank guns of the forward-deployed 1039th and 1053d Artillery-Antitank Battalions, not the seventy-eight Luftwaffe Flak 88s deployed on the Bourguébus Ridge, that inflicted most of the damage. NARA T-311, 17, 7018866, Meyer-Dietring, "Bericht über die O.B.Besprechungs am 20.7.1944 auf dem Gefechtsstand der PzGr. West," 22 July 1944; Janusz Piekalkiewicz, *Die 8.8 Flak im Erdkampf-Einsatz* (Stuttgart: Motorbuch, 1978), 135.

57. Several captured British Shermans spearheaded these attacks and helped to confuse the British defenders. Although Typhoons flew numerous sorties they neither halted the German attacks nor inflicted significant damage. The 124th Typhoon Wing claimed only two kills. Alex Vanags-Baginskis, *Aggressors, Volume 1: Tank Buster vs. Combat Vehicle* (Charlottesville, Va.: Howell Press, 1990), 61.

58. The I SS Panzer Corps lost twenty-seven tanks during GOODWOOD and claimed the destruction of ninety-three. NARA T-311, 17, 7018868, Pz.Gr. West, Tagesmeldung, 21 July 1944.

59. Estimates of British loss figures have varied enormously from 500 (Blumenson) to 271 (Ellis). British forces grossly overestimated the damage they had inflicted, claiming over 100 tank kills on 18 July, and historians have uncritically accepted these inflated claims ever since. Blumenson, *Breakout and Pursuit* (Washington, D.C.: GPO, 1961), 193; J. F. Ellis, *Victory in the West* (London: HMSO, 1960) I, 346–348; John Sweet, *Mounting the Threat: The Battle for the Bourguébus Ridge* (San Rafael, Calif.: Presidio Press, 1977), 115.

60. The biggest distinction between the two sectors was that the St. Lô defenses were shallower and therefore more vulnerable to carpet bombing. USAHD MS

ETHINT 69, Lt. Gen. Fritz Bayerlein, "Panzer Lehr Division at the Start of COBRA" (Germany: 1945), 1–2.

61. German medics projected that 13.5 percent of wounded returned to their units within a month, thus several thousand convalescents had returned to their units by the eve of COBRA.

62. Loss figures included the lightly wounded, who either remained with their units or who quickly returned to duty after treatment at theater dressing stations and field hospitals, while replacement figures exclude at least 5,250 *Waffen SS* and paratroop replacements, as well as personnel absorbed from field replacement battalions (12,000), individually returning convalescents and personnel on leave (5,000), reassigned personnel, men returning from courses and schools, and returning sick. Thus formations in Normandy had absorbed at least 28,000, and probably close to 40,000, replacements by COBRA.

63. For example, the LXXXIV Corps consolidated the shattered 77th and 91st Divisions into Divisional Group *König,* and the 9th and 10th SS Panzer Divisions amalgamated their *panzergrenadier* regiments into single reinforced regiments. Herbert Fürbringer, *9.SS-Panzer Division Hohenstauffen 1944: Normandie-Tarnopol-Arnhem* (Paris: Heimdal, 1984), 336–337.

64. Among the earliest alarm units deployed in Normandy were naval companies from Cherbourg that were deployed to the front in the Cotentin after 10 June. NARA T-78, 672, 000218-25, "Vorlaufiger Gefechtsbericht der 709. Inf. Div. Über die Kämpfe vom 6. bis 30 June 1944"; Ingouf, *Bataille de Cherbourg,* chap. 6.

65. On 1 August, for example, the 1st SS Panzer Division remained 7 percent overstrength and the 21st Panzer and Panzer Lehr Divisions 14 percent and 24 percent understrength, respectively. NARA T-78, 719, Zustandbericht 1. SS-Pz.Div, 1 August 1944, Ia Nr. 351/44 g. Kdos, 3 August 1944; T-78, 718, Zustandbericht 21 Pz. Div. 1 August 1944, Ia Nr. 1862/44 g. Kdos; Ibid., Zustandbericht Pz.Lehr-Div, 1 August 1944.

66. Up to 30 June Army Group B lost 164 tanks (including 10 Tigers), 32 assault guns, 41 tank hunters, and 114 heavy antitank guns. By 20 July it had lost 234 heavy antitank guns, 12 heavy flak guns, and 240 howitzers. NARA T-311 1, 000829, HG B, "Waffenlage Stand 1.7.1944," Ib/WuG Anl. 2 zu Tgb. Nr. 04281/44 geh.; T-78, 726, 6076096-98, OKH GenQu, "Kraftfahrzeuge (gep.) Heer, Westen," 1 October 1944.

67. By 14 July, the 6th Parachute Regiment had been reduced to 20 percent of its authorized heavy weapons. On the eve of COBRA some 30,000 replacements were on their way to the front—sufficient to bring German units back up to full defensive strength. Allied air power thus played a decisive role in sapping German strength. On 1 August, 42 percent of the tanks and assault guns committed (713 of 1,684) remained operational. PRO DEFE 3/61, Ultra Decrypt XL 3301, 24 July 1944; NARA T-312, 1517, 001065-66, BVTO AOK 7, "Zusammenstellung der im Monat July 1944 für die Armee bestimmten Einzeltransporte," TKB 1 July–6 August 1944.

68. NARA T-312, 517, 8116474, 15 AOK. "Mun.-Austattung der 1. SS-LAH," 16 June 1944; T-311, 27, 7033361-64, Anl. 26 zu "Kampfanweisung für die Festung Hoek v. H." [spring 1944]; 312, 517, 8116447, AOK 15 OQu., "Munitionswesen," Anl. 1 zu AOK 15/OQu/Qu.1 Nr. 1500/44 g.Kdos, 4 June 1944; T-311, 24, 7028940, "Mun. Bevorratung im Westen," GenStdH/Gen. Qu./Gr. Mun. I Az. 2359 Nr. I/011 901/44 geh. Kdos., 25 May 1944.

69. T-311, 29, 7183272, OB West, "Betreibstoff Einschränkung," Ia/OQu. West/Qu.1 Nr. 027921/44 g.Kdos., 3 June 1944.

70. That most depots in northwest France were in Brittany complicated this

shortage. Of its 18,748 tons of stockpiled ammunition on 1 June, only 7,172 tons (38 percent) was stored in Normandy. NARA T-312, 1571, 000607, 7 AOK, "Versorgungslage Stand 1.6.1944"; USAHD MS B-827, Maj. Otto Eckstein, "The Activities of the German Quartermaster West Before and During the Invasion," (Germany: 1947), 14–20.

71. During the spring of 1944, its gasoline stocks dropped from 7.450 to 4.663 million liters. To redeploy its reserves required twenty times its available lift capacity. NARA T-312, 1571, 000607, "Versorgungslage AOK 7 Stand: 1.1.1944"; T-311, 1, 7000704-705, "Auszüge aus Versorgungs-Tagesmeldungen," HG B Ib Nr. 0355/44 geh. 18 June 1944; NARA 311, 1, 1000677-78, "Stärke des Transportraumes für Verlastungszwecke," AOK 7 Ia Nr. 2708/44 g. Kdos, June 1944.

72. Incomplete figures for June indicate that the Germans lost 654,000 liters of gasoline, 2,308 tons of ammunition, and 2,225 tons of trucking capacity on resupply operations. Total losses from air and sabotage attacks in the West up to 28 June amounted to 10,042 tons of ammunition, 4,374,000 liters of fuel, and 3,383 tons of transport capacity. Fuel losses (from all causes) in June totaled 7,374,000 liters. Only 37 percent of the munitions dispatched to the Seventh Army had arrived by 28 June. NARA T-311, 14, 7014553 OQu West BdE, 30 June 1944; T-312, 1571, 000841, "Ausfallmeldungen," OQu. AOK 7 Nr. 9654/44 geh., 30 June 1944.

73. Up to 15 June the *Westheer* expended 5,000 tons of munitions but received only 3,000 tons. Against a daily requirement of 4,500 tons of supplies for offensive action, the Seventh Army had only 1,300 tons of transport capacity. NARA T-311, 1, 7000704-5, "Auszüge aus Versorgungs-Tagesmeldungen," HG. B Ib Nr. 0355/44 geh., 18 June 1944; AOK 7, "Beurteilung der Versorgungslage der 7. Armee," OQu. AHQu., 21 June 1944.

74. By 13 June the strategic reserve was down to 27,000 liters. NARA T-311, 14, 7014553 O.Qu. West, "Besonders der Ereignisse," 13 June 1944.

75. During June, the German First Army on the Atlantic coast surrendered 74 percent of its reserve fuel to Seventh Army. NARA T-312, 29, 7537089-90, TKB OQu AOK 1, 21 June 1944.

76. On 19 June, rail travel resumed from Paris to Dreux and Verneuil and across the Loire at Tours as far as Le Mans. The Tours rail bridge remained too badly damaged to allow unrestricted single-track crossing before 29 June, and even then many trains continued to unload south of the Loire. NARA T-78, 611, 000088, General des Transportwesens West Abt. Ib, "Seit Beginn der Invasion wurde folgende Wehrmacht-Transporte in Frankreich-Belgien-Holland gefahren"; T-78, 611, 000089, "Zusammenstellung der Ausladungen der Reichs- u. Basis-züge im Juni 1944," n.d.; ibid., "Ausladungen der Einzelnachschubsendungen innerhalb der besetzten Westgebiete," n.d.; T-78, 611, 000092, Chef Trspw./ vorgesch.Staffel, "Brückenbericht," 23 June 1944; T-78, 613, 000340, General des Eisenbahntruppen, "Zusammenstellung der in der Zeit vom 1.4–30.6.44 im Armee-bereich durchgeführten bewegungen"; T-312, 1571, 000983, AOK 7 BVTO, "Im Monat Juni 1944 gefahrene Nach-, Abschub- und Lazaretten-züge," Anl. 20 zu TKB BvTO AOK 7, n.d.; T-312, 1571, 000766, "Eisenbahn-Nachschubtransporte," OQu. West/ Qu1/ NT BrB.Nr. 03039/44 g.kdos, 22 June 1944.

77. The Seventh Army's supply situation first slightly improved on 29 June. NARA T-311, 14, OQu. West, "Versorgunslage Stand: 29 Juni 1944."

78. The Germans also ferried supplies from the Atlantic ports of Bordeaux and Royan to the Breton ports of Brest, St. Nazaire, Lorient, and St. Malo. But lack of shipping, Allied air attacks, the distances involved, and lack of supplies ensured that this operation contributed little to the German resupply effort. The first Paris barges

unloaded at Elbeuf on 22 June and between 1–10 July delivered an average of 433 tons daily. NARA T-78, 611, 000092, General des Transportwesens West, "Wehrmachttransporte auf Binnenwasserstrassen," Tätigkeitsbericht Juni 1944; T-311, 14, 000551, TKB OQu. West, 29 June 1944; T-311, 15, 9075225-236, "Seineschifffahrt Stand: 10.7.1944," Anl. zu KTB OQu. West, July 1944; T-311, 15, 7015378, Anl. zu KTB OQu. West, July 1944.

79. Up to 15 June one-fifth of the German transport reserve was disabled by air attacks, breakdowns, and accidents. In June Army Group B lost 1,866 trucks, 33 buses, 103 prime movers, and 2,198 other motor vehicles, including on average 30 supply trucks daily. NARA T-311, 1, 7000828, Ob. Kdo. d. Heeresgr. B, "Zusammenstellung der Totalausfälle an Kfz. in der Zeit vom 6.6–30.6.1944," 29 July 1944.

80. The increasing use of divisional truck columns to collect supplies from the interior merely exacerbated truck losses and accelerated the decline in unit mobility. NARA T-311, 15, 7015166ff, OQu. West, "Versorgungsübersicht, Juni–Juli 1944."

81. Between 9 June and 7 July 10,440 tons of supplies passed through Tours, an average of 360 tons a day. The importance of the supply line through Tours can be gauged by the immediate and frantic German effort to rebuild the bridge by erecting a temporary span. NARA T-311, 1, 7009804, TKB HG. B Abt. Qu. Ib BrB. Nr. 090/44 geh., 15 July 1944.

82. Between 8–14 July 48 percent and 43 percent, respectively, of the Seventh Army's fuel and ammunition arrived by rail and water. NARA T-311, 15, 7015322ff, "Versorgungsübersicht," 8–14 July 1944.

83. Average daily fuel dispatched to the Seventh Army fell 22 percent from 49,000 to 38,000 liters. NARA T-311, 15, 7015301ff, OQu West "Versorgungsübersicht Juli 1944."

84. Historians have missed the impact of GOODWOOD on the German logistic situation in assessing its contribution to Allied victory in Normandy. It was in this realm that GOODWOOD made a decisive contribution to COBRA's success. The Seventh Army only maintained its gasoline receipts at 73 percent of pre-GOODWOOD levels by employing most of its own trucks to collect fuel from Le Mans, Alençon, and Dreux. NARA T-311, 15, 7015301ff, OQu West, "Versorgungsübersicht," July 1944.

85. The first fuel train arrived at Le Mans on 25 July, too late to resupply German troops during the decisive first 48 hours in which the Americans broke the German front. PRO DEFE 3/63, Ultra Decrypt XL 3852, 28 July 1944; NARA T-311, 15, 7015466, OQu. West, "Versorgungsübersicht," 25.7.1944; PRO WO 171/376, Guards Armd. Div. Int. Sum. 31, August 1944, apdx. A.

86. Between late June and 24 July, *Kampfgruppe* Kentner's ammunition stocks for machine guns and mortars declined by 64 percent and 75 percent, respectively. On the eve of COBRA, *Kampfgruppe Kuske* of the 17th SS *Panzergrenadier* Division *Götz von Berlichingen* had only 1,000 rounds per machine gun and thirty rounds per rifle; less than two days' combat at average consumption rates. NARA, WNRC, RG 407, 101–20, FUSA G2 Periodic Rpt. 51, 31 July 1944, Anx.; NARA T-354, 156, 3800792, "Tagesmeldung Kampfgruppe Kuske," 23 July 1944.

87. "Bewegungen stark behindert," the Seventh Army reported. NARA T-311, 1, 70009824, Tagesmeldung HG B Abt Qu Ib, 25 July 44. For lack of flak munitions, see PRO DEFE 3/62, Ultra Decrypt XL 3568, 27 July 1944.

88. Von Kluge had replaced von Rundstedt on 3 July as commander in chief in the West.

89. PRO DEFE 3/64, Ultra Decrypt XL 4160, 31 July 1944.

90. By 14 July the Germans had lost 1,400 tons of trucking capacity on the

British sector alone. In June German losses amounted to 4,200 motor vehicles, including 1,866 trucks. By the end of August German motor vehicle losses exceeded 20,000. NARA T-311, 28, 7034542, "Bericht über die Fahrt des Herrn Feldmarschall zur Pz.Gr.West u. d. I. SS-Pz.Korps am 14.7.1944"; T-311, 1, 7000828, OQu. Heeresgr. B, TKB, 29 July 1944; Richard L. DiNardo, "Germany's Panzer Arm: Anatomy and Performance," Ph.D. diss., City University of New York, 1988, 27.

91. The XLVII Panzer Corps on 7 August fielded 248 tanks, 164 howitzers, 59 antitank guns, and 40 assault guns. PRO DEFE 3/116, Ultra Decrypt XL 5600, 11 August 1944.

92. Only one of the attack divisions, the 116th Panzer Division was at all fresh and still strong. PRO DEFE 3/116, Ultra Decrypt XL 5600, 11 August 1944; USAHD MS ETHINT 17, Lt. Gen. Gerhard Graf von Schwerin, "116th Panzer Division in Normandy" (Luxembourg: 1945), 21.

93. Ultra gave Bradley only four hours' warning of the German attack and front-line troops as little as twenty minutes' notice. Ralph Bennett, *Ultra in the West* (London: Hutchinson, 1979), 119; Carlo D'Este, *Decision: The Unwritten Story of Montgomery and the Allied Campaign* (London: Collins, 1983), 415–419; Bradley, *A General's Story* (New York: Holt, 1951), 291.

94. Postbattle analysis confirmed nine German tanks, eleven armored personnel carriers, one armored car, and six trucks destroyed by air attack. PRO WO 106/4348, ORS Rpt. 4, "Air Attacks on Enemy Tanks and Motor Transport in the Mortain Area, August 1944," table II.

95. The Germans might have recaptured Avranches if they had struck further south where there were few U.S. troops, but clearly they could not have held the town for long.

96. As late as 11 August SHAEF still characterized German combat spirit as "excellent" and the tenacity of their defense as "awesome." PRO WO 219/ 161, FID D2 Memo to SHAEF G2, "Reports on Morale of the German Soldier," August 1944; PRO DEFE 3/65, Ultra Decrypt XL 4271, 1 August 1944.

97. Accurate figures are unobtainable due to the loss of German records during the chaotic retreat. The most widely accepted figures are that the Allies encircled 100,000 German troops, killed 10,000 and captured 40,000, while 50,000 escaped. Panzer Group West estimated the last figure on 21 August based on a dubious guess by the III Flak Corps, which had escaped the pocket prior to the desperate breakout battle. USAHD MS A-922, Gen. Hans Eberbach, "Panzergroup Eberbach at Alençon & Its Breakthrough of the Encirclement of Falaise" (Germany: 1946), 36; MS ETHINT 58, Maj. Gen. Frhr. von Gersdorff, "Seventh Army, 25.7–31.8.1944" (Germany: 1945), 5.

98. Actually, the Allies probably surrounded about 80,000 troops, because most service units and some combat elements either escaped from or were pushed aside before the pocket closed. In all two army, four corps, and twelve divisional headquarters were cut off. Allied prisoner estimates are inflated because they are based on aggregate figures from the entire theater. Of the 42,260 prisoners taken between 18–23 August, probably 35,000 came from the Falaise pocket. USAHD MS A-922, 36; William Breuer, *Death of a Nazi Army: the Falaise Pocket* (New York: Stein & Day, 1985); Eddy Florentin, *The Battle of the Falaise Gap* (New York: 1967); James Lucas and J. Barker, *The Killing Ground: The Battle of the Falaise Pocket* (London: Book Club Associates, 1978).

99. Postbattle analysis counted 754 armored fighting vehicles, nearly 1,000 guns, and 7,500 vehicles destroyed or abandoned in the pocket. PRO WO 208/3118, 2 ORS Rpt. 15, "Enemy Casualties in Vehicles and Equipment during the Retreat from Normandy to the Seine," October 1944, apdx. D.

100. German equipment losses in the retreat to the Seine were double those in the Falaise pocket. PRO WO 208/3118, "Enemy Casualties in Vehicles and Equipment," Part III.

101. The Fifth Panzer Army disposed of twenty divisions and 113,000 troops. Michel Dufresne, "Le Succèss allemand sur la Seine," *Revue Historique des Armées* 3 (1987), 51.

102. Between 1 April–31 July engineers built 136 bridges totaling 16,824 meters. NARA T-78, 111, 60344025ff, "Eisenbahnpioniertechnische Auswertung der anglo-amerikanischen Invasion in Frankreich im Summer 1944," Anl. zu Kdr. d. Eisb.Pi.Rgt 6 Abt. I Nr. 505/45 geh. [fall 1944]; NARA T-78, 613, 0000273, Kdr. d. Eisb.Pi. Rgt. 6 Abt. Ia Nr. 2352/44 geh., 2 August 1944.

103. In February 1944, seventeen ferries and one pontoon bridge were in operation on the lower Seine. By 23 July twenty-six ferries were in operation, and by late August there were no fewer than forty. NARA T-312, 519, 8118913, "Fähren u. übersetzmittel Lagekarte," A. Pi.Fü.15 Nr.16/44 geh., February 1944.

104. Wesley F. Craven and James L. Cate, *The Army Air Forces in WWII* (Chicago: University of Chicago, 1951) III, 259–261.

105. From early August on, the XIX TAC screened the southern U.S. flank along the Loire as U.S. forces drove west into Brittany and east toward the Seine. From 25 August on, the USAAF diverted significant air assets to support the struggling U.S. assault on Brest. HERO, *Interdiction from Falaise to Westwall, 14 August–14 September 1944* (Dunn Loring, Va.: n.d); Craven and Cate, *The Army Air Forces in WWII* III, 261–266.

106. Heavy rain and low cloud cover prevented any air operations between 21–23 August. Low cloud cover returned on 28 August followed by heavy rain and poor visibility on 29 August, and intermittent rain on 30 August. The Allies launched 3,902 sorties at the Seine bridges, ferries, and avenues of German retreat in late August, with a peak activity of 1,357 sorties on 25 August. Dufresne, "Succès allemand," 53–58.

107. By late August 12 heavy flak batteries defended the Seine between Elbeuf and Caudebec. Bundesarchiv-Militärarchiv, Koblenz (BA-MA) RH, "Flaklagekarte Luftflotte III Stand: 28 August 1944."

108. The Allies estimated that between 21–29 August the Germans lost 14,000 automobiles and 665 tanks, mostly abandoned due to lack of fuel. This was more than twice their total losses in the Falaise pocket. A British survey identified 223 German tanks between Falaise and the Seine, only 55 of which Allied action had destroyed. It attributed 3,770 of 13,350 abandoned vehicles, 15 of 650 tanks, and 10 of 235 self-propelled guns to air attack. On the banks of the Seine estimated losses due to air attack rose to 33 percent. PR0 WO 106/4348, 2 ORS., "Analysis of German Tank Casualties in France, 6.6–31.8.1944," 203; Dufresne, " Succès allemand," 55–56.

109. The Allies estimated that the Germans extricated 98 percent of the troops and 90 percent of the motor transport that reached the Seine, including 135 armored fighting vehicles. Dufresne, "Succès allemand," 55.

110. Desmond Young, *Rommel: The Desert Fox* (New York: Harper & Row, 1950), chap. 10; David Irving, *The Trail of the Fox* (New York: E. P. Dutton, 1977; Avon Books, 1979), 441–473; Ronald Lewin, *Rommel as Military Commander* (New York: Ballantine, 1970; 1980), 286–287; Friedrich Ruge, *Rommel in Normandy* (London: Macdonald & Jane's, 1979); Hans Speidel, *Invasion 1944: ein Betrag zu Rommels und des reiches Schicksal* (Tübingen: Rainer Wunderlich Verlag, 1949); Siegfried Westphal, *Heer in Fesseln: aus den Papieren des Stabchefs von Rommel, Kesselring und Rundstedt* (Bonn: Athenäum Verlag, 1950).

111. His approach to defense reflected the intellectual legacy of the

Clausewitzian flexible defense taught by the *Reichswehr.* Jehuda L. Wallach, *The Dogma of the Battle of Annihilation: The Theories of Clausewitz and Schlieffen and Their Impact on the German Conduct of Two World Wars* (Westport, Conn.: Greenwood Press, 1986), 283–285.

112. He showed considerable concern for the U.S. sector in June but only because he perceived the strategic importance of Cherbourg, not because he recognized American fighting capabilities.

113. Fighters available to the *Luftflotte Reich* fell from 991 on 1 June to 546 by 1 July. Williamson Murray, *Luftwaffe* (Baltimore, Md.: Nautical & Aviation Press, 1985), 266–270.

114. On D-Day *Luftflotte* III fielded 815 aircraft, of which approximately 600 were operational. Up to 19 June it lost 594 aircraft, or 75 percent of its original establishment. It flew 13,829 sorties in June, one-tenth of the Allied total. Murray, *Luftwaffe,* 265–268.

115. On 10–11, June transports dropped supplies to the 6th Parachute Regiment at Carentan and during late June resupplied Cherbourg. Carell, *Invasion,* 143.

116. During August 1944, *Luftflotte* III averaged 324 operational fighters, 67 night fighters, and 191 bombers. HERO, *Interdiction from Falaise to Westwall,* 193.

117. The IX U.S. TAC lost 80 aircraft from 25 July to 7 August, 73 percent to ground fire and only 7 percent to enemy aircraft. Flak claimed the destruction of 2,024 Allied planes in July 1944 in Western Europe and 2,186 in August. At the same time, antiaircraft guns consumed vast quantities of ammunition—it took on average 5,000 light or 16,000 heavy rounds to down an aircraft—which aggravated German supply shortages. H. A. Koch, *Die Geschichte der Deutschen Flakartillerie* (Bad Nauheim: Podzun, 1954), 655.

118. Janusz Piekelkiewicz, *Die 8.8cm Flak im Erdkampf-Einsatz* (Stuttgart: Motorbuch, 1976), 135–36.

119. The *Luftflatte* III was reluctant to waste the III Flak Corps in ground operations. It resisted army demands to allow the 32d Regiment to fire on ground targets on D-Day at Omaha Beach. The battery that savaged British armor at Cagny during GOODWOOD joined action only at the pistol point of an army officer, and the *OKL* precipitously withdrew the corps on 18–19 August out of the Falaise pocket, which meant that the army could no longer halt the Allied advance. For exaggerated claims of the corps's role in GOODWOOD, see USAHD MS B-597, Gen. Wolfgang Pickert, "III Flak Corps, May–Sep. 1944" (Germany: 1947), 21–24. For a more balanced assessment see Luck, *Panzer Commander,* 158–162.

120. E-boats sank the Norwegian destroyer *Svenner* on 6 June and eight merchant ships in June. David Brown, *Warship Losses In WWII* (London: Arms & Armour Press, 1990); H. T. Lenton and J. J. Colledge, *Warship Losses of WWII by British and Dominion Fleets* (London: Ian Allan, 1965); Wilhelm Harnier, *Artillerie im Küstenkampf* (Munich: J. F. Lehmann, 1969), 119; M. J. Whitley, *German Coastal Forces of WWII* (London: Arms and Armour, 1992); Volkmar Kuhn, *Schnellboote im Einsatz* (Stuttgart: Motorbuch, 1986).

121. Air attacks on Le Havre on 15 June crippled the German naval presence in the eastern English Channel, sinking four large patrol ships and ten E-boats.

122. Of 43 U-boats dispatched, 12 turned back prematurely, 18 were sunk, and only 13 completed their patrols. In all, U-boats sank 7 warships and 16 transports, totaling only 55,000 tons. Ellis, *Victory* I, 295.

123. The Germans launched *Neger* attacks on 5–6, 7–8 and 29–30 July, and on 16–17 August. *Biber* craft attacked on 29–30 Aug, *Linse* on 2–3 and 8–9 August, and fast landing boats (on 15 June. Erich Gröner, *Die Schiffe der deutschen*

Kriegsmarine u. Luftwaffe 1939–45 (Munich: J. F. Lehmanns, 1978) and *Die deutschen Kriegsschiffe* (Stuttgart: Bernard & Graefe, 1983), Vols. 6–8; PRO DEFE 3/62, Ultra Decrypt XL 3540, 26 July 1944.

124. The St. Marcouf battery held up the U.S. advance on Montebourg for five days. In June coastal guns sank two warships and three merchant ships and damaged eighteen vessels. Carell, *Invasion,* 127–133; Ingouf, *Bataille de Cherbourg,* 45–46; Harnier, *Küstenkampf,* 92–97.

125. In June 1944 the Germans sank 261 Allied vessels, including twenty-four warships and thirty-five merchant ships. Mines inflicted the most damage. Harnier, *Küstenkampf,* 118–120.

126. However, because so few German troops fought both the Americans and British prior to the breakout in late July, it was difficult for them to evaluate relative British and U.S. capabilities. Those who did were adamant that the Americans were superior. PRO WO 171/258, I Corps Int. Sum. 26, July 1944, "Combat Report, Panzer Lehr Division," apdx. A.

127. Trevor Dupuy's extensive statistical analysis of divisional combat performance in World War II indicates that German combat superiority diminished as the war progressed. While Dupuy's research is valuable, it is overly reductive and misses the reality that raw combat power per se cannot guarantee combat success and that immediate German combat power was bought at the expense of sustained combat strength. Trevor Dupuy, *Understanding War* (London: Leo Cooper, 1992), table 10-2, 115.

Conclusion

An examination of the performance of the U.S., British, Canadian, and German militaries both prior to and during the 1944 Normandy Campaign demonstrates that the U.S. military generally learned more quickly from its combat experience and thus adapted faster than either its British and Canadian counterparts or its German adversary. At the start of World War II in September 1939, the combat capabilities of the western Allied armed forces remained limited. The British military was marginally better and the Canadian military marginally worse prepared than the U.S. armed forces. Yet none had the ability to project effective military power overseas or to prevail against a Nazi war machine that had embarked upon rearmament years before its opponents.

By the end of the Normandy Campaign, the U.S. military had clearly developed superior combat capabilities compared to its Anglo-Canadian allies. The reasons for this were complex. That the United States did not enter the war until December 1941 gave its armed forces significant advantages. Not only did it allow a more ordered mobilization and expansion, but also permitted study and understanding of, at least in part, the reasons for the dramatic German blitzkrieg victories of 1939–1941 and more effective preparation to meet the impending challenge. Nonetheless, no amount of peacetime preparation could adequately prepare U.S. troops for combat, and, inevitably, the green soldiers initially performed poorly in their first combat in North Africa over the winter of 1942–1943 during Operation TORCH. But the fundamental soundness of U.S. doctrine, tactics, and equipment combined with the army's determination both to learn from its experience and to retrain in the field during ongoing combat operations ensured that the army would learn relatively quickly from combat in Tunisia, Sicily, and Italy. The U.S. Army learned from past mistakes, dismissed incompetent commanders, enhanced interarm and interservice cooperation, refined tactics and techniques, and improvised better weapons. In consequence, this military steadily enhanced its combat effectiveness.

The process of rapid adaptation continued during the Normandy Campaign as U.S. forces learned through trial and error to overcome the difficulties of fighting in the Norman hedgerows and against enemy defenses in depth. The Americans also mastered the air-ground battle during the campaign as armored column cover forged the most intimate and effective air-ground coordination yet seen in the war. By the end of the campaign not only were the combat capabilities of the U.S. Army clearly superior to those of its allies, they were also superior to those of its enemy.

Anglo-Canadian ground forces considerably enhanced their capabilities during the war, but the pace of reform was generally slower and only gained momentum during the middle of the war. Rigidly committed to a strategy of attrition, lacking sound doctrine, and suffering the ravages of interwar neglect, the British Army struggled early in the war both to draw appropriate lessons from its combat experience and to improve its capabilities. Such flaws had contributed to a series of reverses during 1940–1942 unparalleled in Britain's history. During 1942–1943 the British Army slowly developed an operational approach, based upon firepower attrition, that proved capable of defeating the Germans. Gradual honing of offensive art finally led British forces to develop an all-round military proficiency during the last year of the war. In 1944, however, real limitations still existed. British offensive art remained unimaginative, mechanistic, and inflexible; at the same time the limitations of its weaponry, the deficiencies in interarm and interservice cooperation, and the need to minimize casualties all ensured that it was difficult for the British military either to inflict sustained damage or penetrate enemy defenses.

The Canadian military, on the other hand, had suffered severe neglect between the wars and thus its fighting potential at the start of the war was marginal at best. Such neglect initially forced the Canadian military into dependence on Great Britain. The resulting anglicization of the Canadian Army, however, turned it into an inferior clone of its British counterpart as the Canadian military struggled to reform and reorganize without a solid base of expertise and experience. At the same time, the Canadian government's reluctance to risk its troops in combat, largely for domestic political reasons, circumscribed the army's preparation. In consequence, lack of combat exposure ensured that the Canadian Army's combat capabilities remained limited in June 1944. It was only during the latter stages of the Normandy campaign that the Canadian military developed a basic proficiency.

The combat capabilities of the German military in September 1939 were far superior to those of its opponents. Germany had begun rearmament several years before its enemies, and the political climate in interwar Germany provided a clear mandate for reform and expansion. The effectiveness of the German Army, the *Heer,* early in the war was predicated on sound, realistic doctrine and training grounded in its Great War experience, the professionalism of its officer corps, the quality of its weaponry, a determination to examine and enhance combat performance at every turn, the martial qualities of German society, and the ideological appeal of National Socialism. These strengths allowed the *Heer* to harness the tank within an aggressive strategic doctrine of deep penetration by mechanized forces to paralyze and overwhelm underprepared militaries before enemies could mobilize their demographic and industrial strength. The unpreparedness of Germany's opponents, however, obscured serious deficiencies that existed in German military capabilities and preparation. The *Heer* suffered from excessive and rushed expansion, it was short of commissioned and non-commissioned officers, had an inadequate service tail, possessed few mechanisms for interservice cooperation, and was inexpert at defense. Nazi racism had also begun to inflate a sense of German superiority and distort accurate assessment of enemy capabilities. But most seriously of all, Germany simply lacked the strategic base for Hitler's quest for world domination.

Adolf Hitler, however, ultimately committed Germany to war against much of the globe. Of necessity, the German Army had to structure and organize itself to maximize its battlefield effectiveness and enhance its qualitative edge. Such measures ensured that one to one, the *Heer* invariably outfought its opponents until very late in the war. Yet, against such overwhelming odds German battlefield superiority could not ultimately surmount marked numerical and material inferiority. As the Allied nations mobilized their economies and manpower, they also began to learn from their combat experience and thus developed greater military proficiency. Improved Allied combat effectiveness inexorably narrowed the German qualitative edge. All the same, that it took the Allies almost six years to overwhelm Nazi Germany testifies to the German military's ability to adapt operationally, tactically, and technically throughout the war. German wartime adaptation appears less pronounced in absolute terms in comparison to its opponents because the *Heer* started in September 1939 from a broad base of general competence and expertise. Thus, in most cases, all the *Heer* required was fine tuning of doctrine, tactics, and equipment rather than more fundamental reform that the British and Canadian Armies required. But, as the tide of the war turned, the pace of German adaptation steadily increased. The net effect of constant adaptation was to postpone inevitable defeat and to greatly increase the price of the Allied victory.

The reasons for the divergent pace of adaptation among these four armies were many and complex. An intricate interplay of circumstances, combat realities, military cultures, broader cultural characteristics, geostrategic considerations, and personalities explain the relative pace and character of adaptation exhibited by the U.S., British, Canadian, and German militaries. Explanations clearly have multiple causes and are inherently difficult to discern. Assessing the relative impact of individual influences is particularly hard. Nevertheless, it is possible to draw some generalized conclusions: prevailing military culture and doctrine exerted the greatest impact on the ability of these military institutions to adapt during World War II.

Cultural factors go some way toward explaining the greater flexibility and adaptability of the U.S. and German militaries. In fact, prevailing military culture profoundly influenced institutional capacity to adapt. The Americans exhibited a managerial and scientific approach to war that reflected the interwar spread of modern business management techniques and notions of professionalism. The Germans, on the other hand, viewed war as an art. It, therefore, championed individual initiative and a flexible command tradition through which its General Staff and officer corps promoted a practical approach to war that emphasized both military education and the need to learn from combat experience.

In interwar Britain, however, officership remained the preserve of elite society and afforded a vehicle for social advancement. Few Britons, both in and out of the military, regarded officership as a profession that required full-time education and preparation. As a result, the army exhibited an amateur approach to professional development that denigrated theory and education and instead elevated improvisation and pragmatism. Class concerns also created an enormous gulf between officers and men that hampered the army's ability to learn and to adapt from the bottom up, the fastest and most effective means of adaptation. British military culture also valued and rewarded loyalty to one's superiors above honesty. Such a rigidly hierarchical culture did not foster the honest self-criticism necessary for rapid and effective adaptation. On the other hand, the culture of the U.S. and German armies proved more receptive to criticism and honest self-appraisal (though for different reasons), which facilitated easier, faster, and more accurate identification and dissemination of lessons learned.

The British Army's long and illustrious history also deeply ingrained traditionalism. The British regimental system had fostered both excellent esprit de corps and a parochial tribalism since Napoleonic days. In the twentieth century, however, its drawbacks threatened to outweigh its benefits: modern warfare demanded greater interarms and interservice coordination. During World War II, however, regimental tribalism hampered the British Army, and to a lesser extent the U.S. and Canadian Armies, from developing combined-arms proficiency. Regimentalism also promoted an intellectual parochialism that inhibited British reevaluation of strategic fundamentals and hindered doctrinal development.

Historical factors also clearly played a major role. World War I profoundly shaped the character, development, and performance of the combatants during World War II, and exerted a baneful effect on the interwar development of the British and Canadian militaries. Societies' reactions to the enormous loss of life created a climate in which both militaries not only had difficulty simply existing but in which they felt compelled to jettison the knowledge of modern war that they had gained at such bitter cost in Flanders. Defeat, on the other hand, energized Germany between the wars to re-create an effective military to eradicate the stigma of failure and achieve the world power status that Imperial Germany had sought. Such a climate proved a powerful stimulus to reform and innovation. The Great War had less effect on the U.S. military. Because the United States entered late, World War I was far less costly or damaging to the country and thus had only a limited influence on the development of strategy, military policy, or the fundamental character of the army. While the nation returned to its historic isolationism, the U.S. military absorbed the lessons of the Great War into revised doctrine between the wars. As a result, it entered World War II with a doctrine that was essentially sound, which greatly aided the army both in distilling correct lessons from its combat experience and in quickly enhancing its proficiency.

Geography and geostrategic considerations also played their part. That both Canada and the United States were able to raise and prepare their ground forces at home free from direct enemy attack facilitated an ordered enhancement of combat capabilities. Great Britain faced its enemy across the English Channel, and until 1943 its maritime lines of communication were imperiled and the nation was subject to disruptive air attacks. Such proximity mandated considerable diversion of resources from the primary task of preparing the armed forces to assume the offensive and crush the enemy. That Germany, on the other hand, was a continental power shaped the pattern of interwar innovation and directed it toward ground warfare against obvious enemies—Poland and France—which made the task of military reform easier.

Domestic political realities also played an important role in shaping relative combat capabilities. The political climate in interwar Germany was conducive to reform as successive German governments gave their military a clear mandate to prepare for ground war against its enemies. The political climate in the United States, Britain, and Canada between the wars was inimical to reform and badly circumscribed the degree of innovation possible. As a result, these militaries had limited capabilities in September 1939. Political considerations also strongly influenced British preparation in the late 1930s as the government geared rearmament to deter German aggression rather than prepare for war. Interwar neglect, followed by hasty and ill-conceived rearmament left the British Army incapable of meeting the military obligations that its government rashly committed its armed forces to fulfilling in 1939. This quixotic quest for deterrence contributed to the unprecedented series of defeats experienced between 1940–1942 from which the army never fully recovered. The legacies of defeat profoundly influenced the development and performance of the British Army throughout the war.

Defeat provided impetus for reform to reverse British fortunes, but at the same time significantly shaped the process and pattern of adaptation that materialized. Defeat entrenched the army's reluctance to evaluate openly its performance as senior commanders censored lessons-learned material to maintain current morale and combat effectiveness in a effort to halt the string of defeats. But censorship, deemed necessary to maintain the current combat proficiency, hampered efforts to enhance future combat effectiveness.

Unappreciative of the need to learn from experience, lacking mechanisms to disseminate lessons, and unwilling to reassess strategic and doctrinal fundamentals, the army was slow to learn from combat. At the same time, enormous political pressure for success led to a series of rash British counteroffensives in the desert campaigns in 1941–1942. Ironically, the quest for victory got in the way of British efforts to enhance combat effectiveness. Premature offensive action dissipated scarce resources and, more seriously, left commanders little time to contemplate larger strategic and doctrinal issues. Thus the British Army muddled its way through, slowly learning the hard way by costly trial and error, until in 1942 in North Africa it gradually discovered a recipe for success—a single approach that proved capable of defeating the Germans. This approach was the de facto operational doctrine of firepower dominance in which artillery smashed one's own infantry into the enemy lines and beat down the enemy in grim, slow, cautious, attritional warfare. At the core of this approach lay recognized British strengths—artillery, logistics, and administration.

Although the victories of 1942–1943 began to restore troop morale, it remained fragile. Such fragility led both the War Office and senior commanders to continue to dominate the lessons-learned process and to censor reports that, deemed too critical, might damage morale. The army high command endeavored to keep the troops ignorant of unpalatable realities, such as the inferior quality of Allied armor, in an effort to maintain what there was of morale and combat effectiveness. Whatever the merits of such motives, the consequence was a hampering of the army's ability to build its future combat effectiveness. The unwillingness to identify problems openly and honestly gravely handicapped the army's efforts to rectify the problems that confronted it.

Defeat also slowed the preparation of the Canadian armed forces. The most fundamental problem of the Canadian military on the eve of Operation OVERLORD in June 1944 was its lack of battle experience. Few Canadian soldiers had seen combat, and for most of those that had this amounted to a single day in the disastrous 1942 Dieppe raid. Defeat at Dieppe both promoted and hindered innovation within the Canadian military. The debacle provided impetus for a much needed shakeup of the Canadian Army during 1942–1943, but it also reinforced the Canadian government's reluctance to commit troops to combat for fear of heavy casualties that might have precipitated a domestic political crisis. With so little experience under its belt, the Canadian Army was unable to generate broad military proficiency before June 1944, and thus it was only during the Normandy campaign that Canadian troops began to grope their way slowly and painfully toward military effectiveness.

If British commanders had sought to shield their troops from unsavory realities, the German High Command and its officer corps resorted to a far more systematic and warped distortion of reality to maintain the fighting power of its armed forces. Nazi racism, inculcated through ideological indoctrination, crippled intelligence efforts to assess accurately the capabilities and potential of enemies, especially the "subhuman" Soviet peoples and the "mongrel" Americans. Such racism hampered German adaptation at every turn and hastened defeat. Yet this German self-deception proved highly effective in maintaining morale, cohesion, discipline and fighting power, even during the dying days of the war when defeat was imminent.

Tactically, operationally, and technically, the *Heer* constantly adapted throughout the war. In consequence, the Western Allies experienced great difficulty in countering the qualitative edge that the *Heer* possessed in 1939. This reality helps to explain both why the Allies required six years to defeat Germany, and why even in 1945 they were still rarely able to prevail on the battlefield without marked numerical and material superiority. Extensive combat experience underpinned German adaptation. Germany went to war in 1939 with essentially sound doctrine rooted in its World War I experience. The first-line German divisions were relatively well trained and had gained valuable operational experience from the occupations of the Rhineland, Austria, Sudetenland, and Czechoslovakia. One of the great strengths of the *Heer* was that, even though the brilliant victories of 1939–1941 provided little incentive for substantial innovation, it never equated success in battle with effectiveness in performance. In consequence, the *Heer* continually evaluated its performance at every stage through extensive, and often highly critical, battle reports. It also drew widely upon the experience of even junior officers in collecting after-action reports and quickly absorbed recent battle experience into revised doctrine and training.

Its approach to learning was certainly less scientific, less formal, and less institutionalized than that of the British and Americans. Yet its extensive and broad-based combat experience gave the German General Staff and officer corps the expertise to extract accurate and appropriate combat lessons. That the Germans also maintained close ties between the field and replacement armies facilitated adaptation as decorated combat veterans were routinely rotated through the replacement army to disseminate their experience, which brought periodic revision of training syllabuses. So even in 1944, German basic training remained more realistic and thorough than that of its opponents.

Throughout World War II the *Heer* also maintained the interwar reputation it had gained for technical innovation as it introduced numerous high-quality weapons. Technical innovation maintained the German firepower edge until late in the war and powerfully reinforced morale, cohesion, and combat resolve (however, the nazi regime poorly orchestrated technological innovation so that its war machine dissipated considerable energy, creativity, and resources in the pursuit of unrealistic projects of marginal utility). Organizationally, too, the army repeatedly refined its force structure and organization to become a leaner, tougher combat organization.

The outcome of the 1944 Normandy Campaign, though, clearly illustrated the ascendancy of the law of numbers. Modern military history indicates that the side with a marked superiority in resources typically prevails. More efficient organization, better equipment, superior training and doctrine, and ideological indoctrination can partially offset inferiority. However, past a certain point the enemy's superiority becomes overwhelming because armed forces can rarely sustain a significant combat advantage due to the very process of battlefield innovation. Consequently, Hitler's invasion of the Soviet Union on 22 June 1941 probably sealed Germany's fate; certainly, Hitler's declaration of war on the United States on 7 December 1941 doomed Germany to defeat.

Effective military adaptation also requires accurate evaluation of the capabilities of the enemy. Anglo-Canadian troops were slow to adapt in part because they poorly appraised the character and capabilities of their enemy. In fact, Commonwealth forces often displayed an alarming ignorance of their opponent, particularly of German defensive doctrine. Thus, in Normandy Anglo-Canadian forces continued to be taken by surprise by German reverse-slope positions that had been the foundation of German defensive techniques since 1917.[1] The U.S. Army also had found its tactics poorly attuned to German defensive techniques during the Normandy Campaign. But U.S. troops gradually learned to attack the full depth of enemy defenses and exploit rapidly any penetration of the German front before the enemy troops had time to react and plug the gap as they invariably did when confronted with more mechanistic British or Canadian attacks.

What this study demonstrates is that militaries whose peacetime doctrines are not fundamentally flawed can adapt effectively, given sufficient combat exposure, as long as they do not suffer decisive defeat. Where an army's basic doctrine is fundamentally flawed however, not only is effective adaptation unlikely, but defeat may follow. Without a correction of fundamental doctrinal flaws, other areas of innovation—organizational and training reforms or better weaponry—can only marginally improve an army's combat capabilities.

The doctrines of the German and U.S. Armies in World War II were essentially sound because they were rooted in careful examination of the lessons of World War I. But British, and by derivation Canadian, doctrine had serious flaws because the British military, in its efforts to exorcise the ghosts of the Somme and Paschendaele, failed to preserve its experience of the Great War. Such failure prevented the British Army from effectively adapting new technology—the tank and the airplane—between the wars, or from perceiving how these new weapons would transform the nature of warfare. Flawed doctrine, therefore, both contributed to the unprecedented series of defeats the army suffered during 1939–1941 and, at the same time, British efforts to draw appropriate lessons from defeat. Fragile morale and a desire to maintain combat capabilities in turn led the War Office and senior British officers to insulate their troops from the truth during the desperate days of 1940–1942 when the specter of defeat loomed. So British forces throughout the war generally adapted more slowly than the Americans. Moreover, flawed doctrine and the army's unwillingness to reevaluate strategic fundamentals blunted the impact that improvements in British organization, equipment, and training brought; the British Army, therefore, did not develop all-round military proficiency until late in the war. Finally, powerful political pressure for success, combined with the concern over morale, meant that as soon as the British Army found a battle-winning formula—Montgomery's *Materialschlacht*—future innovation concentrated on perfecting these elements in which the British Army had already exhibited proficiency.

The U.S. Army, by contrast, learned to apply doctrine more flexibly.[2] U.S. forces minimized and surmounted the inevitable, manifold deficiencies that existed in their organization, tactics, equipment, and training early in the war by an unusual variety of tactical and technological innovations. The process of innovation in the army was rapid because it came largely from the bottom up, as opposed to the top-down adaptation process that characterized the British Army. This receptivity to feedback from enlisted personnel and junior officers was an important strength that facilitated rapid adaptation. At the same time, the U.S. Army exhibited a determination to retrain on the battlefield to enhance its effectiveness.[3]

U.S. and Commonwealth forces displayed distinctive operational styles in Normandy that reflected divergent historical and cultural development. The former attacked more frequently and more continuously, on a broader front, with less artillery and logistic support.[4] As a result, the Americans brought more of their fighting power to bear and applied it more often and for longer. This operational style reflected the United States' limited experience of "total war" that resulted in an approach to combat by which the U.S. military sought to apply overwhelming force to destroy the enemy, in classic Clausewitzian terms, as quickly as possible in battle. U.S. forces were, thus, more given to attacking in bad weather and without strong air, artillery, or logistic support and to press the attack for longer, despite heavy losses, to obtain the objective. The benefits of this approach in Normandy was that it bled the enemy dry and created conditions conducive to a successful breakout. Such an approach, while flawed, was well attuned to the nation's demographic and material strength and allowed Americans to be profligate with resources in a way that was impossible for either allies or the enemy.

For both the British and Canadians and the Germans manpower was always more limited. Because of manpower concerns, rooted in their Great War experience, casualty conservation—the minimization of losses—dominated Commonwealth operations in northwest Europe. This imperative helped reinforce the cumbersome, unsubtle, attritional British approach to operations in which firepower endeavored to smash the enemy and troops occupied the devastated ground. Slow, ponderous, mechanistic, and controlled, such approach left little to chance and kept losses down. It brought success—with such overwhelming firepower it was virtually impossible not to gain ground. But such an approach meant that Anglo-Canadian forces could neither gain much ground quickly nor maintain offensive operations for long. It also meant that the army could not keep up continuous pressure, because it required extended breaks between operations for the logistic buildup needed to guarantee victory. The British approach reflected the army's history, especially the legacy of the Great War slaughter in the trenches, sustained neglect of the interwar years, damaging defeats in the early years of World War II, painful recovery, growing war weariness, and meager manpower reserves. The British approach controlled the battle and made defeat highly unlikely, but at the price of leaving the enemy damaged but intact.[5] However, British operational art was in tune with overall British political-strategic objectives that sought to defeat nazism at tolerable cost and retain the empire, for which Britain required an intact army.

Both approaches by the Western Allies had their merits and drawbacks. Neither operational approach was particularly effective in surmounting German defenses in depth, but there was a narrow advantage in the U.S. approach. The slow, ponderous battle of attrition fought by the British meant that they were unable to exploit an unanticipated opportunity quickly. The battle's mechanistic nature brought about fatal delays that allowed the enemy to recover. Firepower dominance was thus a recipe that could defeat the enemy, but that denied decisive success. This attack doctrine, therefore, ensured that Anglo-Canadian forces were incapable of effecting a breakout from Normandy.

The U.S. forces' approach, on the other hand, provided better opportunities for maneuver, but often lacked sufficient strength or concentration for decisive penetration, and hastened troop fatigue due to constant combat and the shortage of reserves.[6] Broad-front attacks also dispersed strength and slowed the advance. The approach reflected an exaggerated optimism and a stubborn faith in the efficacy of continued offensive action. Thus the Americans butted against strong enemy defenses in adverse terrain, for example in the bocage during June and July 1944 and again later over the winter of 1944–1945 in the Huertgen Forest, and bled themselves dry. But, at least this approach to operations sapped German strength faster and left the enemy susceptible to penetration when the Americans finally concentrated their strength during Operation COBRA in late July and shattered the German defense of Normandy.

The least understood facet of the U.S. Army's performance in the European Theater, however, was its growing operational flexibility that complemented its tactical and technical ingenuity. The greater flexibility of the army allowed it to recognize flaws in its operational art more quickly and subsequently to refine its capabilities. One of the key changes in U.S. attack methods during summer 1944 was a gradual shift toward narrower attack frontages and greater concentration. This shift began with the break-out across the Cotentin Peninsula in mid-June 1944 to isolate Cherbourg and hasten its fall. This development continued with the COBRA breakout in late July south of St. Lô and became increasingly prevalent in the last nine months of the war.[7] Concentrated offensives provided greater opportunities for both tactical and operational maneuver that took advantage of the dwindling mobility of the enemy. When coupled with speed and boldness, a narrow-front assault completely undid the German defense south of St. Lô in late July. U.S. forces gradually learned through trial and error to bring greater and better coordinated firepower to bear on the full depth of enemy defenses, and in this regard these attack methods were clearly ahead of those of the British by August 1944.

The performance of the protagonists in the 1944 Normandy Campaign exemplifies the ingredients necessary for military effectiveness. These ingredients include, first and foremost, the development of a sound, unambiguous, and realistic doctrine that emphasizes flexibility, adaptability and critical self-appraisal, and, second, the need for rigorous and honest peacetime preparation for war. The experiences of the U.S., British, Canadian, and German militaries during World War II clearly demonstrate how difficult it is for military institutions to perfect organization, force structure, equipment, doctrine, and tactics during wartime, especially in the face of parallel enemy adaptation in light of their own combat experience.

Notes

1. Timothy Lupfer, *Dynamics of Doctrine: The Changes in German Tactical Doctrine during the First World War* (Fort Leavenworth: U.S. Army Command and General Staff College, 1981).

2. Michael Doubler, *Closing with the Enemy: How G.I.s Fought the War in Europe* (Lawrence: University of Kansas Press, 1994), passim.

3. Ibid.

4. Hart, *Montgomery,* 125–127.

5. Bradley contrasted the British and U.S. approaches as follows: "When Montgomery prepared to attack he dragged up everything he had for an all out campaign. . . . We Americans, on the other hand, constantly nibbled away at key positions of an enemy and sought to prevent him from entrenching himself in position. We constantly kept him knocked off balance." Letter, Bradley to Eisenhower, 29 June 1944 quoted in Carlo D'Este, *Decision in Normandy: The Unwritten Story of Montgomery and the Allied Campaign* (London: Collins, 1983), 340.

6. Montgomery recognized the drawbacks of the U.S. approach. He wrote that "owing to continuous fighting without relief, the American troops rapidly tired; man-management was bad, the infantry were very wet and tired, and some men did not have a hot meal for four days running." And with his typical tactless conceit he dismissed the U.S. approach as "futile doctrine." IWM BLM 78/1, "Notes on the Campaign in North-West Europe," para. 11.

7. General Patch's U.S. Seventh Army, in its advance from southern France to the German frontier during fall 1944, increasingly attacked on narrower frontages and devised concentric envelopment tactics that allowed it to overcome strong defenses with only marginal numerical and material superiority. Keith Bonn, *When the Odds Were Even: The Vosges Mountains Campaign* (Novato, Calif.: Presidio Press, 1994).

Bibliography

Primary Sources—Unpublished

Modern Military Branch, National Archives, Washington, D.C.

RG 332 ETOUSA Historical Division Records

Washington National Records Center, Suitland, Md.

RG 407   WWII Operational Reports, 1940–1948

U.S. Army Military History Institute, Carlisle Barracks, Pa.

FUSA. *Battle Experiences, 1944.* 1944.
G–2, Tank Destroyer Center. *Tank Destroyer Combat Reports from Theaters of Operations.* February 1944.
General Board U.S. Forces in the ETO. *Reports on Ops. 1944–45.*
Observer Board, European Theater of Operations, U.S. Army, Army Ground Forces. *Reports of the AGF Observers Board ETO 1944–45.*

Public Record Office (PRO), Kew, London

AIR 37	Allied Expeditionary Air Force Papers
IR 40	Air Ministry Papers
CAB 44	Narratives for the Official Histories
CAB 106	Historical Section, Archivist and Librarian Files
DEFE 2	Combined Operations HQ: Reports
DEFE 3	Ultra Messages
PREM 3	Prime Minister's Private Office: Operational Papers
WO 33	War Office "O" and "A" Papers
WO 73	Monthly Returns
WO 106	Directorate of Military Operations and Intelligence
WO 162	Adjutant General's Papers
WO 163	War Office Council and Army Council Records
WO 166	UK Home Forces War Diaries

WO 171	Twenty-First Army Group: Unit War Diaries 1944
WO 179	War Diaries, Dominion Forces
WO 193	War Office Council Records
WO 199	UK Home Forces Papers
WO 205	Headquarters Papers, Twenty-First Army Group
WO 208	Directorate of Military Intelligence
WO 212	Order of Battle Charts
WO 216	CIGS Papers
WO 219	Supreme Headquarters Allied Expeditionary Force Papers
WO 223	Staff College, Camberly Records
WO 231	Directorate of Military Training
WO 232	Directorate of Tactical Investigation
WO 233	Directorate of Military Intelligence
WO 241	Directorate of Army Psychiatry
WO 277	Department of the Permanent Under Secretary, C–3 Branch
WO 285	Dempsey Papers
WO 291	Army Operational Research Group

Department of Documents, Imperial War Museum, London

AL	Enemy Documents Section
BLM	Bernard Law Montgomery Papers
IWM	Lieutenant General Bucknall and Major General de Guingand Papers

Liddell Hart Centre for Military Archives, Kings College, London

| LHP | Liddell Hart Papers |
| AP | Field Marshall Viscount Alanbrooke Papers |

RAF Museum, Hendon, London

RAF Bombing Analysis Unit, *The German Retreat Behind the Seine, August 1944.* November 1944.

Canadian Public Archives, Ottawa

| CP | Crerar Papers |
| RG 24 | Department of National Defense Papers |

Brigadier Churchill Mann Papers
Colonel Ralston Papers
Lieutenant-General Kenneth Stuart Papers

Captured German Records Collection,
National Archives Washington, D.C.

T–77	Records of the German Armed Forces High Command (*OKW*)
T–78	Records of the German Army High Command (*OKH*)
T–311	Records of Commander in Chief West, Army Group B and Army Group G
T–312	Records of the First, Seventh and Fifteenth Armies

T–313   Records of Fifth Panzer Army
T–314   Records of the LVIII Panzer, LXXIV, LXXX, and LXXXIV Corps
T–315   Records of the 346th, 709th, 711th, and 716th Divisions
T–354   Records of the *Waffen SS*
T–501   Records of the Military Governor Belgium-North France

*U.S. Army Historical Division Foreign Military Studies
Collection, National Archives, Washington, D.C.*

A, B, C, D, P, and ETHINT Series Manuscripts

Primary Sources—Published

Brooks, Stephen, ed. *Montgomery and the Eighth Army*. London: Bodley Head, 1991.

Colby, Elbridge. *The First Army in Europe, 1943–45*. Washington, D.C.: 91st Congress, 1st Session, Doc. 91–25, 1969.

FM 1–5. *Employment of the Aviation of the Army*. Washington, D.C.: GPO, April 1940.

FM 18–5. *The Organization and Tactics of Tank Destroyer Units*. Washington, D.C.: GPO, 16 July 1942.

FM 31–35. *Aviation in Support of Ground Forces*. Washington, D.C.: GPO, April 1942.

FM 100–5. *Field Service Regulations (Tentative), Operations, 1939*. Washington, D.C.: GPO, 1939.

FM 100–5. *Field Service Regulations*. Washington, D.C.: GPO, 1941.

FM 100–20. *Command & Employment of Air Power*. Washington, D.C.: GPO, 1942.

FUSA. *Report of Operations, October 1943–1 August 1944*. [Paris: FUSA, 1944].

FUSA. *Report of Operations, 1 August 1944–22 February 1945*. Washington, D.C: GPO, 1946. 5 vols.

FUSA. *Report of Operations, 22 February 1945–8 May 1945*. Washington, D.C: GPO, 1946. 3 vols.

FUSA. *First United States Army Combat Operations Data: Europe, 1944–45*. Washington, D.C.: GPO, 1948.

OKH. Kampferlebnisse auf Polen. Berlin: Offene Worte, 1940.

OKW. Kampf um Norwegen: Berichte und Bilder vom Kriege Gegen England. Berlin: Zeitgeschichte Verlag, 1940.

Schramm, Percy E., ed. *Kriegstagebuch des Oberkommandos der Wehrmacht*. Frankfurt: Bernard & Graefe, 1961–69. 4 vols.

SHAEF. *Report by the Supreme Commander to the Combined Chiefs of Staff on the Operations in Europe of the Allied Expeditionary Force, 6 June 1944 to 8 May 1945*. Washington, D.C.: GPO, 1946.

TUSA. *After Action Report, 1 August 44–9 May 45*. [Germany]: TUSA, 1945.

TUSAG. *Twelfth Army Group Report of Operations, Final After Action Report*. Germany: TUSAG, 1945. 12 vols.

War Department. *Lessons from the Tunisian Campaign*. Washington, D.C.: GPO, October 1943.

———. *Lessons from the Sicilian Campaign*. Washington, D.C.: GPO, 1943.

———. *Lessons from the Italian Campaign*. Washington, D.C.: GPO, 1944.

War Office: *Mechanized and Armoured Formations, 1929*. London: HMSO, 1929.

————. *Field Service Regulations, Vol. I.* London: HMSO, 1930.

————. *Infantry Training, 1932.* London: HMSO, 1932.

————. *Field Service Regulations, II-III* London: HMSO, 1935.

————. *Military Training Pamphlets.* London: HMSO, 1938–1945.

————. *Current Reports from Overseas.* London: HMSO, 1939–1945.

————. *Lessons from Theatres of War.* London: HMSO, 1942–1945.

————. *Lessons of Dieppe.* London: HMSO, 1943.

————. *The Tactical Handling of the Armoured Division.* London: HMSO, 1943.

————. *Lessons Learnt from the Tunisian Campaign.* London: HMSO, July 1943.

Memories and Autobiographies

Belchem, David. *All in the Day's March.* London: Collins, 1978.

Bradley, Omar N. *A Soldier's Story.* New York: Holt, 1951.

Bradley, Omar and Clay Blair. *A General's Life.* London: Sidgewick and Jackson, 1983.

Brereton, Lt. Gen. Lewis H. *The Brereton Diaries: The War in the Air, 1941–45.* New York: Morrow, 1946.

Burns, Lt. Gen. Eedson L. M. *General Mud: Memoirs of Two World Wars.* Toronto: Clarke and Irwin, 1956.

Butcher, Harry, C. *My Three Years with Eisenhower.* London: Heinemann, 1946.

Carver, Michael. *Out of Step: The Memoirs of Field Marshall Lord Carver.* London: Hutchinson, 1989.

Churchill, Winston. *The Second World War.* London: Cassell, 1948–1954.

Collins, Joseph L. *Lightning Joe: An Autobiography.* Baton Rouge: Louisiana State University, 1979.

Dalgleish, John. *We Planned the Second Front.* London: Gollancz, 1945.

De Guingand, Maj. Gen. Francis. *Operation Victory.* London: Hodder and Stoughton, 1947.

————. *Generals at War.* London: Hodder & Stoughton, 1964.

Eisenhower, Dwight D. *Crusade in Europe.* New York: Da Capo Press, 1948.

Fuller, J. F. C. *Memoirs of an Unconventional Soldier.* London: Ivor Nicholson and Watson, 1936.

Gale, Gen. Sir Richard. *With the 6th Airborne Division in Normandy.* London: Sampson Low, Marston, 1948.

————. *A Call to Arms.* London: Hutchinson, 1968.

Gavin, James M. *On to Berlin: Battles of an Airborne Commander, 1943–1945.* New York: Viking, 1978.

Grigg, Percy J. *Prejudice and Judgement.* London: Jonathon Cape, 1948.

Guderian, Heinz. *Panzer Leader.* London: Joseph, 1952.

Horrocks, Sir Brian. *A Full Life.* London: Collins, 1960.

————. *Corps Commander.* London: Sidgewick and Jackson, 1977.

Ismay, Lord. *The Memoirs of Lord Ismay.* London: Heinemann, 1960.

Kitching, Maj. Gen. George. *Mud and Green Fields: The Memoirs of Major General Kitching.* Langley, British Columbia: Battleline, 1986.

Leinbaugh, Harold P. and John D. Campbell. *The Men of Company K: The Autobiography of a WWII Rifle Company.* New York: William Morrow, 1985.

Liddell Hart, Basil H. *Memoirs of Captain Liddell Hart.* London: Cassell, 1967, 2 vols.

Luck, Col. Hans von. *Panzer Commander: The Memoirs of Hans von Luck.* London: Praeger, 1989.

Manstein, Erich von. *Lost Victories.* Chicago: H. Regency Co., 1958.

Mellenthin, Friedrich W. von. *Panzer Battles 1939–45: A Study of the Employment of Armor in WWII.* London: Cassell, 1955.

Montgomery, Bernard L. *Normandy to the Baltic.* London: Hutchinson, 1947.

———. *El Alamein to the River Sangro.* London: Hutchinson, 1948.

———. *Memoirs.* London: Collins, 1958.

———. *The Path to Leadership.* London: Collins, 1961.

Morgan, Gen. F. *Overture to Overlord.* London: Hodder and Stoughton, 1950.

———. *Peace and War.* London: Hodder and Stoughton, 1961.

Patton, George S. *War as I Knew It.* Boston: Houghton Mifflin, 1947.

Pope, Maurice. *Soldiers and Politicians: The Memoirs of Lieutenant-General Maurice Pope.* Toronto: University of Toronto Press, 1962.

Ridgway, Matthew B. *Soldier.* New York: Harper, 1956.

Roberts, Maj. Gen. G. P. B. *From the Desert to the Baltic.* London: Kimber, 1987.

Ruge, Friedrich. *Rommel in Normandy.* London: MacDonald and Jane's, 1979.

Senger und Etterlin, Frido von. *Neither Hope nor Fear.* London: MacDonald, 1960.

Slim, F. M. Viscount. *Defeat into Victory.* London: Cassell, 1956.

Speidel, Hans. *Invasion 1944: ein Betrag zu Rommels und des reiches Schicksal.* Tübingen, Rainer Wunderlich Verlag Hermann Leins, 1949.

———. *We Defended Normandy.* London: Herbert Jenkins, 1951.

Tedder, Air Marshall Arthur. *With Prejudice: The War Memoirs of Marshall of the RAF, Lord Tedder, GCB.* Boston: Little Brown, 1966.

Thompson, Reginald W. *Men Against Fire.* London: Macmillan, 1945.

Vokes, Maj. Gen. Chris. *My Story.* Ottawa: Gallery Books, 1985.

Westphal, Siegfried. *Heer in Fesseln: aus den Papieren des Stabchefs von Rommel, Kesselring und Rundstedt.* Bonn: Athenäum Verlag, 1950.

Zuckerman, Solly. *From Apes to Warlords: The Autobiography of Solly Zuckerman.* London: H. Hamilton, 1978.

Theses and Dissertations

Daley, John L. S. "From Theory to Practice: Tanks, Doctrine, and the U.S. Army, 1916–1940." Ph.D. diss., Kent State University, 1993.

DiNardo, Richard L. "Germany's Panzer Arm: Anatomy and Performance." Ph.D. diss., City University of New York, 1988.

Dowd, Dennis D. "The Battle of the Falaise Pocket: Differing Interpretations." M.A. thesis, Creighton University, 1982.

Gabel, Christopher. "The U.S. Army GHQ Maneuvers of 1941." Ph.D. diss., Ohio State University, 1981.

Hacker, Barton C. "The Military and the Machine: An Analysis of the Controversy over Mechanization in the British Army, 1919–39." Ph.D. diss., University of Chicago, 1968.

Hart, Russell A. "The Metamorphosis of the German Army in the West, June 1943-August 1944." M.A. thesis, Ohio State University, 1992.

Hart, Stephen A. "Montgomery, Twenty-First Army Group and the Campaign in Northwest Europe." Ph.D. diss., Kings College London, 1995.

Hutchinson, William. "Test of a Corps Commander: General Guy Granville Simonds, Normandy 1944." M.A. thesis, University of Victoria, 1983.

Lewis, Samuel J. "A History of the Operations of the German First Army in the Withdrawal to the Moselle River (August 12–September 1, 1944)." M.A., California State University, 1972.

Mansoor, Peter. "The Development of Combat Effective Divisions in the U.S. Army During WWII." M.A. thesis, Ohio State University, 1992.

Mansoor, Peter. "Building Blocks of Victory: American Infantry Divisions in the War Against Germany and Italy, 1941–45." Ph.D. diss., Ohio State University, 1995.

Odell, Arthur. "The Origins, Development, and Utilisation of the 5th Canadian Armoured Division." M.A. thesis, University of Victoria, 1976.

Quintett, R. L. "Hitler's Political Officers: The National Socialist Leadership Officers." Ph.D. diss., University of Oklahoma, 1979.

Sauer, Robert J. "Germany's I SS Panzer Corps: Defensive Armored Operations in France, June–September 1944." Ph.D. diss., Boston College, 1992.

Stewart, William F. "Attack Doctrine in the Canadian Corps, 1916–1918." M.A. thesis, University of New Brunswick, 1982.

Thompson, David. "From Neutrality to NATO: The Norwegian Armed Forces and Defense Policy, 1905–55." Ph.D. diss., Ohio State University, 1996.

Wilson, David A. "The Development of Tank-Infantry Co-operation Doctrine in the Canadian Army for the Normandy Campaign of 1944." M.A. thesis, University of New Brunswick, 1992.

Biographies

Ambrose, Stephen. *The Supreme Commander.* New York: Doubleday, 1970.

Baynes, John. *The Forgotten Victor: General Sir Richard O'Connor.* London: Brassey, 1989.

Blumentritt, Günther. *Rundstedt: The Soldier and the Man.* London: Odhams, 1952.

Bond, Brian. *Liddell Hart: A Study of His Military Thought.* London: Cassell, 1977.

Farago, Ladislas. *Patton: Ordeal and Triumph.* New York: Dell, 1963.

Fraser, David. *Alanbrooke.* London: Collins, 1982.

Graham, Dominick. *The Price of Command: The Biography of General Guy G. Simonds.* Toronto: Stoddart, 1993.

Hamilton, Nigel. *Monty: The Making of a General 1887–1942,* London: H. Hamilton, 1982.

———. *Monty: Master of the Battlefield 1942–1944.* London: H. Hamilton, 1983.

———. *Monty: The Field Marshal 1944–76.* London: Hamilton, 1986.

———. *Monty: The Man Behind the Legend.* London: Sphere, 1988.

Horne, Alistair, and Brian Montgomery. *The Lonely Leader: Monty 1944–1945.* London: Macmillan, 1994.

Howarth, T. E. B., ed. *Monty at Close Quarters: Recollections of the Man.* London: Leo Cooper/Martin Secker & Warburg, 1985.

Irving, David. *The Trail of the Fox.* London: Weidenfeld and Nicholson, 1977.

Jackson, Gen. William G. F. *Alexander of Tunis as Military Commander.* London: Batsford, 1971.

Keegan, John, ed. *Churchill's Generals.* London: Weidenfeld and Nicolson, 1991.

Lamb, Richard. *Montgomery in Europe 1943–45: Success or Failure?* London: Buchan and Enright, 1983.

———. *Churchill as War Leader: Right or Wrong?* London: Bloomsbury, 1991.

Lewin, Ronald. *Rommel as Military Commander.* New York: Ballantine, 1970.

———. *Montgomery as Military Commander.* London: Batsford, 1971.

———. *Slim: The Standard Bearer.* London: Pan, 1978.

Macksey, Kenneth. *Armoured Crusader: A Biography of Major-General Sir Percy Hobart.* London: Hutchinson, 1967.

Mearsheimer, John. *Liddell Hart and the Weight of History.* London: Brassey, 1988.

Messenger, Charles. *The Last Prussian: A Biography of Field Marshal Gerd von Rundstedt, 1875–1953.* London: Brassey, 1991.

Moorehead, Alan. *Montgomery.* London: H. Hamilton, 1946.

Orange, Vincent. *Coningham: A Biography of Air Marshal Sir Arthur Coningham.* Washington, D.C.: Center for Air Force History, 1992.

Raugh, Harold E., Jr. *Wavell in the Middle East, 1939–1941: A Study in Generalship.* London: Brassey, 1993.

Reid, Brian Holden. *J. F. C. Fuller: Military Thinker.* London: Macmillan, 1987.

Roy, Reginald H. *For Most Conspicuous Bravery: A Biography of Major-General George R. Pearkes V.C., Through Two World Wars.* Vancouver: University of British Columbia Press, 1977.

Ryder, Roland. *Oliver Leese.* London: H. Hamilton, 1987.

Sixsmith, Maj. Gen. Eric K. G. *Eisenhower as Military Commander.* New York: Da Capo Press, 1973.

Thompson, Reginald W. *The Montgomery Legend.* London: Allen & Unwin, 1967.

———. *Montgomery the Field Marshal: A Critical Study.* London: Allen and Unwin, 1969.

Trythall, Maj. Gen. Anthony J. *"Boney" Fuller: The Intellectual General.* London: Cassell, 1977.

Warner, Philip. *Horrocks: The General Who Led From the Front.* London: H. Hamilton, 1984.

Whiting, Charles. *Bradley.* New York: Ballantine Books, 1971.

Winton, Harold R. *To Change an Army, General Sir John Burnett-Stuart and British Armoured Doctrine, 1927–1938.* Lawrence: University of Kansas Press, 1988.

Young, Desmond. *Rommel: The Desert Fox.* New York: Harper and Row, 1950.

Unit/Regimental Histories

Abrams, Joe I. *A History of the 90th Division in WWII, 6 June 1944–9 May 1945.* Baton Rouge: Army-Navy Publishing, 1946.

Anon. *Taurus Pursuant: The History of 11th Armoured Division.* Hamburg: British Army of the Rhine (BAOR), 1945.

Baker, Maj. A. H. R., and Maj. B. Rust. *A Short History of the 50th Northumbrian Division.* Yarmouth: 50th Division, 1966.

Barclay, Cyril N. *History of 53 (Welsh) Division in the Second World War.* London: William Clowes & Sons Ltd., 1956.

Blake, George. *Mountain & Flood: The History of the 52nd (Lowland) Division 1939–46.* Glasgow: Jackson and Son, 1950.

Brown, John Sloan. *Draftee Division: The 88th Infantry Division in WWII.* Lexington: University Press of Kentucky, 1986.

Brownlie, W. Steel. *Proud Trooper: The History of the Ayrshire Yeomanry.* London: Collins, 1964.

Clay, E. W. *The Path of the 50th: The Story of the 50th (Northumbrian) Division in the Second World War.* London: Gale and Polden, 1950.

Colby, John. *War From the Ground Up: The 90th Division in WWII.* Austin, Tex.: Nortex Books, 1991.

Duncan, Nigel W. *The 79th Armoured Division: Hobo's Funnies.* Windsor: Profile Publications, 1972.

Ewing, Joseph. *29, Let's Go: A History of the 29th Division in WWII.* Washington, D.C.: Infantry Journal Press, 1948.

Featherstone, Alwyn. *Saving The Breakout: The 30th Division Stand at Mortain, August 7–12, 1944.* Novato, Calif.: Presidio Press, 1993.

Fitzroy, Olivia. *Men of Valour: The Third Volume of the History of the VIII Kings Royal Irish Hussars, 1927–1958.* Liverpool: C. Tinling & Co., 1961.

Fletcher, David. *Vanguard of Victory: The 79th Armoured Division.* London: HMSO, 1984.

Forty, George. *Patton's Third Army at War.* New York: Scribners, 1978.

Fürbringer, Herbert. *9SS-Panzer Division Hohenstauffen 1944: Normandie-Tarnopol-Arnhem.* Paris: Heimdal, 1984.

Futter, Geoffrey W. *The Funnies: The 79th Armoured Division & Its Specialized Equipment.* Hemel Hempstead: Model & Allied Publications, 1974.

Gill, Ronald, and John Groves. *Club Route in Europe: The Story of 30 Corps in the European Campaign.* Hannover: W. Degener, 1946.

Graham, Andrew. *Sharpshooters at War.* London: Sharpshooters Regimental Association, 1964.

Günther, Helmut. *Das Auge der Division: mit der Aufklärungs-Abteilung "Götz von Berlichingen" von Normandie zum Rhein 1944–45.* Neckargemünd: K. Vowinckel, 1967.

Hammerman, Gay M., and G. Sheridan. *The 88th Infantry Division in WWII: Factors Responsible for its Excellence.* Dunn Loring, Va.: HERO, 1982.

Hastings, Max. *Das Reich: The March of the 2nd SS Panzer Division Through France.* New York: Holt, Rinehart and Winston, 1981.

Hewitt, Robert L. *Workhorse of the Western Front: The Story of the 30th Infantry Division.* Washington, D.C.: Infantry Journal Press, 1946.

Johnson, Brig. Roy F. *Regimental Fire! The Honourable Artillery Company in WWII, 1939–1945.* London: Williams Lea and Co., n.d.

Kurowski, Franz. *Die Panzer Lehr Division.* Bad Nauheim: Podzun, 1964.

Lehmann, Rudolf, and Ralph Tiemann. *Die Leibstandarte.* Osnabrück: Munin, 1986. 4 vols.

Lucas, James. *Das Reich: The Military Role of the 2nd SS Division.* London: Arms & Armour Press, 1991.

Luther, Craig W. H. *Blood and Honour: The History of 12th SS Panzer Division "Hitler Youth" 1943–1945.* San Jose, Calif.: Bender, 1987.

McNish, Robin. *Iron Division: The History of the 3rd Division.* London: Ian Allen, 1978.

Meyer, Hubert. *Kriegsgeschichte der 12SS-Panzerdivision "Hitlerjugend."* Osnabrück: Munin Verlag, 1982.

Neillands, Robin. *The Desert Rats.* London: Weidenfeld and Nicholson, 1991.

Norwood, Arthur, and Leonard Rapport. *Rendezvous with Destiny: A History of the 101st Airborne Division.* Washington, D.C.: Infantry Journal Press, 1948.

Rissik, David. *The D.L.I. at War.* Durham: Durham Light Infantry Regiment, 1953.

Rütgen, Helmut. *Die Geschichte der Panzer Lehr Division im Westen.* Stuttgart: Motorbuch, 1979.

Salmud, J.B. *The History of the 51st Highland Division.* Edinburgh: W. Blackwood, 1953.

Sandars, John. *The Guards Armoured Division.* London: Osprey, 1979.

Scarfe, Norman. *Assault Division.* London: Collins, 1947.

Sydnor, *Soldiers of Destruction: The SS Death's Head Division, 1933–1945.* Princeton, N.J.: Princeton University Press, 1977.

Werthern, Wolfgang. *Geschichte der 16 Panzer Division 1939–1945.* Bad Nauheim: Podzun, 1958.

Wolfgang, Paul. *Geschichte der 18 Panzer Division 1940–43 mit Geschichte der 18. Artillerie Division 1943–44.* Reutlingen: Preussischer Verlag, 1995.

Secondary Sources—General Thematic

Bailey, Jonathon B. A. *Field Artillery and Firepower.* Oxford: Military Press, 1989.

Barnett, Corelli. *The Desert Generals.* London, Kimber 1960; Allen and Unwin, 1984.

Barnett, Corelli, et al. *Old Battles and New Defences: Can We Learn from Military History?* London: Brassey, 1985.

Beck, Philip. *Oradour.* London: Leo Cooper, 1979.

Belchem, David. *Victory in Normandy.* London: Chatto & Windus, 1981.

Bennett, Ralph. *ULTRA in the West: The Normandy Campaign 1944–45.* London: Hutchinson, 1979.

Bennett, Ralph. *Ultra and Mediterranean Strategy.* New York: W. Morrow, 1989.

Blumenson, Martin. *The Duel for France, 1944.* Boston: Houghton Mifflin, 1963.

———. *The Battles of the Generals: The Untold Story of the Falaise Pocket—the Campaign that Should Have Won WWII.* New York: W. Morrow, 1993.

Brookes, Andrew J. *Photoreconnaissance.* London: Ian Allen, 1975.

Brown, David. *Warship Losses In WWII.* London: Arms and Armour Press, 1990.

Carver, Michael. *Twentieth Century Warriors: The Development of the Armed Forces of the Major Military Nations in the Twentieth Century.* London: Weidenfeld and Nicholson, 1987.

Chapman, Guy. *A Passionate Prodigality.* London: Nicolson and Watson, 1933.

Clifford, Kenneth J., *Amphibious Warfare Development in Britain & America from 1920–1940.* Laurens, NY.: Edgewood, 1983.

Cooling, Benjamin F. ed. *Case Studies in the Development of Close Air Support.* Washington, D.C.: Office of Air Force History, 1990.

Creveld, Martin van. *Supplying War: Logistics from Wallenstein to Patton.* Cambridge: Cambridge University Press, 1977.

Cross, Robin. *Citadel: The Battle for Kursk.* New York: Barnes & Noble, 1993.

Cruickshanks, Charles. *Deception in WWII.* Oxford: OUP, 1979.

Cushman, John. *Challenge and Response: Military Effectiveness, 1914–1945.* Washington, D.C.: National Defense University, 1988.

Derry, T. K. *The Campaign in Norway.* London: HMSO, 1952.

D'Este, Carlo. *Decision in Normandy: The Unwritten Story of Montgomery and the Allied Campaign.* London: Collins, 1983.

———. *Bitter Victory: The Battle for Sicily, 1943.* New York: Dutton, 1988.

———. *Fatal Decision: Anzio and the Battle for Rome.* New York: HarperCollins, 1991.

Devereaux, Tony. *Messenger God of Battle: Radio, Radar, Sonar: The Story of Electronics in War.* London: Brassey, 1991.

Doughty, Robert. *The Seeds of Disaster: The Development of French Army Doctrine, 1919–1939.* Hamden, Conn.: Archon Books, 1985.

Dunn, Walter S. Jr. *Second Front Now!* Tuscaloosa: Alabama University Press, 1980.

———. *Hitler's Nemesis: The Red Army, 1930–1945.* Westport, Conn.: Praeger, 1994.

Dupuy, Trevor N. *Understanding War: History and Theory of Combat.* New York: Paragon, 1987.

Eisenhower Foundation. *D-Day: The Normandy Invasion in Retrospect.* Wichita: University Press of Kansas, 1971.

Ellis, John. *Brute Force: Allied Strategy and Tactics in World War II.* New York: Viking, 1990.

English, John A. *On Infantry.* New York: Praeger, 1981.

Essame, H. *Normandy Bridgehead.* New York: Ballantine, 1970.

Essame, H., and Belfield, Eversley. *The North-West Europe Campaign 1944–45.* Aldershot: Gale & Polden, 1962.

Fergusson, Bernhard. *The Watery Maze: The Story of Combined Operations.* New York: Holt, Rinehart & Winston, 1961.

Glantz, David. *Soviet Defensive Tactics at Kursk, July 1943.* Fort Leavenworth: CSI, U.S. Army Command and General Staff College, 1986.

———. *Soviet Military Deception in the Second World War.* London: F. Cass, 1989.

———. *From the Don to the Dnepr: Soviet Offensive Operations, December 1942-August 1943.* London: F. Cass, 1990.

———. *Soviet Military Intelligence in War.* London: F. Cass, 1990.

———, and Jonathon House. *When Titans Clashed: How the Red Army Stopped Hitler.* Lawrence: University of Kansas Press, 1995.

Graves, Robert. *Goodbye to All That.* London: Jonathon Cape, 1929.

Graves, Robert, and Alan Hodge. *The Long Weekend: A Social History of Great Britain, 1918–1939.* New York: Norton, 1963.

Hallion, Richard P. *Strike from the Sky: The History of Battlefield Air Attack, 1911–1945.* Washington, D.C.: Smithsonian Institute Press, 1989.

Harris, J. P., and F. H. Toase, eds. *Armoured Warfare.* New York: St. Martin's Press, 1990.

Hastings, Max. *OVERLORD: D-Day and the Battle of Normandy.* London: Joseph, 1984.

Haswell, Jock. *D-Day Intelligence & Deception.* London: Times Books, 1979.

Healy, Mark. *Kursk 1943: Tide Turns in the East.* London: Osprey, 1992.

Historical Evaluation Research Organization (HERO), *Interdiction from Falaise to Westwall, 14 August–14 September 1944.* Fairfax, Va.: HERO, n.d.

HERO. *Opposed Rates of Advance of Large Forces in Europe.* Dunn Loring, Va.: HERO, 1966.

Horne, Alistair. *To Lose A Battle: France 1940.* London: Macmillan, 1969.

Howard, Michael. *The Continental Commitment: The Dilemmas of British Defense Policy in the Era of the Two World Wars.* London: T. Smith, 1972.

Ingouf, Paul. *La Bataille de Cherbourg.* Bayeux: Editions Heimdal, 1979.

Irving, David. *The War Between the Generals.* London: Allen Lane, 1981.

Jackson, Gen. Sir William G. F. *Overlord: Normandy 1944.* London: Batsford, 1978.

Johnson, Hubert C. *Breakthrough: Tactics, Technology and the Search for Victory on the Western Front in World War I.* Novato, Calif.: Presidio Press, 1994.

Keegan, John. *Six Armies in Normandy.* New York: Viking Press, 1982.

———. *The Battle for History: Re-fighting World War II.* New York: Vintage Books, 1996.

Kennedy, Paul. *The Rise and Fall of the Great Powers.* New York: Random House, 1987.

Knox, Macgregor. *Mussolini Unleashed, 1931–1941: Politics and Strategy in Fascist Italy's Last War.* New York: Cambridge University Press, 1982.

Lenton, H. T., and J. J. Colledge. *Warship Losses of World War II: British and Dominion Fleets.* London: Ian Allan, 1965.

Lewin. R. *Ultra Goes to War: The First Account of World War II's Greatest Secret Based on Official Documents.* New York: McGraw-Hill, 1978.

MacIntyre, Donald G. F. W. *Narvik.* New York: Norton, 1960.

Macksey, Kenneth. *Tank Warfare: A History of Tanks in Battle.* London: Rupert-Hart Davis, 1971.

———. *Battle.* London: MacDonald and Jane's, 1974.

———. *Military Errors in WWII.* London: Arms and Armour Press, 1987.

———. *For Want of a Nail: The Impact on War of Logistics and Communications.* London: Brassey, 1989.

Marshall, S. L. A. *Men Against Fire: The Problem of Command in Future War.* New York: W. Morrow, 1947.

Masefield, John. *Gallipoli.* London: Heinemann, 1916.

McKale, Donald. *Rewriting History: The Original and Revised World War II Diaries of Curt Prüfer, Nazi Diplomat.* Kent, Oh.: Kent State University, 1988.

Mead, P. *The Eye in the Air: History of Air Observation and Reconnaissance for the Army, 1785–1945.* London: HMSO, 1983.

Messenger, Charles. *The Tunisian Campaign.* Shepperton: Ian Allen, 1982.

Miller, Russell. *Nothing Less than Victory: The Oral History of D-Day,* London: Penguin, 1994.

Millet, Allan R., and Williamson Murray, eds. *Military Effectiveness.* Boston: Unwin & Allen, 1988. 3 vols.

Millet, Allan R., and Williamson Murray, eds. *Innovation in the Interwar Period.* Washington, D.C.: Office of Net Assessment, Department of Defense, 1994.

Mitchum, Samuel W, and Friedrich von Stauffenberg. *The Battle for Sicily: How the Allies Lost Their Chance for Total Victory.* New York: Orion Books, 1991.

Morgan, Gen. Frederick E. *Overture to Overlord.* London: Hodder and Stoughton, 1950.

Mowat, Charles. *Britain Between the Wars, 1918–1940.* London: Metheun, 1955.

Murray, Williamson, *The Change in the European Balance of Power: The Path to Ruin.* Princeton, N.J.: Princeton University Press, 1984.

———. *Luftwaffe.* Baltimore: Nautical and Aviation Press, 1985.

Ogorkiewicz, Richard M. *Armour: The Development of Mechanized Forces and Their Equipment.* London: Atlantic Books, 1960.

———. *Armoured Forces.* London: Arms & Armour Press, 1970.

Parotkin, Ivan. *Kursk.* Moscow: Progress Publishers, 1974.

Perry, F. W. *The Commonwealth Armies: Manpower and Organisation in Two World Wars.* Manchester: Manchester University Press, 1988.

Posen, Barry. *The Sources of Military Doctrine: France, Britain and Germany Between the World Wars.* Ithaca, N.Y.: Cornell University Press, 1984.

Remarque, Erich Maria. *All Quiet on the Western Front.* London: Heinemann, 1929.

Rosen, Stephen P. *Winning the Next War: Innovation and the Modern Military.* Ithaca, N.Y.: Cornell University Press, 1991.

Roskill, Stephen. *Naval Policy Between the Wars.* New York: Walker, 1968, 1976.

Ross, G. MacCleod. *The Business of Tanks.* Ilfracoombe: Arthur H. Stockwell, 1976.

Ryan, Cornelius. *The Longest Day.* London: Victor Gollancz, 1960.

Salisbury, Harrison. *The 900 Days: The Siege of Leningrad.* New York: Harper Row, 1969: Da Capo Press, 1985.

Schulman, Milton. *Defeat in the West.* London: Secker and Warburg, 1947; Ballantine, 1968.

Shores, Christopher F. *Ground Attack Aircraft of WWII.* London: MacDonald and Jane's, 1977.

Stevens, William G. *Bardia to Enfidaville.* Wellington: War History Branch, Department of Internal Affairs, 1962.

Stouffer, Samuel A. et al. *Studies in Social Psychology in World War II.* Princeton, N.J.: Princeton University Press, 1949.

Strachan Hew. *European Armies and the Conduct of War.* London: Allen and Unwin, 1983.

Strawson, John. *The Battle for North Africa.* New York: C. Scribners, 1969.

Vanags-Baginiskis, Alex. *Aggressors, Vol.1: Tank Buster vs. Combat Vehicle.* Charlottesville, Va.: Howell Press, 1990.

Wark, Wesley K. *The Ultimate Enemy: British Intelligence and Nazi Germany, 1933–1939.* Ithaca, N.Y.: Cornell University Press, 1985.

Watt, Donald C. *Too Serious a Business.* Berkeley: University of California Press, 1977.

Weeks, John. *Men Against Tanks: The History of Antitank Warfare.* New York: Mason/Charter, 1975.

———. *Assault from the Sky: The History of Airborne Warfare.* Newton Abbott: David & Charles, 1988.

Whiting, Charles. *Poor Bloody Infantry 1939–45.* London: Arrow Books, 1989.

Wilmot, Chester. *The Struggle for Europe.* London: Collins, 1952.

Wilt, Alan. *War From the Top: German and British Military Decision Making during WWII.* London: Taurus, 1990.

Winterbottom, Frances W. *The Ultra Secret.* London: Weidenfeld and Nicolson, 1974.

Secondary Sources—U.S. Military

Allen, Robert S. *Lucky Forward: The History of General Patton's Third U.S. Army.* New York: Vanguard Press, 1947.

Baily, Charles M. *Faint Praise: American Tanks and Tank Destroyers in World War II.* Hamden, Conn.: Archon Books, 1983.

Balkoski, Joseph. *Beyond the Bridgehead.* Harrisburg, Pa.: Stackpole Books, 1989.

Beck, Alfred M. et al. *The Corps of Engineers: The War Against Germany.* Washington, D.C.: USACMH, 1985.

Blumenson, Martin. *Breakout and Pursuit.* Washington, D.C.: OCMH, 1961.

———. *The Patton Papers 1940–45.* Boston: Houghton Mifflin, 1972.

———. *Kasserine Pass.* New York: Tower, 1966.

Bonn, Keith, *When the Odds Were Even.* Novato, Calif.: Presidio Press, 1994.

Braim, Paul F. *The Test of Battle: The American Expeditionary Forces in the Meuse-Argonne Campaign.* Newark: University of Delaware Press, 1987.

Brophy, Leo P., Wyndham D. Miles, and Rexmond C. Cochrane. *The Technical Services: The Chemical Warfare Service: from Laboratory to Field.* Washington, D.C.: GPO, 1959.

Challener, Richard. *United States Military Intelligence: Weekly Summaries.* New York: Garland, 1978.

Colby, Elbridge. *The First Army in Europe.* Washington, D.C.: GPO, 1969.

Coles, Harry L. *The War of 1812.* Chicago: Chicago University Press, 1965.

Coll, Blanche D, Jean E. Keith, and Herbert H. Rosenthal. *The Corps of Engineers: Troops and Equipment.* Washington, D.C.: OCMH, 1958.

Craven, Wesley F., and James L. Cate. *The Army Air Forces in WWII.* Chicago: University of Chicago, 1951. 7 vols.

Davis, Richard G. *Tempering the Blade: General Carl Spaatz and American Tactical Air Power in North Africa.* Washington, D.C.: Center for Air Force History, 1989.

Doubler, Michael. *Busting the Bocage.* Fort Leavenworth: CSI, U.S. Army Command and General Staff College, 1988.

———. *Closing with the Enemy: How G.I.s Fought the War in Europe.* Lawrence: University of Kansas Press, 1994.

Dower, John. *War Without Mercy: Race and Power in the Pacific War.* New York: Pantheon Books, 1986.

Futrrell, R. F. *Ideas, Concepts, Doctrine: A History of Basic Thinking in the United States Air Force, 1907–62.* Maxwell Air Force Base, Ala.: The Air University, 1971.

Gabel, Christopher. *Seek, Strike, and Destroy: The Evolution of American Tank Destroyer Doctrine in World War II.* Fort Leavenworth: CSI, U.S. Army Command and General Staff College, 1985.

Garland, Albert N., and Howard Smyth. *Sicily and the Surrender of Italy.* Washington, D.C.: GPO, 1965.

Gillie, Mildred H. *Forging the Thunderbolt: A History of the Development of the Armored Force.* Harrisburg, Pa.: Military Service Publishing, 1947.

Granier, Maj. Thomas R. *Analysis of Operation Cobra and the Falaise Gap Maneuvers in World War II.* Maxwell Air Force Base, Al.: Air Command Staff College, Air University, n.d.

Greenfield, Kent R. et al., eds. *The Organization of Ground Combat Troops.* Washington, D.C.: History Division, Department of Army, 1947.

Greenfield, Kent R. et al., eds. *Army Ground Forces & the Air-Ground Battle Team.* Washington, D.C.: Historical Division, AGF, 1948.

———. *Command Decisions.* New York: Harcourt, Brace, 1959.

———. *American Strategy in WWII: A Reconsideration.* Baltimore: Johns Hopkins University Press, 1963.

Greer, Thomas H. *The Development of Doctrine in the Army Air Arm, 1917–41.* Washington, D.C.: 1983.

Griffith, Robert K. Jr. *Men Wanted for the U.S. Army: America's Experience with an All-Volunteer Army between the World Wars.* Westport, Conn: Greenwood Press, 1982.

Grimsley, C. Mark. *The Hard Hand of War.* Oxford: Oxford University Press, 1995.

Harrison, Gordon. *Cross Channel Attack.* Washington, D.C: OCMH, 1951.

Heller, Charles, and William Stofft, eds. *America's First Battles, 1776–1965.* Lawrence: University of Kansas Press, 1986.

Holley, L. B. Jr. *General John Plamer, Citizen Soldiers, and the Army of a Democracy.* Westport, Conn.: Greenwood Press, 1982.

Howe, George F. *Northwest Africa: Seizing the Initiative in the West.* Washington, D.C.: OCMH, 1957.

Hughes, Thomas. *OVERLORD: General Pete Quesada and the Triumph of Tactical Air Power in World War II.* New York: Free Press, 1995.

Hunnicutt, R. P. *Sherman: A History of the American Sherman Tank.* San Rafael, Calif.: Taurus Enterprises, 1978.

Isley, Jester A., and Phillip A. Crowl. *The U.S. Marines and Amphibious War.* Princeton, N.J.: Princeton University Press, 1951.

Karamales, Lloyd, J. et al. *U.S. Antitank Defense at Mortain, France (Aug. 1944).* McLean, Va.: Science Applications International Corporation (SAIC), 1990.

Kaufmann, J. E., and H. W. *The Sleeping Giant: American Armed Forces Between the Wars.* Westport, Conn.: Praeger, 1996.

Kennett, Lee. *G.I.: The American Soldier in WWII.* New York: Charles Scribner & Sons, 1987.

Kohn, Richard H. *Eagle and Sword: The Federalists and the Creation of the Military Establishment in America, 1783–1802.* New York: Free Press, 1975.

Krepinevitch, Andrew F. *The Army and Vietnam.* Baltimore: Johns Hopkins University Press, 1986.

Langley, Lester. *Banana Wars: An Inner History of American Empire, 1900–1934.* Lexington: Kentucky University Press, 1983.

Lerwill, L. *The Personnel Replacement System in the United States Army.* Washington, D.C.: Department of the Army, 1954.

Lewin, Ronald. *The American Magic: Codes, Ciphers and the Defeat of Japan.* New York: Farrar Straus Giroux, 1982.

MacDonald, Charles B. *The Mighty Endeavor: The American War in Europe.* New York: Oxford University Press, 1969.

———. *Company Commander.* New York: Bantam, 1982.

MacPherson, James. *Battle Cry of Freedom.* New York: Oxford University Press, 1988.

Mahon, John K. *History of the Militia and National Guard.* New York: MacMillan, 1983.

Marshall, S. L. A. *Men Against Fire: The Problem of Battle Command in Future Wars.* Gloucester, Mass.: Peter Smith, 1947.

———. *Night Drop: The American Airborne Invasion of Normandy.* Boston: Little Brown, 1962.

Mayo, Lida. *The Ordnance Department: On Beachhead and Battlefront.* Washington, D.C.: GPO, 1968.

McKenney, Janice E. ed. *Field Artillery: Regular Army and Army Reserve.* Washington, D.C., USACMH, 1992.

Miller, Edward S. *War Plan ORANGE: The U.S. Strategy to Defeat Japan, 1897–1945.* Annapolis: Naval Institute Press, 1991.

Millett, Allan R. *Semper Fidelis: The History of the United States Marine Corps.* New York: Macmillan, 1980.

Morison, Samuel E. *History of United States Naval Operations in World War II.* Boston: Little Brown, 1947–1962. 15 vols.

Palmer, Robert R. et al. *The Army Ground Forces: The Procurement and Training of Ground Combat Troops.* Washington, D.C.: OCMH, 1948.

Patton, George S. *War as I Knew It.* Boston: Houghton Mifflin, 1947.

Pogue, Forest C. *The Supreme Command.* Washington, D.C.: OCMH, 1954.

Richardson, Eudora Ramsey, and Sherman Allen. *Quartermaster Supply in the European Theater of Operations in WWII.* Camp Lee, Va.: The Quartermaster School, 1948–1950, 10 vols.

Rohmer, R. *Patton's Gap.* London: Arms and Armour Press, 1981.

Ross, William F., and Charles F. Romanus. *The Quartermaster Corps: Operations in the War Against Germany.* Washington, D.C.: OCMH, 1965.

Ruppenthal, Roland G. *Logistic Support of the Armies* Washington, D.C.: OCMH, 1953. 2 vols.

Rutherford, Ward. *Kasserine: Baptism of Fire.* London: MacDonald & Co., 1970.

Spector, Ronald, ed. *Listening to the Enemy: Documents on Communications Intelligence in the War with Japan.* Wilmington, Del.: Scholarly Resources Inc., 1988.

Stanton, Shelby L. *World War II Order of Battle.* New York: Galahad Books, 1991.

Starr, Chester G. *From Salerno to the Alps.* Washington, D.C.: U.S. Army, OCMH, 1948.

Stoufer, Samuel A., et al. *The American Soldier: Combat and Its Aftermath.* Princeton, N.J.: Princeton University Press, 1949.

Sunderland, Riley. *Evolution of Command and Control Doctrine for Close Air Support.* Washington, D.C.: Office of Air Force History, 1973.

Swanborough, Gordon, and Peter Bowers. *United States Military Aircraft since 1908.* London: Putnam, 1971.

U.S. Army, Dept. of the Army, Quartermaster School. *Storage and Distribution of Quartermaster Supplies in the Eastern Theater of Operations in World War II.* Fort Lee, Va.: Quartermaster School, 1962.

Waddell, Steve R. *U.S. Army Logistics: The Normandy Campaign, 1944.* Westport, Conn.: Greenwood, 1994.

Weigley, Russell F. *History of the United States Army.* New York: Macmillan, 1967.

———. *The American Way of War.* Bloomington: Indiana University Press, 1977.

———. *Eisenhower's Lieutenants: The Campaigns of France and Germany 1944–45.* London: Sidgewick & Jackson, 1981. 2 vols.

Whiting, Charles. *Kasserine: First Blood.* New York: Military Heritage Press, 1984.

Wilson, Dale E. *Treat 'Em Rough: The Birth of American Armor, 1917–1920.* Novato, Calif.: Presidio Press, 1989.

Secondary Sources—British Military

Badsey, Stephen. *The Breakout from Normandy.* Sandhurst: Department of War Studies Campaign Study, Royal Military Academy, n.d.

———. *Normandy 1944.* London: Osprey, 1990.

Barnett, Correlli. *The Desert Generals.* London: W. Kimber, 1960.

———. *Britain and Her Army, 1509–1970: A Military, Political, and Social Survey.* London: Penguin Press, 1970.

Beddell Smith, Walter. *Eisenhower's Six Great Decisions: Europe 1944–45.* New York: Longmans, Green, 1956.

Belchem, Maj. Gen. David. *Victory in Normandy.* London: Chatto & Windus, 1981.

Belfield, E., and H. Essame. *The Battle for Normandy.* London: B. T. Batsford, 1965.

Bellis, Malcom A. *Brigades of the British Army.* Crewe: M. A. Bellis, 1986.

———. *British Tanks and Formations, 1939–1945.* Crewe: M. A. Bellis, 1987.

———. *Divisions of the British Army.* Crewe: M. A. Bellis, 1987.

———. *Twenty-First Army Group Order of Battle.* Crewe: M. A. Bellis, 1991.

Bidwell, Shelford. *Gunners at War: A Tactical Study of the Royal Artillery in the Twentieth Century:* London: Arms and Armour Press, 1970.

Bidwell, Shelford, and Graham, Dominick. *Fire-Power: British Army Weapons and Theories of War 1904–1945.* London: Allen and Unwin, 1982.

Blaxland, Gregory. *The Plain Cook and the Great Showman.* W. Kimber, 1977.

Bond, Brian. *British Military Policy Between the Two World Wars.* Oxford, Clarendon Press, 1980.

Brett-Smith, Richard. *The 11th Hussars.* London: Leo Cooper, 1969.

Bryant, Arthur. *Triumph in the West.* London: 1959.

Butler, Sir James M. *Grand Strategy.* London: HMSO, 1964.

Collier, Basil. *The Defence of the United Kingdom.* London: HMSO, 1957.

Courtney, G. B. *SBS in WWII.* London: Hale, 1983.

De Guingand, Maj. Gen F. *Operation Victory.* London: Hodder and Stoughton, 1947.

———. *Generals at War.* London: Hodder and Stoughton, 1964.

Dennis, Peter. *Decision by Default: Peacetime Conscription and British Defense, 1919–1939.* London: Routledge and Kegan Paul, 1972.

Ehrman, J. *Grand Strategy.* London: HMSO, 1956. vols. V-VI.

Ellis, John. *The Sharp End: The Fighting Man in WWII.* London: David and Charles, 1982.

Ellis, John. *Brute Force: Allied Strategy and Tactics in the Second World War.* London: Viking, 1990.

Ellis, Maj. L F. *The War in France and Flanders, 1939–1940.* London: HMSO, 1953.

———. *Victory in the West.* London: HMSO, 1960, 1968. 2 vols.

Fletcher, David. *The Great Tank Scandal: British Armour in WWII.* London: HMSO, 1989.

Florentin, Eddy. *Montgomery Franchit la Seine.* Paris: Presses de la Cité, 1987.

Fraser, David. *And We Shall Shock Them.* London: Hodder and Stoughton, 1983.

Golley, John. *The Day of the Typhoon: Flying with the RAF Tankbusters in Normandy.* Cambridge: P. Stephens, 1986.

Griffith, Paddy. *British Fighting Methods in the Great War.* London: F. Cass, 1996.

Grigg, John. *The Victory that Never Was.* New York: Hill and Wang, 1980.

Hampshire, Cecil. *On Hazardous Service.* London: Kimber, 1974.

Higham, Robin. *Armed Forces in Peacetime: Britain 1928–1940, A Case Study.* Hamden, Conn.: Archon Books, 1962.

Hinsley, Francis. *British Intelligence in The Second World War.* London: HMSO, 1978–79. 3 vols.

How, J. J. *Normandy: The British Breakout.* London: W. Kimber, 1981.

Howard, Michael, ed. *The Theory and Practice of War.* London: Cassell, 1965.

———. *The Continental Commitment.* London: Maurice Temple Smith, 1972.

———. *The British Way in Warfare: A Reappraisal.* London: Cope, 1975.

Howarth, David. *Dawn of D-Day.* London: Collins, 1959.

Joslen, H. F. *Orders of Battle 1939–45.* London: HMSO, 1960.

Keegan, John, ed. *Churchill's Generals.* London: Weidenfeld and Nicholson, 1991.

Ladd, James D. *Commandos and Rangers of WWII.* London: MacDonald and Jane's, 1978.

Larson, Robert H. *The British Army and the Theory of Armoured Warfare, 1918–1940.* Newark: University of Delaware Press, 1984.

Liddell Hart, Capt. Basil H. *The Real War, 1914–1918.* London: Faber and Faber, 1930.

———. *The British Way in Warfare.* London: Faber and Faber, 1932.

———. *The Tanks.* London: Cassell, 1959. 2 vols.

Luvaas, J. *The Education of an Army: British Military Thought 1815–1940.* Chicago: Chicago University Press, 1964.

Mackenzie, J., and Brian Holden Reid. *British Army and the Operational Level of War.* London: Tri Service Press, 1988.

Macksey, Kenneth. *For Want of a Nail: The Impact on War of Logistics and Communications.* London: Brassey's, 1989.

Maule, Henry. *Caen: The Brutal Battle and the Break-out from Normandy.* London: Purnell, 1976.

Molony, C. J. C. et al. *The Mediterranean and the Middle East. Volume V: The Campaign in Sicily, 1943 and the Campaign in Italy, 3rd September 1943 to 31st March 1944.* London: HMSO, 1973.

Parham, Maj. Gen. H. J., and Eversley M. G. Belfield. *Unarmed into Battle: The Story of the Air Observation Post.* Winchester: Warren and Sons, 1956.

Parker, H. M. D. *Manpower—A Study of Wartime Policy and Administration.* London: HMSO, 1957.

Pemberton, A. L. *The Development of Artillery Tactics and Equipment.* London: War Office, 1951.

Phillips, C. E. Lucas. *Cockleshell Heroes.* London: Heinemann, 1956.

Pitt, Barrie. *Special Boat Squadron.* London: Century, 1983.

Playfair, I S. O. *The Mediterranean and Middle East* (London: HMSO: 1966). Vols. I–IV.

Postan, Michael M. *British War Production.* London: HMSO, 1952.

Reid, Brian H., ed., *American Studies: Essays in Honour of Marcus Cunliffe.* New York: St. Martin's, 1991.

Sandars, John. *The Sherman Tank in British Service, 1942–45.* London: Osprey, 1982.

Seymour, William. *British Special Forces.* London: Sidgewick and Jackson, 1985.

Shaw, W. B. Kennedy. *Long Range Desert Group.* London: Collins, 1945.

Shay, Robert P. *British Rearmament in the Thirties.* Princeton, N.J.: Princeton University Press, 1977.

Sweet, J. John. *Mounting the Threat: The Battle of the Bourguebus Ridge, 18–23 July 1944.* San Rafael, Calif.: Presidio Press, 1977.

Tout, Ken. *Tank!.* London: Robert Hale, 1985.

Timothy Travers, *The Killing Ground: The British Army, the Western Front, and the Emergence of Modern Warfare, 1900–1918.* London: Allen and Unwin, 1987.

———. *How the War Was Won: Command and Technology in the British Army on the Western Front, 1917–1918.* London: Routledge, 1992.

Young, Brig. Peter. *Commando.* New York: Ballantine, 1969.

Secondary Sources—Canadian Military

Berton, Pierre. *The Invasion of Canada, 1812–1813.* Toronto: McClelland & Stewart, 1980.

———. *Flames Across the Border, 1813–1814.* Toronto: McClelland & Stewart, 1980–1981.

Burns, Eedson L. M. *Manpower in the Canadian Army, 1939–1945.* Toronto: Clarke Irwin, 1956.

Copp, Terry, and Robert Vogel. *Maple Leaf Route: Caen.* Alma, Ontario: Maple Leaf Route, 1983.

———. *Maple Leaf Route: Falaise.* Alma, Ontario: Maple Leaf Route, 1983.

Dancocks, Daniel G. *Spearhead to Victory: Canada and the Great War.* Edmonton: Hurtig, 1987.

Douglas, William A. B., and Brereton Greenhous. *Out of the Shadows: Canada in the Second World War.* Toronto: Oxford University Press, 1977.

Dziuban, Col. Stanley W. *Military Relations Between the U.S. and Canada, 1939–1945.* Washington, D.C.: OCMH, 1959.

English, John A. *The Canadian Army and the Normandy Campaign: A Study in the Failure of High Command.* London: Praeger, 1991.

Goodspeed, Donald J. *The Road Past Vimy: The Canadian Corps, 1914–1918.* Toronto: Macmillan, 1969.

Granatstein, J. L. *Canada's War: The Politics of the Mackenzie King Government, 1939–1945.* Toronto: Oxford University Press, 1975.

Granatstein, J. L., and Desmond Morton. *Bloody Victory: Canadians and the D-Day Campaign 1944.* Toronto: L. and O. Dennys, 1984.

Granatstein, J. L., and J. Mackay Hitsman. *Broken Promises: A History of Conscription in Canada.* Oxford: Oxford University Press, 1977.

Griffin, John, and Samuel Kosstenik. *RCAF Squadron Histories and Aircraft, 1924–1968.* Toronto: Stevenk, Hakkert, 1977.

Harris, Stephen J. *Canadian Brass: The Making of a Professional Army, 1860–1939*. Toronto: University of Toronto Press, 1988.

Hitsman, J. Mackay. *Military Inspection Services in Canada, 1855–1950*. Ottawa: Department of National Defence, 1962.

———. *The Incredible War of 1812: A Military History*. Toronto: Toronto University Press, 1965.

Hunter, Lt. Col. T. Murray. *Canada at Dieppe*. Ottawa: Balmuir, 1982.

Hutchinson, Lt. Col. G. S. *Machine Guns: Their History and Tactical Employment*. London: Macmillan, 1938.

Morton, Desmond. *Canada at War: A Military and Political History*. Toronto: Butterworth's, 1981.

———. *A Military History of Canada*. Edmonton: Hurtig, 1985.

Nicholson, Col. Gerald W. L. *Official History of the Canadian Army in the First World War: The Canadian Expeditionary Force, 1914–1919*. Ottawa: Queen's Printer, 1962.

———. *The Gunners of Canada: A History of the Royal Regiment of Canadian Artillery, Vol. 2*. Toronto: McClelland & Stewart, 1972.

———. *The Canadians in Italy*. Ottawa: Clotier, 1959.

Pickersgill, J. W., ed. *The Mackenzie King Record*. Toronto: University of Toronto Press, 1962. 4 vols.

Robertson, Terence. *The Shame and the Glory: Dieppe*. Toronto: MacClelland & Stewart, 1962.

Roy, Reginald. *1944: The Canadians in Normandy*. Ottawa: Macmillan, 1984.

Smith, Widred I. *Code Word CANLOAN*. Toronto: Dundurn Press, 1992.

Snowie, J. Allan. *Bloody Buron: The Battle of Buron, Caen 8 July 1944*. Erin, Ontario: Boston Mills Press, 1984.

Stacey, Col. Charles P. *The Military Problems of Canada: A Survey of Defence Politics and Strategic Conditions Past and Present*. Toronto: Ryerson Press, 1940.

———. *The Victory Campaign*. Ottawa: The Queen's Printer, 1960.

———. *Arms, Men and Governments: The War Policies of Canada*, Ottawa, Queen's Printer, 1970.

———. ed. *Historical Documents of Canada*. New York: St. Martin's Press, 1972.

———. *Canada and the Age of Conflict: A History of Canada's External Policies*. Toronto: Macmillan, 1981.

Stacey, C. P., and Barbara M. Wilson. *The Half-Million: The Canadians in Britain, 1939–1946*. Toronto: University of Toronto Press, 1986.

Stanley, G. F. G. *Canada's Soldiers: The Military History of an Unmilitary People*. Toronto: Macmillan, 1974.

———. *The War of 1812: Land Operations*. Toronto: Macmillan, 1983.

Swettenham, John A. *To Seize Victory*. Toronto: Ryerson Press, 1965.

———. *McNaughton*. Toronto: Ryerson Press, 1968–1969. 3 vols.

———. *Breaking the Hindenburg Line*. Ottawa: Canadian War Museum, 1986.

Turner, W. B., and Morris Zaslow, eds. *The Defended Border: Upper Canada and the War of 1812*. Toronto: Macmillan, 1964.

Wallace, John. *Dragons of Steel: Canadian Armour in the Two World Wars*. Burnstown, Ontario: General Store Publishing, 1994.

Whitaker, W. Denis, and Shelagh Whitaker. *The Battle of the River Scheldt*. London: Souvenir Press, 1985.

Wigley, Philip G. *Canada and the Transition to Commonwealth: British-Canadian Relations, 1917–1926*. Cambridge: Cambridge University Press, 1988.

Williams, Jeffrey. *The Long Left Flank: the Hard Fought Way to the Reich, 1944–45*. Toronto: Stoddart, 1988.

Secondary Sources—German Military

Abbott, Peter & Nigel Thomas. *Partisan Warfare 1941–45.* London: Osprey, 1983.

Addington, Larry. *The Blitzkrieg Era and the German General Staff, 1865–1941.* New Brunswick, N.J.: Rutgers University Press, 1971.

Air Ministry. *The Rise and Fall of the German Air Force.* London: Air Ministry, 1948.

Bartov, Omer. *The Eastern Front, 1941–45, German Troops and the Barbarisation of Warfare.* New York: St. Martin's Press, 1988.

———. *Hitler's Army: Soldiers, Nazis, and the Third Reich.* Oxford: Oxford University Press, 1991.

Behrendt, Hans-Otto. *Rommel's Intelligence in the Desert Campaign 1941–43.* London: W. Kimber, 1985.

Beinhauser, Eugen. *Artillerie im Osten.* Berlin: W. Limpert, 1944.

Benoist-Mechlin, Jacques. *Histoire de L'Armée allemande.* Paris: Editions Albin Michel, 1938. 3 vols.

Bernhardt, Walter. *Die Deutsche Aufrüstung, 1934–1939.* Frankfurt: Bernard & Graefe, 1969.

Breuer, William. *Hitler's Fortress Cherbourg: The Conquest of a Bastion.* New York: Stein & Day, 1984.

———. *Death of a Nazi Army: the Falaise Pocket.* New York: Stein & Day, 1985.

Buchner, Alex. *Narvik: die Kämpfe der Gruppe Dietl im Fruhjahr 1940.* Neckargemünd: K. Vowinckel, 1958.

Busch, Eric. *Die Fallschirmjäger Chronik, 1935–1945.* Dorheim: Podzun-Pallas, 1983.

Caidin, Martin. *The Tigers are Burning.* Los Angeles: Pinnacle Books, 1974.

Calhoon, Christopher. *German Air Anti-Armor Operations on the Eastern Front: Lessons for Tomorrow's Army.* Carlisle Barracks, Pa.: U.S. Army War College, 1987.

Carrell, Paul [Paul Karl Schmidt]. *Sie Kommen! Der deutsche Bericht über die Invasion und die 80-tagige Schlacht um Frankreich.* Oldenburg and Hamburg: Gerhard Stalling, 1960.

———. *Invasion—They're Coming!* London: Ballantine, 1962.

———. *Hitler Moves East, 1941–1943.* Boston: Little, Brown & Co., 1964.

Carsten, F. L. *The Reichswehr and Politics, 1918–1933.* Oxford: Clarendon Press, 1966.

Castellan, Georges. *Le Réarmament Clandestin du Reich, 1930–1935.* Paris: Librarie Plon, 1954.

Chazette, Alain, and Alain Destouches. *1944: le Mur de L'Atlantique en Normandie.* Bayeux: Editions Heimdal, 1986.

Chew, Allen F. *Fighting in the Russian Winter: Three Case Studies.* Fort Leavenworth: CSI, U.S. Army Command and General Staff College, 1981.

Choltitz, Dieter. *Soldat unter Soldaten.* Konstanz: Europa, 1951.

Citino, Robert M. *The Evolution of Blitzkrieg Tactics: Germany Defends Itself Against Poland, 1929–1933.* Westport, Conn.: Greenwood, 1987.

Cooper, Matthew. *The German Army 1939–45: Its Military and Political Failure.* London: Macdonald & Jane's, 1978.

———. *The Phantom War: The German Struggle Against Soviet Partisans 1941–1944.* London: MacDonald & Jane's, 1979.

Corum, James. S. *The Roots of Blitzkrieg: Hans von Seeckt and German Military Reform.* Lawrence: Kansas University Press, 1992.

Craig, Gordon A. *The Politics of the Prussian Army, 1640–1945.* Oxford: Oxford University Press, 1964.

Creveld, Martin van. *Hitler's Strategy 1940–1941: The Balkan Clue.* London: Cambridge University Press, 1973.

———. *Fighting Power: German and US Army Performances, 1939–1945.* London: Arms & Armour Press, 1983.

Dallin, Alexander. *Deutsche Herrschaft in Russland 1941–1945: Eine Studie über Besatzungpolitik.* Dusseldorf: Atheneum Droste, 1958.

Deichmann, General Paul. *German Air Force Operations in Support of the Army.* Maxwell Air Force Base, Ala.: USAF Historical Division, Research Studies Institute, Air University, 1962.

Deist, Wilhelm. *The Wehrmacht and German Rearmament.* Toronto: Toronto University Press, 1981.

———. *The German Military in the Age of Total War.* Dover, N.H.: Berg, 1985.

Department of the Army, Publication 20–291. *Effects of Climate on Combat in European Russia.* Washington, D.C.: GPO, 1952.

Department of the Army, Publication 104–5. *Terrain Factors in the Russian Campaign.* Washington, D.C.: CMH, 1982.

Department of the Army, Publication 104–15. *Operations of Encircled Forces: German Experiences in Russia.* Washington, D.C.: CMH, 1982, 1988.

Detweiler, Donald. *German Military Studies.* New York: Garland, 1979.

DiNardo, Richard L. *Mechanized Juggernaut or Military Anachronism? Horses & the German Army in World War II.* Westport, Conn.: Greenwood Press, 1991.

Dunnigan, James F. ed., *The Russian Front: Germany's War in the East 1941–1945.* London: Arms & Armour Press, 1978.

Dupuy, Trevor N. *Numbers, Prediction and War.* Fairfax, Va.: Hero Books, 1985.

———. *A Genius for War: The German Army and General Staff, 1807–1945.* Englewood Cliffs, N.J.: Prentice-Hall, 1984.

Downing, David. *The Devil's Virtuosos: German Generals at War 1940–1945.* London: New English Library, 1977.

Edwards, Roger. *Panzer: An Evolution in Warfare, 1939–1945.* London: Arms & Armour Press, 1989.

Ellis, Chris, and Hilary Doyle. *Panzerkampfwagen: German Combat Tanks, 1933–1945.* Kings Langley: Bellona Publications, 1976.

Emde, Joachim. *Die Nebelwerfer: Entwicklung u. Einsatz d. Werfertruppe im 2. Weltkrieg.* Friedberg: Podzun-Pallas, 1979.

Engelmann, Joachim, and Horst Scheibert. *Deutsche Artillerie 1934–45.* Limburg: 1974.

Engelmann, Joachim. *Zitadelle: die grosste Panzerschlacht im Osten 1943.* Friedberg: Podzun-Pallas, 1980.

———. *German Artillery in World War II.* Pitglen, Pa.: Schiffer, 1995.

Florentin, Eddy. *The Battle of the Falaise Gap.* New York: Elek Books, 1967.

———. *Der Rückmarsch: La 5ᵉ Pz Armée retraite en Normandie.* Paris: Presses de la Cité, 1974.

Fretter-Pico, Maximilian. *Missbrauchte Infanterie: deutschen Infanterie division im osteuropäischen Grossraum 1941 bis 1945.* Frankfurt: Verlag für Wehrwesen, 1957.

Gamelin, Paul. *Les Bases Sous-Marins allemandes de L'Atlantique et leurs Defenses, 1940–45.* La Baule: P. Gamelin, 1981.

Gander, Terry, and Peter Chamberlain. *Small Arms, Artillery and Special Weapons of the Third Reich.* London: MacDonald and Jane's, 1978.

Gatzke, Hans von. *Stresemann and the Rearmament of Germany.* Baltimore: Johns Hopkins University Press, 1954.

Gröhler, Olaf. *Krieg im Westen*. Berlin: Deutscher Militär-verlag, 1968.

Gröner, Erich. *Die Schiffe der deutschen Kriegsmarine u. Luftwaffe 1939–45*. Munich: J. F. Lehmanns, 1978.

———. *Die deutschen Kriegsschiffe*. Stuttgart: Bernard & Graefe, 1983.

Grove, Eric. *World War II Tanks: The Axis Powers*. London: Orbis Publishing, [1971].

Gudmundsson, Bruce. *Stormtroop Tactics: Innovation in the German Army, 1914–1918*. New York: Praeger, 1989.

Halder, Franz. *Kriegstagebuch*. Stuttgart: W. Kohlhammer, 1962–1964, 7 vols.

Harnier, Wilhelm von. *Artillerie im Küstenkampf*. Munich: J. F. Lehmann, 1969.

Hass, Gerhart et al. *Deutschland im zweiten Weltkrieg*. Cologne: Pahl-Rugenstein, 1974.

Haupt, Werner. *Heeresgruppe Nord*. Bad Nauheim: Podzun, 1967.

———. *Heeresgruppe Mitte, 1941/43*. Dorheim: Podzun, 1968.

———. *Das Ende im Westen 1945: Bildchronik vom Kampf in West-deutschland*. Dorheim: Podzun [ca. 1972].

———. *Rückzug im Westen*. Stuttgart: Motorbuch, 1978.

Heer, Hannes, and Klaus Naumann. *Vernichtungskrieg: Verbrechen der Wehrmacht, 1941–1944*. Hamburg: Hamburger Edition, 1995.

Hesse, Erich. *Die sowjetrussische Partisankrieg 1941 bis 1944 im Speigel deutsche Kampfanweisungen und Befehle*. Göttingen: Musterschmidt, 1969.

Hinze, Rolf. *Die Zusammenbruch der Heeresgruppe Mitte im Osten 1944*. Stuttgart: Motorbuch, 1988.

Hirschfeld, G., ed., *The Politics of Genocide: Jews and Soviet Prisoners of War in Nazi Germany*. Longdon: Allen & Unwin, 1986.

Hoffmann, Joachim. *Die Ostlegionen 1941–1943*. Freiburg: Rombach & Co., 1976.

Hogg, Ian. *The German Army Order of Battle 1944*. New York: Hippocrene Books, 1975.

———. *German Artillery of WWII*. London: Arms and Armour Press, 1975.

Hubatsch, Walter. *Die deutschen Besatzung von Dänemark und Norwegen 1940*. Göttingen: Musterschmidt, 1952.

Jäckel, Eberhard. Herbert Arnold, transl. *Hitler's Weltanschauung: A Blueprint for Power*. Middletown, Conn.: Wesleyan University Press, 1972.

Jacobsen, H. A., and Rohwer, J., eds. *Decisive Battles of the Second World War: The German View*. London: Andre Deutsch, 1965.

Jars, Robert. *La Campagne de Pologne (Septembre 1939)*. Paris: Payot, 1949.

Jünger, Ernst. *Storm of Steel: From the Diary of a German Storm Troop Officer on the Western Front*. London: Chatto & Windus, 1929.

Jurado, Carlos C. *Foreign Volunteers of the Wehrmacht, 1941–45*. London: Osprey, 1983.

Keilig, Wolf. *Das Deutsche Heer, 1939–1945*. Bad Nauheim: Podzun, 1956, 3 vols.

Kennedy, Robert M. *The German Campaign in Poland 1939*. Washington, D.C.: OCMH, 1956.

Kershaw, Robert J. *It Never Snows in September: The German View of Market Garden and the Battle of Arnhem, September 1944*. Ramsbury, England: Crowood Press, 1990.

Klein, Burton H. *Germany's Economic Preparations for War*. Cambridge, Mass.: Harvard University Press, 1957.

Klink, Ernst. *Das Gesetz des Handelns, "Zitadelle" 1943*. Stuttgart: Deutsche-Verlags Anstalt, 1966.

Klöss, Erhard. *Die Invasion 1944: Aus der Kriegstagebuch der Oberkommandos der Wehrmacht*. Munich: Deutscher Taschenbuch, 1984.

Koch, H. A. *Die Geschichte der Deutschen Flakartillerie.* Bad Nauheim: Podzun, 1954.

Kuhn, Volkmar. *Schnellboote im Einsatz.* Stuttgart: Motorbuch, 1986.

Kurowski, Franz. Joseph G. Walsh, transl. *Deadlock Before Moscow: Army Group Center, 1942–43.* West Chester, Pa.: Schiffer Publishing, 1992.

Kurowski, Franz, and Gottfried Tornau. *Sturmartillerie Fels in der Brandung.* Herford: Maximilian, 1965.

Kurowski, Franz, and Gottfried Tornau. *Sturmartillerie 1939–45.* Stuttgart: Motorbuch, 1977.

Lefevre, Eric. *Panzers in Normandy: Then and Now.* London: Battle of Britain Prints, 1983.

Lewis, Stephen. *Forgotten Legions: German Army Infantry Policy.* New York: Praeger, 1985.

Liddell Hart, Capt. Basil H. *Defence of the West: Some Riddles of Peace and War.* London: Cassell, 1950.

———. *The Other Side of the Hill: Germany's Generals, their Rise and Fall, with their Own Account of Military Events, 1939–45.* London: Cassell, 1951.

———, ed. *The Rommel Papers.* London: Collins, 1953.

Lucas, James. *Panzer Army Africa.* London: MacDonald and Jane's, 1977.

———. *War in the Desert: The Eighth Army at El Alamein.* New York: Beaufort, 1982.

Lucas, James, and Barker, J. *The Killing Ground: The Battle of the Falaise Pocket.* London: Batsford, 1978.

Lupfer, Timothy. *The Dynamics of Doctrine: The Changes in German Tactical Doctrine during the First World War.* Fort Leavenworth: U.S. Army Staff and Command College, 1981.

Madej, W. Victor, *The War Machine—German Weapons and Manpower, 1939–1945.* Allentown, Pa.: Game Publishing, 1984.

———. *German Order of Battle: The Replacement Army.* Allentown, Pa.: Game Publishing, 1984.

Marwan-Schlosse, Rudolf. *Rommels Flak als Pak: das Flak Regiment 135 als Ruckgerat des deutschen Afrikakorps.* Wiener Neustadt: Wellberg, 1991.

Mehner Kurt, ed. *Die Geheimen Tagesberichte der deutschen Wehrmachtfuhrung im Zweiten Weltkrieg, 1939–1945.* Osnabrück: Biblio, 1984.

Militärgeschichtliches Forschungsamt (MGFA), *Handbuch zur deutschen Militärgeschichte, 1648–1939.* Stuttgart: Bernard & Graefe, 1978.

Milward, Alan. *The German Economy at War.* London: Athlone Press, 1965.

Mitcham, Samuel W. Jr. *Hitler's Legions: The German Army Order of Battle, World War II.* New York: Stein & Day, 1985.

Morrow, John. *German Air Power in World War I.* Lincoln: University of Nebraska Press, 1982.

Morzik, Maj. Gen. Fritz. USAF Historical Study 167. *German Air Force Air-lift Operations.* USAF Historical Division Research Studies Institute, Air University, 1961: New York: Arno Press, 1968.

Müller, Klaus-Jürgen. *Das Heer und Hitler: Armee und National-sozialistisches Regime, 1933–1940.* Stuttgart: Deutsche-Verlags Anstalt, 1969.

Müller-Hillebrand, Burkhardt. *Das Heer, 1939–1945.* Frankfurt: E.S. Mitler, 1954–69, 3 vols.

Nehring, Walther. *Die Geschichte der Deutschen Panzerwaffe 1916 bis 1945.* Berlin: Propylaen, 1969.

Ose, Dieter. *Entscheidung im Westen 1944: Der Oberbefelshaber West und die Abwehr der allierten Invasion.* Stuttgart: Deutsche Verlags-Anstalt, 1982.

Ottmer, Hans-Martin. *Weserübung: der deutsche Angriff auf Dänemark und Norwegen im April 1940.* Munich: Oldenburg, 1974.

Paschall, Rod. *The Defeat of Imperial Germany, 1917–18.* Chapel Hill, N.C.: Algonquin, 1989.

Phillpott, Bryan. *The Encyclopaedia of German Military Aircraft.* London: Bison, 1981.

Picker, Henry. *Hitler's Tischgespräche im Führerhauptquartier, 1941–42.* Stuttgart: Seewald, 1963.

Piekelkiewicz, Janusz. *Die 8.8cm Flak in Erdkampf-Einsatz.* Stuttgart: Motorbuch, 1988.

Plocher, Lt. Gen. Hermann. *The German Air Force versus Russia, 1942.* Maxwell Air Force Base, Ala.: USAF Historical Division, Air University, 1966; New York: Arno Press, 1968.

Pritchard, David. *The Radar War: Germany's Pioneering Achievement, 1904–1945.* Wellingborough: P. Stephens, 1989.

Proctor, Raymond. *Hitler's Luftwaffe in the Spanish Civil War.* Westport, Conn.: Greenwood Press, 1983.

[Raus, Col. Gen. Erhard]. *Russian Combat Methods in World War II.* Washington, D.C.: Department of the Army 1950.

Reinhardt, Klaus. *Moscow—The Turning Point: The Failure of Hitler's Strategy in the Winter of 1941–42.* Oxford: Berg, 1992.

Richter, Klaus C. *Die Feldgrauen Reiter: Die berittenen und bespannten Truppen in Reichswehr und Wehrmacht.* Stuttgart: Motorbuch, 1986.

Röhricht, Edgar. *Probleme der Kesselschlacht.* Karlsruhe: Kondor, 1958.

Ruge, Friedrich. *Rommel in Normandy.* London: MacDonald and Jane's, 1979.

Schulman, Milton. *Defeat in the West.* London: Ballantine, 1968.

Schumann, Wolfgang et al. *Deutschland im zweiten Weltkrieg.* Cologne: Pahl-Rugenstein, 1985.

Seaton, Albert. *The Russo–German War, 1941–45.* London: Arthur Barker, 1971.

———. *The Battle for Moscow.* New York: Stein & Day, 1971.

———. *The German Army, 1933–1945.* New York: Meridian Books, 1982.

Showalter, Dennis. *From Railroads to Rifles: The Influence of Technological Development on German Military Thought and Practice, 1815–1866.* Hamden, Conn.: Archon Books, 1975.

Speidel, Hans. *Invasion 1944: ein Betrag zu Rommels und des reiches Schicksal.* Tübingen: Rainer Wunderlich Verlag Hermann Leins, 1949.

Stone, Norman. *The Eastern Front, 1914–1917.* New York: Scribners, 1976.

Streim, Alfred. *Die behandlung sowjetischer Kriegsgefangener im "Fall Barbarossa": eine Dokumentation.* Heidelberg: Müller, Juristischer Verlag, 1981.

Streit, Christian. *Keine Kameraden: die Wehrmacht und die Sowjetischen Kriegsgefangenen, 1941–45.* Stuttgart: Deutsche-Verlags Anstalt, 1978.

Taylor, Telford. *March of Conquest: The German Victories in the West, 1940.* New York: Simon & Shuster, 1958.

Tessin, Georg., and Hans-Joachim Neufeldt. *Zur Geschichte der Ordnungspolizei, 1936–1945.* Koblenz: n.p., 1957.

Tessin, Georg. *Formationsgeschichte der Wehrmacht, 1933–1945.* Boppard am Rhein: Boldt Verlag, 1959.

———. *Verbände und Truppen der deutschen Wehrmacht und Waffen SS, 1939–45.* Osnabrück: Biblio Verlag, 1960–1996, 16 vols.

Toppe, Maj-Gen. Alfred. *German Experiences in Desert Warfare during WWII.* Washington, D.C.: U.S. Marine Corps Department of the Navy, 1990.

Trevor-Roper, Hugh R., ed. *Blitzkrieg to Defeat: Hitler's War Directives, 1939–45.* New York: Holt, Rinehart, & Winston, 1964.

Turney, Alfred W. *Disaster at Moscow: von Bock's Campaign, 1941–42.* Albuquerque: University of New Mexico Press, 1970.

Umbreit, Hans. *Deutsche Militarverwaltungen 1939–39: Die militärische Besetzung der Tschechoslowakei und Polens.* Stuttgart: Deutsche Verlags-Anstalt, 1977.

Urba, Leopold. *Kursk: die Letzte deutsche Panzer-Offensive in Russland.* Rastatt: Moewig, 1986.

U.S. War Department. *German Military Intelligence.* Frederick, Md.: University Publications of America, 1984.

Wagener, C. *Moskau 1941: Der Angriff auf die russische Hauptstadt.* Bad Nauheim: Podzun, 1966.

Wallach, Jehuda L. *The Dogma of the Battle of Annihilation: The Theories of Clausewitz and Schlieffen and their Impact on the German Conduct of Two World Wars.* Westport, Conn.: Greenwood Press, 1986.

Wegemüller, Hans. *Die Abwehr der Invasion: Die Konzeption des Oberbefehlshaber West 1940–44.* Freiburg im Breisgau: Rombach, 1979.

Westphal, Siegfried. *Heer in Fesseln: aus den Papieren des Stabchefs von Rommel, Kesselring und Rundstedt.* Bonn: Athenäum Verlag, 1950.

———. *The German Army in the West.* London: 1950.

Whaley, Barton. *Covert German Rearmament, 1919–1939: Deception and Misperception.* Frederick, Md.: University Publications of America, 1984.

Wheeler-Bennett, John W. *The Nemesis of Power.* London: Macmillan, 1961.

Wilt, Alan. *The Atlantic Wall.* Ames: University of Iowa Press, 1975.

Wray, Maj. Christopher. *Standing Fast: The Development of German Defensive Doctrine, Prewar to Spring 1943.* Fort Leavenworth: U.S. Army Command and General Staff College, 1986.

Zabecki, David. T. *Steel Wind: Colonel Georg Bruchmüller and the Birth of Modern Artillery.* Westport, Conn.: Praeger, 1994.

Zayas, Alfred M. de. *The Wehrmacht War Crimes Bureau, 1939–1945.* Lincoln: University of Nebraska Press, 1989.

Ziemke, Earl. *The German Northern Theater of Operations, 1940–1945.* Washington, D.C.: GPO, 1959; CMH, 1989.

———. *Stalingrad to Berlin: German Defeat in the East, 1943–45.* Washington, D.C.: GPO, 1968.

Zimmerman, R. Heinz. *Der Atlantikwall von Dünkirchen bis Cherbourg.* Munich: Schild-Verlag, 1982.

Articles

Anon. "The Employment of Corps Artillery." *Military Review* 23, 2 (May 1943), 56–57.

Anon. "Reinforcing Artillery Employed in Mass." *Military Review* 23, 3 (June 1943), 59–60.

Anon. "The Important Factor in Infantry-Artillery Co-operation." *Military Review* 23, 7 (October 1943), 80–81.

Anon. "Battle of the Falaise Pocket." *After the Battle Magazine* 8 (May 1975).

Armstrong, Lt. Col. A. G. "Army Maneuvers, 1935." *Journal of the Royal United Services Institute* 80 (November 1935), 520.

Bartov, Omer. "The Conduct of War: Soldiers and the Barbarisation of Warfare." *Journal of Military History* Special Issue: Resistance Against the National Socialist Regime, 1991.

Bartov, Omer. "Indoctrination and Motivation in the Wehrmacht: the Importance of the Unquantifiable." *Journal of Strategic Studies* 9 (March 1986), 16–34.

Bazeley, Lt. Col. H. C. "The History and Development of C. B. Operations by Air O. P." *Journal of the Royal Artillery* 73, 1 (January 1948), 31–44.

Beaumont, Roger, A. "Wehrmacht Mystique Revisited." *Military Review* 70, 2 (February 1990), 64–75.

Benz, K. G. "Fire and Manoeuvre—the German Armoured Corps and Combined-Arms Operations." *International Defence Review* 4 (1984), 473–478.

Bidwell, Brig. Roger G. S. "The Development of British Field Artillery Tactics 1920–1939: Reform and Reorganization." *Journal of the Royal Artillery* 94 (1967), 13–24.

———. "The Development of British Field Artillery Tactics 1940–1943." *Royal Artillery Journal* 95, 1 (March 1968), 1–13.

———. "Monty: Master of the Battlefield or the Most Overrated General?" *JRUSI* 129 (1984), 28–31.

Bellamy, Chris. "Trends in Land Warfare: The Operational Art of the European Theatre." *Royal United Services Institute and Brassey's Defence Yearbook 1985.* London: Brassey, 1985, 227–263.

Bittner, Donald F. "Britannia's Sheathed Sword: The Royal Marines and Amphibious Warfare in the Interwar Years—A Passive Response." *Journal of Military History* 55 (July 1991), 345–364.

Blakely, H. W. "Artillery in Normandy." *Field Artillery Journal* 39 (March–April 1945), 42–48.

Blumenson, Martin. "The Most Over-rated General of World War II." *Armor* (May–June 1962), 9ff.

———. "The Forgotten Corps Commanders." *Army* 13 (July 1963), 40–45.

Boucher, Maj. Gen. C. H. "Infantry Tactics." *The Army Quarterly* 61 No.2 (July 1948), 246ff.

Bovee, D. "Hedgerow Fighting." *Infantry Journal* 55 (October 1944), 8–18.

Brooks, Stephen. "Monty and the Preparations for Overlord." *History Today* (June 1984), 18–32.

Burns, Lt. Col. E. L. M. "The Defence of Canada." *Canadian Defence Quarterly* 13, 4 (July 1936), 341ff.

Busch, Everett. "Quartermaster Supply of Third Army." *Quartermaster Review* 26 (November–December 1946), 71–72.

Butler, James J. "Individual Tank-Infantry Communications." *Armored Cavalry Journal* (July–August 1947), 43–45.

Carsten, F. L. "The Reichswehr and the Red Army, 1920–33." *Survey: A Journal of Soviet & East European Studies* (1962), 44–45.

Cerami, Joseph R. "Training: The 1941 Maneuvers." *Military Review* 67 (October 1987), 34–43.

Cole, Col. A. G. OBE. "German Artillery Concentrations in WWII." *Journal of the Royal Artillery* 75, 3 (1948), 196–199.

Copp, Terry. "Scientists and the Art of War: Operational Research in Twenty-First Army Group." *Journal of the Royal United Services Institute* 136, 4 (Winter 1991), 65–70.

Copp, Terry, and Richard Vogel. "No Lack of Rational Speed: 1st Canadian Army Operations, September 1944" *Journal of Canadian Studies* 16 (Fall–Winter 1981), 145–155.

Corkhill, Lt. Col. W. G. R. "The Effectiveness of Conventional Field Branch Artillery in General War in North-West Europe." *Journal of the Royal Artillery* 94, 2 (September 1967), 117–123.

Davies, Arthur. "Geographical Factors in the Invasion and Battle for Normandy." *Geographical Review* 36 (October 1946), 613–631.

Desch, John. "The 1941 German Army/The 1944–45 U.S. Army: A Comparative Analysis of Two Forces in Their Primes." *Command Magazine* 18 (September–October 1992), 54–63.

Dick, Charles J. "The Goodwood Concept—Situating the Appreciation." *Journal of the Royal United Services Institute* 127, 1 (March 1982), 22–26.

DiNardo, Richard L., and Austin Bay. "Horse-Drawn Transport in the German Army." *Journal of Contemporary History* 23 (1988), 129–142.

Dufresne, Michel. "Le Succès Allemand sur la Seine, Août 1944." *Revue Historique des Armées* 176 (September 1989), 48–60.

Dupuy, Trevor N. "The Current Implications of German Military Excellence." *Strategic Review* 4, 4 (Fall 1976).

Erickson, John. "The Soviet Response to Surprise Attack: Three Directives, 22 June 1941." *Soviet Studies* 23 (April 1972), 549–553.

Exton, Hugh M. "Armored and Infantry Cooperation in the Pursuit." *Field Artillery Journal* 39 (July–August 1949), 155–59.

Faulkner, Richard S. "Learning the Hard Way: Coordination Between Infantry Divisions and Separate Tank Battalions During the Breakout from Normandy." *Armor* 99 (July–August 1990), 24–29.

Förster, Jürgen. "Zur Rolle der Wehrmacht im Krieg gegen die Sowjetunion 1941." *Aus Politik und Zeitgeschichte* 45, No 8 (November 1980), 3–15.

Ganz, Harding, A. "Questionable Objective: The Brittany Ports, 1944." *Journal of Military History* 59, 1 (January 1995), 77–95.

Gatzke, Hans. "Russo-German Military Collaboration during the Weimar Republic." *American Historical Review* 63 (1958), 565–597.

Gessner, Capt. William G. "TORCH: Unlearned Logistics Lessons." *Army Logistician* 15 (November–December 1983), 28–32.

Gjelseteen, Col. E. B. "Massing the Fire of Division and Corps Artillery." *Field Artillery Journal* 33, 6 (June 1943), 426–429.

Glantz, David. "Soviet Mobilization in Peace and War, 1924–1942." *Journal of Soviet Studies* 5 (September 1992), 9–31.

Gooderson, Ian. "Allied Fighter-Bombers versus German Armour in North-West Europe 1944–45: Myths and Realities." *Journal of Strategic Studies* 14 (June 1991), 210–231.

Graham, Dominick. "Sans Doctrine: British Army Tactics in the First World War." in Timothy Travers and Criston Archer, eds. *Men at War: Politics, Technology, and Innovation in the Twentieth Century.* Chicago: Precedent, 1982.

Groehler, Olaf. "Zur Einschätzung der Roten Armee durch die faschischten Wehrmacht im ersten Halbjahr 1941." *Zeitschrift für Militärgeschichte* 6 (1968), 724–738.

Gunzenhäuser, Max. "Die Bibliographien zur Geschichte des Zweiten Weltkrieges." in *Jahresbibliographie: Bibliothek für Zeitgeschichte (Weltkriegsbücherei).* Frankfurt: Bernard & Graefe, 1963.

Hains, Peter C., III. "Tanks in Tunisia." *Cavalry Journal* 52 (July–August 1943), 13–17.

Harris, J. P. "British Armour and Rearmament in the late 1930s." *Journal of Strategic Studies* 11, 2 (June 1988).

Hart, Russell A. "Understanding German WWII Divisional Tables of Organization and Equipment." *World War II Historical Journal* 38 (1994), 11–18.

———. "Feeding Mars: The Role of Logistics in the German Defeat in Normandy, 1944." *War in History* 3, 4 (Fall 1996), 418–435.

Hennicke, Otto. "Zu den Menschenverlusten der faschistischen deutschen Wehrmacht im zweiten Weltkrieg (Dokumente)," *Zeitschaft für Militärgeschichte* 2 (1967), 195–208.

Herwig, Holger. "Clio Deceived: Patriotic Self-Censorship in Germany after the Great War." *International Security* (Fall 1987).

Heyward, N. "GOODWOOD." *Household Brigade Magazine* (Winter 1956–57), 171–177.

Howard, Michael. "Military Science in the Age of Peace." *Journal of the Royal United Services Institute* 119 (March 1974), 3–9.

———. "Monty and the Price of Victory." *Sunday Times,* 16 October 1983.

Huston, James A. "Tactical Use of Air Power in World War II: The Army Experience." *Military Affairs* 14 (Winter 1950), 171–175.

———. "Tactical Air Doctrine and AAF Close Air Support in the European Theater, 1944–45." *Aerospace Historian* 27, 1 (March 1980), 35–49.

Jacobs, W. A. "Air Support for the British Army, 1939–1943." *Military Affairs* 46, 4 (December 1982), 174–182.

Jaggi, Major O. "Normandie 1944: Auswirkung der allierten Luftüberlegenheit auf die deutsche Abwehr." *Allegemeine schweizerische Militärzeitschrift* 124, 5 (1958), 333–361.

Kern, Wolfgang, and Erhard Moritz. "Lehren des faschistischen deutschen Oberkommandos des Heeres auf der bewaffneten Intervention in Spanien 1936–39." *Militärgeschichte* 15 (1976).

Kershaw, Robert. "Lessons to be Derived from the Wehrmacht's Experience in the East, 1939–45." *Journal of the Royal United Services Institute* 132, 3 (September 1987), 61–68.

Kingseed, Maj. Cole C. "The Falaise-Argentan Encirclement: Operationally Brilliant, Tactically Flawed." *Military Review* (December 1984), 2–11.

Kohn, Richard R. "The Scholarship on World War II: Its Present Condition and Future Possibilities." *Journal of Military History* 55, 3 (July 1991), 365–394.

Krancke, Theodore. "Invasionsabwehrmassnehmen der Kriegsmarine in Kanalgebiet 1944." *Marine Rundschau* LXVI (June 1969), 171–172.

Lehman, Milton. "We Learned in Tunisia and Sicily." *Infantry Journal* 54 (February 1944), 11–14.

Liddell Hart, Basil. "Army Manoeuvres." *Journal of the Royal United Services Institute* 70 (1925) 647–55.

Liebermann, S. F. "The Evacuation of Industry in the Soviet Union during World War II." *Soviet Studies* 35 (1983), 90–102.

Lossow, Lt. Col. Walter von. "Mission-Type Tactics Versus Order-Type Tactics." *Military Review* 57, 6 (June 1977), 877–891.

Luttwak, Edward N. "The Operational Level of War." *International Security* 5 (Winter 1980–1981), 61–79.

MacBrien, Maj. Gen. J. H. "The British Army Manoeuvres September 1925." *Canadian Defence Quarterly* 2 (January 1926), 132–150.

MacGregor, Col. E. M. K. "In Defence of Battledrill." *Canadian Defence Quarterly* 1, 4 (Spring 1972), 24–29.

Madej, W. Victor. "Effectiveness and Cohesion of the German Ground Forces in World War II." *Journal of Political and Military Sociology* 6 (1978), 233–248.

Mark, Edward. "A New Look at Operation Strangle." *Military Affairs* 52, 4. (October 1988), 176–184.

Maycock, Thomas T. "Notes on the Development of AAF Tactical Air Doctrine." *Military Affairs* 14 (1950), 186ff.

McAndrew, William J. "Fire or Movement? Canadian Tactical Doctrine, Sicily 1943." *Military Affairs* 51, 3 (July 1987), 140–145.

McKenney, Janice. "More Bang for the Buck in the Interwar Army: The 105mm Howitzer." *Military Affairs* 42, 2 (April 1978), 80–85.

Montgomery, Bernard. "Twenty First Army Group in the Campaign in North-West Europe 1944–45." *Journal of the Royal United Services Institute* 78, 1 (February 1969), 46–51.

Moritz, E. "Die Einschätzung der Roten Armee durch den faschischten deutschen Generalstab von 1935 bis 1941." *Zeitschrift für Militärgeschichte* 2 (1969), 154–170.

Murray, Williamson, "The German Response to Victory in Poland: A Case Study in Professionalism:," *Armed Forces and Society* 7, 2 (Winter 1981), 285–298.

North, John. "Lessons of the North African Campaign." *Military Review* 8 (Fall 1944).

Osmanski, Frank A. "The Logistic Planning of Operation Overlord." *Military Review* 29 (November 1949), 31–40; (December 1949), 40–48; (January 1950), 50–62.

Owen, W. V. "Transportation and Supply at Anzio." *Infantry Journal* 58 (March 1946), 32–38.

Powers, Stephen T. "The Battle of Normandy: The Lingering Controversy." *Journal of Military History* 56 (July 1992), 455–471.

Price, Alfred. "The 3-inch Rocket: How Effective Was It Against the German Tanks in Normandy?" *Royal Air Force Quarterly* 15, 2 (Summer 1975), 127–131.

Rippe, Maj. S. T. "Leadership, Firepower and Manoeuvre: The British and the Germans." *Military Review* 65 (October 1985), 32–39.

Rosen, Milton. "Forest Fighting." *Infantry Journal* (1945), 8–10.

Rotundo, Louis. "The Creation of Soviet Reserves and the 1941 Campaign." *Military Affairs* 50, 1 (January 1986), 23ff.

Roy, Reginald. "Black Day for the Black Watch," *Canadian Defence Quarterly* 3 (Winter 1982–1983), 34–42.

Ruse, C. H. "Smoke—Tactical Weapon of WWII." *Armored Cavalry Journal* (February 1947), 52–54.

Sams, James D. "Ordnance Improvisation in the Combat Zone." *Military Affairs* 28 (May 1949), 32–36.

Samuels, Martin. "Operation Goodwood: 'The Caen Carve-Up'." *British Army Review* 96 (December 1990), 4–13.

Savole, T. A. "Deception at the Operational Level of War." *Army* 37, 4 (April 1987), 30–40.

Schweppenburg, Leo Frhr. Geyr von. "An Old German War-Horse Reviews the British Army, Part II." *The Territorial Magazine* 31, 7, (July 1961), 9–11.

Scott, Maj. G. L. "British and German Operational Styles in World War II." *Military Review* 65, 10 (October 1985), 37–41.

Shils, Edward, and Morris Janowitz. "Cohesion and Disintegration in the Wehrmacht in WWII." *Public Opinion Quarterly* 12 (1948), 280–315.

Spencer, Henry Grady. "Hedgerow Fighting: Baptism in the Hedgerows." *Infantry Journal* 55 (October 1944), 10–11.

Stein, George H. "Russo-German Military Collaboration: The Last Phase 1933." *Political Science Quarterly* 77 (1962–1963).

Stella, Amnon. "Red Army Doctrine and Training on the Eve of the Second World War." *Soviet Studies* 27 (April 1975).

Stewart, Richard W. "The 'Red Bull' Division: The Training and Initial Engagements of the 34th Infantry Division, 1941–43." *Army History* 25 (Winter 1993), 1–10.

Stolfi, Russel H. S. "Equipment for Victory in France 1940." *History* (February 1970).

Sullivan, John J. "The Botched Air Support of Operation Cobra." *Parameters* 18 (March 1988), 97–110.

Sunderland, Riley. "Massed Fire and the FDC." *Army* 8 (August 1958), 54.

Taylor, Maj. John M. "North African Campaign: Logistics Lessons Learned." *Military Review* 63 (October 1983), 46–55.

Terraine, John. "Who Bore the Brunt: What Contribution Did Britain's Armed Forces Really Make?" *World War II Investigator* 1 (April 1988), 22ff.

Thoholte, Gen. Karl. "A German Reflects on Artillery." *Field Artillery Journal* 35, 12 (December 1948), 709–714.

Walker, Fred. "Siege Methods: 1945." *Infantry Journal* (January 1945).

Waqyne, Lt. Col. "Armoured Division's Combat Commands." *Cavalry Journal* 55 (March–April 1946), 43.

Welch, David. "Propaganda and Indoctrination in the Third Reich: Success or Failure?" *European History Quarterly* 17, 4 (1987).

Wilhelmsmeyer, H. "From Invasion to Breakout—Normandy 1944: Part II: Breakout." *British Army Review* 75 (December 1983), 66–78.

Wilson, Maj. H. R. G. "Monty: A Review Article." *British Army Review* 77 (August 1984).

Acronyms and Abbreviations

AAA	Antiaircraft artillery
AF	U.S. Armor Force
AGCRA	Army Group, Royal Canadian Artillery
AGCT	U.S. Army General Classification Test
AGF	U.S. Army Ground Forces
AGRA	Army Group, Royal Artillery
AP	Armor-piercing
ASC	Air support control/U.S. Air Support Command
ASF	U.S. Army Service Forces
ASTP	U.S. Army Specialized Training Program
BAI	Battlefield interdiction
BEF	British Expeditionary Force
C3	Command, control, and communication
CAF	Caribbean Amphibious Force
CAO	Canadian Army Overseas
CAR	Canadian Army Reserve
CAS	Close air support
CASF	Canadian Active Service Force
CEF	Canadian Expeditionary Force (World War I)
CGS	Chief of the General Staff
CIGS	Chief of the Imperial General Staff
CMHQ	Canadian Military Headquarters
CRA	Canadian Royal Artillery
CRAC	Canadian Royal Armoured Corps
CRU	Canadian Reinforcement Unit
DND	Canadian Department of Defence
DOA	Department of the Army
DOD	Department of Defense
DZ	Drop Zone
EAC	Eastern Air Command

ETO	European Theater of Operations
FAC	Forward air controller
FASL	Forward air support link
FMS	U.S. Army Foreign Military Studies
FO	Forward observer
FUSA	First U.S. Army
GBUSFET	General Board U.S. Forces in the European Theater
GHQ	U.S. Army General Headquarters
GPO	Government Printing Office
HC	Hollow-charge
HE	High-explosive
HMSO	His/Her Majesty's Stationary Office
IWM	Imperial War Museum, London
IWM EDS	Imperial War Museum Enemy Documents Collection
KTB	German daily war diary (*Kriegstagebuch*)
LHCMA	Liddell Hart Center for Military Archives, Kings College London
LRDG	Long Range Desert Group
MEC	Middle East Command
MGFA	Militärgeschichtliches Forschungsant
NAC	National Archives of Canada, Ottawa
NARA	National Archives Records Administration, Washington, D.C.
NATAF	Northwest Africa Tactical Air Force
NCO	Noncommissioned officer
NDA	National Defense Act
NPAM	Non-Permanent Active Militia
NRMA	National Resources Mobilization Act
OCMH	Office of the Chief of Military History
OKH	German Army High Command
OKL	German Air Force High Command
OKM	German Navy High Command
OKW	German Armed Forces High Command
OSS	Office of Strategic Services
PAM	Permanent Active Militia
POW	Prisoner of war
PRO	Public Record Office, Kew, London
RA	Royal Artillery
RAC	Royal Armoured Corps
RCOC	Royal Canadian Ordnance Corps
RCT	Regimental combat team
ROTC	Reserve Officer Training Corps
SHAEF	Supreme Headquarters Allied Expeditionary Force
TAC	U.S. Tactical Air Command
Tacair	Tactical aviation

TAF	British Tactical Air Force
TD	Tank destroyer
TFAG	21st Army Group
TKB	German tactical report (*Tätigskeitsbericht*)
TO&E	Table of organization and equipment
TUSA	Third U.S. Army
TUSAG	12th U.S. Army Group
USAAC	U.S. Army Air Corps
USAAF	U.S. Army Air Force
USACGSC	U.S. Army Command and General Staff College
USACMH	U.S. Army Office of the Chief of Military History
USAGFOB	U.S. Army Ground Forces Observer Board
USAHD	U.S. Army Historical Division
USAMHI	U.S. Army Military History Institute, Carlisle Barracks, Pennsylvania
VD	*Volksdeutsch*
WD	War diary
WDAF	Western Desert Air Force
WDF	Western Desert Force
WDHD	War Department Historical Division
WO	British War Office
WP	White-phosphorous artillery round

Index

About the Book

Clash of Arms examines how the Western Allies learned—on the battle-field—to defeat the Nazi war machine.

Beginning with an investigation of the interwar neglect that left the Allied militaries incapable of defeating Nazi aggression at the start of World War II, Hart examines the wartime paths the Allies took toward improved military effectiveness. He also explores the continuous German adaptation that prolonged the war and increased the price of eventual Allied victory. Central to his comparative study is the complex interplay of personalities, military culture, and wartime realities that determined how accurately the combatants learned the lessons of war, and how effectively they enhanced their battle capabilities.

Russell A. Hart is an associate professor and specialist in modern military history at Hawai'i Pacific University. He is coauthor of *German Tanks of World War II, Weapons and Fighting Tactics of the Waffen-SS, Panzer: The Illustrated History of Germany's Armored Forces in WWII, The German Soldier in World War II,* and *The Second World War, Part Six: Northwest Europe, 1944–1945.*